Mary Ann Abodeely

HOPE AND HEALING

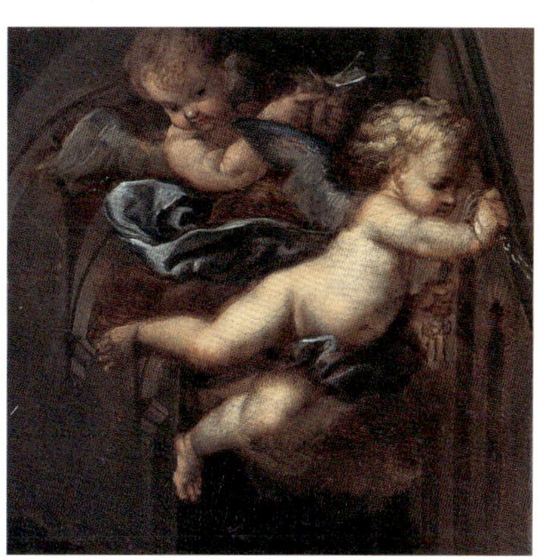

Painting in Italy in a Time of Plague 1500-1800

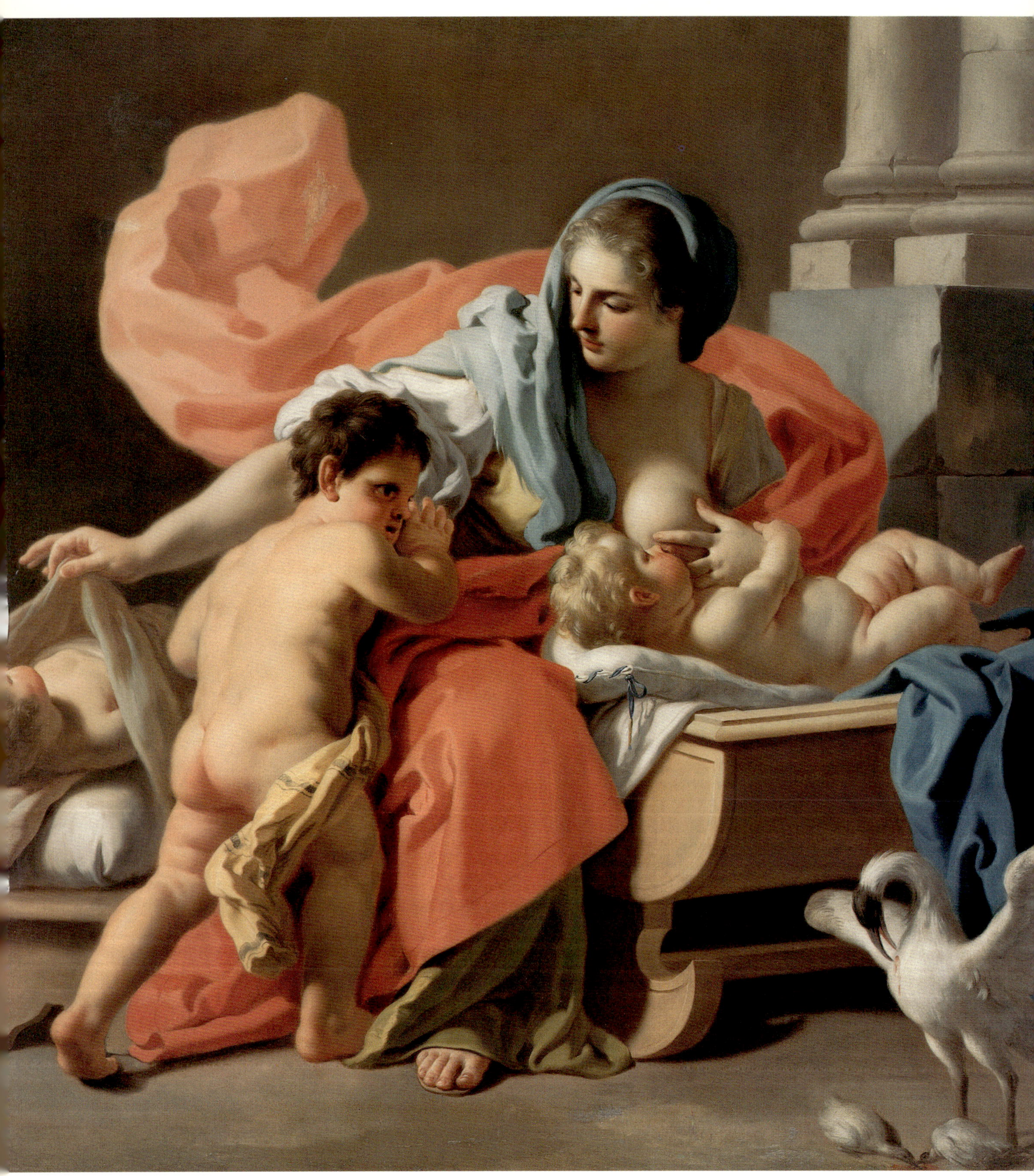

HOPE AND HEALING

Painting in Italy in a Time of Plague
1500–1800

Edited by Gauvin Alexander Bailey, Pamela M. Jones,
Franco Mormando, Thomas W. Worcester
with contributions by
Sheila C. Barker, James Clifton, Andrew Hopkins

Clark University
College of the Holy Cross
Worcester Art Museum

Distributed by the
University of Chicago Press

Published in conjunction with the exhibition *Hope and Healing: Painting in Italy in a Time of Plague, 1500-1800*, held at the Worcester Art Museum, 3 April – 25 September, 2005.

The exhibition and catalogue have been made possible by generous contributions from Atlantic Tele-Network, Inc.; Allen M. Glick, Clark University Class of 1963; a grant from the Old Masters in Context program of the Samuel M. Kress Foundation; and are supported in part by an award from the National Endowment for the Arts, which believes that a great nation deserves great art.

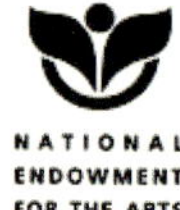

Additional funding for the catalogue has been provided by The Gladys Krieble Delmas Foundation.

ISBN 0-936042-05-2

Produced by Museum Publishing Partners
Editor: Cynthia Purvis Designer: Carl Zahn

Type set in Adobe Jenson and Trajan by Carl Zahn and Frances Presti-Fazio

Cover: Pierre Mignard, *Saint Charles Borromeo Among the Plague-Stricken of Milan*, ca. 1647, Musée des Beaux-Arts de Caen (cat. 25)
Frontispiece: Francesco de Mura, *Allegory of Maternal Love (Charity)*, ca. 1743-44 (detail), Art Institute of Chicago, Preston O. Morton Fund for Older Paintings (cat. 9)

Printed and bound by CS Graphics, Singapore

Gauvin Alexander Bailey, associate professor of art history, Clark University

Pamela M. Jones, associate professor of art history, University of Massachusetts, Boston

Franco Mormando, associate professor of Italian studies and chair, Department of Romance Languages and Literatures, Boston College

Andrew Hopkins, research professor, University of l'Aquila

Thomas W. Worcester, associate professor of history, College of the Holy Cross

James Clifton, director of the Sarah Campbell Blaffer Foundation, Houston, and curator of Renaissance and Baroque Painting, Museum of Fine Arts, Houston

Sheila C. Barker, an independent scholar

Contents

Lenders to the Exhibition

Art Gallery of Ontario
Art Institute of Chicago
Bob Jones University Museum and Gallery
Columbia Museum of Art
Francis Lehman Loeb Art Center, Vassar College
Greenlease Gallery, Rockhurst University
Iris and B. Gerald Cantor Center for Visual Arts at Stanford University
J. Paul Getty Museum of Art
John and Mabel Ringling Museum of Art
Los Angeles County Museum of Art
Mary Jane Harris
Maryland Province of the Society of Jesus at the Jesuit Center
Milwaukee Art Museum
Musée des Beaux-Arts de Caen
Museum of Fine Arts, Boston
Museum of Fine Arts, Houston
National Gallery of Art, Washington
National Gallery, London
New Orleans Museum of Art
Philadelphia Museum of Art
Princeton University Art Museum
Private collection, New York
Richard L. Feigen & Co.
Springfield Museums
The Menil Collection, Houston
The Metropolitan Museum of Art
Toledo Museum of Art
Virginia Museum of Fine Arts
Wadsworth Atheneum Museum of Art
Williams College Museum of Art
Worcester Art Museum

Director's Foreword

When Rev. Michael C. McFarland, S.J., president of the College of the Holy Cross, approached the Worcester Art Museum about the possibility of organizing an exhibition on the plague's influence on the art of early modern Italy, we were responsive to the opportunity to explore an aspect of art history that had been little researched. We were particularly attracted to the interdisciplinary approach of the scholars who had conceived the exhibition and had recently spearheaded the exhibition, *Saints and Sinners: Caravaggio and the Baroque Image*. One of the scholars, Thomas Worcester, serves on the faculty at Holy Cross. With another of the scholars, Gauvin Bailey, on the faculty of Clark University, we were delighted when Clark's president, John Bassett, embraced the project and joined the partnership.

Hope and Healing: Painting in Italy in a Time of Plague, 1500-1800 is the first exhibition outside of Italy to explore the influence of the plague on the fine arts. We are grateful for the opportunity to partner with two other Worcester institutions in examining the role that art and religion played in society's response to the plague during this 300-year period. We hope that the exhibition and catalogue will stimulate ideas and provoke discussion. We are particularly pleased to present the exhibition in Worcester, home to a major medical community whose members play such an important role in combating the plagues of our time.

We would like to express our deep appreciation to Clark University and the College of the Holy Cross, especially their presidents, John Bassett and Fr. McFarland, for their commitment to and generous financial support of this landmark exhibition. We are also grateful for support received from Atlantic Tele-Network, Inc.; Allen M. Glick, Clark University Class of 1963; the Old Masters in Context program of the Samuel H. Kress Foundation; the National Endowment for the Arts; and The Gladys Krieble Delmas Foundation.

We would like to thank the curators of the exhibition, Gauvin Bailey, Pamela Jones, Franco Mormando, and Thomas Worcester, who created the concept for the exhibition and undertook the research for both the exhibition and the catalogue. It has been the pleasure of the Worcester Art Museum staff to work with these four scholars. We would also like to acknowledge Sheila Barker, James Clifton, and Andrew Hopkins, who contributed essays to the catalogue. We join the curators of the show in expressing special thanks to Mary Jane Harris for help at various stages of the project, Andrea Bayer of The Metropolitan Museum of Art for her help and advice, and Anne Guité of Richard L. Feigen & Co.

This catalogue and exhibition would not have been possible without the generous loans from institutions and individuals worldwide. We are extremely grateful for the opportunity to bring to Worcester so many wonderful works of art in an effort to learn more about their creation.

Finally, the exhibition would not have been possible without the professionalism and dedication of the Worcester Art Museum staff. We would like to especially thank Allison Berkeley who coordinated this project in its early stages, and Marie Costello, who succeeded her and brought the project to fruition. It has been a joy to work with both of them. It is the hope of all who have worked on this exhibition and catalogue that this collaborative project will shed new light on one of the most exciting periods in the history of painting.

James A. Welu
Director, Worcester Art Museum

Presidents' Letter

The *Hope and Healing* exhibition is a most welcome opportunity for close collaboration between Clark University, the College of the Holy Cross, and the Worcester Art Museum. Exploring how painting in early modern Italy responded to epidemics of plague, the exhibition brings together a superb collection of paintings never before seen together. We are pleased that our institutions are the principal sponsors of this exhibition, hosted and organized by the Worcester Art Museum. We join Jim Welu, the director, in encouraging scholars, students, teachers, and a broad range of other audiences to enjoy and learn from it.

A major loan exhibition such as *Hope and Healing* requires several years of preparation through scholarly research, complex planning and negotiation, and persistent attention to many details. We congratulate and thank the four curators of the show: Gauvin Bailey (Clark University), Thomas Worcester, S.J. (College of the Holy Cross), Franco Mormando (Boston College), and Pamela Jones (University of Massachusetts/Boston). They conceived and developed this project as an innovative and interdisciplinary effort, focusing on paintings, but studying them not only in order to shed light on important art historical questions, but also on a broader range of critical issues regarding fears and hopes, illness and healing, life and death, religion and society. Together with three other scholars whose essays they commissioned, the curators have also created this catalogue. Working as a team, professors Bailey, Worcester, Mormando, and Jones began work on the exhibition in 2001, and they have succeeded masterfully in carrying it through to fruition.

Michael McFarland, S.J.
President, College of the Holy Cross

John Bassett
President, Clark University

Introduction: Response to the Plague in Early Modern Italy: What the Primary Sources, Printed and Painted, Reveal

Franco Mormando

> "Will you believe such things, oh posterity, when we ourselves who see them can scarcely believe them and would consider them dreams except that we perceive them awake and with our eyes open and that after viewing a city full of funerals we return to our homes only to find them empty of our loved ones?"
>
> Francesco Petrarca, *Rerum familiarum libri,* VIII:7, Letter to His "Socrates" on the Black Death[1]

1. *Plague and Art: The Subject of this Exhibition*

Dateline, New York City, Thursday, 7 November, 2002: "A 53-year-old New Mexico man was in critical condition last night at Beth Israel Medical Center with bubonic plague, the rare and deadly disease that once decimated Europe, health officials said. His wife, a 47-year-old woman, remains under observation at Beth Israel as tests for the disease are conducted." This report from the *New York Times,*[2] repeated in newspapers across the country, took many Americans by surprise: bubonic plague, in their minds, had been relegated to the realm of the remote past and of the almost-legendary. In fact, this ancient enemy, the scourge of Europe for more than three hundred years, has never been completely wiped from the face of the earth. Nowadays, thanks to antibiotics, wonder drugs unavailable to medieval and early modern Europeans, bubonic plague is easily treated and no longer a grave public health threat.

Yet, even with the availability of modern wonder drugs, human society remains to this day threatened by other forms of deadly, contagious disease for which there exists no effective "silver bullet" treatment. In the closing decades of the twentieth century and in the dawn of the twenty-first, several other new "plagues" haunt us: AIDS, Ebola, Hanta, West Nile, "Mad Cow," and SARS. Fortunately, with the sad exception of AIDS, these are diseases we have thus far, through great and anxious effort, managed to contain. Then, in the wake of September 11, 2001, there came the terrifying specter of terrorist-disseminated plagues, most notably anthrax and smallpox. For months this threat kept the American population in a state of anxiety, if not near panic.[3] This nightmarish collective experience of impending doom and helplessness in the shadow of an unseen yet seemingly omnipresent biological enemy gave us our closest approximation to the psychological state of medieval and early modern Europeans who, from the mid-fourteenth to the early eighteenth centuries, lived through wave after wave of bubonic plague. For these nearly four centuries, the plague struck so often and in so many localities that when the inhabitants of any given town or city were not actually living through an active outbreak of plague, they were anxiously awaiting and preparing for its certain return, knowing that there was little they could do to protect themselves.

Hope and Healing takes as its central theme the response of the visual arts to this omnipresent fact of everyday European life – bubonic plague – focusing on Italy during the sixteenth, seventeenth, and eighteenth centuries. In this period, with its busy international ports of trade and other centers of commerce with the East, Italy fell victim to this scourge with extraordinary and devastating frequency. Not surprisingly, we find, in fact, that the plague, explicitly or implicitly, directly or indirectly, partially or entirely, informed and influenced a massive number of works of art produced in Italy in the course of these years. At the same time, as we shall see, many works of devotional art created with no intended reference to the plague, featuring certain traditionally depicted themes (such as the Lamentation over the Dead Christ or memento mori) inevitably acquired new plague-related resonances in the wake of the contagion. Yet despite the crucial importance of its theme in art, *Hope and Healing* represents the first major exhibition outside of Italy devoted to this endemic fact of daily, lived experience of early modern Europe.[4] Exploring the ways in which Italian society responded to this recurring, unpredictable disaster, *Hope and Healing* will illuminate a wide variety of aesthetic, social, and religious concerns that preoccupied artists, patrons, and the general population alike during the ages of the Renaissance and Baroque, and that found expression through art – indeed, helped to shape that art. Our exploration of these issues will be interdisciplinary: a wide variety of contemporary documents – including diaries, personal correspondence, medical and devotional treatises, chronicles and broadsides, poetry, sermons, chapbooks, and biblical commentary – will be examined to illuminate the paintings on display and the themes of the exhibition.

II. *The Role of Art in Times of Disaster*

Unlike the chroniclers (medical or otherwise) of the period, early modern painters did not primarily seek to document the gruesome effects of the contagion, its horror and destruction. This was deemed alien to the nature and purposes of what we now call "fine art." Rather, during these times of social crisis, the role of plague-related art – whether commissioned by confraternities, communes, or private citizens – was, above all, to be an instrument of healing and encouragement, a mirror and a channel of society's search for solace and cure from the heavens, that is, from God and the saints. While inevitably reflecting society's anxieties and sufferings in the face of the unconquerable scourge, art served to remind the viewer of the necessity, availability, and efficacy of the various "celestial cures" at their disposal, thus offering comfort and hope in times of despair.[5] Furthermore, specifically ex-voto works of plague art (e.g., cats. 7, 28, 36) rendered another form of comfort and hope, inasmuch as they represented for the faithful effective, oblational offerings to God or the saints. Let us note that even those works commissioned by civic authorities are explicitly religious in nature, the products of a society utterly defined by Roman Catholicism.[6]

Drawing from a wide reading of the abundant primary sources, this essay will look at early modern Italian beliefs surrounding the nature and cause of the plague and examine the varied, pro-active measures recommended by civil, medical, and ecclesiastical authorities in the face of the plague or threat thereof. In contemporary parlance, these measures were called "*rimedi*" (remedies) and we find them repeatedly described in the most widely disseminated, influential primary sources in print. Plague *rimedi* fall into two categories: "temporal" or "human" remedies (*rimedi temporali, umani*), that is, medical-social-political measures taken to contain the epidemic, and "spiritual remedies" (*rimedi spirituali*), those enunciated and mandated by the Church. Among the latter were special prayer to Christ, the Virgin Mary, and other heavenly intercessors and protectors against plague; confession and public penitential processions; fasting; almsgiving and other acts of charity (the traditional "corporal works of mercy"); and prayerful meditation upon the inevitability and omnipresence of death and the vanity of this world as well as reward and punishment in the next life. All of these *rimedi spirituali*, in turn, we find depicted or alluded to in many of the plague-related images produced in the period for, again, such was the role of art in time of plague, to remind viewers of these efficacious ecclesiastical *rimedi* at their disposal.

Scholarship on the plague has been largely epidemiological or sociological in nature, focused primarily on temporal remedies, that is, public health measures (quarantine, sanitation, hospitals, law enforcement, etc.) and political-economic consequences of the pandemics. This in spite of the fact that there was virtual unanimous agreement among early modern Italians that the only really effective remedies were spiritual. These spiritual remedies have received far less attention in modern scholarship than they receive in the primary sources, printed and painted. This essay – and indeed this catalogue and the exhibition – strives to correct the balance by focusing on the *rimedi spirituali* considered central in the sixteenth, seventeenth, and eighteenth centuries.

III. *Terminology, Symptomatology, and Diagnostic Quandaries*

Before we look at the specific content of the primary sources at our disposal, the "remedies" they advise, and the reflection of these remedies in art, some preliminary historical and medical data will be useful. First among them is the issue of terminology. The plague-related primary sources produced in early modern Italy simply refer to bubonic plague as *peste* or *pestilenza* (in Latin, *pestis* or *pestilentia* and, occasionally, *lues*), "plague" or "pestilence," without any qualifying adjective, bubonic (*bubbonica*) or other. We cannot be certain that the calamitous disease that contemporary writers call *peste* or *pestilenza* (or their Latin equivalents) was in reality bubonic plague. Early modern usage of the two terms is characterized by a widespread and constant ambiguity.[7] This ambiguity, in turn, derives from two factors. The first is the tendency in these centuries to refer to *any* extremely contagious epidemic disease resulting in high mortality as "*the* plague" or "*the* pestilence" – and not, simply and figuratively, as "*a* plague" or "*a* pestilence," with the implication then being that the real "plague," properly and strictly speaking, is specifically the bubonic plague.

In this usage, however, early modern Italians were simply emulating the example of the great ancient Greek medical authority, Galen, and in our own speech today we find the same terminological phenomenon.[8] A virulent epidemic disease in early modern Italy can be labeled "the plague," even in the absence of the most characteristic symptoms of bubonic plague, the buboes, described below. (Yet, at the same time, as we shall see, not every form of bubonic plague produces buboes and not every disease producing buboes is bubonic plague.) In many cases it is now suspected that the disease described is likely to have been either of the two other principal biological killers of these centuries, typhus and typhoid fever, identified as one disease in early modern Italy called *tifo*.[9] Whether or not the disease in any given image or text is indeed bubonic plague, the fact is that the various beliefs surrounding any virulently epidemic disease and the varied responses to it on the part of early modern Italians remained the very same.

The second reason for the uncertainty we face in interpreting early modern descriptions of the plague is the medical establishment's inability to correctly diagnose bubonic plague on all occasions. Bubonic plague can manifest itself in three different forms, according to the mode of entry of the microbe into the body. Each form displays differing symptoms that both vary in severity and are common to other diseases. The most common form of bubonic plague is characterized by the formation of the so-called buboes (in Italian, *bubboni*). These are the often greatly swollen and agonizingly painful pus-filled lymph glands in the armpits, neck, and groin.[10] In the septicemic form of the disease (which occurs when the bacillus enters and rapidly multiplies directly in the bloodstream) and the pneumonic form (in which the airborne pathogen enters the body through the lungs, for example through the inhalation of infected sputum), the buboes do not have time to form since death is these cases can occur within just a day or two. Furthermore, even within the same form of the plague, as George Deaux points out, "[t]he illness varies greatly among individuals and all degrees of severity have been observed, from a mild indisposition which may hardly be noticed to extreme violence equaled only by fulminating cholera." The account of the 1656 Roman plague epidemic included in Jesuit cardinal and historian Sforza Pallavicino's *Vita di Alessandro VII* underscores this fact as one of the "five indisputable truths" concerning this most confounding of medical conditions.[11]

In the face of this bewildering multiplicity of symptoms, early modern doctors lived in a chronic state of diagnostic perplexity, even after centuries of medical experience, treatment, and technical description of the plague. As Giovanni Targioni Tozzetti points out in the survey of plague treatises included in his 1750 work on the "progress of the physical sciences" in seventeenth-century Tuscany: "It is well known from the history books that the Lord God, desiring to punish a population with the scourge of plague, permitted on certain occasions that the most accredited doctors, endowed with great learning and experience, were shamefully deceived in diagnosing the disease and did not recognize it for what it was, and thus, when consulted by government officials, dissuaded the latter from taking the necessary precautionary measures."[12] Such was the case in Rome 1656 at the beginning of the contagion: Sforza Pallavicino reports that the 1656 calamity could have been avoided had there been greater diagnostic expertise on the part of the doctor from the Ospedale di San Giovanni assigned to examine the body of a Neapolitan fisherman who, according to other eyewitnesses, had died with all of the "*rei signali*," sinister signs, of plague.[13]

However, there may have been another reason for such hesitation on the part of both doctors and government officials in acknowledging initial cases of the plague: fear of the disastrous economic consequences that would inescapably follow such an official pronouncement. In the ensuing wide-scale quarantine and prohibition of commerce necessary to contain the disease, the economies of entire towns and regions came to a crashing halt.[14] To the horror of the contagion or threat thereof was thus added the misery of unemployment, food rationing, and general scarcity of goods and services. Hence, one could understand the reluctance to sound the plague alarm until greater certainty about its actual presence was obtained. But, by then, it was tragically too late.

IV. *Plague Statistics: Chronology, Historical Memory, Mortality*

Human misjudgment often rendered impossible what was already a Herculean task, given the state of health, hygiene, and civic institutions in the era: the prevention or effective containment of a plague epidemic. With regard to both the frequency of the outbreaks and subsequent mortality, the statistics emanating from early modern Italy are indeed grim. In their accounts of plague incidence in sixteenth- and seventeenth-century Italy, many modern studies simply refer to the epidemics of 1575, 1630, and 1656, but these were merely the most virulent and widespread among the scores of outbreaks that occurred in those centuries, and even these three pandemics lasted in most localities far more than one calendar year. Biraben, Corradi, and Del Panta all offer statistics on the chronology and location of specific outbreaks in Italy for our period and beyond, the most extensive list being that of Corradi.[15] In view of such statistics, again, it is no exaggeration to claim that when early modern Italians were not actually living through an active outbreak of plague, they were anxiously awaiting its all-too-likely return. During the sixteenth century and for three quarters of the seventeenth, there was hardly a significant period during which the peninsula was completely free of plague.

Even when early modern Italians might be medically free of plague, psychologically they were certainly never free from its grip.

Geographical distance, furthermore, was only of small comfort: knowing how porous was the blanket of protection between them and plague and how rapid the disease's migration, the Genoese or Bolognese, for example, would have had every reason to begin to tremble when they heard of pestilence even in far-off Palermo. Early modern Italians were well aware of the peninsula's exceptional susceptibility to the plague, a susceptibility which they believed (erroneously) to be greater than that of all other localities on the European continent. Girolamo Gastaldi (d. 1685), Alexander VII's Commissioner of Health during the Roman outbreak of 1656, attributes the greater incidence of contagion in his homeland to the peculiarities of the Italian climate as well as the peninsula's easy access to foreigners by land and by sea.[16] In fact, the contagion came to Italy most frequently from abroad, often from the Levant with which the various Italian port cities, especially Venice, engaged in extensive trade.

Commissioner Gastaldi further claims that of all localities in Italy, the city of Rome was "the most frequently infected," basing this judgment on the accumulated data concerning the dates and locations of outbreaks in the Western world, drawn from a wide variety of ancient and modern authorities.[17] Beginning with the year 2443 B.C. with the plagues of Egypt and Ethiopia and ending with his own lifetime, Gastaldi's extensive list is not unique among plague treatises of the late sixteenth and seventeenth centuries.[18] Some authors enter into further discussion of the specifics of individual outbreaks, most especially the famous plague of 431 B.C. in Athens described by Thucydides in Book Two of his *History of the Peloponnesian War*, an account that had great and lasting influence on painted depictions of plague in Italy.[19] At least one source, the *Discorso di peste* of Andrea Gratiolo (Graziali) di Salò (Venice, 1576) even advertises in its title the fact that his work specifically contains a "catalogue of all the most notable plagues from times past," along with its "most useful speculations regarding the nature, causes and cures of the plague."

The prominence given to the inclusion of such chronological lists and the frequency with which one encounters them in our primary sources – especially in those treatises that simply include them with no further reference thereunto or processing of the data therein – causes us to wonder about their ultimate purpose. Historical curiosity and conscientiousness are no doubt part of the explanation, but I suspect there are further, perhaps psychological, factors. Did it give comfort to contemporary readers who were either living through another deadly outbreak or contemplating its imminent return to know that their suffering was not unique? As these lists demonstrated, in all parts of the globe, humankind had been visited throughout history by this dreadful affliction, which, however terrifying and lethal, had never succeeded in extinguishing human society. Despite the slaughter, life and civil order endured.

Returning to the outbreaks specifically of early modern Italy, as far as the actual number of deaths is concerned, accurate statistics are hard to come by. Suffice it to say that the population loss was frequently, as the Italians say, "*di proporzioni bibliche*," that is, apocalyptically catastrophic, even though the specific figures offered by contemporaries are impressionistic and usually the result of hearsay. We do know that the city hardest hit was Naples.[20] The learned Jesuit polymath Athanasius Kircher (1602-80) tells us that 300,000 Neapolitans died within a five-month period during the height of the 1656 outbreak in that city.[21] The plague had beset the city for a much longer period, and Kircher's estimation, like that of other contemporaries, may mistakenly include those who fled the city of their own accord. As Christopher Black reports, "[m]ore rational calculations suggest that the city's population in 1657-8 was two-fifths what it had been in 1654-5, with 240-270,000 persons out of 400-450,000 in Naples and its vicinity dying of plague and allied causes."[22] Genoa, during the same outbreak, lost about 90,000 of its citizens, diminishing in population from 440,000 to

350,000. Venice's population in 1624, before the pandemic of 1630, stood at 142,804, whereas at the time of the next accurate count in 1634, that is, post-plague, it had been reduced to 98,804.[23]

Having experienced brief outbreaks of the plague from 1524 through 1529, Rome escaped the great pandemic of 1630 unharmed. Furthermore, during the next pandemic, in 1656, thanks to the timely and stringent measures adopted by Pope Alexander VII, the Eternal City suffered a relatively low rate of mortality. Writing shortly after the plague had subsided, Gastaldi reports a loss of only 14,473 lives out of the little more than 100,000 residing in the city, whereas Pallavicino claims that figure to be less than 8,000. Modern estimations of Roman mortality in this outbreak place the loss of life at a higher rate, calculating 20,000 deaths out of a pre-plague population of 120,000. In reporting his mortality statistics, by the way, Cardinal Pallavicino adds, with a seeming air of satisfaction, the fact that "almost all of these deaths were from the ordinary masses, with few civil heads, and not one illustrious head, having been lost. One of those lost "civil heads," we might mention, was a brother of artist Gian Lorenzo Bernini, another of whose stricken brothers was, however, saved by ingesting, "con fede," the miraculous "bread (*pagnotella*) of Saint Nicholas of Tolentine."[24]

Florence escaped the plague of 1656 entirely, "partly through timely action of the secular authorities to block any commerce with the infected regions of Genoa and the South."[25] During the earlier pandemic of 1630, although struck by plague, the city was nonetheless fortunate, for the same reason of quick governmental response: the *virtù eroica* of Ferdinand II Grand Duke of Tuscany, together with *la Divina Pietà* and the Virgin Mary's "*pietosa intercessione*," is credited by eyewitness chronicler, Francesco Rondinelli (Ferdinand's librarian and "one of the most illustrious letterati of his age"),[26] with having spared the city from the catastrophic mortality rate experienced by other infected cities. Rondinelli reports a total of circa 12,000 deaths in 1630, with 1,600 to 1,800 additional ones in the re-visitation of the plague in 1633. The Florentine author's figures reflect modern calculations, which put the population loss at only 12 percent of about 76,000 souls. In comparison, during the same outbreak of 1630, Verona and Parma saw the disappearance of more than 50 percent of their populations, as did Milan whose population decreased from 130,000 to approximately 66,000. In Brescia, between 40 and 49 percent of the city was lost to the plague while in Venice, mortality amounted to about 33 percent.[27]

v. *The End of the Outbreaks and of a Medical Mystery*

The great pandemic of 1656-57 was the last virulent, widespread outbreak of plague on the Italian peninsula. Thereafter, only a few small, local, sporadic outbreaks are recorded.[28] The reasons for this abatement have never been identified with complete certainty, but it seems reasonable to conjecture that improved sanitary conditions, more efficient governmental vigilance, acquired immunity among surviving populations and their offspring, and the lessened virulence of the pathogen itself all contributed to the phenomenon. Late seventeenth- and eighteenth-century contemporaries, of course, had no way of knowing that they were now living in the post-plague era: the shadow of that great invisible enemy still hung over them. Fear was readily renewed whenever reports of plague came from abroad: for instance, in the second decade of the eighteenth century, Lodovico Muratori (1672-1750), famed historian and librarian-archivist of the d'Este family in Modena, was moved to write one of the best-known plague treatises in Italy, *Del governo della peste*, and thus prepare authorities for the contagion that had struck beyond the Alps:

> Great apprehension and fear, o most illustrious Lord Conservators of the city and health of Modena, if we want to confess it openly, was provoked in us last year, in 1714 by rumors of plague. After it had penetrated into Austria from Hungary, striking Prague, Ratisbon [i.e., Regensburg, Bavaria], and other cities, and after at the same time, another plague – a different one, I believe – awoke in Hamburg, this horrendous disease, causing wretched slaughter among these peoples, also wrought sheer terror in all neighboring areas. The less courageous souls already imagined it advancing through the regions of Italy and began to make plans for escaping it. ...[29]

Muratori goes on to report that Rondinelli's *Relazione del contagio stato in Firenze l'anno 1630 et 1633*, was being republished "since lately it was noticed that it strangely had become rare and the authorities wanted to better prepare for the future."[30] This better preparation was rewarded and Italy lived through those years with no major harm from plague, as it did during the very last great outbreak in Europe, which assailed Marseille and environs in 1720-22. Nonetheless, the threat was still felt beyond that date: in 1740 we find the Jesuit Athanasius Kircher's plague treatise, the *Scrutinium physico-medicum contagiosae luis quae dicitur pestis* (first edition, Rome 1658) being reprinted yet again, this time in Graz, Austria.[31]

Although, after a nearly four-hundred-year reign, bubonic plague, for all intents and purposes, disappeared from Western Europe after 1722, the biological nature of the contagion and the mechanism of its transmission would continue to remain medical mysteries for more than a century and a half. In 1894, in the wake of the new germ theory of disease (thanks to the work of Pasteur, Lister, and Koch), young Swiss medical student Alexandre Yersin identified in Hong Kong the pathogen responsible for bubonic plague, a bacillus he named *Pasteurella pestis* (renamed in 1970 *Yersinia pestis*). Shortly thereafter, in 1897, another vital piece of the puzzle was solved with the discovery that bubonic plague, primarily a disease of rodents (and, most notoriously, rats) was transmitted to humans by the bite of fleas escaping from the corpses of their dead rodent hosts.[32] Always in great abundance and in intimate proximity to human beings in early modern Italy, neither fleas nor rats were ever seen as suspects in the outbreaks of plague. Rats are included in Poussin's *Plague at Ashdod* and Caroselli's copy thereof (cat. 1) because of their mention in the biblical story upon which the paintings are based, but neither the biblical author nor the artists understood the connection between plague and rodents.

One person in early modern Italy did effectively anticipate Pasteur's germ theory by three hundred years, Gerolamo Fracastoro of Verona (1478-1553), the "founder of modern pathology." In his *De contagione et de contagiosis morbis et curatione* (Venice, 1546), Fracastoro hypothesized that the contagion was actually disseminated by an invisible living agent, which he called *virus*. Later, thanks to the seventeenth-century development of the microscope, what was formerly invisible became visible. The ingenious, if at times fanciful, scientist Kircher took up Fracastoro's intuition and with his new lenses discovered the strange, unimagined world of microscopic organisms (which he called *corpuscula minima* and *seminaria*), multiplying rapidly in organic liquid material taken from plague victims: "so tiny, so slender and subtle, that they elude the senses' every power of comprehension."[33] According to Kircher, these organisms (which he also called *vermicula* "worms," because of their wiggling movement and shapes) were the true source of plague. What Kircher saw under his microscope – no one is quite sure to what specific organisms he is referring – was not the source of the contagion, that is, the bacterium *Yersinia pestis*, which would remain elusive to scientific eyes until 1894. Nonetheless, Kircher had identified the only proper, efficacious avenue for further research into the disease's etiology.

VI. *Causes of Plague and Its Transmission: Early Modern Scientific Explanations*

Unfortunately, no one pursued Kircher's indications and the traditional explanations of the cause of the plague and its diffusion continued to prevail. In the absence of knowledge of the germ theory of disease and of the existence of the pathogen *Yersinia pestis* and its passage from rodent to human via fleas, what then did the early modern Italian believe about the etiology and dissemination of "this most deceiving contagious serpent" (as one seventeenth-century author calls the disease)?[34] Early modern society still clung to explanations formulated, centuries before, by the ancients: simply stated, the plague, along with numerous other diseases, was caused and spread by "corrupt air." The famous "miasma theory of disease" was first expressed in the ancient Greek medical text, *On Airs, Waters, and Places,* by Hippocrates (ca. 460-377 B.C.), who posited excessive humidity as a cause of disease-bearing miasma. Important elaborations by Galen (ca. A.D. 130-200) and Avicenna (A.D. 980-1037) added the putrefaction of organic materials and the escape of underground gases, respectively, as contributing factors.[35]

Thus, much attention in early modern Italy was devoted to ever-changing meteorological conditions in an attempt to predict and prepare for the arrival of plague. At the same time, early modern scientists taught – and the masses of people accepted the teaching – that astrological factors also played an important role in generating this scourge. In an age when everyone, from pope to peasant, sincerely believed in the direct influence of the stars and planets on human health and destiny, "evil conjunctions" of planets were commonly accepted as further generators of miasma, with certain astronomical phenomena, such as comets and falling stars, readily interpreted as presages of earthly calamity, especially pestilential epidemics. Furthermore, once plague had arrived in a locality, it was widely believed – and seemingly confirmed by daily experience – that the mechanisms and vehicles of transmission available to the contagion were frighteningly numerous: not only by touch, but also by breath; indeed, by hearing, sight, imagination, and fear as well, not to mention by deliberate spreading on the part of evil men, a fact acknowledged, for example, by both the already-cited Gastaldi and his younger contemporary, Filiberto Marchini (see Section VII below).[36] As Neapolitan Jesuit poet Giacomo Lubrano (1619-1693) laments in one of his eloquent grief-filled compositions, even the medicines offered to cure the plague could be responsible for its dissemination since they themselves were so easily infected by the mere breath of the already stricken.[37]

Perhaps frustrated by the incapacity of the medical establishment to identify effective remedies, some early modern Italians were not at all satisfied with the official etiological explanations offered by scientific textbooks. Thus, Bolognese medical doctor and professor of science, Giovanni Antonio Bumaldi (alias of Ovidio Montalbani, 1601-1671) begins his 1656 treatise, the *Pestifugo esculapio,* impatiently proclaiming that he will not even bother to enter into a discussion of the causes of the plague because it is simply a waste of time. Even Roman Commissioner of Health Gastaldi admits that "there is nothing that taxes the minds of doctors more than this topic" – the causes of the plague – a further indication that even the medical establishment was dissatisfied with its own received wisdom.[38] However, let us note, the medical-scientific community was simply attempting to pinpoint what they called the "natural causes" of the plague. As we shall see, most everyone in early modern Italy, scientist and layperson alike, acknowledged that the ultimate, the "real" cause of the plague, its Aristotelian "*causa finalis*" (as Gastaldi terms it),[39] was to be found not on the natural or physical plane, but rather on the spiritual: it was a response of God himself to the wickedness of humanity.

We have spoken of the difficulty that medical personnel faced in recognizing bubonic plague in their patients because of the confusing multiplicity of its symptoms. But what about artists? How did they convey the presence of bubonic plague to the viewers of their canvases? The most characteristic visual cues indicating the presence of bubonic plague are the buboes, located either in the groin, neck, or armpits of the victims. In early modern Italian art, decorum dictated that groin buboes be shown instead on the upper thigh, as in many a representation of Saint Roch. More frequently, explicit representation of the buboes was avoided altogether. Artists resorted to a more discrete visual allusion to the buboes, one that was readily understood by their contemporaries, namely, "the gesture of exposing the underarm region ... to the gaze of attendants,"[40] as we see in Tintoretto's *Saint Roch Ministering to the Plague Victims* (1549, church of S. Rocco) or Luca Ferrari's *Saint Dominic Interceding with the Virgin for the Liberation of Padua from the Plague* (1630s, Cassa di Risparmio di Padova e Rovigo).[41]

Plague scenes in art also invariably show figures holding their noses closed with their fingers in an attempt to protect themselves from the horrible stench emanating from the pus-filled bodies of the dead and the dying. This is the second most common visual cue given by artists to indicate the presence of bubonic plague and indeed the horrible stench is one of the most common features of the disease described in the printed sources. Seventeenth-century Roman doctor Giovanni Pressi, who served in two of the city's lazarettos (plague hospitals) during the 1656 outbreak, for instance, reports that the stench given off by the dead body of "that father confessor from San Lorenzo lingered in the air for three days so that any of us who encountered it ... almost fell in a dead faint because of it."[42] Stench was also caused by the corpses of the many unburied victims: these were left to decay wherever they happened to fall since personnel was in woefully short supply to attend to their proper burial, "so that the stench of the dead kills the living," as Giovanni Baldinucci (1577-1656), an eyewitness to the 1630 pandemic in Florence, writes in his diary.[43] Since stench was considered a sign of the "corrupt air" believed to be the origin of plague and most other disease, eliminating the stench by burying dead bodies was of utmost importance. This, together with Christian charity and respect for the earthly remains of a human being, the temporary dwelling place of the soul, accounts for the great emphasis in this period on the corporal work of mercy of "burying the dead," as we shall see among the *rimedi spirituali* depicted in art and exhorted in the printed sources.

Another sign of the plague repeatedly mentioned in the primary sources is the darkening of the body of the victim, a condition that we now know to be caused by widespread subcutaneous hemorrhaging brought on by the infection. We turn again to our Roman doctor Pressi, who reports, for example, that the cadaver of one of his patients, a fifty-year-old friar from San Grisogono "turned horridly black, swollen, and foul-smelling."[44] Aesthetic and moral decorum prevented painters from repugnantly accurate depictions of this blackening of the body; instead, they showed victims' bodies in a state of grayish pallor, such as that of young woman held in the arms of (presumably) her husband at the extreme left of Pietro Bernardi's *Saint Carlo Borromeo Praying Among the Plague Victims* (1610s, Verona, church of S. Carlo).[45] Knowing this, we wonder: did Nicolas Poussin wish to refer, indirectly but explicitly, to the bubonic plague by means of the exceedingly blackened body of the dead Christ in his *Lamentation*, a canvas executed in Rome right in the midst of, or immediately after, the great pandemic of 1656-57? Even if this were not the case (the current state of Christ's body in the canvas could be simply the result of oxidation), given the years in which the painting was completed, it is hard to imagine that the plague could have absent from the mind of the artist or of contemporary viewers. How could this wrenchingly pathetic scene of death and mourning not vividly recall for them the horrors of the plague? How, furthermore, could they not see in it a reflection of their own grief and suffering caused by the plague surrounding them on every side? As is well known, Christians traditionally used scenes of the Passion of Christ precisely in this cathartic, vicarious way: as a mirror of their own personal suffering and as a vehicle for the expression of their own private grief. Francesco Cozza's *Pietà* (Rome, Galleria Nazionale d'Arte Antica, Palazzo Corsini), for example, a painting done in Rome in the same period as the Poussin *Lamentation*, was commissioned by Carlo Antonio dal Pozzo in memory of his older brother, Cassiano, who died in October, 1657.[46]

Of the several other medical manifestations of plague infection – exceedingly high fever, skin rash, delirium, great thirst, headache, vomiting, and utter prostration – only the last sign, the extreme lassitude brought upon its victims, is generally rendered explicit in art. Plague scenes will almost always include a large grouping of men, women, and children with no apparent signs of contagion visible in or on them except their deathly prostrate or otherwise dazed, languishing condition (cats. 1, 2, 5, 6, 25). However, in the absence of actual plague victims within a scene, other, non-medical cues alert the viewer either to the presence of plague within a canvas or to the relevance, direct or indirect, of that disease to the painting. These include arrows, swords, and lances (symbols of divine wrath being vented through plague); dark clouds (a reference to the miasma, corrupt-air theory of plague causation, which may perhaps explain their conspicuous presence in Carlevarijs's *Feast of S. Maria della Salute* [cat. 33]); astronomical or astrological signs and symbols (stars and planets, as already mentioned, considered either causes of the plague or omens of its imminent arrival, such as the comet in Raphael's *Madonna of Foligno*); and an angel holding a flagellum or scourge, symbol par excellence of the plague.[47] Finally, there are, of course, the many plague saints – heavenly intercessors and protectors against the contagion – to also serve as visual clues.

Contemporary viewers would have readily recognized all of these visual cues, whereas we may overlook the significance of some of the more subtle among them. Hence, we may fail to recognize the relevance of the plague to the subject and meaning of a canvas. For example, nothing is known of the provenance of Tintoretto's recently rediscovered *Raising of Lazarus* (cat. 37), which, for stylistic reasons, scholars have dated to the years 1556-57.[48] There is every reason to suspect that this devotional work (whose size suggests a private residence as its original intended destination) may have in fact been an ex-voto in time of plague. To be sure, the raising of Lazarus from the dead – the most spectacular of Jesus's miracles – was one of the most popular subjects in Christian art from the catacombs onward, reminding Christian viewers of the promise of resurrection after their own death. However, this specific subject would have had greater appeal in time of plague, not only for its generic reminder of the Christian belief in the universal resurrection of the saved souls, but also because of its central character, the young *miracolato*, Lazarus. Unbeknownst to many viewers today, "Saint Lazarus" was in fact a plague saint: beginning in the eleventh century this New Testament figure acquired a new role as heavenly protector against leprosy and the plague, thanks to the medieval melding of the identity of the sore-covered beggar of that same name in Jesus's parable recounted in Luke 16:19-31 with that of the brother of Martha and Mary, raised from the dead as recounted in John 11 and depicted in Tintoretto's canvas. Visual cues serve to reinforce the association between this painting and the plague. Despite the absence here of blemishes of any sort, the languishing state of body of Lazarus would have called to mind the prostrate posture of plague victims as depicted in many other works of plague art. An even more vivid reminder of the plague, however, would have been the eyewitnesses in the background holding clothes to their noses in an attempt to protect themselves from the expected stench emanating from Lazarus's body. The years in which this painting is believed to have been executed, 1556-57, coincide precisely with another outbreak of the plague. Although not as deadly as those of 1575-77 or 1630, this mid-century epidemic nonetheless claimed thousands of victims in the artist's hometown, Venice.

Saint Michael the Archangel, Plague Icon

Giovanni Battista Moroni's *Two Donors in Adoration before the Madonna with the Child and Saint Michael* (cat. 21) presents a similar situation. Nothing is known of the earliest history of this work, except for its origins in the north-Italian town of Brescia. Although perhaps not the *podestà* of Brescia and his wife, as a nineteenth-century British exhibition catalogue identified them,[49] the two sitters are nonetheless edifying models of Christian piety: by their (painted) example they encourage the viewer to emulate their devotion to the Madonna, the Christ Child, and Saint Michael the Archangel. The sitters' austere black clothing (characteristic of the Hispanizing tastes of Counter-Reformation Lombardy) and Saint Michael's scales (with which to "weigh" the relative virtue and vice of each soul at the hour of judgment) suggest that the painting is an invitation to meditate upon the inevitability of death and the eternal fate of one's soul. However, looking at this canvas through plague "lenses," we wonder if indeed we may have before us another ex-voto piece commissioned in time of contagion.

To begin with, Mina Gregori's generally accepted dating of the work to 1557-60 corresponds to the later phase or immediate aftermath of the outbreak of the plague just mentioned in connection with the Tintoretto canvas. Apart from this chronological fact, there are visual clues as well, the most compelling of which is the presence of Saint Michael the Archangel. Though, of course, there could be other reasons for his inclusion – for instance, he may be the "name saint" of the male donor – we find Saint Michael most often performing two specific symbolic roles in the art of our period: that of a militant icon of the Catholic Church's struggle against Protestantism and other external enemies – not likely a relevant issue in what would appear to be a domestic devotional canvas – and that of a plague icon, either in his role as unleasher of God's punishing scourge or as beneficent protector. This well-documented connection between Michael and the plague has its ultimate foundation in the Book of Revelation. Revelation, the final book of the New Testament, describes the Apocalypse, the end times of humanity and the final cosmic struggle between good and evil, in which Michael plays an important role as agent of God's revenge and justice and as conqueror of the "ancient serpent," Satan (Revelation 12:7). These end times, the text specifies, will be marked by the slaughter of a fourth of the earth "with sword, famine, and pestilence" (Revelation 6:8) – hence the apocalyptic associations that plague has always had in the imagination of Christian Europe since the Middle Ages. Although Revelation does not identify the sword-bearing soldier of God, Saint Michael, as deliverer specifically of the plague, his overall role as dispenser of God's vengeance and agent of God's will in this cosmic struggle makes the association between the archangel and pestilence natural, if not, indeed, inevitable.[50]

A more specific association between the archangel and plague dates to a sixth-century outbreak in Rome: on that occasion, as we see in a canvas by Jacopo Zucchi (ca. 1540-96) now in the Vatican Pinacoteca. The severity of the contagion induced the pope himself, Gregory the Great, to lead a penitential procession through the streets of Rome, bearing one of the city's miraculous ancient icons, housed in the basilica of S. Maria Maggiore, of the Madonna and Child – who, let us note, are also present in the Moroni canvas. When the procession reached the precincts of Hadrian's Tomb, Saint Michael suddenly appeared atop the monument, seen in the act of replacing his sword in its sheath – a further attribute present in Moroni's *Two Donors in Adoration* – signifying the appeasement of God's wrath and the end of the scourge. In gratitude for this miraculous deliverance, the ancient monument was renamed

"Castel Sant'Angelo" and eventually a statue of Saint Michael, with sword in hand, was placed at its summit. Recounted in that medieval best-seller, Jacopo da Voragine's *Golden Legend*, this tale firmly established Michael as plague icon in all of Western Christendom.[51] We find him, for example, occupying the front center position on the elaborately ornate title page of *Belli divini* (Florence, 1633), a major early modern Italian plague text rich with historical, theological, canonical, and medical information by the Barnabite theologian, Filiberto Marchini (1586-1636).

Returning to the Moroni canvas, we find another detail that may have been evocative of the plague to its original viewers, the gray clouds filling the upper portion of the canvas. As we have already seen, in plague-related paintings dark, thick, gray clouds can often function as a visual cue, reminding the viewer of the then universally accepted "miasma" (corrupted air) theory of plague etiology. Even though in the present canvas, it is most likely that the clouds serve simply as a partition between the heavenly and earthly realms and as a platform for the saintly personages, it is not unreasonable to imagine their serving also, if only unintentionally, as reminder to the viewer of the plague and its cause. Now, to be sure, taken alone, the presence of gray clouds or any single piece of evidence, chronological or visual, is not sufficient to identify a canvas as a plague ex-voto, but taken all together, as we here find, the evidence is indeed compelling. Thus, the somber black clothing worn by Moroni's two sitters may not be merely an example of Hispanizing austerity of fashion, but rather an expression of mourning after the recent outbreak in the town from which the two grateful donors escaped through the intersession of Mary, Jesus, and Saint Michael the Archangel. Even if not specifically a plague ex-voto, the artist's, the sitters' and the original viewers' all-too-proximate experience of massive contagion-caused mortality would have rendered the scene's implied invitation to a pious meditation on death and judgment all the more urgent.

Sweerts's Plague in an Ancient City: *Deciphering the Enigma*

Plague in an Ancient City (cat. 6) by Michael Sweerts, painted in Rome ca. 1650, presents a more difficult hermeneutical problem: there is no doubt at all that what we have before us is a scene of plague, but is it an actual historical plague?[52] If so, which one and to what purpose is it here depicted? Unfortunately, nothing certain is known of the provenance of the work before its arrival in England in the early nineteenth century. The most ambitious canvas of Sweerts's entire production, its debt to Nicolas Poussin's celebrated *Plague at Ashdod* (1630, Louvre) is clear and has been frequently discussed.[53]

But what is its subject? As late as 1984 when on the London art market, the painting was thought to depict the fifth-century B.C. Athenian plague described at length by ancient Greek historian, Thucydides, in Book Two of his *Peloponnesian War*. However, when we compare carefully text and canvas, we find that, despite the painting's classical setting, the similarities are, in the end, too few to make a convincing argument. Furthermore, there is much taking place within Sweerts's scene that the Greek text is simply incapable of explaining. Indeed, no compelling match can be made between this painted scene and any of the more famous written accounts of plague outbreak, be they classical, biblical, or early Christian. In recent years, scholars have uncovered much new information about Sweerts's life and work, filling many a lacuna in our knowledge of his biography and artistic production. Alas, none of it has brought us any closer to deciphering the enigma of this canvas's subject and, hence, its intended message. All that commentators have been able to say with confidence about its subject is what the painting's current title declares: we are witnessing a scene of an outbreak of plague in a city of ancient times. Some have speculated that the artist may be using a generic classical scene to depict and comment upon a contemporary Italian plague, most obviously, that which struck Rome in 1648-50. Others are of the opinion that Sweerts's *Plague in an Ancient City* is not "in any way a documentary work: rather a meditation on the disease's effects on mankind assuaging its horrors through art."[54]

These two theories do not take into consideration the various, specific, and puzzling elements that Sweerts – a serious, learned artist working in lofty ecclesiastical and intellectual circles – has deliberately chosen to include. These features are not simply borrowed from conventional plague iconography and used merely to fill the stage with visually interesting but fundamentally insignificant, generic ornamentation. Rather, they seem to work in express concert to evoke a distinct historical episode, moment, or situation and thus communicate a specific message.

The canvas is divided into two distinct and, apparently, opposing sectors, each of which features a man-made structure of contrasting architectural form and physical condition. On the left, we see what we can, for convenience's sake, call the "Black Temple," dark, gloomy, and time-worn, and on the right (and more "noble") side of the canvas, the luminous and fully intact, if only partially visible, "White Temple." The dramatic chiaroscuro emphasizes this contrast and opposition between the two structures: moving from left to right, from Black to White Temple, we progress from deep darkness to full light. The strong diagonal crossing the canvas from the lower left to the upper right emphasizes the division.

The second distinguishing feature of Sweerts's canvas is the presence of the three gesturing, attention-focusing figures. Prominently positioned close to the very physical center of the canvas, we see an elderly, bearded, distinguished male figure in a brilliant blue toga. This standing male figure – let us call him the "Blue Prophet" – points downward with his left hand to one of the dead women at his feet, while his right hand points to the White Temple. On the steps before that temple stands another solemn male figure – we shall call him the "White Prophet" – shrouded, head and all, in a voluminous, radiant white garment, who points in the same direction as his counterpart in blue. This same gesture is repeated by yet a third figure, located farther in the background (just left of center and closer to the obelisk), a female dressed in white, with covered head, only sketchily rendered but clearly and deliberately singled out by the light. These three figures all focus our attention on the White Temple and what it contains or represents. The distinctive "orans" (raised, extended hands) prayer pose of two of the figures before the temple suggests that it is a Christian church. In historically conscious seventeenth-century Rome, learned artists and learned viewers would have known that this, the "orans" form of prayer, was a defining feature of early Christian worship.[55]

The third notable feature of the canvas concerns the "sun-worshipers" and the obelisk. Scattered in the middle- and backgrounds, especially left and center, we see numerous figures facing and intently gazing at the sun. In the center of the piazza in which many of them stand or sit rises conspicuously an Egyptian obelisk. As Sweerts and his contemporaries in Rome all knew, thanks to the abundant archeological studies published in the late sixteenth and seventeenth centuries, the ancient obelisk was a religious icon, a public structure erected in honor of the Sun God, whose beneficent, omnipresent rays the monolith's very form was meant to represent. This was true not only for their makers, the Egyptians, but also the ancient Romans who transported several of these granite monuments to their capital city.[56] Given the presence of this conspicuous symbol and the demeanor of the sun-fixated figures, I believe it is safe to conclude that the men and women are actively worshiping the sun (probably at dawn, as was conventional in ancient pagan religion), and not mere passively looking in its direction. Some of the same men and women, it would appear, are also processing into the Black Temple, suggesting it is connected to their form of religiosity.

It would be easy to jump to the conclusion that what we are witnessing within the Black Temple are funeral rites for victims of the plague. However, given the acute fear of contagion, plague victims in actual ancient and early modern practice were simply not given this sort of formal, ritualized burial. The highly infectious cadavers of the disease's victims were never paraded around in public, especially in the presence of large gatherings of people, much less in such close confined spaces as the interior of the Black Temple. Moreover, even if all fear and caution had somehow been miraculously overcome, in the midst of a virulent outbreak of deadly plague such as we see outside the Black Temple, hundreds of men, women, and children died on a daily basis: why then do we only see one litter here? Thus, if a burial is indeed taking place therein, it is, most likely, not of victims of the plague. Does the ritual, instead, somehow pertain to the sun-worshiping religion whose devotees we see outside the temple or processing into it?[57]

Let us note that at the apex of the interior ramp of the temple, there is an unseen room or other area from which rays of the sun are pouring forth into the darkness of the temple. Is this simply another exit leading out of the temple? If the latter is the case, then why is no one exiting from the lower right, piazza-side ramp of the temple? Even if the people on the ramp in the upper right are indeed simply exiting the temple, the fact they are exiting in the direction of the sun, and not away from it (i.e., onto the piazza below by means of the lower ramp) would seem to bear some significance.

Also relevant to the identification of the temple is its single and thus highly conspicuous decorative element, a caryatid, incorporated into the left arch, an architectural feature born in pagan antiquity and, in early modern Italy, bearing only and overtly pagan connotations. The subject of a famous digression in Vitruvius's *Ten Books on Architecture* (1:1), caryatids were standard ornamental features of the classicizing gardens of early modern Italian villas. Such gardens became popular in the sixteenth century, especially the rustic fountain grottoes thereof, built in imitation of ancient Roman nymphaea. Nymphaea in ancient lore were originally and literally "gardens of the Nymphs," dwelling places of the pagan female water deities. However, according to Oratorian archeologist Antonio Bosio in his monumental work of 1632, *Roma sotterranea*, the term "nymphaea" in both ancient pagan and early Christian usage came to mean simply places where fountains, streams, and other sources of water were present.[58] At the same time, as Andrea Palladio explains in his *Four Books on Architecture* (4:1), natural sites marked by the presence of fresh water sources were precisely the settings chosen by the ancients for the construction of temples dedicated to their gods of healing. Given all of the preceding visual evidence and historical information, it is reasonable to conclude (even though no sign of water is discernible therein) that the Black Temple is pagan in nature and probably has as its function the pursuit of healing. The pursuit of healing would not, of course, be at all surprising, given the massive presence of disease and death at the very doorstep of the temple. Furthermore, the temple's cavernous, rotund massive form bears a generic resemblance to a well-known ancient Roman monument, the Temple of Minerva Medica. The latter ruin, in Sweerts's day and for a long time thereafter, was believed to be pagan place of worship, due to the putative rediscovery there of the famous *Minerva Giustiniani* (now in the Vatican), an ancient statue of the goddess in her healing aspect, that is, holding in her hand a snake, the same attribute of the ancient god of healing, Aesculapius.[59]

In view of the highly specified features enumerated above, Sweerts's *Plague in an Ancient City*, I would maintain, is neither merely a generic "meditation on the disease's effects," nor a representation of a contemporary, recently experienced Roman plague disguised in more fashionable classical garb, nor an artistic exercise "simply painted to demonstrate his [technical] capabilities."[60] Sweerts, I believe, is here contrasting two religious responses to the plague: one pagan (the Black Temple, left); the other, Christian (the White Temple, right). If this hypothesis is correct and assuming that Sweerts has not dispensed completely with historical accuracy or verisimilitude, we must then ask the question: At what point in actual history did both religions, paganism and Christianity, exist, side by side, legally and freely practiced by their respective adherents? Paying close attention to the visual detail supplied by Sweerts, we must further refine the question to ask not only when the two religions co-existed, but also when Christianity, in fact, enjoyed a greater state of well-being (v. the fine, intact White Temple), while paganism had lapsed into a state of partial decay (v. the dilapidated conditions of the Black Temple). But, there is a further element to factor into our interrogation. We must also, and finally, ask: With these two just-described conditions obtaining, when did, furthermore, a violent plague strike the Roman Empire as well?

The only answer possible turns out to be: in the first half of the fourth century A.D., during the brief but memorable reign (361-63) of Emperor Julian, "the Apostate," enemy par excellence of the Christian faith. Although not one of the better-known plagues of western history, the Julian plague was duly reported by two much circulated texts in early modern Italy, Possevino's *Cause et rimedii della peste* (see Section IX below) and, Possevino's own source, the *Ecclesiastical History* of Nicephorus Callistus Xanthopoulus (ca. 1256-ca.1335), the latter textbook all but forgotten today but much consulted in early modern Europe.[61] But, why, in 1650, choose this particular episode from church history as subject for a painting? What relevance did it have for the contemporary state of religious affairs?

The ultimate aim of Sweerts's *Plague in an Ancient City*, I would suggest, is to celebrate Roman Catholicism as the "one, true faith" by recalling an episode of early Christian history, the reign of the "impious" emperor Julian, in which God responded to the persecution of his people by sending a castigating plague and other natural calamities (as well as by the premature, inglorious death of the young emperor). This was, in the eyes of apologists, a further example of the divine favor enjoyed by their faith. (The same apologetic message is also inherent in the most famous plague painting of seventeenth-century Rome, Poussin's *Plague at Ashdod*, a source of direct inspiration to Sweerts in the creation of the present canvas.)

In 1650, in the wake not only of yet another dreadful visitation of the plague in Rome, but also of the humiliating, massive defeat – political, religious, and economic – of the papacy and the entire Catholic Church in the form of the 1648 Peace of Westphalia, it is not difficult to see how reassuring such a message would have been to Catholics (especially the family of the reigning pope, Innocent X Pamphilij, for whom Sweerts was working while he was creating the present canvas). Indeed, as we shall see in Section IX, "heresy [i.e., Protestantism] as plague" was a recurring topos of early modern Catholic literature.[62] On a more immediate level, of course, Sweerts's work, like many other early modern plague paintings, served as a warning, not only to "heretics," but to lapsed or lukewarm Catholics as well: Cling faithfully and devotedly to the "one, true faith" or else expect dire consequences!

VIII. *The Temporal Remedies: "Mox, Longe, Tarde"*

Like Moroni's *Two Donors in Adoration*, many Italian paintings in our period invite meditation upon death and final judgment, such meditation representing one of the spiritual remedies commonly recommended by ecclesiastical authorities in time of plague. However, before we turn to these spiritual remedies, a quick word about the other, so-called temporal remedies is in order. After centuries of experience with the plague, early modern Italians had arrived at the conclusion that despite all the pills, poultices, and potions offered by doctors, pharmacists, superstitious healers, and practitioners of folkloric medicine, the only sure form of protection against the plague was to simply remove oneself from sources of the contagion, that is, to flee infected or possibly infected people, objects, homes, and towns. "Save your money and don't bother with the remedies of the *fisici* for they are worthless," advises the Florentine Rondinelli, while our Roman doctor Pressi is obliged to admit that given the profession's ignorance as to the true anatomy of the disease, no sure treatment can be identified, and so everyone invents his or her own.[63] However, above all, as Lodovico Muratori informs us, most people made recourse to "the pill of the three [Latin] adverbs," "*Mox, longe, tarde,*" as "the most certain and effective remedy and prophylactic known;" that is to say, they followed the advice of the collective wisdom of humanity, born out of long experience with the contagion, that counseled them to "flee immediately" (*cede mox*), "stay far away" (*recede longe*), and "be late in returning" (*redi tarde*).[64]

Of course, not all the inhabitants of an infected city or town had the means to flee or a suitably isolated, secure place to which to flee. For those who remained, a stringent regime of quarantine had to be endured. City gates were closed to all but certifiably safe traffic; letters and documents arriving through the mail were fumigated; assemblages of people were prohibited; the air was cleansed by the burning of bonfires; streets, buildings, clothing, and any possibly contaminated surfaces were disinfected with vinegar or sulfur or otherwise destroyed by fire; beggars and prostitutes were rounded up; and dogs were massacred as suspected spreaders of the contagion.[65] Homes in which persons had died of the plague (or were suspected to have died of it) were placed under immediate quarantine. In Florence, all women and children, even of those families free of plague, were forbidden to leave the confines of their homes unless they were wealthy enough to afford a sealed carriage for transport; this regulation, Baldinucci reports, "greatly afflicts the poor women who in hot weather suffer house confinement and deplore this partiality."[66] In Rome, the unfortunate residents of an entire neighborhood, Trastevere, where the first cases of plague erupted in 1656, found themselves literally walled in overnight by the authorities in a (failed) attempt to prevent the contagion from spreading to the rest of the city.[67]

These remedies were bitterly resented and resisted by the very people they were meant to protect. However, no "remedy" provoked more resistance than the forced confinement to the lazaretto, the public plague "hospital" where victims (or suspected victims) of the plague were sent either to recover or, more likely, to die from the contagion. The lazarettos – dirty, malodorous, overcrowded, crime-ridden, unrelievedly wretched – inspired sheer terror in the minds of early modern Italians. Doctor Pressi, who spent many days serving in the lazarettos of Rome, confessed to diarist Carlo Cartari that he was

> shocked and amazed that people in Rome [outside the lazarettos] could actually be laughing, much less playing music and singing, for if they stayed in [a lazaretto] for just one day, they would come out very different people and would not feel like laughing any more... All the babies sent there died; at times they were fed goat's milk with sugar to quiet them at night because they cried continuously, while the wailing of the women, who had lost loved ones, pierced one's heart with compassion.[68]

Muratori, who offers one of the most vivid descriptions of the lazarettos and the physical and emotional horror they represented, tells us that the mere thought of being dragged off from one's home and sent to the lazaretto caused people to fall into desperation or some other severe fit, or "passione straordinaria d'animo." The lazarettos, he adds, were often run "by people of little or no charity ... with horrible faces, bizarre dress, and frightening voices."[69] As Gastaldi reminds his readers, "even the imagination merely frightened by the plague is enough to bring on the disease."[70]

IX. *The True Cause and Meaning of the Plague: "Divine War" Against Sinful Humanity*

Even though much ink was spilled in early modern Italy in an attempt to identify and dissect the scientific causes of the plague, most people seem to have accepted the Church's consistent and adamant explanation regarding the ultimate cause and fundamental meaning of this disease: it was, simply, God's punishment of a sinful disobedient humanity. "Pestis est flagellum et sagitta Dei ob peccata hominibus immissa," the plague is a wrathful God's "scourge and arrow," Kircher declares at the beginning of what is otherwise a scientific investigation of the plague.[71] So great is God's wrath and so fierce is his response that, as Muratori mentions, indeed, "some call [the plague] a divine war" against humankind. Furnishing the title of Marchini's 1633 treatise, this blunt description, *"bellum divinum,"* also represents one of the dominant images used in a 1493 "fire and brimstone" sermon on the plague by the zealous Observant Franciscan, Bernardino Tomitano of Feltre, who cites fourteenth-century legal scholar, Bartolus of Sassoferrato, as source of the expression.[72]

Muratori, Marchini, and Tomitano appear not the least bit uneasy with the idea of God the Father and Creator waging war on his own children. Indeed, this same fundamental understanding of the plague echoes everywhere in the primary sources, be they written by ecclesiastics or laymen. Florentine diarist Giovanni Baldinucci writes in 1631, "Our Lord God seems to have unsheathed his sword against Italy, bringing hunger, war, plague and a flood of rivers. Let it please his Majesty not to punish us according to our deserts, but according to his sacred mercy."[73] In a famous exchange of letters on the plague from which Alessandro Manzoni will later draw for his *I Promessi sposi* and *Storia della Colonna Infame*, noted Bolognese poet, jurist, and letterato Claudio Achillini writes in the same year to his similarly learned friend in Rome, Agostino Mascardi:

> I now turn to you and say that, rather than deploring the current castigations, you should use your angelic talent to instead call attention upon the abominable corruption of the present century; if you do so, you will then not only cease to marvel over the ferocity of these calamities, but, rather, will be dumbfounded at the fact that, indeed, all those things which rain down to us from Heaven are not the plague, and are not, instead, arrows aimed, like rays of the sun, at us.[74]

Despite the apparent unanimity among the published voices of early modern Italy regarding the ultimate theological understanding of the plague, the fact that contemporary preachers and other spiritual authorities spend so much time forcefully delivering and strenuously defending this message – the angry God is punishing you for your sins – would suggest that many people in the audience were still in need of persuasion in this regard. Seventeenth-century Capuchin preacher Paolo Bellintani da Salò implies as much when, beginning his catalogue of the divinely sent punitive plagues of Scripture, he exclaims, "Hold it for certain truth that the plague is a scourge from God and that whoever thinks otherwise is grossly deceiving himself."[75] Almost the entire first part of a 1577 sermon to the Bolognese on the plague by famed Franciscan preacher Francesco Panigarola is devoted to a detailed philosophical defense of the notion that even the eternal, ever unchanging, Supreme Being is capable of anger and "just" revenge, followed by an equally detailed exposition of the strategies employed by Satan to deceive humans into believing that the plague has only natural causes.[76]

Even those Christians who fundamentally accepted the Church's explanation still needed enlightenment and reassurance as to how this notion of a genocidally wrathful, vengeful God, whose merciless plague every few years killed thousands of innocent babies along with the guilty, could be reconciled with the "Good News" of Jesus Christ, that is, with the New Testament message of a just, wise, merciful, and, above all, paternally loving God. A long response to this perplexity, coming in the first person from the mouth of God himself, is offered by Antonio Possevino, the already-mentioned sixteenth-century Jesuit author of *Cause et rimedii della peste*, published anonymously and only recently attributed to the Jesuit.[77] Likewise, most of Tomitano's aforementioned sermon on "why tribulations are to be patiently endured" ("De tribulationibus patienter tolerandis") is devoted to the same theme of theodicy, that is, a defense of the goodness and justice of God in the face of a world of pandemic, invincible evil and incessant, atrocious suffering.

Having identified the primary cause of the plague, some spiritual authorities proceed to identify the specific sins responsible for this pestilential "war of God" against humanity, each one doing so according to his own prejudices and personal experiences. For example, Marchini lists five plague-provoking sins in *Belli divini*: the violation of justice and unpunished killing of the innocent; the usurpation of ecclesiastical goods and property; the pride and ambition of the nobility; the refusal to pay tithes and other monies due to the Church and its representatives; and, finally, participation in devil worship, magic and superstition, profane comedies, and other theatrical performances and spectacles.[78] The earlier list promulgated by Tomitano is much longer, beginning generically with all forms of "injustice and rebellion" against God. However, the friar quickly becomes more specific in his accusations, naming as special culprits those who engage in "acts against nature" and other forms of *luxuria*; blasphemers and idolators; usurers and those who support or welcome usurers, especially Jewish ones; as well as, finally, those who refuse hospitality to strangers, the mendicant preacher having himself been a victim of this crime.[79]

Five is also the number of egregious sins, or rather categories of sin, for which God sends the plague, according to Possevino's *Cause et rimedii*.[80] Possevino includes such already-mentioned offenses as pride and arrogance, *luxuria*, usury and theft of property; but, of special interest in an art historical context is his fifth category of plague-provoking sins. This covers all forms of immoral entertainment which, the Jesuit claims, lead to more explicit forms of carnality and lust: "immodest madrigals and songs," "lascivious dances," "lewd books," and, finally,

> the use of nude images in which under the pretext of artistic expression, the world is easily roused to every sordid form of concupiscence. Moreover, with pictures recalling from Hell the memory of the evil and wicked persecutors of the Christian Church, people have now decorated their rooms, and have placed on equal or superior footing these [profane] statues with those of Our Lord Jesus Christ and of his Saints. Therefore it was against all of these barbaric impieties reviving the idolatry of the ancients, for their destruction and so that their very memory be eradicated from the earth, that the Holy Martyrs of Christ bravely exposed their lives to every form of cruelty and that now come, like magistrates of justice and executioners, the Plague and other scourges that castigate the world.[81]

Writing in the midst of the Counter Reformation, Possevino, we are not surprised to find, includes prominently (number 2 on his list) the sin of heresy and indeed, in Jesuit painting of early modern Europe, we encounter the same connection between heresy and plague. The latter is employed as a visual metaphor for the former, as, for example, in Rubens's altarpiece of 1617, *The Miracles of Saint Francis Xavier*, commissioned for the Jesuit church of Antwerp.[82] However, the association between heresy and plague was not merely a Jesuit topos: in his

Bolognese sermon on the plague, Franciscan preacher Panigarola discusses at length the successful dissemination of the "heretical doctrines" of Luther, Calvin, Zwingli, and the other Protestant reformers as a recent scourge sent by an angry God to punish the sinful Catholic world. (Yet another scourge of late, he adds, is the ever-growing military victory of the Turks.) This *flagello* began, the friar says, in 1517 when "the wicked Luther mounted his cathedra of pestilence" and promulgated his "ninety-five false axioms," which "immediately persuaded" the masses.[83]

The source of this explanation of the divine source and punitive-vindictive nature of the plague was, of course, the Bible, the foundational text (at least, in theory) of all Christian doctrine. As preachers and spiritual writers routinely point out, there is abundant proof in Sacred Scripture that, yes, indeed, God is moved to anger and vengeance by the sins of humankind, and that, furthermore, the plague is one of his preferred instruments of castigation and vengeance. Panigarola claims in his Bolognese sermon that the wrath of God is so omnipresent a theme in the Bible that, in fact, "Scripture seems to be a dialogue between man and God in which they speak of nothing else but God's anger. "The preacher goes on to give an extensive account of this "dialogue," having previously catalogued for any skeptical listeners the many biblical examples of divine punishment for sin, beginning with Adam and Eve. All of Panigarola's examples come from the Old Testament, but one could also cite New Testament texts encouraging a similar view of divine retribution for sin. As Deaux points out, even Jesus Christ reinforced belief in the connection between disease and sin: "Jesus himself before commanding a lame man to walk first announced his forgiveness of the victim's sins; on another occasion, he enjoined those whom he had healed to 'sin no more lest a worst thing befall thee.'"[84]

x. *The Plagues of the Bible: Ashdod, King David, Moses and the Brazen Serpent*

In both the Old and New Testaments we find various references to "plague" (of whatever form) as tool of divine punishment,[85] the most familiar perhaps being "the ten plagues of Egypt" recounted in the Book of Exodus. Most of these biblical "plagues" clearly did not specifically involve the bubonic plague; our early modern sources, including preachers and ecclesiastical writers understood this. They nonetheless cited and discussed these episodes as relevant to their own contemporary experiences of pestilence, especially with regard to the question of the divine mechanism of justice and retribution.

The most conspicuous and most frequently cited example of plague as divine castigation was an episode in the life of King David, recounted in both 1 Chronicles 21 and 2 Samuel 24. During his reign as king of the Israelites, David decided to take a census of the people; for reasons that the texts never adequately explain (Yahweh himself orders a census in Numbers 1), this was deemed a most grievous contravention of the will of God. Infuriated at this act of pride – this is how our early modern Italian preachers and spiritual writers identify the sin in question[86] – God sends the prophet Gad to announce the coming castigation. God offers the king, however, his choice of punishment: war, famine, or plague. David chooses what he considers the least of the three evils, plague, and in the ensuing outbreak, 70,000 of the king's people lose their lives. Among the spared, however, is the king himself, who shows himself properly remorseful and carries out public acts of contrition. Our early modern sources, like the Bible itself, are not excessively troubled by the fact that a multitude of innocent people died for a single ill-advised act committed by their ruler, an act that, in turn, was rather harmless in its intent; they accepted in the divine sovereign what they routinely experienced in their earthly ones. Of all of the sources consulted in the course of my research only one even raises the issue: popular Franciscan preacher, Bernardino de' Busti (1450-1513/15) defends

Yahweh's actions, explaining in his plague sermon that King David's subjects were, in effect, his possessions and God does punish evil-doers by taking away their possessions. Furthermore, the preacher reassures his audience, even though they were innocent of this one sin, the slaughtered mass of Israelites were nonetheless guilty of others; in any case, it was better for them to die "because if they had lived, they would have become evil or worse, and would have suffered even greater damnation."[87]

By virtue of this incident, David "became the most important biblical figure associated with pestilence,"[88] and for this reason we find him, for example, prominently placed on the title page of Marchini's *Belli divini* (along with Michael the Archangel and Carlo Borromeo) as well as in the vignette illustrating the allegory of pestilence in the 1758-60 Hertel edition of Cesare Ripa's famous handbook, the *Iconologia*. Among the rare painted depictions of this Old Testament episode is the predella of an altarpiece completed in 1536 by Giorgio Vasari, commissioned by the Confraternity of Saint Roch of Arezzo, Tuscany.[89] Another is Luca Giordano's *The Prophet Gad Offering King David the Choice of Three Punishments: Famine, Civil War, or Plague* (fig. 1), now in Australia. Nothing is known of the provenance of the latter canvas, nor of the second treatment of the theme by the same Giordano in a larger canvas whose date of execution may or may not coincide with a fresco of this episode that Giordano included in the scenes from the life of David done for the monastery church of San Lorenzo at the Escorial.[90] The Escorial fresco series, we might mention, was commissioned by King Charles II, "known for his exaggerated piety." As Meyer explains, this "choice of subject responded to an identification between leaders and events in the Old Testament and the reign of the Spanish Hapsburgs, culminating with the construction of the Escorial in relation to the final victory over the Muslims in Spain."[91]

This identification on the part of sovereigns and other nobility was encouraged by contemporary spiritual authorities, who used this scene from David's life to make an admonitory connection between the scourge of plague and the misdeeds of temporal rulers. Marchini's *Belli divini* interprets the episode as a noteworthy example of God's punishment of "the pride and excessive ambition of the nobility."[92] One wonders if that message was grasped by the famous but erratic and extravagant Gaspar de Haro y Guzman, 7th Marqués del Carpio (1629-87), Spanish Ambassador to Rome and enthusiastic patron of artists. According to a 1682 inventory taken in Rome on the eve of his departure for Naples as the new Viceroy, Don Gaspar's own extensive collection of paintings included a canvas by (or, at least, then attributed to) Luca Giordano depicting the same episode, described in the inventory as "King David weeping for his sins in the presence of the prophet [Gad] and the Angel who is placing his sword back in its sheath."[93]

Another Old Testament episode that involved God's recourse to pestilence in order to punish disobedience or opposition to his will was the Plague of Ashdod sent in retaliation for the Philistine's capture of the Ark of the Covenant, recounted in 1 Samuel 5 and made famous in art by Poussin's great epic canvas of the scene. Already cited for its influence on Michael Sweerts (Section VII), Poussin's work was copied by contemporary artist, Angelo Caroselli (cat. 1), apparently during the very execution of the French artist's original. (Caroselli's copy is believed to show the original state of Poussin's composition.)[94] At Ashdod it was a plague of "tumors" (which may or may not be the buboes of the bubonic plague) that afflicted the enemies of God. Another chastising plague is recounted in the Book of Numbers 21: 4-9, where Yahweh sends a plague of poisonous, "fiery" serpents to punish the Hebrews for murmuring against him and their leader, Moses, during the uncomfortable forty years of wandering in the desert. As Panigarola comments in his plague sermon, "The Jews sinned a thousand times in the desert and God, turning from mercy to justice, made them pay dear for it, once with the armies of the 'Levitici' [*sic*], another time with fire, another time with serpents... O justice, o

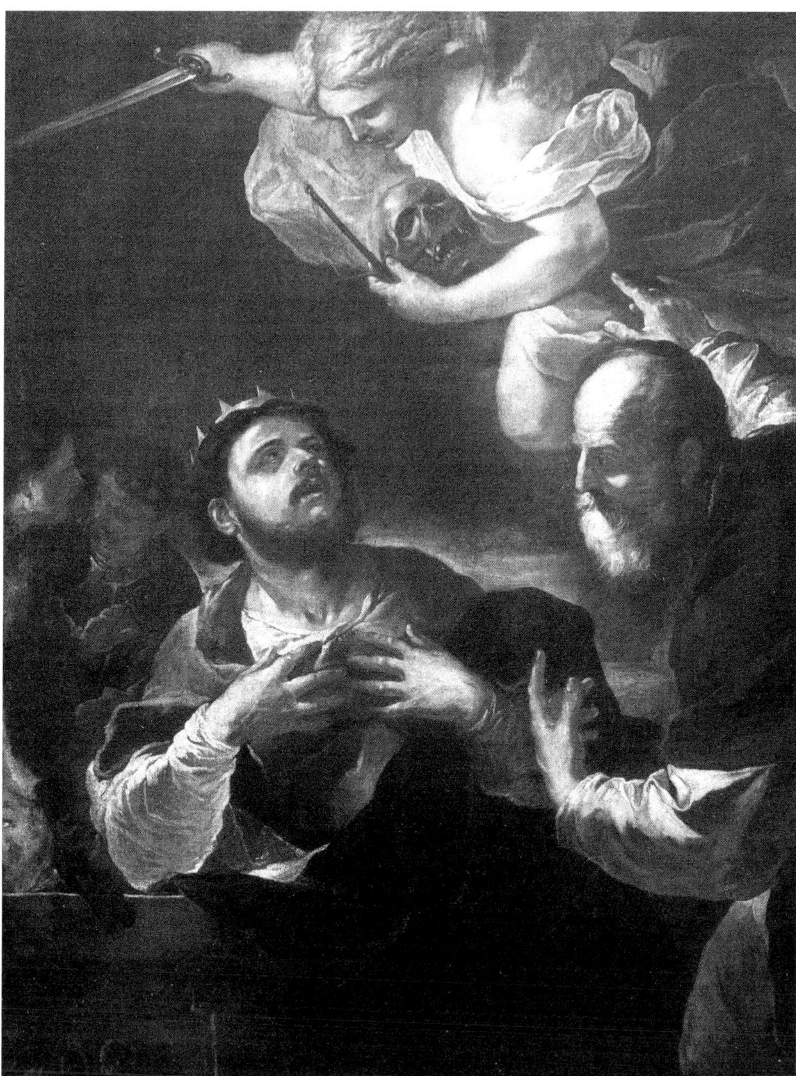

1. Luca Giordano, *The Prophet Gad Offering King David the Choice of Three Punishments: Famine, Civil War, or Plague*. Oil on canvas. On loan from Private collection, 1990. Art Gallery of Western Australia.

chastisement, o scourge, o wrath of God!"[95] In this case, just as God sends the affliction, he also sends the remedy, instructing Moses to create the image of a serpent – fashioned in bronze – and hoist it up on a staff, so that "everyone who is bitten shall look at it and live." Centuries of biblical exegesis have attached many different layers of meaning to this story, but in the Christian tradition, it was seen, consistently and above all, as a prefigurement of the salvific act of Christ's death on the cross, of the health and healing – of both body and soul – that comes through Jesus the crucified Savior.[96] This association was made in the New Testament itself by the Gospel of John 3:14-15. One late seventeenth-century Italian preacher, Jesuit General Gian Paolo Oliva, in a sermon to the Confraternity of Nobles at the church of the Gesù in Rome, adds a footnote to this same message by pointing out that the episode proves that the way to cure evil-doers of their evil is to frighten them with images of horror, an observation of obvious relevance to contemporary audiences' experience of the plague.[97]

In times of plague, images of Moses and the Brazen Serpent acquired greater relevance and resonance for the double message contained therein – epidemic as divine castigation, Jesus as source of healing. Not surprisingly we find the scene occupying a place of central importance in Tintoretto's decoration of the ceiling of the Sala Grande Superiore of the Scuola di San Rocco, a building that represents one of the most eminent monuments to early modern Italian response to the plague.[98] Tintoretto's rendition of the scene, executed during an actual outbreak of the plague in Venice, is coupled with two other Old Testament scenes, *The Gathering of the Manna* and *Moses Striking Water from the Rock*. These three narratives depict forms of service to the sick, the dying, and the otherwise needy, "all charitable activities to which the Scuola was committed"[99] and which, in fact, the Church encouraged, both in print and in paint (as this exhibition illustrates) on the part of all the Christian laity during times of epidemic.

For renowned Jesuit biblical commentator Cornelius a Lapide, writing in the early seventeenth century, the Brazen Serpent episode (or more specifically John's citation thereof) offered an opportunity to emphasize the polemical Tridentine Catholic message that eternal life is gained by active effort, that is, by good works, in addition to grace and repentance.[100] (Of interest to art historians, we might add, is Lapide's anti-Protestant comment in the same context that Pope Adrian I's "first epistle to Charles the Great ... proves that the use of images is lawful from [Moses's use of] this serpent.")[101] Finally, despite thorough catechizing of the early modern masses by Christian spiritual authorities, it is highly likely that the presence of the snakes in this canvas also recalled in the mind of contemporary viewers the pagan god of healing, Aesculapius, whose principal attribute was the serpent and whose fame and sculpted image (especially in the form of ancient statues recovered from long-burial under the streets of Rome) lived on in early modern Italy. The widespread recourse to superstitious remedies to the plague like magic scrolls and amulets bearing the likeness of animals, denounced in our sources, is yet another reminder of how vital and enduring was the "pagan" culture and mentality of early modern Italians under their Christian veneer.[102]

The current exhibition includes a strikingly beautiful rendition of the Brazen Serpent scene (cat. 3) by Giovanni Domenico Ferretti, who "should be considered the leading Florentine artist of the eighteenth century."[103] The canvas comes from a private collection, now being seen for the first time in public since the completion of recent conservation work. Little is known of the origins of the canvas: it is signed and dated, 1736, and may have belonged to the Marchese Andrea Gerini and been exhibited in Florence in 1737 for the feast of Saint Luke the evangelist, traditionally believed to have been a medical doctor as well as a painter. Interesting for our purposes is the fact that a portion of its composition, specifically the tumbled mass of plague-stricken bodies, derives from an explicit plague painting, Marcantonio Franceschini's altarpiece of 1701 depicting Carlo Borromeo and the 1576 Milanese plague (Modena, church of S. Carlo Borromeo).[104] Here, the vertical orientation and the cross-like configuration of the uplifted pole around which entwined the brazen serpent emphasize the episode as a prefigurement of the Crucifixion.

XI. *"Spiritual Remedies" for "Plague of the Soul"*

In a 1576 pastoral letter written while his diocese was under threat from the plague, Cardinal Gabriele Paleotti, bishop of Bologna, reminded his flock that the plague is not a physical ailment, but rather "a plague of the soul."[105] All of the spiritual authorities of the day – and most of the believing lay ones as well – agreed with Paleotti's assessment and hence joined voices in identifying and publicizing the only truly effective response to this disease, the *rimedi spirituali*. These "spiritual remedies" took various forms – special penitential litanies and other prayers, confession, Masses, processions, public collective vows, charitable works – but they all had the same ultimate goal: to rid the land of plague by "placating" God's anger, God's anger being placated through earnest repentance for one's sin and sincere emendation of one's life.

Save your money and don't bother with the medications of the *fisici*, we have already heard Rondinelli declare, and the same scholar goes on to advise: "the true remedy is the correction of one's ways and public prayer, done with faith and perseverance, because if God does not safeguard the city, in vain do these others seek to do so, with all their diligence. ..." Muratori similarly reminds his readers that the most important remedies are those that regard the soul and God, for in time of plague, it is urgent to "make recourse to God and to placate Him."[106] "Even the pagans knew enough to turn to their gods," remarks Rondinelli, while Tomitano cites Livy's *History of Rome* in which Lucius Postumius advises the Romans that, since the plague "comes from God, it is necessary to make peace with God."[107]

The two Franciscan preachers, Bernardino de' Busti and Panigarola, both point out in their plague sermons that the spiritual remedies have their symbolic counterparts in the temporal ones (e.g., physical separation from infected localities is meant to remind us of the necessity of fleeing from sin).[108] However, despite the insistence upon the superiority of the spiritual over the temporal, to my knowledge, there is no preacher or spiritual authority who counsels his audiences to simply ignore the temporal remedies, although the zealous and at times fiery Bernardino Tomitano comes close to it.[109] Both forms of response, the spiritual sources say outright or imply, are to be attended to. Pope Alexander VII's wise, thorough and bi-frontal (spiritual and temporal) attack on the plague in Rome in 1656 is recounted in detailed and approving fashion by Pallavicino in his biography of that pontiff. In their own plague treatises, the Capuchin Bellintani da Salò and the Jesuit Possevino freely intermingle remedies of both types in their recommendations. In the midst of his traditional spiritual counsels in the *Dialogo della peste*, Bellintani, for example, reminds authorities to stock up on food supplies as well as to sequester all beggars and prostitutes, the latter being a "causa fortissima" of contagion. Likewise, in the same breath that he discusses spiritual remedies, Possevino advises readers to burn any infected piece of clothing or other personal article that might spread the contagion so that a single person does not become "the occasion of death for an entire province."[110]

At the top of his list of "Pestis Remedia Spiritualia," Barnabite theologian Marchini places public "acts of repentance," citing the Old Testament case of King David. Among more recent examples, Marchini observes, is the famous penitential procession of Carlo Borromeo, cardinal of Milan, who, with bare feet and a noose around his neck, processed through the streets of his city holding a cross bearing one of the Holy Nails of the Crucifixion, one of Milan's prized relics (see cat. 24).[111] The civil authorities of Borromeo's Milan had vigorously opposed this procession, fearing (correctly) that such a massing of people would only spread the plague. But, the strong-willed Borromeo prevailed: in enacting this particular form of public devotion, Carlo was emulating the example of Pope Gregory the Great (section VII above) during the great Roman plague of 590. Among the earliest recorded in Christian history, that outbreak is memorialized in the late sixth-century *History of the Franks* (10:1) by Gregory of Tours, and, with legendary embellishments, by *The Golden Legend*. On that occasion Gregory mandated a huge procession – called "the sevenfold litanies" because it included representatives from seven sectors of the city's population – terminating in the "basilica of the blessed Mary, ever Virgin," Santa Maria Maggiore. In doing so, Gregory gave start to what was to become a long tradition in times of collective calamity, the solemn public processing of clergy and laity, with the former bearing sacred icons, relics, or banners depicting the Virgin and Child or tutelary saints. One such rare surviving processional banner (*gonfalone*) from the sixteenth century, by Jacopo Bassano featuring Our Lady of Mercy and Saints Roch and Sebastian (cat. 12), is included in this exhibition.

XII. *Memento Mori and Vanitas*

According Gregory of Tours's *History of the Franks*, Pope Gregory began his sermon on the occasion of the 590 penitential plague procession in this fashion:

> Most beloved brethren, those scourges of God which we ought to dread when they are yet to come should be feared all the more when they are upon us and we have felt their power. May our sorrows open to us the way of conversion; may this punishment which we endure soften the hardness of our hearts, as indeed it was foretold by the prophet: "The sword reacheth unto the soul." Behold how all the people is smitten by the sword of divine wrath; one after another, they are swept away by sudden death. ... The blow falleth; the victim is snatched away before he can turn to bewail his sins and to repent. Consider, therefore, in what guise he shall appear before the stern Judge of all, having no respite in which to lament his deeds. ... Houses are left void, parents behold the funerals of their children, and their heirs go before them to the grave. Let every one of us therefore betake himself to lamentation and repentance before the blow is fallen and while time yet remaineth to weep.[112]

Setting the tone for much of all subsequent pastoral response to epidemic, Gregory's speech thus begins with a note of terror, the terror of death. For early modern Catholics, in fact, the greatest form of terror, especially in time of plague, was that of sudden death, death without proper sacramental preparation, especially the confession of one's sins to a priest. There could be no greater calamity than this, for, according to Catholic doctrine, dying in a state of unabsolved mortal sin meant certain, eternal damnation in Hell.[113]

For early modern viewers, this fear inevitably resonated from Giovanni Martinelli's *Death Comes to the Banquet Table* (cat. 4). This startling Florentine Baroque canvas represents a variation on the traditional and popular themes of memento mori ("Remember you shall die") and *vanitas* (vanity).[114] Another strikingly explicit, darkly melancholy Italian Baroque canvas belonging to the same genre is Salvator Rosa's *Humana Fragilitas*, painted in response to the pandemic of 1656, which killed both the artist's son and brother. The thoroughly pessimistic message of the painting, inscribed by the child on the parchment – "Conception is Sinful; Birth, a Punishment; Life, Hard Labor; Death, Inevitable" – derives from medieval Latin sacred poet Adam of Saint Victor. It was communicated to the artist in a sonnet written for him by his philosopher friend, G.B. Ricciardi. The same message is echoed in a contemporary poem, "Tratta de le miserie humane" (On the Misery of the Human Condition), by Rosa's fellow Neapolitan and celebrated man of letters, Giambattista Marino (1569-1625): "At the moment of his birth into this life full of misery, wretched man first opens his eyes not to the sun but to tears, and as soon as he is born, he is made prisoner of tenacious bindings ...In the end a narrow rock encloses his remains, in such haste, that with a sigh I say: From the cradle to the tomb is but a brief step."[115]

The eerie, melodramatic nature of Martinelli's and Rosa's canvases has its counterpart as well in the written plague treatises of early modern Italy. There is perhaps no passage that matches the coarsely blunt, indeed, ghastly means used by a certain Capuchin friar to preach this memento mori message to a group of men and women who, confined to the lazaretto of Milan, had decided to throw a party to relieve the gloom of their forced enclosure. The scene is described by fellow Capuchin, Paolo Bellintani da Salò, in his *Dialogo della peste* (1580s):

> One night some people were having a little party, dancing with each other, in order to keep their spirits up, in one of the rooms of the lazaretto, even though I had prohibited such things under the threat of most grave punishment. Fra Andrea, remembering that the day before among those who had died he had unloaded from a wagon a stout old lady, decided to go and find her body and use it to put an end to the party and inspire some terror among the dancing men and women. After night had fallen, without a lamp, he went to the grave pit in the center of the lazaretto where the dead bodies are discharged and went diligently searching there: finally he found the aforementioned old lady. In hoisting her over his shoulder, he happened to compress her belly so that the air that was in her belly come out through her mouth with a great noise. Who would have not been frightened to death? But not he; instead, calm and confident, he said to her in our Milanese dialect, "Hey, keep quiet, grandma, silence; I'm taking you to go dancing." He went to the door of the room where the dancing was going on and knocked. Some one inside asked: "Who's there?" He didn't answer as we [Capuchins] usually answer, "*Deo gratias*!" and instead said: "We're friends and we want to dance." The door was opened. He went in and threw the body of the old lady at the feet of those who were dancing, shouting out: "Hey, here, make her dance too." Then he added, "Is it possible that having seen death face to face, you are here fooling around and offending God?"[116]

Although somewhat shocking and repellant to us today, these incessant, omnipresent warnings about the plague as a punishment from God and the transitory nature of the world served a useful, positive role during time of plague. Not only did the *vanitas* theme remind those caught in the midst of the horror of an outbreak that "this, too, shall pass," but the ecclesiastical explanation at least "fit the plague into some rational and orderly framework" at a time when "it must have seemed to many that the very fabric of rational order in nature had been destroyed."[117] In other words, the plague "could be understood as part of a coherent divine plan."[118]

Preachers and spiritual writers also imparted consolation in a more directly positive fashion. The greatest consolation for early modern Christians was, of course, the doctrinal belief in Christ's victory over death through his own Resurrection and his promise of life after death for the virtuous, be one's death due to plague or any other illness. The Resurrection was a popular subject for artists in all periods of Christian history, and it comes at no surprise to discover that Sebastiano Ricci's treatment of that theme (cat. 35), was commissioned for the chapel of the Royal Hospital at Chelsea, England. According to Catholic belief, Christ's mother, the Virgin Mary, like her son, had the distinct privilege of entering heaven in her intact, uncorrupt body, and thus, depictions of her Assumption, such as that of the same Ricci in the present exhibition (cat. 34), would have conveyed a hopeful message to pious viewers about the Christian triumph over death and physical decay. (A reminder of the same triumph over death is likewise contained in Jacopo Tintoretto's *Raising of Lazarus* [cat. 37], discussed in section VII.) The eternal bliss awaiting virtuous souls in Heaven in the presence of God, Christ, the Virgin Mary, and the saints is similarly evoked in the many Renaissance and Baroque representations of the celestial realms and their choruses of saintly inhabitants including Vaccaro's *Madonna and Child with Saints Roch, Sebastian, and Francis Xavier* (cat. 18). Such reminders of the virtuous Christian's posthumous destiny in Paradise in a new glorified body were especially welcome in times of pestilence, to which Vaccaro's canvas makes explicit reference through prominent placement of these three male plague saints in the foreground.[119]

As far as written sources are concerned, for these and other messages of consolation in time of contagion, early modern Italians turned (after Scripture, of course) most readily to the oldest and perhaps the most influential Christian treatise written in response to suffering in time of plague. *De mortalitate* is an extended sermon composed in 252 A.D. by Saint Cyprian, bishop of Carthage, while contagion raged throughout the Roman empire. Never out of circulation in the Christian world, Cyprian's work was reprinted in Padua in 1577 during the sixteenth century's most virulent outbreak and is cited in many of the plague sources in our period. Possevino includes *De mortalitate* in his list of "books of spiritual consolation" to be read during the trying times of contagion, while Marchini reprints several entire pages of text from the sermon in *Belli divini*.[120] Reminding his readers of the promise of the Resurrection and the glories of heaven, Cyprian declares that death is not to be feared but embraced as liberation from this world of trial with its vain joys. The traditional Christian theme of *contemptus mundi*, disdain for earthly things, resounds throughout *De mortalitate*: "So many persecutions the mind endures daily, by so many dangers is the heart beset. And does it delight to remain here long amidst the devil's weapons, when we should rather earnestly desire and wish to hasten to Christ aided by a death coming most speedily, since He Himself instructs us, saying, 'Amen, amen, I say to you ... you shall be sorrowful but your sorrow shall come into joy'?"[121] Cyprian encourages Christians to triumph in spirit over the ravages of the plague, even as their bodies are brutally assailed. This experience represents a salutary test of their faith, he declares, at the same time that he delivers a detailed description of the disease's gruesome symptomatology:

> That now the bowels loosened into a flux exhaust the strength of the body, that a fever contracted in the very marrow of the bones breaks out into ulcers of the throat, that the intestines are shaken by continual vomiting, that the blood-shot eyes burn, that the feet of some or certain parts of their members are cut away by the infection of diseased putrefaction, that, by a weakness developing through the losses and injuries of the body, either the gait is enfeebled, or the hearing impaired or the sight blinded, all this contributes to the proof of faith. What greatness of soul it is to fight with the powers of the mind unshaken against so many attacks of devastation and death. ...[122]

XIII. *Charity and the "Corporal Works of Mercy"*

During the same plague outbreak that moved him to write *De mortalitate*, Cyprian composed another extended sermon whose message was likewise destined to echo across the centuries, especially in time of plague, the *De opere et eleemosynis*, "Works and Almsgiving." In Cyprian's time, as during all outbreaks of pestilence, masses of people were reduced to utter destitution in the ensuing collapse of trade and commerce and the overwhelming of all normal public service to the poor, needy, sick, and dying. Always a major threat to European populations even in the absence of plague, famine was a guaranteed consequence of epidemic outbreaks, when indeed it was not their immediate precursor and contributing cause.[123] Bringing commerce between town and countryside to a virtual halt, the contagion also brought death to massive numbers of both urban and farm workers, drastically reducing agricultural production. Cyprian reminds his readers that almsgiving and other works of charity benefit not only those in need but also the souls of those who perform them: "The remedies for propitiating God have been given in the words of God himself; divine instructions have taught that God is satisfied by just works, that sins are cleansed by the merits of mercy. And in Solomon we read:

'Shut up alms in the heart of the poor, and it shall obtain help for thee against all evil.'"[124]

Cyprian's message, repeated and amplified by a host of early modern preachers and spiritual writers, found its visual counterpart in a prodigious number of paintings depicting what have come to be known as the "corporal works (or acts) of mercy" – feeding the hungry, clothing the naked, giving drink to the thirsty, etc. (cats. 9-11). Deriving from Jesus's admonitions in Matthew 25, the list was enlarged in the Middle Ages, specifically because of the plague, to include a further work of mercy, that of burying the dead.[125] Some painters, such as Michael Sweerts, depicted the entire series of acts of mercy (including *Burying the Dead* [cat. 11]).[126] The works of mercy were also illustrated in the form of engravings, such as, most notably in our period, the *Icones operum misericordiae*, first published in Rome, 1586, with commentary by Giulio Roscio. In this popular work, under the rubric, "Mortuos Sepelire Explicatio," Roscio praises the Christians of ancient Alexandria for gathering the corpses of plague victims, closing their eyes and mouths, carrying them on their shoulders, washing, dressing, and giving them proper burial.[127] Also imparting the same message through the medium of the painted image are the many allegorical renditions of the theological virtue of charity, usually depicted as a young mother nursing three infants (cat. 9).[128] Preacher Bernardino Tomitano mocks the plague antidote, the "pill of the three adverbs" ("mox, longe, tarde"), declaring that "it comes from Hell" since it violates the divine precept of loving and serving one's neighbor.[129]

Printed sources (e.g., Possevino and Marchini, to cite only two examples)[130] often detail and extol the charity of specific historical figures, usually canonized saints, in the hope that readers will be inspired to "go and do likewise." Indeed, many of them did, especially as members of the numerous charitable confraternities in operation in early modern Italy. One such confraternity, that of the Misericordia in Liguria, which buried plague victims as part of their service to society, commissioned Caravaggio's *Saint John the Baptist*, now in the Nelson-Atkins Museum, Kansas City. According to Bishop Pier Francesco Costa, son of the artist's patron, Ottavio, the melancholy nature of John's visage is due to his contemplation of "human miseries" and "moves not only the brothers, but also visitors to penitence."[131] In early modern Italy perhaps the most celebrated exemplar of charity was Carlo Borromeo of Milan, whose reputation was greatly helped by the proliferation of painted images of his work on behalf of the plague stricken (cats. 24, 25).

Other individuals celebrated in the printed plague sources include the fifteenth-century Franciscan preacher-reformer, Saint Bernardino of Siena, whose heroic service as a young man during a violent outbreak in his hometown in 1400 earned him a place of prominence in the early modern catalogues of charitable exemplars.[132] In his sermon on the plague, Bernardino Tomitano, the Sienese saint's namesake and fellow Franciscan preacher, cites the elder Bernardino's scolding of those who ran from those in need during the outbreak: "Oh, what should I say of those who in the time of plague abandoned parents, brothers, sisters, neighbors, and left them to die in desperation, like dogs, without provision for either body or soul?"[133] Tomitano also reminds his audience of Bernardino of Siena's promise that service to the plague-stricken will earn you heaven even if you are guilty of "innumerable sins," while recommending (as does Muratori) the Sienese's special devotion to the Holy Name of Jesus (as encapsulated in the IHS monogram of the saint's own design) as an especially powerful prophylactic against or cure of the plague.[134]

Even non-canonized figures were held up as role models for the public: the fourteenth-century Olivetan monk, Bernardo Tolomei (cat. 2) is seen in Crespi's *modello* ministering with his companions to the plague-stricken while a solemn procession (on the left) arrives to bring Holy Communion to them.[135] Aristocrat-turned-Jesuit ascetic, Luigi (Aloysius) Gonzaga (1568-91), recently declared patron of victims of AIDS, is depicted in Batoni's oval devotional portrait of ca. 1744 (cat. 19). Gonzaga labored on behalf of plague victims in Rome during the 1591 outbreak, going so far as to carry them on his own back to the Roman hospitals of Santa Maria della Consolazione and Spirito Santo, as we see him depicted in Zoboli's altarpiece in the Roman church of Santi Carlo ed Ambrogio al Corso. The young Jesuit eventually died from the consequences of such incessant labor, though of "fever," not of the plague.

Although Gonzaga had been canonized twenty years by the time Batoni executed this canvas, even as a *beato*, that is, long before his canonization, he had been presented as an icon of charity in time of plague, especially in Jesuit sources. For instance, famed Jesuit orator Paolo Segneri (1624-96), dedicated one of his widely read *panegirici sacri* to the not-yet-canonized Gonzaga declaring him a veritable "martyr."[136] In Batoni's portrait, we observe the saint in prayerful contemplation of a crucifix lovingly cradled in his left arm. His right hand rests on his heart, a reminder of the emotional and spiritual intensity of his devotion to the Passion of Christ. Luigi wears a white surplice denoting his status as an acolyte, one of the minor orders leading to priesthood, which premature death prevented him from attaining. In the foreground, a skull is a reminder of Luigi's *contemptus mundi* (disdain for the "vain" transient things of this world) and of the inevitability of death, while a bouquet of lilies recalls the perpetual virginity the youth vowed to the Blessed Virgin in 1578 and again at the conclusion of his Jesuit novitiate in 1587.

Though conventionally referred to, even today, as the Jesuit "boy saint," Luigi actually died at the age of twenty-five, which in the sixteenth century would have been considered adulthood. Nonetheless, mirroring the hagiographic tradition promoted by the Jesuits right from the time of Gonzaga's death, Batoni here represents him as a tender adolescent, thus emphasizing the dramatic contrast between his youthful, diminutive exterior and his heroic, spiritual stature. Luigi's youthfulness would have been heightened in order to also facilitate greater identification with him on the part of Catholic adolescent boys (whose patron the Church had officially designated him), especially the students in the Jesuits' numerous secondary schools throughout Europe.

XIV. *Heavenly Protectors Against the Plague, Universal and Local*

Many of these saintly exemplars of charity in time of epidemic became, in turn, tutelary saints against contagion as well, even though they may not have cured anyone during their lifetimes. Bernardino of Siena is memorialized, for instance, in a late fifteenth-century panel by Benozzo Gozzoli, *Saints Nicholas of Tolentine, Roch, Sebastian, and Bernardino of Siena with Kneeling Donors*, now at the Metropolitan Museum of Art, whose inscription identifies the four personages as "saintly defenders against pestilence."[137] Bernardino is just one of many such patron saints; in fact, as Christine Boeckl rightly observes, "[p]lague saints are legion."[138] This profusion is due to the fact that all of the various towns and cities of Italy (and indeed all of Catholic Europe) invoked their own local celestial patrons and canonized heroes and heroines for protection against the deadly scourge – as did, for example, the town of Este in commissioning Tiepolo's Saint Thecla altarpiece (cat. 7) – and did not restrict their recourse to just the few universally recognized tutelary saints.

The Virgin Mary

Among plague saints of universal reputation, the most famous, most invoked in prayer, and most frequently depicted in art are the Virgin Mary (cats. 13, 18, 21, 28,34, 36), Sebastian (cats. 12, 13, 16, 19), and Roch (12, 13, 14, 15, 17, 18).[139] Always one of the prime intercessors between heaven and earth, the Virgin Mary naturally became the object of even more intense attention during times of contagion. When civic authorities decreed the pronouncement of a

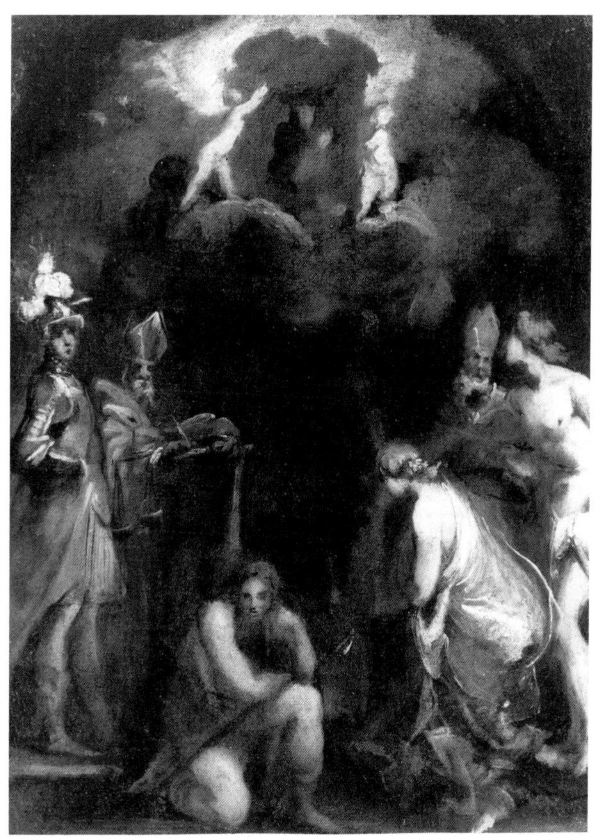

2. Zanobi Rosi, *The Madonna of Impruneta with Saints Sebastian, Roch, Michael the Archangel, Two Bishop-Saints, and a Barefoot Female Saint*. Oil on canvas. Collection of Mary Jane Harris, New York.

solemn vow to heaven for liberation from the plague, it was usually directed to Mary, in any one of her various avatars (most notably, the Madonna della Misericordia).[140] The pronouncement of a public vow was frequently accompanied by the commissioning of a church, painting, or other lasting visual memorial. In our period, among the most famous of these ex-voto works of art devoted to Mary both have their origins in the pandemic of 1630-31: Baldassare Longhena's church of Santa Maria della Salute in Venice and Guido Reni's silken processional banner, the *Pallione del voto*. The latter image was dedicated to the Madonna of the Rosary, a "surprising" choice, as Puglisi points out, inasmuch as it represented the supplanting of the two, older and more revered Bolognese Marian cults, the Madonna of Succor and the Madonna of Saint Luke. In the eyes of early modern Italians, not all Madonnas were created equal: some were deemed more powerful than others.[141]

For the Florentines, instead, two Madonnas were more powerful than one. While besieged by plague in the early 1630s, not only did the entire city gather to make a solemn public vow to their cherished "Santissima Annunziata" at her shrine in the center of town, but it also took the extraordinary measure of bringing into Florence itself the most venerable, miraculous image of the Madonna of Impruneta, an ancient icon normally housed in a small church in a village outside Florence. This temporary *traslatio* occurred *processionalmente* in stages over the course of four days in late May 1633, and at the end, many valuable treasures in the form of jewelry in gold, silver, and precious stones were offered to the Madonna. Rondinelli claims that as a result of this display of devotion on the part of the Florentines, "the plague immediately calmed down and soon thereafter was completely extinguished."[142] *The Madonna of Impruneta with Saints Sebastian, Roch, Michael the Archangel, Two Bishop-Saints, and a Barefoot Female Saint* (fig. 2), a hitherto unpublished *bozzetto* by Zanobi Rosi, for an unidentified work that was either never executed or lost over the centuries, may have, in fact, been created to commemorate this event.[143] At the very least, the work was meant to expressly invoke the Madonna's intercession in time of the contagion, as the inclusion of the universal plague icons, Sebastian, Roch and Michael, suggest.[144]

Saint Sebastian

After the Virgin Mary, the heavenly helper whose assistance was most often sought was the early Christian martyr Sebastian. The concluding entreaty of Carlo Borromeo's 1576 anthology of special plague prayers, *Antiphonae, psalmi, preces, et orationes, ad usum supplicationum temporum pestis,* is emblematic of the special status enjoyed by the saint, invoking Sebastian (and, by name, only Sebastian) right alongside the Virgin Mary in its plea to God for rescue from the scourge: "Heed our prayer, o God of our health and salvation, and through the intercession of Mary the blessed and glorious Mother of God, together with your martyr the blessed Sebastian and all the saints, free your people from the terrors of your wrath. ..."[145] As in prayer, so, too, in painting: in plague-related "Sacra conversazione" scenes, Sebastian is inevitably one of the patron saints depicted in the company of the Virgin, either by himself or with other saintly intercessors (cats. 13, 18). Although much has already been written about this saint, it will be useful to here recall the basic facts of the life and cult of this prodigiously popular saint, who also enjoys the august title (given him by Gregory the Great) of "Defensor Ecclesiae Romanae" and privileged status as one of the three official patrons of the city of Rome.[146]

As is the case with so many of the paleo-Christian and medieval saints, the facts of Sebastian's life are shrouded in centuries of pious legend, although the fact that he existed and died for his faith has itself never been a matter of doubt. The earliest legend is the *Passio Sancti Sebastiani,* for many years believed (even by the Bollandists) to be the work of Saint Ambrose, but in reality a mid-fifth-century composition ("an historical romance")[147] by someone writing in Rome or at least knowing that city very well. According to the *Passio,* Sebastian was a member of the elite Praetorian guard under the Emperors Maximian and Diocletian; though a Christian, Sebastian kept his faith a secret in order to use his military status to help imprisoned Christians. His religious loyalties were discovered and he was sentenced to death at the hands of the imperial archers, who left his body in a field, pierced with so many arrows that, according to the *Passio,* he resembled a hedgehog: "quasi ericius ita esset irsutus ictibus sagittarum."[148] Under the cover of night, his fellow Christians rescued the almost-martyr, who was nursed back to life by a Roman matron, Irene, and her maidservant. "Sebastian healed by Irene," became a favorite subject of Baroque painting (cat. 15. 16), thanks to the re-publicizing of the Sebastian legend in Cardinal Cesare Baronio's *Annales ecclesiastici.*[149]

Once recovered, Sebastian refused to flee the city for his own safety. He became so emboldened in his defense of the faith, that he dared reproach the emperor himself, face to face, for his crimes against the Christians. This time, the imperial death decree was effectively carried out: beaten to death, Sebastian's body was thrown into the Roman sewer, the Cloaca Maxima. The actual form of his martyrdom, "less noble and less picturesque" than the first attempt on his life in the field, Réau explains, "artists have preferred to ignore."[150] One of the few artists to treat the theme was Ludovico Carracci, in a canvas, now in the Getty Museum, commissioned in 1612 by Maffeo Barberini, the future Pope Urban VIII.[151] However, this was not the end of the saint's story: a subsequent apparition by Sebastian to yet another Roman matron revealed the location of his body – on the spot now occupied by the Church of Sant'Andrea della Valle containing the Barberini family chapel for which the same Carracci canvas had been originally intended. Sebastian's recovered body was given proper burial in the catacombs on the Via Appia where now stands a church in his honor, the physical center of his Roman cult. Over the course of the centuries, Sebastian's remains were divided into smaller relics that ended up in various parts of Europe. Rome, of course, kept a substantial portion for itself: St. Peter's Basilica boasts possession of what has been publicized as the saint's head – in reality, as Réau points out, only a fragment of his skull – housed, not at the St. Sebastian altar, but in the sacristy.[152]

Nowhere in the *Passio* or in any of the hagiographic sources of Sebastian's life before the eighth century do we find mention of the plague. So how did Sebastian acquire his role as tutelary plague saint? This was a question raised in early modern plague literature as well, in particular by Marchini for whom it represents one of many historical-theological-medical "problemata" posed by the plague. Marchini's answer is that the role was likely given to Sebastian because of the ancient association in both pagan literature and Christian Scripture between arrows and the plague as punishment inflicted by a wrathful divinity (i.e., Apollo and Yahweh).[153] The later Jesuit hagiographers, the Bollandists, however, disputed Marchini's answer: in the *Acta Sanctorum*[154] they point instead to the account given by Paulus Diaconus (ca. 720-ca.799?) in his *History of the Lombards* (VI:5), and repeated, with the usual fanciful modifications and deformations, in *The Golden Legend*. According to Paulus's somewhat confusing text, during an outbreak of the plague in 680 in Rome (and Pavia ["Ticinum"], capital of the Lombards), "it was revealed to a certain person that the plague would not cease until an altar was erected in honor of Saint Sebastian the Martyr in the Basilica of St. Peter in Chains." The instructions of the divine messenger were carried out and the city was liberated from the plague, the same miraculous liberation occurring (we assume, even though Paulus does not say it explicitly) in Pavia, which had immediately sent for relics of Sebastian.

One of the oldest representations of Sebastian in the city of Rome, in fact, dates to the same outbreak of the plague described by Paulus, as Gregory Martin's 1581 pilgrim's guidebook, *Roma sancta,* points out (and as indeed appears to be the case), and is located in the same church mentioned by Paulus and Martin, St. Peter in Chains (S. Pietro in Vincoli).[155] Yet, this representation, a mosaic, is rather curious inasmuch as it represents the martyr, not as the young athletic Praetorian guard that he was, but rather as a grave, sedate, white-bearded old man, dressed in Byzantine fashion, much as we find in an earlier mosaic in S. Apollinare Nuovo, Ravenna. Whatever the reason for this iconographic choice, according to Réau,[156] it held sway until the fifteenth century. With Renaissance humanism's rediscovery of the beauty of the human body and of the classical gods, Sebastian is increasingly depicted as a young, handsome, athletic hero, usually naked or nearly so. Cannata cites, in accounting for the change, an eighth-century legend in which Sebastian in the form of an ephebe appears to the bishop of Laon; however, among the more usual explanations for this iconographical switch is the desire on the part of artists to display their talent for a realistic depiction of human anatomy.[157] Another, and not unrelated, explanation is the Renaissance grafting of the iconography of Apollo – one of the handsome young athletic types of classical art – onto that of Sebastian. This transference is most apt, given the ancient god's association with the plague: in ancient literature we find Apollo invoked as both wrathful sender of and beneficent protector against deadly pestilence.[158]

More recently, however, some scholars, specifically Louise Marshall and Ellen Schiferel, have contested this Sebastian-as-Apollo thesis, inasmuch as it does not take into proper consideration the sincerely Christian mindset of the original patrons and viewers of the early modern images of Sebastian. For these Christian viewers, they argue, Sebastian, was seen not as a pagan god, but as an *alter Christus*, another Christ, who fulfills the same expiatory, salvific role as does the Savior: he does this by taking upon his innocent shoulders the sins of the people and in his suffering, like a true scapegoat, makes effective reparation for their transgressions in the eyes of God.[159] The basis of Marshall and Schiferel's claim is the undeniable similarity between the numerous representations of Sebastian's first "martyrdom" (via arrows tied to a tree or column in the field) with that of Christ's flagellation or Crucifixion, as most notably in St. Peter's Basilica in the work by Domenichino and in Strozzi's *Saint Sebastian Tended by Saint Irene and Her Maid* (cat. 16).[160] While the argument is extremely compelling and entirely reasonable, these scholars do not offer non-visual corroboration, that is to say, proof in the written texts of the period – sermons, sacred drama, and other devotional/spiritual literature – demonstrating explicitly or implicitly, this assumption of a salvific, Christ-like role by Sebastian in the eyes of early modern viewers. I myself have not yet found any such verification in the texts examined for this essay. What instead one does find in the primary sources regarding the early modern image of the young athletic – and scantily clad – Sebastian, is alarm and censure over the potential temptation to the sin of lust that these and all depictions of naked flesh, even or especially in religious art, represent. One famous expression of this concern is contained in the seventeenth-century moralizing treatise by Jesuit Giovanni Domenico Ottonelli and master painter-architect Pietro Berrettini da Cortona against the "abuses" of painters and sculptors who depict "immagini immodeste e ignude."[161] The erotic depictions of Sebastian in the works by Regnier, Solimena, and Strozzi (cats. 15, 16, 29) would have certainly have raised the eyebrows of such ecclesiastical censors.[162]

Saint Rosalie of Palermo

To examine a final case of tutelary plague saint, we turn to an example of a once purely local intercessor whose cult underwent prodigious expansion during our period throughout Europe, Rosalie (Rosalia) of Palermo, made famous in art by the series of canvases executed by Anthony van Dyck (cats. 30, 31). Rosalie's story is yet another variation on a conventional hagiographical scenario: daughter of Sicilian nobility, at the age of sixteen, the girl refused marriage and renounced her life of privilege, retreating instead to a life of penitential solitude and self-discipline in nearby caves. Death came several years later (1160 being the traditional date) on Monte Pellegrino three miles above Palermo.[163] Before 1625 few people outside of her native Sicily had heard of the twelfth-century hermit, and even in Sicily she was far from renowned among the island's canonized citizens, despite the churches dedicated to her there. Rosalie's name was not even included in the litany of saints prayed to during a solemn penitential plague procession conducted by the bishop of Palermo in 1624.[164] More importantly, "she was not mentioned in any of the ancient martyrologies, and there were no accounts of her life older than the end of the sixteenth century." As a result, whatever we know of her has been "put together from the evidence of local tradition, inscriptions, and paintings."[165]

What changed Rosalie's fortunes was the finding of her body – thanks to a supposed apparition of the saint herself – several months after the same 1624 procession, in a grotto on Monte Pellegrino while the plague still raged in Palermo. Her relics were carried *processionalmente* through the city, an act of devotion that resulted in the cessation of the plague soon thereafter, according to the pious belief of the saint's *devoti*. Luckily for Rosalie, Palermo was home to a large Jesuit community, which was soon won over to the cult of the newly disinterred virgin hermit. The Jesuits (in particular Giordano Cascini) set to publicizing, through printed hagiographies and preached sermons, the life, virtue, and thaumaturgic power of the aristocratic young virgin, not only in Sicily, but throughout the order's international network. That network included, of course, Rome (and, notably, Flanders and France as well). In Rome, Urban VIII himself had a particular devotion to Rosalie: "inflamed with love for the saint," the pontiff had written a poem in her honor and wore on his person one of the saint's relics, a tooth, given to him by one of the major promoters of her cult, the pious Duke of

Montalto, Antonio de Moncada y Aragona. On January 26, 1630, another plague year on the peninsula, Urban VIII further demonstrated his devotion to the Sicilian maiden by ordering the addition of Rosalie's name to the *Roman Martyrology*.[166] This designation formally marked the official elevation of her cult from the mere local to the universal.

It was most likely in these years of active promotion of her cult in Rome that was preached the Latin *Oratio Sanctae Rosaliae*, a hitherto overlooked printed sermon held in the Casanatense Library in the same city. Now unfortunately shorn of its title page and bereft of any indication of where, when, by whom, and to whom it was delivered, the physical evidence, however, clearly suggests that it came from a seventeenth-century Italian press. I strongly suspect that this text is the "oratio latina in laudem S. Rosaliae" described by the Bollandist Johannes Stilting in the *Acta Sanctorum*. Delivered at the Roman College on April 6, 1628, during a "*festivitas*" organized by the Jesuits, "with a magnificent apparatus," and the whole-hearted approval of Urban VIII (who paid for the publication of the oration), this stately, eloquent discourse in honor of Rosalie was written by the Jesuit Angelo Galluccio. However, for reasons unknown to us, it was, instead, on that occasion delivered (in the presence of the "most eminent papal nephew, Antonio Barberini and other Cardinals and Princes") by a "young nobleman," Giovanni Maria Roscioli, a Lateran canon.[167] Whatever its provenance, the sermon offers us a valuable glimpse into how the cult of the Sicilian saint was "marketed" in seventeenth-century Italy, in this case, as so often with ancient and medieval saints, largely on the basis of pure legend accumulated over the centuries.[168]

As required by the *vitae sanctorum* conventions of the day, the *Oratio Sanctae Rosaliae* relies on the traditional stock of hagiographical themes, most especially that of *contemptus mundi*, in describing (or rather, imagining) the external behavior and psychology of the young woman, in order to assure the ecclesiastical authorities and pious laity that she indeed fit the tried-and-true, orthodox mold of Catholic sainthood. At the same time, to give her some distinguishing features among so many other penitential female hermits, the author of the *Oratio* emphasizes her Palermitan roots and makes recurrent use of the floral topos, Rosalie/rose: for example, Rosalie among her familial riches was a rose among thorns while Urban VIII's devotion to Rosalie is likened to the work of bees – a reference to the bees of the Barberini coat of arms – drawn to the rose, resulting in the production of sweet honey. (This association between the saint and the flower is also seen in devotional art of our period [cats. 30, 31] as a useful cue for the identification of the saint.) Like other saints in the period, however, the aristocratic Rosalie also represents in this sermon a convenient political-diplomatic vehicle with which to render due homage to similarly aristocratic patrons and potential patrons, especially those of Spanish connection at a time when Rome was under the heavy-handed influence of Spain.[169] Delivered to a patrician audience (it begins with an address to "Illustrissimi Principes" – the above-mentioned Antonio Barberini and his princely peers?) the *Oratio* is effusive in its praise for not only Urban VIII, but also the island of Sicily and the city of Palermo, and the Spanish noble families of that city.[170]

Further enhancing the early seventeenth-century expansion of Rosalie's cult was the fact that a foreign artist of great talent and social connection happened to be in Palermo on the occasion of the discovery of her body. In the spring of 1624, Anthony van Dyck was invited by the Sicilian viceroy, Emanuele Filiberto of Savoy to visit Palermo, already host to a Genoese community of substantial financial means.[171] Rosalie was van Dyck's principal artistic occupation during his Sicilian sojourn: "confronted with a figure rarely represented in art ... it was he who established the iconography of the saint,"[172] producing several portraits of the saint, now scattered across the globe, two of which are included in the present exhibition (cat. 30, 31). When Rosalie is depicted alone, as in most of van Dyck's series, the saint's iconography is essentially that of the traditional penitential hermit, seen in the wilderness, skull at her feet. A wreath of roses around her head refers not only to her name, but also, as Barker points out, to "her protection against the 'foul air' of pestilence."[173] Bernardo Strozzi's portrait of the saint now at the Musée des Beaux-Arts, Caen, adds a more explicit reference to the plague, showing an arrow in Rosalie's right hand. A powerful new protectress was thus given to the universal church, visualized, immortalized, and publicized by the brush of the masters. However, as Amore observes,[174] as early as 1625, there had been serious challenges to the claims made about Rosalie and her relics at the time of her "resurrection": "In all honesty, it must be confessed that the circumstances surrounding [the] discovery [of her remains] are the cause of grave doubts regarding the authenticity of the body that was found, doubts that are evident in the accounts given even by those involved in the affair." These doubts, in the end, did nothing to dampen the enthusiasm of her *devoti*, including the learned Jesuits of Palermo, Rome, and elsewhere, and the Supreme Pontiff himself.

XV. *Conclusion: "Will you believe such things, oh posterity?"*

The unquestioning alacrity with which early modern Italians, and indeed, Europeans – even those far removed from the geographical center of the Sicilian maiden's cult – embraced the rehabilitated Rosalie in her new role as tutelary plague saint may be for us today the object of incredulity, if not derision. Yet, as this exhibition and catalogue demonstrate, the cultic enthusiasm for Rosalie, Sebastian, and the other heavenly helpers of early modern Italians, as well as the various other forms in which they responded to the plague, becomes completely understandable in light of the theological, psychological, social, and medical reality of that age. That reality was marked by fear, horror, and anxiety, so eloquently expressed by Italian humanist-poet Petrarch, whose famous letter on the plague of 1347-50, quoted in the epigram to this article, gives faithful voice to the emotions of three hundred years of survivors of the contagion. Such were the emotions generated by the assault of an invisible enemy whom science was largely impotent to conquer and who could be effectively combatted and overcome, early modern Italians believed, only by invisible, that is, spiritual means – the various *rimedi spirituali* preached by ecclesiastics and depicted by painters.

"Contemplating the calamitous and desolate state of these our most turbulent and most perilous times, with so great a grief in our heart...": with these words, on 28 October of the pandemic year of 1576, Pope Gregory XIII announced a special "jubileum," a period of extraordinary indulgences, graces, dispensations, and absolutions to offer further spiritual and psychological support, hope, and consolation to the Christian masses mercilessly afflicted by virulent plague.[175] Although Gregory's and the other *rimedi spirituali* described in this essay and given vivid visual form by artists of the period did not eradicate, prevent, or even abbreviate the epidemics, it is clear from the testimony of the contemporary sources that they were, nonetheless, efficacious sources of healing and renewal. During the plague-tormented years of early modern Italian history, thanks in no small part to the power of images, ultimately, hope and courage won out. In the end, as Emile Mâle reminds us, even out of horror and terror there came forth beauty: "Thus, as in the Middle Ages, the great plagues have multiplied the paintings, the frescoes, and the statues ... From these catastrophes that terrified mankind, there remains today a bit of beauty."[176]

1. Petrarca, 417.
2. Thursday, 7 November, 2002, p. A26.
3. The conception of the present exhibition, however, preceded the events of 11 September, 2001, having its origins in 2000 in the participation of the current writer in the re-discovery of Tintoretto's *Raising of Lazarus* (cat. 37), most likely an ex-voto in time of plague (see Mormando 2000).
4. In 1979 the city of Venice organized a multi-genre exhibition entitled *Venezia e la peste, 1348-1797*, while in 1990 at the Invalides, Paris, Henri Mollaret and Jacqueline Brossollet compiled the historical visual survey, *Images de la maladie: La peste dans l'histoire*. The latter exhibition featured only photographed reproductions of the original works of art. In 1994 Boston's Isabella Stewart Gardner Museum presented a small exhibition, *Art's Lament: Creativity in the Face of Death*, devoted to "artistic response to epidemic catastrophe" (*Art's Lament*, Preface) across several centuries, national boundaries, and artistic media.
5. Our research confirms Louise Marshall's conclusions, based on her study of a smaller sampling of Italian (Renaissance) plague art, that is to say, its fundamentally hopeful, positive, and self-confident nature: "In setting up hierarchical relationships of mutual obligation between worshipper and image, those who lived during the pandemic were not neurotic and helpless, but were taking positive – and in their eyes effective – steps to regain control over their environment" (Marshall 1994, 488). See also Marshall 2000, 20: "Far from collapsing into neurotic guilt and helpless despair, as is so often assumed, those who lived under the constant shadow of plague responded to their situation with energy and hope. The invention and ritual manipulation of a wide range of prophylactic images testifies to contemporaries' confidence in their ability to access the sources of supernatural power."
6. For a discussion of the Catholicism of early modern Italy, see Worcester 2002.
7. Another common term for the disease is *febbre pestilenziale*, pestilential fever. The anonymous reviewer of a Paduan medical treatise on the plague (*Dissertatio therapeutica de peste habita in Archi-Lycaeo Patavino à Car. Patino*) in the *Journal des savants* (1683: 234) observes that a distinction must be made between "plague," "pestilence," and "pestilential fever," even though the "ancient doctors (*anciens Medicins*) have confused the three terms;" however, he acknowledges the fact that the word "plague" (*peste*) is often "used in a more universal sense to refer to any disease from which few escape alive." Similarly, Alfonso Corradi, author of the massive *Annali delle epidemie occorse in Italia dalle prime memorie fino al 1850*, separates cases of "peste o peste bubonica" from those of "pestilienza" in the chronological lists of outbreaks at the end of his study, although some of the latter cases might indeed involve bubonic plague (Corradi, 5:647-68).
8. Deaux, 12. Lucenet, 15, quotes Galen as saying: "When a disease affects a great number of people it is an epidemic; when most of these victims die from it, it is a plague."
9. Black, 24. In his study of the fourteenth-century "Black Death," Samuel Cohn has come to the conclusion that this medieval killer "was not the same rat-based bubonic plague whose agent (*Yersinia pestis*) was first cultured at Hong Kong in 1894" (Cohn 2002, 703; see also Cohn 2003).
10. The information about the medical aspects of the disease in the paragraphs that follow and in the next section of this essay is taken from Biraben, 1:7-12; Boeckl 2000, 7-12; Deaux, 64-66; McGrew, 36-46; Sobel, 200-201.
11. Deaux, 65; Pallavicino, 12-13; see also Wills, 80.
12. Targioni Tozzetti, 3:131.
13. Pallavicino, 11-12. For all aspects of the history of the plague in Rome and much of the related art, especially that of the seventeenth century, Sheila Barker's exhaustive doctoral dissertation is indispensable; see also her essay in the present catalogue.
14. Black, 23.
15. Biraben, 1:394-400; Corradi, 5:652-59 ("peste o peste bubbonica"), 667-68 ("pestilenza"); Del Panta, 138-78.
16. Gastaldi, 18.
17. Gastaldi, 9ff. The commissioner includes this catalogue of outbreaks and sources ("Celebriores pestilentiae totius orbis, quarum extat memoria, per tempora et loca recensentur") in chapter two of his lavishly illustrated and conscientiously documented account of the city of Rome's response to the plague of 1656, the *Tractatus de avertenda et profliganda peste politico-legalis* (Bologna, 1684), which we have just quoted.
18. For other such chronological lists, see, e.g., Bumaldi, 28-32; Kircher, 132-48; Rondinelli, 219-30.
19. For a discussion of Thucydides's account in the primary sources, see, e.g., Marchini, *Belli divini*, 4-5, with a long extract given in his *Philosophica de pestilentia problemata*, 5-8.
20. For the plague in Naples, see James Clifton's essay in the present catalogue.
21. Kircher, 148.
22. Black, 23.
23. For the plague in Venice (and further mortality statistics for the Veneto region), see Andrew Hopkins's essay in the present catalogue.
24. See Black, 23 for modern calculations of the Genoese and Roman population loss in 1656; Black, 220 for that of Venice (as well as Preto, 97-98); Corradi, 5: 654 for plague in Rome, 1625-29; Gastaldi, 116; Pallavicino 17: "quasi tutto di plebe con poche teste civili, niuna illustre." The report about Bernini's brothers comes from the seventeenth-century diary of Roman lawyer, Carlo Cartari, 252.
25. Litchfield, 100.
26. The quotation is from the biographical preface (pp. v-vi) supplied by the anonymous editor of the 1714 edition (Florence: Jacopo Guidicci e Santi Franchi) of Rondinelli's *Relazione*.
27. Rondinelli, "A' lettori (unpaginated preface to his *Relazione del contagio*) for the population figures; 3-4 for Ferdinand's heroic virtue; Dooley, 184 for modern statistics for Florence, Verona, Parma, Brescia, and Venice; Marino, 65 for the Milanese statistics.
28. Del Panta, 179-90.
29. Muratori, 432.
30. Muratori, 436. The value of Rondinelli's treatise is underscored by Targioni Tozzetti, 3:131.
31. Graeci: typis Haeredum Widmanstadii. For the Jesuits and the plague, see Sheila Barker's and Gauvin Bailey's essays in the present catalogue.
32. The 1897 discovery was made by Masanori Ogata and Paul Louis Simond, working independently. For all these nineteenth-century medical developments, see Wills, 71-85; and McGrew, 44-45. Wills notes, "After decades of controversy, it is now universally agreed that Yersin and not Kitasato was the discoverer of the plague bacillus" (75).

33. Kircher, 141, as quoted and translated by Rowlands, 105, cat. no. 116; for Fracastoro and Kircher, see also Capanna, 175-76.
34. Bumaldi, 6.
35. Gazzaniga, 53; Smoller, 173-74.
36. Marchini, *Philosophica de pestilentia problemata*, Problemata 23, 24, and 25; Gastaldi, 678-80.
37. Lubrano, "L'Eraclito, sfogo di malinconie per la peste di Napoli," 148, vv, 83-84, "E spargono ammorbati a gli antidoti stessi il Tosco i fiati."
38. Bumaldi, 5; Gastaldi, 641.
39. Gastaldi, 640.
40. Marshall 1994, 986.
41. See *Venezia e la peste*, 243-44, fig. a16 and color plate IV for the Tintoretto canvas; for Ferrari's ex-voto work, see the same catalogue, 269-70, fig. a44 and color plate V.
42. Quoted in Cartari, 249. Brighetti reproduces the same report in full (261-64; 263 for the stench reference) giving the doctor's name as "Ressi;" however since in his diary Cartari makes several references, by name, to "Pressi" as a man of his personal acquaintance, I assume this is the correct spelling of his family name.
43. In Dooley, 197.
44. Cartari, 249; Brighetti, 263.
45. See *Scienza e miracoli*, 341-42 and color plate D39 for Bernardi's altarpiece.
46. For the Cozza painting, see Fumaroli, 105 and fig. 82.
47. For these, see Boeckl 2000, 46-47, 54, 96-97.
48. For a complete discussion of the provenance and subject of this painting, see Mormando 2000.
49. See *Giovan Battista Moroni (1520-1578)*, scheda 23, 118; for this painting see also *Age of Caravaggio*, 70-72, cat. no. 8; and *I pittori bergamaschi*, 100.
50. For Michael and the plague, see *Scienza e miracoli*, cat. D46, 349-50; Mercalli; Sheila Barker's essay in the present catalogue, and, in particular for Michael as apocalyptic warrior in the context of plague iconography, see Barker, 243-45. For the plague and the Apocalypse in general, see Smoller.
51. The earliest historian to describe the 590 A.D. plague procession, Gregory of Tours (539-94), does not mention any angelic apparition in his *History of the Franks*. Michael's connection to the story is a later medieval accretion, Jacopo da Voragine's text representing "one of the earliest surviving accounts" of the legend (Barker, 14). See Barker, 14-17 for Saint Michael's association with the Roman fortress named after him.
52. For the most current research and complete bibliography on Sweerts, see the essays in Jansen and Sutton, especially that of Bikker; for *Plague in an Ancient City*, see cat. XIII, 113-17 of the same work.
53. *Plague in an Ancient City* is believed to have been executed toward the end of Sweerts's stay in Rome. The artist arrived in the city in the mid-1640s and was there until at least 1652; by July 19, 1655 he had returned to Brussels (Bikker, 25, 31). The earliest documented notice of the painting is the news of its sale in 1804 at Christie's London (Jansen and Sutton, 117). For Poussin's *Plague at Ashdod* as "Sweerts's primary visual source," see Jansen and Sutton, 113, citing Roberto Longhi. Until Longhi's 1934 essay, the canvas had been attributed to Poussin. According to Longhi's later and now generally accepted thesis, the architectural setting of the painting comes from the hand of Viviano Codazzi, a specialist in the genre (Jansen and Sutton, 116).
54. Jansen and Sutton, 116. See *Dutch and Flemish Paintings*, cat. 49, for the opinion that in his *Plague* canvas Sweerts "was clothing in antique garb reference to the contemporary plague that raged in Rome from 1649 to 1650."
55. The fact was given wide publicity through (among other channnels) the *Annales ecclesiastici*, that vastly influential apologetic history of the church by Oratorian cardinal, Cesare Baronio (d. 1607); see Baronio, Vol. 1, annus Christi 58, cc. 109-11. The "orans" prayer pose is a prominent feature, as well, of Caravaggio's *Entombment* (1603-4), originally created for Filippo Neri's Chiesa Nuova, a painting that, according to Alessandro Zuccari, gives evidence of the Oratorian "recovery of paleo-Christian typologies" (Zuccari, 55, n. 17)
56. The presence of the obelisk, thus, does not necessarily identify the setting of Sweerts's scene as an Egyptian city, such as Alexandria, the thriving, celebrated capital of Graeco-Roman Egypt, struck by plague in both the third and sixth centuries. Alexandria is, in any case, a port city, as Sweerts and his contemporaries well knew, and there is no sign of a port or any body of water in *Plague in an Ancient City*. It is possible that the artist may not have intended to invoke any one city in particular.
57. The Black Temple's now oxidized interior is more legible in the early nineteenth-century engraving by James Fittler. Fittler's engraving can be found in Forster, no. 31.
58. Bosio, 414. We can exclude the possibility, by the way, that the Black Temple is meant to represent a Christian catacomb. By the time Sweerts painted this canvas, many Christian catacombs had been extensively explored and their contents thoroughly inventoried and illustrated in Bosio's celebrated volume. Sweerts's Black Temple contains none of the visual details we find in Bosio.
59. There were conflicting reports about the true site of the rediscovery of the Minerva Giustiniani; see Haskell and Penny, 269-71, cat. 63.
60. Jansen and Sutton, 114.
61. Possevino, 6r-6v; Nicephorus, 10:35. The Emperor Julian was an ardent devotee of the Sun God, a readily known fact in seventeenth-century Europe.
62. It may be pertinent to the meaning of Sweert's canvas that one of the principal victors at Westphalia was France, who proved to be no friend of Pope Innocent X or the papcy, and whose king at the time was Louis XIV, "the Sun King." The space restrictions of the present catalogue do not allow me to here enter into a detailed exposition of these hypotheses or of any of the preceding observations concerning Sweerts's canvas, but this I shall be supplying in a separate publication, along with more extensive bibliographic citation.
63. Rondinelli, in the unpaginated "A' lettori" prefatory material; for the Pressi opinion, see Pressi, 262.
64. The popular proverb was communicated in the couplet: "Haec tria tabificam tollunt pestem / mox, longe, tarde, cede, recede, redi." See Muratori, 446; and Gazzaniga, 52.
65. These are among the typical measures taken by cities and towns of our period, as repeatedly described in many of our sources, e.g., Baldinucci, Cartari, Gastaldi, Marchini, Pallavicino, and Rondinelli. The detail about the elimination of the dogs comes from Baldinucci, 193. The most complete description of these measures, accompanied by numerous detailed illustrations, is that of

Gastaldi. Among the many secondary sources discussing this topic, see the most recent Benvenuto. For further discussion of dogs and the plague, see Thomas Worcester's essay in the present catalogue.

66. Baldinucci, 199.
67. Pallavicino, 6.
68. Cartari, 248.
69. Muratori, 470.
70. Gastaldi, 680.
71. Kircher, 1.
72. Tomitano, 267-68: "Bartolus dicit: quid credis sit pestis, nisi bellum Dei contra nos?" For Marchini's title, see his discussion, "Tituli explicatio: cur divinum bellum," included in the "Apparatus ad tractatum," the unpaginated preface to his *Belli divini.*
73. Baldinucci, 194. Later (202) Baldinucci cites as proof of this belief the fact that "no nuns or friars have so far died from the contagion, except for those who looked after the afflicted and a few others."
74. Mascardi and Achillini, 14-15. For Manzoni's borrowings from these letters, see Bellini, 31-32.
75. Bellintani da Salò, 3738.
76. Panigarola, 264v-272r. For the dissemination of this and other works by Panigarola in France, see Thomas Worcester's essay in the present catalogue.
77. Possevino, 19r-23r. The attribution to Possevino was made by J. Patrick Donnelly, according to A. Lynn Martin, 89, n. 1. Possevino's text was widely disseminated in our period: first published in Macerata in 1576 by episcopal order, it was reprinted in Florence in the following year and then again in Milan in 1630.
78. The list is given in the unpaginated preface, "Apparatus ad tractatum," to Marchini, *Belli divini.*
79. Tomitano, 268-77.
80. Possevino, 12v-19r.
81. Possevino, 17r, v.
82. For this topos in art, see Boeckl 1996. For the discussion of heresy in *Cause et rimedii*, see 13v-14r; see also A. Lynn Martin, 95.
83. Panigarola, 272-74 for both the Protestant and Turkish threats. Plague is used as an image for heresy also in that best-selling inquisitional encyclopedia of early modern Europe, the *Malleus Maleficarum* (The Hammer of Witches, first publ. 1485): see, e.g., Part 3, Question 29.
84. Deaux, 6. The unidentified New Testament episodes to which Deaux refers are, I presume, Matthew 9:1-8 and John 5:1-14.
85. For a list of scriptural references to the plague, see, e.g., Day, 659; and Fuller, Index, s.v., "Plague."
86. See, e.g., Possevino, 11v-12r and 13r. Other references to the punishment of David in the plague literature are Panigarola, 265; Bellintani da Salò, 3738; and Marchini, *Belli divini*, unpaginated preface ("Apparatus ad tractatum").
87. Busti, 166-67.
88. Boeckl 2000, 54.
89. Marshall 1994, 518 and figs. 15-16.
90. The undated canvas (154.5 x 117.5 cm), now in a private collection in Australia and on extended loan to the Art Gallery of Western Australia, West Perth, is not listed in Ferrari's complete catalogue of Giordano's works. For the second larger and horizontal version (164 x 207 cm.), see Ferrari 1992, I, entry A372 and figure 481, where it is listed as "art market, Madrid" and given the date 1685, "presumed to be from [Giordano's] Spanish period since the same subject appears in the Escorial decoration; however, the painting would seem to have been executed before [his] departure for Spain." (See n. 93 below regarding a Giordano King David inventoried in Rome in 1682.) For the Escorial fresco, see Ferrari 1992, I, entry A525, p. 333 and fig. 663. A copy of the Australian Giordano, formerly property of the Rose Art Museum, Brandeis University, bore an attribution to Giordano's disciple, Paolo de Matteis, at the time of its sale at Sotheby's, New York, *Important Old Master Paintings*, June 7, 1978, lot 195. However, the canvas, presently in the Bob Jones University Museum, is now attributed to August Heyn (1837-1920), on the basis of what appears to be his signature inscribed on the reverse (personal communication from John Nolan, BJUM Curator, August, 2003).
91. Meyer, 122; the remark about the king's piety comes from Carr, 49. For David as a model for early modern princes, see also Polleross.
92. Marchini, *Belli divini*, unpaginated preface ("Apparatus ad tractatum"), "nobilium virorum superbia ac ambitio inordinata."
93. See Burke and Cherry, 1:746, item n. 300 of Inventory n. 109. Although the description does not completely match either of the already-cited Giordano King David canvases, it is, nonetheless, very close and could in fact be referring to one of them, any discrepancy being due, perhaps, to hasty observation on the part of the compiler of the inventory. In any case, there is no other known treatment of this King David subject by Giordano. Burke and Cherry do note that "some evidence ... suggests that many of Don Gaspar's pictures bore unrealistic attributions" (1:727); however, Giordano himself was present in the city at the same time and hence such a mistake in attribution would seem strange. For a brief biography of Don Gaspar (also known as the Marqués de Eliche, or Heliche or Liche), see Burke and Cherry, 1:462; and the *Grove Dictionary of Art*, s.v., "Carpio, Marquéses de."
94. Poussin's composition is believed to have been changed after Caroselli's copy had been completed. For discussion of the Poussin and Caroselli canvases see Barker, 297-303, as well as her essay in the present catalogue; for both Poussin and Caroselli, see *Roma 1630*, 162-71.
95. Panigarola, 265.
96. For a typical early modern exegesis of the Brazen Serpent story, see that of the great Jesuit biblical commentator, Cornelio a Lapide (1567-1637), in his *Commentaria in Scriptura Sacra*, "Commentaria in Numeros," 2:304-06.
97. Oliva, "Sermone detto nell'Oratorio de' Nobili al Giesù, l'Ultima Domenica dopo la Pentecoste," *Sermoni detti*, 789-70, s. 630. In the same passage, Oliva refers to the "corpi apestati" (*sic*), the bodies of the plague-stricken victims of the fiery serpents, further reminding us of the ready connection that the early modern imagination made between this Old Testament story and plague epidemics.
98. For the Scuola di San Rocco, see Howard, 156-59; and Andrew Hopkins's essay in this catalogue.
99. Kaminski, 256.
100. Lapide, *Great Commentary*, Saint John's Gospel, 112. On the same page Lapide inserts another polemical swipe against the Protestants, commenting: "From all that has been said, it will appear how foolish is Calvin's interpretation that this lifting up of Christ is not His Crucifixion but the preaching of His Gospel." For Lapide's commen-

tary on the Old Testament text of the Brazen Serpent episode, see n. 96 above. For another seventeenth-century commentary on the same Old Testament episode, see Segneri, 1:334-38.
101. Lapide, *Great Commentary*, Saint John's Gospel, 111. The anti-iconoclastic implications of the episode had been pointed out by second-century Christian apologist, Justin Martyr, long before the virulent controversies surrounding the legitimacy of devotional images of the eight- and ninth-century Byzantine Church and later of the Protestant Reformation,. In his *Dialogue with Trypho*, commenting upon the Brazen Serpent episode, Justin asks rhetorically, "Tell me, did not God, through Moses, forbid the making of an image or likeness of anything in the heavens or on earth? Yet didn't he himself have Moses construct the brazen serpent in the desert?" (quoted in Lienhard, 241).
102. For the use of amulets as plague remedies, see Kircher, 113-14; see also Smoller, 173-74; and Baldwin. Regarding the Roman god of healing, Aesculapius, it was in part because of the plague, we might point out, that the ancient Romans imported him to their city (Shelton, 367-68).
103. *Twilight of the Medici*, 220, entry 128, on which my discussion of the canvas here depends, as well as Baldassari, 175-76.
104. Baldassari, 176. For the provenance of the canvas, see *Twilight of the Medici*, 220; and Baldassari, 175-76.
105. *Copia di una lettera pastorale di monsig. illustrissimo cardinal Paleotti vescovo di Bologna al popolo suo nel pericolo della peste*, 1576, quoted by Zanette, 447.
106. Rondinelli, "A' lettori," unpaginated; Muratori, 518.
107. Rondinelli, 234; Tomitano, "De peste," 267. Jesuit preacher Gian Paolo Oliva instead mocks the pagans who turned to their false god, Apollo, in time of plague and perished nonetheless: "Predica detta nella Basilica di San Pietro, la Domenica corrente fra le ferie dell'Epifania," *Aggiunta a' quaranta sermoni*, 180-81.
108. Busti, 174-85; and in summary fashion, Panigarola, 27
109. Tomitano, "De peste," 266.
110. In Pallavicino, see, e.g., 15-16; Bellintani da Salò, 3745-46; Possevino, 36r-v.
111. Marchini, *Belli divini*, unpaginated prefatory section, "Apparatus ad tractatum." For the relic of the Holy Nail, see Pamela Jones's essay in the present catalogue.
112. Gregory of Tours, 2:426 (Book 10:1).
113. For the topic of sudden death in early modern Catholicism, see Worcester 1999, 90.
114. For the painting (of which another version exists in the Snite Museum, University of Notre Dame), see Spear 1971, 88-89; for this theme in art and in Italian culture in general, see Scalabroni; and Scaramella.
115. For the complete original text, see *Antologia della poesia italiana: Seicento*, 60. For Rosa's canvas and his personal experiences in this period of his life, see Scott, 108-17; *Treasures from the Fitzwilliam*, cat. 99; *Salvator Rosa* (exh. cat. Hayward Gallery), cat. 27; and Scaramella, 85 (74-85 for the Baroque period in general). For the same pessimistic view of human existence, see Fioravanti, bk. 1, chap. 57, pp. 60v-61r.
116. Bellintani da Salò, 3757.
117. Deaux, 5. Deaux is here specifically referring to the experience of the Black Death of 1348 but the psychological reaction holds true for subsequent outbreaks as well.
118. Marshall 1994, 516.
119. For Francis Xavier as plague saint, see Clifton, 491-94; and Boeckl 2000, 129-30. Xavier also appears in Guido Reni's famous ex-voto plague banner, the *Pallione del voto*, 1630, discussed later in this essay.
120. Possevino, 34v; Marchini includes his extracts from Cyprian among the unpaginated prefatory materials in *Belli divini*. Muratori also offers a list of specific works of spiritual consolation (539-40) but his list mostly comprises modern titles.
121. Cyprian, *Mortality*, chap. 5, 202-3.
122. Cyprian, *Mortality*, chap. 14, 210.
123. For statistics on the chronic food crises of early modern Italy, see Black, 25; for the problem of famine, see also Thomas Worcester's essay in the present catalogue.
124. Cyprian, *Works and Almsgiving*, 231.
125. Jansen and Sutton, 81.
126. For Sweerts's Seven Acts of Mercy series, see Jansen and Sutton, 81-93.
127. Roscio, 41.
128. For the allegories of charity in early modern painting, see *L'allégorie dans la peinture*.
129. Tomitano, 271.
130. Possevino, 23r-29r; Marchini, *Belli divini*, 268-310.
131. Quoted by Ward in Townsend and Ward, 13. For confraternities and their art in time of plague, see, e.g., Marshall 2000.
132. Marchini, *Belli divini*, 275. For Bernardino and the plague of 1400 in Siena, see Mormando 1999a, 34.
133. Tomitano, 271-72; for the full quotation from Bernardino of Siena, see his *Opera omnia*, 3:173.
134. Tomitano, 272, 273; Muratori, 543. As Thomas Worcester explains in his essay in the present catalogue, Saint Roch also invoked the Holy Name of Jesus to cure cases of the plague.
135. For this *modello*, see Spike, who instead claims that the scene depicts a penitential plague procession, in which Bernardo successfully intercedes for the cessation of the plague, that cessation being signaled by the angel at the center of the composition seen in the act of departure (Spike, 116).
136. Segneri, no. 13, 2:608, col. 2. For further discussion of Gonzaga as plague saint, as well as of the Batoni portrait and the controversial question of the saint's "martyrdom," see Sheila Barker's essay in the present catalogue.
137. Information from the website of the Metropolitan Museum of Art, metmuseum.org.
138. Boeckl 2000, 40.
139. For Saint Roch, see Thomas Worcester's essay in this catalogue.
140. For the plague and the Madonna della Misericordia, see Marshall 1994, 506-15.
141. For the history behind and iconography of Reni's *Pallione*, see Puglisi (411 for the reference to the supplanted Madonnas). For Longhena's Santa Maria della Salute, see Andrew Hopkins's essay in the present catalogue.
142. This extraordinary event is described in detail by at least three contemporaries: see Baldinucci, 199-201; Rondinelli, 276-84, in the long appendix (247-84) to his *Relazione del contagio*, entitled *Breve Relazione della Madonna dell'Impruneta*; and Sobel, 265-68, who quotes the letters of eyewitness, Suor Maria Celeste Galilei. Rondinelli's claim is in his Impruneta Appendix, 275; at the very end of the same appendix can be found an itemized catalogue of the gifts made to the Madonna on this occasion.

143. The attribution of the small *bozzetto* (37 x 28 cm., oil on canvas) to Rosi was made privately by Roberto Contini (and confirmed by Mina Gregori) to its owner, Mary Jane Harris (personal communication from M.J. Harris). Rosi (ca. 1585/89-1633) was one of Cristofano Allori's most devoted pupils and most intimate collaborators; it was he in fact who completed many of Allori's works left unfinished while Allori was all but incapacitated by an illness that led to his premature death in 1621. For Rosi, see Contini (121 for the conjectured dates of birth); Thiem, 32; and Pizzorusso, 31, 33, 54; the date of Rosi's death is given by Brooks, 36.

144. The identification of the Marian icon here depicted was made privately by Mina Gregori to its owner (personal communication from M. J. Harris). Under the clouds at the right, let us note, appears the faint outline of yet another episcopal miter. In black and white photographs Roch might be easily mistaken for John the Baptist, but in the full-color *bozzetto* itself, the red bubo on his upper right leg and the white shell of Saint James on his pilgrim's staff are clearly discernible. I have identified the saint on the extreme left as Michael the Archangel: although he does not bear wings, his military apparel and the balances in his hand – both traditional attributes of the saint – strongly suggest this identification. The blond, barefooted female saint is likely to be Mary Magdalene, a popular model of repentance, one of the most important of the *rimedi spirituali* for the plague. Supporting Gregori's identification of the Impruneta icon is the thick wrap of cloth surrounding the image, which the *putti* have just raised to expose the image to the viewer: as Baldinucci reports in his diary (201), "This most holy image of Impruneta is covered with many cloths and is never exposed; and they say ... that God desires it to remain hidden, because anciently some prelates wished to expose it and lost their eyesight in various accidents and as soon as they put the cloths back on they were made whole again." See also Rondinelli, 250, who confirms this fact: "in so many centuries of being hidden [from human sight], there is no memory of anyone who has ever seen [the Madonna's image]." Hence, the icon in Rosi's *bozzetto* does not represent an accurate representation drawn from the actual image (of late Gothic style), still extant and now on public display, fully uncovered, at Impruneta.

145. *Antiphonae*, 22.

146. For the cult of Sebastian, see the *Acta Sanctorum*, "De S. Sebastiano Mart.;" *Butler's Lives*, Jan. 20th, 242-44; and Gordini. For his iconography, see Cannata; Jones, 31-36; Marshall 1994, 488-500; Schiferel; Réau; Zupnick; and, especially for Rome, Barker, 13-14, 51-52, 60-65, 70-78, 113-14, 253-83, as well as her essay in the present catalogue.

147. Gordini, 777.

148. *Acta Sanctorum*, "De S. Sebastiano Mart.," 642.

149. Réau, 1197. For Baronio and Sebastian, see von Henneberg, 138-41.

150. Réau, 1191.

151. For Barberini's devotion to Sebastian, see Schütze, 92; and Rice 1997, 192-93.

152. Réau, 1191; Rice 1997, 96n.68; Gordini, 785; Gregory Martin, *Roma sancta*, 28, 32. For the location of the saint's relics, see *Acta Sanctorum*, "De S. Sebastiano Mart," 625-28.

153. Marchini, *Philosophica de pestilentia problemata*, Problemata VIII, 17. For the arrows as symbol of divine wrath in pagan mythology and the Bible, see Deaux, 15; Marshall 1994, 493-95; Schiferel, 211.

154. *Acta Sanctorum*, "De S. Sebastiano Mart.," 624.

155. Gregory Martin, 42; see also Frutaz, 6; Réau, 1192-93; and Cannata, 793.

156. Réau, 1192.

157. See Cannata, 794, for both the eighth-century legend and for Sebastian as a "pretext for a free anatomical virtuosity."

158. For Sebastian and Apollo, see Deaux, 38; Freedman, 9-10; Marshall 1994, 491-93; Schiferel, 209; Zupnick, 217-18.

159. Marshall 1994, 491-500; Schiferel, 215-17. Note that Marshall and Schiferel base their observations only on Renaissance (i.e., fifteenth-century) representations of Sebastian. Barker (253-83) notes the same explicit Christological casting of Sebastian in Roman art of the sixteenth and seventeenth centuries, although, again, contemporary textual confirmation is wanting.

160. Domenichino's original altarpiece was replaced by a mosaic copy and placed in the church of Santa Maria degli Angeli; for the altarpiece, see, Rice 1997, 192-97; Barker, 272-81. The Strozzi canvas was recently reunited with its long-missing upper portion (containing the putti); see Temin.

161. Ottonelli and Berrettini devote many pages to this theme; references to Sebastian can be found on pp. 42 and 289. For the same concern about nudity of the saints in art, see Mormando 1999b, 117-18; and Brown, 281-90. For the Ottonelli-Berrettini treatise, see Bailey, 171.

162. For a discussion of sexuality in Reni's several depictions of Sebastian and in the artist's own life, see Spear 1997, 67-76.

163. For Rosalie's life and cult, see *Acta Sanctorum*, "De S. Rosalia Virgine;" Amore; *Butler's Lives*; Collura, 9-78.

164. Amore, 428.

165. *Butler's Lives*, "Saint Rosalia, virg.," 49. For the events of 1624-25 leading up to the rediscovery of Rosalie's body and the subsequent renaissance of her popular cult, see Collura, 79-92; and Bailey's essay in this volume.

166. *Acta Sanctorum*, "De S. Rosalia Virgine," 349, for Urban's devotion to Rosalie, his poem in her honor, and the relic given to him by the Duke. (The running marginal note to this *Acta Sanctorum* essay reads "Auctore J.S.," that is, Johannes Stilting, S.J..) See Collura, 84 for the date of the papal brief, "Scriptam in caelesti," announcing Rosalie's insertion in the Roman Martyrology. It is here appropriate to note, by the way, that, contrary to previous report (Boeckl, 57), Pope Urban never contracted the plague in Palermo or in any other locality.

167. *Acta Sanctorum*, "De S. Rosalia Virgine," 349-50. Stilting therein says (350) the oration was published in "Cascini, p. 51 seq." – most likely referring to Cascini's posthumous *Di Santa Rosalia, romita palermitana, palesata con libri tre .... nelli quali si spiegano l'inventione delle Sacre Reliquie, la vita solitaria, e gli honori di lei con aggiunta di Tre digressioni historiche, del Monte Pellegrino, ove visse e morì, di suo parentado, ch'ebbe discendenza dall'imperatore Carlo Magno, e d'alcuni componimenti in sua lode* (Palermo, 1651), which, unfortunately, I have not been able to consult in order to compare the oration texts in question. For this 1651 work, see Collura, 118.

168. Rome, Biblioteca Casanatense, Vol. Miscellanee 1370, no. 1.

169. For the Spanish "occupation" of Rome in our period, see Dandelet.

170. *Oratio Sanctae Rosaliae*, 7. Specifically mentioned are the "nobilissimiae gentis de Aragona et Moncada" and Antonio duke of Montalto (the same *devoto* of Saint Rosalie, mentioned by the Bollandist Stilting), as well as "Ioannam de Lacerda Medinae Caeli Ducis filiam." Saint Teresa of Avila is also cited here.
171. For van Dyck's Rosalie paintings, see Gauvin Bailey's essay in the present catalogue, as well as Martin and Feigenbaum. For Rosalie in art, see also Collura, 95-95-114, 125-82, figs. 1-99 and pls. 1-24. The *Acta Sanctorum* entry on Rosalie contains many illustrations and reproductions of her image in art, especially those of pre-1600 vintage.
172. Martin and Feigenbaum, 126.
173. Barker, 304, n. 242.
174. Amore, 428.
175. Gregory XIII, *Jubileum ad avertenda pestis pericula* ("Calamitosum e miserabilem huius nostri"), publicatum Bonomiae die 28 octobris 1576, M. Datarius Cal. Glorierius A. de Alexiis, apud Alexandrum Benatium.
176. *L'art religieux après le Concile de Trente* (Paris: Colin, 1932, 383), quoted by Barker, Preface, iv.

Bibliography

Acta Sanctorum. "De S. Rosalia Virgine eximia contra pestem patrona . . . Commentarius Praevius." ["Auctore J.S.," i.e., Johannes Stilting.] Septembris, tom. 2 (Sept. 4): 278-380. Paris, 1868.

—. "De S. Sebastiano Mart. Romanae Eccl. Defensore." Januarius, tom. 2 (Jan. 20): 622-60. Paris, 1863.

The Age of Caravaggio. Exh. cat. New York and Milan, 1985.

L'allégorie dans la peinture. La représentation de la charité au XVIIe siècle. Exh. cat. Ed. Alain Tapié. Caen, 1986.

Amore, Agostino. "Rosalia, patrona di Palermo, santa." In *Bibliotheca sanctorum*, 9:427-33.

Antiphonae, psalmi, preces, et orationes ad usum supplicationum tempore pestis. Caroli S.R.E. Presb. Card. S. Praxedis Archiepiscopi jussu editae. Milan, 1576.

Antologia della poesia italiana: Seicento. Ed. Cesare Segre and Carlo Ossola. Turin,2001.

Art's Lament: Creativity in the Face of Death. Exh. cat. Boston, 1994.

Bailey, Gauvin A. "The Jesuits and Painting in Italy, 1550-1690: The Art of Catholic Reform." In *Saints and Sinners*, 151-78.

Baldassari, Francesco. *Giovanni Domenico Ferretti*. Milan, 2002.

Baldinucci, Giovanni. *Memoirs of the Plague in Florence*. In Dooley, 183-207, 646-49.

Baldwin, Martha R. "Toads and Plague: Amulet Therapy in Seventeenth-Century Medicine," *Bulletin of the History of Medicine* 67 (1993): 227-47.

Barker, Sheila. "Art in a Time of Danger: Urban VIII's Rome and the Plague of 1629-1634." Ph.D. thesis. Columbia University, Department of Art History and Archeology, 2002.

Baronio, Cesare. *Annales ecclesiastici*. 37 vols. Barri-Ducis, 1865.

Bellini, Eraldo. *Agostino Mascardi tra "ars poetica" e "ars storica."* Milan, 2002.

Bellintani da Salò, Paolo. *Dialogo della peste*. In *I Frati Cappuccini: Documenti e testimonianze del primo secolo*. 5 vols. in 6. III/2:3735-61. Ed. Costanzo Cargnoni. Perugia, 1988-93.

Benvenuto, Grazia. *La peste nell'Italia della prima età moderna. Contagio, rimedi, profilassi*. Bologna, 1996.

Bernardino of Siena. *Opera omnia*. Ed. Johannis De la Haye. 5 vols. Venice, 1745.

Bibliotheca Sanctorum. 13 vols. Rome, 1961-70.

Bikker, Jonathan. 2002. "Sweerts's Life and Career – A Documentary View." In Jansen and Sutton, 25-36.

Biraben, Jean-Noël. *Les hommes et la peste en France et dans les pays européens et méditerranéens*. Paris, 1975.

Black, Christopher F. *Early Modern Italy: A Social History*. London, 2001.

Boeckl, Christine M. *Images of Plague and Pestilence: Iconography and Iconology*. Kirksville, Missouri, 2000.

—. "Plague Imagery as Metaphor for Heresy in Rubens' *The Miracles of Saint Francis Xavier*." *Sixteenth Century Journal* 27 (1996): 979-95.

Bosio, Antonio. *Roma sotterranea opera postuma ... Compilata, disposta, e accresciuta dal M.R.P. Giovanni Severani*. Rome, 1632.

Brighetti, Antonio. *Bologna e la peste del 1630*. Bologna, 1968.

Brooks, Julian. "Drawing in Florence, c. 1600: The Studio and the City." In *Graceful and True: Drawing in Florence, c. 1600*. 22-39. Exh. cat. Oxford, 2003.

Brown, Beverly Louise. "Between the Sacred and the Profane." In *The Genius of Rome, 1592-1623*, ed. Beverly L. Brown. 274-303. Exh. cat. London, 2001.

Bumaldi, Giovanni Antonio [*alias of Ovidio Montalbani*]. *Il pestifugo esculapio cioè regole più secure per iscampare da ogni contagioso pericolo*. Bologna, 1656.

Burke, Marcus B. and Peter Cherry. *Collections of Paintings in Madrid Collections*. Ed. Maria L. Gilbert. The Provenance Index of the Getty Information Institute; Spanish Inventories, I. 2 vols. Los Angeles, 1997.

Busti, Bernardino de'. "Sermone del Rev. Bernardino Busti milanese dell'Ordine di Santo Francesco. Tradotto in toscano dal Reverendo Don Silvano Rozzi monaco di Camaldoli. Nel quale si tratta dei segni, cause e rimedii della pestilenza." Published with the Florence, 1577 edition of Possevino, *Cause et rimedii.*

Butler's Lives of the Saints. "St. Rosalia, Virg." Ed., rev., and supplemented by H. J. Thurston and D. Attwater. 4 vols. September 4: 9:49-50. Allen, Texas, 1995.

Cannata, Pietro. "Sebastiano, santo, martire di Roma: Iconografia." In *Bibliotheca sanctorum*, 11:789-801.

Capanna, Ernesto. "Zoologia kircheriana." In *Athanasius Kircher. Il museo del nondo.* Exh. cat. Ed. Eugenio Lo Sardo. 176-77. Rome, 2001.

Carr, Dawson. "The Fresco Decorations of Luca Giordano in Spain." *Record of the Art Museum, Princeton University* 41 (1982): 42-55.

Cartari, Carlo. *Diario.* In Cesare D'Onofrio, *Roma val bene un'abiura. Storie romane tra Cristina di Svezia, Piazza del Popolo e l'Accademia d'Arcadia.* 223-58. Rome, 1976.

Cause et rimedii della peste, see Possevino, Antonio.

Clifton, James D. "Mattia Preti's Frescoes for the City Gates of Naples." *Art Bulletin* 76 (1994): 479-501.

Cohn, Samuel K. "The Black Death: The End of a Paradigm." *American Historical Review* 107 (2002): 702-38.

—. *The Black Death Transformed: Disease and Culture in Early Renaissance Italy.* Oxford, 2003.

Collura, Paolo. *Santa Rosalia nella storia e nell'arte.* Palermo, 1977.

Contini, Roberto. "Pittori minori – ma veramente tali? – per il cabinet Doré." In *Le "siècle" de Marie de Médicis.* Actes du Séminaire de la Chaire Rhétorique et Société en Europe (XVIe-XVIIe siècles) du Collège de France. Ed. Françoise Graziani and Francesco Solinas. 118-124. (Special issue of *Franco-Italica*, 2002, nn. 21-22.) Paris, 2002.

Corradi, Alfonso. *Annali delle epidemie occorse in Italia dalle prime memorie fino al 1850 compilati con varie note e dichiarazioni.* 5 vols. Bologna, reprint 1972.

Cyprian (bishop of Carthage), Saint. *Mortality (De mortalitate). Works and Almsgiving (De opere et eleemosynis).* In *Saint Cyprian: Treatises.* Trans. and ed. Roy J. Deferrari. Washington, DC, 1977.

Dandelet, Thomas J. *Spanish Rome, 1500-1700.* New Haven, 2001.

Day, A. Colin. *Roget's Thesaurus of the Bible.* San Francisco, 1992.

Deaux, George. *The Black Death 1347.* New York, 1969.

Del Panta, Lorenzo. *Le epidemie nella storia demografica italiana (secoli XIV-XIX).* Turin, 1980, ristampa 1986.

Dooley, Brendan, ed. and trans. *Italy in the Baroque: Selected Readings.* New York, 1995.

Dutch and Flemish Paintings from New York Private Collections. Ed. Ann Jensen Adams. New York, 1988.

Early Modern Italy 1550-1796. Ed. John A. Marino. Oxford, 2002.

Ferrari, Oreste. *Luca Giordano. L'opera completa.* 2 vols. Naples, 1992.

—. "De Matteis, Paolo." *The Dictionary of Art.* Ed. Jane Turner. 20:841-43. New York, 1996.

Fioravanti, Leonardo. *Il reggimento della peste.* Venice, 1626.

Forster, Edward. *The British Gallery of Engravings.* London, 1807.

Freedman, Luba. "Saint Sebastian in Veneto Painting: The 'Signals' Addressed to 'Learned' Spectators." *Venezia Cinquecento* 8 (1998): 5-20.

Frutaz, A.P. *Basilica di S. Pietro in Vincoli.* Revisione storico-archeologica di S. Ciofetta. Rome, 2001.

Fuller, Reginald, ed. *A New Catholic Commentary on Holy Scripture.* Rev. ed. London, 1969.

Fumaroli, Marc. *Nicolas Poussin: Sainte Françoise Romaine.* Paris, 2001.

Gastaldi, Geronimo. *Tractatus de avertenda et profligandis peste politico-legalis.* Bologna, 1684.

Gazzaniga, Valentina. "*Mox, longe, tarde, cede, recede, redi.* Epidemie di peste nell'Italia del Seicento." In *Scienza e miracoli*, 52-59.

Giovan Battista Moroni (1520-1578). Exh. cat. Bergamo,1979.

Gordini, Gian Domenico. "Sebastiano, santo, martire di Roma." In *Bibliotheca sanctorum*, 11:775-89.

Gregory of Tours. *History of the Franks.* Ed. O.M. Dalton. 2 vols. Oxford, 1927.

Gregory XIII. *Jubileum ad avertenda pestis pericula* ("Calamitosum e miserabilem huius nostri"). Bologna, 1576.

Haskell, Francis and Nicholas Penny. *Taste and the Antique: The Lure of Classical Sculpture, 1500-1900.* New Haven, 1981.

von Henneberg, Josephine. "Cardinal Caesar Baronius, the Arts, and the Early Christian Martyrs." In *Saints and Sinners*, 136-50.

Howard, Deborah. *The Architectural History of Venice.* Rev. ed. New Haven, 2002.

Jansen. Guido and Peter C. Sutton. *Michael Sweerts (1618-1664)*. Exh. cat. Ed. Duncan Bull. Amsterdam, 2002.

Jones, Pamela. "The Power of Images: Paintings and Viewers in Caravaggio's Italy." In *Saints and Sinners*, 28-48, 81-86.

Kaminski, Marion. *Venice: Art and Architecture*. Cologne, 2000.

Kircher, Athanasius. *Scrutinium physico-medicum contagiosae luis quae dicitur pestis*. Rome, 1658.

Lapide, Cornelius a. *Commentaria in Scriptura Sacra*, "Commentaria in Numeros, cap. XXI." 2:304-09. Paris, 1866.

—. *The Great Commentary*. Vol. 5: St. John's Gospel, Chapters I-XI. Trans. Thomas W. Mossman. Edinburgh, 1908.

Lienhard, Joseph T., ed. *Ancient Christian Commentary on Scripture. Old Testament, III: Exodus, Leviticus, Numbers, Deuteronomy*. Downer's Grove, Illinois, 2001.

Litchfield, R. Burr. "The social world: cohesion, conflict, and the city. In *Early Modern Italy 1550-1796*, 87-103.

Longhi, Roberto. "Per Michiel Sweerts (1934)." In *'Me pinxit' e quesiti caravaggeschi 1928-1934*, 177-81. Vol. 4, *Opere Complete*. Florence, 1968.

Lubrano, Giacomo. *Scintille poetiche*. Ed. Marzio Pieri. Ravenna, 1982.

Lucenet, Monique. *Les grandes pestes en France*. Paris, 1985.

Marchini, Philibertus. *Belli divini sive Pestilentis temporis accurate et luculenta speculatio theologica, canonica, civilis, politica, historica, philosophica*. Florence, 1633.

—. *Philosophica de pestilentia problemata quibus eiusdem signa, causae, effectus, duratio, desitio, symptomata, remedia spiritualia, caracteristica, naturalia proponuntur et examinantur* (bound with the preceding).

Marino, John A. "Economic structures and transformations." In *Early Modern Italy 1550-1796*, 51-68.

Marshall, Louise. "Confraternity and Community: Mobilizing the Sacred in Times of Plague." In *Confraternities and the Visual Arts in Renaissance Italy: Ritual, Spectacle, Image*. Eds. Barbara Wisch and Diane Cole Ahl. 20-45. Cambridge, 2000.

—. "Manipulating the Sacred: Image and Plague in Renaissance Italy." *Renaissance Quarterly* 47 (1994): 485-532.

Martin, A. Lynn. *Plague? Jesuit Account of Epidemic Disease in the 16th Century*. Kirksville, Missouri, 1996.

Martin, Gregory. *Roma sancta (1581)*. Ed. George Bruner Parks. Rome, 1969.

Martin, John Rupert and Gail Feigenbaum. *Van Dyck as Religious Artist*. Exh. cat. Princeton, 1979.

Mascardi, Agostino and Claudio Achillini. *Due lettere, l'una del Mascardi all'Achillini, l'altra dell'Achillini al Mascardi sopra le presenti calamità*. Bologna, 1631.

McGrew, Roderick. *Encyclopedia of Medical History*. New York, 1985.

Mercalli, Marica. "L'Angelo di Castello: La sua iconografia, il suo significato." In *L'Angelo e la città*. Exh. cat. Vol. 1. Rome, 1987.

Meyer, Joachim. "A Drawing by Luca Giordano from the 'Cabinet de Solimene.'" *Paragone/Arte* 47, nn. 551-555 (1996): 118-26.

Mormando, Franco. *The Preacher's Demons: Bernardino of Siena and the Social Underworld of Early Renaissance Italy*. Chicago, 1999. [Mormando 1999a]

—. "Teaching the Faithful to Fly: Mary Magdalene and Peter in Baroque Italy." In *Saints and Sinners*, 107-35. [Mormando 1999b]

—. "Tintoretto's Recently Rediscovered *Raising of Lazarus*." *Burlington Magazine* 144, issue 1171 (2000): 624-29.

Muratori, Lodovico. *Trattato del governo della peste*. In *Lodovico Muratori, Annali d'Italia ed altre opere varie*. 5 vols. 5:432-559. Orig. pub. Modena, 1714. Milan, 1838.

Oliva, Gian (Giovanni) Paolo. *Aggiunta a' quaranta sermoni detti in varii luoghi sacri di Roma*. Rome, 1675.

—. *Sermoni detti in varii luoghi sacri di Roma*. Bologna, 1680.

Oratio Sanctae Rosaliae. n.d., n.p. Rome, Biblioteca Casanatense, Vol. Miscellanee 1370, item #1.

Ottonelli, Giovanni Domenico, and Pietro Berrettini. *Trattato della pittura e scultura, uso et abuso loro*. Orig. pub. Florence, 1652. Ed. Vittorio Casale. Treviso, 1973.

Pallavicino, Sforza. *Descrizione del contagio che da Napoli si comunicò a Roma nell'anno 1656 e de' saggi provedimenti ordinati allora da Alessandro VII estratta dalla Vita del medesimo pontefice che conservasi manuscritta nella Biblioteca Albani opera inedita*. Rome, 1837.

Panigarola, Francesco. "Predica intitolata La Peste. Per essersi fatta in San Petronio di Bologna, a tempo, che quella Città era in grandissimo pericolo di infettione." In *Prediche di Monsig. Reverend.mo Francesco Panigarola Vescovo d'Asti fatte da lui straordinariamente e fuor de' tempi quadragesimali in vari luoghi et a varie occasioni* ... Venice, 1599.

Paulus Diaconus (Paul the Deacon). *Historia Langobardorum*. Scriptores Rerum Germanicarum in usum scholarum ex Monumentis Germaniae Historicis recusi, vol. 9. Hanover, 1878.

Petrarca, Francesco. *Rerum familiarum libri I-VIII.* Trans. Aldo S. Bernardo. Albany, 1975.

I Pittori Bergamaschi dal XIII al XIX. III: Il Cinquecento. Bergamo, 1979.

Pizzorusso, Claudio. *Ricerche su Cristofano Allori.* Florence, 1972.

Polleross, Friedrich. "Mas exemplar, que imitador de David: zur Funktion des Identifikationsporträts zwischenTugendspiel und Panegyrik." *Wolfenbütteler Arbeiten zur Barockforschung* 25 (1995): 229-45.

[Possevino, Antonio.] *Cause et rimedii della peste, et di qualsivoglia altra infermità ...* Macerata, 1577.

Pressi (Pressius), Giovanni. *Considerazioni e consigli sulla peste* (Rome 1656). In Brighetti (under the mistaken name of Ressi), 261-64; excerpts also included in Cartari, *Diario*, 248-49.

Preto, Paolo. "Peste e demografia. L'età moderna: le due pesti del 1575-77 e 1630-31." In *Venezia e la peste*, 97-98.

Puglisi, Catherine R. "Guido Reni's *Pallione del Voto* and the Plague of 1630." *Art Bulletin* 77 (1995): 403-12.

Réau, Louis. "Sébastien (20 janvier)." In *Iconographie de l'art chrétien.* 3 vols in 6. III/3:1190-99. Paris, 1955-59.

Rice, Louise. *The Altars and Altarpieces of New St. Peter's: Outfitting the Basilica, 1621-1666.* Cambridge, 1997.

—. "Urban VIII, the Archangel Michael, and a forgotten project for the apse altar of St. Peter's." *Burlington Magazine*, 134, issue 1072 (1992): 428-34.

Roma 1630. Il trionfo del pennello. Exh. cat. Académie de France à Rome. Milan, 1994.

Rondinelli. Francesco. *Relazione del contagio stato in Firenze l'anno 1630 e 1633. Con un breve ragguaglio della miracolosa Immagine della Madonna dell'Impruneta.* Florence, 1634.

Roscio, Giulio. *Icones operum misericordiae.* Rome, 1586.

Rowlands, Ingrid D. *The Ecstatic Journey: Athanasius Kircher in Baroque Rome.* Exh. cat. Chicago, 2000.

Saints and Sinners: Caravaggio and the Baroque Image. Exh. cat. Ed. Franco Mormando. Chestnut Hill, Mass., 1999.

Salvator Rosa. Exh. cat. Hayward Gallery, London. London, 1973.

Scalabroni, Luisa. *"Vanitas." Fisionomia di un tema pittorico.* Turin, 1999.

Scaramella, Pierroberto. "The Italy of Triumphs and of Contrasts." In Tenenti, 25-98.

Schiferel, Ellen. "Iconography of Plague Saints in Fifteenth Century Italian Painting." *Fifteenth Century Studies* 6 (1983): 205-26.

Schütze, Sebastian. "San Sebastiano" In *Bernini scultore. La nascita del barocco in casa Borghese.* Ed. Anna Coliva and Sebastian Schütze. 78-95. Rome, 1998.

Scienza e miracoli nell'arte del '600. Alle origini della medicina moderna, 52-59. Ed. Sergio Rossi. Milan, 1998.

Scott, Jonathan. *Salvator Rosa: His Life and Times.* New Haven, 1995.

Segneri, Paolo. *The Manna of the Soul. Meditations for Every Day of the Year.* 2 vols. Second ed. London, 1892.

—. "Panegirico sacro XIII in onore del Beato Luigi Gonzaga." In *Opere.* 2:601-09. Venice, 1773.

Shelton, Jo-Ann. *As the Romans Did: A Sourcebook in Roman Social History.* New York, 1998.

Smoller, Laura. "Of Earthquakes, Hail, Frogs, and Geography: Plague and the Investigation of the Apocalypse in the Later Middle Ages." In *Last Things: Death and the Apocalypse in the Middle Ages.* Eds. Caroline Walker Bynum and Paul Freedman. 156-87, 316-37. Philadelphia, 2000.

Sobel, Dava. *Galileo's Daughter: A Historical Memoir of Science, Faith and Love.* New York, 1999.

Spear, Richard E. *Caravaggio and His Followers.* Cleveland, 1971.

—. *The Divine Guido: Religion, Sex, Money and Art in the World of Guido Reni.* New Haven, 1997.

Targioni Tozzetti, Giovanni. *Notizie degli aggrandimenti delle scienze fisiche accaduti in Toscana nel corso di anni LX del secolo XVII.* Orig. publ. Florence, 1780. Bologna, 1967.

Temin, Christine. "Reunited: A masterwork is restored, and a historic puzzle (partly) solved." *Boston Globe*, Sunday, March 28, 2004, Living/Arts section, N1 and 11.

Tenenti, Alberto, ed. *Humana Fragilitas: The Themes of Death in Europe from the 13th to the 18th Century.* Clusone (Bergamo), 2002.

Thiem, Christel. *Florentin Zeichner des Frühbarock.* Munich, 1977.

Tomitano da Feltre, Bernardino. *Sermoni del Beato Bernardino Tomitano da Feltre.* Nella redazione di Fra Bernardino Bulgarino da Brescia. Ed. Carlo Varischi da Milano. 3 vols. "De tribulationibus patienter tolerandis," 1:353-65. "De peste," 11:265-74. Milan, 1964.

Treasures from the Fitzwilliam. Exh. cat. Cambridge, 1989.

Twilight of the Medici: Late Baroque Art in Florence, 1670-1743. Exh. cat. Florence and Detroit, 1974.

Venezia e la peste. 1348/1797. Exh. cat. Comune di Venezia, Assessorato alla Cultura e Belle Arti. Venice, 1979.

Ward, Roger. "Caravaggio and His *Saint John the Baptist* for Ottavio Costa." In Richard P. Townsend and Roger Ward, *Caravaggio and Tanzio: The Theme of St. John the Baptist.* 1-19. Tulsa and Kansas City, 1995.

Wills, Christopher. *Plagues: Their Origin, History, and Future*. London, 1996.

Worcester, Thomas. "Trent and Beyond: Arts of Transformation." In *Saints and Sinners*, 87-106.

—. "Introduction." *From Rome to Eternity: Catholicism and the Arts, ca. 1550-1650.* 1-16. Eds. Pamela M. Jones and Thomas Worcester. Leiden, 2002.

Zanette, Laura. "Tre pedicatori per la peste: 1575-1577." *Lettere italiane* 42 (1990): 430-59.

Zuccari, Alessandro. "La cappella della 'Pietà' alla Chiesa Nuova e i committenti del Caravaggio." *Storia dell'arte* 47 (1983): 53-56.

Zupnick, Irving L. "Saint Sebastian in Art." Ph.D. thesis. Columbia University, Dept. of Art History and Archeology, 1958.

Plague Art in Early Modern Rome: Divine Directives and Temporal Remedies

Sheila Barker

> In times of plague (God save us) everyone who wishes to take part in this life [of service] must promise to serve the plague victims if he is commanded to do so by the Superior [of the order], however it is the very misssion of this Company to assist plague victims, both as Priests and as Layfolk.
>
> Saint Camillo of Lellis, *Rule of the Company of the Ministers of the Sick* (1584)

> When one seeks to serve God in serving his neighbor, it is a most supremely noble form of charity, sometimes more deserving of heaven's mercy than so many other acts of devotion.
>
> Lodovico Antonio Muratori, *Del governo della peste e delle maniere di guardarsene* (1714)

When Bernardo Bellotto, a stranger to Rome and its history, chose his vantage point for *The Tiber with the Church of San Giovanni dei Fiorentini, Rome* (cat. 20), he unwittingly placed himself in the midst of a setting once blighted by memories of plague. Trastevere, the neighborhood immediately adjacent to him as he contemplated his view, had been walled in like a giant tomb one night without warning during the plague of 1656 to prevent its residents from spreading the contagion to the rest of the city. The church of S. Giovanni dei Fiorentini that Bellotto painted in the right foreground was the home of the confraternity of the Pietà established in 1448 "when after a great eclipse of the sun Rome was left devastated by earthquakes and pestilence, and no one could be found to bury the dead, especially the poor among them."[1] Castel Sant'Angelo, the massive structure dominating the center of his canvas, had given scarce shelter to the papal court from the plague introduced by Charles V's army in 1527. At the fortress's peak, Raffaello da Montelupo's sculpture commemorated the angel that, according to later legends, had appeared in the sky during the plague of 590, sheathing its bloody sword to signal the end of the plague as Pope Gregory I led a procession across the river.[2] This miracle is depicted in numerous Roman images all sharing the same configuration of fortress, river, and sky seen in Bellotto's canvas, including Giovanni de' Vecchi's painting at S. Maria in Aracoeli, Giovanni Battista Montalto's fresco once at S. Angelo ai Corridori di Borgo (now in the church of the Annunziatella), a fresco in the SS. Trinità dei Monti by an assistant of Michelangelo, Jacopo Zucchi's painting formerly in S. Maria Maggiore (now in the Pinacoteca Vaticana), Giovanni Battisti Ricci da Novara's fresco in S. Gregorio al Celio, and an anonymous fresco in the atrium of that same church (fig. 3) which also depicts the Tiber River's infestation of snakes, then considered both a symbol and natural cause of pestilence.[3]

This river, placid and beguiling in Bellotto's view, for millennia had engirded the city with danger, periodically unleashing bouts of pestilence. The populace sought to protect itself in antiquity by lining the shores with a phalanx of cults propitiating such health deities as Febris, Apollo, and Esculapius.[4] These prophylactic cults were suppressed in the Christian era, but the river continued to be feared as a source of contagious diseases. Rome's physicians warned during the Renaissance that usage of the Tiber for drinking water "brings plague and

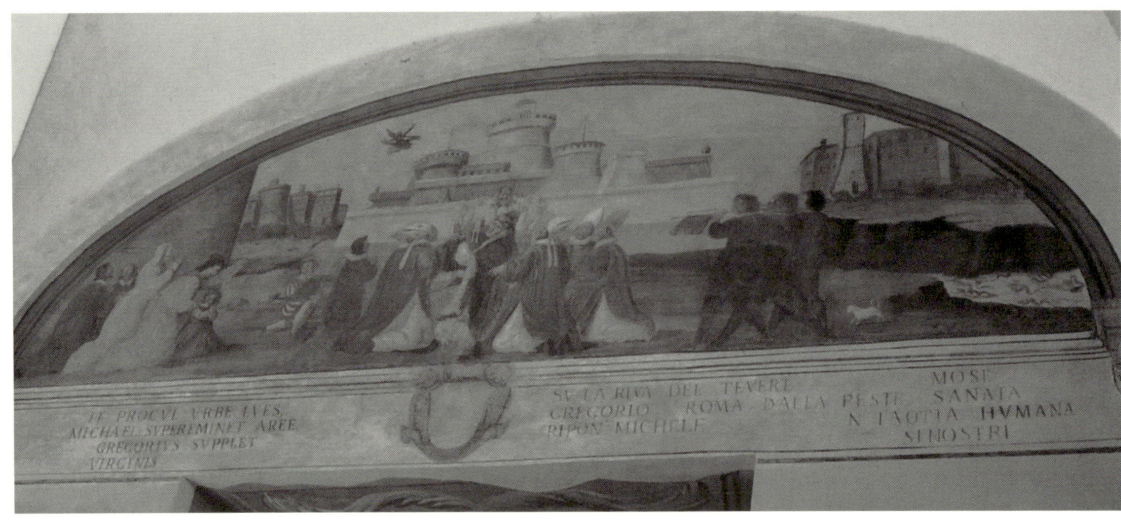

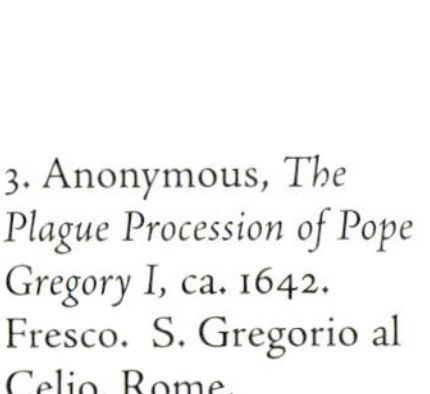
3. Anonymous, *The Plague Procession of Pope Gregory I*, ca. 1642. Fresco. S. Gregorio al Celio, Rome.

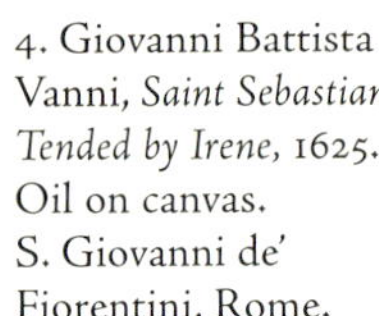
4. Giovanni Battista Vanni, *Saint Sebastian Tended by Irene*, 1625. Oil on canvas. S. Giovanni de' Fiorentini, Rome.

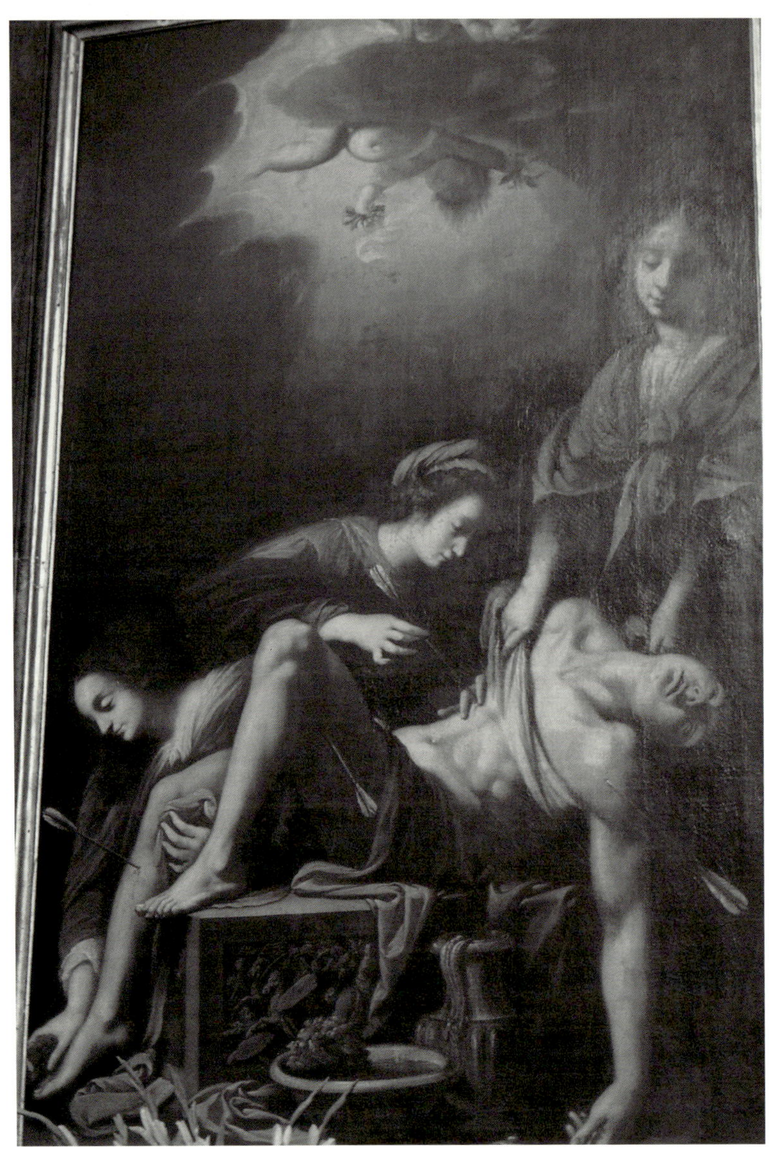

ruin to this city," and a slew of fountains fed by repaired aqueducts were built to provide a safer alternative.[5] When bubonic plague swept through Italy in 1630, giant chains were hoisted from bank to bank at night to protect the city from surreptitious arrivals of contaminated cargo and travelers. These measures came too late during the plague of 1656, when a single Neapolitan fisherman sailed up this artery and debarked with a disease that killed more than 8,000 Romans, clogging the Stygian waterway with the traffic of little boats carrying blackened corpses to the mass grave near St. Paul's Basilica. (See Andrew Hopkins, p. 141 in this volume, on how a traveler from Trent brought the plague to Venice.)

Arriving in Rome in 1741 – the same year that epidemic fevers broke out for the first time in New York[6] – Bellotto encountered a society with an ancient history of epidemic disease and a plague culture quite distinct from that of his native Venice. However, over the preceding hundred years, advances in public health had spawned changes in the themes and functions of plague art, not only in Rome, but in other European capitals as well. As a result, obsolete now were many of the traditions and practices developed when plague was still seen from a position of almost total vulnerability. Even the disease itself was practically obsolete: plague had not touched Rome since 1696, and by the time of Bellotto's visit, Italy had endured its final outbreak of bubonic plague, aside from a limited outbreak affecting Messina in 1743.[7] In this essay, we will examine plague art from the years leading up to Bellotto's arrival to Rome in light of the dramatic adaptations in the social response to epidemic disease. What role this cultural transformation might have played in the disappearance of bubonic plague from Europe so long before the true cause of the disease and its vectors were discovered is a question left for others to pursue.

The first significant evidence of this cultural transformation in plague art can be found in the early seventeenth-century depictions of Saint Sebastian – a universal plague saint to be sure, but one with particularly strong ties to Rome, where he was almost killed, then cured, then martyred, and finally buried. The traditional iconography of the saint depicts the first, unsuccessful attempt on his life: with origins in the tenth century and familiar throughout the European continent, it features Sebastian bound to a post and left to die after being shot with arrows by Diocletian's guard, as in *Madonna and Child with Saints Sebastian and Roch*, by Bernardino Luini (cat. 13). The image of the nude, wounded youth suspended on a column or a tree bears certain pictorial similarities to the Crucified Christ, especially in light of the knowledge that he will be restored to health; at the same time, in popular culture those arrows lodged in Sebastian's flesh retained their pagan association with plague. Both of these factors contributed to the folkloristic appeal of this traditional image of Sebastian, and to its superstitious use as a powerful shield against epidemic diseases: according to homeopathic magic as well as the ancient principle of totem sacrifice, the icon of a man inflicted with flesh wounds was commonly believed to repel and cure all those maladies blamed on the invisible, airborne arrows of divine anger.

By the time the plague of Palermo reached Rome in 1625, an alternative iconography for Sebastian had emerged. An altarpiece completed that year by Giovanni Battista Vanni (fig. 4), shows Irene and her assistants carefully extracting the arrows from Sebastian's flesh and covering his open wounds with medicinal ointments, working under the cover of darkness as they contravene Diocletian's death sentence and risk discovery by the imperial guards. Contemporary works of the same subject include *Saint Sebastian Attended by the Holy Women* attributed to Nicolas Regnier (cat. 15) and Bernardo Strozzi's *Saint Sebastian Tended by Saint Irene and her Maid* (cat. 16), with its strongly christological imprint recalling traditional images of Sebastian.

Two important changes are represented by this new iconography. First, as a history rather than a static icon, the representation of the Cure of Sebastian largely displaces the saint's intercessory function with a moral or didactic emphasis; second, in depicting the care lavished on Sebastian's wounds, these images constitute a pronounced endorsement of temporal medicine in the treatment of bodily suffering. This emphasis on the role of medical intervention in Sebastian's cure links all the early morphologies of the subject, including those in which angels provide medical assistance (such as Giovanni Baglione's *Saint Sebastian Cured by an Angel*, executed in Rome in 1601), and those in which a male surgeon leads Irene and a male helper in the saint's cure (as in the case of Giovanni Francesco Guerrieri's *Cure of Saint Sebastian*, executed in Rome ca. 1615-18); it is clearly the most significant aspect of the new iconography.[8]

Images of the Cure of Sebastian seem to have served as the special insignia of laymen who volunteered to assist the sick, especially plague victims, at Rome's hospitals.[9] Vanni's image, for example, was made for the church of S. Giovanni dei Fiorentini, which by this time had its own hospital, managed by the confraternity of the Pietà noted above; likewise, Giovanni Baglione painted his *Cure of Saint Sebastian by Angels* (1624) for a chapel at the church of S. Maria dell'Orto, the seat of a confraternity that oversaw the operations of a hospital annex staffed by doctors, priests, and assistants, as well as a pharmacy.[10] As attested by one confraternity's sixteenth-century charter, the members of such brotherhoods were not only "motivated by piety," they were also "mindful of their own salvation."[11] Images of the Cure of Sebastian conceivably served functions corresponding to these two concerns. By showing Irene tenderly dressing wounds of the young, handsome, and unyielding Christian martyr, Baglione's and Vanni's paintings fostered piety toward an ideal patient so that the charitable caregivers might follow this example and "without any feelings of disgust look upon the sick."[12] The image also evoked direct comparisons between the confraternities that succored Rome's sick and their saintly (or angelic) prototypes who had aided Sebastian; by implication, both groups of caretakers might hope for the saint to reciprocate by interceding for their eternal salvation.

The Cure of Sebastian was – along with the Good Samaritan, Caritas Romana, and Tobias Curing his Father's Blindness – one of a handful of subjects available for the representation of medical assistance as a work of piety, an interpretation emphasized by the fact that Irene and her helpers are often referred to in the titles of such images as "*pie donne*," pious women. Yet among the subjects of this type, the Cure of Sebastian is most closely associated with contagious epidemics, since Sebastian's arrows retain their identity as metaphors for plague, and his caregivers risk their own lives to help their patient – just as in plaguetime. Altarpieces depicting the Cure of Sebastian therefore qualify as the first ever to figure within the sacred space of Rome's churches the goals and means of charitable medicine in association with plague.[13]

What is the significance of this? In effect, with these altarpieces depicting the Cure of Sebastian, the Church was redefining its role in relation to the problem of disease, especially epidemic disease. Stated most simply, these images signal a shift of emphasis from the bodily needs of the patient to the spiritual motives of the healer. The imagery of the older but still vital paradigm had addressed the afflicted in the form of miracle-working icons or thaumaturgic saints that promised spiritual cures for temporal ailments – a stance that, over the centuries, increasingly brought the Church into competition with other available therapeutic systems, such as pharmaceutical medicine and public medicine, while doing little to suppress the more heterodox systems of astrology, folk medicine, and witchcraft.[14] The imagery of the new paradigm resolved this competition with temporal remedies by addressing instead the community of the healthy, spurring them to practice Christ-like charity toward the sick, and advocating natural medicines as one means of carrying out this spiritual mission.[15]

The incursion of an iconography of "temporal remedies" into the images decorating

Rome's churches is the result of important medical developments that took place in the sixteenth century, and that were connected to the general inclination toward reform then prevalent within the Catholic Church. The way for these advancements was in a large sense laid by the Capuchin order, the strictest followers of the Franciscan Rule, who became independent in 1528 as the Fratres Minores de vita eremitica. Clearly, the notion of eremitism explicit in their official title did not stop them from coming to the aid of the laity. They earned admiration for their selfless care of syphilis patients at Rome's hospital of S. Giacomo degli Incurabili (where they collaborated with the laymen of the Compagnia del Divino Amore, established at that hospital in 1515 under Ettore Vernazza), and for their devoted care of plague victims during the epidemics of 1577 and 1630.[16]

In assisting the sick, the Capuchins conformed to the precepts of scientific medicine with sanitary practices that included the purification of the foul-smelling air of the lazaretto with incense and the frequent changing of patients' bed linens; they also furnished medicines including the famous "Capuchin Syrup" at their Roman pharmacy, opened in 1633.[17] Clearly, though, their service at the lazaretto transcended the concern for preserving the life of the body, especially when it came to their own bodies. Paradigmatic in this sense is Vittore da Milano's indifference to the risk of contracting disease at the Milanese pesthouse during the plague of 1630, which was modeled after Saint Francis of Assisi's zealous service among the lepers of Gubbio. According to one Capuchin witness,

> Every day, even though extremely busy, he celebrated Mass, administered the Holy Eucharist, and gave sacramental Absolution to many out of heartfelt concern. In fact, this father was so full of charity and affection that, like a loving mother, he rushed to meet the carts arriving with the infected victims, and with his own hands helped to unload the sick and place them on the grass; he provided each with a place in the shelter, and with words overflowing with divine wisdom he encouraged them to bear the pain of the contagious disease while remitting their sins, and many of these victims would die in his arms.[18]

Thus, even as they sought to minimize the physical discomfort of the patients using medicinal remedies, the Capuchins were distinguished from the physicians with whom they worked in these lazarettos by their ultimate concern for their own and the patients' souls in preparation for the death that was sometimes postponed, but nonetheless inevitable.

An anecdote from the Palermo plague of 1624 describes how the friars addressed the universal malady that the physician's medicine can never cure, our mortal nature. At a lazaretto run by the Capuchins, a plague victim asked a doctor why God should allow the Capuchin fathers, his faithful servants, to die as they carried out their charitable work. The doctor replied, "Medicine did not educate me to investigate the judgments of God, but I can say this: that the Capuchin fathers teach us in life how we ought to live, and here in death they teach us how we ought to die; they die before us, with our same disease, and thus we learn, may it please God, that a true Christian dies resigned to obey God's will, contrite and humble, just as we have seen his servants the Capuchins die."[19] This exchange dramatically illustrates how strictly Capuchins lived, and died, by the Catholic teaching that disease – even plague – has a place within the economy of salvation: it creates an opportunity for the caregiver to express his divine devotion through works of selfless charity, as well as an opportunity for both the victim and the caregiver to submit to the operation of divine grace.[20] Indeed, the numerous surviving accounts of the order's service to plague victims testify to the fact that despite their employment of "human" or "temporal" remedies to protect patients from the ravages of disease and to lessen their suffering, the Capuchins conceived of their mission as a religious one rather than a medical one, and were thus readily disposed to sacrifice their own bodies in order to save others' souls and give spiritual comfort.[21]

Though the Capuchins used temporal remedies in their care for the victims of plague and other contagious diseases, there is no indication of this aspect of their service in the imagery of their church of S. Maria della Concezione in Rome, built with the generous patronage of Urban VIII Barberini and his family. Construction of the church began just after the plague of Palermo receded, and the altarpiece commissions were determined in the wake of the next plague of 1630.[22] However, aside from two altarpieces in this church depicting miraculous healings – Andrea Sacchi's *Saint Anthony of Padua Reviving a Dead Man* and Pietro da Cortona's *Ananias of Damascus Cures Saint Paul's Blindness* – it is difficult for the modern visitor to recognize in the other altarpieces (depicting christological subjects, the Virgin of the Immaculate Conception, Saint Francis, Saint Michael, and Saint Felix of Cantalice) any relation to the impact of plague. Only once it is understood that this order addressed disease foremost as a consequence of sin – the first cause of all human suffering – do the other subjects of christological devotion and Capuchin intercessors cohere logically into a single decorative program guided by the contingencies of plague.[23]

To give an example of how these other images in the church of the Concezione reflect a unified response to the danger of epidemic disease, we ought to consider its most celebrated altarpiece, Guido Reni's *Saint Michael the Archangel Overcoming Satan* (fig. 5), whose composition is repeated in Giovanni Andrea Sirani's painting of the same name (cat. 22).[24] In Reni's work, Michael appears as the warrior angel of Revelation 12:7-9, conquering evil at the end of

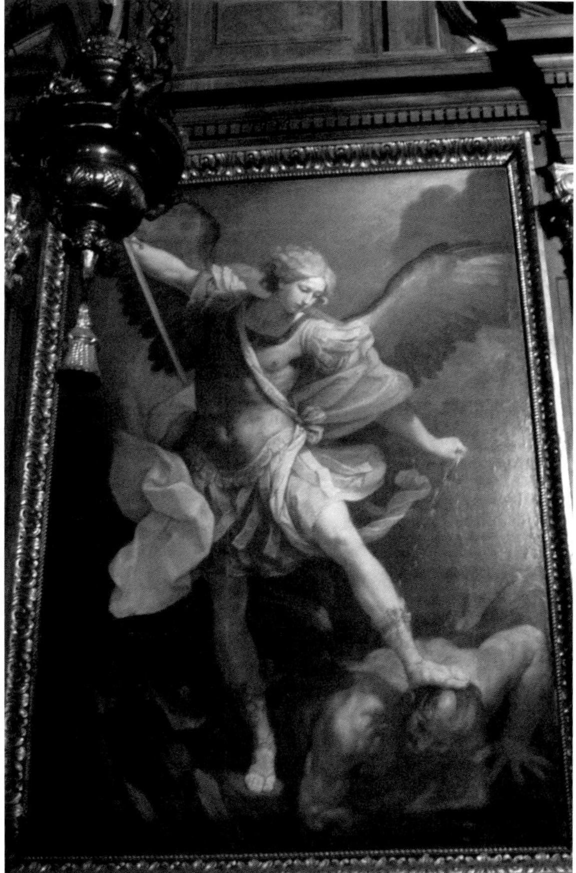

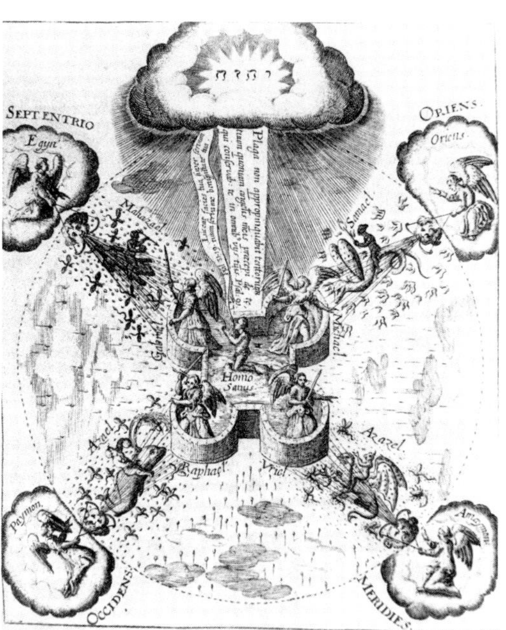

5. Guido Reni, *Saint Michael the Archangel Overcoming Satan*, ca. 1635. Oil on canvas. S. Maria della Concezione, Rome.

6. Robert Fludd, *Munimenti, nostri sanitatis*, 1631. Woodcut *Integrum morborum mysterium: sive medicinae catholicae*, I:338. Photograph: Biblioteca Nazionale Centrale di Roma.

time. It was then an unusual subject in Rome, especially when compared to the more prevalent image of Michael as the plague-rescinding angel who visited the city during the procession of Saint Gregory the Great.[25] These two roles of the archangel, however, are closely related, especially with regard to their cultic significance in times of plague: since sin was designated by theologians as the precipitating cause for God's punishing plagues, Michael's apocalyptic victory over evil is complementary as well as necessary to his historical role as a plague-rescinding agent.

The cult of the archangel as Satan's conqueror promised divine protection against plague and other diseases – and not just because plague represented the microcosmic enactment of celestial Armageddon ("Heaven's invisible intestinal war," as Mattia Naldi, a contemporary physician, put it).[26] Salutary aspects of the warrior angel's cult in Italy can be traced back to Saint Michael's shrine at Monte Gargano, which had long been known for miraculous cures when Saint Francis visited the sanctuary.[27] In Rome, the cult of the warrior angel may date back as early as 530; however, there is no evidence of the cult's specific connection to plague until the outbreak of 1427-33, when the first Roman lay organization dedicated to serving the sick formed under the name of San Michele Arcangelo.[28]

Though the Counter-Reformation Church had used the Archangel's apocalyptic triumph over evil as a standard for its battle against Protestant heresy, Saint Michael's cult in the seventeenth century still embraced the idea of temporal triumph over disease. The persistence of the cult's salutary aspects is most evident in popular devotions to the Archangel, such as the Palermitan chapbook prayer that promises Michael will cure a mountebank's roster of ailments, preserving his devotees "from sickness, and evil, from fever, misfortune, and deformity, and from every other great pestilence."[29] It can also be surmised from the decoration of the end wall of the Old Ward of the Lateran Hospital once painted with Gaspare Celio's (now lost) fresco of Saint Michael, and, likewise, from the decoration of a room of the Jesuit infirmary at the Roman novitiate with an image of Saint Michael victorious over sin, displayed alongside allegorical images comparing pride to epilepsy, avarice to fever, lust to sanguinary excesses, and the cardinal virtues to medicinal remedies.[30]

A vague reference to Saint Michael's salutary powers occurs in the prayer "Te splendor et virtus Patris" that Pope Urban VIII composed for the Roman Breviary of 1632, in which Michael and his fellow angels are beseeched to defend "our life on earth." Urban VIII's actions, however, spoke even louder: he dedicated his papacy to Saint Michael after recovering from malarial fever, and, in December of 1630, he went to Saint Michael's altar in St. Peter's Basilica in order to extend the Jubilee concession in light of the dangers of famine, war, and plague.[31] (See Thomas Worcester's essay, p. 165, for more on Pope Urban VIII and the plague.) Given this pope's interest in the natural sciences, he probably entertained the humoral and mechanical explanations of the angelic role in disease professed by such esoteric physicians as Levinus Lemnius, who blamed certain fevers on "perverse Spirits" and attributed their vanquishment to the internal action of "good ... Spirits, that is, salutary Angels," or Robert Fludd, whose cabalistic medicine describes four evil angels (Samael, Azazel, Azael, and Mahazael) who assail the individual with maladies and four good angels (Michael, Gabriel, Uriel, and Raphael) who defend the individual, as figured in the marvelous illustrations to Fludd's book (fig. 6).[32]

In a cultural climate in which there were even "scientific" corroborations of the hygienic aspects of Saint Michael's cult, we can be certain that the laurel branches painted on the ceiling of Saint Michael's chapel at S. Maria della Concezione (fig. 7), just above Reni's altarpiece, are more than a simple proprietary declaration of Barberini patronage. Clustered around placards invoking the warrior angel's protection, this vegetative motif refers as much to the laurel wreath of victory as to the medicinal uses of laurel to repel the plague, simultaneously

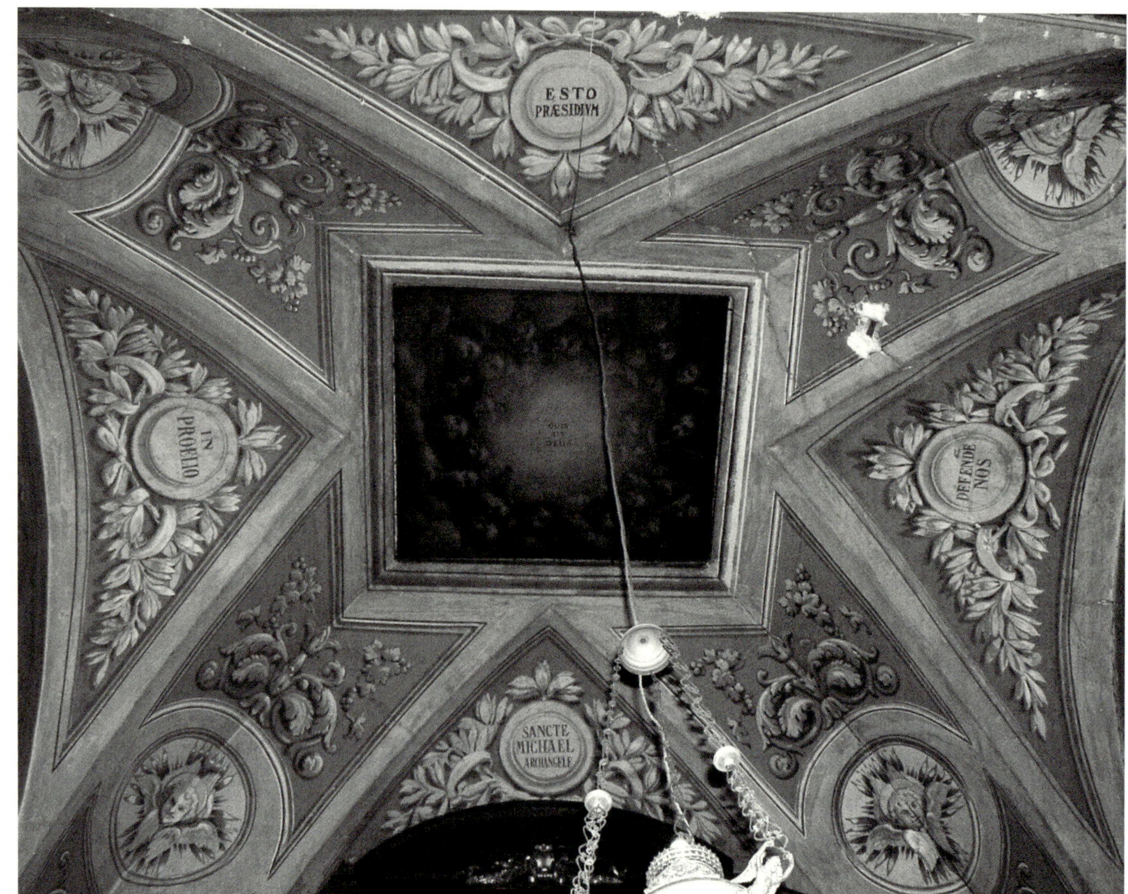

7. Anonymous, Ceiling ornament of the chapel of St. Michael, S. Maria della Concezione, Rome.

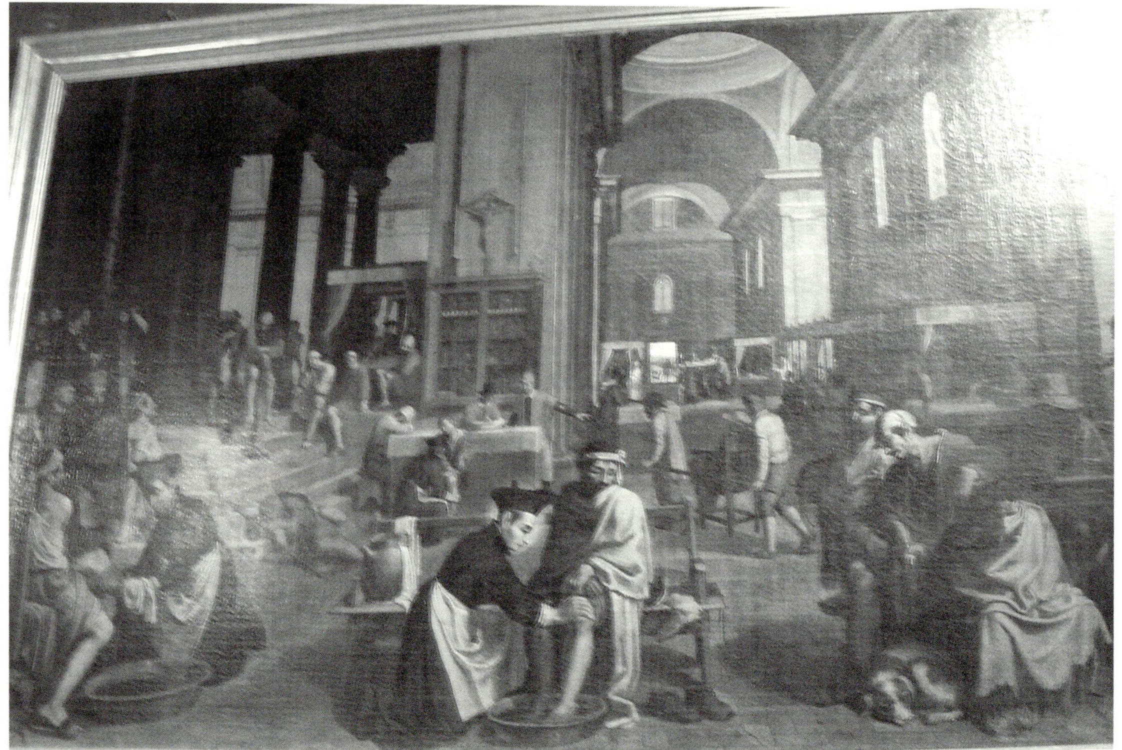

8. Anonymous, *Jesuits Helping the Sick*, ca. 1620-50. Oil on canvas. Oratory of St. Luigi Gonzaga, Rome.

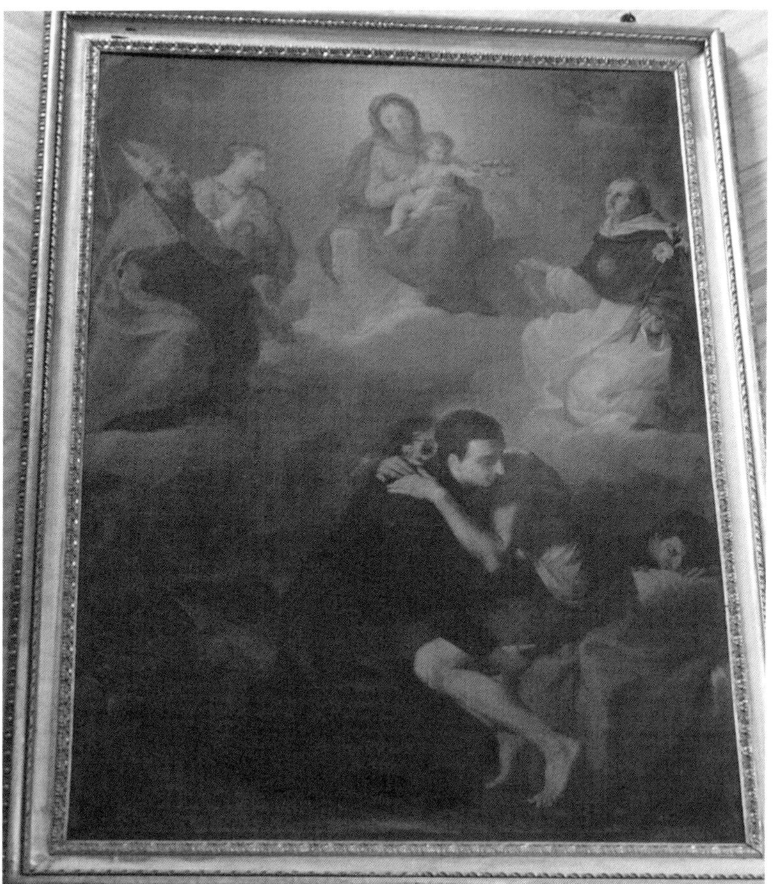

9. Giacomo Zoboli, *Saint Luigi Gonzaga Helping a Plague Victim*, 1726. Oil on canvas. SS. Carlo e Ambrogio, Rome.

invoking the two special roles of the archangel figured in Reni's altarpiece below: victor over sin, and defender of health. Let us be clear, though: Reni's altarpiece attests to the power of divine remedies; by contrast, natural cures – aside from the medicinal simple decorating the ceiling of Saint Michael's chapel – have no place in this Capuchin church's decorative program, despite the order's liberal provision of temporal remedies in their service in Italy's hospitals and lazarettos.

The same is true of the Roman churches belonging to another order founded in the sixteenth century, the Society of Jesus. Following the approval of their order in 1540, the Jesuits soon demonstrated their zeal for the charitable assistance of the sick, eclipsing the Capuchins in the use of scientific medicine and introducing to Europe new remedies and drugs discovered in the course of their missionary work around the world. At the Collegio Romano, the Jesuits operated a pharmacy (best known for its fresco decorations by Andrea Sacchi and Emilio Savonanzi) that distributed medicaments to the sick under the supervision of physicians, and their novices staffed all of Rome's most important hospitals.[33] Such myriad public-health activities are represented in a painting in the oratory of Saint Luigi Gonzaga at the Collegio Romano (fig. 8), where Jesuits are shown treating patients in a fantastic setting more reminiscent of a great church than a hospital.

Yet despite the centrality of the assistance of the sick to the Jesuit mission in Baroque Rome, not a single altarpiece in the churches of the order makes allusion to their activities in this realm. Instead, it is an altarpiece in the basilica of SS. Carlo e Ambrogio al Corso where testimony is given of the Jesuits' efforts to allay suffering through charitable medicine. Giacomo Zoboli's 1726 *Saint Luigi Gonzaga Helping a Plague Victim* (fig. 9) depicts the young novice of high birth who, disregarding his own health, carried a plague victim he found lying in the streets of Rome to S. Maria della Consolazione, the hospital where he was posted as part of his Jesuit training. As a result of his contact with the sick man, Luigi contracted a plague fever followed by the consumptive fever that killed him in June of 1591.

Zoboli's painting shows the saint assisting a plague victim within a hospital while three saints above – presumably Augustine, Catherine of Alexandria (though perhaps alluding to Catherine of Siena, seen with her pen in the contiguous altarpiece also by Zoboli), and Thomas Aquinas – observe as the Christ Child on the Virgin's lap holds a crown of roses above Luigi's head. This interpolation of a *sacra conversazione* within the secular space of a hospital is no less an iconographic novelty than the presence of a hospital scene within the sacred space of a Roman church. Among the works leading up to Zoboli's noteworthy image is an anonymous work (fig. 10) in the oratory of Saint Luigi Gonzaga in the Collegio Romano, executed in a simple, anecdotal style, perhaps by a follower of Giovanni Francesco Guerrieri. It shows Luigi striding briskly through Rome with the plague victim slung over his shoulder in a heroic pose that has been justly compared to depictions of Aeneas carrying Anchises.[34] Walking directly behind him with marked worry, an older Jesuit companion holds up the berretta that has fallen off Luigi's head, but Luigi is too consumed with his mission to consider his own dignity, appearance, or even safety, with his bare head leaving him all the more exposed to contagion and to the elements. Despite the fact that this image makes no explicit reference to medicine, it nevertheless speaks to the Jesuit order's enthusiastic provision of temporal remedies to the most needy: on the one hand it testifies to Luigi's resolve to bring his charge to a hospital where his health will be overseen by physicians, and, on the other, it demonstrates that Luigi's assistance was in itself a "temporal remedy," which neither transcended his limited mortal abilities nor involved miraculous interventions of a divine nature.

In the following years, probably around 1710, French sculptor Pierre Le Gros gave dra-

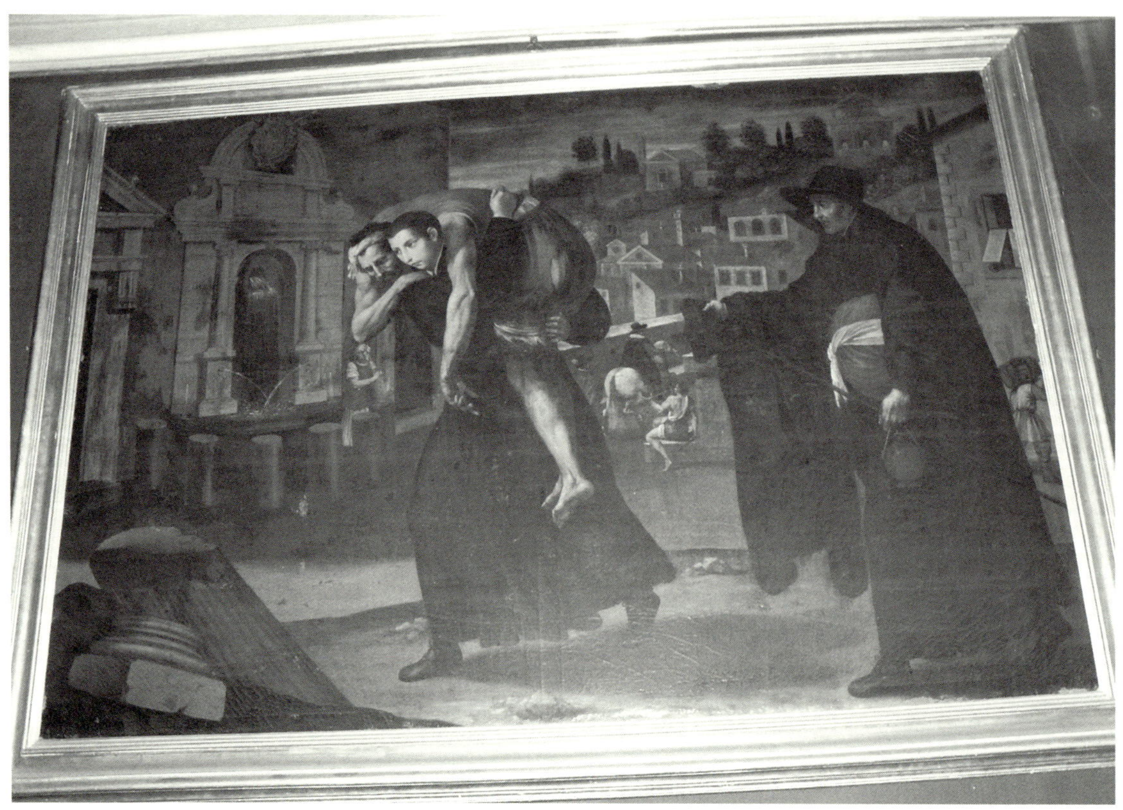

10. Follower of Giovanni Francesco Guerrieri, *Saint Luigi Gonzaga Helping a Plague Victim*, ca. 1610-15. Oil on canvas. Oratory of Saint. Luigi Gonzaga, Rome.

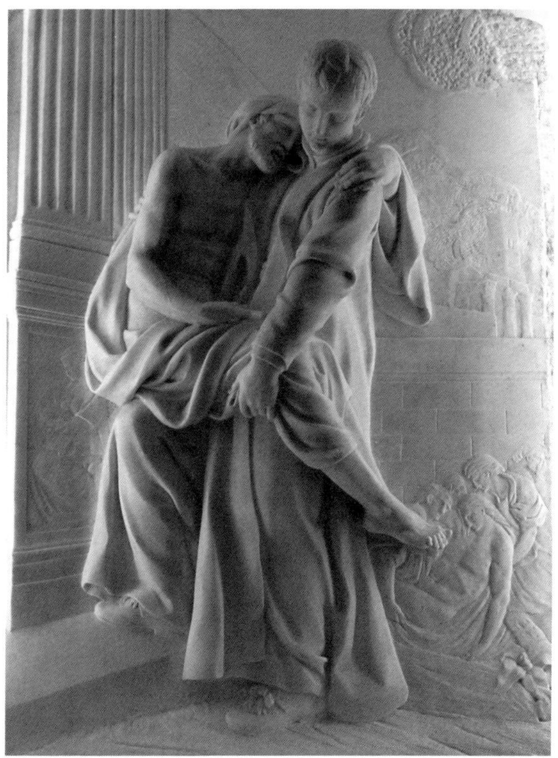

11. Pierre Le Gros, *Saint Luigi Gonzaga Helping a Plague Victim*, ca. 1710. Marble.
Hospital of S. Spirito in Saxia, Rome.

matic emphasis to Christian spirituality in the marble *Saint Luigi Gonzaga Helping a Plague Victim* (fig. 11) he produced for the hospital of the Consolazione, now at the hospital of S. Spirito in Sassia.[35] Dispensing with humanistic narratives of heroic action, Le Gros sought instead to depict in monumental fashion the profound devotion that motivated Luigi's compassionate act. Key to this portrayal is the way that Luigi's large, ponderous figure envelopes the fragile, half-naked body of the invalid, unmistakably invoking such christological images as Michelangelo's marble *Pietà* in St. Peter's. With this pose, the artist unites two men's faces so closely that their breath must dangerously commingle; he also allows Luigi to look upon the man in his arms with such tenderness and depth of feeling that one understands that in this dejected, soiled, and diseased mortal, Luigi recognizes Christ himself. Unperturbed by the revolting sight and smell of plague, Luigi appears even to pause at the threshold of the hospital with his burden, as if to savor the wellspring of Christian love that bonds him to this pitiful creature.

Inspiration for Le Gros's remarkable portrayal may have come in part from the hagiographies of one of Luigi's immediate models of charity toward the sick, Saint Filippo Neri. Canonized in 1622, Filippo had worked for many decades in Rome's hospitals alongside the greatest physicians of his age; along with Cesare Baronio and Francesco Maria Tarugi, he helped to establish the Istituto della Santissima Trinità for the care of poor convalescents and pilgrims; he also succeeded in inducing local nobility to work at the city's hospitals performing tasks that not even the lowest-ranking paid staff would deign to do.[36] It is said that once, when Giovanni Battista Salviati, cousin of the queen of France, was neglecting his hospital duties in order to pray in the church of S. Spirito, Filippo and a sick patient walked up behind him and dressed him in a white apron to remind him of his oath to "to leave aside God for God" (*lasciar Iddio per Iddio*), that is, to seek Christ not at the altar but in the sick, who are made in his image.[37] In likening the plague victim in Luigi's arms to the dead Christ, Le Gros reminds us of this teaching.

As for the assimilation of Luigi in his mercy to Mary, Mother of God, Le Gros was echoing the teaching of yet another religious healthcare reformer working in the hospitals of Rome: Saint Camillo of Lellis (1550-1614), founder of the order of the Ministers of the Sick. Camillo, who was canonized in 1746, left writings indicating the nature of his contribution to public healthcare, including the "Rules and practices to be followed in the hospitals when caring for the indigent sick" appended to the Rule he wrote for his order in 1584. The twenty-seventh item directs clerics to undertake their work in the hospitals with motherly compassion for the sick: "First, each one must ask for the Lord to bless him with a maternal affection for his neighbor, so that he might serve him with all the charity of his soul and his body, because we desire, with God's grace, to serve all the sick with the same affection that is shown by a loving mother when her only child falls sick."[38] This instruction to offer the patient maternal love, when coupled with Saint Filippo Neri's exhortation to seek Christ among the sick, suggests that the Virgin Mary, and particularly Mary of the Pietà, served as an ideal model for the caregiver's affective state.

When Le Gros's marble relief was moved in 1936 to its present location in the hospital of S. Spirito in Sassia, an inscription was added identifying Luigi as a "victim of Christian charity" (*victima christianae caritatis*).[39] This phrasing confirms the Church's new focus on the caregiver's administration of temporal remedies as an act of sacrificial compassion. It also implies Luigi's status as a martyr – a designation that had become the focus of heated debate in the decades following Luigi's death, when some theologians began clamorously arguing that those who died in the course of caring for victims of the plague deserved the crown of martyrdom.[40] One of these proponents of plague martyrdom, Francesco Antonio Sarri of the order of the Ministers of the Sick, wrote a treatise that narrowly avoided condemnation, the *Glorioso trionfo d'invitta morte di carità, emulatrice di vero martirio nel quale al vivo si dimostra la molta somiglianza ch'è fra la morte de' Santi Martiri, e di coloro, ch'in serviggio dell'appestati per la Carità Christiana muoiono* (Naples, 1632); other treatises, like Teofilo Raynaud's *De Martirio per pestem* (Lyon, 1630) and Barnabite Filiberto Marchini's *Belli divini, sive pestilentis temporis* (Florence, 1633), were put on the Roman Inquisition's Index of prohibited books for declaring that those who died serving the sick "are to be declared martyrs and counted among them."[41]

The refusal of the Church to qualify Luigi as a martyr proved no impediment to his canonization in 1726, the same year that Zoboli completed the altarpiece (fig. 9) for SS. Carlo e Ambrogio. In Zoboli's work, emphasis is moved from the motives that compelled Luigi's actions to their profound consequences. As Luigi fulfills his rescue mission by gently setting the blue-skinned plague victim in his hospital bed, the two figures are momentarily bound in a sweet embrace. The interlocking of their limbs underscores their interlocking fates as two mortals who would both soon succumb to death; this idea of their shared destiny is echoed by the nearly symmetrical mirroring of their arcing torsos. Without dismissing Le Gros's earlier assimilation of the rapport between Luigi and the plague victim to a meditation upon the dead Christ, Zoboli's composition calls attention to Luigi's own mortal nature, as well as his own imminent transformation into a dying patient.

If Luigi is meant to be seen here as a man contemplating his own death, then Zoboli has shown him to be utterly at peace with these thoughts, painting Luigi with a smooth brow and a subtle veil of a smile. He freely offers his own arms to give a small bit of comfort to the wretched plague victim, surely thinking upon the eternal comfort that awaits them both in the arms of the Creator. In a letter to his mother, written in the final days of his illness, Luigi expressed himself in terms that reverberate strikingly with Zoboli's image:

> The violence of the fever at the height of its course and fervor has somewhat eased up, and [the sickness] had proceeded slowly in me up until the

> glorious day of the Ascension. Beginning then, however, a great flow of phlegm took hold of my chest, such that, bit by bit, I am making my way toward the sweet and tender embraces of the Celestial Father, on whose breast I hope to rest safely forever.[42]

In this letter, we see how Luigi's experience as a health worker allowed him to monitor the progress of his disease; the letter also demonstrates that Luigi's knowledge of his body's accelerating material demise was accompanied by the perception of his soul's rapid advance toward eternal life. In this way, Luigi's last days exemplify the chiastic relationship between spiritual growth and physiological death that was the crux of such religious treatises on the plague as Jesuit Etienne Binet's *Sovrani et efficaci rimedi contro la peste e morte subitana,* translated into Italian in 1656, which teaches that to find consolation in plague time one must "live dying," that is to say, through mortification and the frequent meditation upon death, deadly fears of death are overcome, and the way to eternal life is made clear.[43] (See Thomas Worcester's essay, p. 164, for more on Binet and the plague.)

Later images of Luigi frequently refer to these very sorts of meditations that prepared the Jesuits for the consequences of an active life of sacrificial service. A particularly exquisite example is the 1744 portrait, *Saint Luigi Gonzaga,* by Pompeo Batoni (cat. 19). Luigi's death at the tender age of 23 vividly exemplified the pious conviction, expressed by Binet, that "Living a long life is of little consequence, since what matters most is dying well."[44] Batoni's work contrasts the healthy, pink bloom of Luigi's youthful countenance with death's skull beside him, an alarming reminder that it is never too early to begin preparing for the next world.

Batoni's painting carries an additional message, suggesting with its subtle poetics that these spiritual preparations can take on a physical expression as well. If we consider the imagery carefully, we can see how fully Luigi is engaging his body in his meditations, cradling the crucifix against his breast (with the same gentleness he would later direct toward the plague victim), setting his supporting arm directly atop the skull as if to enact Christ's triumph over death, and gesturing emphatically to his chest with his other arm to declare his willingness to suffer with Christ in order to join him in eternal life. The expressive physicality of Luigi's devotional exercises reminds the viewer that these were directly related to his mission in the world, embodying the kind of self-discipline considered indispensable to the practice of charitable medicine by reformers such as Saint Camillo of Lellis. As Camillo explained in an address of 1599 to the members of his order, the Ministers of the Sick:

> If someone inspired by the Lord God should want to practice charitable works, both corporeal and spiritual, though our institution, let him be aware that he must be dead to all the things of this world, including family, friends, possessions, and even himself, and he must live only in the Crucified Jesus, under the gentle yoke of perpetual poverty, chastity, obedience, in service to the poor sick, even should they be stricken with plague, in their corporeal and spiritual needs, both day and night, according to whatever is commanded of him, which tasks he will carry out for love of God, and as penitence for his sins.[45]

Batoni's portrait of Luigi not only alludes to the rare spiritual gifts required of this new breed of religious caregivers, it also depicts the rigorous devotional exercises by which they honed these gifts, "dying" to themselves in order to serve Christ in the world.

In the years just preceding Batoni's creation of this masterful portrayal of the spiritual basis for charitable medicine, Rome's artistic glorification of its practical and corporeal dimen-

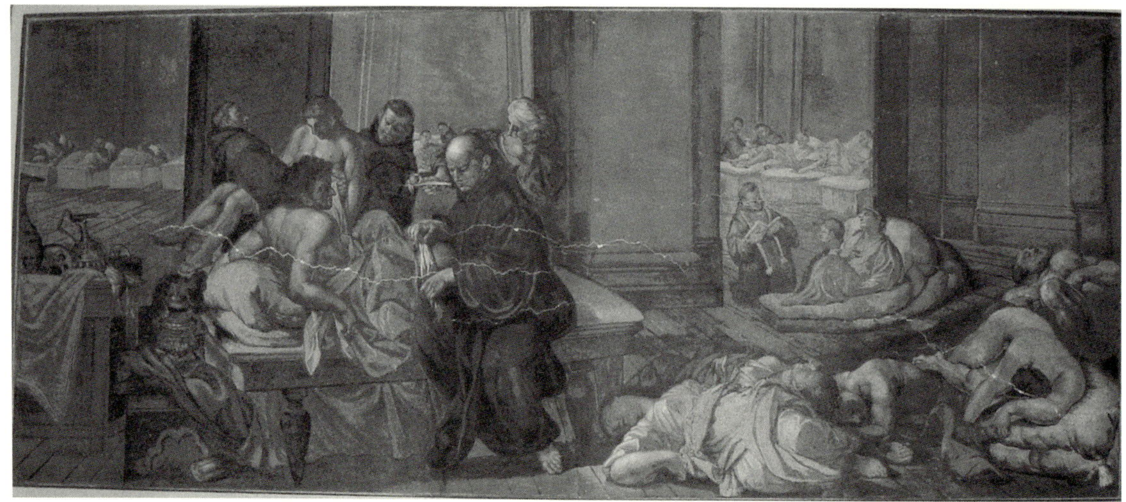

12. Lazzaro Baldi, *Saint John of God Attending Plague Victims*, 1690. Fresco. S. Giovanni Calabita, Rome.

sion reached both a literal and metaphorical pinnacle. This moment was in 1742, when Corrado Giaquinto completed the fresco spanning the ceiling of the nave of S. Giovanni Calabita, *Glory of Saint John of God* (fig. 13).

Saint John of God made his impact on the reform of public medicine as the founder of the order of the Hospitaller Brothers in Granada in 1539; of all the religious orders dedicated to the assistance of the sick, this one boasted the greatest number of physicians, surgeons, and pharmacists, many of whom received their professional training within the order itself.[46] In Rome, where the order was popularly known as the Fatebenefratelli, Saint John of God's followers first organized a modest hospital in the Piazza di Pietra before founding the hospital of the Tiber Island, which served as the city's primary intramural lazaretto during the plague of 1656.

When John was canonized in 1690, the Roman branch of the order celebrated by commissioning Lazzaro Baldi to fresco the ceiling of the sacristy of the Tiber Island church given to them in 1640, S. Giovanni Calabita. Baldi's image of *Saint John of God Attending Plague Victims* (fig. 12) shows members of the order in their black habits giving medical assistance to plague victims.[47] In the foreground, a barefoot Hospitaller Brother sits next to a patient in order to apply unguents and bandages to his leg, while two others carry a plague victim into this room where he will join the other new patients lying on the floor, waiting for treatment; only the young assistant in lay clothing covers his hand to protect himself from the pestilential air, whereas the Hospitaller Brothers seem accustomed to the ubiquitous danger and unpleasant smells, from which the smoking incense burner in the foreground provides partial protection. In the background we see patients recovering in neatly ordered beds, receiving medical attention from the solicitous brothers. Astoundingly, there is in this whole scene only one detail that indicates a priestly activity: on the right side of the composition in the middle ground, a Hospitaller Brother with a stole around his neck kneels on the floor before a prostrated patient and her child, presumably holding a Sacramentary and administering the sacrament of Last Rites.[48] Other than this one vignette, however, the activities depicted are exclusively medical.[49]

Though we have already seen in the discussion of paintings at the Collegio Romano how the ancillary spaces of church complexes might contain strong endorsements of public medicine, nothing in Rome compares to the fresco that the Hospitaller Brothers of Rome commissioned for the ceiling of the nave of their recently restored church. Here, in the lower zone of Corrado Giaquinto's *Glory of Saint John of God* (fig. 13), the order's founder is depicted tending to plague victims on the steps outside a hospital, offering a bowl to a patient with one arm and reaching with the other for the medicines on a tray supported by a helper in elegant clothes. Also on these steps is the Archangel Raphael, directing other angels above to distribute bread to the sick – a miraculous incident recorded in the same hagiographies that claim Raphael once appeared to the saint saying, "John, you and I have the same task."[50] In the upper zone, John appears in heaven as he receives a crown of thorns from Mary and Christ; bearing witness to the celestial scene are three saints, Sebastian (Rome's stalwart intercessor against plague, and the saint whose feast marks the day that John experienced his "conversion" in 1537), Augustine (the author of the order's rule), and Giovanni Calabita (to whom the order's Roman church is dedicated).[51] John's activities in the earthly realm below, which are dialectically paired with his reception into heaven, involve the provision of food and medicine to the sick. These are, of course, strictly temporal remedies, based on secular science; this point is emphasized by the fact that John's assistant is not dressed as an acolyte, but rather as a fashionable courtier. The celestial coronation of a brother who serves the sick with the layman's cures rather than the priest's is nothing short of revolutionary; it is an apotheosis of charitably administered temporal remedies, triumphantly brandished across the length of a church.

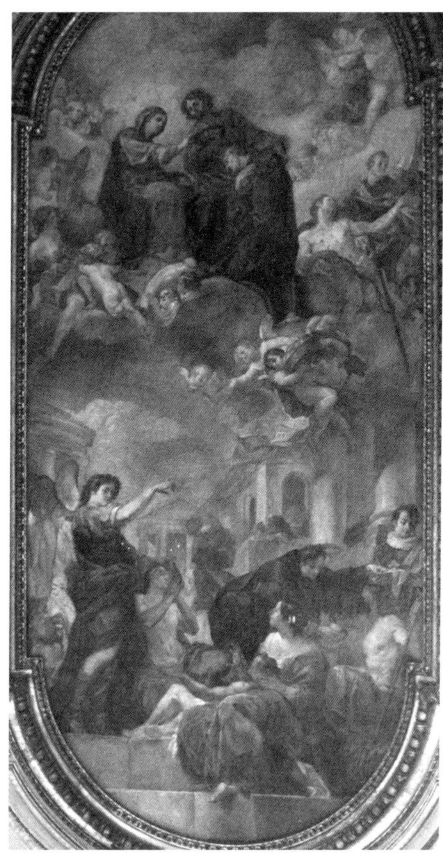

13. Corrado Giaquinto, *Glory of Saint John of God*, 1741-42. Fresco. S. Giovanni Calabita, Rome.

With Pompeo Batoni's portrait of Saint Luigi Gonzaga and Giaquinto's fresco, *The Glory of Saint John of God*, this discussion of Rome's plague art returns to its point of departure: the years when Bernardo Bellotto briefly alighted in Rome. Bellotto arrived just as charitable medicine received its supreme pictorial "placet" in the Hospitaller Brothers' church of S. Giovanni Calabita, culminating more than a century of experiments with iconographies for the depiction of the new alliance between temporal remedies and spiritual directives. Though no one had yet realized it, this was also the moment when public healthcare reforms initiated by such great religious leaders of the sixteenth century as Filippo Neri, Carlo Borromeo, Gaetano of Thiene, Camillo of Lellis, and John of God had – along with other contributing factors – permanently disrupted the cyclical outbreaks of bubonic plague in Italy.

Bubonic plague may have been only one of the diseases that confronted these religious reformers of public medicine, but as the most fierce, violent, and terrifying illness known to Europe, it challenged these men to muster their greatest spiritual gifts, and to reshape the ideologies that conditioned and limited social response to such crises. The art examined in this essay documents these changing ideologies in Rome, and in some circumstances, it may have served as a stimulus of such changes. Accompanying these epistemological developments was the rise of new orders who worked in concert with the medical community to make temporal remedies available on a city-wide scale. Their interventions introduced new themes and protagonists to plague art, but more importantly, they helped to bring a close to Rome's long history of living in the shadow of plague.

1. Totti, 244-45; see also Micheloni, 281-308.
2. The first sculpture of a plague angel may have been elevated to the top of Castel Sant'Angelo before the reign of Nicholas III Orsini, i.e. before 1277; the present plague angel is Pietro Verschaffelt's 1752 version (D'Onofrio 1978, 166-72).
3. Titi, 377, attributes the Trinità de' Monti fresco to "un siciliano, che serviva Michel'Angelo Bonarroti."
4. On water and health in Roman religion, see Adanti, 36. The original *apollinar* of Veiovis / Soranus, later identified with Apollo, was on the north shore of the Tiber in Campo Marzio near the church of S. Giovanni de' Fiorentini (Coarelli, 377-78; and Gagé, 72). On Febris, see Gagé, 72; and Adanti, 19. On Esculapius's cult on the Tiber Island, see Kerényi, 16-17; and Wickkiser, passim.
5. Lack of spring water in Renaissance Rome obliged many to rely on the Tiber for drinking water even though such physicians as Alessandro Traiano Petroni, Giovan Battista Modio, and Andrea Bacci debated its safety. See Pecchiai, 9; and *Roma la città dell'acqua*, 36-37.
6. Riley, 93.
7. On the plague that infested Rome's rione of the Borgo in 1696, see Pazzini, 385-86. Preto, 1-3, mentions several plagues that struck Europe in the eighteenth century.
8. On Baglione's *Saint Sebastian Cured by an Angel* (Harris Collection, promised gift to the Palmer Museum of Art, Pennsylvania State University), see Smith O'Neil, 203-4. See also Henneberg, 140, for its possible relation to the patronage of charitable institutions, as well as Jones, 31-35, for its iconographic relation to the cult of guardian angels. On Guerrieri's *Cure of Saint Sebastian* (Milan, Pinacoteca di Brera), see *Giovanni Francesco Guerrieri*, 90-91.
9. One image of the Cure of Sebastian was made for a church where there was no organized assistance for the sick: Baglione's 1630-32 *Saint Sebastian Tended by Irene and Her Assistant* for the basilica of Quattro Santi Coronati (only later in Urban VIII's reign would an orphanage be established here); in this case, the patron, Cardinal Girolamo Vidone, may have wished to edify the crowds who flocked to the saint's relics beneath the image with an example of pious charity.
10. The hospital at S. Giovanni de' Fiorentini was organized in 1606 to serve the poor sick among that nation. S. Maria dell'Orto's hospital and pharmacy served the guilds that in turn staffed and funded these facilities. See Maroni Lumbroso and Martini, s.v. "Arciconfraternita di S. Giovanni Battista della Pietà dei Fiorentini" and s.v. "Arciconfraternita di S. Maria dell'Orto"; Biblioteca Vallicelliana, 17, 22, 29; and Fanucci, 51-52. For the history of charitable assistance in Rome, see Da Villapadierna. Baglione's altarpiece at S. Maria dell'Orto decorates the chapel of Saint Sebastian, where an inscription stone notes the patronage of Luciano Brancalleo, a fruit vendor, in 1624; see Guglielmi, 319; Barroero, 95-97; and Smith O'Neil, 224.
11. See Sannazzaro, 34.
12. See Gentilcore, 132.
13. Before the Christian endorsement of human remedies was depicted in churches, it could be seen in Rome's hospitals and pharmacies, such as the pharmacy of the Collegio Romano, frescoed in 1629 by Andrea Sacchi and Emilio Savonanzi. Also relevant is the ca.1600 cycle of decorations in the Jesuit infirmary at the novitiate of S. Andrea al Quirinale, described in Richeôme, 2:422-58.
14. Images of the old paradigm sometimes coexisted with those of the new paradigm. At S. Maria dell'Orto, where Baglione's *Cure of Saint Sebastian by Angels* encouraged Christians to aid the afflicted to the best of their human abilities, there was also a miraculous image, the Madonna dell'Orto. The cult of this healing icon, which dates to 1488 when it cured a woman's disease, induced locals to build the namesake church (Barroero, 17-18). On the complex–and sometimes conflicting – coexistence of various therapeutic systems in Italy, see Cipolla, passim and Gentilcore, passim.
15. Expressing this view of human remedies, Francisco di Castro in 1585 wrote that for Saint Camillo of Lellis, "the medicine of the body was the means of [furnishing] that of the soul" (Russotto 1958, 40).
16. On the Compagnia del Divino Amore in Rome, see Canezza, 204-6; and Biblioteca Vallicelliana, s.v. "Arciconfraternita di S. Maria del Popolo e di S. Giacomo." The Capuchins' work at the hospital of S. Giacomo degli Incurabili began in 1529 at the instigation of Vittoria Colonna (Canezza, 207-8, 215). For the Capuchins' care of plague victims, see *I frati cappuccini*, 3/2.5; D'Alatri, 84-88; Cordovani, 31ff; and *Annales minorum*, 27: 298-304. Additional bibliography is found in the *Lexicon capuccinum*, 1339-43. For the Capuchin perspective on the theology of disease, see for example "Il ragguaglio della fondazione del Ven.o Monasterio delle Monache Cappuccine ad Monte Cavallo," B.A.V., Vat. Lat. 9162, f.45, in which plague is defined as a "corruption of the air that men draw into themselves when they breathe and respire that contaminated air, which upon penetrating the veins poisons the blood, generates acute and pestilential fevers, and since there is no punishment from God more universal or more severe than this [plague], it thus happens many times that those who have sought out the evil acts of humans as [contributing causes] find the proof."
17. Pellegrino da Forli, 1:17.
18. *I frati cappuccini*, 3/2: 3694.
19. *I frati cappuccini*, 3/2: 3706.
20. The Church's fundamental teachings on disease can be traced back to Saint Cyprian's "De mortalitate" from the third century, discussed extensively in the essay by Franco Mormando in this catalogue. For general accounts of the conception of disease in the Catholic Church, see Palmer, passim; Maggioni, passim; and Amundsen, passim.
21. See for example Da Seggiano, 1-10; and *I frati cappuccini*, 3/2: 3694.
22. Da Isnello, 79-82, recounts the history of these commissions.
23. The christological subjects in the original program, including Mario Balassi's *Transfiguration of Christ*, Baccio Ciarpi's *Christ in the Garden*, and Andrea Camassei's *Pietà*, may reflect the fact that for Capuchins, the invocation of Christ was foremost among the "exercises of piety and devotion...practiced as a religious prophylactic against plague" (*I frati cappuccini*, 3/2: 3859 n. 7). These same christological subjects also figure among the paintings in the Jesuit infirmary at S. Andrea al Quirinale. The Concezione's altarpiece program and its relation to the plague are discussed at greater length in Barker, 242-55.
24. The altarpiece's patronage and its pertinence to the plague are discussed in *Scienza e miracoli*, 348. On the sources for Reni's altarpiece, see Pepper, 32, 281; and Guarino, 83-92.

25. Earlier examples include Giovanni de' Vecchi's altarpiece (see n. 28 below) and the fresco that once decorated the altar wall of the sixteenth-century Chateauvillain Chapel of the Trinità dei Monti. The Triumph of Saint Michael over Satan was repeated later in the century in Francesco Mola's altarpiece at S. Marco and in Sebastiano Conca's for S. Maria in Campitelli. There are no Barberini commissions of Raphael as the plague-rescinding angel; I suspect that the Barberini doubted the authenticity of the story that arose six centuries after the event. In Torrigio's study of Saint Michael dedicated to Francesco Barberini, the plague-rescinding angel is treated only as a subject of art, not as an historical event.
26. "Guerra intestinal invisibile dal Cielo" (Naldi, 2).On the sanitary and militant aspects of Michael's protection, see Guarino, 84, 91-2; Mercalli, 96; and Rice, 429. They are traced to the Archangel's cult in Byzantium and its Hebraic origins in Rohland, 9-33 and 75-104. In popular imagination, Michael's foe, Satan, was associated with the plague and with its dissemination; see Rinaldi, 81.
27. At the cave of Monte Gargano, where the militant Saint Michael had been worshipped since the early middle ages, pilgrims gathered stones believing these would repel and cure illness. On this tradition, as well as Saint Francis's pilgrimage to this site, see Mâle, 376, 491; D'Onofrio, 1978, 163; and Guarino, 110.
28. According to Severano, 3, (a treatise dedicated to Card. Francesco Barberini), Boniface II erected a church dedicated to "S.t'Angelo" in 530. The confraternity of San Michele Arcangelo, founded in 1432, established a hospital called the Angelorum, as well as the church mentioned above, Sant'Angelo ai Corridori di Borgo (which was destroyed during the reign of Alexander VI and rebuilt in 1564); see Lombardi, 346; also Hülsen, 527; Totti, 24; and Fioravanti Martinelli's "Roma Ornata" in D'Onofrio, 1968, 19. In this church, Giovanni de' Vecchi's painting, *Saint Michael Vanquishing Satan* stood at the high altar while a scene of Gregory I's plague procession was relegated to a side chapel; the arrangement suggests that the image at the high altar encompassed all aspects of the angel's cult, including the historical manifestation as Rome's plague-rescinding angel.
29. *La devotissima oratione del Glorioso Santo Michaele Archangelo*, fol.1-2.
30. On the hospital of S. Giovanni in Laterano in the seventeenth century, see Mola, 78; and Curcio, 119, 122. Celio's fresco is mentioned in Titi, 473. On the decoration of the Jesuit infirmary, see Richeôme, 2:455-58.
31. On the Pope's sickness and the dedication of his reign to Saint Michael, see Rice, 428-29. On the solemnity of 1630, see the *avviso* of December 13,1631, B.A.V., Ott. 3338, 218v.
32. "Perversos Genios," "bonos...Genios, seu Angelos salutares." Lemnius, 134-37. Fludd, 1:333-39.
33. The Jesuit novices were particularly active at the hospital of the Consolazione, designated for the treatment of plague victims. Their work here is noted in the entry for "pestilence" in Moroni, 52: 227: "Jesuit novices stayed, for all but a few days of the month of October, at the above-mentioned hospital [of the Consolazione] in order to do pious works, both spiritual and corporeal, among the sick."
34. The allusion to Aeneas and Anchises is noted by Arcari and Padovani, 2:81, where it is also noted that the two fountains seen in the image were built by Paul V in 1612-13, establishing a *terminus post quem*. The fountains thus may indicate Borghese patronage of the painting, and this in turn supports the association with Guerrieri, who was working for the Borghese in these same years.
35. This work appears in Bissell's catalogue raisonné as no. 27. It was probably displayed at the hospital of the Consolazione near another low-relief sculpture also transported to S. Spirito, this one in terracotta, representing of Camillo of Lellis assisting the sick. See Da Riese, 38; and Pericoli, 79.
36. Filippo owned all the books written by Andrea Cesalpino, his own doctor, and learned about pharmacy from his friend, botanist Michele Mercati. His adherents were taught to offer the sick a range of human remedies, from words of hope and comfort, to foods determined according to their illness, to hygienic care that included shaving their beards, cleaning their beds, and washing their feet. See Canezza, 102-4.
37. This incident is described in nearly these very words in Canezza, 103.
38. "Ordini et modi che si hanno da tenere nelli hospitali in servire li poveri infermi," published in Vanti 1965, 64-66.
39. The inscription is visible in fig. 48 in Bissell; it is no longer displayed near the relief.
40. On this debate, see Vanti 1944, 120; also Sannazzaro, 136-38. The Church may have opposed the designation of this new class of martyrs so as not to encourage the convocations of people near the corpses of those religious who died of plague while manning the lazarettos. Similar questions regarding "martyrdom for hospitality" continue into the present: on October 25, 1992, the 71 Hospitaller Brothers assassinated in Spain while carrying out their mission were beatified under Pope John Paul II. According to a statement on the event posted on the website of the Order of the Hospitaller Brothers (www.oh-fbf.it), "With the beatification of these 71 Hospitaller martyrs the Catholic martyrology has been enriched in a significant manner. This is not so much by reason of their number, but more for the precise and special way they died as martyrs of hospitality."
41. "martyres esse iudicandos et inter martyres recensendos." Filiberto Marchini, *Belli divini*, cited in Vanti 1944, 120.
42. "La violenza della febbre nel maggior corso e fervore allentò un poco, e m'ha condotto lentamente fino al giorno glorioso dell'Ascensione. Dal qual tempo per un gran concorso di catarro al petto si rinforzò, talchè a mano a mano m'avvio ai dolci e cari abbracciamenti del celeste Padre, nel cui seno spero potermi riposare con sicurezza e per sempre" (Letter of 10 June, 1591, in Canezza, 217).
43. "Per consolatione dell'anime atterite dal timore della morte...si vive morendo"; "...morendosi vivo, vive" (Binet, 63).
44. "Il vivere gran tempo, poco rilieva, importa ben molto il muorir bene" (Binet, 87). One of the most popular seventeenth-century treatises on the earthly preparation for Final Judgment is Roberto Bellarmino's *Art of Dying Well*, first published in Rome in 1620; on this work, see Worcester, 87-106.
45. "Se alcuno inspirato dal Signore Iddio vorrà esercitare l'opere di misericordia, corporali, et spirituali secondo il Nostro Istituto, Sappia che ha da esser morto a tutte le cose del mondo, cioè a Parenti, Amici, robbe, et a se stesso, et vivere solamente a Giesù Crocifisso sotto il suavissimo

giogo della perpetua Povertà, Castità, Obedienza, et Servigio delli Poveri Infermi, ancorché fussero Appestati" (from the "Formula di Vita" as presented at the 9th Congregation of the order on June 19, 1599, published in Vanti 1965, 97).

46. On Saint John of God and his legacy of healthcare reform, see Pazzini; and Russotto 1969. The professional preparation of the order is discussed in Russotto 1969, 2: 94-96.

47. One memorial sketch of the composition, attributed to Baldi's assistant Giovan Battista Lenardi, is in the Fagiolo Collection; another is in the Galleria Spada.

48. I thank Franco Mormando for his assistance with the reading of this image.

49. In contrast to this imagery of secular remedies, Francesco Solimena's ca. 1690 painting of *A Miracle of Saint John of God* in the present exhibition (cat. 29) emphasizes spiritual remedies, especially of the type that occurred after the saint's death. In particular, Solimena's image may represent the miraculous cure of 16-year-old Isabella Arcelli, a patient at the lazaretto on the Tiber Island during the Roman plague of 1656 who, after being treated surgically by the Hospitaller P. Pasquale, recovered overnight through the spiritual intervention of John of God, to whom she had prayed before going to sleep. It is one of two miracles officially recognized in the saint's canonization proceedings and detailed in Russotto 1969, 2: 219-220.

50. The several miracles involving Raphael are noted in Russotto 1969, 1: 28. In Hebrew, Raphael's name signifies "God heals, " and he is associated with healing because he instructed Tobias on how to cure his father's blindness (importantly, though, this spiritual intervention produces a cure by means of a "natural remedy, " the fish oil).

51. Information on the commission of Giaquinto's work and the iconography comes from Huetter, 56-59, and Russotto 1950, 34-35.

Bibliography

Adanti, Guido. *Le divinità della salute nell'antica Roma.* Milan, 1966.

Amundsen, Darrel W. *Medicine, Society, and Faith in the Ancient and Medieval Worlds.* Baltimore and London, 1996.

Annales minorum seu trium ordinum a S. Francesco institutorum. Vol. 27. Ed. Aniceto Chiappini (1628-1632). Quaracchi, 1934.

Arcari, Gianluigi and Umbert Padovani. *L'immagine a stampa di san Luigi Gonzaga*, 2 vols. Mantua, 2000.

Baglione, Giovanni. *Le vite de' pittori, scultori, architetti, ed intagliatori, dal pontificato di Gregorio XIII. del 1572. fino a' tempi di papa Urbano VIII.* Rome, 1642.

Barker, Sheila Carol. "Art in a Time of Danger: Urban VIII's Rome and the Plague of 1629-1634." Ph.D. Diss. Columbia University, 2002.

Barroero, Liliana. *S. Maria dell'Orto.* Le chiese di Roma illustrate, 130. Rome, 1976.

Biblioteca Vallicelliana. *Quelli che servono gli infermi: assistenza e medicina a Roma nei secoli XVI e XVII: mostra bibliografica: Roma 18 maggio-18 giugno 1987.* Rome, 1987.

Binet, Étienne (Stefano Binetti). *Sovrani et efficaci rimedi contro la peste e morte subitana.* Rome, 1656.

Bissell, Gerhard. *Pierre Le Gros 1666-1719.* Chippenham, 1997.

Canezza, Alessandro. *Gli arcispedali di Roma nella vita cittadina nella storia e nell'arte.* Rome, 1933.

Cipolla, Carol. *Faith, Reason, and the Plague in Seventeenth-Century Tuscany*, trns. Muriel Kittel. Ithaca, 1979.

Cordovani, Rinaldo. *I Cappuccini a Montefiascone.* Montefiascone, 1982.

Curcio, Giovanna. "L'Ospedale di S. Giovanni in Laterano: funzione urbana di una istituzione ospedaliera II." *Storia dell'arte* 36-7 (1979):103-130.

D'Alatri, Mariano. *I Cappuccini della Provincia di Roma.* Rome, 2000.

Da Isnello,Domenico. Il convento della S. Concezione de' Padri Cappuccini in Piazza Barberini. Viterbo, 1923.

Da Riese, Fernando. *Santa Maria della Consolazione.* Rome, 1968.

Da Seggiano, Ignazio. "La medicina, coefficiente dell'attività missionaria dei Cappuccini nel sec. XVII." *Italia Francescana* 23 (1948):1-10.

Da Villapadierna, Isidoro. "L'età moderna." In *La carità cristiana in Roma.* Ed. Vincenzo Monachino. Bologna, 1968.

La devotissima oratione del Glorioso Santo Michaele Archangelo. Palermo, 1604.

D'Onofrio, Cesare. *Castel S. Angelo e Borgo tra Roma e Papato.* Rome: 1978.

—. *Roma nel Seicento.* Rome, 1968.

Fanucci, Camillo. *Trattato di tutte le opera pie dell'alma città di Roma.* Rome, 1601.

Fludd, Robert. *Integrum morborum mysterium: sive medicinae catholicae.* Frankfurt, 1631.

I frati cappuccini. Documenti e testimonianze del primo secolo. Ed. Costanzo Cargnoni. Perugia, 1991.

Gagé, Jean. *Apollon romain. Essai sur le culte d'Apollon et le développement du 'ritus Graecus' à Rome des origines à Auguste.* Bibliothèque des Écoles françaises d'Athènes et de Rome, 182. Paris, 1955.

Gentilcore, David. *Healers and Healing in Early Modern Italy.* Manchester, 1998.

Giovanni Francesco Guerrieri. Un pittore del Seicento fra Roma e la Marche. Exh. cat. Ed. Marina Cellini and Claudio Pizzorusso. Venice, 1997.

Guarino, Sergio. "Aspetti dell'iconografia di Michele Arcangelo tra XV e XVIII secolo." In *L'angelo e la città*. Ed. Francesco Sisinni. Rome, 1987.

Guglielmi, Carla. "Intorno all'opera pittorica di Giovanni Baglione." *Bollettino d'arte* 39 (1954):311-326.

Henneberg, Josephine von. "Cardinal Cesare Baronius, the arts, and the Early Christian Image." In *Saints & Sinners: Caravaggio & the Baroque Image*. Exh. cat. Ed. Franco Mormando, 136-50. Boston, 1999.

Hülsen, Christian. *Le Chiese di Roma nel medioevo. Cataloghi ed appunti*. Hildesheim and New York, 1975.

Huetter, Luigi. *S. Maria dell'Orto in Trastevere*. Rome, 1955.

Jones, Pamela. "The Power of Images: Paintings and Viewers in Caravaggio's Italy." In *Saints & Sinners: Caravaggio & the Baroque Image*. Exh. cat. Ed. Franco Mormando, 28-86. Boston, 1999.

Kerényi, Carl. *Asklepios. Archetypal Image of the Physician's Existence*. Trns. Ralph Manheim. New York, 1959

Lemnius, Levinus. *De miraculis occultis naturae libri III*. Frankfurt, 1611.

Lexicon capuccinum. Promptuarium historico-bibliographicum Ordinis fratrum minorum capuccinorum, 1525-1950. Rome, 1951.

Maggioni, Bruno. "Gesù e la Chiesa primitiva di fronte alla malattia." In *Il sacramento dei malati. Aspetti antropologici e teologici della malattia*. Turin, 1975.

Mâle, Émile. *L'art religieux après le Concile de Trente*. Paris, 1932.

Maroni Lumbroso, Matizia, and Antonio Martini. *Le confraternite romane nelle loro chiese*. Rome, 1963.

Mercali, Maria. "L'angelo di castello: la sua icononografia, il suo significato." In *L'angelo e la città*. Exh. cat. Ed. Francesco Sisinni. Rome, 1987.

Micheloni, Placido. "L'ospedale romano di S. Giovanni de' Fiorentini. (Documenti d'archivio)." *Humana Studia* 1, no. 6 (1949):158-184.

Mola, Giovanni Battista. *Breve racconto delle miglior opere d'architettura, scultura et pittura fatte in Roma et alcuni fuori di Roma* (1663). Ed. Karl Noehles. Berlin, 1966.

Moroni, Gaetano. *Dizionario dell'erudizione storico-ecclesiastica*. Venice, 1840-1861.

Naldi, Mattia. *Regole per la cura del contagio*. Rome, 1656.

Palmer, Richard. "The Church, Leprosy, and Plague in Medieval and Early Modern Europe." In *The Church and Healing*. Ed. W. J. Sheils. Oxford, 1982.

Pazzini, Adalberto. *Assistenza e ospedali nella storia dei Fatebenefratelli*. Torino, 1956.

Pecchiai, Pio. *Acquedotti a fontane di Roma nel Cinquecento*. Rome, 1944.

Pellegrino da Forli. *Annali dell'Ordine dei Frati Minori Cappuccini*. Milan, 1882-85.

Pepper, Stephen. *Guido Reni. L'opera completa*. Novara, 1988.

Pericoli, Pietro. *L'ospedale di S. Maria della Consolazione di Roma dalle sue origini ai giorni nostri*. Imola, 1859.

Preto, Paolo. "Il 'Governo della peste' e la realtà politico-sanitaria dell'Italia del primo '700." In *Il buon uso della paura: per una introduzione allo studio del trattato muratoriano 'Del governo della peste.'* Florence, 1990.

Rice, Louise. "Urban VIII, the Archangel Michael, and a Forgotten Project for the Apse Altar of St. Peter's." *The Burlington Magazine* 134 (1992):428-434.

Richeôme, Louis. *Les oeuvres du R. père Louis Richeôme*. 2 vols. Paris, 1628.

Riley, James C. *The Eighteenth-Century Campaign to Avoid Disease*. New York, 1987.

Rinaldi, Stefania Mason. "Le immagini della peste nella cultura figurativa veneziana." In *Venezia e la peste: 1348-1797*. Exhibition Catalogue. Ed. Commune di Venezia. Venice, 1980.

Rohland, Johannes Peter. *Der Erzangel Michael, Arzt und Feldherr: zwei Aspekte des vor- und frühbyzantinischen Michaelskultes*. Leiden, 1977.

Roma la città dell'acqua. Exh. cat. Ed. Angela Adriana Cavarra. Rome, 1994.

Russotto, Gabriele. "Lineamenti di una iconografia." In Piero Chiminelli, etc., *Per il IV centenario della morte di S. Giovanni di Dio, 1550-1950*. Rome, 1950.

—. *San Giovanni di Dio e il suo Ordine Ospedaliero*. 2 vols. Rome, 1969.

—. *Spiritualità ospedaliera*. Rome, 1958.

Scienza e miracoli nell'arte del '600 alle origini della medicina moderna. Exh. cat. Ed. Sergio Rossi. Milan, 1998.

Severano, Giovanni. *Historie delle chiese di Roma, e particolare delle sette*. Rome, 1675.

Smith O'Neil, Maryvelma. *Giovanni Baglione. Artistic Reputation in Baroque Rome*. Cambridge, 2002.

Titi, Filippo. *Descrizione delle pitture, sculture e architettura esposte al pubblico in Roma*. Rome, 1763.

Torrigio, Francesco Maria. *Narratione dell'origine dell'antichissima chiesa di Santi Michel'archangelo, e magno vescovo, e martire*. Rome, 1629.

Totti, Pompilio. *Ritratto di Roma moderna*. Rome, 1638.

Un uomo venuto per servire: Camillo de Lellis nell'antica cronanca di un testimone oculare. Ed. R. Corghi and G. Martignoni. Milan, 1984.

Vanti, Mario. *I Ministri degli Infermi nella peste del 1630 in Italia*. Rome, 1944.

—. *Scritti di san Camillo de Lellis*. Rome, 1965.

Wickkiser, Bronwen. "The Appeal of Asklepios and the Politics of Healing in the Greco-Roman World." Ph.D. Diss. University of Texas at Austin, 2003.

Worcester, Thomas. "Trent and beyond: Arts of Transformation." In *Saints & Sinners: Caravaggio & the Baroque Image*. Exh. cat. Ed. Franco Mormando, 87-104. Boston, 1999.

San Carlo Borromeo and Plague Imagery in Milan and Rome

Pamela M. Jones

Carlo Borromeo, Reformer and Plague Saint

Carlo Borromeo (1538-1584) was the only sixteenth-century Italian, later canonized, whose cult was inextricably linked with the plague. Born into a noble Milanese family, Borromeo was educated in preparation for an ecclesiastical career, ultimately receiving a law degree from the University of Pavia in 1559. Almost immediately thereafter he was called to Rome by his uncle Gian Angelo de' Medici, who had just ascended the papal throne as Pius IV. In 1560, Pius appointed Carlo to the cardinalate. Cardinal Carlo Borromeo, the papal nephew, distinguished himself as Prefect of the Secretariate of State; in that capacity, for example, he helped direct the last session (1562-63) of the Council of Trent, which decreed reforms of the Roman Catholic Church. These decrees were intended to be implemented by individual bishops, who were required to reside in their sees. Although Carlo had been appointed Archbishop of Milan in 1564, Pius, who relied heavily on his nephew, did not allow him to take up residence in Milan until October 1565.

As archbishop, Carlo Borromeo immediately began reforming the Diocese of Milan in accordance with his interpretation of the Tridentine decrees. Wietse de Boer, who called Carlo's diocesan reform "an extraordinary social experiment," characterized it as a system of discipline that aimed at the sanctification of everyday life by governing the lives of all kinds of people.[1] At the heart of Carlo's reform program was the sacrament of Penance, through which he sought to transform individuals and society in general. As we will see, this penitential approach characterized Carlo's ministry during the virulent outbreak of the plague in Milan in 1576-77, familiarly known as "Carlo Borromeo's plague." Borromeo's diocesan leadership during the plague combined private and public penitence with selfless, personal ministry to the afflicted. As a result, many of his contemporaries – not least the legions of poor Milanese who were trapped in the city, and who suffered and died in the lazaretto – considered Carlo not merely a dedicated archbishop, but a living saint.

From Beatification to Canonization: Establishing the Main Narrative Themes of Carlo Borromeo's Plague Iconography, 1602–10

Carlo Borromeo's iconography was first codified in a cycle of twenty paintings commissioned by the Veneranda Fabbrica of the Duomo (the Cathedral Chapter) of Milan to celebrate his beatification on 4 November 1602.[2] Canon Alessandro Mazenta oversaw the project, but Ernesto Brivio has suggested that Federico Borromeo, Carlo's younger cousin and successor as Archbishop of Milan, may have provided the program.[3] On the day of Carlo's beatification, the complete cycle was first displayed in the Duomo. The paintings–which are known as the "Quadroni"(large paintings) due to their scale – were hung between the pillars of the nave. One of Milan's leading artists, Giovanni Battista Crespi, called Il Cerano, designed the entire cycle, which achieves a unified effect despite the fact that a team of artists of varying talents painted the individual works. In reproductions the paintings' theatrical late Mannerist compositions and gestures and their bright tempera colors seem quite heavy handed. When seen across the vast space of the dark Gothic nave, however, the figures' gestures seem less emphatic and the paintings' colors more natural.[4] Four of the twenty scenes treat Carlo's plague min-

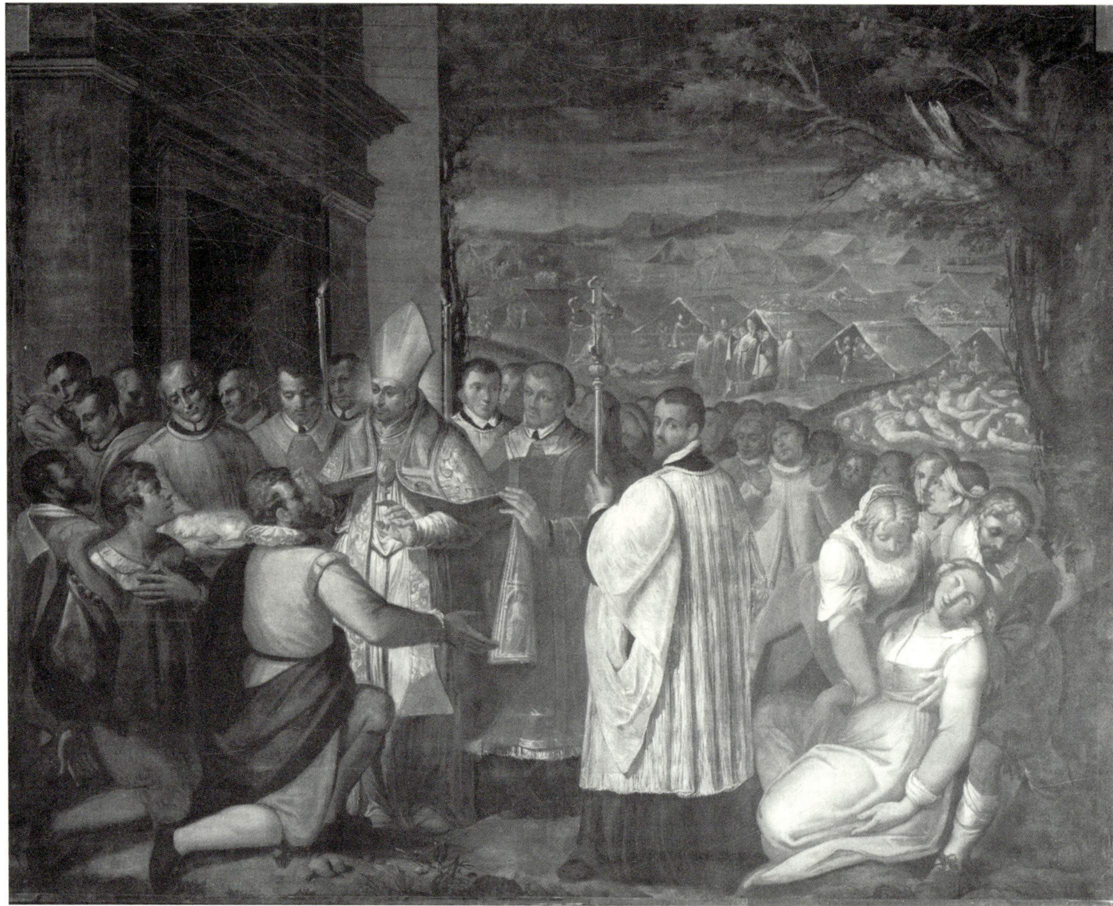

14. Camillo Landriani, called Il Duchino, *Carlo Borromeo Administers the Sacraments to the Plague-Stricken*, 1602. Tempera on canvas. Cathedral, Milan.

istry, which had given rise to his popular cult.[5]

Camillo Landriani, called Il Duchino, a mediocre Lombard artist, painted *Carlo Borromeo Administers the Sacraments to the Plague-Stricken* (fig. 14) in 1602 after a design by Cerano.[6] Although the Quadroni series established the standard narratives of Carlo's plague iconography, it is easy to see why Duchino's image – which despite some engaging details is rather dry and stilted – failed to set an aesthetic standard for emulation among later artists who treated this theme. For example, Pierre Mignard, in his beautiful and much later painting on the same theme (cat. 25), borrowed no figures or motifs from Duchino.

Duchino's painting, however, merits careful attention for what it shows us about the conditions under which Archbishop Carlo ministered to plague victims. The scene is set at Milan's lazaretto, or plague hospital, which had been built between 1488 and 1513 in a huge field outside the city walls near Porta Orientale (the present-day Porta Venezia).[7] The complex consisted of a rectangular, porticoed building containing numerous separate rooms for the afflicted; this building enclosed an enormous interior courtyard. In the center of the courtyard stood the church of S. Gregorio, named for Pope Gregory the Great, who led an expiatory plague procession in Rome in 590.[8] The entire Milanese complex was consequently often referred to simply as S. Gregorio.[9] A moat filled with water was constructed around the lazaretto complex in an attempt to minimize the spread of the contagion. Although the lazaretto was large, the plague that struck Milan in 1576 was so deadly that various camps of tent-like huts had to be set up in the countryside beyond the city walls to house the enormous overflow of plague victims who could not be accommodated in the lazaretto itself.[10]

When the plague arrived in Milan in late July 1576, the civic administration immediately went to work to contain it. The Tribunale della Sanità (Health Tribunal) cordoned off a safe area, and guards were posted at Milan's gates to prevent persons from plague-infested areas from entering the city. The Spanish governor, the Marquis d'Ayamonte, forbade gentlemen holding public office from leaving the city without his explicit permission, and established punishments for anyone who helped spread the plague, for instance by re-using belongings of the afflicted.[11] Most affluent Milanese, including many magistrates, fled the city, whereas those without means were left stranded in the city, hungry and without work due to the mandatory closing of shops and businesses. Although the civic officials quickly distributed as many provisions as possible, they could not meet the needs of the populace. Carlo Borromeo stepped in to provide for the material needs of his flock, spending most of his own income on them and soliciting donations from the wealthy. But he was also determined to provide for his parishioners' spiritual needs in the lazaretto and camps. At first the Health Tribunal hesitated to allow Carlo to visit these facilities. Ostensibly, as Marco Bendiscioli remarked, this was to protect him from the contagion, but the tribunal was also reluctant to set a precedent in favor of ecclesiastical jurisdiction over a pious institution that the civic government claimed as its own.[12] Times were desperate, however, and the lazaretto was beset by organizational, provisional, and criminal problems – not to mention that there was no medical cure for the plague. In short, overwhelmed by these predicaments, the civic authorities granted Archbishop Carlo permission to carry out a full-fledged plague ministry inside the lazaretto and the camps. (See Andrew Hopkins's essay, pp. 137-38 of this volume, on lazarettos and containment in Venice.)

To return to Duchino's painting, in the left foreground we see Archbishop Carlo in episcopal vestments standing with clerical assistants near the stone portal of S. Gregorio. In his plague chronicle the Jesuit priest Paolo Bisciola recorded that the archbishop visited the lazaretto and hut cities every day, personally administering the sacraments to the ill without fear for his own health.[13] Carlo's attempt to enlist the assistance of the secular and regular clergy in his ministry in the lazaretto was controversial, however. The Jesuit Provincial, Francesco Adorno, balked at Carlo's request because he believed that sending his priests into Milan's lazaretto was tantamount to condemning them to death.[14] Despite this, in addition to the diocesan clergy, members of the Capuchin, Barnabite, and other religious orders – including Jesuits – did assist Carlo in the lazaretto and outlying camps. Although many of the clergy died, Carlo did not. This enhanced his reputation as a holy man.

Duchino's composition juxtaposes the horror of the plague with the Roman Catholic message of hope for salvation. In the foreground Archbishop Carlo is shown anointing the forehead of an ill man.[15] Although Carlo fearlessly touched plague victims in order to administer the sacraments, as a precautionary measure he and his priests washed their hands in vinegar or perfumed them after direct contact with the infected. In Duchino's painting a priest standing to the left of Archbishop Carlo holds out a tray on which lies a fluffy white cloth, which Carlo could later use to cleanse his hands.[16] The man whom Carlo anoints gestures toward the right side of the composition, where an expiring woman – presumably the man's wife – is in dire need of receiving Last Rites. She is carefully helped to the ground.[17] In the distance behind the pitiful semi-recumbent woman a heap of nude corpses awaits burial in a mass grave. Beyond the dead, stretching far into the distance, is a hut city filled with desperately ill people. To underscore Carlo's tireless ministry, Duchino also included the figure of the archbishop in this area of the composition: he is seen ministering to the ill before a hut depicted slightly to the left of the pile of corpses.

Amid so much death, a message of hope is prominently rendered in the central foreground. As the plague-stricken man kneels before Carlo and entreats his assistance for the

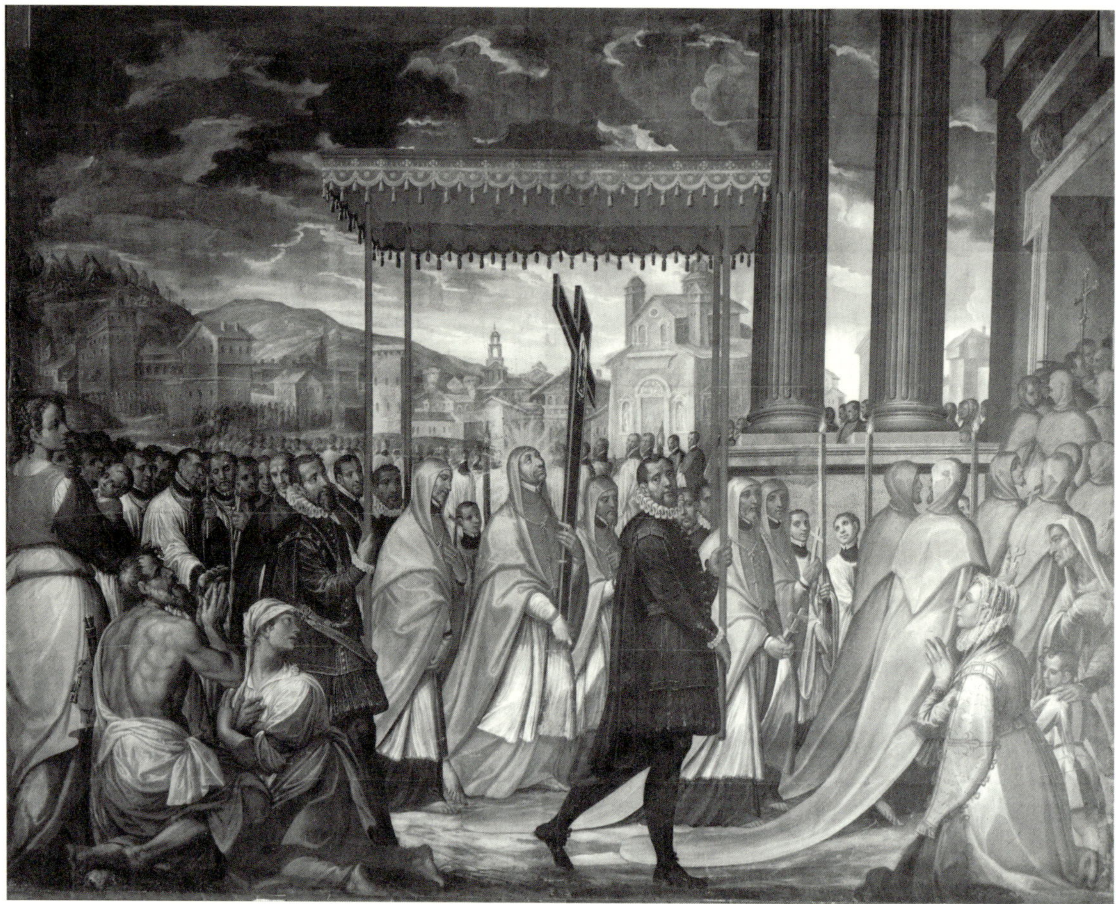

15. Gian Battista della Rovere, called Il Fiammenghino, *Carlo Borromeo's Procession of the Holy Nail*, 1602. Tempera on canvas. Cathedral, Milan.

dying woman, Carlo gives him the sacrament; all the while, a priest holds aloft a gleaming crucifix, a beacon of hope that unites the two areas of the composition. The priest holding the crucifix is turned toward Carlo and the ill man, but rotates his head to look out at viewers of the painting. He beseeches beholders in the cathedral of Milan to witness the administration of the sacraments. Worshipers in the cathedral knew that the sacraments depicted in the painting involved confession of one's sins, that is, penitence. Indeed, Carlo had encouraged more frequent confession and Communion than was typical during his time.[18] In Duchino's painting, the priest in the foreground also draws viewers' attention to the crucifix to convey the redemptive message of Christ's sacrifice.

Another plague scene in the Quadroni cycle, *Carlo Borromeo's Procession of the Holy Nail* (fig. 15), was executed in 1602 by Gian Battista della Rovere, called Il Fiammenghino.[19] This painting represents a public penitential procession that Borromeo led in Milan in October 1576. As we have noted, Carlo's systematic diocesan reform program was founded on public and private penance.

The procession of the Holy Nail was given considerable emphasis by Borromeo himself, his early biographers, and plague chroniclers. In addition to figuring in pictorial narratives beginning with that of Fiammenghino, the procession – and the cult of the Holy Nail itself – played a vital role in related devotional images of San Carlo. Indeed, Grammatica's devotional painting of about 1619-21 (cat. 24) is one such example. That Fiammenghino's painting depicts Carlo Borromeo walking in a procession under a ceremonial canopy surrounded by members of the clergy and laity is perfectly clear. But a brief historical account of the procession and cult–including important details that have been overlooked entirely or given insufficient emphasis – will help us understand more fully the key elements of Carlo Borromeo's persona as plague saint. (See the essays by James Clifton and Andrew Hopkins in this volume, on Neopolitan and Venetian processions and the plague.)

As mentioned previously, the plague struck Milan at the end of July 1576. Its intensification in October led Carlo to organize public penitential processions to entreat God's mercy. At first the civic authorities opposed the idea for fear that the processions would spread the contagion, and, indeed, according to Bisciola, the processions did have that effect.[20] Yet, as noted by Giovanni Pietro Giussano, whose biography of the saint was published in 1610, Archbishop Carlo persuaded the civic government to allow his processions by citing the efficacy of Gregory the Great's procession during Rome's plague of 590.[21] As a result, Carlo was allowed to organize various public penitential processions during the plague. He led the first three between 3 and 6 October. Since plenary indulgences were granted to everyone who took part in these processions, it is not surprising that the general public – including about 1,000 *disciplinati*, who flagellated themselves continuously – participated in great numbers. Borromeo himself encouraged everyone to fast on the days of the three processions, and to walk barefoot in them.[22] Each procession began at the cathedral, went to a major Milanese church, and then returned. In these carefully orchestrated processions Carlo played a special penitential role, as described by various biographers, including Giussano, who wrote that the archbishop:

> [w]ore a purple [*pavonazza*] pontifical cape in token of penitence, drawing the hood down to his eyes, his train sweeping the ground instead of being carried in state. Round his neck he bore a rope like the halter of a condemned criminal; in his hand he carried a crucifix (preserved to this day in the sacristy of the cathedral [of Milan]) on which he kept his eyes fixed throughout the whole way, like a malefactor led forth for execution. He considered himself to bear upon his shoulders the burden of the sins of his people, and offered himself in sacrifice to God for them, well content to receive the chastisement due to them if only they might be spared what yet remained to fill up the measure of their retribution.[23]

Although Giussano's description of the plague procession was written later, and thus had no influence on Fiammenghino's painting, his account can help us appreciate the Christ-like persona that Carlo intended to convey during the procession, for Fiammenghino presented it in a strikingly similar way. The painting is set outdoors near the cathedral, which is seen through the canopy; it is rendered in accordance with the then current facade plan of Pellegrino Tibaldi and Francesco Maria Ricchino.[24] The single difference between Giussano's description and Fiammenghino's painting concerns Borromeo's garments. Fiammenghino, who was of course concerned that his figure of Carlo would be immediately recognizable, did not cover his face; he also depicted him not in penitential purple, but in the scarlet cassock and mozzetta and white rochet that readily identify him as a cardinal. To underscore the penitential purpose of the procession, Fiammenghino instead portrayed Borromeo and the prelates surrounding him wearing great capes made of sackcloth. The prelates are also shown barefoot.[25]

Both Giussano and Fiammenghino emphasize Carlo's humble, Christ-like role in the procession. In the painting, Carlo's appearance and demeanor correspond very closely with Giussano's later account: he is seen barefoot with the noose around his neck, his train dragging on the ground as he gazes at the crucifix. Fiammenghino included yet another detail that had been recorded earlier by plague chroniclers and slightly later by biographers: an injury to Carlo's foot incurred on the first of these penitential plague processions. In his account of Milan's plague published in 1577, Bisciola described the effect Carlo's injury had on the faithful during the plague processions:

> [w]hat most moved the populace to tears, penitence, and sadness, was the Most Illustrious Cardinal in a funereal and lugubrious aspect, that great black Cross on which was carried the Holy Nail; that blood, which issued from the foot of His Illustrious Lordship. [26]

Similarly, Giussano recounted in 1610 that,

> It pleased God during the procession, to accept the oblation of His servant [Carlo], and to lay upon him some part of the suffering for which he had offered himself. As he walked along with bare feet, carrying a large crucifix in his hand, rapt in contemplation of the passion of Jesus Christ, his foot caught in an iron grating, so that one of his nails was torn off to the quick. He would not, however, stop to apply any remedy, but bore the pain without flinching. ...[27]

Fiammenghino depicts Carlo, blood flowing from his foot, walking stoically in the company of ecclesiastical and lay participants, while others watch from both sides, some of them kneeling in prayer. The very long procession winds into the distant background, where the horizon meets a stormy sky, effectively evoking the turbulent times.

Thus far, we have considered only the first two processions, but Fiammenghino actually represents the third one, which went from the Duomo to S. Maria presso S. Celso and back. It was distinctive because in it all of Milan's relics were carried, and to Carlo, the most important of these was the Holy Nail, reputedly one of the nails used to affix Christ's body to the cross.[28] Due to his particular devotion to the Passion of Christ, Carlo sought to enhance the cult of the Holy Nail. He therefore had the nail attached to the wooden processional cross in time for the third procession, that of Saturday, 6 October. In Fiammenghino's painting, the Holy Nail, which centuries earlier had been shaped into a horse's bit–hence its odd shape, is seen mounted in a crystal container on the black cross. When he led the procession of the Holy Nail, Carlo again walked barefoot with the noose around his neck, humbly allowing his train to drag on the ground. Because he would not wear bandages on the toe he had injured three days earlier, it continued to bleed during the third procession. How he must have welcomed that flowing blood, for it helped reinforce the christological significances of his penitential act!

When the procession returned to the cathedral, the archbishop preached on the instruments of Christ's Passion, and then placed the Holy Nail on the high altar for the celebration of the Forty Hours Devotion. Normally this popular Eucharistic devotion centered on the display of the host in a monstrance on the altar for forty hours, in commemoration of the number of hours that Christ spent in his sepulcher.[29] Carlo put the Holy Nail on display for forty hours so that the entire populace could pray for salvation; every hour he led a new meditation on one of the mysteries of the Passion.

Viewers of Fiammenghino's painting – whether during the celebration of Carlo's beatification in 1602 or his feast day every year beginning in 1610 – would have understood immediately the penitential and salvational messages of this theme.[30] The facsimiles of the Holy Nail that Carlo had made and distributed to the faithful during the plague to increase their

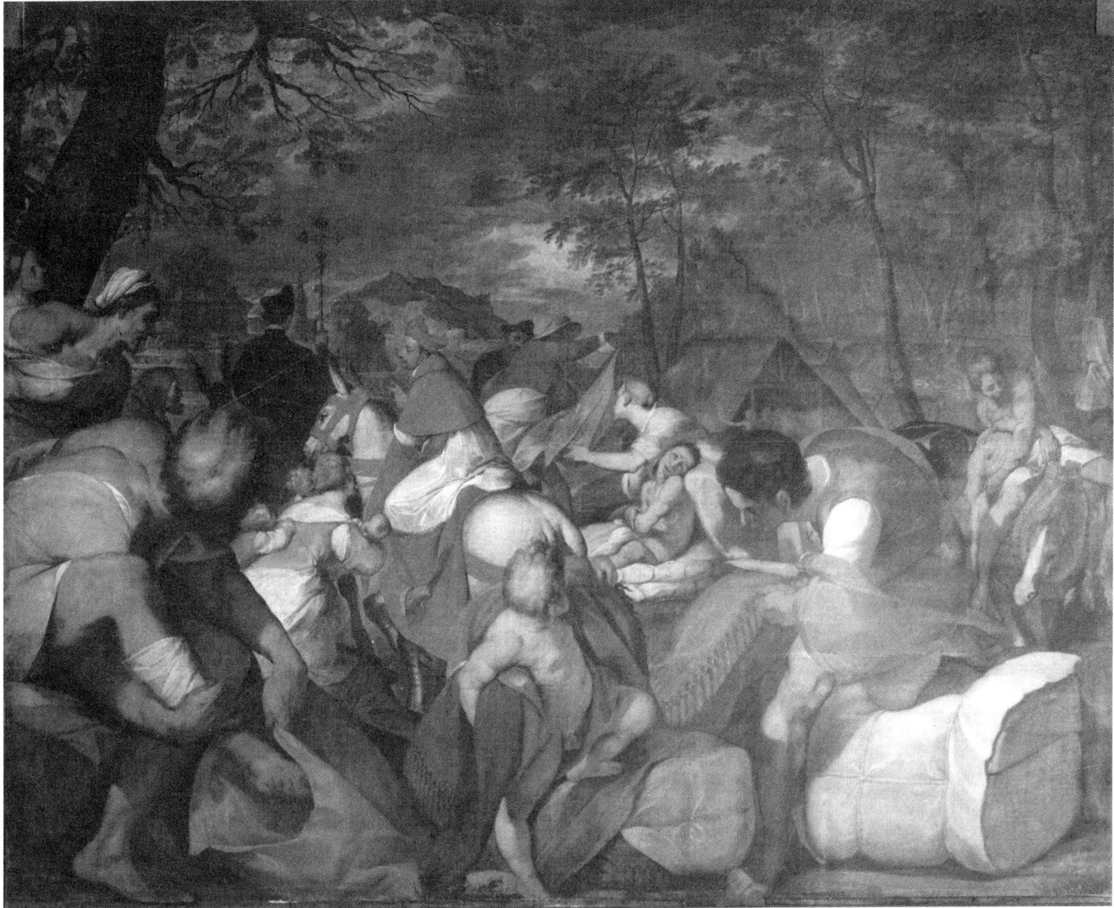

16. Giovanni Battista Crespi, called Il Cerano, *Carlo Borromeo Distributes His Clothing and Furnishings to the Plague-Stricken*, 1602. Tempera on canvas. Cathedral, Milan.

devotion no doubt also continued to serve as sites for meditation and remembrance, both of the processions themselves, which were undertaken annually beginning in 1577 – the year that Carlo established the annual feast of the Holy Nail – and of paintings of them.[31]

As we have seen, Cerano conceptualized the entire Quadroni series, and the scenes that he painted himself are the most famous – although not necessarily the most influential – among them. In his painting *Carlo Borromeo Distributes His Clothing and Furnishings to the Plague-Stricken* (fig. 16), Cerano treats Carlo's charity toward the poor plague victims as cold weather encroached in late fall of 1576.[32] As recorded by plague chroniclers and the saint's biographers, Carlo donated his own furnishings and garments to the afflicted, keeping only a few old clothes and the vestments required of his episcopal office. He even stripped the Archiepiscopal Palace virtually bare of its tapestries and other furnishings to have clothing made for the suffering masses.[33] Then he personally oversaw the distribution of these provisions in the lazaretto and camps.

Cerano captures the urgency of the situation and the people's gratitude for Carlo's charity. The scene is set outdoors amid trees with leaves just starting to change color against a glowering sky. Carlo and two clerks regular in black vestments help distribute clothing in a camp outside the S. Gregorio complex, which is seen in the left background.[34] In the center of the composition, Carlo, riding a white horse, blesses a mother and her children, who kneel before him in thanksgiving. Behind Carlo to the right, a man holds out a sheet to a woman so that she may cover the nude body of a man, whose neck is bent to the side in a pose common to plague victims in the advanced stages of the disease.[35] The foreground is populated by, on the left, people hastily donning clothes and gathering up blankets, and, on the right, a man leaning on a pack of cloth while using scissors to cut a large piece in two. Behind him, a man on horseback struggles to carry a corpse. This subject was also included in the later painting cycle that decorated St. Peter's in Rome on the occasion of Carlo Borromeo's canonization in 1610, but in the long run it was somewhat less popular than the two themes previously discussed. [36] Depictions of the saint's charity are numerous indeed, but they are as likely to show San Carlo donating clothing to the lame and poor as to the plague-stricken.[37] (See Andrew Hopkins's essay, pp. 140-41 for more on the theme of charity and the plague.)

In 1603 Cerano painted another plague theme for the Quadroni cycle: *Carlo Borromeo Blesses the Crosses Erected Outside for Provisional Altars*.[38] Although it is unclear whether Cerano's scene is meant to take place during or after the pestilence, it is unquestionably plague-related. Various quarantines were imposed in Milan when the plague became especially acute, and at such times people could not leave home to attend Mass; therefore, the archbishop had columns erected at prominent intersections in the city and crosses placed atop them.[39] Temporary altars were constructed beside the columns so that quarantined persons could hear Mass by looking out their windows. This theme never became popular, and indeed failed to be included in the cycle for Carlo's canonization ceremony at St. Peter's.

In short, at the beginning of the seventeenth century the Quadroni established the main narrative themes of Carlo Borromeo's plague iconography. The overall view of his plague ministry presented at the time of his beatification by and for members of his own diocese was not altered significantly in the official imagery created for his canonization apparatus in St. Peter's in Rome.

Carlo Borromeo's canonization ceremony was celebrated at St. Peter's on 1 November 1610. As in the case of the Quadroni series for the beatification, the Veneranda Fabbrica of the Duomo of Milan paid for the decorations. [40] Canon Mazenta oversaw their production for Archbishop Federico Borromeo. The church's facade received a temporary painted triumphal decoration, but what interests us is the painting cycle that decorated the temporary twelve-sided structure – the theater or apparatus – built inside the chancel of St. Peter's. This cycle consisted of thirty-nine paintings rendered in gold chiaroscuro by Antonio Tempesta. Intended as ephemera, they do not survive. Several visual sources discussed and illustrated by Niels Rasmussen record the general appearance of the apparatus, but not its painting cycle.[41] Yet we know all of the paintings' themes due to Marco Aurelio Grattarola's detailed description, published in 1614.[42] Tempesta's cycle included scenes of both San Carlo's life and miracles. The plague figures only in the part of the series dedicated to the saint's life. Rasmussen has discussed in detail how this decoration functioned within the liturgy of the canonization ceremony; I will therefore focus solely on the plague iconography incorporated in it.

The St. Peter's cycle included twenty-three scenes of San Carlo's life. The cycle's three plague themes had all been included in the Quadroni series: San Carlo administering the sacraments to the plague-stricken, his penitential plague procession, and his charitable donations of clothing and furnishings to the afflicted. Only the Quadroni's scene of Carlo blessing the outdoor altars erected during the plague was omitted from the St. Peter's apparatus.

A partial visual record of the ephemeral decorations of St. Peter's is provided by an image designed by Tempesta and engraved by Raphael Guidi, the *Vita et Miracula San Caroli Borromei* (fig. 17) made in 1610 to commemorate the canonization.[43] This engraving consists of a portrait of San Carlo surrounded by twenty vignettes. Instead of three plague scenes, as in the St. Peter's apparatus, the very selective print contains only one. On the right side, it is the third vignette from the bottom, and its inscription reads, "He visits the plague-stricken and administers the holy sacraments to them." In this scene, Carlo appears on the right under a canopy held by attendants; at the lower left two corpses are seen along with a hut and two

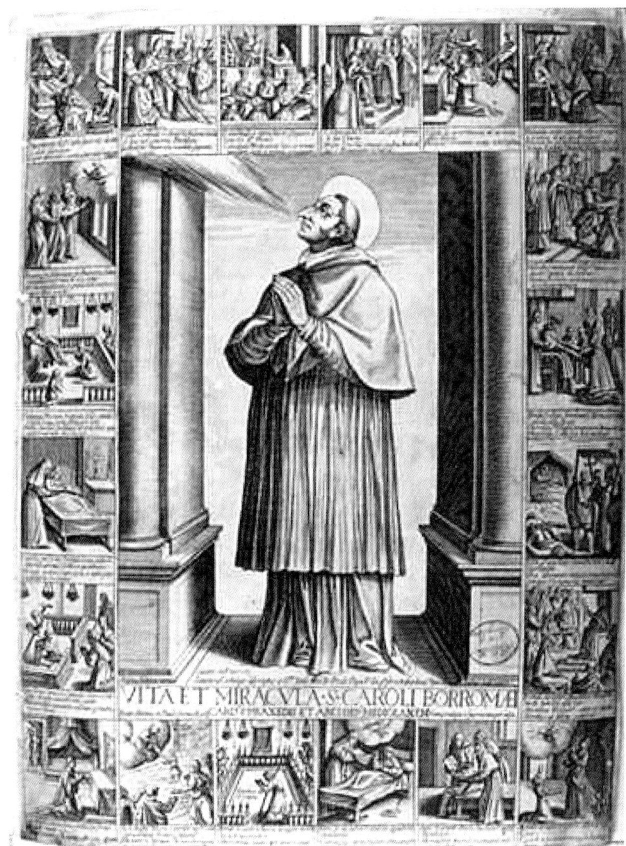

17. Raphael Guidi after Antonio Tempesta, *Vita et Miracula San Caroli Borromeo*, 1610. Engraving. Biblioteca Angelica, Rome.

plague-stricken persons. Compositionally, this scene has nothing in common with Duchino's painting in the earlier Quadroni series; perhaps none of Tempesta's plague scenes borrowed compositional motifs directly from the Quadroni.

Prints of varying quality and size – such as that of Tempesta – helped disseminate San Carlo's official plague imagery to wide audiences. Smaller and less expensive than paintings, prints were thus affordable by many more people, who could buy them in print shops or from vendors. In addition to Tempesta's engraving, Floriano Greuter's eight-page book of engravings entitled *Vita, et Miracoli di San Carlo Borromeo* deserves mention. It was also produced in Rome in 1610 to commemorate the saint's canonization.[44] Folio four, which focuses on San Carlo's charity in general, has as its central scene Carlo's selling of titles in order to give money to the poor. Four of the six flanking scenes concern the plague, and three of them are the very ones depicted in both the Quadroni and the apparatus in St. Peter's. Greuter's fourth scene shows Carlo making a will in favor of the poor at the time of the plague, that is, bequeathing his money to the Ospedale Maggiore (Great Hospital), an institution for the poor. Although an atypical pictorial choice, it was a widely known episode in the saint's life.[45]

The prints that we have been discussing were by accomplished artists and Greuter's was sold in the form of a small book, so they would not have been the cheapest options for potential buyers. Typically for religious prints of the era, both artists' engravings contain multiple inscriptions explaining the subjects. The inscriptions in Greuter's book are provided only in Italian. But those on Tempesta's engraving (fig. 17) appear in both Latin – the universal language of the Roman Catholic Church – and Italian, which indicates that it was meant for a diverse viewing public comprised of pilgrims from all over Europe who had come to Rome to celebrate the saint's canonization. Assuming that they could afford to buy such prints–which may not be the case – people who were illiterate could benefit from the visual imagery on the single-sheet engraving or in the book, but could also have memorized the short captions after having heard them read aloud. Although Greuter's book was dedicated to Ranuccio Farnese, Duke of Parma, this did not preclude a wider audience for it; indeed, it was listed among numerous engravings of San Carlo on a variety of formats available for sale in the 1614 print shop inventory of the Vaccari brothers in Rome.[46]

Experiencing Images of Carlo Borromeo as Plague Saint

San Carlo was an exceedingly popular saint, and once his plague iconography had been established, it spread quickly throughout the Catholic world. In the following discussion, I will examine a few important plague narratives, but will accent devotional themes because they are better represented in the exhibition. Some of these devotional paintings depict Carlo Borromeo as plague saint, while others depict themes that were focal points for penitential prayers undertaken in the Diocese of Milan to appease God during the pestilence.

Plague Narratives

By far the most commonly depicted plague narratives were the three treated in both the Quadroni and canonization apparatus: the saint administering the sacraments to the plague-stricken, leading the procession of the Holy Nail, and his distribution of clothing to the afflicted. A discussion of each of these narrative themes, one produced in Pavia and the other two in Rome, will help us appreciate the ways in which such imagery could function in different viewing contexts.

Borromeo's plague imagery was used in Northern Italy well before his canonization in 1610.[47] A famous example is Cesare Nebbia's *The Plague of Milan* (fig. 18), a fresco painted in 1604 for the Collegio Borromeo in Pavia.[48] Nebbia's painting combines two of the three most popular narratives of the saint's plague iconography: on the right, Carlo gives Extreme Unction to a dying man, while in the central middle ground, he carries the Holy Nail in procession under a canopy. At the lower left one sees the corpses of plague victims being buried in a mass grave, while behind them, in the distance, clergy tend to the plague-stricken in Milan's lazaretto.

In 1602, at the time of Carlo's beatification, this painting was commissioned by Archbishop Federico Borromeo of Milan. Unlike the Quadroni and many other plague narratives, it decorates not a church, but a public room in the Collegio Borromeo, a residential college at the University of Pavia.[49] Carlo Borromeo had established various educational institutions – including the Collegio Borromeo, founded in 1561 in the diocese of Pavia – as a way to achieve the reform of morals. The Collegio Borromeo was founded for the benefit of young noblemen of straitened circumstances who wanted to study at the university but live in a morally upstanding environment, that is, apart from dissolute students. It contained a refectory, chapel, separate rooms for the fellows, and administrative and public rooms. The main public room was the Aula Magna, also called the Sala Maggiore, in which, for example, the college's academy met and students' laureates were conferred. Federico Borromeo commissioned Cesare Nebbia and Federico Zuccaro – who had received important papal commissions in Rome in the immediately preceding decades – to paint a fresco cycle on two walls and the ceiling of the room consisting of scenes from Blessed Carlo's life. Federico must have intended this cycle to promote both Carlo's memory and his cause for sainthood.

Nebbia's *The Plague of Milan* and Zuccaro's *Carlo Borromeo Raised to the Cardinalate*, painted on facing walls, are far larger, thus more prominent, than the paintings on the ceiling. In

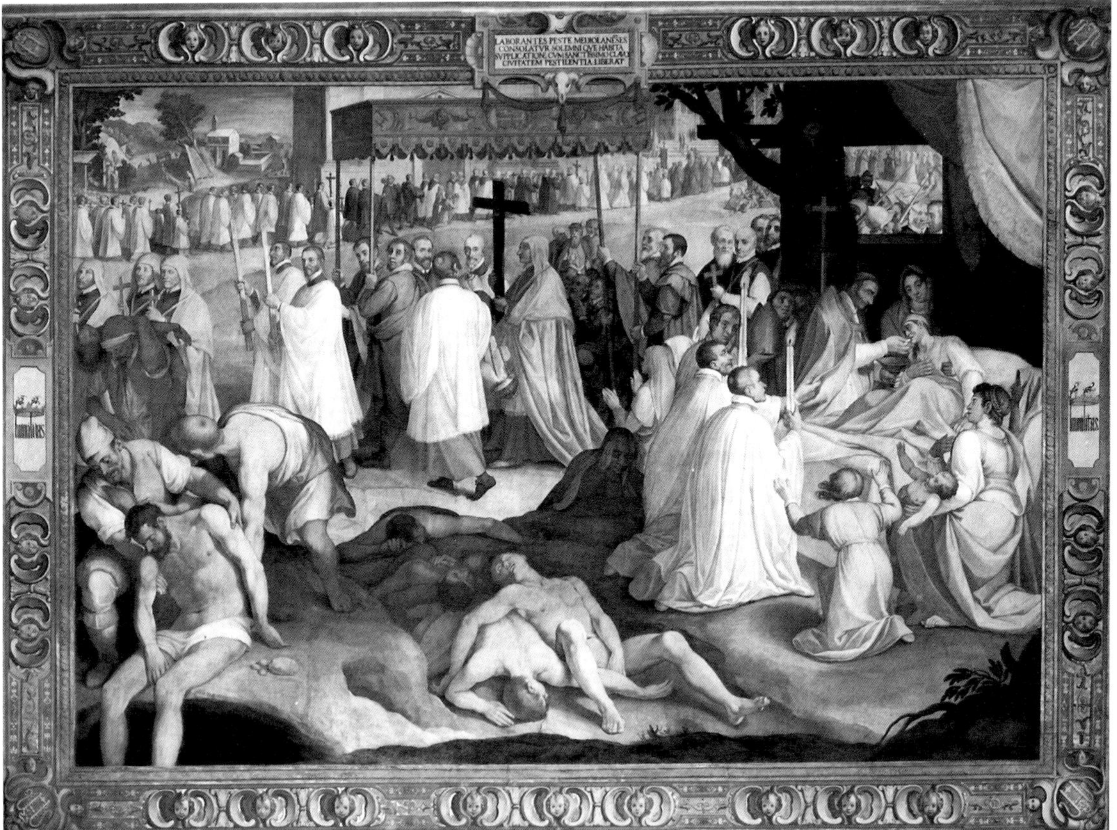

18. Cesare Nebbia, *The Plague of Milan*, 1604. Fresco. Collegio Borromeo, University of Pavia.

presenting Blessed Carlo as a role model for students endeavoring to live morally upright lives, Federico Borromeo accented not simply Carlo's choice of an ecclesiastical career but the exemplary way in which he had carried out his office as Cardinal Archbishop, as demonstrated by his charity toward poor plague victims.

It seems that most students had already embarked on their career paths by the time they arrived at the Collegio Borromeo. When viewing Nebbia's *The Plague of Milan*, students who had chosen ecclesiastical careers saw in unflinchingly forthright terms precisely what Blessed Carlo had expected of the secular and regular clergy: personal ministry to poor, ordinary Christians no matter what the circumstances. This included risking one's life through physical contact with the afflicted, and the unglamorous duties of comforting dying persons, working amid heaps of fetid corpses, and abasing oneself and suffering in imitation of Christ when leading or participating in penitential processions and other devotions to beseech God's mercy.

For students who had chosen secular careers, Nebbia's fresco of Carlo's pastoral care underscored the importance of Christian charity in general. According to Roman Catholic teaching, charity not only helped one gain salvation while assisting others, but also helped prevent such punishments meted out by God as war, famine, and plague (see Thomas Worcester's essay in this volume.). In *The Plague of Milan* Nebbia conveys this in purely visual terms. In addition, however, a Latin inscription in a cartouche above his fresco states the subject for its learned audience. It reads, *LABORANTES PESTE MEDIOLANE[N]SES CONSOLATVR SOLEMNIQVE HABITA SUPPLICATIONE CUM SANCTISSIMO CLAVO CIVITATEM PESTILENTIA LIBERAT* (He consoles the Milanese people suffering from the

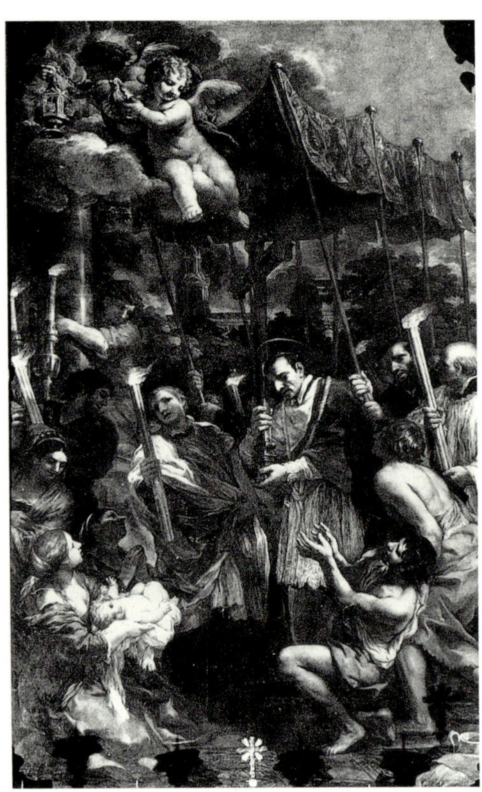

19. Pietro da Cortona, *San Carlo's Procession of the Holy Nail*, 1667. Oil on canvas. S. Carlo ai Catinari, Rome.

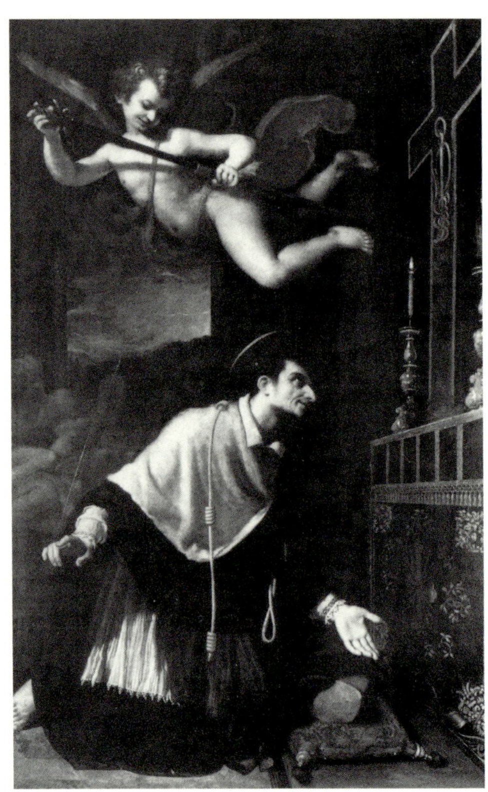

20. Andrea Commodi, *San Carlo Venerating the Holy Nail*, ca. 1621-22. Oil on canvas. S. Carlo ai Catinari, Rome.

plague, and with a solemn prayer having been held, and with the Holy Nail, he frees the city from the pestilence).

Of course most plague narratives treating Carlo Borromeo were produced after his canonization. Pierre Mignard's *Saint Charles Borromeo Among the Plague-Stricken of Milan* of about 1647 (cat. 25), is a particularly fine and influential example of the theme of the saint's administration of the sacraments. It was painted in Rome as a *modello*, or sketch, for a competition for the commission of the high altarpiece of the Barnabite church of S. Carlo ai Catinari.[50] The Clerks Regular of Saint Paul, familiarly known as the Barnabites after their mother church of S. Barnaba in Milan, originated in that city in 1530. During his episcopacy Carlo Borromeo frequented S. Barnaba for devotions and promulgated the Barnabites' constitutions in 1579. S. Carlo ai Catinari was the Barnabites' first church in Rome and also the first Roman church dedicated to the saint.[51] A Roman church with Milanese roots, it was an extremely important site of Borromean plague imagery. Indeed, this is to be expected since the Barnabites were proud of having directly participated in Carlo's plague ministry during the pestilence in Milan.[52]

In addition to Mignard's *modello*, which the Barnabites rejected, I will consider two other paintings executed for the church: Pietro da Cortona's *San Carlo's Procession of the Holy Nail* of 1667 (fig. 19), which won the competition and is still in situ on the high altar, and Andrea Commodi's considerably earlier *San Carlo Venerating the Holy Nail* of about 1621-22 (fig. 20), which Cortona's painting replaced. Mignard's theme of San Carlo giving Communion to the plague-stricken was included in both the Quadroni and the canonization apparatus, but his famous composition, executed much later, draws artistic inspiration from neither of the earlier works. Instead, in its monumentality and arrangement of the principal figures, Mignard's painting (cat. 25) resembles images of *The Last Communion of Saint Jerome* by Agostino Carracci and Domenichino.[53] Mignard depicts Carlo standing in the center of the composition with clerical assistants. He offers the host to a dying woman, who is tenderly supported by (presumably) her husband, while her child clings to her in desperation. This touching motif, which was meant to evoke pity in the hearts of viewers of the public altarpiece, derives from a famous composition by Raphael that was engraved by Raimondi (cat. 5).

The pathos of Mignard's scene is enhanced by languid plague-stricken figures lying helplessly in beds on the left and right sides of the painting. Several of them gaze mournfully at the saint or gesture toward him in hopes of receiving spiritual nourishment. Above Carlo's head are two putti, one of whom uses a thurible to cense the air. In this era, incense was used to purify miasmic air considered a cause of the plague, as viewers of Mignard's painting would have known. But in Mignard's picture, the presence of the incense also accompanies the administration of the sacrament, thus underscoring Carlo's concern with the care of souls.

Mignard's composition was particularly influential, and Christine Boeckl has explained its popularity partly on the basis of its sacramental theme, which of all the plague themes associated with San Carlo was the most highly charged in terms of doctrinal issues.[54] In response to Protestant challenges, the Council of Trent – which Carlo Borromeo helped direct – decreed that the sacraments and the clergy who administered them were needed to gain salvation. After the council ended, Carlo presided over the compilation of the Roman Catechism, which taught this doctrine to Catholics worldwide. For Carlo Borromeo, Protestantism was a real threat, because the diocese of Milan extended into the Swiss Cantons where Protestantism was widely practiced.[55] Carlo provided confessors for the plague-stricken and personally gave Communion and Last Rites to the ill. He also baptized infants born at S. Gregorio and in the camps. In addition, because many adults in his diocese had not been confirmed, he also administered that sacrament to throngs of them, healthy and ill alike.[56] Indeed, special emphasis was given to the sacraments in Carlo's diocesan reform program as a whole. Thus, Mignard's composition emphasizes the Eucharist, which priests offer to persons who have confessed as part of a good life and in preparation for a good death, one leading to eternal life.

In around 1657 Mignard returned to France.[57] Reproductive engravings – particularly the one produced in Italy by Mignard's friend François de Poilly – disseminated his design throughout Europe.[58] Boeckl has shown that Mignard's treatment of the sacramental subject found particularly receptive audiences among Catholics living north of the Alps, where confessional diversity was the norm.[59] But Italian audiences also appreciated his composition, as demonstrated by a painted copy apparently based on Poilly's engraving that is attributed to Emilio Taruffi and is now in the Galleria Nazionale in Parma. The small size of Taruffi's painting leaves no doubt that it was made to be displayed in a private setting.[60]

The reasons why Mignard did not receive the commission for S. Carlo ai Catinari are undocumented.[61] Cortona won the competition, and we have noted that his painting represents a different plague theme: *San Carlo's Procession of the Holy Nail* (fig. 19). Perhaps the competing artists were allowed to choose the specific themes themselves, or, alternatively, the Barnabites may have changed their minds about the theme midstream. In any case, a main factor conditioning the Barnabites' ultimate choice of Cortona's theme over that of Mignard must have been liturgical: on San Carlo's feast day the Barnabites displayed their cherished relics on the high altar, and those relics included both a shaving of the Holy Nail and part of the noose, or Holy Rope, that the saint wore during the penitential plague procession in which the nail was carried.[62] These two relics – the nail and the noose – figure prominently in both Cortona's painting and the one by Commodi that it replaced. Neither relic, however, appears in Mignard's image.

Let us now turn our attention to Pietro da Cortona's *San Carlo's Procession of the Holy Nail* (fig. 19) of 1667, which won the competition and remains on the high altar of S. Carlo ai

Catinari.[63] The Barnabites endeavored to reform society through missions and by the example of their own penitential lives. Whereas Mignard's painting lacks a penitential dimension, Commodi made explicit references to Carlo's penitential prayers and to his procession of the Holy Nail, which itself is the central theme of Cortona's painting. Cortona shows Carlo wearing a large noose around his neck and walking in procession under a *baldacchino* surrounded by clerical assistants. He carries the heavy black processional cross with the Holy Nail facing outward toward the viewer, and he wears bluish-violet penitential garb rather than the scarlet cardinal's vestments widely used in paintings of the theme. The primary sources agree that during the plague procession, Carlo wore dark penitential vestments, the color of which they describe as *pavonazza* – deep violet.[64] Cortona followed the precedent that his master Commodi had set years earlier in his high altarpiece (fig. 20) for the same church in depicting Carlo in a dark penitential garb. In Cortona's painting, Borromeo wears a bluish-violet cassock, white rochet, and bluish-violet great cape. The Barnabites must have stipulated that Borromeo be depicted this way.

In his biography of Borromeo published in 1592, Carlo Bascapè, General of the Barnabite order, wrote that the saint had worn dark violet vestments in the procession.[65] Later, in a letter of 1614, Bascapè expressed dissatisfaction with a design for a painting of the saint for a Lombard church precisely because in it Borromeo was wearing scarlet, but should have been portrayed in dark violet.[66] In his letter Bascapè acknowledged the usefulness of scarlet vestments as immediate signifiers of Borromeo's office as cardinal, but suggested that having one of his companions hold his scarlet biretta (cardinal's cap) should suffice in that regard. Remarkably, this is precisely what Cortona did many years later; in his painting Carlo wears penitential vestments and a black-clad cleric on the left holds his scarlet biretta. Dark violet vestments were important, for they conveyed Borromeo's penitence. Cortona turned this liturgical necessity to brilliant advantage: he based his entire palette on the contrast between deep blue-violets, blues, reddish golds, and golds with occasional white accents. The result is an image of majestic grandeur that carries well down the long nave of the Barnabite church.

Although he emphasized the penitential aspects of San Carlo's care of the plague-stricken, Cortona also creatively incorporated into his altarpiece references to Mignard's theme, the saint's administration of the sacrament. At the upper left of Cortona's composition are two angels, one of whom censes the miasmic air, while the other holds the pyx in which the *viaticum* is carried to the ill. In front of Carlo, toward the left, several women beseech his aid. On the right, a plague-stricken man supported by a youth stretches out his hands toward the sacrament held aloft by the angel above.

Another long neglected aspect of Cortona's painting is the key role that Barnabites play in it. In addition to having helped Carlo Borromeo administer the sacraments to the afflicted, the Milanese Barnabites had taken part in Carlo's procession of the Holy Nail.[67] In his high altarpiece for the order's Roman church, Cortona gives prominent places to two Barnabites who were well known for having lost their lives in November 1576 – the month following Carlo's procession of the Holy Nail. In Cortona's painting, two men carrying candles flank Archbishop Carlo. They wear white surplices over black cassocks with white collars, habits that identify them as clerks regular.[68] Jesuits, who are also clerks regular and thus wore very similar habits, likewise assisted in Carlo's plague ministry, but there are good reasons for identifying the figures in Cortona's painting as two specific Barnabite priests. Soon after having taken charge of the camp set up between Milan's Ludovican and Ticinese gates in November 1576, the Barnabite fathers Cornelio Croce and Giacomo Maria Berna died of the plague. That Cortona intended to depict these particular Barnabite priests is likely because the nobleman Croce, whom Carlo first charged with the administration of the camp, was only twenty-six years old, whereas his colleague and successor, Berna, was nearly seventy.[69] In Cortona's painting we see that the clerks regular flanking Carlo are individualized figures of distinctively different ages; Croce is depicted as a sweet-faced youth on Borromeo's right, and Berna as an aging bald man on his left. Francesco Barelli da Nizza, who wrote an encomiastic Barnabite history in 1703, emphasized both men's selfless ministry to plague victims.[70] Croce and Berna, although not official saints, were Barnabite plague martyrs, eminently suitable figures for inclusion in Cortona's altarpiece.[71]

Cortona's painting (fig. 19) has a more devotional, less movemented, effect than the two works on the same theme that we have already considered, those by Fiammenghino (fig. 15) and Nebbia (fig. 18). Because neither of the earlier paintings was an altarpiece, emphatic horizontal processional movement was an effective choice for each. By contrast, after experimenting with a somewhat more movemented composition in his preparatory work for the high altarpiece of S. Carlo ai Catinari, Cortona ultimately executed a more static final painting. Alessandra Anselmi suggested that the more movemented design of Cortona's *modello* would have better suited the architectural framework of the altar, which refers to ephemeral processional *apparati*.[72] Yet the Barnabites are likely to have seen the static quality of Cortona's final painting, which endows the theme with a more timeless, devotional character, as a positive attribute. After all, Andrea Commodi's *San Carlo Venerating the Holy Nail* (fig. 20), which Cortona's painting replaced in the new, much larger architectural framework created in the mid-seventeenth century, was likewise a static devotional painting. It is thus possible that the Barnabites requested the changes seen in Cortona's final design, wherein San Carlo's action is effectively stopped, giving the clerical patrons and lay worshipers alike the opportunity to contemplate at length the significances of personal sacrifice and penitence to human redemption, which was reenacted before the painting every time Mass was celebrated.

Devotional Paintings

To turn to devotional imagery, Andrea Commodi's *San Carlo Venerating the Holy Nail* of about 1621-22 (fig. 20) is the painting that Cortona's replaced on the high altar of S. Carlo ai Catinari. It was commissioned by the Barnabites as a replacement for a now lost painting by Gaspare Celio, which was the church's first high altarpiece.[73] The precise theme of Celio's altarpiece is unknown, but it did portray San Carlo. Giovanni Baglione reported in his *Vite* (*Lives*) of 1642 that, for reasons unspecified, the altarpiece by his rival Celio did not please the Barnabites.[74] Whatever the other inadequacies of Celio's painting may have been, it must have been in poor condition by the time Commodi's replacement was commissioned, because it had been displayed in an area of the unfinished church that lacked a ceiling.[75] Commodi's *San Carlo Venerating the Holy Nail* in S. Carlo ai Catinari is one of several nearly identical versions of the theme by him, the earliest of which, now in Soriso, is signed and dated 1613.[76] Commodi's paintings on the theme were highly influential due to their innovative iconography and beauty. As Maurizio Fagiolo dell'Arco remarked, Commodi's painting for S. Carlo ai Catinari is rather Lombard in feeling on account of its *morbidezza*, or softness, and its subtle effects of light and dark.[77] These qualities heighten its affective power.

As a devotional painting Commodi's image could be freed from the temporal and spatial concerns often expected of narratives, and in it the artist combined several aspects of Carlo's plague ministry in a compelling visual medley. San Carlo is seen kneeling in prayer before an altar with lit candles on which is placed the Holy Nail mounted on the black processional cross. The saint looks toward the relic with an expression of sublime sweetness, disregarding his wounded foot, from which blood flows profusely. Carlo, barefoot, wears the noose around his neck. Commodi depicts Carlo wearing dark penitential robes with a white rochet, as did Cortona in his much later painting for the same church.[78] Despite his humble appearance,

Carlo's status as a saint is conveyed by a thin gold halo and his status as a cardinal by his scarlet biretta, which lies on a pillow before the altar. The latter detail recalls Bascapè's suggestion in the letter of 1614 mentioned above that depicting the biretta would be enough to indicate Borromeo's ecclesiastical rank.

Commodi's painting was intended to elicit in viewers' minds the messages behind Carlo's penitential plague procession. In placing the Holy Nail on an altar, he refers as well to the relic's prominent role in the following Forty Hours Devotion. Although by Commodi's day the Forty Hours Devotion was well established in Rome, the Barnabites took credit for having instituted the devotion many years earlier in Milan, so this detail heightens the order's role in a penitential devotion of particular importance to the saint.[79] Commodi indicates that the procession and Forty Hours Devotion have been efficacious by depicting at the top of the painting the figure of an angel sheathing his sword. This a reference to the vision that Gregory the Great had experienced during his penitential procession in Rome in 590: Saint Michael the Archangel had appeared to him over Hadrian's Tomb – henceforth to be known as the Castel S. Angelo – and had sheathed his sword as a sign that God's ire had been placated.

Carlo Borromeo's plague procession of the Holy Nail took place in the streets of Milan and the subsequent Forty Hours Devotion inside the cathedral; Commodi's setting alludes to both. On the right side of the composition the altar is set against a dark wall, which evokes a church interior, as does the pavement on which Carlo kneels. On the left side of the painting – which is damaged – a stack of corpses lies in the middle ground in front of a landscape with a threatening reddish sky.[80] This part of the composition evokes, in a general way, the lazaretto and camps. Despite damage to the painting's left side, in a good light one can still make out the figure of a nude man in the heap of corpses who is either rising up – or perhaps falling down. This detail recalls a well-known anecdote about a good Christian death in the lazaretto. An expiring man, given up for dead, was placed in a pile of corpses. When he heard the bell ringing to indicate that a priest was offering the *viaticum*, the man rose up and knelt at his feet, asking to receive Communion; after receiving it, he immediately relinquished his spirit to God.[81]

In its setting in S. Carlo ai Catinari, Commodi's painting met the liturgical needs of the Barnabites by focusing on San Carlo and their church's relics, parts of the Holy Nail and Holy Rope.[82] The painting served the needs not merely of the Barnabite patrons, however. It must also have given hope to poor, sick members of the general public who beheld it. The Barnabite visitation report of 1620, which recorded such persons as frequenting the church in great numbers, decreed that the Barnabite confessors "should willingly carry in the Holy Rope when it is requested by the ill, even if they are poor."[83]

Antiveduto Grammatica's dramatic *Saint Charles Borromeo and Two Angels* of about 1619-21 (cat. 24) is one of many Italian paintings of the seventeenth and eighteenth centuries that seem to have been inspired, either directly or indirectly, by Commodi's altarpiece for S. Carlo ai Catinari – or by one of his other versions of the theme.[84] The original patron of Grammatica's painting is unknown, but the work's small size and horizontal format indicate that it was intended not for display as an altarpiece in a public church, but for private devotion. Indeed, Grammatica has brought the figure of San Carlo in very close proximity to the beholder by eliminating Commodi's setting and showing the saint half-length against a dark background. Gone are the details which had special relevance to the Barnabites of S. Carlo ai Catinari: the references to the Forty Hours Devotion and to the lazaretto where they had worked alongside the saint. Nor does Grammatica dress the saint in the violet penitential garb dear to the Barnabites. Instead, Grammatica's figure wears a scarlet cloak lined with penitential sackcloth.[85]

In his creative reinterpretation of the theme, Grammatica depicts San Carlo wearing the noose around his neck meditating on the Holy Nail mounted on the processional cross. Rather than being placed on an altar, however, the cross is now held, indeed, lovingly embraced, by an angel, who points to the nail while gazing at the saint. San Carlo's right hand is placed in acceptance over his heart. Grammatica follows Commodi in including the figure of an angel sheathing the sword to signify that the saint's penitential acts have had their intended effect and the plague has run its course.

In addition to Commodi and Grammatica, other artists, such as Domenico Fiasella and Orazio Gentileschi, created compelling devotional images on this theme based on historical events recorded in official biographies of the saint and in plague chronicles.[86] Grammatica's interpretation of the theme is among the most appealing, for its bold chiaroscuro effects and highly tangible figures create a strong impact despite its relatively small size.

The theme of San Carlo Venerating the Holy Nail was the most popular devotional subject in the repertory of the saint's plague iconography. We have seen that it was used for both public altarpieces and private devotional paintings. Both as a public altarpiece and in the form of prints the subject also figured in the *Sette Chiese* (Seven Churches) devotion in Rome, one of the most popular Catholic pilgrimages of the early modern era. The *Sette Chiese* devotion consisted of penitential visits to the seven great basilicas of Rome – St. Peter's, St. John Lateran, St. Mary Major, The Holy Cross in Jerusalem, St. Paul Outside the Walls, St. Lawrence Outside the Walls, and St. Sebastian on the Appian Way – in order to pray before their main relics and altars.[87] Numerous indulgences were promised for anyone who made the pilgrimage, and rich and poor alike were encouraged to make these Roman pilgrimages on foot, preferably barefoot. Pilgrims flocked to Rome every year during Holy Week, and in the hundreds of thousands during the Papal Jubilee or Holy Years, which normally took place every twenty-five years during the sixteenth and seventeenth centuries. Special Jubilees of a few weeks' duration were also decreed during calamitous times.

Then as now, guidebooks, spiritual manuals, prints, medals, and other mementos were produced for the pilgrims in large numbers. Giovanni Maggi's set of ten engravings of about 1614-19 entitled *Visita alle Sette Chiese di Roma* was one such memento.[88] The prints in Maggi's series provided pilgrims with a detailed visual itinerary. His engraving *S. Sebastiano in Via Appia* (fig. 21) depicts the pilgrimage church in the center in a landscape punctuated by pilgrims. Around the perimeter are represented the individual chapels to be visited inside the church. This large, impressive engraving was no doubt rather expensive, and its Latin captions were intended for an educated, pan-European audience. Although the survival rate is low for inexpensive prints of this type bearing inscriptions in vernacular languages, many were doubtlessly produced for less affluent and educated pilgrims.

As investigated at length in the exhibition and its catalogue, Saint Sebastian, the patron saint of the pilgrimage church seen in Maggi's print, was worshiped as a plague intercessor throughout the Catholic world. Maggi's engraving demonstrates that within a few years of Carlo Borromeo's canonization, his plague iconography was incorporated into the *Sette Chiese* pilgrimage devotion at S. Sebastiano in Via Appia. This is hardly surprising since Carlo was famous for having performed the *Sette Chiese* pilgrimage with particular humility during the Holy Year of 1575.[89] Moreover, it was widely known that in 1579 Carlo had spent the entire night of Saint Sebastian's feast day in prayer in the catacombs below S. Sebastiano in Via Appia.[90]

The second vignette from the bottom on the left side of Maggi's engraving depicts the altar of S. Carlo in S. Sebastiano. Maggi does not record the name of the artist who painted the altarpiece, which is still in situ, but he is identifiable as Marcantonio Bassetti of Bologna.[91] In his vignette of Bassetti's painting, Maggi provides just enough detail for pilgrims to locate the altarpiece in the church: Maggi shows San Carlo with the noose around his neck and

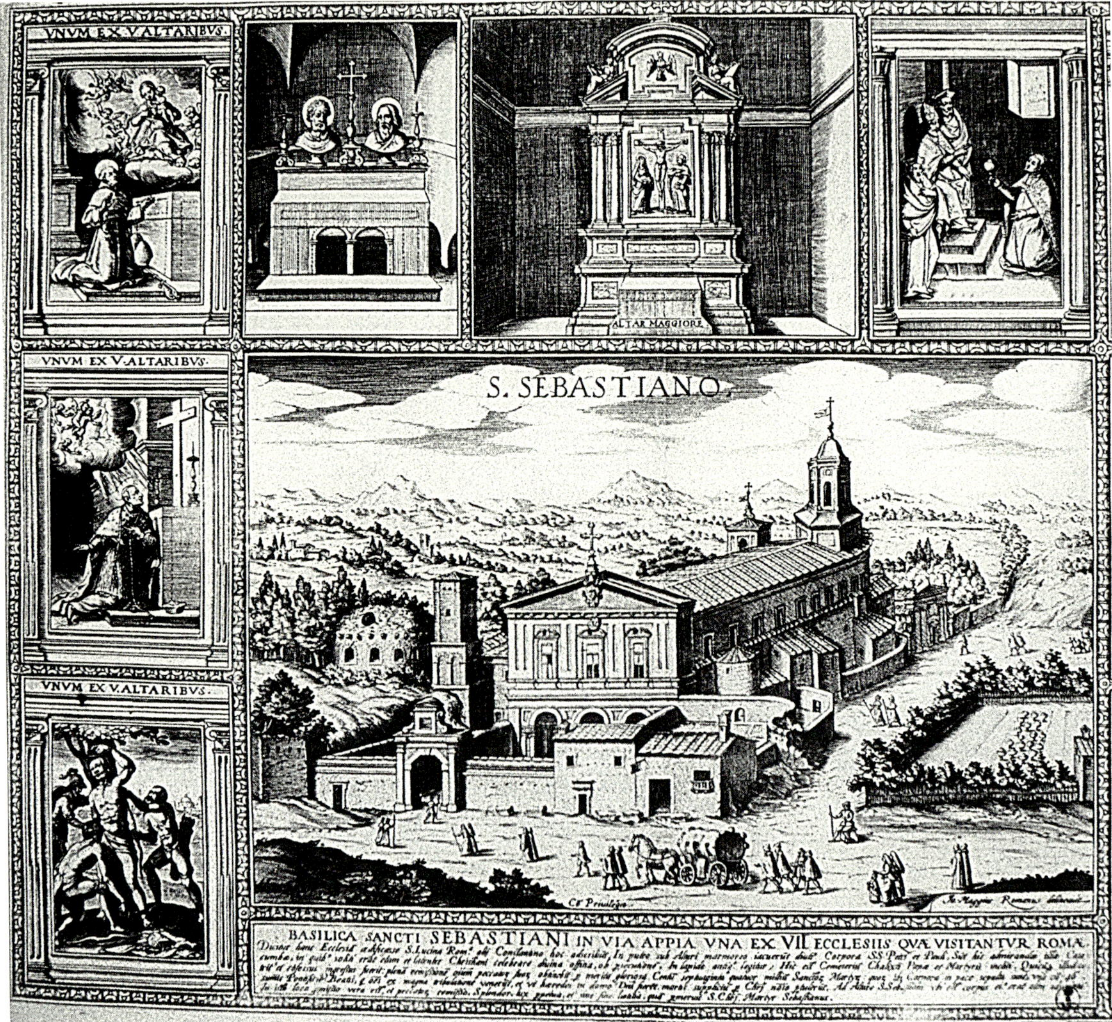

21. Giovanni Maggi, *Visita alle Sette Chiese di Roma: S. Sebastiano in Via Appia*, ca. 1614-19 (detail). Engraving. Biblioteca Nazionale Centrale, Rome.

blood issuing from his toe while kneeling before an altar. Once pilgrims located the original painting, they would see further details, such as the saint's grayish-violet penitential vestments, the Holy Nail on the altar, and the nude bodies of plague victims on the ground at the left. Both Bassetti's painting and Maggi's print must have been seen by thousands of pilgrims from various geographical areas and walks of life, who would have used the images as aids in prayer when beseeching San Carlo's intercession.

Pilgrims and other persons in Rome and in the diocese of Milan also saw images of San Carlo as plague saint while traveling through streets and piazzas. Outside shrines and murals were very common in the early modern period, but relatively few survive in good condition, and the precise circumstances of their production are often unknown. A good example of this kind of art is the anonymous Lombard *Madonna of Mercy with Saints Sebastian, Roch, and Carlo, and a Donor* of 1630, a mural on a building in the Viccolo Laghetto adjacent to the Ospedale Maggiore (Great Hospital) in Milan. At the top of the painting the Madonna of Mercy stands with two angels who hold up her cloak in a protective gesture. She is flanked by two plague saints, Sebastian and Roch. The kneeling figure of San Carlo entreats their intercession, just as he had done through prayers and devotions during his lifetime.[92] San Carlo looks upward at them while gesturing toward a view of Milan's lazaretto at the bottom of the painting. On the right, a patron of the work is depicted kneeling in prayer. An inscription provides his name, now illegible, and title, "Prior." The date "1630" is also clearly seen. Somewhat more information can be gleaned from a reproductive engraving of this mural, the inscriptions of which are clearer.[93] In the print, the donor is recorded as "*Bernardo Cottone Priore,*" and the date is given as "*a dì 30 Decem. 1630.*" At the bottom of the print beside the view of the lazaretto one reads on the left, "*dalla peste,*" and on the right, "*per carità di Dio preservato.*" This indicates that the prior was giving thanks for having survived the plague. According to Paolo Galimberti, although popular tradition holds that the mural was commissioned as an ex-voto during Milan's plague of 1630 by the Corporazione dei Tencitt, or stone-cutters of the Duomo, this cannot be established for certain.[94]

Yet it is not necessary to know the exact details of the commission to appreciate how the mural would have functioned as an ex-voto. The artist successfully juxtaposed the universal and the particular across time and space in order to provide a message of hope and salvation during troubled times. The Madonna of Mercy is naturally given the most exalted place at the upper center of the composition, with the two early plague saints placed near her, above the heads of beholders. On the left side of the painting, saints Sebastian and Carlo are paired because Sebastian, although born in Narbonne, lived in Milan, and Carlo was a Lombard. San Carlo, by far the most recent saint, is rendered most immediate by being placed lower in the composition, closer to the eye level of beholders on the street. Even closer to their eye level is the view of the lazaretto, the final earthly destination of many plague victims. This is the place where, with San Carlo's help, many had died a good Christian death during the plague of 1576-77 and where others had died during a subsequent plague that had just abated when this mural was painted in 1630. It is easy to imagine grateful survivors praying in the street before this image, thanking the Virgin and saints Sebastian, Roch, and Carlo for having interceded on their behalf before God.

In the devotional paintings considered thus far San Carlo is connected to the plague in explicit ways. But other popular devotional themes, such as San Carlo praying before the body of Christ and the lamentation of Christ, are also related to Carlo's plague, although indirectly. These themes treat the subjects of prayers that the saint encouraged members of his diocese to recite during the plague, and bespeak the penitential bent of Carlo's own personal piety, which centered on Christ's Passion.

A deeply moving image, *San Carlo Meditating by the Body of Christ,* attributed to Morazzone and datable to about 1618 (fig. 22), depicts Carlo Borromeo praying in the Chapel of the Holy Sepulcher at the Sacro Monte (Holy Mountain) of Varallo, a popular shrine near Lake Orta in Piedmont.[95] Established in the late fifteenth century by the Milanese Franciscan Bernardino Caìmi as a safer and more accessible pilgrimage destination than the Holy Land, the Varallo shrine consists of separate chapels dedicated to individual moments in Christ's Passion. The shrine continued to grow and receive further embellishments for centuries.[96] Then as now, when worshipers reached a given chapel, they looked through an opening in the wall onto a Passion scene incorporating life-size sculptures of the protagonists positioned in a room with a painted background resembling a theater set. Morazzone himself had worked on several of the chapels at Varallo, so it was a setting with which he was very familiar. But the impact of the painting attributed to him depends not on accurately reproducing the physical appearance of the Chapel of the Holy Sepulcher, but instead on evoking the profound spiritual experience that San Carlo had had in it.

Carlo Borromeo's spiritual retreat at Varallo was described by his early biographers, including Giussano, who recounted that shortly before his death in 1584 Carlo Borromeo, who sensed that he was soon to die, went to the Sacro Monte to prepare for a good death.[97] His spiritual advisor, the Jesuit priest Francesco Adorno, accompanied him.[98] Bascapè reported that at Varallo Carlo chose a cell for his room and began severe mortifications of his body,

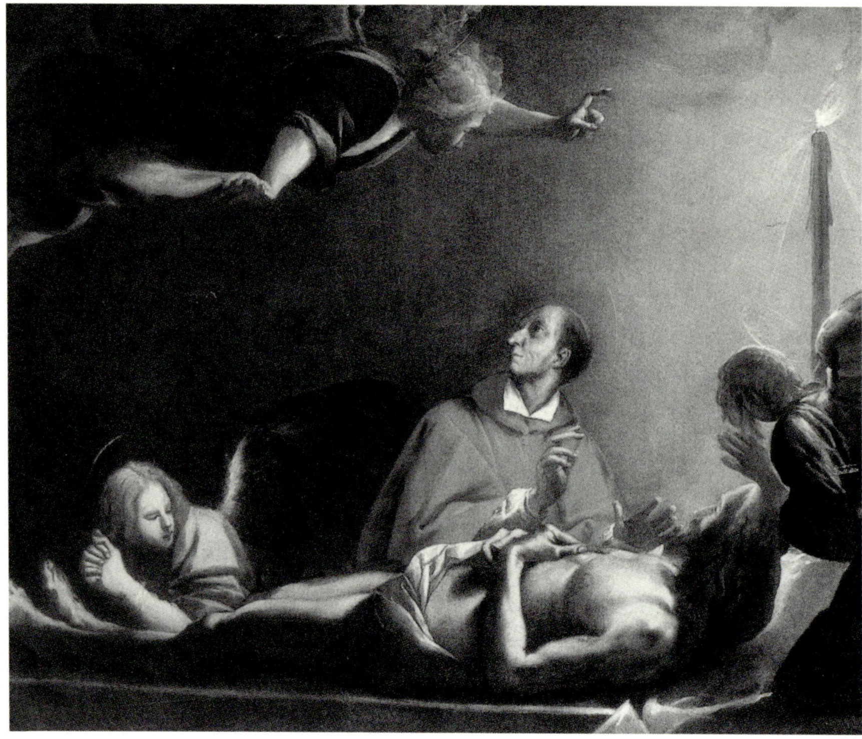

22. Attributed to Pier Francesco Mazzuchelli, called Il Morazzone, *San Carlo Meditating by the Body of Christ*, ca. 1618. Oil on canvas. Private collection.

including sleeping on a wooden plank and whipping himself so severely that his shirt was stained with blood. As usual, he consumed only bread and water. Bascapè added that Carlo spent most of his time either preparing to make a general confession of his life or praying alone in the chapels, particularly in that of the Holy Sepulcher.[99]

In the painting attributed to Morazzone, Carlo is depicted praying at night in the Chapel of the Holy Sepulcher. The body of Christ is laid out before him, and two angels pray at Jesus's head and feet. Carlo has brought a large candle to illuminate the chapel, but its flame wavers wildly as an angel flies in abruptly from the upper left, his arms outstretched. Carlo turns his head toward the intruder and raises his hands in surprise, as does the angel by Christ's head. The flying angel points insistently toward the flickering flame, to indicate that it is about to go out, that is, that Carlo is about to die and be united with the Lord.

All three of Milan's leading painters of the early Seicento – Morazzone, Cerano, and Giulio Cesare Procaccini – helped popularize this subject, and there are several versions of this composition either by or indebted to Morazzone.[100] This painting attributed to Morazzone (fig. 22) is a particularly poignant rendition of the theme, and its soft, painterly strokes and broad gestures belie its small size. The beholder is invited to join San Carlo in meditating on Christ's sacrifice.

The appeal of this devotional subject extended beyond knowledge of Borromeo's two trips to the Sacro Monte at Varallo in 1578 and 1584 – trips that enhanced the shrine's popularity. Indeed, Carlo Borromeo exhibited a lifelong devotion to Christ's Passion. Not just at Varallo, but also during the plague of 1576-77, Carlo practiced a heightened form of asceticism in imitation of Christ in order to atone for the sins of humankind.[101] At the same time, he exhorted members of his flock to pray regularly.[102] In various directives compiled in the *Acta Ecclesiae Mediolanensis* (*Acts of the Church of Milan*), Carlo put forth a detailed devotional program for members of his diocese. Let it suffice to note that during the plague Carlo required the clergy to teach and persuade his flock "at least to recite the seven [penitential]

Psalms, or the Litanies, and other prayers that they know best, which are in the Office of the Madonna, or to say devoutly the *Corona*, or other devotions."[103] Archbishop Carlo even published a little book of prayers that he had widely distributed throughout his diocese for this purpose.[104]

Borromeo was especially concerned with ensuring that everyone would spend their time in pious devotions during periods of quarantine when they could not leave home and thus had extra time to fill. On 20 October 1576, the archbishop directed these admonitions to heads of households:

> To better pass this time to good effect, take into consideration every day that this quarantine is like another holy time of Lent: and just as Our Lord fasted for forty days in the desert – far from any conversation of men, interacting only with God through prayer – each father of a family should ensure that in this public time of sadness and solitude, not only do members of his family retreat from conversation outside their house, but even more that they retreat inside themselves in prayer, in holy meditations, in examining their consciences, in consideration of judgments of God, their own death, universal and individual judgment, the sufferings of hell, the glory of paradise, and other similar things. ...[105]

Of special interest for us is Carlo's establishment during the quarantine of seven periods of daily prayer, corresponding to the seven canonical hours. He explained that seven is a mystical number because the Lord suffered torments during those seven hours. In addition to prayers such as the seven penitential Psalms discussed in the little book distributed to his flock, during the quarantine Carlo entreated the faithful to meditate on the seven principal times that Christ spilled his blood for love of humankind: the circumcision, agony in the garden, flagellation, crowning of thorns, nailing of his hands to the cross, nailing of his feet to the cross, and when his side was pierced.[106] Among prayers of this type, which focused on Christ's Passion according to seven points and thus could constitute a week-long program, Borromeo explicitly recommended meditations on Christ's Passion by the Jesuit Gaspare Loarte and the Dominican Luis de Granada.[107] It will be recalled that Borromeo also mentioned the *Corona* as one of the prayers suitable for times of pestilence.

There were various prayers called the *Corona*, or crown, but given the penitential plague context in which Carlo recommended it to his parishioners, it is possible that he meant the *Corone spirituali* (Spiritual Crowns) of the Capuchin friar Mattia Bellintani da Salò.[108] Fra Mattia's *Corone spirituali* were written especially for Carlo Borromeo. Even if in his directives for prayer of 1576-77 Borromeo was not referring to Fra Mattia's *Corone*, they are important for us. During Carlo's day the prayers were not yet published, but later printed editions of them underscored their connection with the saint.[109] Indeed, in the four-line title of a 1616 edition of Fra Mattia's *Corone spirituali*, it is explicitly stated that Carlo Borromeo had practiced the prayers. The preface notes that Carlo had requested that the Capuchin preacher write a "devout composition about prayer" for him and that Fra Mattia responded by telling Carlo that he had written some "*Corone* in order to hold the collection in one's mind for a [spiritual] voyage."[110] When using Fra Mattia's *Corone spirituali*, Carlo and others could imitate Christ's suffering over the course of a week. The prayer began on Monday with the agony in the garden and reached a crescendo on Saturday with Christ's death and entombment, only to end on Sunday with reflections on the blessings that the Savior's sacrifice brought to humankind.

It was common knowledge both during and after Carlo Borromeo's lifetime that through-

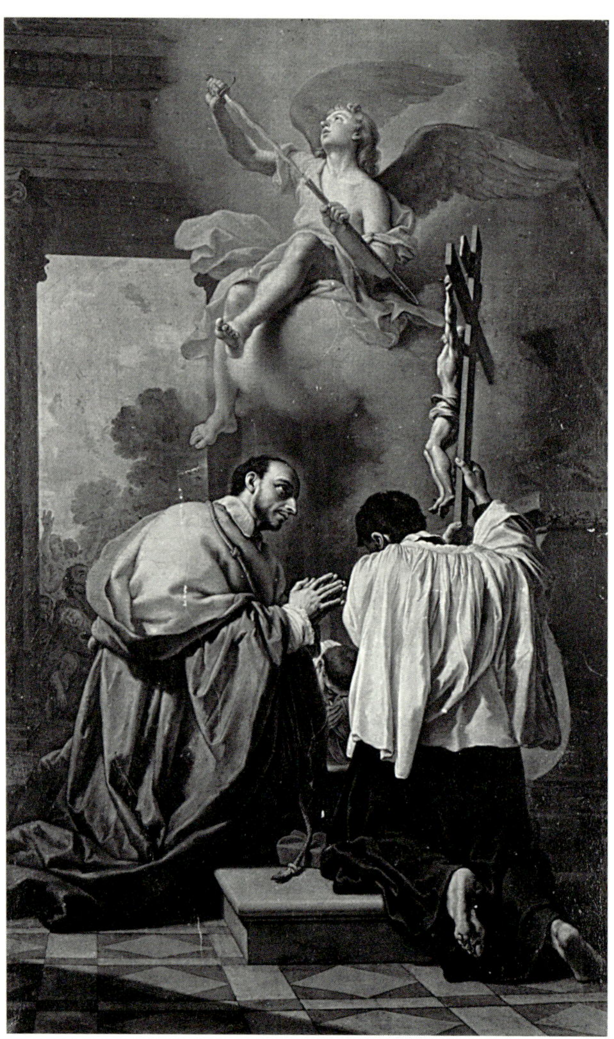

23. Stefano Parrocel, *San Carlo Praying for the End of the Plague*, 1739. Oil on canvas. S. Prassede, Chapel of S. Carlo Borromeo, Rome.

out his life his penitential prayers had centered on the Passion.[111] It was also known that Carlo had used the figurative arts – including individual paintings of Passion scenes and the chapels at Varallo – as focal points for his devotions. Passion imagery was therefore inextricably linked to San Carlo's cult in general and to his persona as plague saint in particular.

The *Lamentation* of ca. 1610-14 (cat. 23) attributed to Cerano's brother, Ortensio Crespi, exemplifies early seventeenth-century Lombard treatments of the theme, in which an earthy naturalism, a Flemish inspired landscape, and a strong appeal to the emotions are combined to create an affective devotional painting that is both intimate and dramatic.[112] A striking feature of Crespi's *Lamentation* is the pathos with which he renders the suffering of Christ and his mother.

In Crespi's painting, Joseph of Arimathea supports the Savior's body, which is placed in closest possible proximity to the viewer. Joseph's gaze is directed downward at an indeterminate angle surely intended to indicate interior reflection. Meanwhile an anguished Mary Magdalene helps support the unstable figure of the Virgin Mary, whose head is thrown backward and mouth is agape in agony, mirrowing both her son's pose and his suffering. Rather than emphasizing Christ's divinity by idealizing his body, Crespi emphasizes his earthly suffering by paying close attention to his wounds. Spattered blood appears on the Lord's shoulders and coagulates around the livid, open gash in his side. Rings of flesh rise up around the holes in his hands, where more blood has collected. His eyes have rolled back in their partially open sockets, and his flesh is beginning to turn green. According to Christian theology, Christ's sacrifice made human salvation possible, and Crespi stresses the brutality of his death and the horror it instilled in his mother and followers.

In the *Corone spirituali*, one of Carlo Borromeo's preferred penitential prayers, Fra Mattia likewise engaged the worshiper with the horror of Christ's wounds in graphic detail. Much of the fifth crown, entitled *Friday. Jesus is affixed to the Cross*, centers on the nails being driven into the Lord's flesh. In this section, Fra Mattia entreats the worshiper to meditate:

> On that so painful & opprobrious crucifixion, considered thus in general, in order to thank the Father & Son together for it all. On his awaiting the blow in his right hand, the executioner already having the nail & the hammer in his hand, & placing the point of the nail in the middle of the palm of the good Jesus, whose senses trembled, & [yet] whose spirit was very constant. On the first blow that the executioner gave, piercing much of his hand. Of the second blow that he gave him, which completely affixed his hand to the wood. Of the pain that he felt at those blows, which was ever harder, ever increasing. Of the blood that he shed for us, flowing in abundance. ...[113]

The resonance of this passage for Carlo's cult would have been obvious to anyone familiar with his plague imagery, in which the Holy Nail had such a vital role. Furthermore, on the sixth day, under the rubric *Saturday. Jesus dies & is buried*, Fra Mattia exhorts the worshiper to praise and thank the Lord,

> [f]or that love, which he showed in making himself a man similar to us. For that grace, which his mother made in serving in such a stupendous and loving work. For those fruits which his very holy and mysterious life produced for us. For the incomprehensible benefit of his holy Passion. For his very bitter crucifixion. For that pain, which he suffered while hanging on the Cross, which was very bitter, on account of the weight that mutilated his hands & feet pierced by the nails; on account of not being able to move, nor turn himself due to the piercings; on account of his whole body having been beaten, & lacerated, & very tired; on account of the punctures of the thorns on his glorious head; & on account of the extreme affliction of his mind. And surely this sadness grew greater every hour; & one has to think about it again, & give thanks for it again. ...[114]

These were the kind of meditations that viewers of the painting attributed to Morazzone (fig. 22) were intended to imagine Carlo saying as he knelt before the body of Christ in the Chapel of the Holy Sepulcher at Varallo. And the *Corone spirituali* were the sorts of prayers that viewers could say themselves – in imitation of San Carlo's penitence – before such paintings as those by Ortensio Crespi and Morazzone. In other words, as objects of prayer the devotional paintings by Crespi and Morazzone depended for their success on evoking horror, pity, penitence, and the desire to suffer with Christ – or suffer with Carlo, as he suffered with Christ.

Of course, because early modern Christians believed that God sent plagues to punish human beings for their sins and that atonement was necessary to bring about God's mercy,

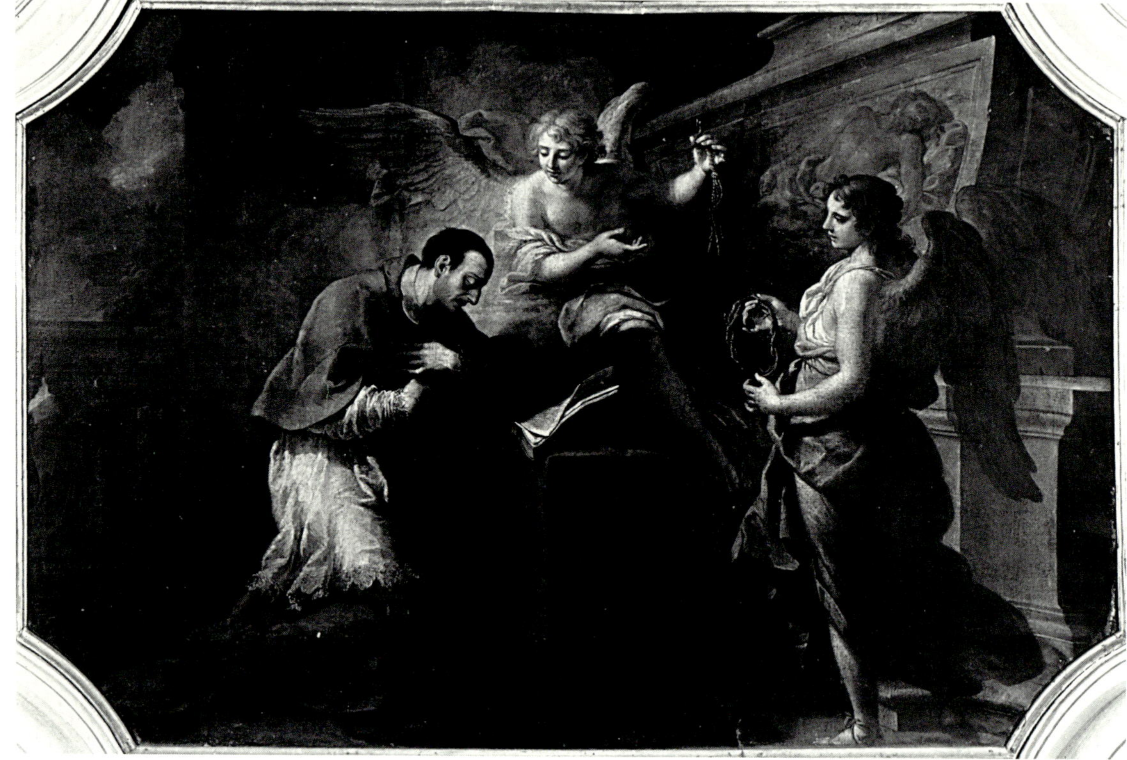

24. Ludovico Stern, *San Carlo Praying Before the Holy Sepulcher at Varallo,* 1741. Oil on canvas. S. Prassede, Chapel of San Carlo Borromeo, Rome.

Passion themes – such as the agony in the garden, crucifixion, and lamentation – were the focuses of penitential devotions during all times of pestilence in all parts of the Catholic world.

We have seen that devotional paintings directly and indirectly connected with San Carlo's cult as plague saint accent his ministry to the afflicted, his penitential devotions in imitation of Christ, and his promotion of the cult of the Holy Nail and its use in the Forty Hours Devotion, all to entreat God's mercy on behalf of the faithful. It is particularly fitting, therefore, that in S. Prassede, Carlo Borromeo's former titular church in Rome, all of these devotional themes come together in a chapel dedicated to the saint that was decorated at the end of the period under consideration in the exhibition.

To sum up our discussion of the devotional dimensions of San Carlo's plague imagery, let us turn to the paintings executed by Stefano Parrocel and Ludovico Stern for the Chapel of San Carlo in S. Prassede. Parrocel's *San Carlo Praying for the End of the Plague* of 1739 (fig. 23) is on the altar. It is flanked, on the left wall, by Stern's *San Carlo Praying Before the Holy Sepulcher at Varallo* of 1741 (fig. 24) and, on the right wall, by Stern's coeval *Ecstasy of San Carlo* (fig. 25).[115] It is noteworthy that whereas many chapels dedicated to the saint contain both devotional and narrative themes, this one contains only devotional themes. Remarkably, despite the great beauty and delicacy of the chapel's three paintings, they have received almost no scholarly attention and their patron or patrons are unknown.

The chapel's altarpiece, *San Carlo Praying for the End of the Plague* (fig. 23) was painted in 1739 by Stefano Parrocel, a Frenchman who had a long career in Rome. The lyrical grace, elegant palette, and tactile refinement of Parrocel's painting are stylistic features that were greatly appreciated in the mid-eighteenth century. By contrast, the unprettified images of Commodi and Grammatica (fig. 20, cat. 24), with their humble figures and earthy colors, characterize an artistic development of the early seventeenth century. At first glance, there-

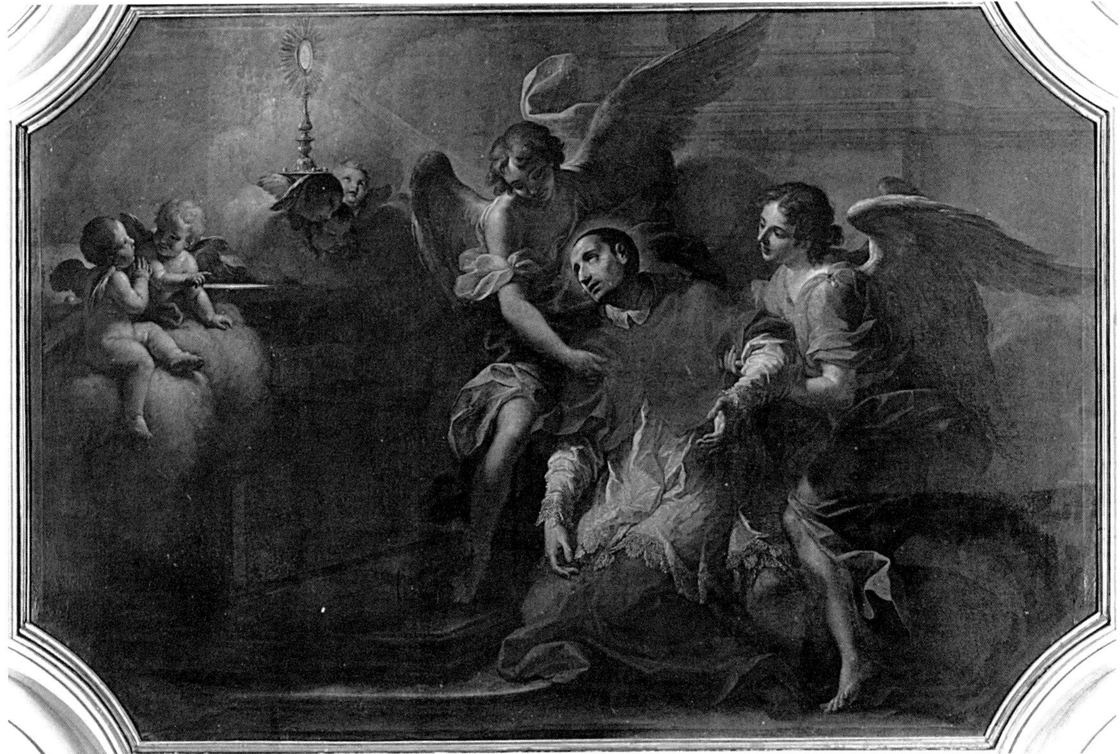

25. Ludovico Stern, *Ecstasy of San Carlo*, 1741 Oil on canvas. S. Prassede, Chapel of San Carlo Borromeo, Rome.

fore, it may appear that although Parrocel's style differs greatly from that of Commodi, their iconography is quite similar. The paintings do have much in common, for like Commodi, Parrocel shows Carlo kneeling in prayer in penitential garb – here it is blue with a mozzetta of sackcloth – with the rope around his neck and his scarlet biretta lying on the step before him. Both artists also depict the angel sheathing his sword. Their settings both combine church interiors on the right with landscapes on the left, in which plague victims are seen. Yet there the similarities end.

In his altarpiece, Parrocel created a new theme by combining elements directly connected to the pestilence – the plague-stricken in the background, the Holy Rope, and the angel sheathing the sword – with an incident indirectly connected to the plague: Carlo's penitential retreat in the Chapel of the Holy Sepulcher at Varallo. Indeed, Parrocel depicts Carlo praying not before an altar but before the sarcophagus of the martyred Savior. One acolyte, facing the viewer, bends his head in prayer. A second acolyte, with his back to the viewer, holds not the Holy Nail mounted on the processional cross, but a crucifix. Parrocel rendered his large figure of Christ on the crucifix in full color rather than as a monochrome sculpture to emphasize his humanity. It was, of course, Christ's humanity – specifically his suffering during the Passion – on which Carlo focused his meditations at Varallo and on which he urged members of his diocese to meditate during the plague.

Yet despite this reference to Christ's Passion, Parrocel's lovely, rather elegaic, altarpiece differs strikingly in mood from Commodi's much earlier painting (fig. 20) because in the later work there is no graphic depiction of suffering. In lieu of Commodi's pile of ugly corpses, in the background Parrocel depicts the unobtrusive figural group of a man carrying a dead child. But Parrocel gives more attention to the adjacent group of persons who react joyfully to the angel's sheathing of the sword. In addition, Parrocel covers Carlo's feet entirely so that no blood is seen pooling under his wounded toe. If Carlo himself had had the brutal details of

Fra Mattia's *Corone spirituali* in mind when praying during the plague and at Varallo, Parrocel certainly did not render them!

On the left wall is Stern's *San Carlo Praying Before the Holy Sepulcher at Varallo* (fig. 24), another creative adaptation of a standard theme in Carlo's iconography. Stern, a Roman artist, portrays San Carlo in scarlet vestments kneeling at a *prie-dieu*. A book is open before him, and his arms are folded on his breast in a gesture of humility. Two angels appear to the saint in a vision as he prays. The angel standing at the right looks toward San Carlo and holds out the crown of thorns, which is dripping with blood. In order to underscore Carlo's humble imitation of Christ, Stern evokes in this part of the composition traditional scenes of the Annunciation, in which Mary humbly accepts her role in human redemption.[116] The second angel hovers beside the *prie-dieu*; he also regards the saint, while holding out the Holy Nail and a scourge, likewise covered with blood. In emphasizing the blood-encrusted instruments of the Passion, Stern recreates more faithfully than does Parrocel San Carlo's penitential spirit, for it will be recalled that at Varallo the saint intensified his self-mortifications, whipping himself so severely that his clothing was stained by blood.

Whereas his painting *San Carlo Praying Before the Sepulcher at Varallo* focuses on bodily suffering (both that of Christ and of San Carlo), Stern's painting on the opposite wall, *The Ecstasy of San Carlo* (fig. 25), focuses on the death of the body and the eternal life of the spirit. This theme cannot be connected with individual episodes recounted in the early biographies, nor had it been treated in the Quadroni or the St. Peter's apparatus. Instead it was conceived to complement the other two devotional scenes in this chapel, and it does so perfectly.

On the left of the painting, Stern depicts an altar with a light blue frontal, above which are three angels. The angels support a brilliant white host in a monstrance, from which a beam of light emanates, moving across the intervening space to illuminate San Carlo's head, around which it forms a radiant white halo. San Carlo, in scarlet garments, gazes toward the host. He is rapt in ecstasy. Like Saint Francis when he received the stigmata, Carlo – another Christ-like saint having a visionary experience – is supported by two angels, for his body has ceased to function and he cannot stand on his own accord. On the left side, stairs painted at the eye level of viewers offer them access to this visionary scene, thereby encouraging them to join two little angels who gesticulate toward the saint and discuss his ecstatic experience.

Like all of the paintings in the chapel, this one focuses on the body of Christ, but this time in the form of the Eucharist, to which San Carlo was particularly devoted. We have seen that during the plague Carlo incorporated the Holy Nail into the Forty Hours Devotion, but throughout his life he also practiced the devotion in its traditional form, which involved praying before the displayed host.[117] This, however, is no ordinary Forty Hours Devotion. Instead, as we have noted, it is a visionary experience. Stern's grace of line, the ethereal golden light that pervades the left side of the painting, and the coupling of Carlo's beatific expression with his slackened body all heighten the transcendent effect of the scene.

In conclusion, we have seen that during the plague of 1576-77 Carlo Borromeo earned a reputation for holiness by courageously ministering to his flock in person. His official image as plague saint centered on three main aspects of his ministry: his administration of the sacraments, charity toward the afflicted, and penitential processions to entreat God's mercy. Together with plague narratives, devotional paintings – such as those just discussed in the Chapel of San Carlo in the Roman church of S. Prassede – presented beholders with Carlo's deeds, or active life, and with his prayerfulness, or contemplative life. Thus, Carlo Borromeo's plague imagery presents him as a penitent, self-sacrificing cardinal archbishop, who concentrated his entire being on ensuring that members of his diocese lived and died well so that they could gain salvation.

1. De Boer, ix; also, ix-xvii, 43-83.
2. The anniversary of Carlo Borromeo's death was 4 November. For color illustrations, see Brivio. The standard study is Rosci 1965.
"Beatification" and "canonization" are technical terms relating to different ranks of officially proclaimed sanctity in the Roman Catholic Church. Although in the early centuries of Christianity sanctity was an unofficial phenomenon, the process of creating saints became progressively more centralized and formalized over the centuries. Following the Council of Trent (1545-63), which was convened to reform the Catholic Church, there was a gap of twenty-five years before any new saints were officially created. Carlo Borromeo's rise to official sainthood was quicker than most of his era, but it was typical in involving two stages. First, Carlo was "beatified," meaning he was officially proclaimed as "blessed." Then, the long process of canonization was initiated, during which Carlo's deeds and miracles were evaluated. At the successful end of the canonization process, he was proclaimed a full-fledged "saint." In the decades following Carlo's canonization, Pope Urban VIII (reigned 1623-44) was instrumental in tightening the policies. In particular, Urban formalized the process of beatification and made it a required preliminary step toward canonization. On the history of beatification and canonization, see Burke.
3. Brivio, viii.
4. In the late seventeenth and eighteenth centuries, six more scenes were added to the cycle. They included stories from Carlo's childhood and youth, which had been included in the St. Peter's apparatus, which is discussed below in the text. Also added to the Quadroni series at that time were new scenes, such as worshipers visiting his tomb in the Duomo. See Brivio, nos. 1, 2, 10, 20, 25, and 26.
5. Rosci 1965, 27-28.
6. See Brivio, no. 16; Rosci 1965, 64-65.
7. See Bascapè; Cattaneo's n. 3 to Bascapè's text (on 922) provides the dates of construction. For an overview of the plague in Milan in 1576-77, see Bendiscioli, esp. 234-40.
8. I am aware of no sources that state the reason for the dedication of the church in the lazaretto to Saint Gregory, but it must be due to his vision during the plague procession.
9. Bascapè, 317. Giovanni Francesco Bascapè (1550-1615) served as Carlo Borromeo's secretary during the plague. When he entered the Barnabite order in 1578, he took the name "Carlo" in homage to Borromeo. Bascapè was elected general of the order in 1586, and again in 1588 and 1591. In 1593 Clement VIII appointed him bishop of Novara, a position he held until his death. See Prodi.
10. See especially, Bascapè, 317, and Giussano 1884. Giussano's vernacular life of Carlo Borromeo was indebted to that of Bascapè, which in 1610 was still available only in Latin. Carlo Borromeo founded Giussano's order–the Oblates of Saint Ambrose–to help carry out his diocesan reform. Significantly, Carlo assigned to the Oblates the Milanese church of S. Sepolcro (the Holy Sepulcher). On the Oblates, see Giussano 1884, II, 22-26. For an overview of the lazaretto including illustrations, see Bendiscioli, 234-47, esp. 237.
Most of the details of Carlo's plague ministry are discussed in a consistent way by all of the early biographers and plague chroniclers; for the sake of brevity, I will merely cite salient examples in each case. Because Giussano's biography is the only early source available in English, for the benefit of non-specialist readers, I will cite it (Giussano 1884) whenever relevant.
The sources consistently refer to the camps of "capanne," or huts, although in paintings they look like tents.
11. Bendiscioli, 235-40; Bisciola, 10-14.
12. Bendiscioli, 240.
13. Bisciola, 8.
14. A.L. Martin, 85, 175-98.
15. Anointing was part of both the sacraments of Confirmation and Extreme Unction. Because the man in the painting does not appear to be at the point of death, Carlo is probably meant to be anointing him as part of the rite of Confirmation. Although Confirmation was not considered necessary to salvation, Carlo confirmed many persons during the plague, on which, see Giussano 1884, I, 423.
16. Bisciola, 10, notes that after giving Communion to persons suspected of having the contagion, priests perfumed or cleansed their hands. Bascapè, 338, mentions that Carlo approved various precautions for priests, including purifying their hands with vinegar or with the flame of a lit candle immediately after having administered the sacraments.
17. At night corpses were carried from S. Gregorio to an adjoining public burial ground known as the Fossone, where they would be interred the next day. On the mass burials, see Giussano 1884, I, 383; also Paolo Bellintani,122. Paolo Bellintani–not to be confused with his brother Mattia, discussed in the text below–was a Capuchin who oversaw care of the sick in the lazaretto. His tract contains much information about such practical issues as how to enforce justice at S. Gregorio, how to purge houses and other belongings, and the laundry system.
18. De Boer, *passim*, and 77-78.
19. Brivio, no. 15; Rosci 1965, 74-75.
20. Bisciola, 6. By contrast, Giussano (1884, I, 396) reports that "[t]he plague made no progress during these [processional] days, as might have been expected...."
21. Giussano 1884, I, 391, 394.
22. Bisciola, 6. For Borromeo's recommendations and indulgences granted (with papal permission), see *AEM*, II, 1313-15.
23. Giussano 1884, I, 392. All quotations are cited in English from Manning's edition. Giussano wrote of Borromeo: "[e]'era vestito della cappa Pontificia pavonazza, e tirato lo cappuccino ne gl'occhi...." There are two important points to note in this description of vesture. First, Giussano's reference to the "cappa Pontificia" indicates that Borromeo was wearing the "cappa magna," a huge ceremonial cape with a large hood, designed to cover the whole body; this was normally fur-lined for warmth. Second, Giussano's use of the word "pavonazza" indicates that Borromeo was wearing penitential vestments reserved for Lent and mourning. The language of vesture, although crucial to understanding Carlo's image as plague saint, has never been brought to bear on the topic. See discussion in the text below, and n. 64, for elaborations of this point. See Giussano 1610, 267. On the "cappa magna" (great cape), see Noonan, 317-18; on penitential garments, 283-375.
24. Brivio, no. 15.
25. As Noonan states (284), technically the orange-red color worn by cardinals is termed "scarlet." The men immediately in front and in back of Carlo are identifiable as

canons regular by the following vestments: black tunics covered by white rochets, and red mozzettas. See Noonan, as in n. 23 above, esp. 283-375. Noonan does not mention the use of great capes made of sackcloth.
26. Bisciola, 6; my emphasis.
27. Giussano 1884, I, 394.
28. According to legend, Saint Helen found in Jerusalem the Holy Cross and the nails used to affix Christ to it. Saint Ambrose, patron saint of Milan, discussed one of the nails in his funeral oration of 395 for the Emperor Theodosius; this nail became known as the Holy Nail. For details on the legend, see, for example, Bugato, 22-23; Bascapè, 345-49.
29. On the Forty Hours Devotion, see Moroni. Also see nn. 30 and 79 below.
30. In 1577, Carlo established the annual Feast of the Holy Nail on 3 May, the Feast of the Invention of the Cross. On the Holy Nail and the Forty Hours Devotion, see Giussano 1884, I, 391-95, 452-55; Bascapè, 341-45, 396-407. Also nn. 29 and 79 herein.
31. Giussano 1884, I, 455, mentions the facsimiles of the Holy Nail that Carlo had distributed during a quarantine. Bascapè, 405, notes that Borromeo sent King Philip of Spain a reproduction of the Holy Nail, which was consecrated by contact with the relic itself.
32. Brivio, no. 17; Rosci 1965, 48-49.
33. Bascapè, 333-37; Giussano 1884, I, 377-78, 389.
34. Perhaps these clerks regular are meant to be the Barnabite fathers Cornelio Croce and Giacomo Maria Berna, who ran one of the camps. See the text below on the paintings in the Barnabite church of S. Carlo ai Catinari in Rome for a full discussion of the Barnabites' role in Carlo's plague ministry.
35. For medical facts and photographs of recent plague victims, see Boeckl, 7-32.
36. An overview of the relative popularity of the various themes is beyond the scope of this study, particularly because the sheer numbers of images involved is so high. Grattarola's mention in 1614 of fifty-two altars and chapels dedicated to San Carlo in Rome alone is an index of how widespread Carlo's imagery became within only a few years of his canonization. Many of these chapels and altars contained plague imagery. See Grattarola, 402-5.
37. This is understandable since Carlo performed charitable acts throughout his life. Good examples of generic treatments of San Carlo's charity are Antonio Carracci's fresco *San Carlo Giving Alms* in the Chapel of S. Carlo in S. Bartolomeo al Isola in Rome, in which two lame men are positioned prominently in the foreground, and Mattia Preti's fresco of the same theme on the entrance wall of S. Carlo ai Catinari. For Carracci's painting, see Pupillo, 41-43; 41 for an illustration; for Preti's painting, see A.M. Erba, 23.
38. Brivio, no. 19; Rosci 1965, 82 and ill. on 83.
39. On the quarantine, see Bisciola, 11; *AEM*, II, 1315-20; Bascapè, 353-55; Giussano 1884, I, 418-22.
40. See Rasmussen, to whom my discussion is indebted.
41. *Ibid.*
42. Grattarola, 224-27.
43. Rasmussen, 132, noted the importance of Tempesta's engraving.
44. Greuter's title page shows San Carlo standing in a niche with personifications flanking him. Each of the following seven pages consists of one large scene flanked by six small ones.
45. See, for example, Giussano 1884, I, 375.
46. Vaccari, 18.
47. On the growth of Carlo's cult before his canonization, see Giussano 1884, II, 267-68.
48. I am grateful to John Alexander for sharing with me his expertise on the Collegio Borromeo, and for offering suggestions on this section of my essay. See Alexander on the college; also see Caravaggi, et al., on the college and its decorations; esp. 9-23 and 47-58.
49. *Ibid.*
50. On Mignard's painting, see: A. Tapié and N. Gallissot in *La Peinture*, 76-77; Anselmi; Fagiolo dell'Arco; Boyer.
51. Premoli 1922; Barelli da Nizza I, 471-86, treats in detail the foundation of the church of S. Carlo ai Catinari in Rome. On Carlo Borromeo and the Barnabites, also see Giussano 1884, I, 70-73.
52. Barelli da Nizza's description of 1703 of the Barnabites' role in Carlo's plague effort is a particularly revealing document of the order's self-image. See Barelli da Nizza I, 563-70.
53. See Fagiolo dell'Arco, 229-31, for discussion and illustrations.
54. Boeckl, 114-15, 123-25. Boeckl (114) erroneously stated that this theme was not included in the original Quadroni series.
55. See De Boer, xi, for a map of the Diocese of Milan.
56. For Carlo's administration of the various sacraments, see Giussano 1884, I, 423-29.
57. On the competition and the reproductive engravings of Mignard's *modello*, see the literature cited in n. 50 above.
58. Poilly's engraving, which reverses Mignard's composition, is known in two states, both of which are illustrated by Boyer on 24.
59. Boeckl, 123-25.
60. Fornari Schianchi, cat. no. 569, 142-44. Taruffi, a Bolognese artist, lived 1633-96; his painting is illustrated on 142.
61. The Barnabite archives in Rome, in which the relevant materials presumably once were kept, were largely destroyed during the Napoleonic period. See the literature cited in n. 50 above for what little is known about the competition.
62. The feast day was first celebrated in the church on 3-4 November 1611. On 26 February 1612, the church's first stone was laid in a public ceremony. The shaving of the Holy Nail and the fragment of the Holy Rope were carried in procession on this occasion. See Barelli da Nizza, I, 483.
63. On this painting, see Fagiolo dell'Arco, Anselmi.
64. According to the following sources, Carlo wore dark violet (*pavonazza*) penitential clothing: Giussano 1884, I, 392; Bugato, 22; Bascapè, 343 (and also his letter cited in note 66 below). The color *pavonazza* was rendered differently by the artists, varying from gray-violet to a much bluer shade of violet. The important point, however, is that violet, purple, or dark blue signified penitential garb as opposed to the standard cardinalitial scarlet.
65. Bascapè, 343. See n. 9 above for biographical information on Bascapè.
66. Bascapè's correspondence is in the Fondo Bascapè of the ASPB in Milan. The letter in question was directed to the Barnabite priest Lorenzo Binagho of Milan on 27 April 1614. See ASPB, Lettere Episcopali, XXV, no. 228. I

am grateful to Eugenio Merzagora for his expert advice on the archival materials.
67. Barelli da Nizza, I, 566.
68. The most comprehensive and well illustrated historical discussion of vestments of the regular clergy is Rocca. On the clerks regular, see: Borràs i Feliu and Cagni, both in Rocca. I am grateful to Karin Wolfe for this reference.
69. On Croce and Berna, see Barelli da Nizza, I, 565-66.
70. Ibid.
71. Neither Croce nor Berna was beatified or canonized. Their names do not appear in the *processi* of the Congregazione dei Riti in the Archivio Segreto Vaticano. Premoli 1913, 279, refers to them as "two martyrs of charity." Croce and Berna are included in their order's official roster of holy persons, the *Menologia dei Barnabiti*; see Levati and Cociago, 232-43.
72. Anselmi, 666.
73. Commodi's Rome version is datable on stylistic grounds to ca. 1621-22, although a somewhat earlier date should not be ruled out. A *terminus ante quem* for its execution was established by Giulio Mancini, who saw Commodi's painting in S. Carlo ai Catinari in about 1623-24. See Mancini, I, 279. The problems surrounding the attribution, dating, and original commissions of Commodi's multiple versions of the theme are too numerous to be discussed here. See the following literature: Boyer; Fagiolo dell'Arco; esp. Papi 1994, 51-63.
74. Baglione 1642, 334.
75. In the report of the Visitation of 26 November 1621, it is remarked that in the winter the choir of the unfinished church must be covered by a large canvas, which will serve as a roof, against which will lean "the painting of s. Carlo." Whether the painting in question was that of Celio or of Commodi is indeterminable. However, it is clear that Celio's painting had been on an unprotected altar for years by the time Commodi's replacement was commissioned. See the ASPB, Milan, G Cartella No. V, Fasciolo unico, No. 118, fol. 1r.
76. Papi 1994, cat. no, 20 on 90-91 and fig. 33; Fagiolo dell'Arco, 219-20 and fig. 1.
77. Fagiolo dell'Arco, 219.
78. Depending on the light, the vestments in Commodi's painting appear to be either black or purplish black. It may be that the vestments were originally purple but have darkened to black.
79. Both Barelli da Nizza, I, 133 and 184, and Premoli 1913, 42-45 – Barnabite authors who wrote in 1703 and 1913 respectively – stated that the Barnabites ideated the Forty Hours Devotion in Milan in the mid-1530s. Barelli da Nizza explicitly noted that Carlo Borromeo subsequently practiced the Barnabites' Eucharistic devotion in churches in Milan. Premoli (1913, 44) went to great pains to argue that the devotion's origin was due to Antonio Maria Zaccaria, the saint and co-founder of the Barnabite order–rather than to the Capuchin Giuseppe da Fermo (to whom its introduction is often attributed). Clearly, wherever the truth may lie, the foundation of the Forty Hours Devotion was very much a part of the Barnabites' self-image in the early modern period–and even much later.
80. On the painting's condition, see Papi 1994, cat. no. 26 on 97-98. Restoration of the Rome version in 1970-71 revealed that its entire left side had been retouched.
81. Giussano 1884, I, 383; Bisciola, 3.
82. In a book currently in preparation, *From Caravaggio to Guido Reni: Altarpieces and Their Viewers in the Churches of Rome*, I will argue on the basis of further documentation that Commodi's iconography was particularly important in a Barnabite context.
83. See the ASPB in Milan, G Cartella No. V, Fasciolo unico, No. 101, fol. 1r; the report is dated 20 December 1620.
84. Grammatica's painting is discussed by Riedl, cat. no. 35 on 142-43; and Papi 1995, cat. no. 44 on 108 and fig. 32 on 171.
85. Because the figure is only half-length it is impossible to determine precisely which kind of cloak he wears. The lining of his cloak, which should be scarlet or violet depending on the liturgical season, here is rendered as made of sackcloth.
86. See Riedl (145) for illustrations of similar paintings attributed to Fiasella and Gentileschi.
87. There is considerable scholarship on the *Sette Chiese* pilgrimage, much of it within studies of the papal Jubilee years. See, for example, Strinati. For sixteenth-century accounts, see Fanucci; G. Martin, 18-20.
88. The series bears no date. However, the engraving of S. Sebastiano post-dates Scipione Borghese's renovations of 1612. On the restoration, see: Baglione 1639, 88-95; Panciroli, 663. Maggi's *Sette Chiese* series also includes an engraving of S.Lorenzo fuori le Mura with a *vignette* of its altar of San Carlo, which was destroyed in 1619 when the side chapels were renovated. On the renovation of S. Lorenzo, see Baglione 1639, 150-51. Contini's dating of Bassetti's painting (depicted in Maggi's image of S. Sebastiano) to ca. 1614 further narrows the date of Maggi's print series to ca. 1614-19. See n. 91 below.
89. See Giussano 1884, I, 341-42.
90. This was exceedingly well known. See Giussano 1884, II, 92.
91. On Bassetti's painting, see Contini, who dates it to ca. 1614. I thank Michael Erwee for this citation.
92. For vows made to Saint Sebastian during "Carlo Borromeo's plague," see, for example, *AEM*, II, 1310-66. When the plague abated, Carlo gave Mass in the Milanese church of S. Sebastiano on 15 October 1577; see Bascapè, 409.
93. For an illustration of the engraving, see Nicolini, 512.
94. I am grateful to Paolo Galimberti for his written communication to me about this mural.
95. For a discussion of the theme and its popularity, see Gregori, cat. no. 32 on 62, which concerns a version then in Gallarate.
96. A well-illustrated introduction to the shrine in English is provided by Debiaggi. Also see Langé and Pensa.
97. Giussano 1884, II, 236-46.
98. *Ibid.*, II, 22-26. Adorno was the same Jesuit who had been reluctant to allow his priests to work in the lazaretto for fear that they would die.
99. Bascapè, 613-25. Carlo's devotions at Varallo lent such prestige to the shrine that in 1772 his prayers were commemorated in a chapel dedicated to him adjacent to the Chapel of the Holy Sepulcher, and in 1776 a statue of San Carlo in prayer was installed in the Chapel of the Agony in the Garden, with which the Passion begins. See Debiaggi, 32, 55.
100. Ibid. See Zani in Caravaggi, et al., cat. no. 112 on 122-23, for an anonymous variant formerly attributed to

Morazzone.
101. Bascapè, 393-95; Giussano 1884, I, 370-71.
102. See *AEM*, II, 1310-19.
103. Ibid., II, 1310.
104. Ibid., II, 1314-15.
105. Ibid., II, 1318.
106. Ibid.
107. Ibid., II, 1317.
108. Another popular prayer, known in multiple versions, was the *Corona di Giesù Christo*. It consisted of meditations on the events of the Savior's entire thirty-three years of earthly life, thus giving less attention to the Passion than did Fra Mattia's prayer.
109. Merelli established that Fra Mattia's *Corone spirituali* first appeared in print no earlier than 1613. Thus, although it was well known to Carlo Borromeo, it may not have been known in his diocese as a whole until 1613. See: Merelli 1986 and Merelli 1984.
110. M. Bellintani da Salò; for the quotations, 10. As indicated in the title, this is not the first edition; however, it is the only one with which I am familiar. Also see the articles by Merelli, as in n.109 above.
111. De Klerck. On Fra Mattia's prayers in relation to a painting by Antonio Campi, see 89 and n. 31. On Carlo's contemplative use of the arts and his penchant for Passion themes, see 79-95.
112. Rosci 2000, cat. no. 219 on 287-88, lists the painting as: "Cerano?" More recently, in a communication to Ann Guité at the offices of Richard Feigen, Rosci has attributed the *Lamentation* to Ortensio Crespi.
113. M. Bellintani da Salò, 74-75.
114. Ibid., 84-85.
115. There are no studies of the chapel itself or of the individual paintings in it. On Parrocel, see Sestieri, I, 141-43. Parrocel was born in Avignon in 1696 and came to Rome in 1717, where he died in 1775. He was a member of the Accademia di S. Luca 1734-62. Sestieri provides bibliography and a checklist of Parrocel's major works. Ludovico Stern was born in Rome in 1709, was a member of the Accademia di S. Luca in 1756, and died in Rome in 1778. For a very brief biography and bibliography, see Rudolph, 803; also see Cat. No. 650 on Stern's *Ecstasy of Saint Carlo* in S. Prassede; although Rudolph records the *Ecstasy* as signed and dated "LUDOVICVS STERN ROM 1741," the signature and date actually appear instead on his painting *San Carlo Praying Before the Holy Sepulcher in Varallo* on the opposite wall. I thank Karin Wolfe for this reference. I have benefited greatly from on-site discussions of these paintings with Karin Wolfe, Carolyn Valone, and Sheila Barker.
116. I thank Sheila Barker for this astute observation.
117. On Carlo's celebrations of the Forty Hours Devotion in Milan, see Giussano 1884, I, 190, 210, 315, 326, 356, 395, 462 (in thanksgiving for the end of the plague); II, 50.

Bibliography

Acta Ecclesiae Mediolanensis A Sancto Carolo Cardinale S. Praxedis Archiepiscopo Condita Federici Cardinalis Borromaei...Vol. II. Milan, 1846. [Cited as *AEM*.]

Alexander, John. "The Collegio Borromeo: A Study of Borromeo's Early Patronage and Tibaldi's Early Architecture." Ph.D. Diss. University of Virginia, 2001.

Anselmi, A. "The High Altar of S. Carlo ai Catinari, Rome." *Burlington Magazine* 138 (1996), pp. 660-67.

Archivio Storico dei Padri Barnabiti, Milan. [Cited as ASPB.]

Baglione, G. *Le Vite de' Pittori Scultori et Architetti*... Rome, 1642.

Baglione, G. *Le Nove chiese di Roma*. Rome, 1639.

Barelli da Nizza, F.L. *Memorie dell'Origine, Fondazione, Avanzamenti, Successi, Ed. Uomini Illustri Della Congregazione De' Chierici Regolari di S. Paolo Chiamati volgaramente Barnabiti*. 2 Vols. Bologna, 1703.

Bascapè, C. *Vita e Opera di Carlo, Arcivescovo di Milano, Cardinale di S. Prassede*. Transl. G. Fassi. Notes E. Cattaneo. Milan, 1965. [Rpt. In Lat. with Ital. transl. of Latin ed., Ingolstadt, 1592.]

Bellintani, Paolo. *Dialogo della peste. Ed. E. Paccagnini. Notes C. Boroni. Centro Studi Cappuccini Lombardi*, XXVIII. Milan, 2001.

Bellintani da Salò, Mattia. *Corone spirituali Del R.P.F. Matthia Bellintani da Salò, Predicatore Capuccino, Per l'attentione in contemplare la Passione del Salvatore. Le quali erano pratticate da S. Carlo, Ristampate di nuovo ad uso dell'Archiconfraternità delle Sacre Stimmate di S. Francesco di Roma*. Rome, 1616.

Bendiscioli, M. "Parte II. Vita Sociale e Culturale. Cap. IX. I Conflitti Giurisdizionali tra L'Arcivescovo Cardinale Borromeo e Le Autorità Pubbliche." In *Storia di Milano. Vol. X. L'Età dei Borromei 1559-1630*. Milan, 1957, pp. 234-40.

Bisciola, Paolo. *Relatione Verissima del Progresso della Peste di Milano*. Bologna, 1577.

Boeckl, C.M. *Images of Plague and Pestilence. Iconography and Iconology. Sixteenth Century Essays & Studies*, Vol. LII. Kirksville, Missouri, 2000.

Bona Castellotti, M., Ed. *Musei e Gallerie di Milano. Quadreria dell'Arcivescovado*. Milan, 1999.

Borràs i Feliu. "In 'non abito' dei Chierici regolari." In *La Sostanza dell'Effimero*, ed. G. Rocca, pp. 103-04.

Boyer, J.-C. "Un cas singulier: le Saint Charles Borromée de Pierre Mignard pour le concours de San Carlo ai Catinari." *Revue de l'Art* 64, no. 2 (1984), pp. 23-34.

Brivio, E. *The Life and Miracles of St. Carlo Borromeo. A Pictorial intinerary in Milan Cathedral.* Transl. E. Upton. Milan, 1995.

Bugato, P. *I Fatti di Milano, Al contrasto della Peste, Over Pestifero contagio: Dal primo d'Agosto 1576. fin a l'ultimo dell'anno 1577. Particolarmente cavati dall'aggiunta dell'Historia del Rever. P. Bugato Milanese, stringamenti posti.* Milan, 1578.

Burke, P. "Ch. 5. How to be a Counter-Reformation saint." In *The historical anthropology of early modern Italy. Essays on perception and communication.* Cambridge, 1987, pp. 48-62.

Cagni, G.M. "Chierici regolari di s. Paolo (Barnabiti). " In *La Sostanza dell'Effimero.* ed. G. Rocca, pp. 454-56.

Caravaggi, G., L. Erba, S. Fugazza, et al. *Almo Collegio Borromeo.* Pavia, 1992.

Contini, R. "Marcantonio Bassetti Sulla Via Appia." *Paragone* 44-46 (1994), pp. 191-96.

Debiaggi, C. *Il Sacro Monte di Varallo.* Varallo, 1998.

De Boer, W. *The Conquest of the Soul. Confession, Discipline, and Public Order in Counter-Reformation Milan. Studies in Medieval and Reformation Thought.* Vol. LXXXIV. Leiden, 2001.

De Klerck, B. *The Brothers Campi: Images and Devotion. Religious Painting in Sixteenth-Century Lombardy.* Transl. A. McCormick. Amsterdam, 1999.

Erba, A.M. *Chiesa di San Carlo ai Catinari Roma.* Rome, 1984.

Fagiolo dell'Arco, M. "L'Altare Colonna in S. Carlo ai Catinari. Gaspare Celio e Andrea Commodi, Martino Lunghi il giovane e Orfeo Boselli, Pierre Mignard e Pietro da Cortona." In *Studi in onore di Giulio Carlo Argan.* Florence, 1994, pp. 218-45.

Fanucci, C. *Regola, et ordini da osservarsi in visitar le Sante Sette Chiese di Roma...* Rome, 1590

Fornari Schianchi, L., Ed. Galleria Nazionale di Parma. *Catalogo delle opere. II Seicento.* Milan, 1999.

Giussano, G.P. *Vita di S. Carlo Borromeo Prete Cardinale del titolo di Santa Prassede Arcivescovo di Milano Scritto dal Dottore Gio. Pietro Giussano Nobile Milanese. Et dalla Congregatione delli Oblati di S. Ambrogio dedicate alla Santità di N.S. Papa Paolo Quinto.* Rome, 1610.

Giussano, G.P. *The Life of St. Charles Borromeo, Cardinal Archbishop of Milan, from the Italian of John Peter Giussano, Priest and Oblate of St. Ambrose.* Pref. H.E. Manning. 2 Vols. London and New York, 1884. [Rpt. of Rome, 1610.]

Grattarola, M.A. *Successi Maravigliosi della veneratione di S. Carlo Cardinale di S. Prassede, & Arcivescovo di Milano.* Milan, 1614.

Gregori, M., Ed. *Il Morazzone. Catalogo della mostra.* Exh. cat. Milan, 1962.

Greuter, F. *Vita, et Miracoli S. Carlo Borromeo Cardinale di S.ta R.a Chiesa del Tit. Di S.ta Prassede.* Rome, 1610.

Langé, S. and A. Pensa. *Il Sacro Monte. Esperienza Del Reale e Spazio Virtuale Nell'conografia Della Passione A Varallo.* Entries by G. Pacciarotti. Milan, 1991.

Levati, L. M. and V.M. Colciago. *Menologio dei Barnabiti. Vol. XI. Novembre.* Genoa, 1938.

Mancini, G. *Considerazioni sulla pittura.* 2 Vols. Ed. A. Marucchi. Rome, 1956. [First publ. of ms. of ca. 1623-24.]

Martin, A.L. *Plague? Jesuit Accounts of Epidemic Disease in the 16th Century.* Kirksville, Missouri, 1996.

Martin, G. *Roma Sancta (1581).* Ed. G. Bruner Parks. Rome, 1969.

Merelli, F. "Carteggio di Mattia e Giovanni Bellintani Da Salò col Cardinale Federico Borromeo." *Collectanea Franciscana* 56/1-2 (1986), pp. 57-108.

Merelli, F. "S. Carlo Borromeo e P. Mattia da Salò cappuccino. Epistolario. " *Collectanea Franciscana* 54/3-4 (1984), pp. 285-313.

Moroni, G. "Quarant'ore." In *Dizionario di Erudizione Storico-Ecclesiastico.* Vol. LVI. Venice, 1852, pp. 113-21.

Nicolini, F. "Parte III. La Peste del 1629-30." In *Storia di Milano. Vol X. L'Età dei Borromei (1559-1630).* Milan, 1957, pp. 497-557

Noonan, J.-C. *The Church Visible. The Ceremonial Life and Protocol of the Roman Catholic Church.* New York, 1996.

Panciroli, O. *Tesori nascosti dell'alma città di Roma...* Rome, 1625.

Papi, G. *Antiveduto Gramatica.* Soncino, 1995.

Papi, G. *Andrea Commodi.* Florence, 1994.

La Peinture Religieuse à Caen, 1580-1780. Exh. cat. Musée des Beaux Arts, Caen, 2000.

Premoli, O. *Storia dei Barnabiti nel Seicento.* Rome, 1922.

Premoli, O. *Storia dei Barnabiti nel Cinquecento.* Rome, 1913.

Prodi, P. "Bascapè, Carlo." In *Dizionario Biografico degli Italiani.* Vol. 7. Rome, 1995, pp. 55-58.

Pupillo, M. *St. Bartholomew's On The Tiber Island.* Milan, 1998.

Rasmussen, N. "Iconography and Liturgy at the Canonization of Carlo Borromeo." *Analecta Romana Instituti Danici* 15 (1986), pp. 119-50.

Riedl, H.P. *Antiveduto della Grammatica (1570/1-1626). Leben und Werk*. Berlin, 1998.

Rocca, G., Ed. *La Sostanza dell'Effimero. Gli abiti degli ordini religiosi in Occidente*. Exh. Cat. Museo Nazionale di Castel Sant'Angelo. Rome, 2000.

Rosci, M. *Il Cerano*. Milan, 2000.

Rosci, M. *I Quadroni di San Carlo Borromeo nel Duomo di Milano*. Milan, 1965.

Rudolph, S. "Stern, Ludovico." In *La Pittura del Settecento*. Milan, 1983.

Sestieri, G. "Parrocel, Stefano. " In *Repertorio della pittura romana della fine del Seicento e del Settecento*. 3 Vols. Turin, 1994.

Strinati, C., Ed. *La Storia dei Giubilei*. 4 Vols. Rome, 1997-2000.

Vaccari, A. and M. *Indice e Nota particolare di tutte le stampe di rame, che se ritrovano al presente nella stamperia di Andrea, e Michel'Angelo Vaccari in Roma*. Rome, 1614.

Zani, V. "Cat. No. 92. Carlo Borromeo adora di notte il Cristo morte di Varallo in imminenza della morte." In *Quadreria dell'Arcivescovado*, Ed. M. Bona Castellotti. Milan, 1999, pp. 122-23.

Art and Plague at Naples

James Clifton

> A city so lovely that it was the delight of Europe, and so populated that it counted eight hundred thousand souls, seemed like a cemetery.
>
> Giuseppe Campanile[1]

A public square is crowded with figures, alive, moribund, dead. Corpses, their bellies swollen from disease, lie in various postures on the ground; others are carried toward their final resting place. Some who live but suffer from the effects of the illness pitch headlong to the ground, gesture wildly in a delirious frenzy, or receive the last sacrament from a religious. Nearby, a gentleman, perhaps the viceroy, sits astride a powerful horse and gestures commandingly, but his direction seems to go unheeded in the confusion. The horror and chaos of the scene are perhaps best exemplified by the overturned cart at the left, from which spill cadavers, discolored, half-nude, with heads hanging and mouths agape. In the sky, the Virgin Mary pleads with her scowling son to stop the carnage; an angel tries to halt the downward motion of his sword. Domenico Gargiulo's famous painting of the Largo del Mercatello (now Piazza Dante) during the plague of 1656 in Naples (fig. 26) accords well with eye-witness accounts of the city suffering nearly unimaginable horror.[2] Carlo Celano described a major Neapolitan thoroughfare clogged with corpses dead from the plague: "There was no more

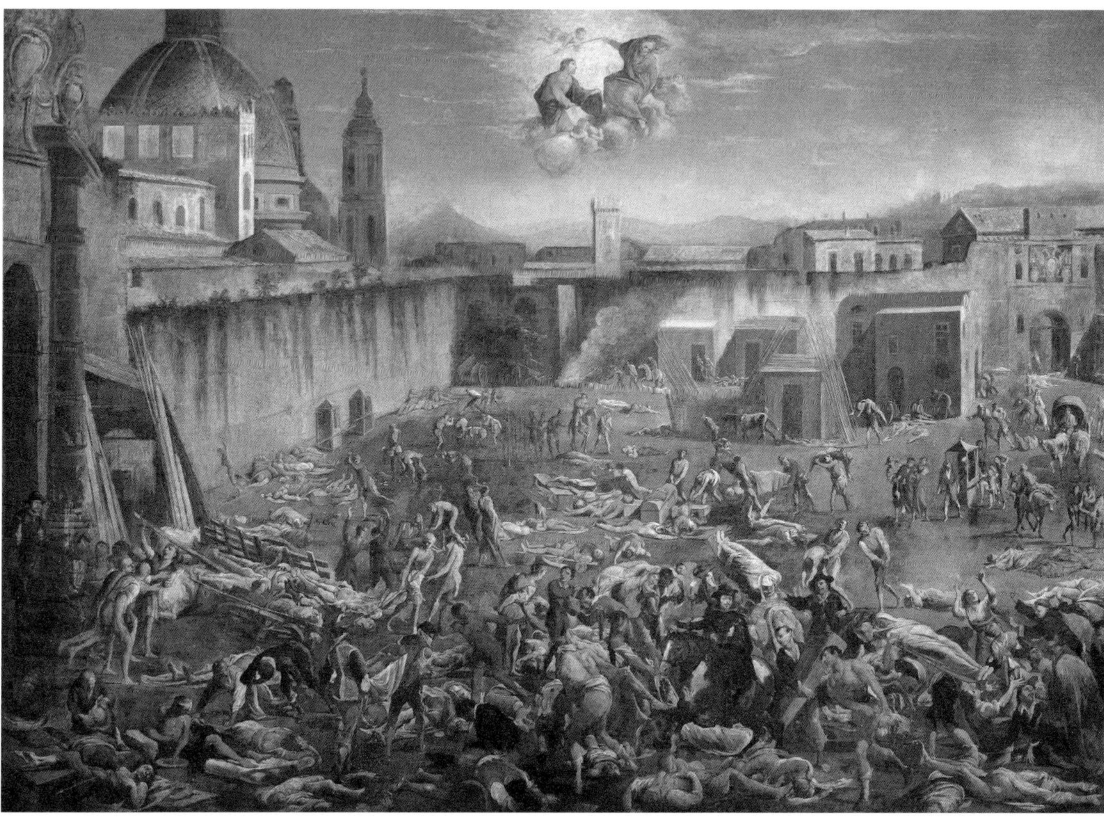

26. Domenico Gargiulo, *Largo del Mercatello during the plague of 1656 in Naples*, ca. 1656-60. Oil on canvas. Museo di S. Martino, Naples.

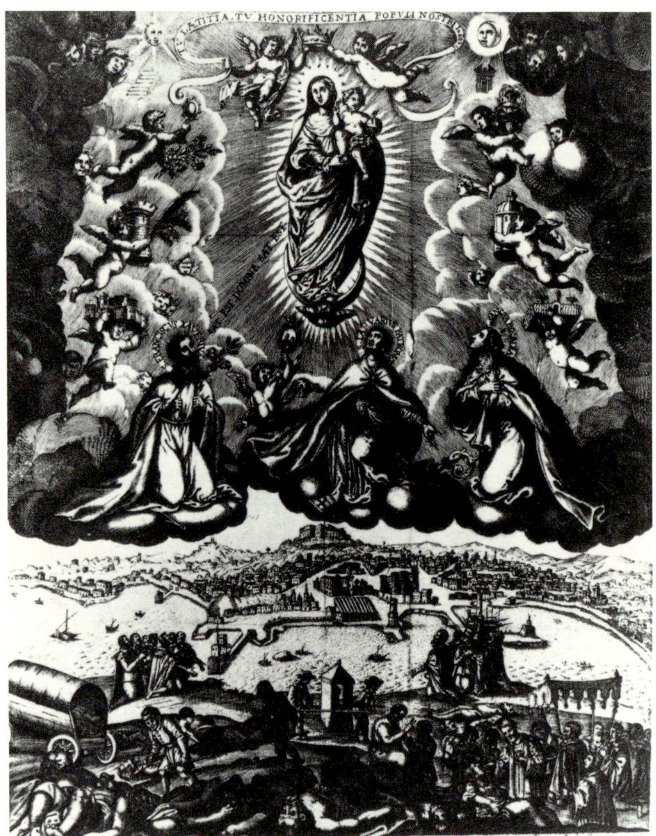

27. Nicolas Perrey, *Immaculate Conception with Saints Januarius, Francis Xavier, and Rosalie,* 1656. Engraving.
Photo: from Giuseppe Galasso, "Napoli nel Viceregno spagnolo dal 1648 al 1696," *Storia di Napoli,* VI, pt. 1, facing p. 208.

room to bury, nor anyone who could bury [the dead]; with my own eyes I saw this strada di Toledo where I lived paved with corpses so that carriages going to the Palazzo [Reale] could not proceed except over baptized flesh. I cannot describe this tragedy further because I could not do so without tears."[3]

In the early months of 1656 people in the poorer quarters of Naples began to die suddenly and unaccountably, in ever increasing numbers. By the time Viceroy Garcia de Avellaneda y Haro, count of Castrillo, officially declared the presence of the plague in May, the epidemic had spread to all parts of the city and was far beyond control. As the summer heat intensified, so too did the plague, killing thousands daily in June and July. In mid-August the disease suddenly released its grip on the Neapolitans, torrential rains cleansed the city streets, and the survivors thanked the heavenly hosts that they were saved. But the plague had done its damage. Whereas Naples had been one of the largest cities in Europe, its numbers were reduced by more than half by the epidemic; famine was rampant afterwards, the city was in dire financial straits, and recovery took generations.

As the plague progressed, the governing bodies of Naples and the Deputati della Salute (deputies of health) took various, seemingly futile steps – such as quarantine – to halt its spread. The measures based on scientific understanding of the plague failed, and the officials had recourse to supernatural agents. To defend themselves from the "three flails of God" – war, pestilence, and famine – Christians often had recourse to saints as intermediaries, to intercede on their behalf to placate the wrath of God (sometimes conceived as God the Father, sometimes as Christ). The wrathful Christ sometimes threatens from on high in paintings such as Gargiulo's. The Virgin Mary was understood to be the most powerful intercessor, but it was a function that could be performed by any saint, and the Neapolitans turned to many. Official invocations of saintly intercession began on 12 May 1656 when the Eletti (syndics) called upon the Virgin Mary (as the Madonna of Constantinople), as well as Saint Anthony of Padua, Saint Januarius (San Gennaro) and the Blessed Cajetan (Beato Gaetano da Thiene). On 12 June, the Deputati della Salute, "having considered and put into practice ... every expedient that could by natural means liberate our city from its present calamity," made several public vows to defend the Immaculate Conception of the Virgin and prayed for her aid in restoring the health of the city.

The Deputati della Salute, the Eletti, and other officials of the city participated fully in, indeed led, public acts of devotion to secure the health of the city – examples of what has been called "civic religion." In civic religion, as Donald Weinstein has described it, laymen are "transmitters of religious values"; religious ritual is no longer reserved for monastic or ecclesiastical space and occurs as well in public, civic space; and "formerly worldly and temporal activities and institutions" (such as those of the Deputati della Salute and the Eletti in Naples) gain religious legitimation.[4] The boundaries between public and private were as permeable as those between religious and lay in responses to the plague. Not only did private individuals participate in communal activities, but the modes and content of their personal activities often overlapped with those of the community. Responses to the plague included the use of visual imagery as prophylaxis, remedy, supplication, and thanks for divine assistance.

A few days after the Deputati's vow to defend the Immaculate Conception, the Neapolitan Eletti determined to have painted above seven of the city gates frescoes of the Immaculate Conception with Saints Januarius, Francis Xavier, and Rosalie. Because the frescoes could not be executed for some time, the Eletti also commissioned a print of the same subject, to be issued as both a woodcut and a copper engraving and to be distributed freely to the people of Naples (fig. 27). The work was undertaken by Nicolas Perrey, a prolific French engraver working in Naples, and was paid for in September 1656. In November, Mattia Preti was commissioned to paint the frescoes, which were completed from 1657 to early 1659. They were severely damaged by an earthquake in 1688 and have since been destroyed.

The compositions of the frescoes are known through two surviving oil sketches (figs. 28, 29), supplemented by documentary evidence.[5] Both sketches adhere to an identical compositional and iconographic format deriving from the instructions of the Eletti: the Virgin Immaculate with the Child is placed centrally, flanked by the saints Januarius, Francis Xavier, and Rosalie. Both also include elements not mentioned by the Eletti: an angel with a flaming sword in the center of each canvas (a traditional figure deriving from Saint Gregory the Great's vision of Saint Michael sheathing a blood-stained sword indicating the end of the Roman plague of 590), and figures of the plague-stricken and those tending to them in the lower portion of each work. Differences between the two paintings, though subtle, are many, suggesting the artist's plan to vary his frescoes within a strictly defined scheme.

Most significant among the figures in Perrey's engraving and Preti's frescoes are, of course, the Virgin and Child. Placed directly along the central vertical axis of each image, the statuesque Virgin towered over all the other figures. The incorporation of the Virgin and Child in large-scale votive paintings in response to a plague was not new. Guido Reni's so-called *Pala della Peste* of 1631, which was carried annually in Bologna as a processional banner, and which Preti may very well have known, is perhaps the most prominent example. The purity of the Virgin – especially when invoked in her *most* pure, that is, immaculately conceived, form – as antithesis to the pestilence occasioned her appearance in votive imagery in Naples as elsewhere. The converse relationship between the Virgin's freedom from original sin and the plague is suggested by the vow of the Deputati della Salute in which original sin, like the plague, is referred to as "common contagion." Father Indico Fiorillo, in a sermon that was part

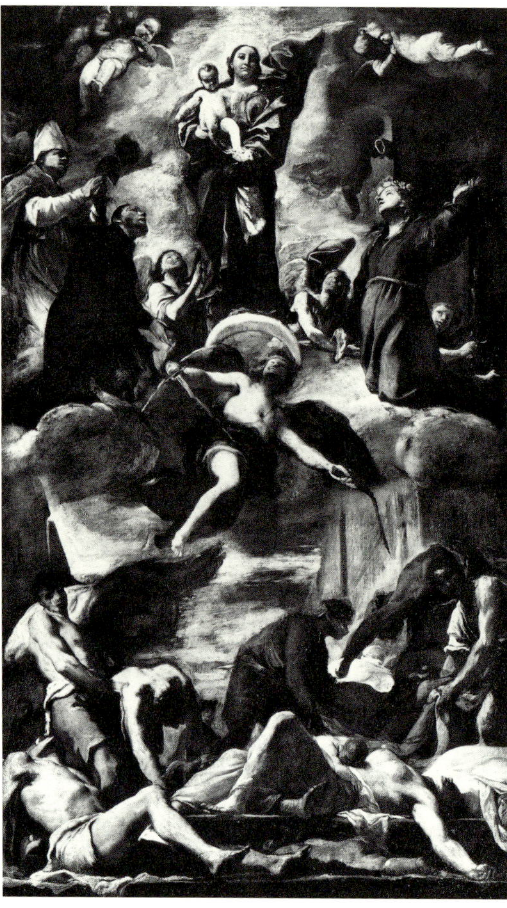

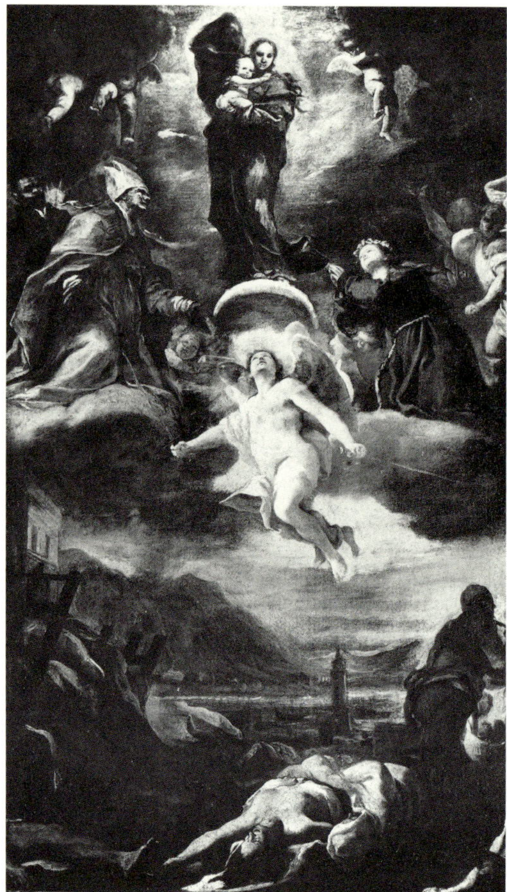

28. and 29.
Mattia Preti, *The Immaculate Conception with Saints*, ca. 1657.
Oil on canvas.
Museo e gallerie Nazionale di Capodimonte, Naples.

of the city's celebration of the feast of the Immaculate Conception in 1659, noted that Naples had invoked Mary, recognizing her "as an impenetrable wall against the Original Plague," and that the plague was the heir of humankind's first sin, introduced in the Garden of Eden.[6] Similarly, the inscription on Perrey's engraving substitutes "plague" (*lues*) for "sin" in alluding to the Virgin's immaculate conception: "To the Virgin who has never experienced the original plague of humankind ... so that they [the Virgin and named saints] may avert the plague from the city, land, and kingdom of Naples." The Virgin and saints all serve as intercessors, but the Virgin's purity accords her special protective powers.

The doctrine of the Immaculate Conception – that from the very first moment of her conception the Virgin Mary was preserved from all stain of original sin – was still controversial in the seventeenth century. In 1618, following trends in Spain, Viceroy Pedro Girón, duke of Osuna, took steps to increase the cult in Naples, vowing publicly to defend the belief and exacting a similar vow from public officials. Following the ceremony on the Feast of the Immaculate Conception (8 December) in the Jesuit church of the Gesù Nuovo, a statue of the Virgin Immaculate was carried in procession. By the time of the plague some forty years later, the cult of the Immaculate Conception was a firmly entrenched part of the civic religion of Naples, enjoying widespread participation. The culmination of the many acts of devotion to the Virgin Immaculate in response to the plague was an extravagant celebration of her feast day in 1659, which included elaborate ephemeral architectural and pictorial decorations throughout the city as well as at the church of S. Lorenzo, a procession of noblemen with a statue of the Virgin Immaculate, and eight sermons over the course of the eight-day celebration. The sermons, delivered by members of different orders, were in part defenses of the doctrine of the Immaculate Conception, suggesting that it may still have been a point of theological controversy, but largely they were hymns of praise to the Virgin Mary, using the particular doctrine of the Immaculate Conception to increase devotion to her.

By the mid-seventeenth century, the iconography of the Immaculate Conception had largely been standardized in accordance with the description of the Apocalyptic Woman: "And a great sign appeared in heaven: A woman clothed with the sun, and the moon under her feet, and on her head a crown of twelve stars" (Rev. 12:1). The Virgin Immaculate was generally surrounded by angels, sometimes with standard Marian symbols, and occasionally accompanied by God the Father. The number of such images, particularly by Neapolitan and Spanish artists, is legion. Preti's compositions adhere to the norm in the inclusion of the moon at the Virgin's feet and her crown of stars, as do all other official Neapolitan images of the Immaculate Conception connected with the plague. Preti's images deviate from the norm, however, in the presence of the Christ Child in the arms of the Virgin Immaculate.

The Eletti, in commissioning Preti's frescoes, clearly specified that the Virgin should be holding the Christ Child in her arms, like the statue carried in procession in 1618, which had a determining effect on the shaping of the Neapolitan plague iconography. That statue was also carried in times of civic stress, namely, the eruption of Vesuvius in 1631, the popular uprising in 1647, and the plague in 1656. The statue was housed in the church of the Immaculate Conception at the hermitage-convent founded by Suor Orsola Benincasa on a hill overlooking Naples, which was one of the churches in which the Eletti made public vows of devotion to the Immaculate Conception during the plague. They also determined to participate twice annually in masses at Suor Orsola's church to mark the Feast of the Immaculate Conception and the anniversary of Orsola's death. In 1616, Suor Orsola had prophesied that tragedy would befall the city of Naples:

> Woe to you, Naples, if this hermitage is not built soon, woe to the whole world. ... [I]f the people of Naples, and in particular the Signori, knew the woe and the castigations that hang over them if this place is not built soon, they would all move to have it done, and they would take bread from the mouths of their own children, and the Signori themselves would carry the chests, and the rocks, and the mortar on their own shoulders; to make it quickly each person would do a little, and everyone would participate in this great good.[7]

The hermitage was indeed still unfinished in 1656 when Orsola's prophecy was published. To many it was clear that the plague was the "scourge of God for the unfulfilled promises in building the church ... of Suor Orsola."[8] As she had stipulated, toward the middle of June, about the time of the vows to the Immaculate Conception, all sectors of society, including the viceroy himself, hurried to contribute financially and physically to the construction of the edifice.

In Preti's images, the statuesque Virgin Immaculate is flanked by saints Januarius, Rosalie, and Francis Xavier, who offer their prayers and supplications for the suffering city. Saint Januarius, bishop of Benevento, martyred at Pozzuoli in 305, was chief patron saint of Naples. From the late fourteenth century the saint's blood, kept in two ampules, has liquefied when brought in proximity to the relic of his head several times each year. In depictions of the saint these vials are often carried by angels, as is visible in one of Preti's *bozzetti*. The aid of Saint Januarius was invoked in Naples during the plague of 1526 and against the threat of the Sicilian plague of 1624, and he was held primarily responsible for saving Naples from a terrifying eruption of Vesuvius in 1631. The efficacy of prayers to him was readily recalled during the plague in 1656. His aid was invoked officially in the earliest vows, on 12 May, in mid-June, and again on 2 July, when the Deputati della Salute vowed to build a hospital for the poor under the protection of saints Januarius and Francis Xavier, which was finished only in 1667. On 3 July, as a sign of celestial appreciation for the vow of the previous day, four hundred of the plague-stricken in the lazaretto of S. Gennaro were healed. Depictions of Saint Januarius in seventeenth- and eighteenth-century Naples – particularly of his martyrdom, with special emphasis on his miraculous blood – are legion, in both public and private contexts. Years after the plague and after Mattia Preti had left Naples, he executed, perhaps for a Neapolitan, a forceful painting of the saint's decapitation (cat. 27), a composition that proved popular, as more than one version exists. Around 1700, Francesco Solimena, described by the eighteenth-century biographer Bernardo De Dominici as "the Cavalier Calabrese [that is, Mattia Preti] ennobled," paired Saint Januarius with the perennial plague saint, Sebastian (whose protection was less frequently invoked in Naples than elsewhere) in another altarpiece (cat. 28). (See Sheila Barker's essay in this volume, for more on the iconography of Saint Sebastian.)

One of the vows to Saint Francis Xavier was made in his chapel in the Gesù Nuovo before a painting by Giovanni Bernardino Azzolino. On 8 May 1653, the appearance of the saint in this painting reputedly underwent a miraculous transformation, becoming pale in the face and sweaty in the brow, and raising and lowering his eyes to the vision of the Madonna depicted above him. This phenomenon continued for several weeks, was investigated by a committee appointed by Cardinal Archbishop Ascanio Filomarino, and was attested to by nearly one hundred witnesses, including several painters. The miracle was later understood as presaging the coming of the plague, and along with Saint Francis Xavier's previous involvement with various plagues – both during and after his actual lifetime – led the Eletti to seek his protection. On a more private level, Francis Xavier's aid in combating the plague was also recognized. Many are the stories of the saint's miraculous healing powers, particularly through images of him, which were sometimes applied to the suffering body, as was oil from his lamps:

> One could measure in moments the life of Father Gennaro Pisa of the Company of Jesus, who had fallen sick from the plague after having been exposed to it in the service of the plague-stricken in the city of Aquila. In that state an image on paper of Saint Francis Xavier was applied to his heart; and this [image], gathering into itself the malign pestilence of the body of the languishing, wonderfully absorbed all those sores that had appeared on his body; and to the marvel of many people, it was seen full of those spots from which the Father remained entirely healed.[9]

In commissioning Preti to depict Francis Xavier above the city gates, the Eletti seem to have slighted the Blessed Cajetan of Thiene, founder of the Theatines. Cajetan's aid was also invoked during the plague, including in the Eletti's vows of 12 May, with apparently impressive results. On 7 August 1656, his feast day, during the height of the affliction, when thousands had been dying each day since mid-July, not one person succumbed in the lazarettos of S. Gennaro or of S. Maria di Loreto, and thereafter the force of the pestilence rapidly diminished. There were many sworn witnesses to this miracle, which played an important role in Cajetan's canonization in 1671. City officials had reason to appreciate not only the supernatural efforts of Francis Xavier and Cajetan but also the terrestrial aid given by members of the Jesuits and Theatines to the people of the afflicted city. In August 1656, letters were sent to officials of the Theatine order and the Society of Jesus, thanking them for the help given to the plague-stricken by their priests. According to one contemporary estimate, of the pre-plague population of nearly three hundred Jesuits in Naples, only eighty survived; of two hundred and fifty Theatines, only seventy. It is easy to imagine that the relatively few surviving members of each order were eager to gain public acclaim, if not directly for their own efforts and sacrifices, then at least vicariously through the glorification of their respective saints. Ultimately, complaints from the Theatines prompted the Eletti to pay for statues of Blessed Cajetan to be placed on the city gates and in front of the Theatine church of S. Paolo Maggiore. In 1662, responding to continuing feuds between the Theatines and Jesuits, the bishop of Acerra noted that Francis Xavier and Cajetan peacefully coexist on the city gates and suggested, among other things, "that both orders preach that the plague of Naples was removed by the intercession of Saint Francis Xavier and the Blessed Cajetan."[10]

The invocation of Saint Rosalie and her subsequent inclusion in Perrey's print and Preti's frescoes derived from her fame as liberator of the city of Palermo from the plague of 1624, as seen in van Dyck's painting (cat. 30). Rosalie was ultimately included among the saints credited with the salvation of Naples from the plague, and to honor her the Eletti had a silver lamp presented at the saint's tomb. (See Gauvin Bailey's essay in this volume for a thorough study of Saint Rosalie and the plague in Palermo.)

The resolution of the Eletti did not call for one of the most significant portions of Preti's compositions, the mortal figures represented in the lower register. This imposing drama of death had a considerable impact on subsequent representations of the plague, including Luca Giordano's altarpiece at S. Maria del Pianto (on which, see below) and Francesco Solimena's *A Miracle of Saint John of God* (cat. 28).[11] Preti's inclusion of these figures was undoubtedly influenced by Perrey's print, which included representations of people engaged in activities common during the plague, as well as a group of noblemen representing the Eletti and Deputati della Salute, who kneel in an attitude commonly associated with donor portraits.

Perrey's inclusion of the topographical view derives from an important aspect of the tradition of votive imagery. Depictions of a city with its protecting saints had been used for such plague-related imagery as Reni's processional banner, but they had also been a common feature of maps and views of various cities, including Naples, since the early Renaissance. Preti does not include the view of the city and the kneeling officials, opting instead for a continuity of time and space throughout each work. The enlargement of the figures, both living and dead, in the lower portion of each *bozzetto*, or sketch (as well as the differences owing to the addition of color), lends the paintings an emotive power absent from the print. And though none of the figures in the lower portions of the *bozzetti* seems aware of the celestial drama enacted above, the two strata are represented as contiguous, suggesting that the figures above and their actions are as real as those so graphically represented below.

It is important to note, however, that the frescoes did not so much eliminate Perrey's view of the city and donor portraits as transform them. The image of the city was expanded in the frescoes not only by the enlargement of the mortal figures but also by the placement of the frescoes on the periphery of the city; an aerial view of the city – simultaneously visited by tragedy and protected by patron saints – has been replaced by the walls of the city itself. As much as the processions of the statue of the Immaculate Conception and the relics of Saint Januarius through the streets of Naples, the painted gates were a celebration of *communitas*.

The location of the frescoes on the city gates emphasizes the communal suffering and salvation of the populace insofar as the gates may be considered a symbolically charged civic space. The presentation to the public of the city as a cohesive entity, unified under the aegis of powerful celestial figures, was of obvious importance to the Eletti – who had responsibility for the gates in quarantining the city during times of plague – as civic leaders. That these leaders did not in fact represent the lower classes (and only minimally the middle class) is obscured by Preti's presentation of the beleaguered Neapolitans as a unified group.

Images of the Virgin and saints depicted on city gates, whether singly or as part of a cycle, invite an understanding of their purpose that was never explicitly stated: that of protecting the city. City gates were almost always intimately bound up with systems of defense. As ports of entry they were lacunae in a massive girdle of defensive walls, and thus called for particular protection in the case of attack. Their maintenance was often provided for by massive bastions flanking them. Images of the *santi protettori* above them would also have assured those approaching, whether hostile or not, that the gate – that is to say, the city itself – was under the special care of powerful celestial figures. But there could be another, more fundamental, function of city-gate imagery: to act literally as talismans against the entry of hostile, evil, and even pestiferous forces into the city. The use of the term "averruncent" ("turn away," used in antiquity in religious contexts) in Perrey's engraving to describe the action of those repulsing the plague is particularly appropriate for figures stationed above the city gates.

It is clear that, for many, images played an important role in combating the plague; moreover, it is worth noting that images of recent manufacture with no history of miracle working were also thought to be efficacious – that is to say, apotropaic images were not limited to miraculous icons. To protect themselves from the plague, individuals wore talismans or amulets made from various materials such as nonoxidizing metals, precious stones, or paper, inscribed or imprinted with prayers, incantations, religious images, crosses, the number 4, or the like. Images of Saint Francis Xavier were not only applied to sores in a curative capacity, as noted above, but were also displayed on the doors to homes in a preventive one. It is likely that the widely disseminated prints of the Immaculate Conception and saints by Perrey were similarly attached to doors or walls with a prophylactic intent. The derivation of the imagery of Perrey's print and Preti's frescoes from a particularly revered statue of the Immaculate Conception would only have enhanced the impression of their supernatural protective qualities. (See Pamela Jones's essay, pp. 73-74, for a discussion of print dissemination and its influence.)

Of the innumerable penitential processions that occurred during the plague, many had as their goal the church of S. Maria di Costantinopoli and the miraculous frescoed image of the Virgin and Child housed therein. On several occasions Giulio Spinola, the papal nunciate to Naples, described the veneration of the image in his reports to Rome, including, on 13 May 1656, the prayers of the Eletti "for divine help for the preservation of this city from every contagious disease."[12] But the veneration of the Madonna of Constantinople was not limited to the civic leaders; on one occasion Spinola noted that the crowd congregating there was innumerable, and late in May he reported that "the processions of poor, barefoot girls and women to the Church of the Madonna of Constantinople continued every day until yesterday."

The Italian cult of the Madonna of Constantinople derives from a miraculous Byzantine icon – the *Hodegetria* – which was probably destroyed in the fall of Constantinople in 1453, although some reports had it safely transported to Italy. An icon in Bari was purported to be the original *Hodegetria*, and numerous miracles were ascribed to it, including the salvation of Bari from the plague in 1657. The veneration of the image in Bari seems to have led directly to the establishment of the cult of the Madonna of Constantinople elsewhere in Apulia, and the cult was widespread in Southern Italy, especially Sicily, where Eastern influence was greatest. Numerous copies and versions of the *Hodegetria* were made, and churches, chapels, and confraternities were dedicated to the Madonna of Constantinople in major centers and smaller towns.

The cult of the *Hodegetria* or the Madonna of Constantinople in Naples may date from as early as the fourteenth century, but it flourished in the sixteenth century. In 1528 the Kingdom of Naples was struck, in the words of the chronicler Gregorio Rosso, with the "three flails of

God, war, plague, and famine."[14] The French under the viscount Lautrec Odet de Foix had invaded the kingdom and laid siege to the city of Naples itself, cutting off the supplies of food and water. The siege was lifted in September and with it the Neapolitans' fears of violence or starvation. But the plague, which had first made itself felt in Naples in September of the previous year, and had grown more potent throughout the course of the siege, continued to rage through the spring of 1529. However, in June of that year – a season when plagues generally increased in intensity – the plague came to a relatively sudden end, owing, according to Rosso and others, like the end of the siege, to the intervention of the Virgin, in this case, made manifest by the discovery of an image of her:

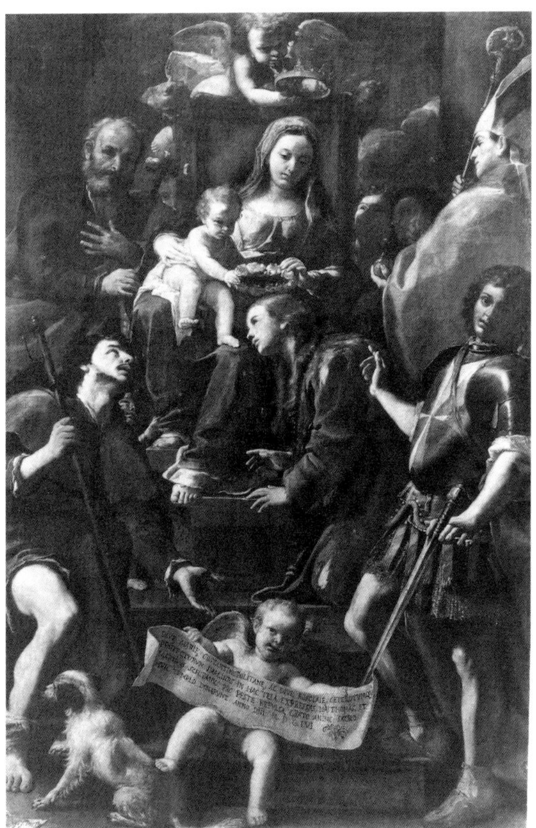

30. Mattia Preti, *Madonna of Constantinople*, 1656. Oil on canvas. S. Agostina degli Scaizi, Naples.

> In the month of June of this year, the third day of Whitsunday, was found close to the walls of the city of Naples an image of the most holy Madonna Mother of God, by the revelation of an old woman who lived close-by, to whom was promised by the Mother of God the end of the Plague, with effect, as one sees; and for that reason the city of Naples began immediately to build a church for the said image, with the title of the Madonna of Constantinople, and one hopes that she will protect it from the said disease in all future times.
>
> And not only did the Madonna of Constantinople liberate Naples from the plague, but also from war, because at the same time peace was concluded between the Emperor and the Pope.[15]

The Madonna of Constantinople was invoked in Naples against the spread of the Lombard plague in 1575 and the Sicilian plague in 1624, and the relics of Saint Januarius were carried to her church during the eruption of Vesuvius in 1631.

The communal iconography of the Madonna of Constantinople was appropriated for a private altarpiece by Mattia Preti, painted for the lawyer Giovanni Tommaso Schipani and his son, Marino Schipani, and placed in the church of S. Maria della Verità (better known as S. Agostino degli Scalzi) in Naples (fig. 30). According to the inscription at the bottom of the painting, it was created as an ex-voto for the Schipani, thanking the Virgin, Saint Rosalie, and other saints for their salvation from the recent plague. The vow is elaborated in the installation contract, which names the other saints represented: Saint Januarius, Saint Roch, Saint Joseph, and Saint Nicasius. Preti was not concerned with the particular formal type of the Byzantine *Hodegetria* or even the miraculous icon discovered in Naples in 1528. Rather it was her title alone that evokes her protective powers. In the installation contract, the patrons were also careful to ensure that the painting "remain always on view, so that the glorious Virgin of Constantinople and the other saints may be more greatly venerated."[16] Unlike his frescoes for

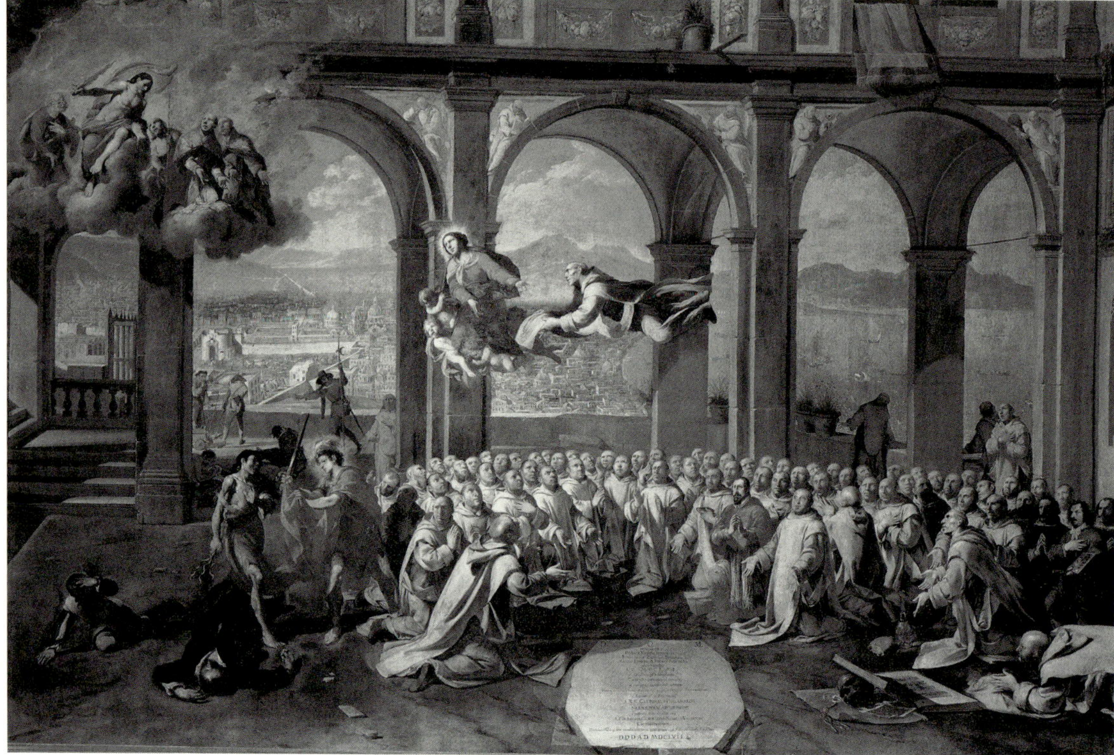

31. Domenico Gargiulo, *Ex-Voto for the Carthusians' Escape from the Plague*, 1657. Oil on canvas. Certosa di San Martino, Naples.

the city gates, Preti's *Madonna of Constantinople* includes no terrestrial narrative, nothing beyond the inscription to tie it specifically to the events of 1656. The viewers of the painting, with whom the Schipani were so concerned, were thus not to be limited to their exact contemporaries; rather, a continuing dialogue with future viewers was also intended. Although Preti's painting is a response to a personally considered, specific historical event, its conception and purpose sought to push it beyond the boundaries of its original context.

Mary is also the featured intercessor in a complex ex-voto painted by Domenico Gargiulo for the Carthusians at the Certosa di S. Martino in the Vomero, on the hill above the city of Naples (fig. 31). In it are represented nearly seventy monks, mostly gathered in a semicircle around the inscribed stone set into the floor, before an arcade, behind which are visible the city and bay of Naples. Easily recognizable among the non-monastic figures represented are Cardinal Archbishop Ascanio Filomarino, in red robes, and Gargiulo himself, clearly identified at the extreme right by his palette and brushes. Among the monks, the features of the prior Andrea Cancelliere are also recognizable in the figure to the right of Filomarino. Above the monks are the Virgin, supported by four cherubs, and Saint Bruno, who flies after her, extending the Rule of his order so that she may gesture toward it in a carefully choreographed aerial show. The Virgin looks up at the wrathful Christ who, though lounging on a bank of clouds, menacingly waves a flaming sword in his right hand while eyeing the desperate group of monks below. Helping the Virgin to reason with Christ are Saint John the Baptist, Saint Peter, and two Carthusian bishop saints, Hugh of Lincoln and Anthelmus of Belley. Striding threateningly toward the group of monks, stepping across a nobleman (the plague spares no one, regardless of age, gender, or station in life, as Cesare Ripa noted) is a pestilential hag, but she is shunted aside by the young Saint Martin of Tours, the titular saint of the monastery.

Though it is not an exact topographical rendering, the landscape visible through the interstices of the architecture approximates a view from a point near, if not actually at, the Certosa di San Martino. The twin peaks of Vesuvius are clearly visible through the central arch, descending into the Sorrentine peninsula to the right. At the left of the painting the Mercatello is depicted on a disproportionately large scale. Unable to provide specific details of human activities in the city on the minute scale of the rest of the background, the artist has chosen to enlarge this single piazza, the same piazza he used to exemplify the life of the plague-stricken city in another painting. The piazza in the Carthusian painting is replete with figures performing functions that find parallels in contemporary written descriptions: priests giving the last rites to the dying, Turks or galley-slaves hauling the white-swathed dead, and so on. Similarly, at the right side of the painting, one sees the bodies of plague victims, dumped into the bay, floating in their linen burial garb among the sailboats.

Once the plague penetrated within the walls of a monastery, its devastation there was often disproportionately severe owing to the communal habits of the religious. In his 1658 description of the Neapolitan plague, Carlo Francesco Riaco, abbot of S. Sapienza di Folina, estimated the numbers of religious who died, order by order.[17] Of some 600 Dominicans, about 400 died, most of the 160 reformed Franciscans perished, and of 190 Capuchins only a bare minimum remained to fulfill the official duties in the monasteries. An exception to the rule of decimation was the order of the Carthusians. Riaco says that more than one hundred of them protected themselves well at the Certosa, being content to offer numerous prayers for the people. Gargiulo's painting asserts that the Carthusians benefited from the Certosa's good location well above the city, the caution exercised by the monks in dealing with potentially plague-ridden outsiders, and divine intervention.

Theoretically, even the religious were not excluded from those lashed by the flail of the plague as the monastic figure in Andrea Vaccaro's *Intercession of the Madonna for the Souls in Purgatory*, painted for the votive plague church of S. Maria del Pianto, makes amply clear (fig. 32). Yet the theme of Gargiulo's painting is in fact that the Carthusians, through special protection, were exempt from the onslaught of the plague.

Saint Martin had no particular reputation as a plague saint, but it seems appropriate to engage such a young warrior as one's protector against attack. He moves toward Plague in a clear attempt to ward her off, yet it is not with his raised sword that he threatens her, rather with his red cloak, newly divided by that sword. Without the requisite beggar recipient of the divided cloak – a standard bit of Saint Martin's iconography – the gesture seems absurd. Nevertheless, Saint Martin's divided cloak is a clear reference to his charitable act, and it is with this symbol of charity that he defends the monks from destruction. The implication that the Carthusian monks were saved from the plague not only by the intercessory efforts of Mary, Saint Bruno, *et alia*, but by their own charitable acts as well (equating the monks of San Martino with their patron saint) may seem surprising, considering that the Carthusians, unlike monks of other orders, remained within their monastic retreat, nor mingling with the inhabitants of the city in order to serve them. However, although the inhabitants of the Certosa could not boast of the physical aid to the plague-stricken offered by other orders, they nonetheless participated in the struggle for the survival of the city in a manner consistent with the solitude emphasized in their Rule: through concentrated prayer. Furthermore, they continued during the plague their practice of giving food to the poor who approached the monastery for that purpose. It is perhaps to this continuous, however limited, intercourse with the poor of the city that not only the gesture of Saint Martin, but also the open gate in the left middleground refers.

Plague, hideous as she is, appears in the painting as a servant of the wrathful Christ. The tradition of explaining epidemics – and any disaster – as the result of divine anger against sinners is certainly an old one, and it is often reiterated in connection with the Neapolitan

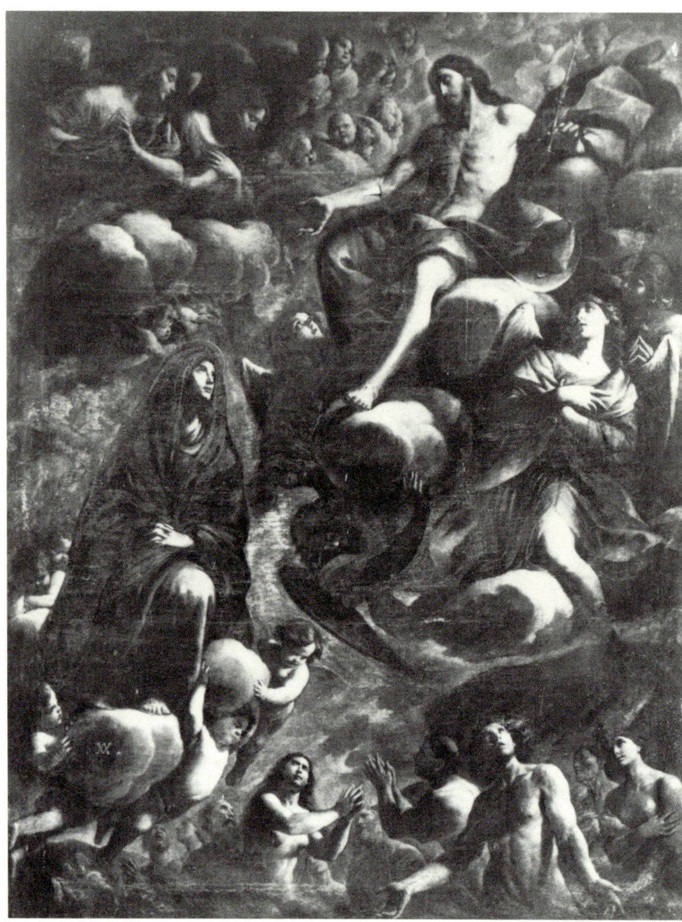

32. Andrea Vaccaro, *Intercession of the Madonna for the Souls in Purgatory*, 1660-62. Oil on canvas.
Museo e Gallerie Nazionali di Capodimonte, Naples.

plague. The Carthusians, however, attributed their salvation not to a lack of sinfulness, but rather, as the lapidary inscription in the foreground of the painting notes, to the intercessions of the Virgin and saints Bruno and Martin.

The prominence in the painting of the Virgin and Saint Bruno with the Rule of the order, and the inclusion of saints Peter and John the Baptist at the upper left allude to a single episode from Carthusian history. At the Grande Chartreuse at Grenoble, in 1093 (only seven years after the founding of the order), some of the monks were beginning to question the necessity of such a strict Rule, which imposed silence and austerity, and suggestions were made to change the constituent precepts of the order to conform with those of more lenient monastic groups. These grumblings were later seen as the work of the Devil, or as Maleagro Pentimalli called him in relating the story in 1622, "that pestiferous and malignant serpent."[18] But the spiritual lives of the monks and the rigor of their order were preserved by miraculous apparition: Saint Peter appeared to the Carthusians of Grenoble exhorting them to honor and devote themselves to the Virgin Mary, and she in return would perpetually intercede with her Son on their behalf. The monks then elected Mary as their advocate and protectress, and, as Pentimalli further explains, were renewed in their vows, from which they were never to deviate.

Saint Bruno was not present at the apparition, but he is connected to the event via his supposed authorship of the Rule of the order. Although Saint Bruno did not in fact leave a written Rule, he is depicted in several instances at San Martino as having done so. Gargiulo focuses attention on the Rule in his painting by locating it near the exact center, framed by a prominent arch, and by using it as a connecting device between two of the major figures: Saint Bruno and the Virgin Mary. With the Rule were naturally associated its major precepts – those questioned by the eleventh-century Carthusians of Grenoble – and it is not surprising that references to these virtues are to be found in Gargiulo's painting. In the lower right-hand corner a monk draws attention to a group of objects by his deeply bowed posture and hands clasped in prayer. This still life, which is further emphasized by the red cloth on which it rests, consists of a skull, a three-stranded flail, and a book. The skull refers to a contemplative, solitary life, and the flail – which functions as balance and antidote to the instrument wielded on the opposite side of the painting by the figure of Plague – is clearly a reference to penitence. Just beyond the still life, another monk gestures to a partial loaf of bread and a flask of water while gazing up at the celestial activity, a reference to the Carthusians' stringent dietary restrictions. The result of a crisis in the community – whether spiritual as in 1093, or physical as in 1656 – was naturally a re-affirmation of the stringency of the Rule and devotion to celestial advocates.

There is some evidence that Gargiulo's painting hung in the Certosa's *forasteria*, which functioned as quarters for distinguished visitors. The *forasteria* belonged to the more internal parts of the monastery, removed from areas where necessary commerce with the outer world occurred. It was described in the seventeenth century as comfortable, its walls hung with numerous paintings. Although no visitor to the Certosa is known to have recorded his impressions of Gargiulo's painting (or indeed of any work in the *forasteria*), we can at least imagine what one was meant to understand from it. Monastic and priestly orders in Naples besides the Carthusians had reason to be proud of the efforts of their members in assisting the plague-stricken of the city; the numbers of their dead can be and have been used as indices of their dedication. The Carthusians, on the other hand, did not circulate among the afflicted and suffered no dead whose devotion could then be extolled. Rather, the pride of their order must have derived from the exactly opposite condition: none of the Carthusians of San Martino died, thanks to their dedication to the Rule and privileged protection by the Virgin and saints. This pride is the motivating force behind the production of Gargiulo's painting, and is articulated not only in the painting as a whole but also explicitly in its inscription. The Carthusians were justifiably proud of the beauty of their monastery and of its location, and Gargiulo's painting manifested for both the Carthusians and their visitors the physical and spiritual salubrity of the Certosa.

The Virgin Mary and other Neapolitan saints play a prominent role in the decoration of the small church of S. Maria del Pianto (Saint Mary of Tears), which was constructed precisely in response to the plague of 1656 – not as an ex voto, like S. Maria della Salute in Venice, for example, but to commemorate and ease the passage of the plague victims through purgatory. The church, which was completed in 1662, sits on a hill in the Poggioreale section of Naples, well outside the seventeenth-century walls, at the entrances of the Grotta degli Sportiglioni (Neapolitan dialect for "bats"), which was the burial site for some sixty thousand.[19]

The most prominent individual patron of the church's construction and decoration was Gaspar de Bracamonte, Count of Peñaranda, viceroy of Naples from 1659. It was he who requested Andrea Vaccaro and Luca Giordano to supply the altarpieces, and he was portrayed in Domenico Antonio Parrino's *Teatro eroico e politico dei governi de' vicerè del regno di Napoli* (1692) with an image of the church as a symbol of his artistic legacy to the city of Naples.[20] Yet the church of S. Maria del Pianto is not the product of a single benefactor. Much like the hermitage of Suor Orsola Benincasa, the church was built with the gifts, if not with the actual physical labor, of a broad cross-section of Neapolitan society. Although the land was provided by a single individual, and the project may ultimately have been guided by the viceroy, funds for the church and its decoration came from a variety of sources.[21] Major contributors included the Flemish merchants and patrons of art, Gaspar Roomer and Jan Vandeneynden. Such institutions as the silk merchants and goldsmiths guilds and the Banco della Pietà also contributed. Furthermore, mendicants circulated in the city collecting funds toward the new church's completion. As the chronicler Innocenzo Fuidoro reports, the church was "built ... with funds from the alms of the faithful Christian Neapolitans, and there [Mass] is celebrated for the souls of the dead from the recent plague of 1656, buried in that grotto and in other places in Naples."[22]

This purpose is explicitly represented in Andrea Vaccaro's *Madonna of Purgatory* (fig. 32), formerly on the high altar of the church. Luca Giordano's paintings from the transept altars, *Saint Januarius Interceding for the Plague Victims* (fig. 33) and *The Crucified Christ with Saints* (fig. 34), also support the theme and, with Vaccaro's painting, form a unified whole.[23] Vaccaro's altarpiece presents nude figures standing waist-deep in flames minimally indicated at the lower edge of the painting. These figures watch a drama of intercession being played above them. The Virgin, kneeling on clouds borne aloft by putti at center left, looks up to Christ, ensconced in a nebulous throne, his gaze and right hand extended toward his mother, his left hand poised on a blue globe and delicately holding a scepter. The sky is filled with cherubs and angels in attitudes of adoration. Giordano's *Saint Januarius* shows the saint, accompanied by putti carrying his bishop's miter and vials of his miraculous blood, kneeling on clouds and looking up to the Virgin and Christ. She kneels at Christ's side, her hands folded in prayer as he turns to her, his back bent under the weight of his cross. Saint Januarius gestures toward the scene below, which is dominated by the discolored bodies of a half dozen victims of the plague, with representations of the removal of other bodies and a city wall and gate in the background. At the upper right an angel sheathes his sword, signifying the end of the plague. Giordano's other altarpiece shows the crucified Christ, his cross leaning dramatically toward five figures clustered at the left side of the canvas: Saint Bacolus, Saint Eufebius, Saint Candida, the Blessed Francis Borgia, and Saint Asprenus.[24] Above them God the Father appears amid a swirl of light, drapery, clouds, and cherubs.

Giordano's two paintings are quite different, yet complementary. The *Saint Januarius* is essentially a narrative painting, the *Crucified Christ* less so – an *Andachtsbild*, as it were. The *Saint Januarius* shows that saint and the Virgin Mary – the two most important intercessors for Naples – actively beseeching Christ on behalf of the plague-stricken city, while the *Crucified Christ* shows five lesser patron saints in attitudes of adoration of the Savior, a reminder of their devotion to and hence intercessory power with him. The bodies littering the foreground of the *Saint Januarius* have become the skulls and bones strewn about the foot of the cross in its companion piece. These skulls constitute an interesting twist on the common motif of the single skull of Adam at the foot of the cross, referring to the tradition that Golgotha was the burial place of the first man. Giordano has revived a pictorial tradition in depicting the blood from the wounds on Christ's feet flowing onto the skull, signifying the power of his spilled blood to redeem man from sin, and he has departed from tradition in depicting a relative multitude of skulls – an obvious reference to the many sons and daughters of Adam buried there in the Grotta degli Sportiglioni.

The plague victims' skulls in the *Crucified Christ* and bodies in the *Saint Januarius* explicitly connect the two paintings to Vaccaro's work on the high altar where those victims are depicted in the flames of purgatory. Two women and two men are featured prominently in the foreground, and, as is typical of such representations, all the figures are nude, emphasizing the fact that death recognizes neither gender, nor class, nor profession – a point that is further stressed by the presence of the soul of a religious (a tonsured monk), so many of whom died in the plague. An unusual feature of Vaccaro's painting is the presence of the adult Christ. In

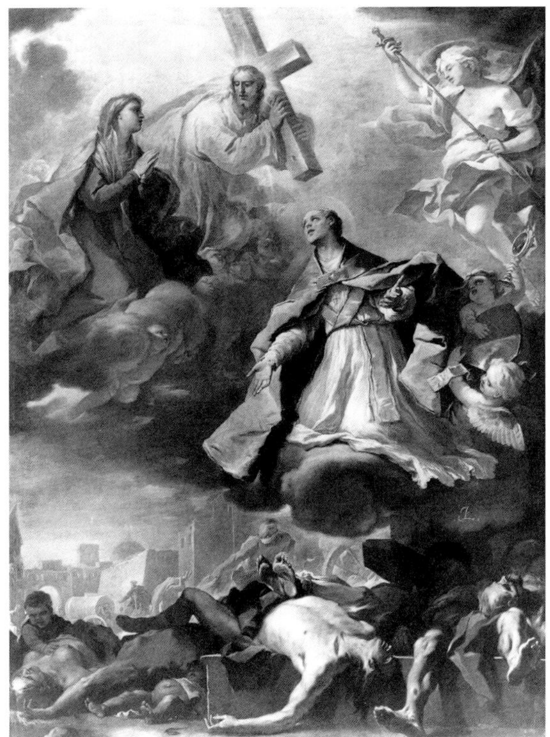

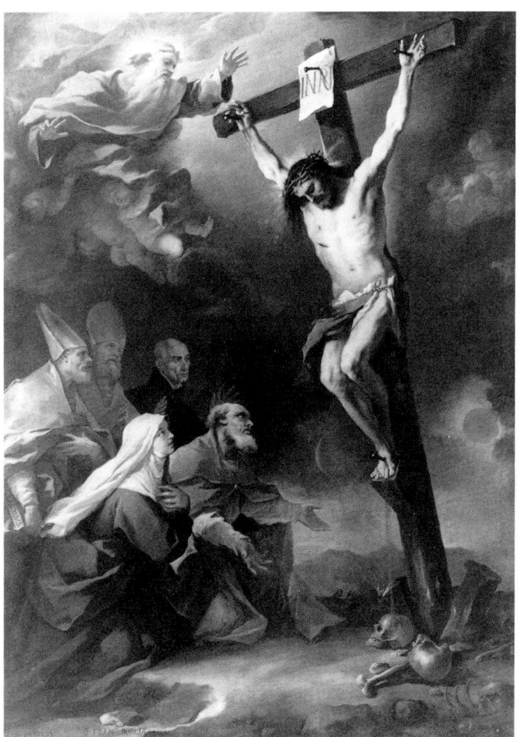

33. Luca Giordano, *Saint Januarius Interceding for the Plague Victims*, ca. 1660-62. Oil on canvas. Museo e Gallerie Nazionali di Capodimonte, Naples.

34. Luca Giordano, *The Crucified Christ with Saints*. ca. 1660-62. Oil on canvas. Museo e Gallerie Nazionali di Capodimonte, Naples.

seventeenth-century Naples, most images of the Madonna of Purgatory represented the souls addressing their pleas to the Virgin and Child. Vaccaro's subordination of the Virgin to Christ, who is represented with scepter and globe as *Salvator mundi*, both emphasizes the ultimate authority in the purgation of sins and reception into heaven and brings the work into accord with Giordano's paintings in the church, both of which feature Christ as the object of adoration and supplication.

In 1745, Bernardo De Dominici described Vaccaro's painting as representing "Our Savior angry at the grievous sins of the Neapolitans, in the act of punishing them with the flail of cruel Pestilence."[25] Similarly, he calls the meek, cross-bearing Christ in Giordano's painting, "the enraged Lord."[26] In fact, none of the three paintings depicts Christ as angered or threatening. In both of Giordano's paintings he is represented explicitly as suffering – with and for the people of Naples – and in Vaccaro's painting he is, at worst, somewhat aloof. De Dominici's mischaracterizations – followed by several writers, even in the twentieth century – may be comprehensible in light of the traditional assessment of the plague as punishment wrought by an angered deity, evident in Domenico Gargiulo's paintings (figs. 26, 31). During the plague of 1656 references were made rather early on to the wrath of God and the punishment of the Neapolitans for their sins, both in official documents and in private accounts. For example, the vow of 12 June to the Immaculate Conception notes that "Divine Justice wants to exercise the rigor merited by our sins," and Carlo Francesco Riaco, who compares the plague to the Last Judgment, describes "Naples target of divine anger, theater of miseries, foyer of disease, field of death, sea of confusion, sepulcher of corpses, Naples judged by the strong arm of the most high."[27] In *La spada della misericordia* ("The Sword of Mercy"), a one-act play of 1657 that takes as its theme the Neapolitan plague of 1656, Francesco Gizzio prefaces the drama with these remarks: "All the punishments of this life are instruments of divine mercy, which flagellates the sorrowful to make them repent and free them from eternal torment, and the just to sanctify them; punish in life, in order not to punish us in death."[28]

With the end of the plague, the mood began to shift. In the celebratory atmosphere the survivors began to forget or block out the pain of the recent past, and the notion of punishment for the wickedness of their ways seemed for many far removed from their present reality. Like a collective sigh of relief, there was a sharp increase in the number of marriages, including unusual ones outside of one's class or with a person considerably older or younger; some took more than one wife. Monks left their orders to marry, and vows to God were forgotten: "many, who in the fervor of the disease had vowed to God to maintain a chaste and penitent life, married, having forgotten their obligation; almost as if the human race stood in danger of being extinguished, and they saw themselves obliged to propagate it."[29] Soon after the plague, the Neapolitans displayed more dissolute and licentious behavior than before. Responding to reports from Melfi in 1660 that three nuns had been raped, Fuidoro wrote: "I can testify that in this kingdom and in [the city of] Naples, there was greater fear of God and of justice before the war of 1647 and the plague of 1656. Now everything is luxury and ostentation, and without substance, and people of the Giudecca [the Jewish ghetto of Naples] keep slaves. Think about it, reader!"[30]

The transformation of Neapolitan mores and even social structure after the plague was the subject of *Napole scontrafatto dapo la pesta*, a lengthy poem in Neapolitan dialect by Giambattista Valentino, first published in 1665.[31]

> Here one saw in fact a change as soon as the plague had finished; each person transformed himself as he wished when he saw the tempest finish, every old shoe was put in shape, at each house there was always a celebration, and the tribulations and weeping having finished, you heard, if not laughter, then music and singing.[32]

The constant revelry that Valentino decries was not limited to private homes, but was everywhere apparent, even at the Grotta degli Sportiglioni, site of the church of S. Maria del Pianto, where a bar of sorts had been erected and the inebriated abounded:

> And that place of eternal memory, I mean the Grotta degli Sportiglioni, that from being a cistern of eternal weeping and wailing became a tavern of so many guzzlers and drunks, as if the dead and the plague-ridden were alive or even resuscitated.
>
> Because six paces from the cemetery there is a lovely eating place where drunkenness reigns and everyone acts capriciously; there one gets from Bacchus every impropriety with music, singing, yells and babble, with thousands and thousands of dishonest women and strumpets curling your hair.
>
> When I saw it, my lord, believe me that I lost my senses and the suffering was such that as if crazed I began to cry, and I said: Oh, crude and heartless people, how can you behave like such rogues, that instead of mourning with sobs, you drink a well of tears?
>
> Then I received a response from a stupid brute, who was short and fat . . . , who among thousands of bacchants seemed as Bacchus; and he raised to his mouth a wine-vessel and said: "Now is not the time for lamentation, since we are not dead from the plague, we always want to make an uproar and celebrate."[33]

There is no accusation of moral culpability in the paintings by Giordano: Christ is not angry but carries his cross or hangs upon it, bleeding for the dead, commiserating with them as if they too were caught as innocents in a destined tragedy. Even in Vaccaro's painting, where the souls must be purged of their terrestrial sins, the sufferings – and thus their guilt–seem minimal. Although the church commemorates the dead, its decoration is clearly directed toward the living, and insofar as the plague could be understood as punishment for the wicked ways of all Neapolitans – including the survivors – the impression given by the paintings is one of absolved guilt. The time for the personal and collective penitence of the Neapolitans ended with the disappearance of the plague. What ensued was a celebration and revived, if also somewhat frenetic and uncontrolled, enjoyment of life – the atmosphere in which the paintings of S. Maria del Pianto were conceived and executed.

The effectiveness of the message of Preti's city gate frescoes and Giordano's *Saint Januarius Interceding for the Plague Victims* – that the horrors of the plague are overcome by celestial intervention – is dependent on a powerful presentation of the dead and dying, especially the giant discolored bodies threatening to tumble into the viewer's space from Giordano's painting. De Dominici took note of the "various cadavers of the plague-stricken so vividly expressed that they inspire horror in the viewers."[34]

No such language characterizes De Dominici's description of the painting of the plague by Domenico Gargiulo that has been connected with the painting of the Largo del Mercatello (fig. 26), although it differs in details. De Dominici emphasizes the naturalism of Gargiulo's work, listing many of the varied activities represented in the painting, implicitly assessing the work as a kind of *reportage*, and Gargiulo is often referred to as a chronicler of his times or is said to have "documented" particular events.[35] In this sense, Gargiulo's work can be related to the host of contemporary accounts of the plague, which consistently stress a first-hand experience: "Of what I write my own eyes have been witnesses, and I would gladly not have experienced it so as not to have seen such misery and so many dead in my afflicted land."[36] But in fact, Gargiulo probably spent rather little time observing closely the effects of the plague on an individual level, especially if he were safely ensconced at the Certosa, and elements in the painting are as conventional here as in the works by Preti, Giordano, and many others. For example, a nursing child at the breast of a dead mother, as Gargiulo depicts at the lower edge of the painting, was said by several writers to have been seen during the plague of Naples,[37] and Salvatore De Renzi went so far to as to assert that Gargiulo had represented one such instance ("among other pitiful scenes, all imitated from reality, but gathered in one visible point").[38] Such a thing may have happened, and Gargiulo might have seen it, but the motif is a literary and artistic convention traceable to antiquity (albeit in reference to battle rather than plague) and often used in the seventeenth century, including Caroselli's copy of Poussin's *Plague at Ashdod* (cat. 1), and the plague scene by Carlo Coppola (cat. 26). Indeed, it recalls Marcantonio Raimondi's *The Plague* (cat. 5), which seems to have been the first instance of its use in the context of the plague and certainly helped popularize the motif.[39] Similarly, in Gargiulo's painting, the broken cart that spills its cargo of corpses to the ground had also appeared in earlier images relating to the plague.[40] Furthermore, Gargiulo has regularized the architecture of the square and displaced the hills above the city to the background where the Bay of Naples should be (and would be blocked by the intervening urban area), rejecting an exact topographical view in the service of a more complete evocation of place. Gargiulo's viewpoint in the painting is unattainably high, resulting in the minimalization of the figures and with it the minimalization (though not trivialization) of the horror depicted. The threatening aspects of the plague are contained by the scene or even by the act of framing the painting.

Thus Gargiulo transforms terror into a precious object for possession. At the time of the

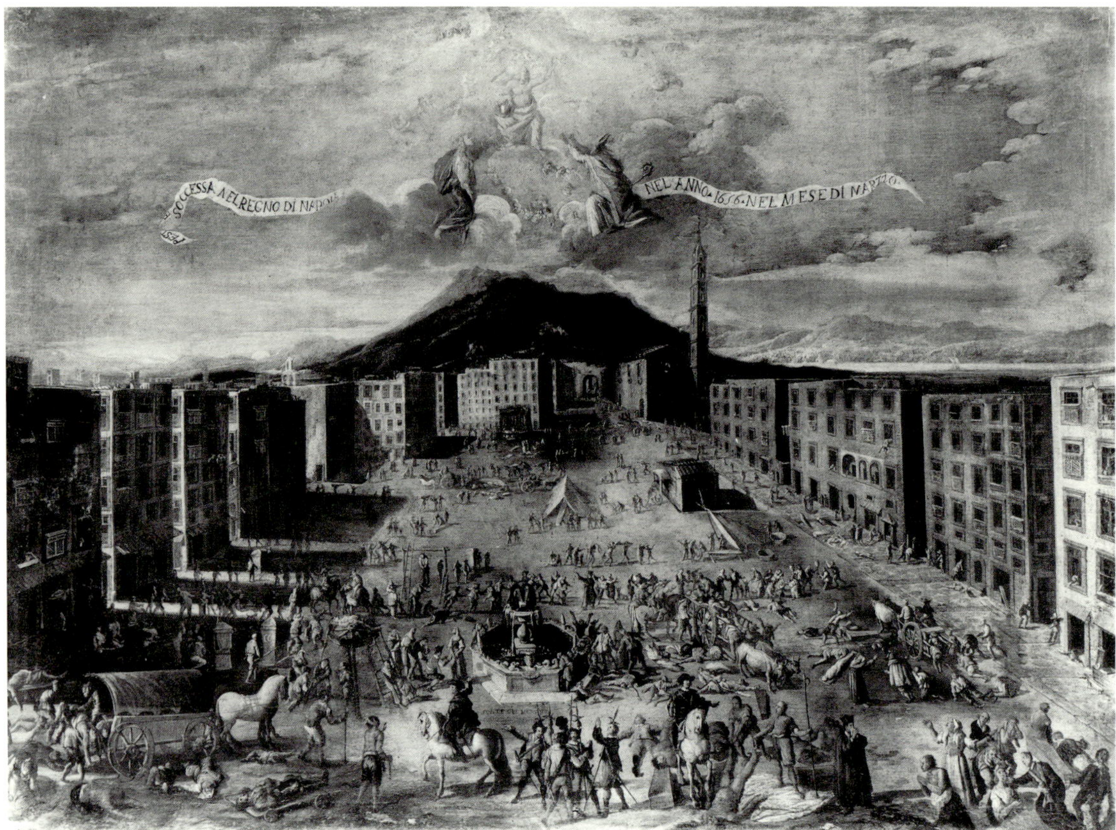

35. Carlo Coppola, *Piazza del Mercato during the Plague of 1656*, ca. 1660. Oil on canvas. Museo di S. Martino, Naples.

plague the individual was threatened with destruction of self, family, and even the civic order as it was then known. Valentino's *Napole scontrafatto dapo la pesta* repeatedly emphasizes the breakdown of societal structure following the plague: religious left their orders, prostitutes married, apprentices suddenly became masters, the lower classes put on the trappings of the upper classes, everyone wanted to be in charge, and no one wanted to obey. Gargiulo did not recall the plague in order to present the threats to the viewer with all their original vigor and terror; rather, he offered it as controllable, non-threatening, rendered impotent, as it were. The putative realism of Gargiulo's painting suggests that seventeenth-century viewers may have read it in the way contemporary audiences read photographs. Thus, as Roland Barthes has argued for photographs, Gargiulo's painting does not provoke a sense of "being there," in which the viewer has the illusion of actually entering the moment the work depicts, but rather of "having been there," recalling the moment, separated by time and distance.[41] Coppola's painting (cat. 26) by contrast, positions the viewer at ground level, near the bodies of the dead as in the compositions by Preti and Giordano, but without their comforting recourse to celestial figures. Gargiulo, on the other hand, separates his viewers from the moment depicted at the same time that he assures them of the veracity of his image. In his ex-voto for the Carthusians (fig. 31), the barriers between "viewer" (the monks) and catastrophic event included the architectural structures separating the Carthusians from the scene below. The explicit separation in the Carthusian picture has become implicit in the *Largo del Mercatello during the Plague* (fig. 26); architectural barriers have been removed, and the artist relies on the high, unnatural viewpoint to assure the viewers of their safe separation from the event.

The effects of such devices are perhaps more evident in a representation of the Piazza del Mercato in Naples during the plague by Carlo Coppola (fig. 35), which is similar to Gargiulo's painting of the Mercatello in size, format, and assumed vantage point. As we would expect, the tiny figures enact the drama of the plague: bodies are loaded onto wagons, a priest gives communion to a dying woman, figures in death throes lurch from upper-story windows, those accused irrationally of disseminating the plague are executed, and so on. Coppola's composition is much more highly ordered than Gargiulo's: the piazza is completely surrounded by buildings, rather than being left open on one side; Coppola's buildings are treated much more regularly and geometrically, and they cast deep, even shadows across the piazza; even the supposedly frantic figures are carefully arranged in rows parallel to the bottom edge of the canvas. Coppola's banderole in the sky above the piazza, which announces that the work depicts "the plague that occurred in the Kingdom of Naples in the year 1656, in the month of March," is a verbal intrusion into the pictorial field that places emphasis on the distance in time of the event, as well as on the artifice of representation. Parts of the image are labeled in block capitals, most noticeably the fountain in the center, again emphasizing the two-dimensional surface, the separation of viewer from event, and giving the viewer an additional means – a verbal one – of controlling the event depicted. If "art is a matter of imposing order on chaos," as E. H. Gombrich has asserted,[42] it is particularly so here. Through artifice, the viewer may gain tangible possession of and control over a threatening, anarchic event.

This essay derives from my Ph.D. dissertation (Clifton 1987), parts of which were published as Clifton 1990, Clifton 1993, and Clifton 1994. In some instances, fuller discussion and documentation may be found in those publications. Unless otherwise noted, all translations are mine.

1. Campanile, 712.
2. On the painting, see Sestieri and Daprà, 294-95; Daprà, 150-51.
3. Celano, 1401-02.
4. Weinstein, 265, 267.
5. A two-sided sheet of chalk sketches of figures relating to the project recently appeared on the market (Colnaghi 1995, no. 21).
6. In Rossa, 13, 48-49.
7. From a copy of the sworn testimony of seven nuns of Suor Orsola's convent, 1656 (Archivio Segreto Vaticano, MS Nunziatura di Napoli, 54, 519v).
8. Pasquale, 29.
9. *Ragguaglio della miracolosa protezione*, 82-83. The curative effects of images of saints are also evident in the painting of *A Miracle of Saint John of God* (cat. 29).
10. Carrafa, 210r, no. 18.
11. See also, for example, Tommaso Fasano's *Madonna del Carmine and a Procession for the Plague* (*Civiltà del Seicento*, 1:269).
12. Archivio Segreto Vaticano, MS Nunziatura di Napoli, 54, 409v.-410r.
13. Archivio Segreto Vaticano, MS Nunziatura di Napoli, 54, 448r.
14. Rosso, 8:7.
15. Rosso, 8:30-31.
16. The contract is transcribed in Clifton 1993, 344-45.
17. Riaco, 184ff.
18. Pentimalli, 81.
19. On the church and its decoration, see Strazzullo; Wethey; *Luca Giordano 1634-1705*, 122-23. Giulio Spinola reported that the cave was already full by 24 June and gave the tally of sixty thousand bodies (Archivio Segreto Vaticano, MS Nunziatura di Napoli, 54, 541r). Campanile, 711, puts the number at fifty thousand.
20. Pointed out by Wethey, 678.
21. For a list of major benefactors, see Strazzullo, 222, and Nappi, 34.
22. Fuidoro, 1:125 (quoted by Strazzullo, 222).
23. The legacy of Bernardo De Dominici's colorful (and erroneous) account of the genesis of the paintings out of a putative competition between Giordano and Vaccaro for the prime location of the high altar (involving not only the Count of Peñaranda but also Pietro da Cortona, Andrea Sacchi, Gianlorenzo Bernini and others as judges) has been that three paintings have not been treated as a coherent iconographic ensemble. See De Dominici 1729, 14-15, and De Dominici 1742-45, 3:145-47, 398-99.
24. The reasons for including these particular saints are unclear. Only Saint Eufebius and Saint Asprenus (as well as Saint Januarius) were among the dozen protector saints of Naples appearing on maps of the city produced by Alessandro Baratta in 1629 (labelled "Patroni Fidelissima Vrbis Neapolitanae"; see *Civiltà del Seicento*, 1:91) and Pietro Miotte in 1648 (see De Seta, 148). Wethey, 681, suggests that the Blessed Francis Borgia may have been particularly admired by the Count of Peñaranda.
25. De Dominici 1742-45, 3:147.
26. De Dominici 1742-45, 3:399, although in his earlier *vita* of Giordano, he had more correctly described "Our Lord Jesus Christ, who carries the cross on his shoulder" (De Dominici 1729, 14).
27. Riaco, 155-56.
28. "La spada della misericordia," in Gizzio, 2:198. For other references to the sins of the Neapolitans and the wrath of God, see Rubino, 696; Campanile, 679; Gatta, 7-9; Pasquale, n. pag. (in the dedication); and "Per la Peste di Napoli," in Gaudiosi, 62.
29. "Relazione del contagio," n. pag.
30. Fuidoro, 1:52.
31. On the poem, see Massa's introduction to the cited edition (Valentino, 1-20), as well as Pironti.
32. Valentino, 30.
33. Valentino, 63-64.
34. De Dominici 1729, 15.
35. De Dominici 1742-45, 3:196-98. The same may be said of De Dominici's comments on Gargiulo's other famous large-scale paintings of recent events, the Eruption of Vesuvius of 1631 and the Revolt of Masaniello of 1647. The assumption by most scholars, including myself (Clifton 1987), that Gargiulo's painting of the Largo del Mercatello during the plague formed part of a series (at least informally) with these two paintings has been corrected on documentary grounds in a stimulating study of his works by Christopher Marshall, who suggests that the plague and Vesuvius paintings may have been associated with each other, apart from the Masaniello painting (Marshall, 483-84 and 495, n. 27).
36. Rubino, 696; cf. "Relazione della pestilenza," 349; Pasquale, 2; Campanile, 710; Celano, 1401-02.
37. Gatta, 25; Pasquale, 58; Campanile, 713; "Relazione Del contagio," n. pag.
38. De Renzi, 78, n. 1.
39. Bellori, 430, writing in regard to Poussin's painting, nicely indicates the affective function of the motif: "another baby, not dead but still breathing, holding its hand on the maternal breast, bringing its mouth to the breast to suck the milk, increases sympathy and the gloomy appearance."
40. Mollaret and Brossollet, 16.
41. Barthes, 44.
42. Gombrich, 94.

Bibliography

Barthes, Roland. "Rhetoric of the Image." In *Image Music Text*, traanslated by Stephen Heath, 32-81. London, 1977.

Bellori, Giovan Pietro. *Le Vite de' pittori, scultori e architetti moderni*, edited by Evelina Borra. Turin, 1976.

Campanile, Giuseppe. "Della Peste di Napoli dell'Anno Bisestile 1656." MS XXVI.D.5, 679-722. Naples, Biblioteca della Società Napoletana della Storia Patria.

Carrafa, Placido. "Capitoli della Gare trà Gesuiti e Teatini nel occasione della famosa Predica S. Ignatio fatta dal P[ad]re Placido Carrafa Eletto Vescovo della Acerra." MS XI.E.19, fols. 208r-211v. Naples, Biblioteca Nazionale.

Celano, Carlo. *Notizie del bello dell'antico e del curioso della Città di Napoli*. 1692. Reprint, edited by A. Mozzillo, A. Profeta, and F. P. Macchia, Naples, 1970.

Civiltà del Seicento a Napoli. Exh. cat. 2 vols. Naples, Museo di Capodimonte and Museo Pignatelli, 1984.

Clifton, James. "Images of the Plague and Other Contemporary Events in Seventeenth-Century Naples." Ph.D. diss. Princeton University, 1987.

—"Micco Spadaro at the Certosa di San Martino in Naples: The Plague Ex-Voto of 1656." *Ricerche sul '600 napoletano* (1990): 85-99.

—"Mattia Preti's *Madonna of Constantinople* and a Marian Cult in Seventeenth-Century Naples." In *Parthenope's Splendor: Art of the Golden Age in Naples*, edited by Jeanne Chenault Porter and Susan Scott Munshower, 336-63. Papers in Art History from The Pennsylvania State University, vol. 7. University Park, Pennsylvania, 1993.

—"Mattia Preti's Frescoes for the City Gates of Naples," *The Art Bulletin* 76 (1994): 479-501.

Daprà, Brigitte. *Micco Spadaro: Napoli ai tempi di Masaniello*. Exh. cat. Naples: Certosa di San Martino, 2002.

[De Dominici, Bernardo.] *Vita del Cavalier D. Luca Giordano*. Naples, 1729.

De Dominici, Bernardo. *Vite de' pittori, scultori ed architetti napoletani*. 3 vols. Naples, 1742-1745.

De Renzi, Salvatore. Napoli nell'anno 1656. 1867. Reprint. Naples, 1968.

De Seta, Cesare. *Napoli*. 2ND ed. Rome and Bari, 1984

Fuidoro, Innocenzo [Vincenzo D'Onofrio]. *Giornale di Napoli dal MCDLX al MDCLXXX*. Cronache e documenti per la storia dell'Italia meridionale dei secoli XVI e XVII, 5. Naples, 1934.

Gatta, Geronimo. *Di vna gravissima peste, che nella passata Primauera, & Estate dell'anno 1656. depopulò la Citta di Napoli, suoi Borghi, e Casali, e molte altre Città, e Terre del suo Regno*. Naples, 1659.

Gaudiosi, Tommaso. *L'arpa poetica*. Naples, 1671.

Gizzio, Francesco. *L'echo armoniosa delle sfere celesti cioè la corrispondenza de' santi con le Virtù, alla Gratia Divina*. 2 vols. Naples, 1693.

Gombrich, E. H. *Norm and Form: Studies in the Art of the Renaissance*. London, 1966.

Luca Giordano 1634-1705. Exh. cat. Los Angeles County Museum of Art, 2001.

Marshall, Christopher R. "Causa di Stravaganze": Order and Anarchy in Domenico Gargiulo's *Revolt of Masaniello*." *The Art Bulletin* 80 (1998), 478-97.

Mollaret, Henri H., and Jacqueline Brossollet. "La Peste, source méconnue d'inspiration artistique." *Koninlijk Museum voor schone Kunsten. Jaarboek* (1965), 3-112.

Nappi, Eduardo. *Aspetti della società e dell'economia napoletana durante la peste del 1656. Dai documenti dell'Archivio Storico del Banco di Napoli*. Naples, 1980.

Pasquale, Niccolò. *A' posteri della peste di Napoli, e suo Regno nell'Anno 1656. dalla redentione del mondo*. Naples, 1668.

Pentimalli, Maleagro. *Vita del gran patriarca S. Bruno cartvsiano*. Rome, 1622.

Pironti, Pasquale. "La peste a Napoli del 1656 nel poemetto di G. B. Valentino." *Il Rievocatore* 18 (1967), 7-9.

Ragguaglio della miracolosa protezione di S. Francesco Saverio apostolo delle Indie verso la Città, e il Regno di Napoli nel contagio del MDCLVI. 1660. Reprint Naples, 1743.

"Relazione del contagio di Napoli, e suo Regno dell'Anno Bisestile 1656, con quanto più di memorabile avvenne in d[ett]o tempo." In "Historia." MS. XV.G.29. Naples, Biblioteca Nazionale.

"Relazione della pestilenza accaduta in Napoli l'anno 1656." Ed. Giuseppe De Blasiis. *Archivio storico per le province napoletane* 1 (1876), 323-57.

Riaco, Carlo Francesco. *Il giudicio di Napoli. Discorso del passato contaggio rassomigliato al Giudicio Vniuersale*. Naples, 1658.

Rossa, Antonio. *Relatione della Sollennissima Festa fatta in Napoli all'Immacolata Co[n]cettione di MARIA per lo scioglimento del Voto fatto dalla medesima Città nell'Anno del contagio 1656*. Naples, 1661.

Rosso, Gregorio. "Istoria delle cose di Napoli sotto l'imperio di Carlo V." In *Raccolta di tutti i più rinomati scrittori dell'istoria generale del Regno di Napoli*, vol. 8. Naples, 1770.

Rubino, Andrea. "Peste crudele in Napoli." *Archivio storico per le province napoletane* 19 (1894), 696-710.

Sestieri, Giancarlo, and Brigitte Daprà. *Domenico Gargiulo detto Micco Spadaro paesaggista e "cronista" napoletano*. Milan, 1994.

Strazzullo, Franco. "Documenti per la Chiesa di S. Maria del Pianto." *Napoli nobilissima* 4 (1965): 222-25.

Valentino, Giambattista. *Napole scontrafatto dapo la peste*. Ed. Sebastiano di Massa. Naples, n.d.

Weinstein, Donald. "Critical Issues in the Study of Civic Religion in Renaissance Florence." In *The Pursuit of Holiness in Late Medieval and Renaissance Religion: Papers from the University of Michigan Conference*, edited by Charles Trinkaus with Heiko A. Oberman, 265-70. Studies in Medieval and Reformation Thought, vol. 10. Leiden, 1974.

Wethey, Harold E. "The Spanish Viceroy, Luca Giordano, and Andrea Vaccaro." *Burlington Magazine* 109 (1967), 678-87.

Anthony van Dyck, the Cult of Saint Rosalie, and the 1624 Plague in Palermo

Gauvin Alexander Bailey

Italian cities often sought deliverance from pestilence by enlisting the help of local saints who subsequently combined the roles of city patron and plague saint. We have seen several examples of this in this catalogue, notably Saint Januarius, patron of Naples, or Saint Charles Borromeo, his counterpart in Milan. Such saints often dated back to Early Christian or medieval times and their cults were only resurrected in the context of the plague in the early modern period. Borromeo, a contemporary figure who played an active role in the post-Tridentine reconstruction of the church, was a famous exception. Yet few saints played such an all-encompassing role in the lives of their home cities as Saint Rosalie, whose name has become almost synonymous with her birthplace, the plague-ridden metropolis of Palermo. Saint Rosalie fit many of the usual categories: she was a medieval saint whose ties with the plague were tenuous at best, yet who enjoyed a carefully orchestrated "rediscovery" during the plague of 1624, and would forever be associated with it. But Rosalie arguably enjoyed – and continues to enjoy – a higher profile in her own city than any other plague saint in Italy. The beloved *Santuzza* has become Palermo's primary patron, outstripping her rivals Christina, Ninfa, Oliva and Agatha; her effigy stares down at visitors from the city's domes and church towers; and the civic calendar culminates in a celebration in her honor between 10 and 15 July. During this Festino di Santa Rosalia, Palermo hosts an extravagant and fiendishly costly procession involving a massive ship on wheels called *il carro* (in 1974 it held as many as fifty musicians), grandiose firework displays, concerts, horse races, and street food ranging from pumpkin seeds and toasted chickpeas sold by the *siminzari* (seed sellers) to a kind of tiny snail called *babbaluci d'u festino*.[1] Even the local football team, Calcio Palermo, wears a very unmanly pink in honor of their patroness.

Only one figure can approach Rosalie's fame in his association with plague in Palermo, and his memory is merged inseparably with Rosalie's own. The Flemish painter Anthony van Dyck (1599-1641) almost single-handedly created Rosalie's iconography as we know it today: the full-figured, blonde or auburn-haired saint wearing a Franciscan habit and crowned with flowers who is still reproduced in holy cards, coral figurines in the dioramas known as *capezzali*, and traditional glass paintings. The young van Dyck spent almost a year and a half in Palermo between the early spring of 1624 and September of 1625 – much longer than is usually attested to in the scholarship – a sojourn that was at once terrifying and extremely good for business. During those plague-ridden months, thanks to a sudden need for an iconography to celebrate the newly rediscovered saint and some friends in high places, van Dyck turned from painting portraits of the viceroy and wealthy Genovese merchants to a series of Rosalie pictures, and developed four main iconographic prototypes for the saint. Nevertheless, he was not the first to work out a new Rosalie imagery, and – contrary to the widely held belief – he studied closely the work of Sicilian artists in developing his imagery, particularly the work of Vincenzo La Barbera (1605-1637), a little-known palermitan artist who may have painted Rosalie's first image during the plague year 1624.

In this chapter I will look at this Sicilian influence and attempt a more precise dating for van Dyck's Saint Rosalie series based on this new evidence. I will also consider a much more surprising legacy enjoyed by one of van Dyck's followers, the virtually unknown Tuscan sculptor Gregorio Tedeschi (late sixteenth century-ca. 1634). Although never recognized as such, Tedeschi's sculpted image of the dying Saint Rosalie at the Santuario di Monte Pellegrino (1625) is the first sculpture of a recumbent dying saint in the history of Italian Baroque sculpture, and I will trace a theoretical link between this work and Bernini's much more famous *Blessed Ludovico Albertoni* (1671-74) via the figure of Melchiorre Cafà (1635-1667), a little-known Maltese sculptor whose recumbent *Saint Rose of Lima* (1665) – named after her namesake from Peru – is generally regarded as the precursor of Bernini's masterpiece.

The historical Saint Rosalie (d. ca. 1160) was allegedly the daughter of Sinibaldo, a nobleman at the court of King Roger of Sicily, niece of William II (1130-1160), and a descendent of Charlemagne.[2] Rejecting marriage at the age of sixteen, Rosalie abandoned the sensual pleasures of the Norman aristocracy and moved to a cave near her parents' home on the top of Monte Pellegrino, where she spent the rest of her life as a recluse, carving her resolution on the wall and receiving a crown of roses from angelic visitors.[3] She probably took the habit of a Basilian nun, since the Greek rite was dominant in Norman Sicily and her earliest icon (fig. 36) comes from the Basilian convent adjacent to S. Maria dell'Ammiraglio (la Martorana).[4] Although Rosalie was largely forgotten in the Middle Ages and her name did not appear in any of the old martyrologies, a few local churches were dedicated to her in the thirteenth century, including a well-known one in nearby Bivona. In the mid-sixteenth century a community of Franciscan anchorites established a small convent on Monte Pellegrino in homage to Rosalie, although it was dedicated to the Virgin of the Immaculate Conception. Living in caves and small huts, these anchorites became known as the Romiti di Montepellegrino. One of them, San Benedetto da Sanfratello (called Il moro, 1525-89), began to research the whereabouts of Rosalie's body in 1585.[5]

As Franco Mormando notes in his introduction to this catalogue, Rosalie's life fell into a common hagiographical pattern: that of the virgin recluse who left a life of riches to live as a hermit, dying in a renunciation of the flesh that was considered a kind of "martyrdom."[6]

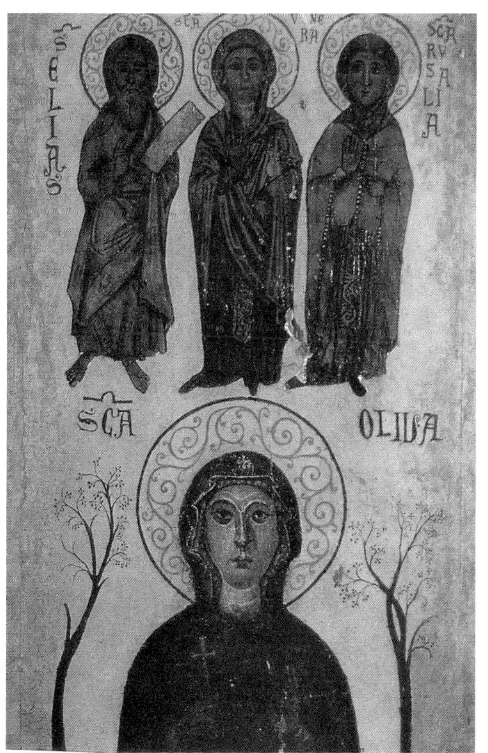

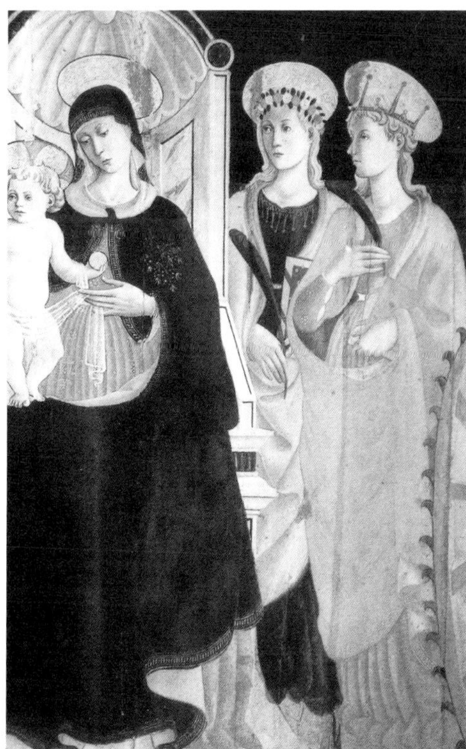

36. *Saints Oliva, Elia, Venera, and Rosalie*, thirteenth century. Italo-Byzantine icon, tempera on panel. Museo Diocesano, Palermo.

37. *Sacra Conversazione with Saint Rosalie*, mid-fifteenth century. Pisan, tempera on panel. Museo Nazionale, Pisa.

However, her rediscovery in early modern times reflected a particular historical phenomenon: the Palaeochristian Revival Movement. This movement first arose in Rome under Pope Gregory XIII and gained momentum under Clement VIII in preparation for the 1600 Papal Jubilee.[7] An ideological restoration of the era of the Early Church, the movement aimed to return to the purity of Christianity's first centuries in the wake of the Council of Trent. In Rome it was marked by the restoration and renovation – often in a heavy-handed manner – of ancient basilicas and churches. Cardinal patrons were especially active in restoring their titular churches, including Cardinal Rusticucci's church of S. Susanna, Cardinal Giustiniani's S. Prisca, and Cardinal Sfondrato's S. Cecilia in Trastevere. One of the most active of these cardinals was the Oratorian Cesare Baronio, whose history of the Church, called the *Annales Ecclesiastici* (1588-1607), begun at the request of Filippo Neri, became the classic text of the Palaeochristian Revival.[8] The movement especially favored the cult of early Christian martyrs. The relics of these often obscure saints would come to light in highly orchestrated "discoveries" – the most famous being that of Saint Cecilia in 1599 – and they would then be borne aloft in spectacular Roman-style triumphal parades, as in the case of saints Nereo, Achilleo, and Domitilla, whose processions passed through the triumphal arches in the Forum on their way to Baronio's titular church in 1597.[9]

Rosalie's "discovery" during the plague of 1624 bore all the earmarks of the Palaeochristian Revival Movement, even though she was a medieval saint herself. The plague was the worst ever to visit the city. Breaking out in June of 1624, it claimed almost ten thousand victims – including the viceroy Emanuele Filiberto – before it ended in May of 1625. All public buildings except churches were closed, as were the city gates, and lazarettos were built outside the city to house the sick, including a particularly large one near the port that also served as a quarantine for visitors.[10] According to legend, a vision led a lone hunter to discover Rosalie's bones in her cave on Monte Pellegrino on July 15, and instructed him that if he carried her bones through the city the plague would end. Civil and ecclesiastical authorities wasted no time in accepting the relics as authentic. On July 27, church officials acknowledged Rosalie as the intercessor and patron of the city, and images of the renewed saint began to proliferate. Half a year later, on February 22, 1625, the Church declared her relics to be genuine, and on the same day the Senate announced that the city would build chapels to Saint Rosalie in the cathedral (to the right of the high altar) and in the cave in Monte Pellegrino.[11] In a solemn procession reminiscent of those of the Palaeochristian Revival in Rome, Saint Rosalie's relics were carried from Monte Pellegrino to the cathedral, a route that is retraced every year during the Festino.[12] The ending of the plague shortly thereafter confirmed Rosalie's cult as a plague saint and patron for the city.

Rosalie's cult flourished in the years that followed. Antonio Cuccia has divided its development into three phases.[13] In the first, between the discovery of Rosalie's bones in 1624 and 1630, when her name was inscribed in the *Martyrologium Romanum*, the cult was promoted not only by civic officials and the Archbishop of Palermo Giovanni (or Giannettino) Doria, but also by the Jesuits, who enjoyed an influential presence in the city.[14] The Jesuits were the first to carry an image of Rosalie in procession (it was housed in the Palermo Gesù) on 1 August 1624, and soon afterward they dedicated a chapel to her in that same church.[15] Their interest in Rosalie stemmed partly from their location, as the neighborhoods near their church, like the Kalsa, were among the worst hit by the pestilence.[16] The Jesuits would later introduce Rosalie's cult into Rome, Antwerp, and Paris.[17]

During the second phase in the development of Rosalie's cult, between 1630 and 1651, the canonic form of her hagiography was firmly established. The year 1651 marks the publication in Palermo of *Di Santa Rosalia romita palermitana...libri tre*, an illustrated reconstruction of her cult from medieval times by Giordano Cascini, the former Jesuit Provincial of Palermo (in office, 1626-29), which resembled the kind of archaeological martyrs' treatises published in Rome by Baronio and others.[18] This book sets forth the story of her life and the subsequent development of her cult. It is an especially important document to art historians, thanks to its fifteen illustrations of Rosalie's rare pre-1624 imagery. The final phase of the cult, much more triumphalist and celebratory in nature, dates from the mid-seventeenth century onward, and witnessed the expansion of her cult into literature, panegyrics, and fully organized festivals.[19]

Pre-1624 Iconography of Saint Rosalie

Even though her cult has medieval origins, very little pre-1624 imagery for Saint Rosalie survives. Nevertheless, the basic elements of her reconstructed iconography were already present in these early depictions. In the Italo-Byzantine icon from la Martorana – the earliest known image of the saint – Rosalie is included in a trio of figures above a much larger image of Saint Oliva (fig. 36). She probably wears the habit of a Basilian nun, a brown cowl with a leather belt, which would frequently be confused with that of a Franciscan or Dominican nun later on, although some scholars maintain that it is a Benedictine habit instead.[20] Rosalie's companions in the painting, saints Elia, Venera, and Oliva, were all founders of monastic orders, and Venera was a plague saint, having been invoked officially during the plagues of 1494 and 1530. Rosalie stands in a fully frontal pose, with her right hand open in the Greek Orthodox sign of benediction and her left hand grasping a Byzantine cross.[21]

Rosalie's image next appears between the late fourteenth to mid-fifteenth century in an unexpected place: Tuscany.[22] The city of Pisa enjoyed sporadic contacts with Palermo from as early as 1064, but with their loss of Sardinia in 1324-25 Pisans increased their investment of capital in Sicily, and an artistic exchange ensued. On one hand, several Pisan paintings were exported to Sicily, along with the occasional artist such as Iacopo di Michele (Gera da Pisa, fl. 1371-95); on the other hand, the cult of Saint Rosalie was exported to Pisa. In Pisan depictions, Rosalie is always blonde, and she usually wears the modest but elegant garment of an aristocratic woman (predominantly pink in color, in reference to her name), although she sometimes appears in the homespun robe of an Augustinian. She usually wears a crown of roses (either pink or a combination of white and red – the red signifying martyrdom), and holds a martyr's palm and a book. In one case she wears a ring on her right ring finger, and sometimes a skull serves as a symbol of her penitence. Four panel paintings survive from local Pisan churches, the oldest of which is a polyptych by Francesco Traini (active 1321-63) in which she appears among the right-hand lateral saints flanking an image of the Madonna and Child. Two others are large *sacre conversazioni* in which she appears as one of a pair of saints on the right side of the Madonna and Child (fig. 37). The latest panel is by Ghirlandaio (1449-1494) in the Museo Nazionale in Pisa.

In the mid-fifteenth century, Sicilian painters took up painting Rosalie again. Antonello da Messina, the most important Sicilian painter of the period, executed a bust portrait of Saint Rosalie reading, *Virgin Mary Reading (?)* (ca. 1445-50), in which a pair of angels lowers a golden crown laced with white and red roses on her head (fig. 38). Antonello here adapts from the iconography of the Virgin Annunciate, a subject he treated in another painting that originally formed part of the same collection.[23] The imagery is so closely related that the only indication that Rosalie is not the Virgin Mary is that she is only wearing a single star of pearls on her mantle instead of the three stars traditional on images of the Madonna. Antonello painted Rosalie again in a version for S. Cassiano in Venice (ca. 1474-75), in which she stands next to Saint Liberalis in a simple but aristocratic gown with a crown of roses in her hair.[24] Tommaso de Vigilia (ca. 1435-1497), the most noteworthy painter of Western Sicily in the fif-

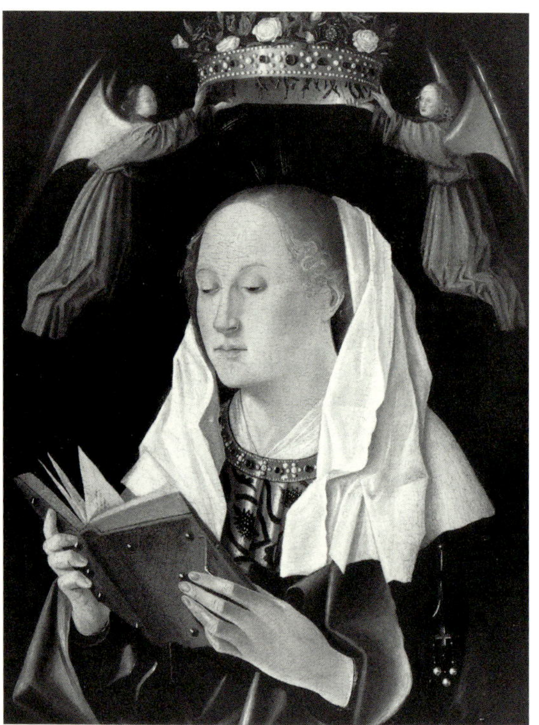

38. Attributed to Antonello da Messina, *Virgin Mary Reading(?)*, ca. 1460-69. Oil on panel. The Walters Art Museum, Baltimore.

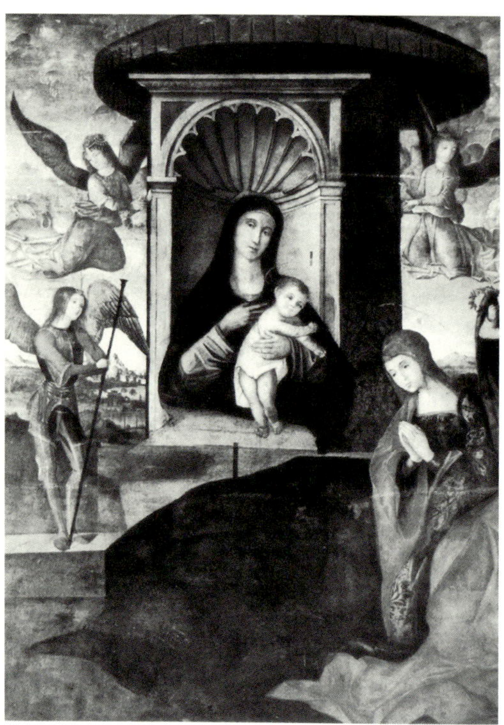

39. Riccardo Quartararo, *Madonna and Child with Saint Rosalie*, 1506. Oil on panel. Galleria Regionale di Sicilia, Palermo.

teenth century, painted two altarpieces entitled *Coronation of Saint Rosalie* in 1494 for the churches of S. Rosalia and S. Agata in Bivona.[25] In these two paintings, preserved as engravings in Cascini's study, Rosalie wears the clothes of a young noblewoman (although in one version the Franciscan cord is visible underneath) and she kneels before the Madonna and Child, while the infant Jesus places a golden crown and crown of roses on her head.

In at least one pre-1624 painting, Rosalie appears in the decorative program of a hospital, foretelling her later association with illness. A lost fresco on the east wall of the entrance hall of the Ospedale Grande di Palermo, now the Palazzo Sclafani, included Rosalie above a scene of the *Last Judgment* as one of the "Five Virgin Saints, Protectors of Palermo" (including Agatha, Christina, Ninfa, and Oliva). All are shown as half-figure portraits above a view of Palermo, Rosalie in the middle crowned with roses and holding her hands together praying for God's intercession.[26] The fresco may have been executed in thanksgiving for protection from the plague of 1529-30, a pestilence that hit Messina but not Palermo. This painting might have merited only a footnote had it not been executed in the same hallway as the famous late fifteenth-century *Triumph of Death* fresco (originally on the west wall) now in the Galleria Regionale della Sicilia.

One of the last pre-1624 Rosalie paintings of note was the *Madonna and Child with Saint Rosalie* (fig. 39) by the Agrigento painter Riccardo Quartararo (1443-1507). Painted in the year of his death and left unfinished, it was executed for the little church of S. Rosalia Inglobata in Palermo, once next to the still-extant chapel of S. Caterina all'Olivella and said to be the location of her family house.[27] The panel shows Rosalie kneeling before an image of the Madonna and Child, dressed as a noblewoman in rich turquoise and red robes, accompanied by an angel who places a crown of red roses on her head. On the opposite side, Saint Michael offers her a staff, either for self-defense or as a symbol of pilgrimage. Especially noteworthy is the fact that it is the first Rosalie image to include a depiction of the two hills associated with her life as an anchorite, Monte Pellegrino and nearby Quisquina.

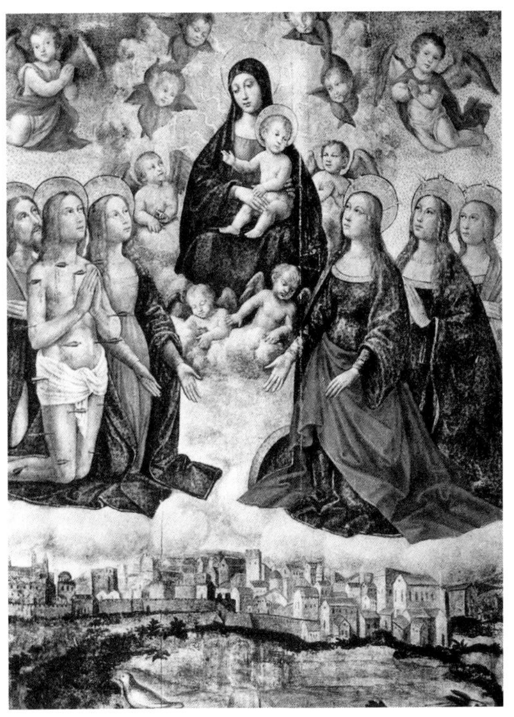

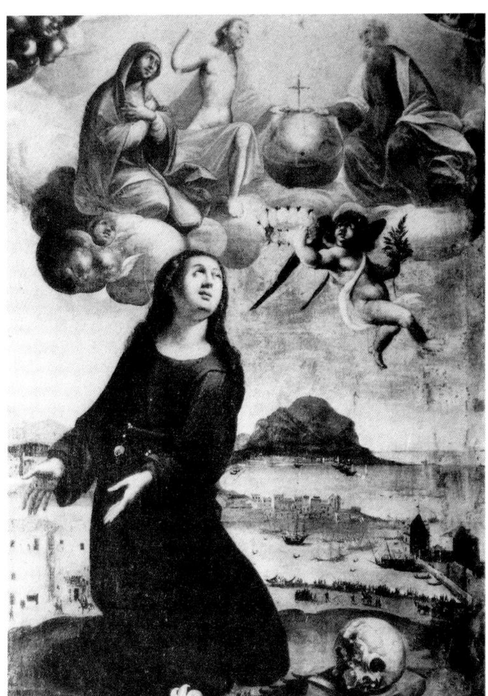

40. Mario di Laurito, *The Holy Protector Saints of Palermo Intercede for the City*, 1530. Oil on panel. Museo Diocesano, Palermo.

41. Vincenzo La Barbera, *Saint Rosalie Intercedes for Palermo*, 1624. Oil on canvas. Museo Diocesano, Palermo.

In the fifteenth century, Rosalie's ties to plague grew stronger. In *The Holy Protector Saints of Palermo Intercede for the City* (1530), now attributed to the Neapolitan painter Mario di Laurito (fl. 1503-36) and commissioned by the palermitan Senate on the occasion of the 1529 plague in Eastern Sicily, eight saints kneel in the clouds above a topographically accurate cityscape of Palermo and below the Madonna and Child (fig. 40).[28] Although Rosalie is one of many saints – including the universal plague saints Sebastian and Roch as well as Venera, Cristina, Ninfa, Agata, and Oliva – and even though she is only barely visible, she is nevertheless clearly associated with deliverance from the plague. Rosalie wears a generic nun's habit, neither Basilian nor Benedictine. A panel and fresco, now lost, that were executed forty-five years later during the 1575 plague in Western Sicily for churches in Mazara (Trapani) and Bivona, are noteworthy in that they also include Rosalie among more traditional plague saints such as Saint Roch and the local Saint Venera. This handful of fifteenth-century works demonstrates an association between Saint Rosalie and the plague even before 1624, although the link was expressed *sotto voce*.[29]

Saint Rosalie's solo debut as a plague saint took place when the Jesuits processed their sixteenth-century painting of Rosalie through the streets of Palermo on 1 August 1624. The procession was a futile attempt to save the life of Viceroy Emanuele Filiberto, who had fallen deeply ill. Although the original of this painting no longer exists, a 1745 copy by Vito D'Anna in the Gesù shows that it was based closely on the original icon in la Martorana, showing the saint in a frontal pose giving the sign of benediction and wearing the habit of a Greek Rite anchorite, although with the addition of an angel holding a crown of red roses in the upper right.[30] Rosalie's debut is very significant for our discussion of van Dyck's contributions to Rosalie imagery. The Jesuits' choice of this older painting for the procession suggests that no new iconography had yet been created, and therefore Teresa Pugliatti proposes this date as the *terminus post quem* for any 1624 imagery of the saint.[31]

The scholarship is unanimous in attributing the next stage in the development of Rosalie's iconography to Anthony van Dyck and his celebrated series of Rosalie canvases, of which two are in the present exhibition (cats. 30, 31). There can be no doubt that van Dyck made the most important contribution to Rosalie's revival in the wake of the 1624 plague, conceiving a rich and original repertoire of imagery for the saint and invigorating the style of palermitan painting for generations to come with his energetic impasto and monumental figure types. Nevertheless, I propose that he was not the first artist to create a new iconography for Rosalie, and my identification of Vincenzo La Barbera as his precursor suggests a new time frame for van Dyck's Rosalie series.

From Termini Imerese, a small town East of Palermo, La Barbera (ca. 1577- ca. 1651) was a little-known architect and painter whose career spanned the transition from late Renaissance to Baroque.[32] La Barbera was invited to Palermo in 1622 to design the *apparati* for the Jesuit celebrations of the canonization of saints Ignatius of Loyola and Francis Xavier, and he played a key role in conceiving the decoration of the interior of the Gesù in the lavish marble *mischio* that makes it one of the most splendid in Sicily.[33] It may have been La Barbera's Jesuit connections that got him the commission from the palermitan Senate to paint the first image of the renewed Saint Rosalie on 27 July 1624, a work that debuted in a procession through the city on 4 September of the same year.

Recently restored for the 2004 re-opening of the Museo Diocesano, this canvas depicts the saint, this time a brunette, kneeling before a splendid panoramic view of Palermo with Monte Pellegrino at the center and the giant lazaretto near the port on the lower left (fig. 41).[34] Rosalie wears the brown habit of a Franciscan with a cord around her waist; at her feet are a white lily (a symbol of virginity and a play on her name: *rosa* + *lilia*) and a book with a skull resting on it. For the first time, the skull here does not merely represent her life of penitence, but symbolizes the plague dead and also her relics, which were at that time being tested by ecclesiastical authorities. It also serves as a *memento mori*, reflecting a resurgence of such symbolism in the lay culture of the period. An example of a secular work on that theme is Giovanni Martinelli's *Memento Mori* (*Death Comes to the Dinner Table*) of ca. 1635-59, in which a skeleton with an hourglass rudely interrupts a lavish banquet (cat. 4).[35] Rosalie's Franciscan garb can be related to the role the Franciscans played in reviving the cult of Monte Pellegrino, and the skull also recalls Franciscan imagery.[36] To Rosalie's right an angel lowers a crown of pink roses onto her head, and above we see the Holy Trinity with the globe of the world and the Madonna praying for intercession. The landscape and the figure of Rosalie are the most accomplished parts of the canvas, while the notably weaker upper part is probably the work of assistants. Recent scholarship has attributed to La Barbera a much poorer quality version of this work (ca. 1625), this time with the saint on the right and a pile of oversized corpses on the left, but its style seems quite different.[37]

La Barbera was not a great painter, and his contribution to early Baroque painting would have been negligible had he not painted this image at the same time that one of the giants of the Baroque, Anthony van Dyck, happened to be in Palermo.[38] The basic story of van Dyck's sojourn in Sicily is well known. In the spring of 1624 – almost certainly before the plague broke out in May – the young Flemish painter left Genoa for Palermo at the invitation of the Viceroy Emanuele Filiberto and probably members of Palermo's prosperous Genovese mercantile community. Van Dyck was invited to Sicily to paint portraits, and one of his most splendid portraits of this period is that of the viceroy himself (1624), now in the Dulwich Picture Gallery in London. Despite what was clearly an extremely productive stay in Palermo, in which van Dyck painted several portraits in addition to his contributions to the iconography of Saint Rosalie, the literature has until recently insisted that he returned to Genoa to escape the plague only a few months after his arrival there, in September 1624.[39] This topos of van Dyck fleeing pestilence begins with his early biographers Giovanni Bellori (1672) and Raffaele Soprani (1674), and it has remained a stubborn fixture in the van Dyck literature, even though Sterling noted as early as 1939 that leaving a city during a plague "was not an easy matter," with all the continental ports maintaining strict quarantine.[40] Recent archival work by Giovanni Mendola has demonstrated that van Dyck remained in Palermo much longer than anyone had believed, not departing for Genoa until after 3 September 3 1625, months after the plague ended and he could do so without hindrance.[41] Mendola's new dating allows us much more leeway for creating a time frame and partial chronology for van Dyck's Rosalie paintings.

Scholars have disagreed about how many of van Dyck's Rosalie paintings were actually executed in Sicily, although there has always been a suspicion that van Dyck painted more pictures there than was possible in the little time that Bellori and Soprani allotted him. Vincenzo Abbate felt that they were almost all painted in Genoa after the artist's return, even though they were likely commissioned by Sicilian patrons.[42] Charles Sterling, on the other hand, contended that van Dyck must have painted – or at least begun – most of them in Sicily, with the exception of the canvas in the Museo de Arte in Ponce (fig. 42), which he maintained was done later in Antwerp.[43] Meanwhile, Erik Larsen was convinced that all of the early Rosalie paintings were done in Sicily, except for the *Madonna of the Rosary* (fig. 47), which was begun in Sicily and finished in Genoa.[44] Most recently, Mendola has provided strong documentary evidence to back up Larsen's claim, with one exception: the *Madonna of the Rosary* was only *commissioned* in Sicily but actually painted on the mainland.[45] If we agree with Mendola that all but one were painted in Palermo, we can therefore date them between 4 September 1624, when La Barbera's canvas was debuted, and 3 September of the next year when van Dyck returned to Genoa – ample time to have done the work.[46]

The question remains as to why van Dyck became involved in the new Rosalie iconography in the first place. I propose that it was not only his obvious prominence in the artistic life of the city that brought him to Rosalie, but also his Genovese connections. The man who declared Rosalie's relics to be genuine in February of 1625, and one of the saint's most prominent promoters, was Archbishop Giovanni Doria (in office 1608-40), the scion of one of Genoa's most prominent families and Emmanuele Filiberto's temporary successor as viceroy.[47] It seems very likely that Doria himself invited van Dyck to contribute to his city's reclamation of the cult of Rosalie. Van Dyck even painted portraits of other members of the Doria family, such as that of Marcantonio Doria, Prince of Angri (a Sicilian title), which may date from his Sicilian sojourn, and Marchesa Geronima Spinola-Doria (ca. 1625), which he painted shortly after returning to Genoa.[48]

Sterling is the only scholar to have attempted an admittedly tentative chronology for van Dyck's Rosalie paintings. While I agree with Larsen that there is very little evidence to allow us to place these works in a definite order, I will hazard a guess as to which one was first. Owing to its close similarity in composition to La Barbera's canvas, I nominate the *Saint Rosalie Interceding for the Plague-Stricken of Palermo* in the Ponce Museum of Art (fig. 42).[49] Here a relatively lithe figure of Rosalie kneels slightly right of center on a rocky outcropping, her hands held out toward a view of the city of Palermo below, including Monte Pellegrino, which she indicates by her right hand. She turns her head toward the right, looking expectantly toward a heavenly light that emanates from the upper right corner. A skull and other human bones are scattered on the ledge below the saint, beneath the cityscape. The cave behind Saint Rosalie represents her grotto on Monte Pellegrino, complete with a rolled-up straw mat on the ground. Rosalie wears a Franciscan cowl, with a knotted rope around her

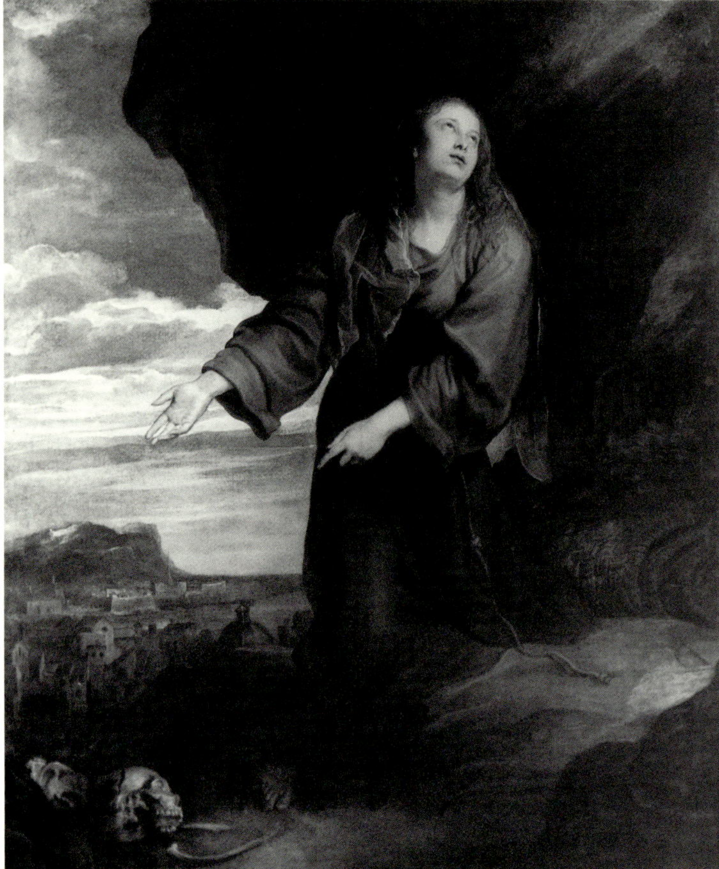

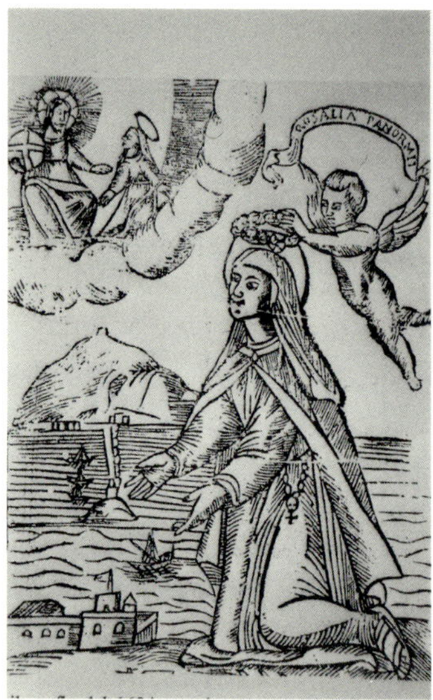

42. Anthony van Dyck, *Saint Rosalie Intercedes for Palermo*, ca. 1624-25. Oil on canvas. Museo de Arte de Ponce, The Luis A. Ferré Foundation, Inc., Ponce, Puerto Rico.

43. *Saint Rosalie Intercedes for Palermo*, 1624, woodcut. After Malignacci, 1991, fig. 100.

waist. Van Dyck's version is more accomplished in every way: While Rosalie's basic pose and facial expression are borrowed from La Barbera, van Dyck's Rosalie is more active, with a fleshier, less rounded face, and more fire in her eyes. Her golden tresses and gossamer veil mark a firm departure from the La Barbera version, and with this painting van Dyck introduces a blonde prototype for Rosalie that would remain the most popular – and one that immediately recalled the Magdalene.

The main difference between the two versions is the position of Rosalie. In the La Barbera she is left of center and indicates the lazaretto specifically, whereas in the van Dyck, her hand gestures encompass the entire city and Monte Pellegrino – a much more satisfactory solution. The location of van Dyck's protagonist echoes that of a crude woodcut made in Sicily around 1624 (fig. 43) – which shares the angel, the Madonna, and God the Father with the La Barbera version – although the two have little else in common.[50] The sky is also a major difference between van Dyck's and La Barbera's works: the powder blue sky of the latter is showered with golden light, and populated by the Trinity, the Madonna, and angels. Van Dyck's sky is much more ominous, with stormy gray clouds echoing the dark interior of the cave behind her. In fact, grays and browns dominate throughout the painting.

Two stylistic features point toward the La Barbera canvas as the model for the Ponce Rosalie. Sterling noted that the painting used much less impasto than van Dyck's other Rosalie canvases, saying that it was unusually "thin and smooth in the surface."[51] This led him to attribute the painting to van Dyck's Antwerp period and therefore after 1629. While Larsen and others have noted that the picture could not have been painted later, since it was copied frequently in Sicily by Sicilian artists (early copies can be found in the Ospedale dei Sacerdoti and Galleria Regionale in Palermo), this stylistic feature does bring the work closer to La Barbera's late Maniera style, with its polished surfaces and careful brushwork. Another stylistic feature unusual for van Dyck's work – as Christopher Brown has noted – is its inclusion of so detailed a topographical section at the lower left.[52] This, too, seems to have been done in homage to La Barbera's painstaking reconstruction of Palermo harbor and the surrounding hills. I propose that Doria contracted van Dyck shortly after the 4 September procession, perhaps because he was unhappy with La Barbera's modest canvas and wanted someone of van Dyck's status to undertake a job that had such far-reaching spiritual and political implications for plague-ridden Sicily.

Despite van Dyck's borrowings from La Barbera, it was the Flemish master who established the main aspects of Rosalie's iconography in the wake of the 1624 plague. He emphasized the Franciscan identity of her cowl, including the knotted cord that was absent in La Barbera's version. He also gave her blonde hair and stressed her role as a contemplative saint – alone, in her anchorite's cell – an identity that has encouraged parallels with the iconography of Saint Francis of Assisi and the Penitent Magdalene.[53] In particular, as noted by Brown, van Dyck was inspired by the *Saint Francis in Ecstasy* that Guido Reni painted for the church of S. Filippo Neri in Naples (after 1622). Rosalie's figure type, blonde hair, and cave-like setting also recall Reni's *Penitent Magdalene* in the Palazzo Corsini.[54] As Abbate pointed out, van Dyck's emphasis on the saint's solitude, meditation, and renunciation of earthly pleasures placed Rosalie in the mainstream of post-Tridentine sacred imagery as a model for an ideal Christian life.[55] The straw mat behind her combined with her gesture toward a distant landscape also recalls the iconography of the Death of Saint Francis Xavier, which enjoyed renewed popularity in the wake of his 1622 canonization and found its ultimate prototype in the 1670s in the work of Maratti and Gaulli in Rome.[56]

Van Dyck's final version of the same scene, now in the Menil Collection in Houston (cat. 30), is worlds apart.[57] This ravishing canvas enlivens the scene considerably, endowing it with a sweeping sense of movement, a stronger, more confident impasto, and a heightened emotion expressed through light, pose, and facial expression. This is a much more self-assured work in which van Dyck revels in the Venetian-inspired brushwork and light effects he had perfected in the earlier part of his Italian sojourn. Here we no longer see the detailed, topographical view of Palermo but merely a nondescript harbor and some low hills. Van Dyck has gone back to the La Barbera picture and introduced the angel with the crown of pink roses, although here the angel approaches from the upper left and is accompanied by another angel who scatters roses at Rosalie's feet. Heavenly approbation plays a much larger role here than in the Ponce canvas: golden sunrays penetrate a roiling cloudburst in the upper right, illuminating the saint's expectant face. Rosalie is a much more sensual figure too, her golden hair spilling over her breast and caressed by her left hand, and the golden highlights are themselves much more emphatic. With her left hand on her breast, signifying her love for the divine, she recalls Magdalene imagery even more suggestively than in the Ponce picture, as in Reni's smaller *Penitent Magdalene* at the Walters Gallery.[58] Maurice Vaes has also noted how similar Rosalie's pose is to that of the ecstatic Saint Francis in Guido Reni's version at S. Filippo Neri in Naples, which van Dyck may have seen during a visit to Reni's studio.[59] Rosalie's fingers are longer and more elegant than in the Ponce version. Even her brown monastic garb is made more sensual through its luxuriant folds and the vivid red veil that gathers over her left thigh and right arm.

There is some doubt about where to place a third, poorer, version of this scene now in the Duke of Wellington's collection at Apsley House (fig. 44). Sterling considered the smaller and more loosely painted Apsley House Rosalie a preliminary sketch for the Menil canvas. It has

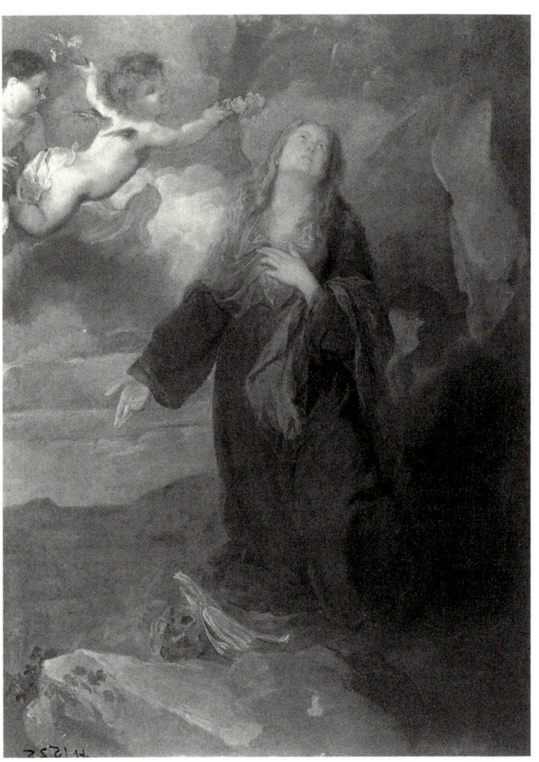

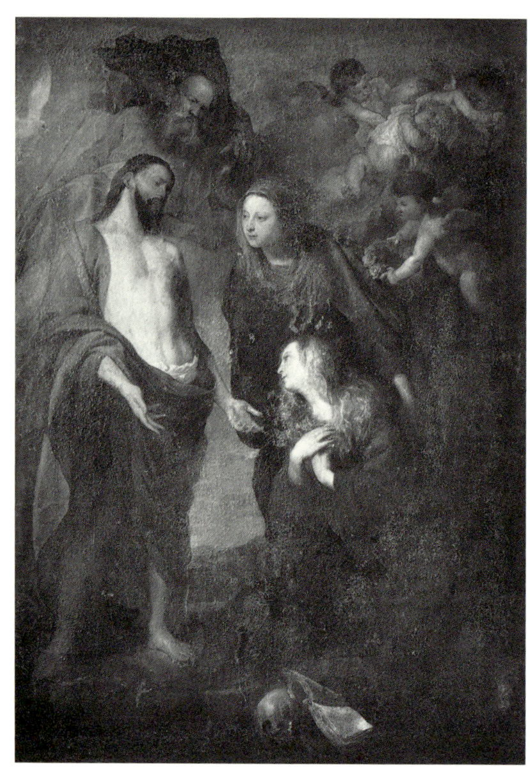

44. Anthony van Dyck, *Saint Rosalie Intercedes for Palermo*, ca. 1624. Oil on canvas. Apsley House, The Wellington Collection, London.

45. Anthony van Dyck, *Saint Rosalie Presented to the Holy Trinity by the Virgin Mary*, ca. 1624. Oil on canvas. Bayerische Staatsgemäldesammlung, Munich.

more in common with the Menil picture than the Ponce version, since it shares the two angels of the former and lacks the detailed landscape of the latter. The main difference is that it places the skull and books in the center, on the rocky outcropping in front of the saint, rather than to the far left. Although Larsen is unwilling to place any of these paintings in order, he does accept the Apsley House version as autograph.[60] I concur with Sterling that this is a first attempt at the Menil painting, especially since it was an early practice of van Dyck's to make a preliminary version of a picture before executing a more finished one.[61]

In summary, I have placed the Ponce picture first, followed by the Apsley House sketch and the Menil version, the most mature and confident of van Dyck's Rosalie Interceding for the Plague-Stricken of Palermo series. I will not attempt to place any of the other Rosalie paintings in chronological order, agreeing with Larsen that to do so without any further documentation is a fool's errand. The rest of van Dyck's Rosalie paintings fall into three categories: those showing Rosalie in Glory being lifted heavenward by angels, Saint Rosalie being presented to the Holy Trinity by the Virgin Mary, and a half-length portrait of the saint being crowned by an angel and holding a skull. In the only full-scale altarpiece in the group, the *Madonna of the Rosary* (fig. 47), Rosalie is merely one of several saints beseeching the Madonna for divine assistance.

With *Saint Rosalie Interceding for the Plague-Stricken of Palermo* in the Metropolitan Museum – the greatest of the Rosalie in Glory series – van Dyck has abandoned all references to La Barbera's composition, and moved in a different direction, this time inspired by the iconography of the Assumption of the Virgin (cat. 34).[62] Larsen maintains that this is the first of this series, in which Rosalie is borne heavenward by angels and clouds, and that her figure is the model for the Rosalie in the *Madonna of the Rosary*.[63] In this canvas, her whole body faces right for the first time, although her hands still point down toward the left, as in the Ponce picture. A single angel remains from the Menil canvas on the left, holding a crown of pink roses over Rosalie's head, and the lights of the city of Palermo and the profile of Monte Pellegrino are

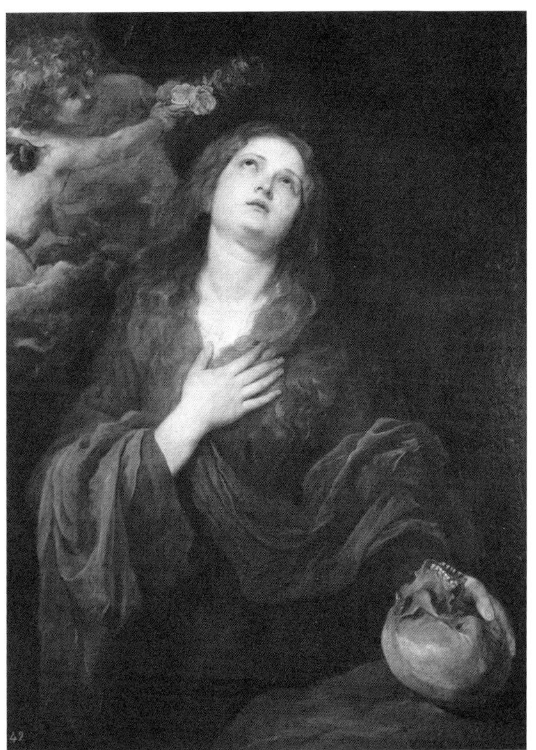

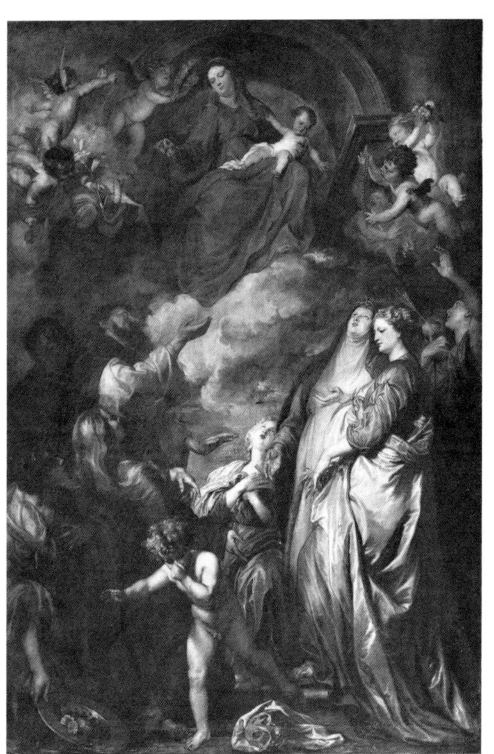

46. Anthony van Dyck, *Saint Rosalie*, ca. 1624. Oil on canvas. Museo del Prado, Madrid.

47. Anthony van Dyck, *Madonna of the Rosary with Saint Rosalie*, 1628. Oil on canvas. Oratorio del Rosario, Palermo.

barely visible in a badly worn passage in the lower right of the canvas. The skull also makes an appearance, borne aloft by an angel on the lower left. Chromatically, this work differs from the other three canvases, in that luminous light blues pierce through the clouds in the background. The satin veil that hangs over Rosalie's right arm and the shock of pink fabric intertwined in the lower pair of angels add a touch of luxury. Investigations during the 1990s using neutron autoradiographs showed that the work was painted directly over a sketch van Dyck had made of a self-portrait. A copy of the Metropolitan canvas in copper is on display at the Galleria Regionale.[64] Van Dyck painted a copy of this canvas, now in the Alte Pinakothek in Munich, whose quality and strong impasto Larsen praises.[65] As Abbate notes, this new prototype of Rosalie in glory served as a model for several Southern Italian and Spanish works, including Jusepe de Ribera's *Assumption of the Magdalene* in the Museo de la Real Academia in Madrid and his *Apotheosis of Saint Januarius* (another plague saint) in the monastery of the Discalced Augustinians in Salamanca, as well as Pietro Novelli's *Apotheosis of Saint Cajetan* in the Theatine church in Palermo.[66]

Van Dyck's third category for Rosalie imagery appears with his *Saint Rosalie Presented to the Holy Trinity by the Virgin Mary* (fig. 45), although the painting is in very poor condition and neither Sterling nor Larsen is ready to make a definite attribution to van Dyck.[67] Here a much more diminutive Rosalie kneels to the right of center, her hands crossed at her breast and her gaze directed upward at a standing figure of Christ. A skull and book rest at her knees. On the left, Christ stands, wearing an ample gown over his lower body, and he reaches down with both hands to accept her. Behind Rosalie the standing Virgin Mary places her hands on the saint's shoulders, gently nudging her forward. God the Father and the Holy Spirit float above Christ, and a group of angels frolics in the upper right, one of them lowering a crown of roses onto Rosalie's head. Although stylistically very different from La Barbera's canvas (fig. 41), this is the only picture of the van Dyck series to share the iconography of the Trinity with that earlier work.

The fourth and final iconographic type created by van Dyck for Rosalie is represented by the slightly more than half-length composition at the Prado (fig. 46). Now with auburn rather than blonde hair, the saint stands in the mirror-image of her pose in the Metropolitan picture, with her right hand on her breast and her left hand held downward, although her head is still tilted toward the right.[68] With her left hand, she rests a skull on a rocky outcropping, that hides her lower body from the viewer. In this closely cropped, intimate pose, she resembles the Magdalene more closely than ever. As in the Menil version, an angel holds a bouquet of pink roses above her head on the upper right. This version has the darkest backgrounds of all, though it is pierced on the upper left by the same luminous blue seen in the Metropolitan version.

The grandest of van Dyck's Rosalie paintings – and the only one still in Sicily – is the monumental altarpiece in the Oratorio del Rosario in Palermo (fig. 47).[69] It is also the only one that can be dated exactly. A contract shows that the work was commissioned on 22 August 1625, by the Confraternity of the Oratorio della Compagnia del Rosario in S. Domenico, less than two weeks before van Dyck's probable departure for Genoa and with the understanding that he would paint it "in the City of Naples, or some other part of Italy."[70] Although Bellori tells us that van Dyck began it in Sicily and took it with him to finish in Genoa, there is now little doubt that it was painted entirely in Genoa (probably by 1627) and sent back to Sicily sometime before April 1628. Most scholars have accepted Bellori's version, including Larsen, who writes that the canvas was painted "as a means of intercession to stop the scourge," even though the plague had abated several months earlier and it turns out to have been painted in thanksgiving.[71]

The *Madonna of the Rosary* is not, strictly speaking, a Rosalie picture; in fact, Rosalie plays a relatively minor role in the canvas, much as she did in the Pisan *sacre conversazioni* from the early Cinquecento (fig. 37). The confraternity contract spelled out which saints were to be included in the canvas, referring specifically to saints Dominic, Vincent, and Catherine, because they were Dominican saints, as well as the patrons of Palermo, and including not only Rosalie but also Cristina, Oliva, Ninfa, and Agata.[72] Bellori described it thus: "He portrayed the Virgin in a glory of angels holding rosaries; and below Saint Dominic with the five virgin saints of Palermo, among whom are Saint Catherine and Saint Rosalie, with a cherub nearby holding his hand to his nose because of the stench of a death's head on the earth, the countersign of the disease from which the city was liberated through the intercession of the saints."[73] In addition, Abbate has identified saints Sebastian and the barely visible Roch at the far right in the background. The appearance of these more traditional plague saints relates this picture iconographically to Luini's *Madonna and Child with Saints Sebastian and Roch* [cat. 13], Bassano's *Saints Sebastian and Roch* (cat. 12), and Vaccaro's *Madonna and Child with Saints Roch, Sebastian, and Francis Xavier* (cat. 18).[74] The cherub with his hand to his nose, a common motif in plague imagery, appears in Caroselli's *The Plague at Ashdod* (cat. 1) and Tiepolo's *Saint Thecla Praying for the Plague-Stricken* (cat. 7), both of which borrowed the motif from Marcantonio Raimondi's famous print after Raphael, *The Plague at Phrygia* (cat. 5). Scholars have disagreed about which figure is Rosalie in the *Madonna of the Rosary*. Brown maintains that the tall figure shown in near profile in the right-hand group is the palermitan patron, while Mendola indicates that Rosalie is the blonde figure in the center background who kneels with her hands on her breast, looking upward in a version of a pose that has become standard in van Dyck's Rosalie imagery.[75] I tend to agree with Mendola's identification. The composition is traditional for a grand altarpiece, with the Madonna and Child in glory in the upper level adored by two groups of full-length saints, and Brown and Larsen have traced it to Rubens's *Madonna and Saints* for the Chiesa Nuova in Rome (the original version of which Rubens took with him back to Antwerp, where van Dyck likely saw it).[76]

After his departure from Sicily, van Dyck returned to the theme of Rosalie once more with his *Coronation of Saint Rosalie*, painted in 1629 for the Antwerp Confraternity of Bachelors, a Jesuit organization that he joined upon his return to Flanders in 1628. Now in the Kunsthistorisches Museum in Vienna, the painting shows a richly dressed, auburn haired Rosalie approaching an enthroned Madonna and Child on her knees, accompanied by saints Peter and Paul, and her now standard symbols of the books, skull, lily, and crown of roses, which the child places on her head.[77]

Van Dyck's Legacy in Stone: The Case of Gregorio Tedeschi

When van Dyck departed Sicily in September of 1625, he left behind one of the island's most enduring and beloved images, a renewed iconography for Saint Rosalie that would last for centuries. In the imaginations of Sicilians, and palermitans in particular, Rosalie would forever be associated with blonde or auburn tresses, a Franciscan-inspired brown cowl, and a full figure. The impact of van Dyck's Rosalie iconography was felt immediately in the work of the leading painters in Palermo, including such Flemish expatriots as Guglielmo Walsgart (1612-1666), and the great *monrealese* painter Pietro Novelli (1603-1647), Sicily's most important painter of the Baroque. Novelli executed many canvases featuring a solo Rosalie wearing a brown habit, and he emphasized her youthful beauty in a way that was reminiscent of Magdalene imagery. Two of his finest treatments of the subject are *Madonna of the Graces with Saints Rosalie and John the Baptist* (ca. 1637) now in the Galleria Regionale, based loosely on the composition of van Dyck's *Madonna of the Rosary*, and *Saint Rosalie Nominated as Patron Protectress Against the Plague for Castiglione delle Stiviere* (ca. 1634), a particularly dramatic work in which the saint (here a brunette) heroically assumes the mantle as patroness as the dead and dying languish below.[78] Castiglione delle Stiviere (near Mantua) was the birthplace of the Jesuit plague saint Luigi Gonzaga, represented in this exhibition by a canvas by Pompeo Batoni (cat. 19). The Jesuits can probably be credited with orchestrating Rosalie's appearance in that far-off Lombard town, since they were major promoters of Rosalie's cult outside of Sicily. Even Pietro's daughter Rosalia Novelli (b. 1628) contributed to the development of her namesake's imagery, in her *Mary Magdalene, Saint Rosalie, and Saint Francis* in Piriano (Messina), which shows Rosalie flanked by the other two saints in front of Monte Pellegrino.[79] The parallel between Rosalie and the Magdalene could not have been made any clearer.

One of the most noteworthy legacies of van Dyck's reconstruction of Saint Rosalie is the virtually unknown Carrara marble sculpture of the recumbent Rosalie by Gregorio Tedeschi in her grotto on Monte Pellegrino (fig. 48).[80] Tedeschi was a florentine sculptor who carved two of the statues on Palermo's famed Quattro Canti (*Spring*, 1620-24 and *Saint Cristina*, 1630), and he also executed a recumbent marble sculpture of the *Dying Saint Lucy* in Siracusa (1634). Like La Barbera, Tedeschi worked on the interior of the palermitan Gesù, on the altar of Saint Francis Xavier (ca. 1622).[81] Carved in 1625, probably on order from the same palermitan Senate who commissioned La Barbera's painting of July 1624, Tedeschi's *Dying Saint Rosalie* depicts a heavy-set woman lying on a slab of rock. She lies in the pose in which her body was reputedly discovered in 1624, and it is also one that is very reminiscent of imagery associated with the Penitent Magdalene, as in Sisto Badaloccio's *Penitent Magdalene* from the 1620s in the Mary Jane Harris Collection.[82] Rosalie grasps her gown with her right hand, turns her head toward heaven in ecstasy, and cups her left hand behind her ear as if straining to hear the word of God. A nearby angel places a crown of lilies on her head. Unfortunately, not much can be made out of the main body of the sculpture, since it was sheathed in silver by order of Carlo III Bourbon in 1748.[83] This pose is entirely unprecedented in Rosalie imagery. A few

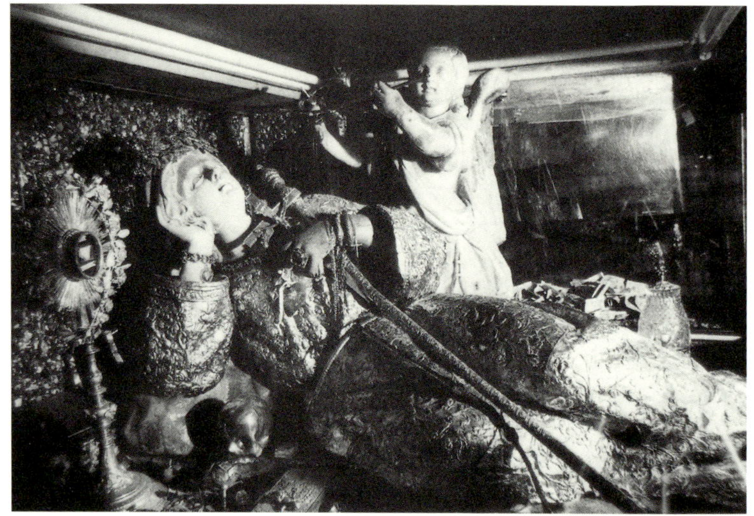

48. Gregorio Tedeschi, *Dying Saint Rosalie*, 1625. Marble. Santuario di Monte Pellegrino, Palermo.

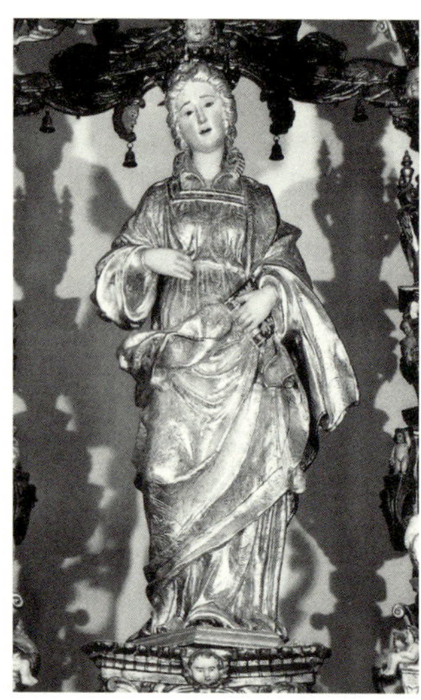

49. *Saint Rosalie*, early seventeenth century. Polychrome wood. Church of S. Rosalia, Bivona.

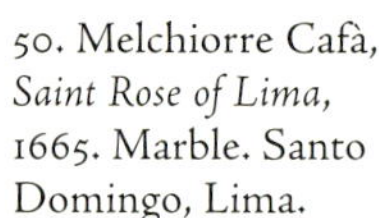

50. Melchiorre Cafà, *Saint Rose of Lima*, 1665. Marble. Santo Domingo, Lima.

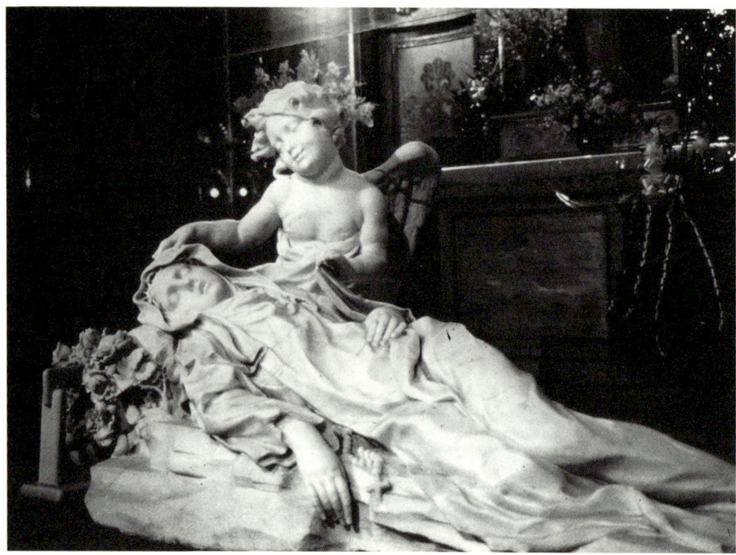

pre-1624 statues of Saint Rosalie survive in wood, one of them a processional statue kept in a *fercolo* (baldachin) in the church of S. Rosalia in Bivona, which has been attributed to the bivonese sculptor Ruggero Valenti (ca. 1601) but is much restored (fig. 49), and another a delicate image of the saint wearing a Franciscan gown and knotted cord in the Galleria Regionale, formerly in Caltavuturo.[84] In both of these examples, she is shown standing, and has a slender, elongated body.

Tedeschi may have referred to a number of models for the pose of his recumbent saint. As a sculpture of a rediscovered saint, it recalls Stefano Maderno's marble Saint Cecilia (1601) at S. Cecilia in Trastevere in Rome, who is also shown recumbent, although already dead. Although their lower bodies are in similar positions, Cecilia's neck is severed and her head is therefore turned away from the viewer and hidden in a shroud. Rosalie's pose also echoes that of Saint Lawrence in Bernini's early sculpture (ca.1614-15). Like Rosalie, Lawrence supports himself on one elbow and tilts his head backward to look for his eternal reward – although he is roasting on a fiery grill and not reclining calmly on a slab of stone. Tedeschi's figure also brings to mind Caravaggio's painting of the *Ecstasy of Saint Francis* (ca. 1595), in which Saint Francis's pose is almost the exact mirror image of *Dying Saint Rosalie*, although Tedeschi's angel is a much more traditional cherub than Caravaggio's adolescent angel, and he stands apart from the main figure.[85] In both the *Saint Francis* and the *Saint Rosalie* one hand rests on the saint's chest, in Francis's case specifically indicating the stigmata but in both versions emphasizing the burning love of the heart.

It becomes clear how revolutionary Tedeschi's sculpture is when we compare it to the next known sculpture of a recumbent dying saint, Melchiorre Cafà's 1665 *Saint Rose of Lima*, a work that depicts a saint with almost the same name (fig. 50). A Roman Baroque sculptor of Maltese origin, Cafà (1635-67) was possibly the greatest sculptor of the generation after Bernini, but came to an untimely death at the age of thirty-two after only a decade of feverish activity. Cafà specialized in ecstatic saints, of which his *Ecstasy of Saint Catherine* in S. Caterina da Siena a Monte Magnanapoli (finished 1667) is his most celebrated Roman work. But his most famous work of all is his *Saint Rose of Lima*, carved in Rome for the Dominican monastery of Santo Domingo in Lima, where it remains.[86] Although Cafà's figure is more passive in appearance, with her head resting on a stone pillow and her right arm dangling by her side, the basic pose of the figure, lying on her side and facing the viewer with her left hand resting on her torso, does recall Tedeschi's *Dying Saint Rosalie*. Like Tedeschi's work, Cafà's group includes a cherub who attends the recumbent saint.

According to Baldinucci, Cafà's *Saint Rose of Lima* was the first Italian sculpture to show a dying saint, and it is widely accepted as an inspiration for Bernini's own *Blessed Ludovica Albertoni* (1672-4). In fact, the Tedeschi is even closer to the Bernini, since in both sculptures the saint supports herself on her right elbow while her left hand rests on her torso, and both of them are shown still alive, in their death throes, with their eyes and mouth still open. Could Cafà have known the Tedeschi? Although I have not been able to find any evidence proving that Cafà visited Palermo, it would have been natural to pass through Sicily on the way between Malta and Rome, a voyage he made for the first time in 1658 and then twice in 1666.[87] If so, perhaps Tedeschi's *Dying Saint Rosalie* is the ultimate inspiration, through Cafà, of Bernini's *Blessed Ludovica*. In any case, Tedeschi's group appears to be the earliest sculpture of a dying saint ever carved by an Italian sculptor, preceding Cafà's innovation by exactly forty years. How unexpected that the most significant legacy of van Dyck's iconography of Saint Rosalie would manifest itself in stone, leaving Baroque sculpture with one of its most enduring motifs.

1. For a recent monograph on the Festino, see Santoro 2003. See also Isgrò 1981-86.
2. Mele 2003; Santino 1999; Gerbino 1991; Collura 1977; Réau 1955-59, 1170-71.
3. Réau 1955-59, 1170-71; Martin and Feigenbaum 1979, 125; Santoro 2003, 15-17; 24-25.
4. Pugliatti 1991, 68.
5. Abbate 1991, 92; Santoro 2003, 25.
6. Pugliatti 1991, 68.
7. On the Paleochristian Revival Movement in general, see Bailey 2003, 123-27; Freiberg 1995, 161-176; Macioce 1990, 9-75; Herz 1988b; Herz 1998a; Zuccari 1984, 31-147; Abromson 1981, 121-219.8. Freiburg 1995, 38; Zuccari 1984, 34-36; Abromson 1981, 123.9. Abromson 1981, 126.10. Santoro 2003, 26, 29-30; Martin and Feigenbaum 1979, 125; Sterling 1939, 53.
11. Santoro 2003, 15-16.
12. Santoro 2003, 9-10.
13. Cuccia 1991, 135.
14. Reau 1955-59, 1170.
15. Giannino 2003, 29-30; Tricoli 2001, 104, 115-16.
16. Tricoli 2001, 83
17. Martin and Feigenbaum 1979, 126; Reau 1955-59, 1170.
18. Salvo 2001, 689.
19. Typical panegyric works from this era include Fabio 1692, and *La giuditta palermitana*, 1671.
20. Pugliatti 1991, 68.
21. Barricelli 1991, 53.
22. Barricelli 1991, 56-7; Reau 1955-59, 1170.
23. Both paintings originally formed part of the Lanza di Traba collection in Palermo (Barricelli 1991, 58).
24. This painting is now lost, but an engraving of it survives in Cascini (Barricelli 1991, 60).
25. Barricelli 1991, 61.
26. Pugliatti 1991, 72-73.
27. Abbate 2001, 30-31; Pugliatti 1998, 35-40.
28. Pugliatti 1991, 79; Pugliatti 1998, 149-52.
29. Pugliatti 1991, 82.
30. Giannino 2003, 29; Tricoli 2001, 104; Pugliatti 1991, 86.
31. Pugliatti 1991, 86.
32. Abbate 1999, 273.
33. Tricoli 2001, 80-82.
34. Abbate 1991, 99; Collura 1977, 96.
35. Abbate 1991, 91.
36. Abbate 1991, 92.
37. Abbate 1999, 66 (fig. 11).
38. On van Dyck's Rosalie paintings, see: Mendola 1999, 88-105; Bonaccorso 1990, 22, 25, figs. 22, 25; Larsen 1988, I, 230-233; Larsen 1988, II, 181-84; Brown 1982, 80-82; Larsen 1980, cat. 442-46, 451, 454; Martin and Feigenbaum 1979, 125-26; Sterling 1939, 53-62; Mastranga 1908, 11-18.
39. Martin and Feigenbaum 1979, 27, 125; Pacciarotti 1997, 98-99; Abbate 1991, 93; Larsen 1988, I, 230.
40. Sterling 1939, 53. People traveling from Palermo were even quarantined in other cities in Sicily (Santoro 2003, 29). Bellori writes: "se ne partì il più tosto come in fuga ed a Genova fece ritorno" (Bellori 1672, 276-77).
41. Mendola 1999a, 97-99; Mendola 1999b, 58-63.
42. Abbate 1991, 94.
43. Sterling 1939, 53-62.
44. Larsen 1988, I, 233.
45. Mendola 1999a, 101.
46. Mendola 1999a, 99.
47. Santoro 2003, 26.
48. The Marcantonio Doria portrait is in Larsen 1988, II, 131 (cat. 318).
49. Larsen 1988, II, 183 (cat 454); Held 1965, 58-59; Sterling 1939, 59-62; Glück 1909, 156.
50. Malignaggi 1979, 180-1.
51. Larsen 1988, II, 183; Sterling 1939, 54.
52. Brown 1982, 82.
53. Mendolaı 999a, 101; Martin and Feigenbaum 1979, 126; Brown 1982, 81.
54. Brown 1982, 82; *Guido Reni* 1988, cat. 47.
55. Abbate 1991, 91.
56. Bailey 1999, fig. 15.
57. Mendola 1999a, 101, 103; Martin and Feigenbaum 1979, 127-29; Larsen 1988, I, 233; Larsen 1988, II, 181 (cat. 451); Brown 1982, 18-82; Sterling 1939, 59-62; Vaes 1924, 201; Di Giovanni 1889, 288.
58. *Guido Reni* 1988, cat. 52; Mormando 1999, cat 8.
59. Vaes 1924, 201.
60. Larsen 1988, II, 191 (cat. 453).
61. Martin and Feigenbaum 1979, 24.
62. Van Dyck's *Assumption* at the National Gallery (1628/32) is very similar in figure type, as Brown notes; Brown 1982, 82. For the literature on this painting, see: Mendola 1999a, 101-02; Larsen 1988, I, 233; Larsen 1988, II, 181 (cat. 449); Brown 1982, 81-82.
63. Larsen 1988, I, 233; Larsen 1988, II, 181.
64. Larsen 1988, II, 181; *Physics Through the 1990s* 1986, 133, fig. 6.3.
65. Larsen 1988, II, 181 (cat. 450); Mendola 1999a, 101; Sterling 1939, 54.
66. Abbate 1991, 95.
67. Larsen 1988, II, 184 (cat. 456); Sterling 1939, 55.
68. Larsen 1988, II, 181 (cat. 455); *Museo del Prado* 1996, cat. 1494.
69. Larsen 1988, II, 181 (cat. 448).
70. Mendola 1999a, 106. The text reads: "et cum conditionibus quibus infra nimirum Depingere nella Citta di Napole o in altro luogo d'Italia." See also Mendola 1999b, 61.
71. Larsen 1988, I, 232.
72. Mendola 1999a, 99; Barnes 1997, 75-76.
73. Larsen 1988, I, 232.
74. Abbate 1991, 94.
75. Brown 1982, 80; Abbate 1991, 99.
76. Larsen 1988, I, 233; Brown 1982, 81.
77. Martin and Feigenbaum 1979, 126; Abbate 1991, 98.
78. Abbate 1999, cat 31.
79. Abbate 1991, 101-106; Mastranga 1908, 15.
80. Sterling was the first to acknowledge Tedeschi's debt to van Dyck, writing that the sculpture "is a faithful reproduction of the type created by van Dyck." (Sterling, 1939, 54)
81. Seta 2002, 117, 315, 317; Giannino 2003, 13; Tricoli 2001, 80.
82. In a published illustrated series of Rosalie's life from 1629 recently attributed to van Dyck, the identification of the scene represented by Tedeschi's sculpture as Rosalie's death is made explicit in the caption: "S. Rosalia virgo, hoc situ corporis cum cruce et rosario, in monte Peregrino iuxta Panormum A.o 1624 inventa est." (Filipczak 1989, 695). For the Badalocchio, see Mormando 1999, plate 7.
83. Cuccia 1991, 137.
84. Cuccia 1991, 136.
85. Puglisi 1998, 124.

86. See Bailey 2002, fig. 6; Boucher 1998, fig. 2.
87. Bacchi 1996, 791-92.

Bibliography

Abbate, Francesco. *Storia dell'arte nell'italia meridionale*. Rome, 2001.

Abbate, Vincenzo. "La città aperta. Pittura e società a Palermo tra Cinque e Seicento." In Vincenzo Abbate, ed., *Porto di Mare 1570-1670: Pittori e pittura a Palermo tra memoria e recupero* (Naples, 1999): 11-56.

Abbate, Vincenzo. "Il '600: Santa Rosalia nella rappresentazione pittorica." In Aldo Gerbino, ed., *La Rosa dell'Ercta* (Palermo, 1991): 91-108.

Abromson, Morton. "Painting in Rome during the Papacy of Clement VIII." Unpublished Ph.D. dissertation, New York University, 1981.
Bacchi, Andrea. *Scultura del '600 a Roma*. Milan, 1996.

Bailey, Gauvin. *Between Renaissance and Baroque: Jesuit Art in Rome, 1565-1610*. Toronto and Buffalo, 2003.

Bailey, Gauvin. "The Jesuits and Painting in Italy, 1550-1690." In Franco Mormando, S.J., ed. *Saints and Sinners: Caravaggio and the Baroque Image* (Boston and Chicago, 1999): 151-78.

Bailey, Gauvin. "Creating a Global Artistic Language in Late Renaissance Rome: Artists in the Service of the Overseas Missions, 1542-1621." In Pamela Jones and Thomas Worcester, eds., *From Rome to Eternity: Catholicism and the Arts in Italy, ca. 1550-1650* (Leiden, 2002): 225-251.

Barnes, Susan J., et al. *Van Dyck a Genova*. Milan, 1997.

Barricelli, Anna. "Imago pittura di Santa Rosalia tra Medioevo e civiltà del Quattrocento." In Gerbino, 1991, 49-64.

Bellori, Giovanni Pietro. *Le vite de' pittori, scultori et architetti moderni*. Rome, 1672.

Bonaccorso, M.T. "L'ultimo dei grandi. Sulla mostra 'Pietro Novelli e il suo ambiente,'" *Quaderni dell'Istituto di Storia dell'Arte Medievale e Moderna, Facoltà di lettere e filosofia Università di Messina*, 14 (1990): 5-30.

Boucher, Bruce. *Italian Baroque Sculpture*. London, 1998.

Brown, Christopher. *Van Dyck*. Oxford, 1982.

Clifton, James. "Mattia Preti's *Madonna of Constantinople* and a Marian Cult in Seventeenth-Century Naples." In Jeanne Chenault Porter and Susan Scott Munshower, eds., *Parthenope's Splendor: Art of the Golden Age in Naples* (University Park, 1993): 337-364.

Collura, Paolo. *Santa Rosalia nella storia e nell'arte*. Palermo, 1977.

Cuccia, Antonio. "L'immagine scolpita di Santa Rosalia vergine palermitana." In Gerbino, 1991, 133-50.

Di Giovanni, Vincenzo. "I Paruta in Palermo e nella Signoria del Castello di Sala di Madonna Alvira, indi Sala di Paruta." *Archivio Storico Siciliano*, new series, XIV (1889), 269-92.

Fabio, Ascenso, *La mano tutta mano di S. Rosalia, vergine palermitana: panegirico Sacro*. Messina, 1692.

Filipczak, Zirka Zaremba. "Van Dyck's Life of Saint Rosalie." *The Burlington Magazine* 131 (1989): 693-98.

Freiburg, Jack. *The Lateran in 1600: Christian Concord in Counter-Reformation Rome*. Cambridge, 1995.

Gerbino, Aldo, ed. *La Rosa dell'Ercta*. Palermo, 1991.

Giannino, A. *La chiesa del Gesù a Casa Professa, Palermo*. Palermo, 2003.

La giuditta palermitana, ovvero la Vergine S. Rosalia, triomfatrice d'Oloferne, cioé della Peste. Palermo, 1671.

Glück, Gustav, ed., *van Dyck, Des Meisters Gemälde*. Stuttgart-Leipzig, 1909.

Guido Reni: 1575-1642. Los Angeles, 1988.

Held, Julius S. *Ponce Art Museum: Paintings of the European and American Schools*. Ponce, 1965.

Herz, Alexandra. "Cardinal Cesare Baronio's Restoration of SS. Nereo ed Achilleo and S. Cesareo de' Appia." *Art Bulletin* 70 (1988): 590-620 [1988a].

Herz, Alexandra. "Imitators of Christ: The Martyr-Cycles of Late Sixteenth Century Rome Seen in Context." *Storia dell'arte* 62 (1988): 53-70. [1988b]

Isgrò, Giovanni. *Feste barocche a Palermo*. Palermo, 1981-86.

Larsen, Eric. *L'opera completa di van Dyck: 1613-26*. Milan, 1980.

Larsen, Eric. *The Paintings of Anthony van Dyck*. 2 vols. Freren, 1988.

Macioce, Stefania. *Undique spendent: Aspetti della pittura sacra nella Roma di Clemente VIII Aldobrandini*. Rome, 1990.

Malignaggi, Diana. "Dentro l'immagine: la rappresentazione iconografica di S. Rosalia attraverso le stampe." In Gerbino, 1991, 177-90.

Martin, John Rupert, and Gail Feigenbaum, *van Dyck as Religious Artist*. Princeton, 1979.

Mastranga, Cesare. "Dipinti di Antonio van Dijck e della sua scuola nel Museo Nazionale di Palermo." *Bolletino d'Arte* II, 1 (1908): 11-18.

Mele, Grazia. *Santa Rosalia: Storia e leggenda della patrona di Palermo*. Palermo, 2003.

Mendola, Giovanni. "Un approdo sicuro: nuovi documenti per van Dyck e Gerardi a Palermo." In Abbate 1999, 88-105. [Mendola 1999a]

Mendola, Giovanni. "Van Dyck in Sicily." In Christopher Brown et al., *van Dyck 1599-1641* (Antwerp 1999): 58-63. [Mendola 1999b]

Mormando, Franco. *Saints & Sinners: Caravaggio & the Baroque Image*. Boston, 1999.

Museo del Prado: Catálogo de las pinturas. Madrid, 1996.

Pacciarotti, Giuseppe. *La pittura del seicento*. Torino, 1997.

Physics Through the 1990s. Washington, 1986.

Pugliatti, Teresa. *Pittura del Cinquecento in Sicilia*. Naples, 1998.

Pugliatti, Teresa. "Rosalia vergine palermitana nelle immagini pittoriche del secolo XVI." In Gerbino, 1991, 65-90.

Puglisi, Catherine. *Caravaggio*. London, 1998.

Réau, Louis. *Iconographie de l'art crétien*. Paris 1955-59.

Salvo, F. "Cascino (Cascini, Accascina), Giordano." In Charles O'Neill and Joaquín M.a Domínguez, ed. *Diccionario histórico de la Compaña de Jesœs: Biográfico-Temático* I (Rome, 2001): 689.

Santino, Umberto. *I giorni della peste: il festino di Santa Rosalia tra mito e spettacolo* Palermo, 1999.

Santoro, Rodo. *Il festino di santa rosalia*. Palermo, 2003.

Seta, Cesare de, et al. *Palermo: Città d'arte*. Palermo, 2002.

Sterling, Charles. "Van Dyck's Paintings of St. Rosalie." *Burlington Magazine* 74 (February 1939): 53-62.

Tricoli, Maria Clara Ruggieri, ed. *Costruire Gerusalemme: Il complesso gesuitico della Casa Professa di Palermo dalla storia al museo*. Milan, 2001.

Vaes, Maurice. "Le séjour d'Antoine van Dyck en Italie (novembre 1621-autumne 1627)." *Bulletin de l'Institut Historique Belge à Rome* IV (1924), 163-234.

Rudolf Wittkower. *Art and Architecture in Italy, 1600-1750*. Harmondsworth, 1991.

Zuccari, Alessandro. *Arte e committenza nella Roma di Caravaggio*. Torino, 1984.

Combating the Plague: Devotional Paintings, Architectural Programs, and Votive Processions in Early Modern Venice

Andrew Hopkins

Saint Mark's face in shadow evokes the devastating effects of the 1510 plague (fig. 51). Physicians Cosmas and Damian gesture to the open sore Roch fingers as he looks to them for help; Sebastian turns from the others, eyes wistfully lowered, his somber visage contrasting with Titian's bravura rendition of his nude torso and billowing drapery.[1] Originally painted for the island church of Spirito Santo, in May 1659 the Saint Mark altarpiece was relocated to the new votive church of S. Maria della Salute, begun as a response to the devastating plague of 1630.[2] Built as an offering to the Virgin, the Salute commemorates what proved to be the last major plague in the city; it was also the last great architectural monument of the Republic and the last significant votive procession to be added to the series the doge and *signoria* performed annually. Looking beyond these rituals of public devotion and ducal procession, however, one finds a republic that had precociously adopted techniques of distribution and enclosure on the monastic model as a practical measure to combat the plague, pioneering the development of island lazarettos to isolate the sick and quarantine the suspect in effective, coercive architecture sited away from public view.[3]

Lazarettos

In the fifteenth century the Venetian government extended its power over the unique topography of the city through the creation of island isolation hospitals with stretches of water separating them from the densely populated center.[4] The first plague hospital was founded by senate decree on 28 August 1423 on the small island of S. Maria di Nazareth, just off the Lido.[5] The architecture of the lazaretto followed the traditional form of the convent in which it was housed. Dedicated specifically to the poor without fixed abode who were infected with the plague, this hospital with twenty rooms (later eighty) enabled individual isolation so that the sick from various places such as the city, the lagoon islands, and incoming ships could be held separately.[6] This lazaretto (later the Lazaretto Vecchio) functioned as a center for quarantine and disinfection and it held in containment those who would otherwise wander through the city seeking charity but also spreading contagion.

This technique of isolation responded to the classical theory of plague generation, then still current, of the circulation of "corrupt air," or the "miasma theory of disease."[7] Isolation proved to be effective, and the authorities soon devised a more elaborate arrangement that not only separated the sick from each other but also from the convalescent and from those merely suspected of being infected. This systematic approach was made possible through the creation, by government decree of 18 July 1468, of the Lazaretto Nuovo on an island vineyard five miles from the city, adjacent to the island of S. Erasmo (fig. 52).[8] The Lazaretto Nuovo had a rectangular cloister-like complex with a church in one corner and two floors containing a succession of wards with numerous entrances that facilitated a strict division between various arriving, convalescing and suspect groups.

At the Lazaretto Nuovo patients were held for forty days convalescence; more coercively, the suspect (*i sospetti*) including the families of the sick and arriving shiploads were held to ascertain if any latent sickness would manifest itself. A system of isolation in wards was

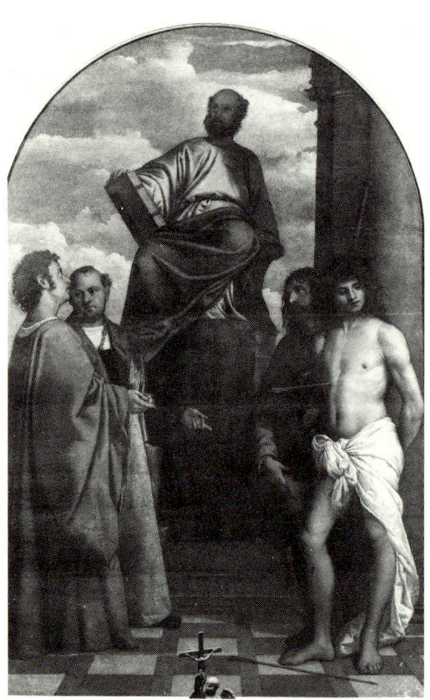

51. Titian, *Saint Mark Altarpiece*, ca. 1510. Oil on canvas. S. Maria della Salute, Venice.

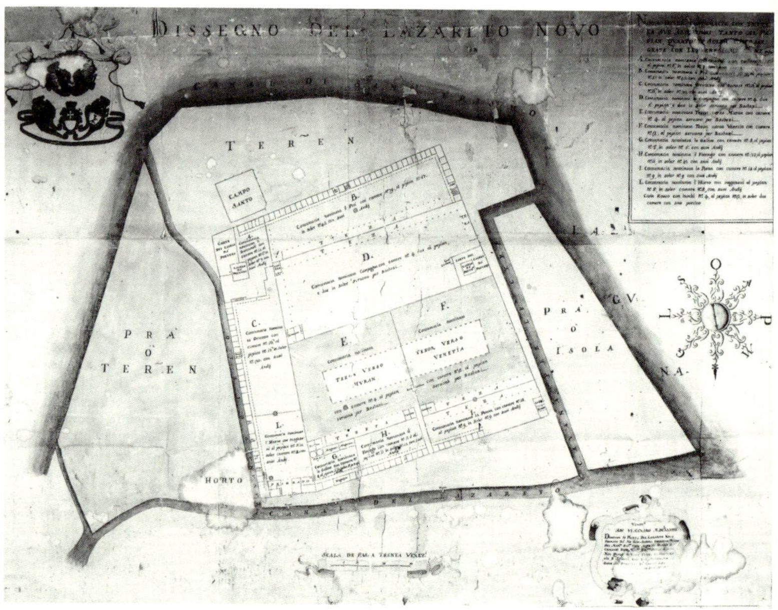

52. Gio. Andrea Cornello, *Map of the Lazaretto Nuovo*, 1637. Pen, black ink on paper on a canvas support. State Archives, Provveditori alla Sanità, Venice.

devised so that each group would ideally progress over forty days to a clean bill of health or complete convalescence. By 1503 there were four quarantine wards in which inmates passed ten days each, thereby progressing through the spaces of the lazaretto in separate groups, whether the crew of a ship or a group of families admitted together.[9] On showing signs of sickness, however, a patient was removed and sent to the Lazaretto Vecchio and the others had to begin quarantine again.[10] Each ward was responsible for burying any of its group that died, as the staff had little contact with patients, part of the system devised following the establishment by senate decree of 20 June 1485 of the Magistrato alla Sanità (Health Office) within the existing Magistrato al Sal (Salt Office). On 7 January 1486, three noblemen were elected as *Provveditori* (directors), initially a temporary and then a permanent office that began with a prior, two doctors, and three servants but that, by 1541, had twenty-seven staff including two priors with responsibility for the lazarettos.[11]

Saint Roch

In concert with these official strategies of control went parallel efforts at encouraging the establishment of popular charitable confraternities dedicated to poor relief to provide an urban focus for popular devotion.[12] The Scuola (confraternity) dedicated to Saint Roch, founded during the plague epidemic of 1478, was the object of a considerable surge of devotion so that already in May 1483 when the landlord of the German friar, Felix Faber, died of suspected plague, the friar "went by water to the church of S. Roch... and invoked the aid of the aforesaid saint, who is the especial helper of those who fear the plague."[13] (See Thomas Worcester's essay for Saint Roch and his cult in relation to the plague.) In 1485 Roch's body was brought from Montpellier, in 1486 his confraternity elevated to the status of a Scuola Grande, and in 1489 a church was begun behind S. Maria Gloriosa dei Frari. Bartolomeo Bon designed the church (later rebuilt) and in 1516, as *proto* (superintendent of works) to the Scuola, began a grand new building that was completed 1527-49 by Antonio Scarpagnino.[14]

The grandest space of the Scuola, the first-floor *sala capitolare* (meeting hall), was reached

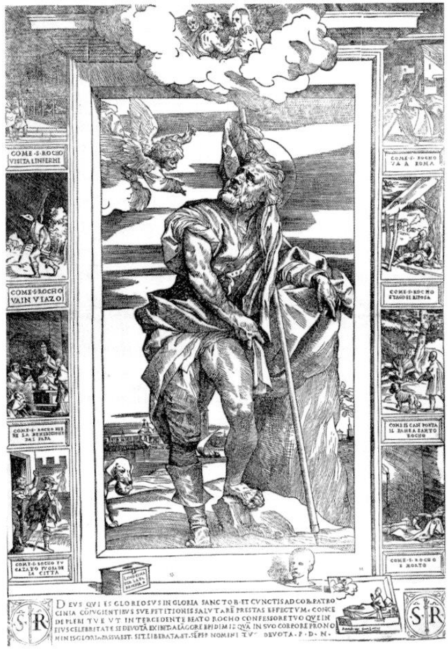

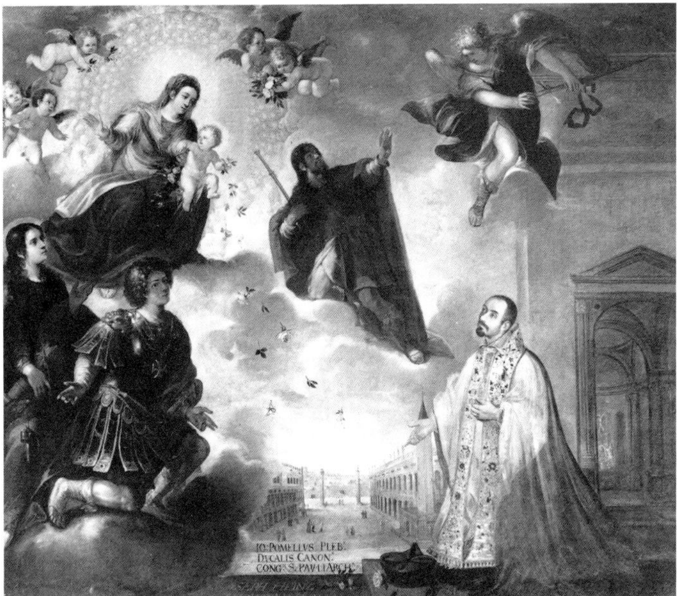

53. Titian, *Saint Roch and the Story of his Life,* 1520s. Woodcut. British Museum, London.

54. Giuseppe Heintz the Younger, *The Parish Priest Pomelli and Saints John the Evangelist, Theodor, and Roch who Implores the Archangel Saint Michael not to Unsheath his Sword,* 1632. Oil on canvas. S. Fantin, Venice.

by Scarpagnino's extravagant "imperial" staircase, with parallel ramps at ground-floor level leading to a broad landing from which a single ramp leads to the upper hall decorated with Jacopo Tintoretto's famed pictorial cycle.[15] The Scuola was the locus for ritual processions in which the staircase played an important part, as did the richly decorated facade covered with colored marbles and large freestanding columns – its function as ceremonial backdrop perfectly captured by Antonio Canaletto's *The Doge Visiting the Church and Scuola di San Rocco* of circa 1735 in the National Gallery of London.[16] Some members of the confraternity believed that the sumptuous and expensive facade belied the role of the Scuola in helping the poor and this led to considerable disagreement, especially with regard to the construction of the staircase, later decorated by Antonio Zanchi in the 1670s with paintings of plague scenes.[17]

Increasing Venetian devotion to Roch can be seen in the Saint Mark altarpiece, painted around the time Giorgione died, probably of plague.[18] It also heralds the ascendancy of Titian to the role of foremost artist in Venice. His woodcut *Saint Roch and the Story of his Life* must have been printed in the 1520s to raise more money for building, as indicated by the collection box above the inscription at the bottom left of the image (fig. 53).[19] Saint Roch is represented wearing a pilgrim's dress and carrying a staff, with his upper thigh exposed to show a decorously located plague buboe, while vignettes framing the image illustrate traditional episodes from his life.[20] The small votive print depicting Roch's apparition to a plague victim at bottom right emphasizes the extent to which popular piety was fundamental to the success of the Scuola di S. Rocco.[21] (See Pamela's Jones's essay, pp. 73-74, for print dissemination and its influence.)

Devotional paintings such as Jacopo Bassano's *Saints Sebastian and Roch* of circa 1551 (cat. 12) present a typical pairing of these two plague saints: Roch, with his traditional beard, hat, and staff, pulls back his cloak to indicate an area of skin in shadow that signifies the presence of a plague buboe. Sebastian leans forward to greet Roch with a bright spurt of blood issuing from the wound in his chest, pierced by his trademark arrow.[22] (See Sheila Barker's essay, pp. 47-48 for more on the transformation of the iconography of Saint Sebastian.) A Venetian context is suggested by the verso of the canvas depicting the Madonna of Mercy together with

Saint Anthony of Padua whose relics and feast day would be celebrated at S. Maria della Salute from 1656, another plague year.[23] Roch also appears in Giuseppe Heintz the Younger's *The Parish Priest Pomelli and Saints John the Evangelist, Theodor, and Roch who Implores the Archangel Saint Michael not to Unsheath his Sword* of 1632 (fig. 54).[24] Pomelli, a canon of S. Marco and parish priest of S. Fantin, appears between a large-scale representation of his own parish church and the centrally located view of the *piazzetta* looking toward the *bacino* of S. Marco. He represents just one of the numerous religious who, during the plague, offered succor to the sick and helped to prevent panic at a local level. Sometimes, however, even the religious fled the city and, following their mid-sixteenth-century change in official policy, during the 1576 epidemic there was a significant exodus of Jesuits to the country villas of Venetian nobles.[25] In 1630 the Benedictines at S. Giorgio Maggiore reaffirmed their exemption from administering the sacraments during times of plague, despite a direct request from the patriarch Giovanni Tiepolo.[26]

Contagion and the poor

In contrast to the predominant belief that plague was sent as a punishment from God, in 1546 the Veronese scholar and physician Girolamo Fracastoro published in Venice his cogent articulation of the theory of contagion.[27] Although his insight was not immediately understood or accepted, given the mildness of the 1555-57 plague, the Health Office in Venice was able to examine individual cases, consult doctors, and even hold a meeting with the doge and senate on 24 August 1556 to examine various theories of causation and begin to posit contagion as the likely method. They also began, at least to some degree, to put in place strategies for the examination and documentation of individual cases.[28]

As was recognized by the sixteenth century, the plague mainly affected the poor: the reduced circumstances of the respectable poor, such as the massive numbers of urban workers who lived on the breadline, deteriorated sharply amid the overall economic chaos in which commerce ceased and the abrupt termination of their employment drove them to starvation.[29] But the plight of the poor was attributed not only to inadequate food and small, filthy houses – made worse when these abodes were quarantined and boarded up – but also to their supposedly immoderate sexual habits.[30] Then there were the unrespectable poor, such as vagrants, criminals, and galley slaves, who were even more likely to be infected with the plague as so many of them took employment arising from it, as undertakers, fumigators, and cleaners and clearers of plague-stricken houses.[31] Those who could, fled the chaos of the city but, ethically, if one was noble, the proper course of action was to remain. The countryside, in any case, had both strongly positive and negative aspects during periods of plague as it was both a refuge and a blockading force that could withhold supplies. It too was the site of thousands of starving peasants, for famine usually preceded plague and eventually drove them into Venice in search of food, where they often congregated in the courtyard of the Ducal Palace.[32] Yet as Pullan has shown, the poor in cities, such as those who acted as undertakers, were not simply objects of fear as incubators and spreaders of disease, but also the objects of charity directed toward them as a supplication for Christ's mercy.[33]

Charity

In this context the representation of Lazarus, recounted in Luke (16:19-31), as the poor, sore-covered beggar who was ignored by the rich man, takes on significant meaning. A number of devotional paintings from this period can be linked to the presence of plague in Venice, such as Jacopo Tintoretto's *The Raising of Lazarus* of circa 1557 (cat. 37).[34] In this recently rediscovered work, Lazarus is dragged from a sarcophagus slab in the right foreground toward the center of the visual field by an unidentified young man, one arm supported by his sister Martha while his other sister Mary turns toward Christ (John 11:32). The miracle of Lazarus's resurrection is conveyed by the pristine beauty of his fine figure, reinforced by the figures of the two men in the central background who hold handkerchiefs to their noses because of the expected stench of death and decay that, in this case, fails to emanate (John 11:39). The smell of death was surely one of the overwhelming urban phenomena during times of plague.

Charity to the poor as an act of placation is also represented by Bernardo Strozzi's *An Act of Mercy* (cat. 10).[35] Strozzi renders the act of feeding the poor (Matthew 25: 35-40), in pure caravaggesque mode, bathing in light the two figures in the front plane but leaving in shadow the young boy and the old man to the left. While the sagging flesh of the old man in profile recalls similar figures in Caravaggio's work, the woman swathed in beautiful fabrics recalls the Gentileschis' art.[36] Strozzi painted this work around a decade before his transfer to Venice in 1630, the year plague devastated the city. As a former Capuchin dedicated to helping the poor and the suffering, he must have been particularly attuned to the needs of plague victims, but the horror that must have confronted him there is well conveyed by another religious observer, the Jesuit Domenico Cosso who wrote from Venice on 18 January 1577, "Oh what very great compassion and grief, together with fear, to see the houses, the shops, and the churches closed and barricaded with crossed planks across the doors as a sign and as a barrier! The city was almost deserted, so that it was unusual to see some poor men in a street, each fleeing the others as if they feared their shadows.... So many, many barges full of dead bodies packed like sardines [*composti come le sardelle*] and so many barges full of infected goods passed by that the wind brought a great stench and stink, even from the lazaretto as a result of the multitude of bodies and the burning of infected goods."[37]

Something of this horror is evident in Domenico Tintoretto's preparatory design of 1631, sketch for a plague banner, *The Virgin Supplicating Christ for Plague-Stricken Venice* (cat. 36).[38] Unlike the final work, with its pious women, in the *modello*, in addition to the undertakers in the middle ground carrying away dead bodies, Tintoretto depicted both dead bodies in the foreground and the terrifying image of a boarded-up house, whose inhabitants were left to their fate.[39]

Fear and denial

The fear of being boarded up and abandoned was one reason any outbreak of plague created such panic throughout the city; often the houses were so tall and narrow that dead bodies could hardly be extracted and were thrown from windows instead.[40] As is well known, in order to avoid isolation the government blatantly tried everything in its power to prevent any declaration of plague – barefaced denial was preferable to being blockaded. Foreign representatives were systematically lied to, somewhat like the dissimulation to Gustav von Aschenbach by the hoteliers and other authorities in Thomas Mann's *Death in Venice*.[41] For once blockades were effected, fear (*paura*) would spread through the city faster than the disease itself.[42]

Denying the existence of the plague, however, seriously delayed effective response and often resulted in a greater epidemic. This was certainly the case for the 1575-77 plague that claimed Titian's son Orazio along with almost fifty thousand other victims.[43] Preceded by years of famine, the 1575-77 plague was one of the worst in Venice's history. It was brought to the city by one Matthio from Trent, who died in the parish of S. Basegio in Venice on 2 July 1575. Disastrously, the clothes he brought with him were sold to pay the expenses of his illness and funeral.[44] This lapse – indeed collapse – in the systematic procedures of the

Provveditori alla Sanità, designed to prevent the origination, importation, and spread of plague in Venice, was due to their being over-burdened in the 1570s with other duties such as the enforcement of poor laws, taking the census of the city's population, and policing the bearing of arms by travelers.[45]

Following the initial declaration of plague, matters were made worse by the senate, which called for additional testimony from medical experts at the University of Padua. These medics – Girolamo Mercuriale and Girolamo Capodivacca – humiliated the *Provveditori* by making a public announcement that there was no plague in city, so that the shutting up of houses and deployment of lazarettos was severely curtailed.[46] The pronouncement by the Paduan medics was well received whereas the *Provveditori* were considered to be exaggerating the case for their own interests.[47] These medics then proceeded to personally inspect the sick in order to offer reassurance but eventually the numerous outbreaks became too widespread and subsequently it was recognized that the movement of the Paduan doctors between the sick and the healthy probably contributed to the enormous scale of the outbreak.[48] Indeed, the practical concern to limit the movement of people and goods repeatedly brought the *Provveditori* into direct conflict with the religious authorities and the state's traditional recourse to devotion and supplication.

Science versus supplication

Science dictated isolation and, in 1576, in addition to the confinement of people in their houses, a plan was hatched for the mass evacuation of ten thousand poor to tents and barracks at Lizzafusina.[49] All assemblies were forbidden and the *sestieri* of Castello, Cannaregio, and S. Marco were placed under an eight-day quarantine.[50] Yet the religious response called for increased numbers of ritual processions through the city to demonstrate repentance for ignoring God's repeated signs of wrath, in hindsight recognized by doge Alvise Mocenigo in the 1569-70 famine, the Arsenale and Ducal Palace fires of 1569 and 1574, and the Turkish wars of 1570-73.[51]

Despite the tight controls on movement and public assembly, an annual votive procession to the Scuola Grande of S. Rocco was instigated by the government in 1576 together with its vow to build a new church and pledge an annual procession to it.[52] This was the context in which Il Redentore was commissioned by the senate on 4 September 1576 and dedicated to Christ the Redeemer.[53] After much debate a site on the Giudecca overlooking the canal was chosen and the architect Andrea Palladio first designed a centralized church.[54] Iconographically, the centralized form was appropriate for a church erected as a votive response to a plague and perfectly expressed Palladio's desire to design architecture based on antique precedent.[55] After this was rejected, Palladio designed a longitudinal church that more effectively accommodated the seating arrangements for the annual visit by the doge and government members as well as the ritual processions of clergy and confraternity members.[56] (See Pamela Jones's essay, p. 55 for Milan's processions and the plague.)

Architectural programs and votive processions

Like other ducal visits, there were two distinct parts to the feast-day procession to the Redentore, as represented by Giuseppe Heintz the Younger (fig. 55).[57] The doge and *signoria* arrived by boat from piazza S. Marco and processed up the magnificent flight of stairs and through the nave of the church to attend a low Mass in the sanctuary. As this group left the Redentore, the members of the *Scuole*, the congregations of priests and other religious, who had processed over the two votive bridges, respectively traversing the Grand and Giudecca

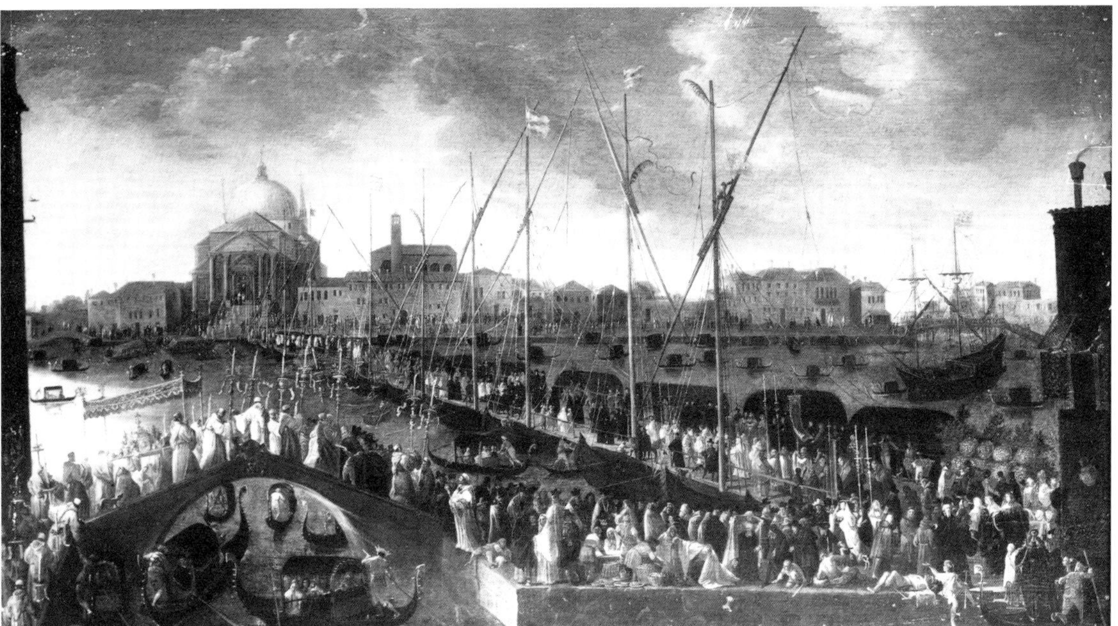

55. Giuseppe Heintz the Younger, *The Procession to the Redentore*, ca. 1630. Oil on canvas. Museo Correr, Venice.

Canals, now processed through the Redentore before returning over the two bridges and passing through the choir of S. Marco before the doge and *signoria*.[58] Similar strategies and ceremonies were adopted to combat the plague of 1630.

In 1630 processions were instigated by the zealous patriarch Giovanni Tiepolo even before plague reached the city.[59] The three *sestieri* of S. Marco, S. Rocco, and S. Pietro di Castello, were declared to be of special holiness and the "holy ashes" of Lorenzo Giustinian, the first patriarch of Venice and a famous healer of the sick in the lazaretto, were displayed at S. Pietro di Castello, the cathedral of Venice. Patriarch Tiepolo also requested Giustinian's canonization at this time, an act that foreshadowed the development of his cult in the seventeenth century as an intercessionary figure with respect to the plague. Following initial, practical decrees to clear areas of Venice of beggars, the government turned to traditional acts of supplication and, with their decree of 22 October 1630, commissioned the new church of S. Maria della Salute and vowed to hold an annual procession.[60]

From the outset, the vow linked the new church to ceremony, as seen in Bernadino Prudenti's *The Virgin and Child with Saint Mark the Evangelist, the Blessed Lorenzo Giustiniani, Saint Roch and Saint Sebastian Expelling the Plague from Venice* (fig. 56). Commissioned on 24 November 1631, the painting was completed in just four days so that it could be displayed from a platform located in front of the porticoes of the Procuratie Nuove during processions.[61] Apart from the familiar profile of Lorenzo Giustinian, Prudenti also represented the church of the Salute according to the winning design by Baldassare Longhena.

After his proposal was selected in June 1631, Longhena revised his design at the request of the deputies appointed to supervise the construction of the building. The church comprises a sequence of interrelated but relatively autonomous spaces including a domed rotunda surrounded by an ambulatory, a domed apsidal sanctuary, and a choir for the conventuals beyond the high altar, which together fulfilled the complex requirements of the Venetian senate that commissioned the building, including the need to accommodate participants in the annual ceremony.[62] Each year, on 21 November, the doge, *signoria*, and senate went in boats to S. Maria della Salute, ascending the magnificent flight of stairs and entering the principal door thrown open to receive the procession. Boschini's engraving *The Doge Nicolò Contarini visiting*

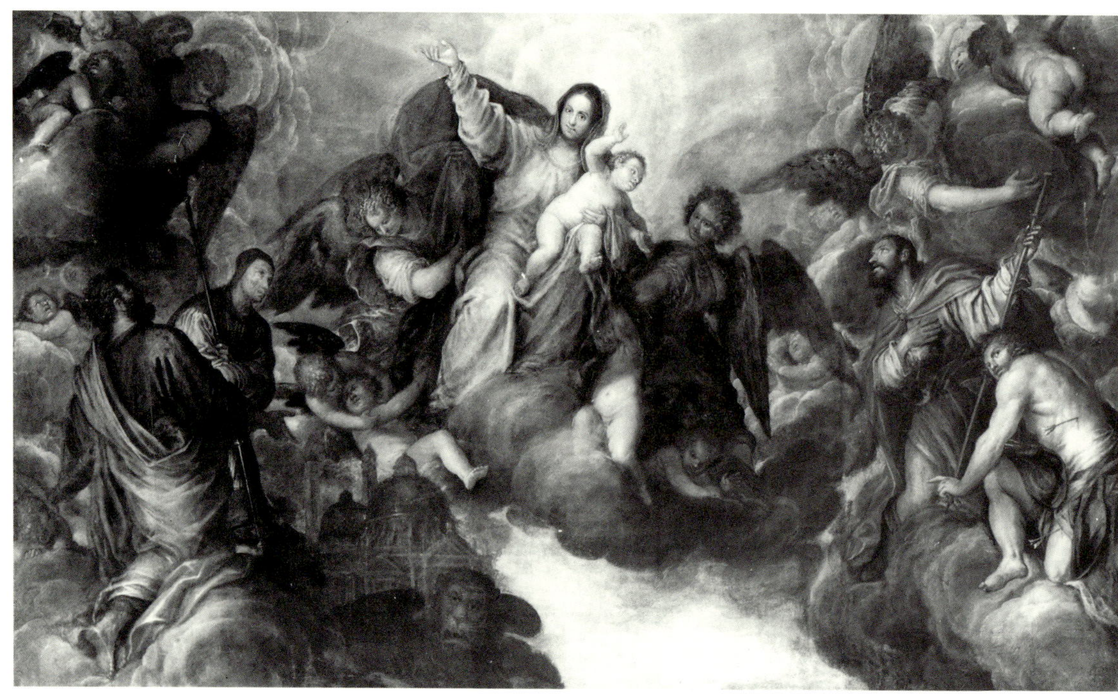

56. Bernadino Prudenti, *The Virgin and Child, with Saint Mark the Evangelist, the Blessed Lorenzo Giustiniani, Saint Roch, and Saint Sebastian Expelling the Plague from Venice*, 1631. Oil on canvas. S. Maria della Salute, Venice.

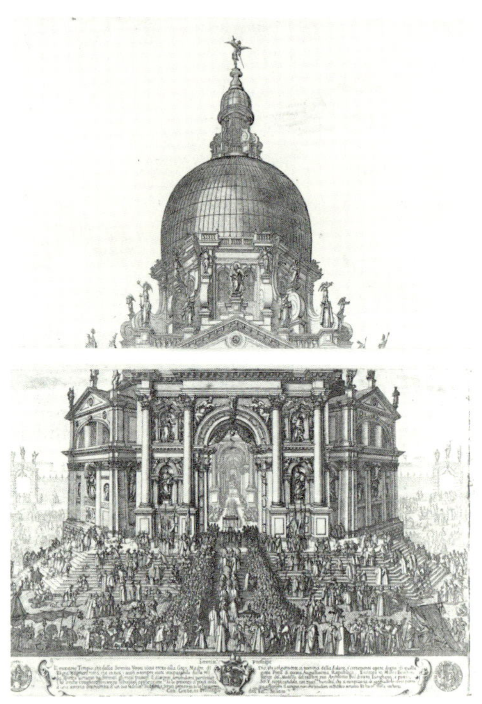

57. Marco Boschini, *The doge Nicolò Contarini visiting S. Maria della Salute in Procession*, 1644. Etching with some engraving in two plates. Den Kongelige Kobberstiksamling, Statens Museum For Kunst, Copenhagen.

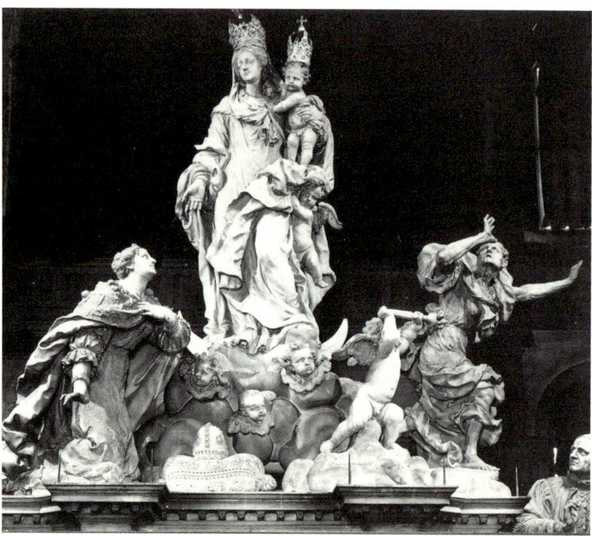

58. Baldassare Longhena and Giusto le Court, *High Altar with Saint Mark, Lorenzo Giustiniani and Venetia, who Implore the Virgin and Child to Expel Plague who Flees their Attack*. Carrara marble. Santa Maria della Salute, 1670. Venice.

S. Maria della Salute in Procession captures the view into the building (fig. 57). Once inside, this group moved directly through the center of the church and into the sanctuary, attending a low Mass before returning in boats to the piazza and hence to S. Marco. Equally significant was the second processional group that included thousands of members of the Scuole Grandi and the regular clergy who came in procession and most probably entered the Salute by one of the small doors, proceeded around the ambulatory of the rotunda, thus passing all six altars of the rotunda and the high altar, before leaving through the other side door and returning over the pontoon bridge to S. Marco. The ambulatory of the rotunda was designed to accommodate this processional movement of the Scuole and religious through the church on its feast day, as Longhena himself stated in his original memorandum accompanying his design: "Between the large nave of the church and the chapels, there will be space for being able to go around and around with the processions of the main feast days without the impediment of the people that one finds in the middle of the church."[63]

Quite a different aspect of this ceremony, the pontoon bridge, became the focus of a splendid large canvas by Luca Carlevarijs, *The Feast of S. Maria della Salute* (cat. 33). Carlevarijs's focus on the bridge thrown across the Grand Canal foreshadows the entire development of Venetian *vedute*. The painting's structure is based, at the left, on the line of palaces of the Grand Canal that funnels the view onto the *bacino* and the line of buildings that stretches along the waterfront all the way to the end of the *sestiere* of Castello. The Grand Canal and the pontoon bridge occupy the center of the painting, enabling Carlevarijs to bring forward the human element in the closely observed genre details, including ladies, nuns, and schoolgirls – all a far cry from the ducal procession with members of the Venetian confraternities represented in Giuseppe Heintz the Younger's work. To the right Carlevarijs depicts Giuseppe Benoni's Dogana da Mar (customs house), built after Longhena's original designs were rejected, with Palladio's highly recognizable Benedictine church of S. Giorgio Maggiore in the distance.[64] Rather curiously, however, Carlevarijs deliberately avoided representing the destination of the votive procession that is the focus of almost every view-painting subsequently executed on this spot in Venice.

Plague concealed and revealed

Just as Carlevarijs's and Heintz's canvases focus on processions rather than plague, so too at S. Maria della Salute only one of the last works to be executed in the decorative program explicitly referred to plague: Giusto le Court's *High Altar with Saint Mark, Lorenzo Giustiniani and Venetia who Implore the Virgin and Child to Expel Plague who Flees their Attack* (fig. 58).[65] This sculptural ensemble executed in 1670 is one of le Court's most powerful works and plague, traditionally represented as a withered old hag with swirling drapery, raises her right arm in an attempt to ward off attack.[66]

The presence of Venetia, together with Saint Mark and Lorenzo Giustinian, gives a local iconography to this work commemorating the 1630 plague, just as Giambattista Tiepolo's *modello* of *Saint Thecla Praying for the Plague-Stricken* (cat. 7) refers to the devastating impact of the same plague on the town of Este in the Veneto.[67] The *modello* and finished high altarpiece in the church of the Grazie at Este were commissioned from Tiepolo following his triumphal return from Würzburg to Venice in 1753. At this time Tiepolo worked for Lodovico Rezzonico, who concurrently employed the architect Giorgio Massari to complete his palace on the Grand Canal, begun in mid-seventeenth century by Longhena.[68] Tiepolo's *modello* was probably painted in 1758, as the finished altarpiece was installed on the high altar on Christmas Eve 1759.[69]

Variations between the *modello* and the final oil include substantial changes to the back-

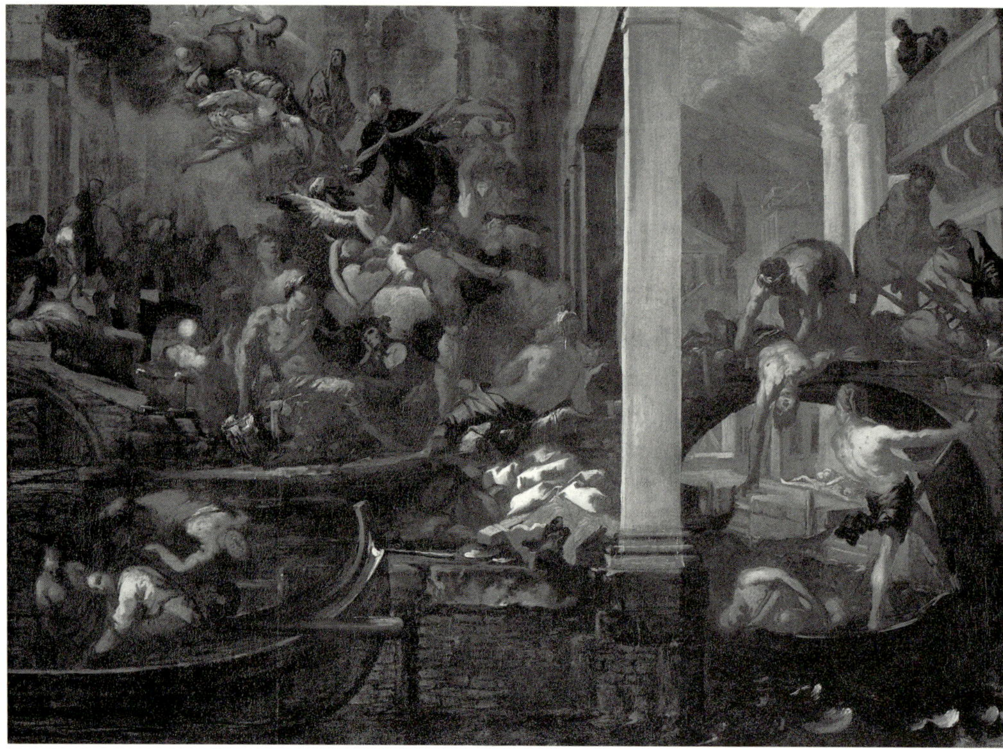

59. Antonio Zanchi, *The Plague in Venice*, 1666. Oil on canvas. Kunsthistorisches Museum, Vienna.

ground view of Este. The addition of a plague-ridden body being carried away more convincingly links the foreground action to the middle ground, where three additional exclaiming figures link Saint Thecla to the left with the city of Este in the background. But the raw action of the *modello* is much subdued in the final painting: gone is the brutal male about to separate the baby clinging rather desperately to its mother. This figure and the adjacent, awkward pair of disembodied legs are eliminated. The unfortunate conjunction in the *modello* of the knees of the demon and the head of Saint Thecla was altered in the finished altarpiece so that the fleeing figure is quite separate. Commissioned and executed for this small but important town whose patron saint was Thecla, Tiepolo's work is a poignant reminder that plague often devastated the countryside with even harsher consequences and greater loss of life. Apart from the wonderfully delicate coloring, this is also Tiepolo's most convincing rendition of spirituality and has great emotional depth.[70]

Later paintings are further testament to the continuing impact of the idea of plague. Antonio Zanchi's *The Plague in Venice* (fig. 59) is preparatory to the full-size works decorating the imperial staircase of the Scuola Grande di S. Rocco, where they would be seen by those processing up to the *sala capitolare* and Tintoretto's masterful cycle. Zanchi's overly dramatic works focus on the horrific results of the plague, including dead bodies being taken away by boat, others being dragged onto the bridge to be lowered into the boat, or simply thrown into the water. The decoration of this staircase complex reminds us of the conflicts and contradictions inherent in the various responses to the plague. Yet again time and money were dedicated to decoration as a demonstration of devotion in the hope of saving the city and its inhabitants. Together with the Virgin on the main dome of S. Maria della Salute, the celebratory nature of the Scuola Grande di San Rocco refers not to the darkest hours of epidemic but rather to Venice's victory over plague through the intercession of its heavenly protectors.

My thanks to the editors of the catalog, to Deborah Howard and all the fellows and staff of Villa I Tatti. A particular debt is owed to Richard Palmer, whose important doctoral dissertation of 1978 was only very partially published but whose research has informed much of this essay, and to the fundamental scholarship of Brian Pullan.

1. Joannides, 148-51. The painting may also allude to the League of Cambrai.
2. Hopkins 2000, 73-74.
3. See the pioneering research on the history of the plague in Venice by Palmer. Preto 1978. Preto 1979, 97-98. Preto 1984, 377-406. Preto 1991, 177-92. The fundamental early work is by J. Howard, 10, who referred to Venice as "the place where lazarettos were first established." (See Pamela Jones's essay, p. 3 in this volume, for lazaretto and containment policies in Milan.). Similar policies of coercive isolation without external recourse were adopted by the US government at Guantanamo bay for HIV-positive Haitian refugees in the 1980s and for so-called enemy combatants since late 2001.
4. *Venezia e la peste*, 363. See the stimulating essay by Cosgrove. For the less attractive side of the Venetian authorities see Queller.
5. The original decree, Archivio di Stato di Venezia (hereafter ASV), Senato Misti, register 54, c.141v, is published in *Venezia e la peste*, 365. See also Palmer, 183-86 for the etymology of "*nazareto = lazzaretto*". Also see Vanzan Marchini.
6. Other patients, such as the infirm and the mad, were deliberately not held at the lazarettos. A good account of the architecture is given by Morachiello, 158. Also see Vanzan Marchini 2004. For a much later period see Bergdoll. Much recent work on hospitals and charity has been done in the Florentine context, for which see the work of Henderson and, for an account and images of the Florentine plague of 1630 see Baldinucci, and Pagliarulo.
7. Zitelli and Palmer. Other possible causes were noted, including planetary conjunctions or sodomy, the latter being, in theory, controllable. During the 1464 plague the *Consiglio dei Dieci* (Council of Ten) discussed "increasing" the punishment for sodomy from decapitation to death by burning, for which see Palmer, 291, and the essay by Mormando in this catalog.
8. The original decree ASV, Senato Terra Registro (hereafter STR) 6, c.29r, is published in *Venezia e la peste*, 366. See also Palmer, 355.
9. Palmer, 190.
10. Palmer, 189-95. See also Bergdoll, 5.
11. ASV, STR 9, c.168r, STR 10, c.189v. Cited in Palmer, 62-64, 73-74. The staff included a *nodaro* (notary), *scrivan* (book-keeper), *capitano* (captain), and *fanti* (servants/infantry). As noted by Palmer, 127-30, 135, the *Provveditori alla Sanità* between 1498 and 1504 also issued other important decrees that recognized the danger of drinking bad water from wells and eating rotten food. They prohibited the emptying of chamber pots from balconies and the discharge of household waste and sewage pipes directly onto the streets, described as a "*cosa oltra che la sii vergognosa et puvolente e etiam pericolosa de generar vari morbi*"; they also insisted upon the importance of cleaning by *scovadori* or *mundadori* (rubbish-collectors) of *scovazze* (rubbish) which was to be taken to *scovazzere* (dumps), although much ended up in the canals, for which see ASV Provveditori alla Sanità, Register 2, cc.25v, 27r-28r. These dumps were hardly satisfactory as indicated by one Tomitano "quei luoghi chiamati in Venetia gattoli. Perciochè io gli ho veduti alle volte si pieni di bruttura, e fetenti per la corruzione delle herbe e scorze di meloni, e altre si fatte cose putride, che io ne ho preso una grande meraviglia, come l'aere ogni anno non venga ad alterarsi e generare delle febbri pestifere," cited by Palmer, 118.
12. Pullan, 1971. Pignatti, 1981.
13. Fabri.
14. Posocco. Palmer, 285-86. D. Howard, 2002, 156-59. Guidarelli.
15. For the staircases see Sohm. For the staircase of the Scuola Grande della Misericordia see Fabbri. Also see Guidarelli.
16. Muir, 216, 227. A recent analysis of the columns applied to the facade can be found in Gaier 2002, 76.
17. Tafuri, 125-54.
18. Anderson, 284.
19. Exemplum held at the British Museum, London (inv. 1860-4-14-140), woodcut in a single block, 56 x 40.2 cm. See Rosand and Muraro, 108-111, cat.12A. *Venezia e la Peste*, 240-41, cat.a14. Howard D. 2002, 156.
20. Rosand and Muraro, 110. Above the main image is the apparition of Christ carrying the cross, modeled on the Scuola's devotional work, probably by Titian, but often given to Giorgione, for which see Ferrara, 168-75. For the symptoms of bubonic plague see Palmer, ix, xvii, citing Mercuriale, 2-3, "*carbunculi, vibices frequentissimae in dorso, maculae nigrae, violaceae, rubeae.*"
21. *Venezia e la Peste*, 240-41. For Roch, see the essay in this catalog by Thomas Worcester.
22. Wyke. Talvacchia.
23. Hopkins 2000, 71-73.
24. Venice, S. Fantin, 350 x 290 cm, signed and dated 1632, inscribed: "*Jo. Pomellus pleb(anus) Ducalis Canon(icus) Cong(regation)is S. Pauli arch(ipresbite)r.*"
25. Martin, 120-23.
26. ASV, San Giorgio Maggiore, busta 53, processo 80, letter from the patriarch, Giovanni Tiepolo, to the Benedictines, "vi facciamo sapere che da noi sieti stati deputati ministrar li sacramenti necessarij nella presente occasione di contaggio in quella parte della Giudecca", together with other "documenti che sta-

biliscono li Monaci Cassinensi non esser obbligati in tempo di peste alla amministrazione di sacramenti."

27. Palmer, 91-96. Fracastoro defined contagion as "an infection that passes from one thing to another," for which see the translation with notes by Wilmer Wright, New York, 1930, 3. Massaria, and the essay by Mormando in this catalog. In 1594 Fynes Morison, who believed that the city's marshy site was unhealthy, compared the canals to the veins in a human body, Morison, I, 163. Also see Cipolla.

28. Palmer, 98-102, 111-12. Notable events during this plague included the deaths of the priors of both lazarettos. Foucault, focused on the later period for his brilliant analyses.

29. Palmer, 114, citing Archivio di Stato di Firenze, Archivio Mediceo del Principato, filza 2971, c.284, 27 June 1556, citing the ambassador: "tutti questi sono poverissimi." See the important work by Geremek, esp. in this context pp.131-36. Also see the essay by Mormando in this catalog.

30. Palmer, 115 cites Nicolò Massa, "Raggionamento," stating that the poor were at risk because they bought the worst food and lived in "casupule piene di figliuoli," c.20r-v, which were then shut up, "stando serrati s'infirmano, perche in quel poco di luogo hanno la scaffa, il necessario, et ogni altra sorte d'immonditie della casa, di tal maniera che l'aere è quasi putrido," c.17v. Palmer, 144, "conoscendosi chiaramente dell'esperienza che tal augmento nasce principalmente perche questo afflito populo si trova per lo più habitar in casette molto ristrette et anguste," citing ASV Provveditori alla Sanità, Register 3, cc.29v-30v.

31. Pullan 1992, 101-23, reprinted in Pullan 1994.

32. Pullan 1992.

33. Pullan 1994, 106-7.

34. Mormando 2000, 625. See also Avagnina, 308-10, cat.24, and the essay by Mormando in this catalog.

35. Milkovitch, 36-36, cat.12. Mortari, 165-66, cat.378.

36. For Caravaggio see Langdon and for Gentileschi see Christiansen and Mann.

37. Martin, 51.

38. The *modello* is at Princeton University (inv. 48-1910) and the final oil at S. Francesco della Vigna in Venice.

39. Narrow houses were especially a feature of the Ghetto. Concina *et al.* Boccato, 111-46.

40. Defoe.

41. Mann. The best early modern account of plague is still Defoe. Also see the essay by Mormando in this catalog.

42. One of the most convincing points made by Samuel Cohn is the rapidity with which plague spread in the past, compared with the extremely slow spread of bubonic plague, Cohn, 1. One suspects that the rapid diffusion of the 1575-77 and 1630-31 plagues would indicate fast and widespread conversion from bubonic to pneumonic plague. Also see the essay by Mormando in the catalog.

43. Preto 1979, 97-98. Although Titian died during the plague, the cause given in his death certificate was "fever" and he did not die in the lazaretto. His son Orazio did die of plague in the lazaretto: communication of Charles Hope for which I am most grateful. Contemporary accounts were written by Lumina, and Benedetti and Lumina.

44. Palmer, 211.

45. Palmer, 123, 213, 219.

46. Palmer, 246.

47. Palmer, 251, 278, noting a similar occurrence in 1630 when Giovanni Battista Fuoli, the physician to the Health Office, was subjected to public hostility and threats to his life when he claimed there was plague.

48. Palmer, 253, 267.

49. Palmer, 144 citing ASV, Provveditori alla Sanità, Register 3, cc.29v-30v.

50. Palmer, 142-43, 301-2, the Scuola Grande di S. Rocco was closed sometimes during the plague as the conflict between the need for prayer and the danger of congregating was recognized.

51. Palmer, 280-82, 303-4, who cites the patriarch Giovanni Trevisan's recognition of God's wrath in his 1576 letter to the people of Venice, "afflitoni che giustamente patimo per la moltitudine di peccati nostri," and further, "per mitigar l'ira del Signor Dio provocata contra di questa città per la poca riverentia che si ha alli sacri tempi," ASV Secreta, Materie miste notabili, Register 95, cc.67r-68r.

52. ASV, Collegio Ceremoniale 1, c.71r, "Ordine tenuto dal Serenissimo Principe il giorno dell'assontion della Vergine e di S Rocho quando esce di Palazzo." Muir, 216.

53. Timofiewitsch.

54. Now see Howard 2003, 306-25. See also Pizzigoni.

55. Sinding-Larsen, in his important study of centralized churches of the Renaissance, listed four principal criteria, relevant from early Christian times onward, for which the centralized form was considered appropriate. These churches were: 1) martyria, sepulchral, or memorial buildings; 2) hospital churches or those dedicated to helpers against the plague; 3) churches dedicated to Christ's death or resurrection; and 4) churches dedicated to the Virgin Mary. Sinding-Larsen, 219. See also the important essay by Niero 1979.

56. Hopkins 1998, 30-48.

57. Museo Correr, 115 x 205 cm. This is one of the two important paintings of the Redentore, the other is by Alessandro Varotari called Padovanino, *The Doge Alvise Mocenigo kneeling before a model of the church of the Redentore*, Venice, collection of Marchesa Olga di Cadaval, cm 168 x 266. See *Venezia e la peste*, 264-65, cat. a38.

58. Ceremonial aspects are dealt with in Hopkins 1998, 30-48.
59. Palmer, 290, 306-309. Pullan 1994. Hopkins 2000, 134-53. The processions were also discussed in detail by Moore.
60. Hopkins 2000, 3-4.
61. Venice, S. Maria della Salute, oil on canvas, approximately 2m x 3m, but cut down from its original size at the bottom because the plague-stricken figures imploring the Virgin, which were originally depicted are no longer there, see *Venezia e la peste*, 263, cat.a37; Hopkins 2000, 9-10, cat.9. For the plague in Bologna in 1630 see Puglisi. The best-known plague painting from the Veneto is that by Antonio Giarola, called the Cavalier Coppa, whose *Verona supplicating the Trinity*, in the chapel of the Conception in the church of S. Fermo at Verona which explicitly shows a landscape covered by numerous corpses, see *Venezia e la peste* 1979, 270, cat.a45. For the Procuratie Nuove see Hopkins 2003b, 125.
62. Hopkins 2000, 134-53.
63. ASV STF 326, cc.12r–v. Hopkins 2000, 132-33.
64. For the Dogana, see, Hopkins 2002, 405-16. Guerra, 276-95.
65. *Venezia e la peste*, 277-78, cat.a52. Niero 1988, 137-40. Guerriero, 48-71.
66. Ripa, 397. Hopkins 2000, 75-81. Boucher, 161-63.
67. Morassi, 34, 151. Christiansen 1996, 317-19, cat.51. Whistler in Christiansen 1996, 189-97.
68. Pavanello.
69. Between July 1630 and October 1631 over 30% of Venice's population died: 46,490 deaths among 142,000 residents. The total number of deaths within the dogado, including the cities of Murano, Malamocco, and Chioggia, was 93,661. In certain cities of the terraferma, such as Padova, up to 60% of the inhabitants perished: 18,375 deaths among 31,988 residents; 17,700 of Vicenza's 31,897 residents died; 32,895 of Verona's 53,533 residents died; and in the province of Brescia approximately 140,000 people died. Within fifteen months between 300,000 and 700,000 inhabitants of Venice and the terraferma perished. Preto 1984. Ulvioni. Piva. Hopkins 2003a. Also see Mormando essay in this catalog.
70. Barcham. Now also see the dissertation by Fassl.

Bibliography

Anderson, Jaynie. *Giorgione: The Painter of "Poetic Brevity."* New York, 1997.

Avagnina, Maria Elisa. "Lazarus and the Rich Man," in *Jacopo Bassano c. 1510-1592*. Exh. cat. , eds. Beverly Brown and Paola Marini. Bologna, 1996, pp. 308-10, cat. 24.

Baldinucci, Giovanni. *Quaderno: peste, guerra e carestia nell'Italia del Seicento*, ed. Brendan Dooley, Florence, 2001.

Barcham, William. *The Religious Paintings of Giambattista Tiepolo: Piety and Tradition in Eighteenth-Century Venice*, Oxford, 1989.

Benedetti, Rocco and Mutio Lumina. *Raguaglio minutissimo del successo della peste di Venetia…* Tivoli, 1577.

Bergdoll, Barry. "The architecture of isolation: M.-R. Penchaud's quarantine hospital in the Mediterranean," *AA files* 14 (1987): 3-13.

Boccato, Carla. "La mortalità nel Ghetto di Venezia durante la peste del 1630," *Archivio Veneto* 140 (1993): 111-146.

Boucher, Bruce. *Italian Baroque Sculpture*. London, 1998.

Christiansen, Keith. *Giambattista Tiepolo*. Exh. cat. New York/Milan, 1996, pp.317-19, cat.51.

Christiansen, Keith and Judith Mann, eds. *Orazio and Artemisia Gentileschi*. Exh. cat. New Haven/London, 2001.

Cipolla, Carlo. *Public Health and the Medical Profession in the Renaissance*. Cambridge, 1976.

Cohn, Samuel. *The Black Death Transformed: Disease and Culture in Early Renaissance Europe*. London, 2002.

Concina, Ennio *et al. La Città degli Ebrei. Il Ghetto di Venezia: architettura e urbanistica*. Venice, 1991.

Cosgrove, Denis. "The myth and the stones of Venice: an historical geography of a symbolic landscape," *Journal of historical geography* 8 (1982): 145-69.

Defoe, Daniel. *A Journal of the Plague Year*. London, 1722.

Fabbri, Gianni, ed. *La Scuola Grande della Miseracordia di Venezia: storia e progetto*. Milan, 1999.

Fabri, Felix. *The Wanderings of Brother Felix Fabri*, trans. Aubrey Stewart. London 1892.

Fassl, Johanna. "Giambattista Tiepolo." PhD diss., Columbia University, 2004.

Ferrara, Daniele. "Christo portacroce," in *Giorgione: "Le maraviglie dell'arte,"* exh. cat. (Venice, Accademia), eds Giovanna Nepi Scirè and Sandra Rossi. Venice, 2003, pp. 168-75, cat. 10.

Foucault, Michel. *Discipline and Punish: The Birth of the Prison*, trans. Alan Sheridan. New York, 1977.

Fracastoro, Girolamo. *De contagione*, Venice, 1546 (translation with notes by Wilmer Wright, New York, 1930).

Gaier, Martin. *Facciate scare a scopo profano: Venezia e la politica dei monumenti dal Quattrocento al Settecento* (*Studi di Arte Veneta* 3). Venice, 2002.

Geremek, Bronislaw. *Poverty: A History*, trans. Agnieszka Kolakowska. Oxford, 1994.

Guerra, Andrea. "Palladio's plan for the church of San Giorgio Maggiore in Venice and its successive vicissitudes," *Journal of the Society of Architectural Historians* 61 (2002): 276-95.

Guerriero, Simone. "'Di tua Virtù che infonde spirto a i sassi': per la prima attività veneziana di Giusto Le Court," *Arte veneta* 55 (1999 [2001]): 48-71.

Guidarelli, Gianmario. *Una giogia ligata in piombo: la fabbrica della Scuola Grande di San Rocco in Venezia 1517-1560*. Venice, 2002.

Henderson, John. "Healing the body and saving the soul: hospitals in Renaissance Florence." *Renaissance Studies* 15/2: 188-216.

Henderson, John, *Piety and Charity in Late Medieval Florence*, Oxford, 1994.

Hopkins, Andrew. "The influence of ducal ceremony on church design in Venice," *Architectural History* 41 (1998): 30-48.

Hopkins, Andrew. *Santa Maria della Salute: architecture and ceremony in Baroque Venice*. Cambridge, 2000.

Hopkins, Andrew. "La Dogana da Mare e l'Isola della Salute: da zona industriale a zona di rappresentanza," in *Architettura: processualità e trasformazione* (*Quaderni dell'Istituto di storia dell'architettura* 34/39), eds. Maurizio Caperna e Gianfranco Spagnesi, 2002, pp. 405-16.

Hopkins, Andrew. "Venezia e il suo dominio," *Il Seicento (Storia della Architettura Italiana)*, 2 vols., ed. Aurora Scotti, Milan, 2003, II, pp. 400-423.

—. "Vincenzo Scamozzi e Baldassarre Longhena," in *Vincenzo Scamozzi 1548-1616*, exh. cat. (Vicenza, Centro Palladio), eds Franco Barbieri and Guido Beltramini. Venice, 2003, pp. 120-127.

Howard, Deborah. *The Architectural History of Venice*, rev. ed. New Haven/London, 2002.

Howard, Deborah. "Venice between East and West: Marc'Antonio Barbaro and Palladio's church of the Redentore," *Journal of the Society of Architectural Historians*, 62 (2003): 306-25.

Howard, John. *An Account of the Principal Lazarettos in Europe*. Warrington, 1789 (2nd ed. 1791).

Joannides, Paul. *Titian to 1518: The Assumption of Genius*. New Haven/London, 2001.

Langdon, Helen. *Caravaggio: A Life*. London, 1998.

Lumina, Mutio. *La liberazione di Vinegia*. Venice, 1577.

Mann, Thomas. *Death in Venice: Complete, Authoritative Text with Biographical and Historical Contexts, Critical History, and Essays from Five Contemporary Critical Perspectives*, ed. Naomi Ritter. Boston, 1998.

Martin, A. Lynne. *Plague? Jesuit accounts of epidemic disease in the sixteenth century*. Kirksville, 1996.

Massaria, Alessandro. *De peste libro duo*. Venice, 1579.

Mercuriale, Girolamo. *De pestilentia*. Venice, 1577.

Milkovich, Michael. *Bernardo Strozzi: paintings and drawings*. Exh. cat. (Binghamton N.Y., University Art Gallery). Binghamton, 1967.

Moore, James. "Venezia favorita da Maria: Music for the Madonna Nicopeia and Santa Maria della Salute," *Journal of the American Musicological Society* 37 (1984): 299-355.

Morachiello, Paolo. "Howard e i Lazzaretti da Marsiglia a Venezia: gli spazi della prevenzione," in *Venezia e la peste*, pp.157-64.

Morassi, Antonio. *G.B. Tiepolo: His Life and Work*. London, 1955.

Morison, Fynes. *An Itinerary*, 4 vols. Glasgow, 1907.

Mormando, Franco. "Tintoretto's Recently Rediscovered Raising of Lazarus," *The Burlington Magazine* 144 (2000): 624-29.

Mortari, Luisa. *Bernardo Strozzi*, 2nd ed. Rome, 1995.

Muir, Edward. *Civic ritual in Renaissance Venice*. Princeton, 1981.

Niero, Antonio. "I templi del Redentore e della Salute: motivazioni teologiche," in Venezia e la peste, pp. 294-98.

Niero, Antonio. "Precisazione e attribuzione a Giusto le Court," *Arte Veneta* 42 (1988): 137-40.

Pagliarulo, Giovanni. "Jacopo Vignali e gli anni della peste," *Artista: critica dell'arte in Toscana*, 1994: 138-198.

Palmer, Richard, "The control of plague in Venice and northern Italy 1348-1600." Ph.D. diss., University of Kent at Cantebury, 1978 (copy at the Kunsthistorisches Institut, Florence).

Pavanello, Giuseppe. "I Rezzonico: committenza e collezionismo fra Venezia e Roma," *Arte Veneta* 52 (1998): 87-111.

Pignatti, Teresio ed. *Le scuole di Venezia*. Milan, 1981.

Piva, Luigi. *La pestilenza nel Veneto*. Padua, 1991.

Pizzigoni, Vittorio. "I tre progetti di Palladio per il Redentore," *Annali di Architettura* 15 (2003 [2004]), pp. 165-178.

Posocco, Franco. *Scuola Grande di San Rocco: la vicenda urbanisctica e lo spazio scenico*. Citadella, 1997.

Preto, Paolo. *Peste e società a Venezia*. Vicenza, 1978.

Preto, Paolo. "Peste e demografia: l'età moderna: le due pesti del 1575-77 e 1630-31," in *Venezia e la peste*, pp. 97-98.

Preto, Paolo. "La società veneta e le grandi epidemie di peste," in *Storia della Cultura Veneta. Il Seicento*, eds Girolamo Arnaldi e Manlio Pastore Stocchi, 4/II. Vicenza, 1984, pp. 377-406.

Preto, Paolo. "Le grandi paure di Venezia nel secondo '500: le paure naturali (peste, carestie, incendi, terremoti)," in *Crisi e rinnovamenti nell'autunno del Rinascimento a Venezia*, eds. Vittore Branca and Carlo Ossola. Florence, 1991, pp.177-92.

Puglisi, Catherine. "Guido Reni's Pallione del Voto and the plague of 1630," *The Art Bulletin* 77 (1995): 402-12.

Pullan, Brian. *Rich and Poor in Renaissance Venice. The Social Institutions of a Catholic State*. Oxford, 1971.

Pullan, Brian. "Plague and perceptions of the poor in early modern Italy," in *Epidemics and Ideas: Essays on the Historical Perception of Pestilence*, eds. Terence Ranger and Paul Slack. Cambridge, 1992, pp.101-23. (Reprinted in Pullan, Brian, *Poverty and Charity: Europe, Italy, Venice, 1400-1700*, Aldershot, 1994.)

Queller, Donald. *The Venetian Patriciate: Reality versus Myth*. Urbana, 1986.

Rosand, David and Michelangelo Muraro. *Titian and the Venetian Woodcut*, exh. cat. (Washington, National Gallery of Art). Washington, 1976.

Ruggeri, Ugo. "Alessandro Varotari detto il Padovanino," *Saggi e memorie di storia dell'arte* 16 (1988): 101-65.

Staale Sinding-Larsen. "Some functional and iconographic aspects of the centralized church in the Italian Renaissance," *Acta ad archflologiam et artium historiam pertinentia* 2 (1965): 203-52.

Sohm, Philip. "The staircases of the Venetian Scuole Grandi and Mauro Codussi," Architectura 7 (1978):125-49.

Tafuri, Manfredo. *Venezia e il rinascimento: religione, scienza, architettura*. Turin, 1985.

Talvacchia, Bette. "The Double Life of Saint Sebastian in Renaissance Art," in *The Body in Early Modern Italy*, eds. Julia Hairston and Walter Stephens. Baltimore, Johns Hopkins Press, forthcoming.

Timofiewitsch, Wladimir. *The Chiesa del Redentore* (*Corpus Palladianum* 3), University Park, Pa., 1971.

Ulvioni, Paolo. *Il Gran castigo di Dio: carestia ed epidemie a Venezia e nella terraferma 1628-1632*. Milan, 1989.

Vanzan Marchini, Nelli-Elena. *Le leggi di sanità della repubblica di Venezia*, 4 vols. Vicenza, 1995-98.

Vanzan Marchini, Nelli-Elena, ed. *Rotte mediterranee e baluardi di sanità: Venezia e I lazzaretti mediterranei*. Milan, 2004.

Venezia e la peste 1348-1797. Exh. cat., Venice, 1979.

von der Malsburg, Raban. *Die architektur der Scuola Grande di S. Rocco in Venedig*. Heidelberg, 1976.

Whistler, Catherine. "Tiepolo as a religious artist," in Christiansen 1996, 189-97.

Wyke, Maria. "Playing Roman soldiers: the martyred body, Derek Jarman's Sebastiane and the representation of homosexuality," in Maria Wyke ed., *Parchments of gender: deciphering the bodies of antiquity*, Oxford, 1998, pp. 243-266.

Zitelli, Andreina and Richard Palmer. "Le teorie mediche sulla peste e il contesto veneziano," in *Venezia e la peste* 1979, pp. 21-28.

Saint Roch vs. Plague, Famine, and Fear

THOMAS WORCESTER

The cult of Saint Roch was as international as it was Italian; it owed much of its development to painting and to the printing press. As Andrew Hopkins has shown, in his essay in the present catalogue, Saint Roch figured prominently among the saints depicted by Venetian painters as offering hope and healing in time of plague. In Venice and indeed over much of the Italian peninsula, Saint Roch was a focus of devotion, a devotion that elicited paintings of Roch that in turn inspired further devotion.[1] In this, the concluding essay of the exhibition catalogue, I shall examine some of the ways in which the cult of Saint Roch developed from the late fifteenth century on, in word and image, not only in Italy but also beyond the Alps, especially in France. Just as the threat of plague, and outbreaks of what was thought to be plague, were both chronologically long and geographically wide, so too was the popularity of Saint Roch.[2]

I shall begin consideration of the cult of Saint Roch with examination of two *vitae* first published in the fifteenth century. Then I shall consider the various roles in which Roch was imagined: as a pilgrim, as ill with plague, as healed by an angel, as fed by a dog, as a saint visiting/caring for the poor and the sick, as a saint paired with Saint Sebastian, and as a saint interceding with Christ and the Virgin. Paintings in this exhibition show Roch in all these roles, as do a number of other paintings I shall consider. Having examined Roch in painting in Italy, I shall examine some of the ways in which the Transalpine cult of Saint Roch prospered, and some of the ways in which the recurrence of plague promoted circulation of ideas and images across national and geographic borders. Finally, I shall examine how this exhibition contributes to on-going debate among historians of early modern Europe on "mentalities" of fear and reassurance. Paul Slack has argued that epidemics of the past "throw a peculiarly sharp light on the ideologies and mentalities of the societies they afflicted."[3] If Slack is right, painting done in the shadow of plague may offer a bright light onto such mentalities.

Lives of Saint Roch

An anonymous life of Saint Roch, probably written around 1430, gained wide attention with the advent of the printing press in the second half of the fifteenth century. Known as the *Acta Breviora*, this life of Roch, written in Latin, has been published in a volume by Angelo Fanelli that includes another life of Saint Roch, Francesco Diedo's *Vita Sancti Rochi*. Diedo was a Venetian, a professor of law at Padua, and governor of Brescia when he wrote this *vita* in 1478, and it was first printed the following year. In 1477 there had been a severe outbreak of plague in Brescia.[4] Diedo's text was published at various times, in Latin and in several translations into the vernacular; other *vitae* of Saint Roch produced in the late 1400s and beyond often relied heavily on the *Acta Breviora* and on Diedo.[5] Whether or not these were historically accurate *vitae* – or indeed whether or not a Roch ever existed at all – is not a question I shall pursue.[6] It is certain that the cult of Saint Roch developed rapidly from the late fifteenth century on, and this is the topic at hand.

The unknown author of the *Acta Breviora* recounts Roch's birth in terms reminiscent of that of Saint John the Baptist (in Luke 1:1-80): Roch is born to pious parents who had long wanted a son. Identified as Joannes and Libera, Roch's parents are overjoyed at his birth; they also find that he was born with a red cross on his chest. Roch's father dies when the boy is but twelve years old, and his mother when he is fifteen. Leaving his native city of Montpellier, in southern France, Roch decides to make various pilgrimages in Christendom (*varias per christianitatem peregrinationes agere*).[7] But, while the reader might expect to hear of Jersusalem, of Santiago de Compostela, or Rome and other pilgrimage destinations popular among late medieval Christians,[8] the only pilgrimage Roch is reported to have made was to Rome. The anonymous *vita* recounts Roch's experiences on his way to Rome, in Rome, and returning from Rome.

In recounting Roch's pilgrimage, the *Acta Breviora* frequently attributes healings from plague to Roch's invocation of the name of the Jesus. The name of Jesus was a devotion that grew rapidly in fifteenth-century Italy; the Observant Franciscan Bernardino of Siena was a key figure in promotion of the Holy Name.[9] On the way to Rome, according to the *Acta Breviora,* there was a "most cruel" plague in Acquapendente. Roch visited the hospital day and night, and touched the people without fear (*impavide*). He blessed them in the name of Christ Jesus, visiting every house infected with plague, and cured everyone whom he touched with the sign of the cross. He also liberated Cesena, long tormented by a plague no less intense, in a short time.[10]

The entire city of Rome was infected with plague, including a cardinal from Angera, "in the Lombard province." Roch made a sign of the cross on the cardinal's forehead; the cross remained on the cardinal's forehead and he was freed from the plague. When the cardinal asked Roch to erase the cross, lest he become a spectacle for the people, Roch exhorted him to always wear the cross in memory of the Passion of the Redeemer, by whom he was delivered from the plague. The cardinal presented Roch to the pope, who gave Roch a plenary indulgence. Roch stayed in Rome with the cardinal for three years, working among the poor and plague-infected.[11]

When the cardinal died, Roch left Rome for Rimini, and then Novara, both cities he liberated from plague. In Piacenza, he spent a long period at the hospital curing the sick. Afflicted with great pain (*gravi dolore*), he withdrew to a wooded place, in a solitary valley not far from Piacenza, where he built a small refuge. There Roch prayed to God, thanking the Savior Jesus for having given him the plague that the others had, and asking him for grace. As soon as he had finished the prayer, a beautiful fountain sprang up and refreshed him.[12]

Biblical stories appear to serve as models for a number of events in Roch's life. A miraculous fountain in the wilderness would have reminded many readers of the biblical story of Moses and water from the rock in the desert (Exodus 17:1-7). In a similar manner, what follows in the *Acta Breviora* could have recalled Jesus calling the rich young man to give up all that he had and to follow him (Luke 18:18-30). Near the woods where Roch was stood the rural residence of a wealthy noble named Gothardus; his dog brought bread daily to Roch. One day Gothardus followed his dog and found Roch. Roch gave thanks to God and exhorted Gothardus to renounce his goods and follow the way of Christ, seeking alms and bread, in his name. Roch was actually more successful with Gothardus than Jesus apparently had been with the rich young man, for Gothardus eventually does what he was called to do.[13]

The *Acta Breviora* concludes with Roch freeing Piacenza from plague, with Roch himself cured of plague by an angel, and with Roch's imprisonment and death in the city of Angera. Roch frees Piacenza from plague, by touching and blessing in the name of Jesus (*in nomine Jesu tangendo et benedicendo*). One day, while Roch is sleeping, Gothardus hears an angelic voice calling out to Roch and telling him that the Lord had heard his prayer and that he was cured of plague, so that he could go back to his fatherland. Gothardus recounts this to Roch; while Roch is returning to his *patria,* he stops at Angera. There he is arrested as a spy and imprisoned for five years. As death approaches, he confesses his sins to a priest; then, before his death an angel comes to him and asks him if he has any request. Roch asks that all those who reverence the name of Jesus be liberated from plague. After Roch's death a table is found upon which in golden letters it is written that God had heard Roch's prayer for the suffering persons. Also after Roch's death, his identity, hitherto unknown in Angera, is revealed by the table's inscription (of his name), and by an elderly woman, who recognizes the cross on his chest, and explains that he is in fact the son of Joannes of Montpellier, and nephew of the "lord" of Angera.[14]

Diedo's *vita* of Saint Roch differs from the *Acta Breviora* in a number of major ways. Diedo provides dates for Roch's birth (1295) and death (1327), and a number of other events.[15] Diedo makes explicit the similarity of Roch's birth to that of John the Baptist: Roch was born of devout, elderly parents as was John the Baptist of Elizabeth and Zechariah (*ut Joannem Baptistam ex Elizabeth et Zacharia*). Diedo cites more-or-less verbatim Luke 12:33, on selling all one has and giving to the poor. Diedo also highlights the dying father's exhortation to the young Roch to adore the suffering Christ, and to assist poor widows, children and especially orphans, and to avoid greed.[16]

As a pilgrim in Italy, Diedo's Roch goes beyond his father's exhortations, gaining a reputation for healing people of the plague, all the while remaining humble. At Acquapendente, those cured of plague consider Roch as sent from heaven (*e caelo missum*), but he implores them not to exalt his name (*ne eius nomen*).[17] Diedo identifies the cardinal Roch cures in Rome, as being from Britain. When the cardinal presents Roch to the pope, the cardinal explains that Roch is the one who had "indelibly" signed him with the cross. Roch prostrates himself on the ground at the feet of the pope, bathing them with his tears, and asking pardon for his sins. The pope declares that he is man of God and does not need pardon .[18] Before leaving Rome, Roch saves the people from plague; they give thanks to God for Roch.[19]

Diedo's version of Roch's stay in Piacenza is quite brief, but his account of Roch and Gothardus is more detailed than that in the *Acta Breviora*. A repentant Gothardus compares himself unfavorably to his own dog: "My dog, to whom nature gave no reason," shows compassion to this poor sick man, finding food for him and offering it to him. "But I, abounding in riches, to whom nature has given reason and the faculty of having compassion," left this man to die "alone and abandoned" in the wilderness.[20] Diedo explicitly compares Roch's experience of being fed in the wilderness with that of the biblical figure of Elijah, fed by a bird (1 Kings 17:6); he also recounts how Roch instructed Gothardus on the teachings of Saint Paul the Hermit, Saint Jerome, Saint Anthony and other hermits.[21] Having cured the sick in the hospital and elsewhere in Piacenza, Diedo's Roch is even sought out by the sick animals; they throw themselves at his feet, seeking a cure. A voice from heaven calls out to Roch, telling him that his prayer has been heard, that he himself is cured, and that he is to return to his native city.[22]

While Diedo's account of Roch's imprisonment and death is much like that in the *Acta Breviora*, he adds not only a date for his death, but an explanation of how devotion to him had spread in the 1400s. Diedo recounts how the Council of Constance met beginning in 1414. A "most cruel" plague (*pestis saevissima*) then broke out in that city, and the Council Fathers decided to leave Constance. But God inspired a young boy to speak to them, telling them that a certain Roch was much venerated by the French, and that all those who turned to him were freed from the plague. Following the boy's advice, the Fathers made a solemn procession through the city, accompanied by the people and by an image of Roch; they made public prayers and "mortified" their bodies with fasting and flagellation. The plague quickly ceased; the inhabitants of Constance as well as the conciliar assembly changed their sadness into joy, and the saint was given the highest honors in Germany.[23] Diedo concludes his *vita* by highlighting Italian devotion to Saint Roch. The Italian Fathers at the Council of Constance brought to us (*ad nos*) Roch's fame, he writes, and it inspired the construction of basilicas, chapels, and churches named after him, where one could see images, statues, and the testimonies of votive offerings.[24]

Such events may or may not have actually taken place during and after the Council of Constance, which met 1414-18.[25] Diedo's text offers important evidence, however, of how the cult of Saint Roch was perceived and promoted in late fifteenth-century Italy. His cult was considered to be international in origin and very effective against the plague. Images and other representations of Roch were believed to be a key part of the cult's effectiveness. Various editions and translations of the two lives of Roch circulated widely in the sixteenth and seventeenth centuries. Other versions of his life appeared. One major variant is the place of Roch's imprisonment and death; according to some texts, he returned to his home of Montpellier, was imprisoned there, and died there.[26]

Painting and the Cult of Saint Roch

André Vauchez states that the cult of Saint Roch spread in southern France and in northern Italy in the 1420s and 1430s; it also developed to the north, in Germany and the Low Countries. In the late 1470s several confraternities dedicated to Roch were founded in Venetian territories; what were said to be Roch's relics were transferred to Venice itself in 1485. In 1490 those relics were moved to a new confraternal church of Saint Roch, dedicated in 1508. In the mid-1500s, Tintoretto decorated the walls with what have become some of the more famous depictions of Roch.[27] Yet if the Venetian confraternity (Scuola di San Rocco) – and more generally Venice – became centers of devotion to Roch, they surely did not go unrivalled.[28]

Paintings of Roch, Venetian and other, tended to emphasize certain themes and episodes in his life; other themes and episodes appeared rarely, if at all. For example, Gothardus, quite prominent in the *Acta Breviora* and in Diedo, seems not to have interested artists (or their patrons) very much. The idea of Roch as pilgrim is central to his iconography. Pilgrimage was a major focus of Catholic piety in the late medieval and Renaissance periods,[29] and painters showed Roch dressed for pilgrimage. Roch was thought to have been a layman, not a priest or a monk or a friar.[30] The vast majority of pilgrims were lay, and they traveled on foot. Like the apostle James, who was usually portrayed as a pilgrim, Roch is often shown with a staff in hand, and wearing a scallop shell, another symbol of pilgrimage, as in Bernardino Luini's *Virgin and Child with Saints Roch and Sebastian* (cat. 13).[31] Sometimes there is a gourd or other container for water or other drink, and a white cloth hanging from the staff or wrapped around what might be food for the journey. Such a cloth is very prominent in Jacopo Bassano's *Saints Sebastian and Roch* (cat. 12), where it seems to echo or parallel the loin cloth worn by the otherwise naked Sebastian.[32] Roch's white cloth may have been intended to remind viewers of the white rod sometimes carried by plague victims (or by those suspected of being infected) in order to warn others of the disease.[33]

Yet in some ways Roch was not a typical pilgrim. He was atypical, of course, in his miracle working. But he was also unusual in that he was not remembered as visiting any shrines of saints, or any specific holy places to which pilgrims in Rome flocked. Falling ill while on pilgrimage must have been a rather common experience, but imprisonment, presumably, was much rarer.

Roch's plague bubo, almost always depicted on his thigh, was very much a favored theme.[34] In Jacopo Bassano's *Saints Sebastian and Roch* (cat. 12), Roch pulls back his garment with his left hand and points to the exposed bubo. Roch makes a similar gesture, with his right hand, in Luini's *Virgin and Child with Saints Sebastian and Roch* (cat. 13); in his left hand, he holds a rosary, for use in praying to the Madonna. Yet Roch does not appear to be terribly

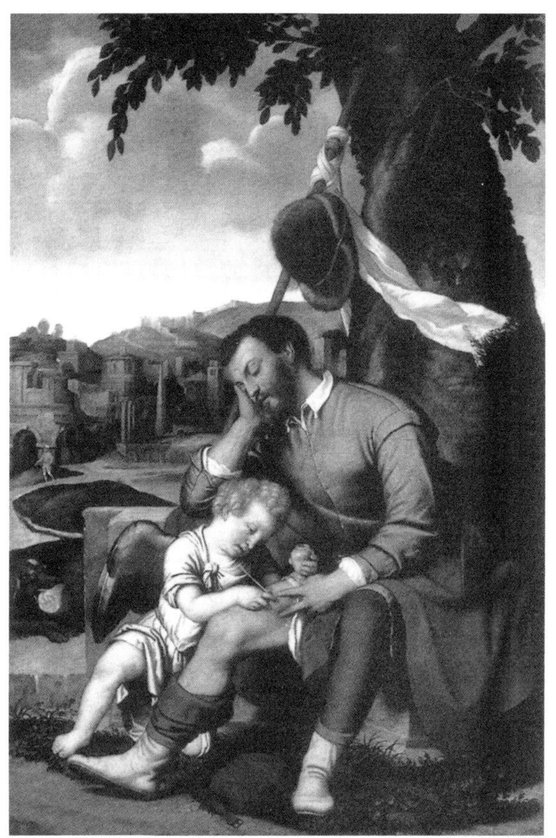

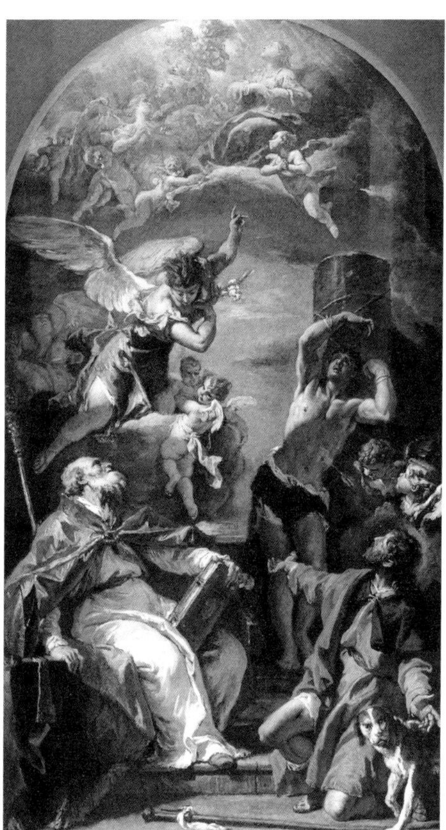

60. Alessandro Bonvicino (known as Moretto da Brescia), *Saint Roch being Cured by an Angel*, ca. 1545. Oil on canvas. Szépmüvészeti Múzeum.

61. Sebastiano Ricci, *A Glory of the Virgin with the Archangel Gabriel and Saints Eusebius, Roch, and Sebastian*, ca. 1724-25. Oil on canvas. Los Angeles County Museum of Art, Gift of the Ahmanson Foundation.

ill: Apart from the bubo, he shows none of the symptoms of plague, which included extreme fever, insomnia, continual vomiting, a horrid stench, a blackened tongue and lips.[35] By showing a healthy-looking Roch, with what often appears as a rather benign bubo, painters could both maintain artistic decorum, and encourage viewers hoping for recovery from the plague.

If certain saints were thought especially efficacious against certain illnesses, such beliefs often took as their point of departure some event in the saint's life that linked her or him with a specific medical problem or group of problems. For example, Saint Apollonia was said to have had her teeth smashed as part of her martyrdom; she became a favorite intercessor for tooth ache sufferers, even though her legends did not include any mention of her teeth being restored.[36] While Roch was by no means the only saint to whom plague sufferers turned for help, he – unlike Sebastian – was believed to have actually had the bubonic plague – and to have recovered.

Some painters showed quite prominently an angel attending to Roch, perhaps even lancing or applying a salve to his bubo. In an altarpiece from the church of Sant'Alessandro in Brescia, *Saint Roch being Cured by an Angel*, (fig. 60) Alessandro Bonvicino (known as Moretto da Brescia)[37] shows a young angel putting salve or ointment into his lanced bubo; Roch appears to sleep peacefully through the treatment. In an age long before effective anesthesia, such an image would have offered hope not only for a cure from plague, but a miraculously painless cure as well.

Saint Roch was very frequently portrayed as accompanied by a friendly dog. In Luini's *Virgin and Child with Saints Sebastian and Roch* (cat. 13), the dog stands close to Roch's exposed leg. In Moretto da Brescia's *Saint Roch being Cured by an Angel* (fig. 60), the dog approaches the scene of healing, carrying bread in its mouth. In Sebastiano Ricci's *A Glory of the Virgin with the Archangel Gabriel and Saints Eusebius, Roch, and Sebastian* (fig. 61), Roch's dog stands in the foreground of a complex composition. The dog looks straight out at the viewer, the only figure in the painting to do so. This painting was a *modello* for an altarpiece commissioned by the House of Savoy for the chapel of a hunting lodge, the *Venaria Reale*, on the outskirts of Turin.[38] In 1730-35, Giovanni Battista Tiepolo did a series of more than twenty paintings of Saint Roch, each for a member of the Venetian Scuola di San Rocco.[39] In these intimate portraits, Roch is portrayed without any other human figures or any angels. Almost all of the portraits, however, include the dog. An excellent example is the version in the Philadelphia Museum of Art (cat. 17). As in Ricci's altarpiece for the *Venaria Reale*, Roch's dog looks outward to the viewer.

In time of plague, civic authorities often ordered the slaughter of dogs, and perhaps other animals as well, as a way of reducing opportunities for the disease to spread. Mark Jenner, in a fascinating essay on "The Great Dog Massacre," points out that this policy was implemented in many European countries, and over the several centuries of plague outbreaks. For instance, in the Florentine plague of 1494, dogs were killed by official order; in the 1603 plague in London, the parish of Saint Margaret's, Westminster, paid for the killing of more than 500 dogs; in Rome and Naples in 1656-57, both dogs and cats were exterminated; in the Marseille plague of 1720, there were "fierce debates" among physicians about the usefulness of such slaughter.[40] Fear of dogs in time of plague was, in some cases, also informed by an astrological theory. In 1631, a Florentine physician argued that the constellation of the Dog was an omen of plague.[41] The central role of a beneficial canine in the iconography of Saint Roch – often depicted as bringing him bread – would surely have encouraged those who criticized extermination practices. Roch's dog not only did him no harm, but it may have saved him from starvation.

Dog defenders in time of plague would also have found support in the legends of Saint Guinefort. Jean-Claude Schmitt has examined how, from the thirteenth century on, there appears to have been confusion between a "martyred" dog in medieval France, and a human martyr in Milan and Pavia from the time of Emperors Diocletian and Maximilian. Both were called Saint Guinefort. The dog was said to have tried to defend a baby from attack by a serpent; the serpent killed the child and wounded the dog. The faithful dog remained by the child's cradle; blamed for the death, the dog was executed. But its burial place became a site where people brought sick children to be healed by a dog they believed to have been innocent and a martyr.[42] The human Guinefort was a Christian preacher beaten, stoned, and shot through with arrows in Milan. He survived, and made his way to Pavia, where he cured the blind and the sick, before his own death and burial there. His legend bore many similarities to that of Saint Sebastian; from the late fourteenth century on, Saint Guinefort was invoked in time of plague.[43]

Understandably, persons suffering from plague were eager for healing from almost any source, human, divine, or animal. As bad as plague was, it was also often accompanied by other afflictions. Famine and plague often went together, along with war. Quarantines and the general disruption of economic life that came with a severe outbreak were causes of hunger and even starvation.[44] Though some of the causes and effects among plague, famine, and war in early modern societies may be debated by historians,[45] they were often experienced as simultaneous or sequential. For example, Giovanni Francesco Prandi, a Jesuit eyewitness to the 1576 plague, claimed that more were dying of starvation in Milan than of the plague.[46] In the seventeenth century, severe plague followed a major crop failure in Italy in 1628.[47]Biblical precedents and predictions also suggested a relationship among these afflictions. In both Old and New Testaments, they are identified together as divine punishments. In the Old Testament, a sinful King David was offered a choice of three punishments from God: famine,

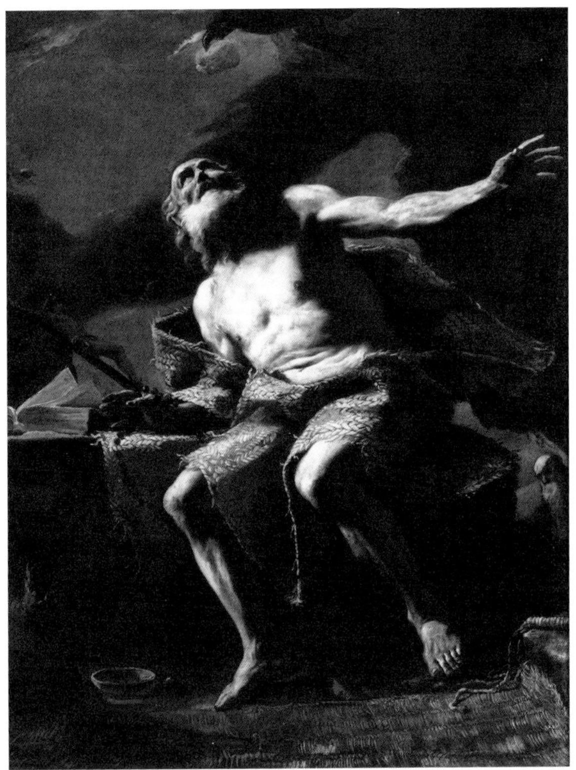

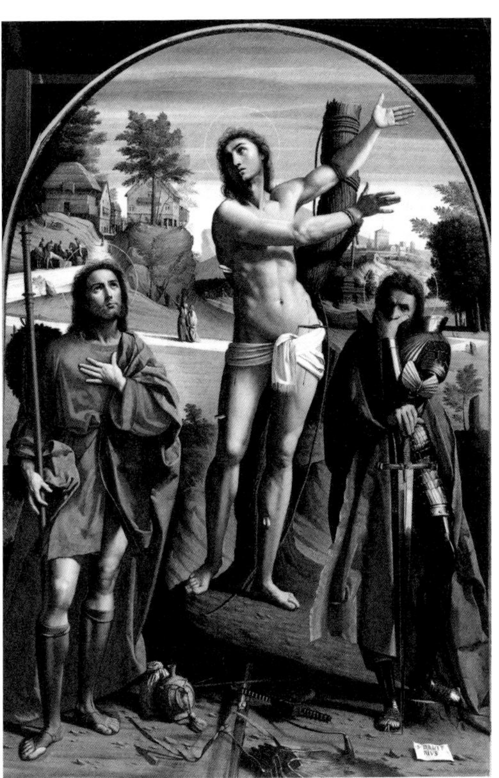

62. Mattia Preti, *Saint Paul the Hermit*, ca. 1656-60. Oil on canvas. Art Gallery of Ontario, Toronto. Purchase, Frank P. Wood Endowment, 1968.

63. L'Ortolano, *Saints Sebastian, Roch and Demetrius*, after. 1516. Oil on wood. National Gallery of Art, London.

war, or plague (in 2 Samuel 24:10-25). In the New Testament, the Book of Revelation envisions death for a sinful world by sword, famine, and pestilence (Revelation 6:8).[48]

While paintings of Saint Roch had little to say about the "sword" or war, they offered hope of healing from plague and, especially when Roch's dog was included, hope of feeding in time of famine. Diedo's life of Saint Roch made explicit comparisons between Roch being fed by a dog and Elijah and Paul the Hermit being fed by birds. The iconography of Saint Paul the Hermit, a fourth-century ascetic who lived in the Egyptian desert, often features a raven or other bird bringing bread; an example of a stunning painting showing such aviary charity is Mattia Preti's *Saint Paul the Hermit* (fig. 62).[49] The painting is thought to have been done in Naples, ca.1656-60, during or shortly after one of the worst outbreaks of plague.

Feeding the hungry was a corporal work of mercy often depicted in painting. An excellent example is Johannes Lingelbach's *Roman Street Scene with Feeding the Hungry* (cat. 8), painted in Rome in the mid-1600s. The giving of drink to the thirsty no doubt often accompanied provision of food, and it, too, was the subject of paintings, including Bernardo Strozzi's *An Act of Mercy* (cat. 10). An adequate supply of clean water was sometimes seen as a key ingredient in prevention of plague outbreaks.[50] In the *Acta Breviora*, Saint Roch himself benefited from both a dog's bread and a miraculous fountain.

Distribution of alms to the poor was closely related to offering food and drink, one part of the legend and iconography of Saint Roch. Like Lingelbach, Jan Miel was a northern artist working in Rome who often painted *bambocciate*, or street scenes of daily life.[51] Miel's *Saint Roch* (cat. 14) shows the saint distributing coins to the poor, while his dog stands attentive. In this intimate image, Miel includes a mother holding an infant child at her breast. Her expression suggests more a constant struggle for survival than the joys of motherhood. Paintings done in the shadow of plague often depicted a mother and infant, the latter frequently unable to nurse at the breast of a dying or dead mother. Such a scene is prominent in the foreground of Raimondi's *The Plague* (cat. 5); it is even more central in Caroselli's *Plague at Ashdod* (cat. 1); it occurs yet again in Mignard's *Saint Charles Borromeo among the Plague-Stricken of Milan* (cat. 25).[52] In paintings such as these, a link between plague and famine, at least for young children, was made abundantly clear.

The dying/dead mother unable to nurse her children was a kind of reverse image of a frequently depicted allegory of Charity. Painters often depicted Charity as a healthy young woman, nursing one or more healthy children. Francesco de Mura's *Charity (Allegory of Maternal Love)* (cat. 9) offers an excellent example. The allegorical figure of Charity was at times depicted as holding an inflamed heart; in Vaccaro's *Madonna and Child with Saints Roch, Sebastian, and Francis Xavier* (cat. 18), Charity holds such a heart in one hand while she embraces an infant with the other. Above, an enthroned Madonna gives a breast to the infant Jesus; the Madonna looks in the direction of Charity, and Charity looks toward her. This *modello* was done for an altarpiece at Santa Maria delle Grazie, in Marigliano, near Naples. The *modello* (and the altarpiece) include four male saints, Francis Xavier, Vito, Sebastian and Roch. In addition to the altarpiece, Vaccaro produced for the same church individual paintings of these four saints. The image of Saint Roch shows him kneeling, pilgrim's staff at his side, before the Madonna and child.[53]

While Saint Roch was sometimes depicted without other saints, he was very often portrayed in a *sacra conversazione* with others, Saint Sebastian and the Virgin Mary in particular. Saint Roch was a relative newcomer as a plague intercessor, at least as compared to Sebastian. In some paintings, Roch seemed to play a secondary or supporting role to Sebastian, as in L'Ortolano's *Saint Sebastian and Saints Roch and Demetrius* (fig. 63) originally an altarpiece for the church of S. Maria at Bondeno, near Ferrara.[54] Demetrius, like Sebastian, was believed to have been a soldier and a martyr for the faith, persecuted under the Roman emperors. In this painting, Demetrius and Roch flank Sebastian, who is raised somewhat above them; Sebastian is tied to a tree, much like Jesus on the cross. Such a composition compared Sebastian to Jesus himself, but Roch and Demetrius to those who stood at the foot of the cross. Vaccaro's painting for Marigliano (cat. 18), some two centuries later, also suggests a supporting or secondary role for Roch.

Yet many other paintings place Roch and Sebastian on a par. In this exhibition, the paintings by Luini (cat. 13) and Bassano (cat. 12) clearly show such equality. Lorenzo Lotto was a Venetian artist who also worked in Treviso, Rome, and Bergamo; he painted *The Virgin and Child with Saints Roch and Sebastian* (fig. 64), for his friend, the physician Battista Cucchi.[55] For the church of S. Rocco at Parma, Veronese (and his workshop) produced an altarpiece showing Christ in heaven stopping the plague by holding back arrows (fig. 65). Below, on earth, Roch and Sebastian intercede for suffering humanity, while in heaven, the Virgin Mary and John the Baptist relay their prayers to Christ.[56]

It would be difficult to overstate the centrality of the Virgin Mary in Catholic piety and painting around 1500. Especially beloved as mother of the infant Jesus, she was also believed to be the intercessor *par excellence* with Christ and God, for every sort of ill, physical and spiritual. Catholicism in the Reformation and post-Reformation eras reaffirmed the importance of Mary, in the face of Protestant criticism.[57] Certainly in Italy, there was little need for such efforts, as she remained as popular as ever. James Clifton, in his essay in this catalogue, shows how important she was as a plague intercessor. By the eighteenth century, however, there was a new emphasis on her assumption into heaven.[58]

An example is Sebastiano Ricci's *Assumption*, painted 1708-12, for a church in Clusone, near Bergamo.[59] In a rather large *bozzetto* (cat. 34) of this work a figure with a pilgrim's staff is among the people gathered around Mary's empty tomb, and watching her on her way to heaven. This is most likely Saint James, a pilgrim and one of the apostles, believed to have

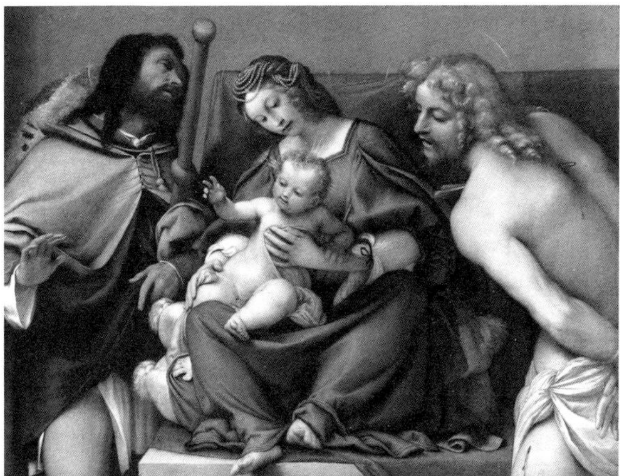

64. Lorenzo Lotto, *The Virgin and Child with Saints Roch and Sebastian,* ca. 1521-22. Oil on canvas. National Gallery of Canada, Ottawa.

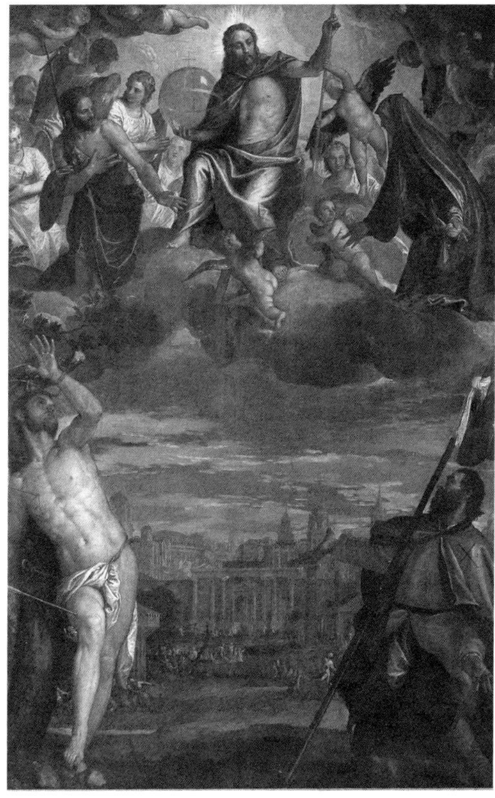

65. Veronese, *Christ Stopping the Plague with the Prayers of the Virgin, Saint John the Baptist, Saint Roch, and Saint Sebastian,* ca. 1580-85. *Oil on canvas.* Musée des Beaux Arts, Rouen.

been present at Mary's assumption into heaven. However, in the *bozzetto*'s foreground stands a dog. Is the pilgrim perhaps Saint Roch rather than Saint James?[60] Some viewers, at least, could have thought so, regardless of the painter's intention. Roch's feast day was 16 August; the Assumption was celebrated on 15 August. Association of Roch with the Assumption would have been easy. Any victims of plague or other illness looking to Roch for healing would have found comfort and reassurance in the Assumption. Mary was believed to have been assumed into heaven, soul *and* body. Like the Resurrection of Christ (see cat. 35), and the raising of Lazarus (see cat. 37), the Assumption of Mary would have offered hope to those seeking a restored, healthy body, here below and in eternity. One of Ricci's later commissions was for an altarpiece in the Karlskirche in Vienna. Built as an ex-voto church after the end of a 1713 outbreak of plague, it was dedicated to Carlo Borromeo. Ricci was commissioned to do an altarpiece of the Assumption;[61] clearly, this theme was thought to be very appropriate for celebration of deliverance from plague.

Mary was imagined as particularly efficacious in presenting to God or Christ the prayers of other saints, both lay and clerical. For example, Vaccaro shows Francis Xavier wearing a surplice and stole, as he gestures toward Marigliano, and looks upward to the Madonna and child in heaven, pleading with her for the city (cat. 18). Xavier was a Jesuit priest, canonized in 1622. Christine Boeckl has argued that after the Council of Trent such lay saints as Roch were sometimes eclipsed in Catholic devotion by clerical saints. The cult of Carlo Borromeo offers some evidence for her point.[62] Yet it is important to stress that the older plague saints did not disappear. Though Roch stands somewhat in the background in this Vaccaro altarpiece, Sebastian is just as prominent as Xavier. Like Xavier, he points to the city of Marigliano, and calls upon the Virgin Mary and Jesus to come to its assistance. Xavier's clerical status, though highlighted by the priest's stole, appears, nevertheless, to give him no advantage over the layman Sebastian as a saintly intercessor.

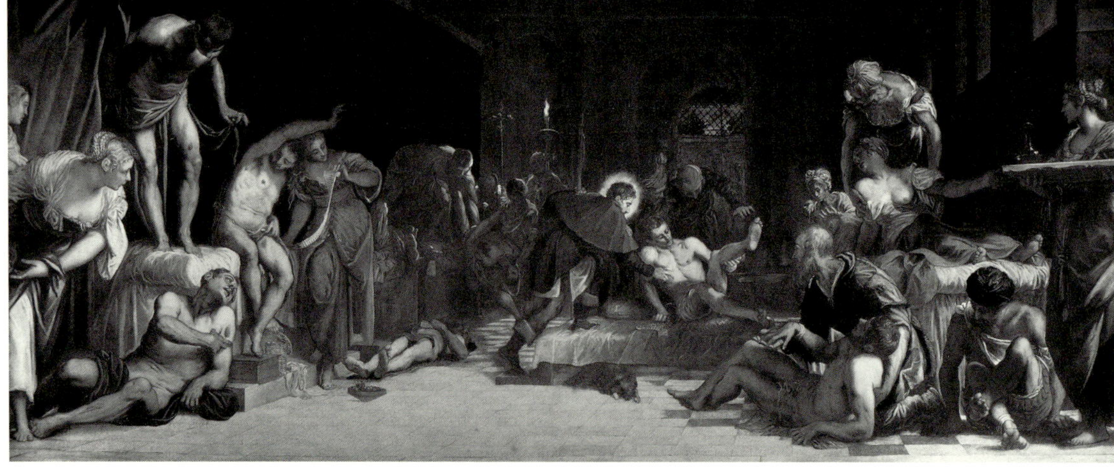

66. Tintoretto, *Saint Roch Curing the Plague-Stricken*, 1549. Oil on canvas. Scuola di San Rocco, Venice.

Christine Boeckl suggests that post-Tridentine iconography increasingly emphasized saints as helping to meet spiritual rather than physical or material needs. To demonstrate this point, she contrasts Tintoretto's 1549 painting, for the Scuola di San Rocco in Venice, of Saint Roch ministering to plague victims (fig. 66), with Mignard's painting, done a century later for a Roman church, of Carlo Borromeo bringing the eucharist to those stricken with plague (cat. 25).[63] While Tintoretto shows Roch treating a plague bubo, Mignard shows Borromeo bringing the spiritual sustenance that only clergy could provide.

It may be that, especially in Rome, center of the papacy and thus of clerical Catholicism, post-Tridentine iconography tended to exalt the clergy, including the role of clerical saints in time of plague. Yet devotion to, and paintings of such well-established lay saints as Sebastian and Roch do not appear to have declined in Italy, 1500-1800. Luini's *Virgin and Child with Saints Sebastian and Roch* (cat. 13), from northern Italy in the early sixteenth century, and Vaccaro's *modello* for the church at Marigliano (cat. 18), from two centuries later in southern Italy, both affirm the efficacy of lay, intercessory saints. Tiepolo's series of images of Saint Roch, done in Venice ca. 1730-35, suggests continued vitality of devotion to Roch, not eclipse by something else, clerical or otherwise.[64] Between the early sixteenth century and the mid-eighteenth century, Catholicism itself, and Catholicism and the arts may have experienced many changes.[65] Some things, however, were largely resistant to change. Devotion to (and painting of) Roch and other lay plague saints were part of that resilience.

Plague International

Plague and fear of plague, from 1500 to 1800, were far larger than the Italian peninsula.In their meticulous study of the "medical world" of early modern France, Laurence Brockliss and Colin Jones use the image of a "shadow" to divide their study into a first part, "Beneath the Shadow of the Plague," on France in the sixteenth and seventeenth centuries, and a second part, "Beyond the Shadow of the Plague," on France, ca.1680-1789.[66] Saint Roch and his cult were not confined to the Italian peninsula. Roch was believed to have been from Montpellier, in southern France, but the stories about him recovering from the plague, averting famine, and ministering to plague victims, all took place in Italy. By about 1500 his cult was widespread in France and Italy.

An excellent example of Roch in an early sixteenth-century French painting is *The Deposition with Saints Sebastian and Roch*, by an anonymous master (fig. 67). Among the women

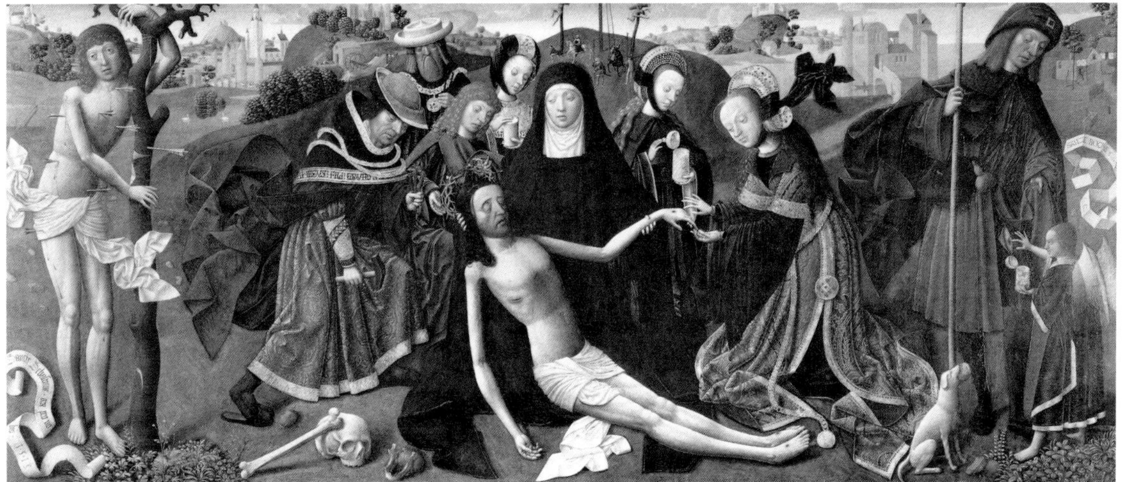

67. Master MM, *The Lamentation*, 1515. Oil on canvas. Springfield Museums, Springfield, MA. The James Philip Gray Collection.

gathered around the dead body of the crucified Jesus is Mary Magdalene, clearly identifiable by her jar of ointment; she is shown preparing to anoint his body. To one side of the central scene stands Saint Roch, carrying a pilgrim's staff, with his dog (bread in mouth) at his feet. An angel, bearing a jar like that of Mary Magdalene, applies a healing ointment to the plague bubo on his thigh. Roch's bubo appears as comparable to the wound in Jesus's side. On the other side of the painting is Saint Sebastian, pierced with arrows, and wearing but a loin cloth, similar to that of Jesus. The tree to which he is bound parallels Roch's staff. The painting suggests, in multiple ways, the parallels between Jesus and the two plague saints.[67]

As Roch had gone from France to the Italian peninsula, and perhaps back to France, his cult also circulated unimpeded by national frontiers. Several of the painters represented in this exhibition made their own artistic pilgrimages to Italy from their more northern homelands, perhaps returning home eventually. The plague itself circulated even more freely; what was perceived as plague was imagined as a local outbreak of a multinational phenomenon.

What one might call print in a time of plague, i.e., written texts produced that were somehow about the plague, often had an international character, even if in the vernacular. In his essay, Franco Mormando examined a number of important Italian plague treatises, sermons, and other writings, some of which went through many editions. One of the authors he treated is Francesco Panigarola (1548-94), a Franciscan, a prolific preacher and writer, and a bishop. Milanese by birth, Panigarola was eventually named bishop of Asti. But he also had considerable experience in France, as a student of theology in Paris in the early 1570s, and later as a legate in France, during the 1589-90 siege of Paris, in the period of the Wars of Religion.[68]

Some of Panigarola's works were published in French versions. A collection of his sermons published in France in 1592 included the plague sermon he had given in Bologna in 1577 (see Mormando's essay); in French it is entitled *Du fléau de la peste*.[69] This collection included a sermon Panigarola had given in Bologna on the twenty-third Sunday after Pentecost, in 1576, on the world as mortal and dying (*Du Monde mortel, mourant et qui meurt*).[70] Sermons the Franciscan had preached in Paris were also included, among them one delivered twenty years earlier, in the presence of King Charles IX and his mother Marie de Medici. In 1572 the young Panigarola had praised the French monarch, celebrating among other things his ability to heal persons suffering from scrofula.[71] Henry IV would receive far less praise from the legate Panigarola! Three of his sermons preached in Paris in 1590, and published in 1592, denounced Henry as a heretic and but as a pretender to the throne.[72]

Heretics were the main focus of a series of discourses Panigarola gave in 1582 in Turin, at the request of and in the presence of Charles Emmanuel, Duke of Savoy and Prince of Piedmont. A French translation of these "Catholic lessons" on church doctrine was published in France.[73] Taking aim at Calvin and Calvin's disciples, Panigarola spoke of the theological "arms" needed to combat the heretics, of how to do harm to the heretics and of how to defend against them.

At least one oration delivered in Italy and in Italian was also published in Italian in France: Panigarola's oration on the death of Carlo Borromeo was published in Paris in 1585. Discoursing at length on Borromeo and his many virtues, Panigarola tells the Milanese that Borromeo loved them (*ti amava, ò Milano*).[74] The Milanese are thus asking themselves, if plague comes again, who will defend us? For in time of plague, when the streets were deserted, when the air was infected, when houses were uninhabited, when the wife fled from the husband, and the husband from the wife, the son from the father, the father from the son, the brother from the sister, and the sister from the brother, in that hour this most holy man (*santissimo huomo*) was there. Without fear, Carlo Borromeo entered into houses and lazarettos; "with his own hand," he gave the sacraments.[75]

These are but a few examples of Panigarola's works, including some of those published after his death. The geographic space within which he worked, and in which his writings were published, was Italian and French. Persons on both sides of the Alps, in the late sixteenth century and beyond, could well have found comfort in his words. If coping with plague – both the literal plague, and the metaphorical plague of heresy – they would have found a sympathetic voice.[76]

Etienne Binet (1569-1639) was a Frenchman who crossed the Alps to join the Jesuits. A native of Dijon, Binet left France in 1590, in the midst of Wars of Religion, to enter the Jesuit novitiate at Novellara (near Mantua). Père Binet returned to France in 1603, when Henry IV allowed the Jesuits back from a period of exile imposed following accusations of Jesuit involvement in an assassination attempt on the king. Binet was a rector of colleges in Rouen and Paris; he was also Jesuit provincial superior. These administrative tasks did not prevent him from publishing nearly fifty books, many of which went through various editions in French and in translation to Italian and other languages.[77] In Italian, he was known as Stefano Binetti.

One of Binet's works (mentioned by Sheila Barker in her essay) was on plague and sudden death: *Remèdes souverains contre la peste et la mort soudaine*. First published in 1628, this work went through various editions; an Italian translation, *Sovrani e efficaci rimedi contro la peste e la morte subitanea*, translated by Giuseppe Fozi, S.J., was published in Rome in 1656, in the midst of one of the worst outbreaks of plague in the early modern period.[78] Binet's plague treatise is still in print in a 1998 edition.[79] Binet sets a very positive tone, insisting that plague does more good than harm: plague makes one scorn the world and its vanities; plague makes one think of salvation and of confessing one's sins; plague serves as purgatory for many persons who then go directly to paradise after death; without the plague there would be less devotion, and fewer alms and prayers.[80] In this Jesuit's view, plague is a time for making saints and martyrs. For him, no preacher ever preached penitence as effectively as does the plague; it "forces" people to become saints and to throw themselves on the "paternal bosom" of God. This God sends the plague because he wishes to send people to paradise. Those who die caring for and helping those suffering from plague are true martyrs. Plague is a time of salvation, a time blessed by God for making saints and martyrs of paradise.[81]

This sort of justification – even celebration – of divinely imposed plague may make one wonder whether Binet really intends to discuss any remedies, as the title suggests. In fact, Binet does discuss what he calls excellent remedies for "killing" the plague. He asserts that, medically speaking, nothing prevents plague better than joyous living; "true joy" comes from true contentment, and perfect contentment is found only in purity of conscience and of heart.[82] Not too surprisingly, Binet repeatedly recommends the sacrament of penance as a kind of purification, and as preparation for a "good" death. He also recommends devotion to intercessory saints, especially such plague saints as Sebastian, Carlo Borromeo, and Roch. To Saint Sebastian, Binet instructs, "make a vow" and offer him a beautiful gift, such as a church, join his confraternity, remember that hundreds of times he has "suffocated" the plague.[83] Père Binet exhorts his readers to "strangle" the plague with the rope of Saint Charles – on this rope, see essay by Pamela Jones – by imitating the humility of the holy cardinal.[84] For Binet, Saint Charles also shows how charity preserves one from the plague. He sold his silverware, his expensive furniture, and his own bed for the sake of the poor; even though he was every day among the plague victims, not only did he not contract the plague, but he never even had a headache.[85] Those seeking remedies for plague, would do well to "make a vow" to Saint Sebastian or to Saint Roch, vowing a quantity of Masses, and to make some gift to these saints whom God has sent to cure (*guérir*) those afflicted with plague or who fear it greatly.[86]

Appended to Binet's text were various prayers to be said in time of plague and other illness. On the title page of a 1629 version, published in Lyon, Binet's rather lengthy subtitle explains the multipurpose of the "remedies" he proposes: "whence devout souls may draw a very gentle consolation, and spiritual recreation, both during the contagion, and in any other affliction or illness." The prayers, some in Latin and some in French, include a lengthy litany of the Virgin Mary, invoked under many titles, *Consolatrix afflictorum* among them. There is also a prayer to Saint Joseph, an act of contrition, several psalms, a litany of the saints, and prayers to the Virgin Mary, Saint Sebastian, and Saint Roch, for use in time of plague.[87]

In the opposite direction of "imports" to Italy, what happened in Rome in times of plague had a widespread resonance elsewhere, in print and otherwise. In her essay, Sheila Barker examined Pope Urban VIII and Rome. Christine Boeckl, in her study of images of plague and pestilence, points out Urban VIII's strong personal devotion to Saint Roch; in 1629, he gave official approval to Roch's cult even though Roch had never been canonized.[88] Quite naturally, within the papal states, Urban's influence was abundant. In Bologna, for instance, a collection of statutes issued in time of plague, and published in 1631, included a summary of a plenary indulgence granted by Urban VIII, on 22 June 1630, both for those serving persons sick with plague, and for those dying of the contagion. Among the former group, those specifically mentioned include priests administering sacraments to the infected or those suspected of being infected (*sospetti o infetti*); physicians; women nursing the children of infected women; those bringing the sick to hospitals; those burying the dead; those giving food, drink, and other necessities to the infected and suspected, or visiting them. In addition, the indulgence is also granted to those who, in any other manner attend to the spiritual or corporal needs of the infected or suspected, and who go to confession and communion, and recite the penitential psalms or a part of the rosary. To those near death (*in articulo di morte*) the indulgence is granted provided that they confess and receive Communion, or if they are unable to do so, at least are contrite and invoke the name of Jesus, aloud if possible, and if not, at least with the heart.[89]

Yet even in France, where a proud tradition of relative independence from papal directives remained strong in the seventeenth century, actions and directives of Pope Urban VIII in combating the plague were noticed and acted upon. The *Mercure françois* was a kind of annual, semi-official journal published in Paris beginning in 1605. It often focused on the great deeds of the French king, but also on other events in France and elsewhere, especially calamities of various kinds, plague included. In a volume published in 1631, plague in Lyon in 1628 received lengthy attention.[90] A volume published in 1632 recounted the jubilee decreed and celebrated by Pope Urban VIII in 1629. The pope, finding that "most of Christendom was afflicted with plague, war, and famine," found it suitable to appease the anger of divine justice, "irritated on account of the sins of Christians." Thus he ordered a "universal jubilee," which was celebrated in Rome "with much ceremony" on 22 November 1629.[91]

The *Mercure françois* also recounted how the jubilee decreed by Urban VIII was celebrated in Paris, for two weeks, beginning on 13 January 1630. The general procession with which the jubilee began was so crowded that some persons were suffocated, and parishes and religious orders could not process in proper order. But the queens showed their devotion and piety, going by foot in the procession. Throughout the two weeks, the king's "truly Christian devotion" was admired, for he visited on foot all nineteen stations established by the archbishop of Paris, even though they were distant from one another. Princes and lords of the court followed the king's example.[92]

Plague and response to plague were local, but they were also international. An outbreak of plague in one city or region could very quickly generate fear in distant places. One of the reasons why fear of plague continued to be a major component of European mentalities well into the eighteenth century is the plague of the early 1720s in Marseille and environs. While it turned out to be a relatively isolated, though extremely lethal outbreak, no one at the time knew that it would be geographically so circumscribed. In eighteenth-century Europe, printing presses and plague literature proliferated at a rapid pace.[93]

One example of such literature is Daniel Defoe's *Journal of the Plague Year*, first published, in England, in 1722. While it was written as if a journal of a London resident during the terrible plague of 1665, Defoe wrote it as reports of plague in Marseille were sowing fear in England and elsewhere. Given the fictive time of 1665, he obviously does not mention the Marseille plague in any direct way. He does, however, explicitly compare the London contagion of 1665 to that of 1656 in Naples; in both cases, Defoe adds that some reports exaggerated the daily mortality, claiming even 20,000 a day.[94] Yet his "journal" does include, lengthy scenes of dying persons, dead bodies, and great fear. Likening plague to "a dark Cloud that passes over our Heads," Defoe imagines it very much as Luca Carlevarijs did in painting (cat. 33).[95] Protestant England did not have anything like the continental Catholic religious culture that supported – and prospered from – religious painting. Yet Defoe's visual imagination, recorded in print, perhaps compensated for the relative dearth of painting. A painting such as Sebastiano Ricci's *Resurrected Christ Surrounded by Angels*, commissioned around 1714 for the Chelsea Royal Hospital (see a *modello*, cat. 35), demonstrates that Italian religious painting was not altogether absent from Defoe's England.[96]

Franco Mormando discussed, in his essay, a plague treatise of Lodovico Muratori (1672-1750), a treatise that went through many editions (and translations), from the first in 1714, and continuing even beyond his death. Muratori makes an appropriate *terminus ad quem* for questions about plague and print, 1500-1800.[97] Some of the editions published after the early 1720s, among them one published in Rome in 1743, include an appended report on the plague at Marseille, attributed to three physicians from Montpellier: Chicoyneau, Verny, and Soullier.[98] Muratori explains that the report was first published in Marseille on 20 December 1720, and "immediately" reprinted in Turin "for the public good;" he has now translated it into Italian for the "instruction" of Italians.[99] To his translation of the report, Muratori adds his own "observations" on prevention and cure of plague.[100]

The texts of Defoe and Muratori suggest a long and wide impact of the Marseille outbreak on European attitudes regarding plague. Historians often speak of the eighteenth century as a time of growing optimism and of improving health; the work of Colin Jones and Laurence Brockliss on the "shadow of the plague" in France, discussed above, reflects that perspective by positing a kind of move "beyond" the fear of plague after about 1680. If there was such a shift, the 1720 contagion must have come as a terrible shock. The mortality of the

Marseille plague was extremely high: Jones and Brockliss estimate 50,000 deaths in a city that had a 1720 population of 90,000.[101] Other towns and cities nearby were also infected, including Aix, Avignon, Orange, and Toulon.[102]

But was the religious and cultural response to plague in Marseille and environs much different from what it had been in the sixteenth or seventeenth centuries, in cities such as Venice, Rome, or Milan? A recent study by Raymond Jonas on France and the history of the cult of the Sacred Heart is very useful in helping to answer this question. Jonas shows how devotion to both Saint Charles and to the Sacred Heart of Jesus was promoted by the bishop of Marseille, Henri François Xavier de Belsunce de Castelmoron. Imitating closely the plague processions of Carlo Borromeo in Milan – see the discussion by Pamela Jones in her essay – Belsunce walked barefoot and in penitential garb through the plague-ridden neighborhoods of Marseille, on 1 November 1720. He wore a cord around his neck and carried a crucifix.[103] Unlike the archbishop of Milan, Belsunce also consecrated the city of Marseille to the Sacred Heart, on 12 June 1722; at the same time, the city's civic and business leaders made a perpetual vow to make an annual votive offering to the Sacred Heart in "reparation" for sin.[104]

Belsunce's carefully scripted imitation of Carlo Borromeo suggests a deliberate continuity in responses to plague, from the late sixteenth century well into the eighteenth. It also suggests continuity across the Alps. But was there also continuity in iconography and painting? In fact, Belsunce was often depicted as a new Saint Charles. For example, a painting of Belsunce by Nicolas-André Monsiau was shown in Paris at the salon of 1819.[105] It showed Belsunce bringing Communion to plague victims, in a composition obviously derived from the work of Pierre Mignard (cat. 25).

Does one also find continued devotion to Saint Roch in France – was he still frequently invoked in time of plague by the eighteenth century? Paintings of Tiepolo and Ricci (discussed above) demonstrate that Roch was still an important and popular saint in Italy. In Rome, in 1780, Jacques-Louis David painted *Saint Roch Interceding with the Virgin for the Victims of the Plague*, a work commissioned by the health department of the city of Marseille, for its chapel. The painting (fig. 68) commemorates the plague of 1720, and shows Roch pleading with the Virgin Mary for plague victims in Marseille. After exhibition in Rome, the painting was delivered to its patrons in 1782.[106]

Another piece of evidence of continued French interest in Saint Roch is the large church dedicated to him in Paris. A church of St. Roch was built on the rue Saint-Honoré in the years 1584-87, in the midst of the Wars of Religion. By the 1620s it was deemed too small. In 1629 the archbishop made the church a parish, but financial difficulties caused delay in building the new structure. Its cornerstone was laid on 28 March 1653 by Louis XIV and Queen Mother Anne of Austria; Jacques Le Mercier, architect of the Sorbonne and of the monastery Val de Grâce, was the architect. Construction was interrupted in the late seventeenth century, but in 1701 Louis XIV authorized a lottery that permitted resumption of work. In 1719, the financier John Law, a convert to Catholicism, gave 100,000 pounds toward completion of the church, on the occasion of his first Communion. The interior was completed in 1723; Robert De Cotte and his son Jules-Robert designed the façade, built in the late 1730s. The church was consecrated in 1740. Among famous parishioners of St. Roch were playwright Pierre Corneille (d. 1684), painter Pierre Mignard (d. 1695), and André Le Nôtre (d. 1700), designer of the gardens at Versailles.[107] Though much of the interior decoration was destroyed or damaged during the French Revolution, the parish church of St. Roch resumed Catholic worship in 1801. One of the first works of art added was a new statue of Saint Roch, sculpted in 1803 by Guillaume Boichor.[108]

In other ways as well, devotion to Saint Roch proved resilient, even in the face of a

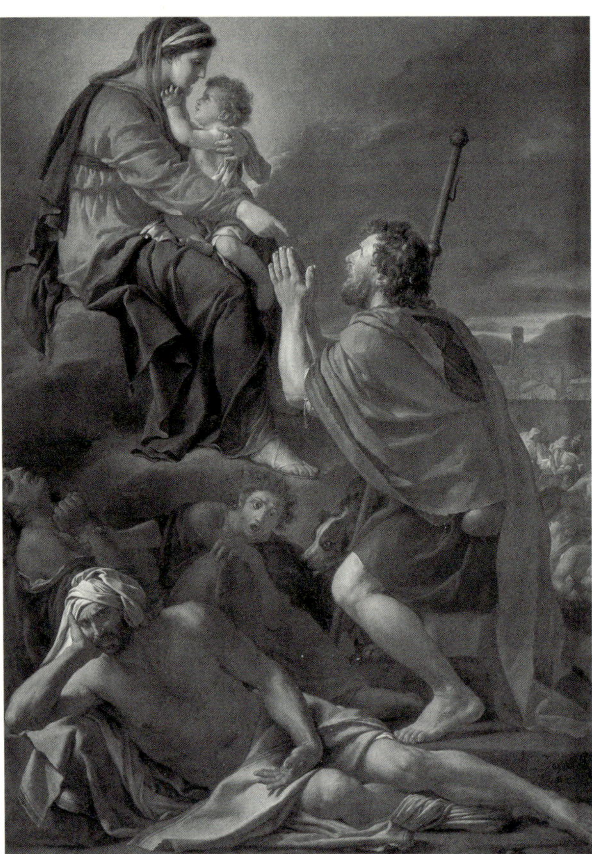

68. Jacques-Louis David, *Saint Roch Interceding with the Virgin for the Victims of the Plague*, 1780. Oil on canvas. Musée des Beaux Arts, Marseille.

dechristianizing Revolution and a disappearance of plague in Europe. Devotion to him outlasted the plagues that made him such a favored saint. In nineteenth-century France, Roch was frequently invoked against other afflictions, cholera in humans, and against phylloxera in vineyards.[109] In Italy, in the twentieth century, there were still some 3,000 churches, chapels, and oratories dedicated to San Rocco.[110] The cult of Saint Roch also crossed the Atlantic with immigrants to America. For instance, some ten miles south of Worcester, Massachusetts, the site of this exhibition, the Catholic parish church in the town of Oxford is dedicated to Roch.

Roch and Reassurance

Richard Palmer has argued that, in sixteenth-century Europe, "thousands could die of typhus or smallpox almost without public comment, whereas a few cases of plague would cause panic."[111] Lynn Martin, in his study of Jesuit accounts of "pest" finds frequent descriptions of fears inspired not only by outbreaks of pest, but by rumors of an approaching pest. Fear and rumor in a town "could reinforce each other and produce panic among the inhabitants."[112] Many other historians have also stressed the fears inspired by plague over several centuries.[113] Colin Jones and Laurence Brockliss, in their study of early modern France, state that "[p]lague killed – and it frightened. Deaths caused by it were so colossal, that mortal fear became a banal reality. Representations of the plague-wracked body became a kind of paroxysmic template of catastrophe, a form of death in life, which shaped how all serious diseases and life threatening events were viewed, and how the body was conceptualized."[114] William Naphy and Andrew Spicer, in a more geographically comprehensive work entitled *The Black Death: A History of Plagues 1345-1730*, offer this conclusion:

> Perhaps the greatest legacy of plague is the memory of its destructive power. Fear is the abiding inheritance of four centuries of pestilence. Fear of disease, fear of pollution, fear of outsiders, fear of diversity, fear of doctors, scientists, and politicians. Sealed in their homes by the state, abandoned by clergy and physicians, cowering on their sickbeds, Westerners learned to distrust and fear the potent power of plague and most attempts to prevent it. If they learned anything it was that the correct response to plague was harsh and draconian quarantine or speedy flight. People feared plague and pestilence and they still do.[115]

Some other historians have emphasized how Catholicism, far from offering solace, offered fear of an angry God, and along with fear of such a deity, fear of eternal punishment in hell. Michel Péronnet has explored how plague was frequently interpreted as a "sign" of God's wrath.[116] Jean Delumeau's two massive tomes on fear and sin in the Christian West, from the late Middle Ages to the Enlightenment, explore a pervasive "mentality" of fear and guilt.[117] Brian Pullan has examined how the poor, in early modern Italy, were at once subjects of pity, recipients of charity, *and* objects of fear. As the latter, they were feared as incubators and spreaders of plague and other diseases.[118] Piero Camporesi, focusing on seventeenth-century Italy, argues that Catholicism in that era "had a formidable capacity to terrorize its followers but was incapable of consoling them."[119] Paul Slack has offered a more mixed assessment of religion and fear in time of plague, in many eras and places. From plague in ancient Athens onward, "people either sought solace in religious practices or fled from Gods which had failed them."[120]

Alleged failures of medicine and government in the face of plague, along with a certain pessimism and despair, have not been accepted by all historians. Samuel Cohn insists that, by the late fourteenth century and beyond, confidence in medical responses to plague grew dramatically; a "change in mentality" took place; the death rate declined and the "despair" that characterized response to the outbreak of plague in the mid-1400s was replaced by use of herbal and other practical remedies.[121] Cohn acknowledges, however, that his arguments may not apply to the seventeenth century. He notes, for instance, that Genoa and Naples lost as much as three-fifths of their populations in the plague of 1656-57, "losses that may have even exceeded those of 1348."[122] Yet some studies of the plague in early modern Italy do argue that physicians and magistrates were not altogether unsuccessful in their efforts to prevent, limit, and control the plague.[123]

As for religious responses to plague, Jean Delumeau's book, *Rassurer et protéger*, explores at length topics such as saints as intercessors as protectors against disease and other misfortune. Delumeau argues that, in Catholic Reformation France, until the third or fourth decade of the eighteenth century, all levels of society sought miracles from the saints. After that, he suggests, the elite classes turned away from such remedies.[124] On the cult of the saints in Italy, Delumeau points out that relics of Carlo Borromeo were requested by many churches in various parts of seventeenth-century Italy.[125] Much has been written on the Catholic Reformation's emphasis on good works, care of the sick among them.[126] David Gentilcore has explained how fear itself was feared in time of plague; fear or fright was believed to be a frequent cause of death.[127] But Gentilcore's book, *Healers and Healing in Early Modern Italy*, explores the many ways in which medicine, the state, *and* religion promoted healing and reassurance in times of plague and other ills.[128]

Despite their rather sweeping claims, Naphy and Spicer do not mention painters or other artists. Were painters, like Naphy and Spicer's physicians, clergy, and governments, absent and/or helpless and ineffectual in the shadow of plague? Central to this exhibition is the question: did painting in Italy, ca. 1500-1800, promote hope and reassurance in the face of plague? Millard Meiss, in a frequently cited work on painting in fourteenth-century Florence and Siena, found a spirituality that was "tortured," and a "strained, disharmonious unity of plane and space, line and mass, color and shape."[129] Even *if* Meiss were correct on Trecento Florentine and Sienese painting, would such an assessment be at all applicable to the Cinquecento and beyond?

In an article on image and plague in Renaissance Italy, Louise Marshall has argued that "the sight of Roch scarred by the plague yet alive and healthy must have been an emotionally charged image of promised cure. Here was literal proof that one could survive the plague, a saint who had triumphed over the disease in his own flesh."[130] I contend that images of Roch functioned in this way, not only in the Renaissance, but through the Baroque period as well, and even beyond. Some of the images in this exhibition show the fear and suffering engendered by plague, 1500-1800. Yet hope for healing in this world and salvation in the next is even more visible in many of the paintings. The cult of Saint Roch played a key role in promoting not fear, but reassurance. Paintings of Roch clearly did this; though I have but mentioned briefly sculpture and architecture, there is an abundance of these arts (along with music, drawings, and other media) dedicated to Saint Roch, in Italy and elsewhere, over several centuries.

This exhibition may thus be significant not only for understanding an important chapter in the history of painting in Italy, but also as a contribution to the history of European mentalities of fear and /or of reassurance and hope. Peter Burke includes, among the characteristics of history of mentalities, "a concern with the structure of beliefs as well as their content, with categories, with metaphors and symbols, with how people think as well as what they think."[131] This exhibition has sought to explore how early modern people (especially in Italy) thought about life and death, illness and health, plague and piety. It has sought to show how painting was a privileged expression of metaphors and symbols, by which painters and their audiences not only coped with plague and the threat of plague, but also expressed their fears and – especially – their deepest hopes for health and salvation in this world and in eternity.

1. On Roman devotion to Saint Roch, see Barker, 44-45, 78-79.
2. See Biraben.
3. Slack, 3.
4. Fanelli, 3-5. Fanelli's volume includes the Latin text and an Italian translation on facing pages. On Diedo, see Marshall 1989, 172-73.
5. On "history" and "legends" of Saint Roch, see Bessodes. The name is Rochus in Latin, Rocco in Italian, Roch or Roche in English. I shall normally use Roch.
6. On the "problem" of a historically accurate Roch, see Fliche 1950, 343-61.See also Marshall 1989, 169-70.
7. *Acta Breviora*, 10-15. Translations into English from this and other texts are my own, unless otherwise indicated in my bibliography. On Montpellier in the late medieval period, see Le Blévec, 20-25.
8. On characteristics of Christian pilgrimages, see Turner and Turner. On late medieval pilgrimages to Rome, see Cardini, 26-33.
9. See Mormando, 103-5.
10. *Acta Breviora*, 14-17.
11. *Acta Breviora*, 16-17.
12. *Acta Breviora*, 16-21.
13. *Acta Breviora*, 20-23.
14. *Acta Breviora*, 22-31.
15. Diedo 1996, 36-37, 76-77. For an interesting hypothesis situating the "historical" Roch in the late 1300s, see Fliche, 343-61.
16. Diedo 1996, 40-43.
17. Diedo 1996, 44-49.
18. Diedo 1996, 48-53. In his gesture of tearful repentance, Roch appears here as a kind of Saint Mary Magdalene.
19. Diedo 1996, 53-53.
20. Diedo 1996, 56-61.
21. Diedo 1996, 58-59, 68-69.
22. Diedo 1996, 64-65.
23. Diedo 1996, 76-79. Fanelli's edition of Diedo gives the date of Roch's death as 17 August 1327. Some other versions of Diedo specify 16 August 1327; see, e.g., Vaslef, 216. The date of 16 August was celebrated as Roch's feast day.
24. Diedo 1996, 80-81.
25. On Constance, see Loomis.
26. See Marshall 1994, 504-05; Fliche, 343-61; and Bessodes.
27. Vauchez 2000, 14
28. See, on the Scuola di San Rocco, Romanelli, 64-66, and Wiel, 67-81.
29. On Christian pilgrimage, see Turner and Turner.
30. Eventually, some friars claimed – without proof – that Roch had been a Third Order Franciscan; see Vauchez 1968, 271.
31. On this painting, see Tomory, 57.
32. This was apparently part of a plague banner, carried in procession in the town of Bassano; see Brown and Marini, 89-90.
33. On the white rod, see Martin, 182.
34. On medical aspects of bubonic plague, see Boeckl, 7-32.
35. For a vivid description from 1630, in France, see Brockliss and C. Jones, 37.
36. See Lebrun, 113-16, on healing and saints. On Apollonia, see Sandoval, 69.
37. Cogeval and Mojzer, 52-53.
38. Conisbee, Levkoff, and Rand, 199-202. Turin was no stranger to outbreaks of the plague; see Pollak, 84-89.
39. Morassi, figs. 154-171; Piovene, 96-97.
40. Jenner, 48-49.
41. Jenner, 51.
42. Schmitt, 1-8.
43. Schmitt, 91-97. For dogs celebrated as offering hope and healing to human beings, Guinefort and Roch's dog do not lack more contemporary company. Balto and a team of other sled dogs gained much attention for their role in bringing diphtheria serum to Nome, Alaska, during a 1925 epidemic. See the 2003 book by Salisbury and Salisbury. Nor has Roch's dog been forgotten by dog lovers. A recent work on dogs in art and literature includes examples of Italian paintings of Roch and his dog; see Zaczek, 324-25.
44. For some examples of famine in time of plague, see, on Florence, Carmichael, 17.
45. On these kinds of questions, see, e.g., Black, 22-27; Livi-Bacci; Walter and Schofield.
46. See Martin, 156.
47. Sella, 144.
48. On these "four horsemen of the apocalypse" as experienced and imagined in the sixteenth and seventeenth centuries, see Cunningham and Grell. Of course, copious food did not guarantee freedom from illness, plague or other disease. Giovanni Martinelli's *Death Comes to the Dinner Table* (cat. 4) shows wealthy, well-fed people confronted by death in the midst of their abundance.
49. See McTavish et al., 73.
50. On such efforts in Urban VIII's Rome, see Barker , 110-115.
51. On Miel and *bambocciate*, see Orr, 53-54, and Sutton, 254.
52. On this theme prior to Raimondi, see Barker, 41-44. On Raimondi and Mignard, see Boeckl, 49-51; on the Caroselli painting, see Wine, 16-23. In eighteenth-century London, William Hogarth used a similar imagery to depict the ravages of gin drinking among the lower classes. See Warner, 195-96.
53. See Teza, 38-45. Vito (Vitus) was, like Sebastian, a martyr from the first centuries of Christianity.
54. Gould, 181-82.
55. Humfrey, 62-64. The work is in the National Gallery of Canada, Ottawa.
56. Bergot et al., 82-83. Since 1803, the altarpiece has

graced the Musée des Beaux-Arts in Rouen, Normandy. One rarely finds Roch portrayed as on an equal footing with the Virgin Mary; an exception is a pair of woodcuts on the title page of a 1577 plague treatise by Jesuit Paolo Bisciola, published in Ancona and Bologna. The woodcuts show Mary standing on the moon, and Roch displaying his bubo, holding his staff, and accompanied by his dog (with bread). The title page is reproduced in Martin, 28.

57. On the history of devotion to Mary, see Graef.

58. For the historical development of this doctrine, see Jugie.

59. Daniels, no. 278.

60. Perhaps Ricci decided that such ambiguity on James/Roch was not suitable in the final version of the painting. In the latter, the dog is gone, and the figure in the foreground holds keys–identifying him as Saint Peter. With the apostle Peter so clearly portrayed, and the dog removed, the pilgrim figure becomes almost certainly the apostle James. On the *bozzetto* and the final version, see Rizzi, 112-13.

61. There also exists a *bozzetto* of the Karlskirche altarpiece, in the Budapest Museum of Fine Arts; see Cogeval, 68-69.

62. Boeckl, 120.

63. Boeckl, 102-04, 120.

64. Piovene, 96-97.

65. Helpful on this point may be the volume edited by P. Jones and Worcester.

66. Brockliss and C. Jones, table of contents.

67. On this painting, see Schmitz-Eichhoff, 321-22.

68. *Dictionnaire de Spiritualité,* II, 157-159.

69. Panigarola 1592, 584-611.

70. Panigarola 1592, 101-124.

71. Panigarola 1592, 612-47.

72. Panigarola 1592, 648-724. For an example of how Panigarola's preaching was 'received' in Paris, see the journal of Pierre de L'Estoile, in Roelker, 197.

73. Panigarola 1597.

74. Panigarola 1585, 21.

75. Panigarola 1585, 22-30.

76. On heresy viewed as a "plague," see Martin, 71-72. On plague as metaphor, see C. Jones.

77. Sommervogel, I, 1488-1505.

78. Sommervogel, I, 1499.

79. Binet 1998.

80. Binet 1998, 18-22.

81. Binet 1998, 26-33.

82. Binet 1998, 46-47.

83. Binet 1998, 49.

84. Binet 1998, 49-50.

85. Binet 1998, 91-92.

86. Binet 1998, 94.

87. Binet 1629, 254-77.

88. Boeckl, 57; see also Vaslef, 143.

89. *Raccolta,* 83.

90. *Mercure françois* 15 (1631), 1-37.

91. *Mercure françois* 16 (1632), 1079.

92. *Mercure françois* 16 (1632), 1-2 (the page numbering in this volume begins again with events of 1630). The queens were almost certainly Queen Mother Marie de Medici, and Queen Anne of Austria, spouse of King Louis XIII.

93. On eighteenth-century print culture, see Chartier.

94. Defoe, 212-16.

95. Defoe, 212.

96. In addition to the *modello* in Columbia, SC, there is one in the Dulwich Picture Gallery, London. See *Collection for a King,* 104-05.

97. On Muratori as a historian, see Cochrane, 153-72.

98. Muratori 1743, *Relazione della Peste di Marsiglia,* i. The years 1742-44 saw an outbreak of plague in Messina; see Biraben, I, 399-400. Muratori identifies Chicoyneau as Chancellor of the University of Montpellier; some texts of Chicoyneau and Verny on plague are reproduced in Hildesheimer 1990, 159-63.

99. Muratori 1743, *Relazione della Peste di Marsiglia,* i-ii.

100. Muratori 1743, *Relazione della Peste di Marsiglia,* xxiii-xlvii.

101. Brockliss and C. Jones, 349. On municipal measure taken to at least contain the Marseille plague, see Hildesheimer, 1980.

102. See Biraben, I, 388.

103. Jonas, 39.

104. Jonas, 43-44. A text of Belsunce on the plague and on the Sacred Heart, dated 22 October 1720, is reproduced in Hildesheimer 1993, 119-121.

105. Jonas, 40.

106. See Bowron and Rishel, 360-61.

107. Dumolin and Outardel, 160-61.

108. Dumolin and Outardel, 161, 164.

109. Vaslef, 154. For how his feast was celebrated liturgically in the nineteenth century, see the 1858 *Office de Saint Roch,* from Montpellier.

110. Vauchez 1968, 270.

111. Palmer, 79.

112. Martin, 145.

113. One very influential (and controversial) study is that of McNeill. He offers a grand synthesis of "plagues" in world history.

114. Brockliss and C. Jones, 20.

115. Naphy and Spicer, 173.

116. Péronnet, 257-68. On plague imagined as the wages of sin and as "a broom in the hands of the Almighty," see Allen, 61-77. On plague as eschatological, see Cunningham and Grell.

117. Delumeau 1978 and 1983.

118. Pullan 1992, 106-7. On perception of the poor as locus of disease, see also Hays, 306.

119. Camporesi, 101.

120. Slack, 4.

121. Cohn 2002, 710. Cohn also argues that what

was often termed plague was in fact some other disease.

122. Cohn 2003, 240.

123. See Benvenuto, and Cipolla 1981. On Venetian efforts to prevent and treat plague in 1576, see Preto.

124. Delumeau 1989, 210 For an assessment of Delumeau's several works on hope and fear, see Worcester , 157-74.

125. Delumeau 1989, 241.

126. See, e.g., the essays edited by Grell, Cunningham, and Arrizabalaga.

127. Gentilcore 1997, 195.

128. Gentilcore 1998.

129. Meiss, 165. For an example of an assessment of Meiss, see Aikema, 103.

130. Marshall 1994, 505.

131. Burke, 439.

Bibliography

Acta Breviora (fifteenth-century anonymous MS on Saint Roch); recent edition in Fanelli, 1996.

Aikema, Bernard. *Jacopo Bassano and His Public: Moralizing Pictures in an Age of Reform, ca. 1535-1600.* Trans. Andrew McCormick. Princeton, 1996.

Allen, Peter Lewis. *Sex and Disease, Past and Present.* Chicago, 2000.

Barker, Sheila. *Art in a Time of Danger: Urban VIII's Rome and the Plague of 1629-1634.* Ph.D. dissertation. Columbia University, 2002.

Benvenuto, Grazia. *La peste nell'Italia della prima età moderna: Contagio, rimedi, profilassi.* Bologna, 1996.

Bergot, François et al. *Musée des Beaux-Arts de Rouen: Guide des Collections XVIe-XVIIe siècles.* Paris, 1992.

Bessodes, Maurice. *Saint Roch: Histoire et légendes.* Turin, 1931.

Binet, Etienne. *Remèdes souverains contre la peste et la mort soudaine.* (original ed. 1628). Lyon, 1629. Most recent version, ed. Claude-Louis Combet. Grenoble, 1998. Seventeenth-century editions include an Italian translation: *Sovrani e efficaci rimedi contro la peste e la morte subitanea.* Trans. Giuseppe Fozi. Rome, 1656.

Biraben, Jean-Noël. *Les hommes et la peste en France et dans les pays européens et méditerranéens.* 2 vols. The Hague, 1975-76.

Black, Christopher. *Early Modern Italy: A Social History.* London, 2001.

Boeckl, Christine. *Images of Plague and Pestilence: Iconography and Iconology.* Kirksville, MO, 2000.

Bowron, Edgar Peters, and Joseph Richel, Eds. *Art in Rome in the Eighteenth Century.* London, 2000.

Brockliss, Laurence, and Colin Jones. *The Medical World of Early Modern France.* Oxford, 1997.

Brown, Beverly Louise, and Paola Marini, Eds. *Jacopo Bassano c. 1510-1592.* Fort Worth, 1993.

Burke, Peter. "Strengths and Weaknesses of the History of Mentalities." *History of European Ideas* 7 (1986): 439-51.

Camporesi, Piero. *The Fear of Hell: Images of Damnation and Salvation in Early Modern Europe.* Trans. Lucinda Byatt. Cambridge (UK), 1991.

Cardini, Franco. "Il pellegrinaggio a Roma ai tempi di San Rocco." In *San Rocco nell'arte.* 26-33.

Carmichael, Ann. *Plague and the Poor in Renaissance Florence.* Cambridge (UK), 1986.

Chartier, Roger. *The Cultural Uses of Print in Early Modern France.* Trans. Lydia Cochrane. Princeton, 1987.

Cipolla, Carlo. *Fighting the Plague in Seventeenth-Century Italy.* Madison, 1981.

Cochrane, Eric. "Muratori: The Vocation of a Historian." *Catholic Historical Review* 51 (1965): 153-72.

Cogeval, Guy and Miklós Mojzer. Eds. *Italian Old Masters from Raphael to Tiepolo: The Collection of the Budapest Museum of Fine Arts.* Montreal, 2002.

Cohn, Samuel. "The Back Death: End of a Paradigm." *American Historical Review*107 (June 2002), pp. 702-38.

—. *The Black Death Transformed: Disease and Culture in Early Renaissance Europe.* New York, 2003.

Collection for a King: Old Master Paintings from the Dulwich Picture Gallery. London, 1985.

Conisbee, Philip, Levkoff, Mary, and Richard Rand. *The Ahmanson Gifts: European Masterpieces in the Collection of the Los Angeles County Museum of Art.* Los Angeles, 1991.

Cunningham, Andrew, and Ole Peter Grell. *The Four Horsemen of the Apocalypse: Religion, War, Famine and*

Death in Reformation Europe. Cambridge (UK), 2000.

Daniels, Jeffery. *L'opera completa di Sebastiano Ricci*. Milan, 1976.

Defoe, Daniel. *A Journal of the Plague Year*. (first ed. 1722). Ed. Louis Landa. Oxford, 1990.

Delumeau, Jean. *Le péché et la peur: La culpabilisation en Occident XIIIe-XVIIIe siècles*. Paris, 1983.

—. *La Peur en Occident (XIVe-XVIIIe siècles)*. Paris, 1978.

—. *Rassurer et protéger: Le sentiment de sécurité dans l'Occident d'autrefois*. Paris, 1989.

Diedo, Francesco. *Vita Sancti Rochi*. (original ed. 1478). Most recent version, with Latin text and Italian translation, in Fanelli (1996). Early modern editions included various translations, among them *La vie et legende de Monsieur Sainct Roch*. Paris, 1619.

Dumolin, Maurice, and Georges Outardel. *Les Eglises de France: Paris et la Seine*. Paris, 1936.

Fanelli, Angelo. Ed. *Le due più antiche biografiche del '400 su S. Rocco*. Conversano, 1996.

Fliche, Augustin. "Le problème de Saint Roch." *Analecta Bollandiana* 68 (1950), pp. 343-61.

Gentilcore, David. "The Fear of Disease and the Disease of Fear." In *Fear in Early Modern Society*. Eds. William Naphy and Penny Roberts. Manchester (UK), 1997. 184-208.

—. *Healers and Healing in Early Modern Italy*. Manchester (UK), 1998.

Gould, Cecil. *The Sixteenth Century Italian Schools*. London, 1987.

Graef, Hilda. *Mary: A History of Doctrine and Devotion*. 2 vols. London, 1963-65.

Grell, Ole Peter, Cunningham, Andrew, and Jon Arrrizabalaga. Eds. *Health Care and Poor Relief in Counter-Reformation Europe*. London, 1999.

Hays, J.N. *The Burdens of Disease: Epidemics and Human Response in Western History*. New Brunswick, 2000.

Hildesheimer, Françoise. *Le bureau de la santé de Marseille sous l'Ancien Régime: Le renfermement de la contagion*. Marseille, 1980.

—. *Fléaux et société: de la Grande Peste au cholera XIVe-XIXe siècle*. Paris, 1993.

—. *La terreur et la piété: L'Ancien Régime à l'épreuve de la peste*. Paris, 1990.

Humfrey, Peter. *Lorenzo Lotto*. New Haven, 1997.

Jenner, Mark. "The Great Dog Massacre." In *Fear in Early Modern Society*. Eds. William Naphy and Penny Roberts. Manchester UK), 1997. 44-61.

Jonas, Raymond. *France and the Cult of the Sacred Heart: An Epic Tale for Modern Times*. Berkeley, 2000.

Jones, Colin. "Plague and Its Metaphors in Early Modern France." *Representations* 53 (Winter 1996): 97-127.

Jones, Pamela, and Thomas Worcester. Eds. *From Rome to Eternity: Catholicism and the Arts in Italy, ca. 1550-1650*. Leiden, 2002.

Jugie, Martin. *La mort et l'assomption de la Sainte Vierge*. Città del Vaticano, 1944.

Le Blévec, Daniel. "La città di Montpellier ai tempi della formazione di san Rocco." In *San Rocco nell'arte*. 20-25.

Lebrun, François. *Se soigner autrefois: Médecins, saints et sorciers aux XVIIe et XVIIIe siècles*. Paris, 1995.

Livi-Bacci, Massimo. *Population and Nutrition: An essay on European demographic history*. Trans. Tania Croft-Murray. Cambridge (UK), 1991.

Loomis, L.R. *The Council of Constance: The Unification of the Church*. New York, 1961.

Marshall, Louise Jane. "Manipulating the Sacred: Image and Plague in Renaissance Italy." *Renaissance Quarterly* 47 (1994): 485-532.

—*Waiting on the Will of the Lord: The Imagery of the Plague*. Ph.D. dissertation, University of Pennsylvania, 1989. Ann Arbor, 1989.

Martin, A. Lynn. *Plague? Jesuit Accounts of Epidemic Disease in the 16th Century*. Kirksville, MO, 1996.

McNeill, William. *Plagues and Peoples*. (first ed. 1976). New York, 1998.

McTavish, David et al. *The Arts of Italy in Toronto Collections 1300-1800*. Toronto, 1981.

Meiss, Millard. *Painting in Florence and Siena after the*

Black Death: The Arts, Religion and Society in the Mid-Fourteenth-Century. (original ed. 1951). New York, 1964.

Mercure françois 15-16 (1631-32).

Morassi, Antonio. *A Complete Catalogue of the Paintings of G.B. Tiepolo*. New York, 1962.

Mormando, Franco. *The Preacher's Demons: Bernardino of Siena and the Social Underworld of Early Renaissance Italy*. Chicago, 1999.

Muratori, Lodovico. *Del governo della peste, e delle maniere di guardarsene*. Rome, 1743.

Naphy, William, and Penny Roberts, Eds. *Fear in Early Modern Society*. Manchester (UK), 1997.

Naphy, William, and Andrew Spicer. *The Black Death: A History of Plagues 1345-1730*. Charleston, SC, 2001.

Office de Saint Roch, pour le jour de sa fête, le 16 août. Montpellier, 1858.

Orr, Lynn Frederic. "The Roman Environment During the Reign of Innocent X (1644-55)." In *Michael Sweerts 1618-1664*. Eds. Guido Jansen and Peter Sutton. Zwolle, 2002. 48-55.

Palmer, Richard. "The Church, Leprosy and Plague in Medieval and Early Modern Europe." In *The Church and Healing*. Ed. W.J. Sheils. Oxford, 1982. 79-99.

Panigarola, Francesco. *Leçons catholiques sur les doctrines de l'Eglise divisees en trois parties*. Trans. G.C.T. Rouen, 1597.

—. *Oratione di Fr. Francesco Panigarola…sopra il corpo dell'Ill.mo Carlo Borromeo*. Paris, 1585.

—. *Les Sermons de R.P.M. François Panigarole*. Trans. Pierre Matthieu. Lyons, 1592.

Péronnet, Michel. "La peste, signe de la colère de Dieu." In *Les signes de Dieu aux XVIe et XVIIe siècles*. Ed. Geneviève Demerson and Bernard Dompnier. Clermont-Ferrand, 1993. 257-68.

Piovene, Guido. *L'opera completa di Giambattista Tiepolo*. Milan, 1968.

Pollak, Martha. *Turin 1564-1680: Urban Design, Military Culture, and the Creation of the Absolutist Capital*. Chicago, 1991.

Preto, Paolo. *Peste e società a Venezia nel 1576*. Vicenza, 1978.

Pullan, Brian. "The Counter-Reformation, Medical Care and Poor Relief." In *Health Care and Poor Relief in Counter-Reformation Europe*. Ed. Ole Peter Grell, Andrew Cunningham and Jon Arrizabalaga. London, 1999. 18-39.

—. "Plague and Perceptions of the Poor in Early Modern Italy." In *Epidemics and Ideas: Essays on the Historical Perception of Pestilence*. Ed. Terence Ranger and Paul Slack. Cambridge (UK), 1992. 101-23.

Raccolta di tutti li bandi, ordini, e provisioni, Fatte per la Città di Bologna in tempo di Contagio Imminente, e Presente, Li Anni 1628, 1629, 1630, & 1631. Bologna, 1631.

Rizzi, Aldo. *Sebastiano Ricci*. Milan, 1989.

Roelker, Nancy. *The Paris of Henry of Navarre as Seen by Pierre de L'Estoile*. Cambridge, MA, 1958.

Romanelli, Giandomenico. "La Scuola Grande di San Rocco." In *San Rocco nell'arte*. pp. 64-66.

Salisbury, Gay, and Laney Salisbury. *The Cruelest Miles: The Heroic Story of Dogs and Men in a Race Against an Epidemic*. New York, 2003.

San Rocco nell'arte: Un Pellegrino sulla Via Francigena. Milan, 2000.

Sandoval, Annette. *The Directory of Saints: A Concise Guide to Patron Saints*. New York, 1996.

Schmitt, Jean-Claude. *The Holy Greyhound: Guinefort, Healer of Children since the Thirteenth Century*. Trans. Martin Thom. Cambridge (UK), 1983.

Schmitz-Eichhoff, Marie-Theres. *St. Rochus: Ikonographische und medizin-historische Studien*. Cologne, 1977.

Sella, Domenico. *Italy in the Seventeenth Century*. London, 1997.

Slack, Paul, "Introduction." In *Epidemics and Ideas: Essays on the Historical Perception of Pestilence*. Eds. Terence Ranger and Paul Slack. Cambridge (UK), 1992. 1-20.

Sommervogel, Carlos. *Bibliothèque de la Compagnie de Jésus*. 9 vols. Brussels, 1890-1900.

Sutton, Peter. *Masters of Seventeenth Century Dutch Genre Painting*. Philadelphia, 1984.

Teza, Laura. "The Worcester Vaccaro: A Modello from Eighteenth-Century Naples." *Worcester Art Museum Journal* 7 (1983-84): 38-45.

Tomory, Peter. *Catalogue of the Italian Paintings before 1800*. Sarasota, 1976.

Turner, Victor and Edith Turner. *Image and Pilgrimage in Christian Culture: Anthropological Perspectives*. New York, 1995.

Vaslef, Irene. *The Role of St. Roch as a Plague Saint: A Late Medieval Hagiographic Tradition*. Washington, D.C.: Ph.D. thesis Catholic University of America, 1984.

Vauchez, André. "Rocco." In *Bibliotheca Sanctorum*, vol. XI. Rome, 1968. 264-73.

—. "San Rocco: tradizioni agiografiche e storia del culto." In *San Rocco nell' arte*, 2000. 13-19.

Walter, John and Roger Schofield. Eds. *Famine, Disease and the Social Order in Early Modern Society*. Cambridge (UK), 1991.

Warner, Jessica. *Craze: Gin and Debauchery in an Age of Reason*. New York, 2002.

Wiel, M.A. Chiari Moretto. "Il culto di san Rocco a Venezia: la Scuola Grande, la sua chiesa, il suo tesoro." In *San Rocco nell'arte*. 67-81.

Wine, Humphrey. *The Seventeenth Century French Paintings*. London and New Haven, 2001.

Worcester, Thomas. "In the Face of Death: Jean Delumeau on Late-Medieval Fears and Hopes." In *Death and Dying in the Middle Ages*. Ed. Edelgard DuBruck and Barbara Gusick. New York, 1999. 157-74.

Zaczek, Iain. *Dog: A Dog's Life in Art and Literature*. New York, 2000.

Catalogue of the Exhibition

Entries by Gauvin Alexander Bailey and Pamela M. Jones

1

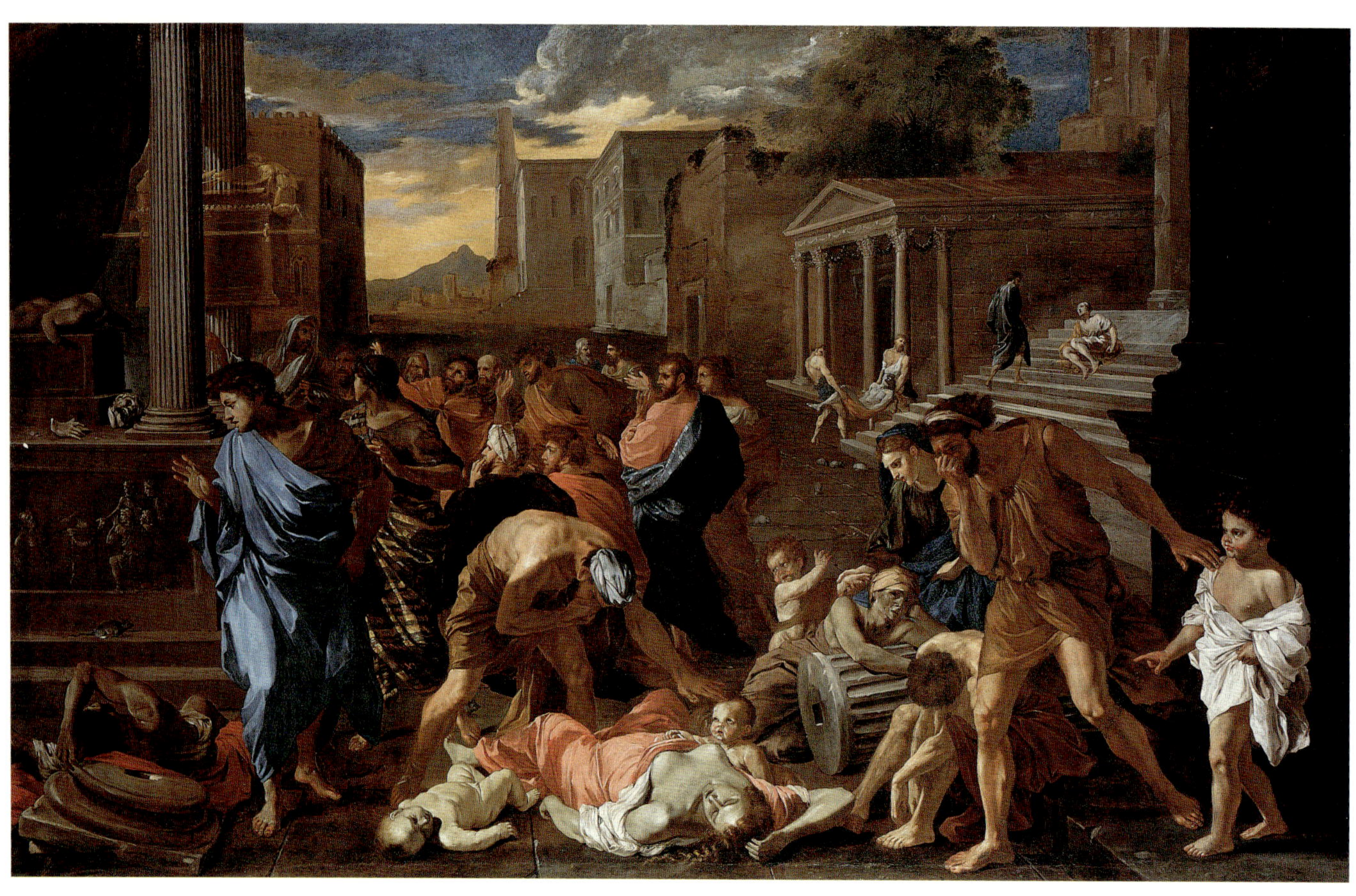

1.
ANGELO CAROSELLI, *The Plague at Ashdod*: Copy after Poussin, 1630
Oil on canvas, 128.9 x 204.5 cm
National Gallery, London

The Roman painter Angelo Caroselli (1585-1652), brother-in-law of the painter and draughtsman Filippo Lauri (1623-1694), was a self-taught artist, and he worked as a copyist and restorer. In 1608 he was a member of the Accademia di S. Luca. Early on Caroselli was known primarily as a caravaggesque painter and he created his own naturalistic interpretation of Caravaggio's work, which was characterized by intense effects of light and emphatic volumes. In the 1630s, however, Caroselli moved away from caravaggism to develop a more dynamic, Baroque style.

Caroselli's *Plague at Ashdod* is a copy after Poussin's painting of the same theme, but it is more than a mere copy. Caroselli's painting was commissioned in 1630 by the Sicilian art collector Fabrizio Valguarnera while Poussin's version, also commissioned by Valguarnera, was still underway. This painting is considered one of Caroselli's finest works and it is one of the most distinguished reminders of the plague of 1630 in Rome. The theme is based on an episode in the Old Testament book of I Samuel 5:1-6, which concerns a plague that God wrought upon the Philistines in vengeance after they captured the Ark of the Covenant and placed it in the temple of the idol Dagon in Ashdod.

Like Poussin's original, Caroselli's painting vividly represents the horrors of plague. The motif of the man raising a handkerchief to his nose and the group at the foreground including the infant suckling its dead mother derive from Marcantonio Raimondi's famous print after Raphael, *Il Morbetto* (cat. 5), itself a much copied paradigmatic plague image. The print, Poussin's painting, and Caroselli's copy can all be traced to Pliny's description of a battle scene by Aristeides. Following Poussin, Caroselli gave his scene biblical style garb and a classical cityscape derived from Sebastiano Serlio's design for a Tragic Stage from Book II of the *Architettura* (Paris, 1545), reflecting his determination to provide the theme with an appropriately tragic setting.

For *The Plague at Ashdod*, Poussin created a setting for tragic theater composed primarily of receding architectural forms with various groups of figures disposed at intervals throughout the deep space. Poussin conveys the horror of the plague by juxtaposing the dead, the dying, and the healthy, and by depicting an array of poses and emotional responses. In Caroselli's copy, the predominantly cool palette underscores the melancholy theme. There are some significant differences between the architectural settings of the copy by Caroselli and the original by Poussin. For example, the enclosed shrine and grand palace on the right in Poussin's version are replaced in Caroselli's copy by a Corinthian temple front and a much smaller building that lacks the grand loggia of Poussin's palace structure. Caroselli's architectural setting is thought perhaps to preserve Poussin's original idea for the background.

2

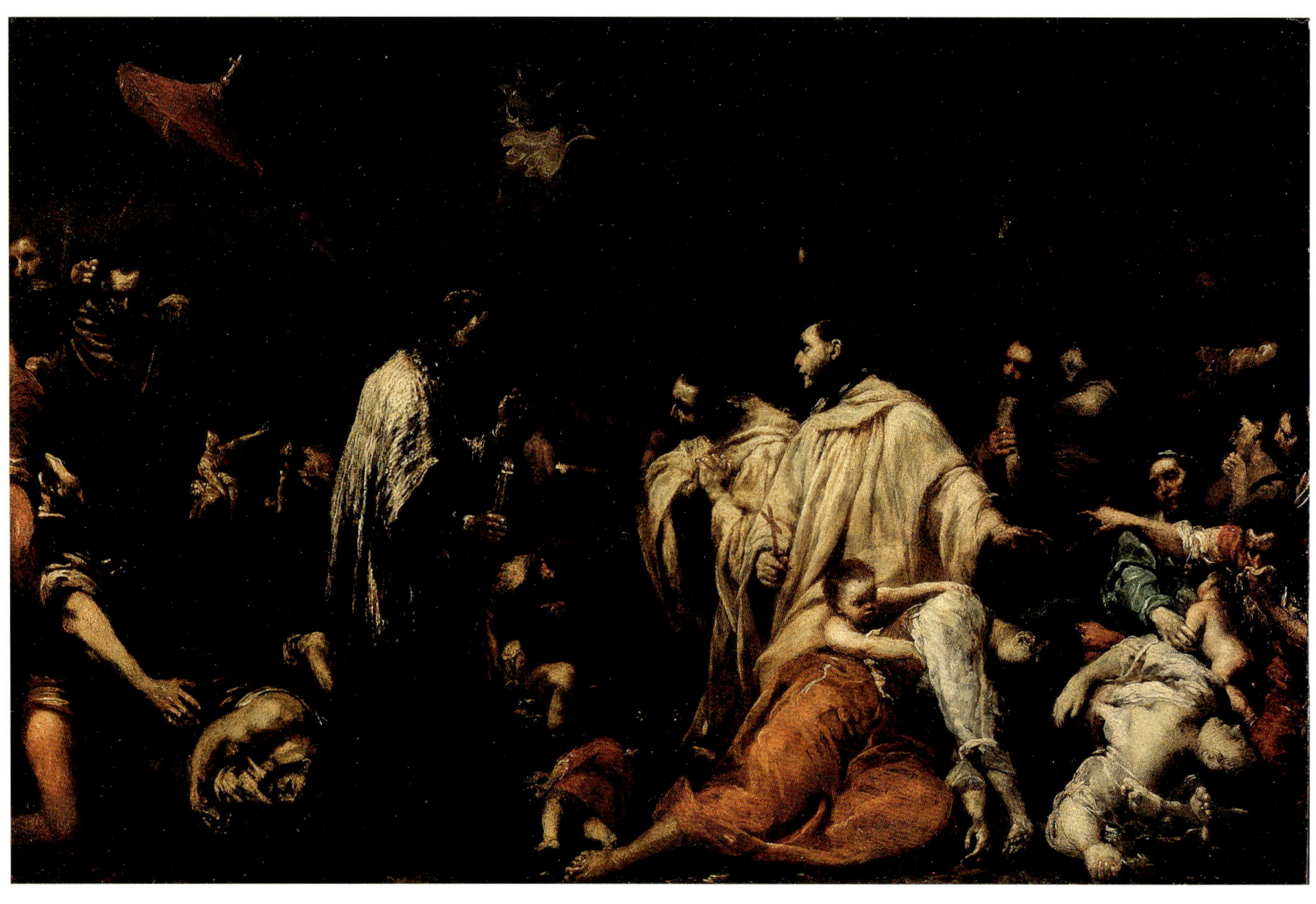

2.
GIUSEPPE MARIA CRESPI, *The Blessed Bernardo Tolomei Interceding for the Plague Victims in Siena in 1348*, 1734
Oil on copper, 42.7 x 66.68 cm
The J. Paul Getty Museum of Art, Los Angeles

The Bolognese painter Giuseppe Maria Crespi (1665-1747) was trained in the academic tradition, but became especially known for genre subjects characterized by striking chiaroscuro effects, in which he pitted bright colors against dark and murky backgrounds. After working in Bologna as a fresco painter, Crespi earned important commissions in Florence at the beginning of the eighteenth century, where he worked for Grand Prince Ferdinando de' Medici. There he painted genre scenes of kitchens and other domestic interiors, peasant scenes, and marketplaces – rivaling his Flemish colleagues who also specialized in these genres. Crespi also earned a reputation as a leading portrait painter and teacher, and his students included Giovanni Battista Piazzetta and Pietro Longhi.

Crespi's painting depicts the young lay brother's selfless care of the plague-stricken of Siena during the dreaded Black Death of 1348, from which Tolomei himself died. Whereas in his youth Crespi gained fame as a genre painter, this work is typical of his late years, during which he became increasingly devout and worked mainly on religious themes. In this expressive painting the small-scale figures characteristic of Crespi's late style are rendered with his distinctive feathery brushwork, and the composition is animated by a powerful play of light and dark across the surface, leading the viewer's eyes from the left, where a priest enters, to Brother Bernard just right of center, who holds a cross and gestures toward his dying patients on the right. Because Brother Bernard's heroic virtue was demonstrated by his ministering to plague victims, it is probable that the Olivetan Abbot Corsi commissioned Crespi's painting to promote the Sienese lay brother's canonization. Yet Tolomei was never canonized, and he was beatified only several decades later, in 1768.

3

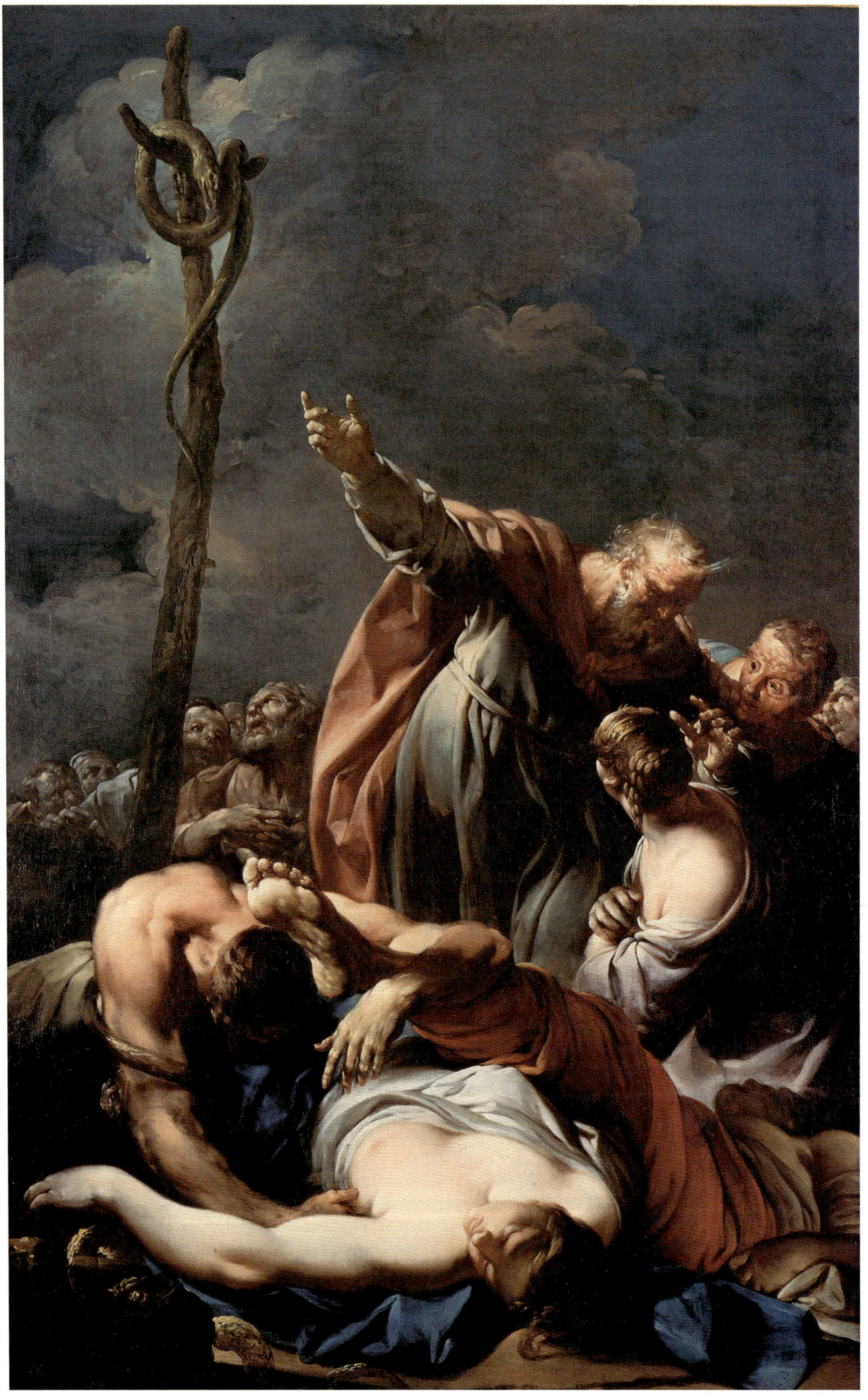

3.
GIAN DOMENICO FERRETTI, *The Brazen Serpent*, 1736
Oil on canvas, 150 x 95.5 cm
Collection of Mary Jane Harris, New York, promised gift to the Palmer Museum of Art, Pennsylvania State University

The Florentine painter Gian Domenico Ferretti (1692-1768) was a leading Settecento artist whose style was indebted to the late classicizing manner of the Bolognese painters Marcantonio Franceschini and Giovan Camillo Sagrestani.

The Brazen Serpent is a pendant to Ferretti's *Liberation of Saint Peter* in Berlin and depicts a well-known episode from the Old Testament book of Numbers (21: 4-9): God sent a plague of poisonous serpents to the Israelites as a punishment for speaking out against him, and, as a result, many Israelites were bitten and died. But God instructed Moses to place a fiery serpent on a pole so that everyone who gazed upon the serpent would be cured.

Ferretti fully exploits the dramatic potential of the miraculous theme, creating a compact, vertical composition in which Moses's theatrical gesture toward the serpent contrasts with the prone bodies of the dead and dying in the foreground. The serpent raised high on the pole calls to mind the figure of Christ on the Cross and indeed the theme of the Brazen Serpent was seen as a prefiguration of Christ's Crucifixion. Thus the scene was meant to give viewers a message of hope during times of tribulation such as outbreaks of plague. Preachers and spiritual writers of the early modern period taught that Christ's sacrifice brought the possibility of human salvation.

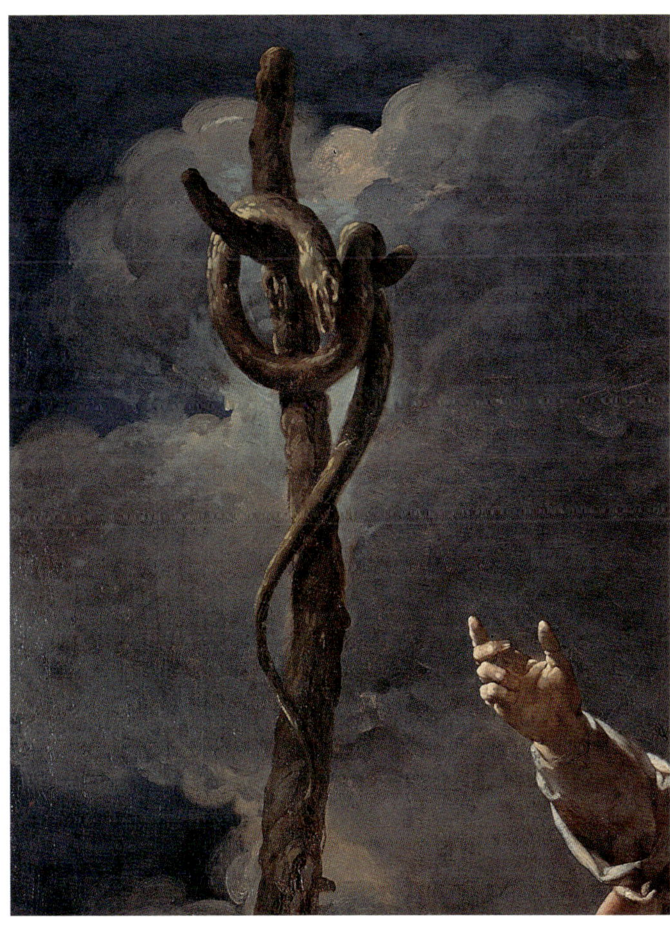

4

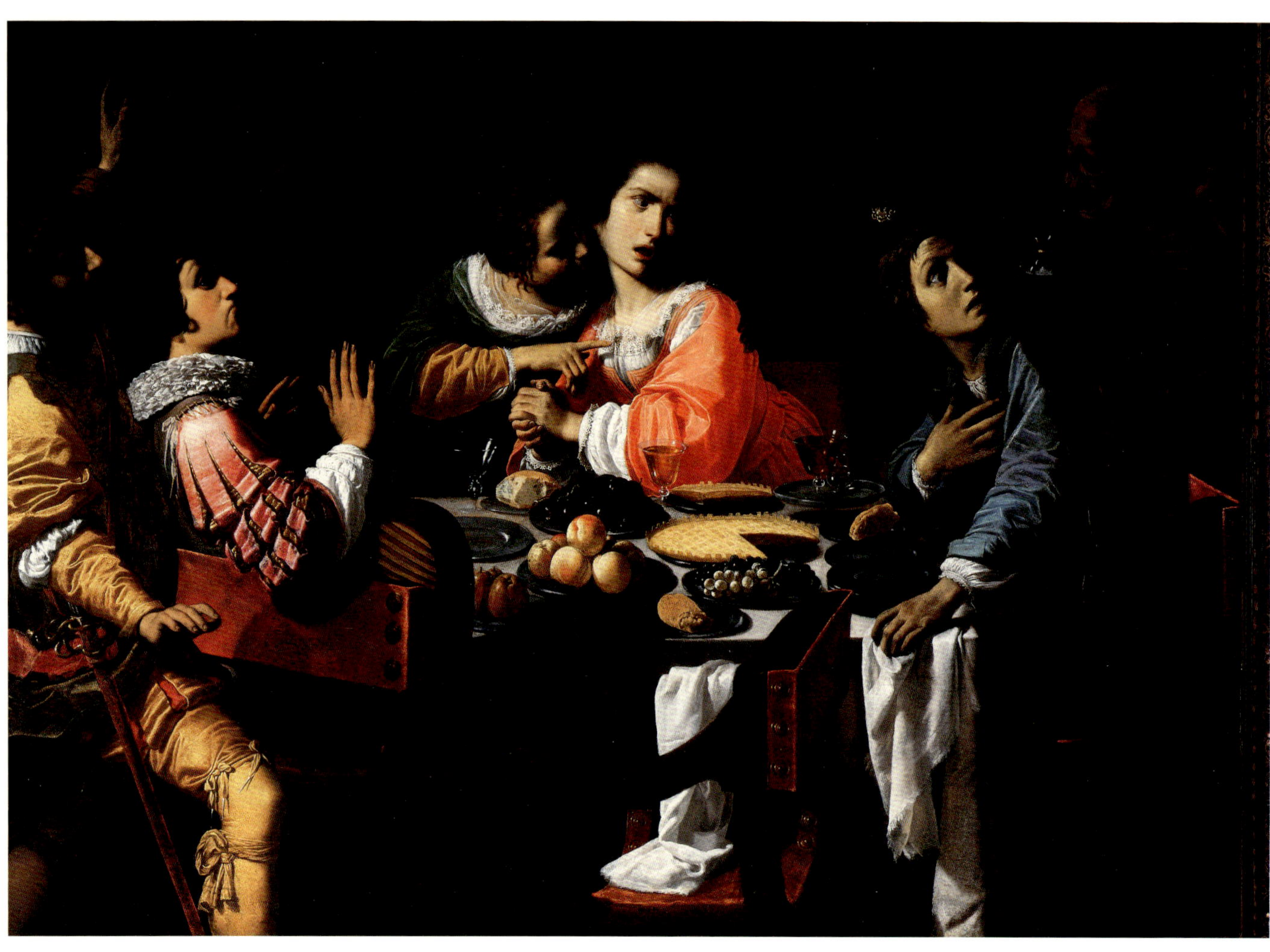

4.
Giovanni Martinelli, *Memento Mori (Death Comes to the Dinner Table)*, ca. 1635
Oil on canvas, 123.15 x 174 cm
New Orleans Museum of Art: Gift of Mrs. William G. Helis, Sr., New Orleans, in memory of her husband

The early career of the Florentine painter Giovanni Martinelli (1600 or 1604-59) remains relatively unknown. He moved to Florence from Arezzo by 1621. Among his earliest surviving works is a cycle of frescoes dated 1634 in Pistoia, and he is known to have been a member of the Accademia del Disegno in Florence in 1635. His frescoes in Pistoia betray the influence of the clear narrative style of Santi di Tito and his use of shimmering, sharp colors recalls that of his compatriots Bernardo Poccetti (who also frescoed at Pistoia) and Cesare Dandini. Martinelli's works of the 1630s, including the *Memento Mori*, are similar in style to those of the Florentine painters Filippo Tarchiani and Anastagio Fontebuoni. Throughout his career, Martinelli continued to paint moralizing allegories, although in the 1640s and 1650s he also received commissions for altarpieces.

Martinelli's colorful and dramatic painting underscores the unpredictable and swift arrival of death. Its Latin title, *Memento Mori*, means "Remember, you shall die." A group of expensively and modishly dressed men and women cavorting around a table laden with lush fruits and pastries is suddenly interrupted by the appearance on the extreme right, in dark shadow, of a skeleton holding an hourglass. The once happy banqueters react with dramatic gestures and call out in surprise. The contrast between the youthful revelers enjoying mundane pleasures and the macabre reality of death was only too real in times of plague, since the pestilence often arrived without warning, attacking affluent and poor alike.

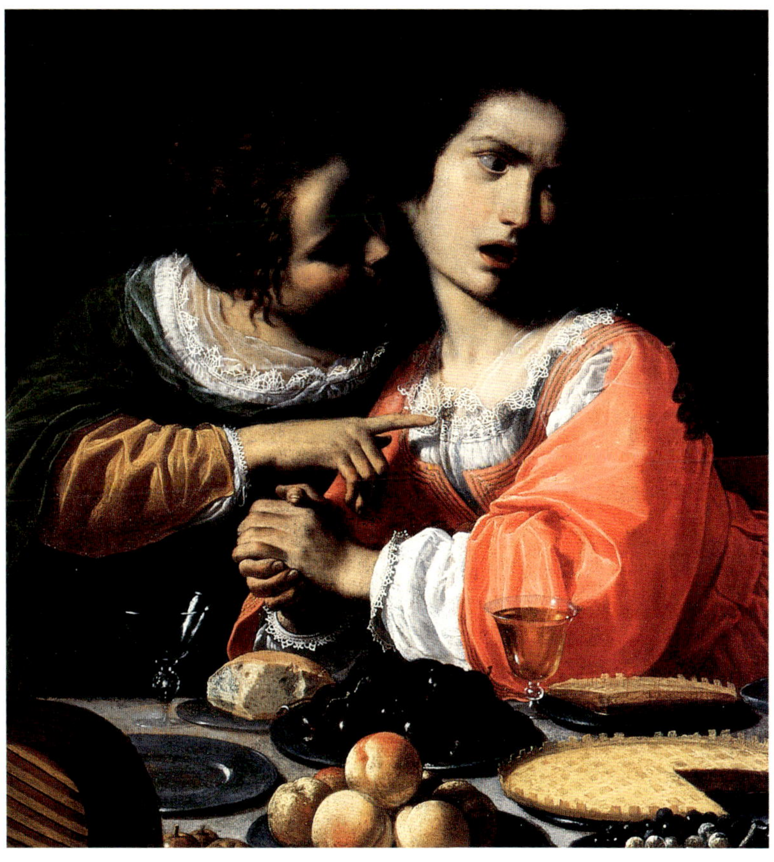

5

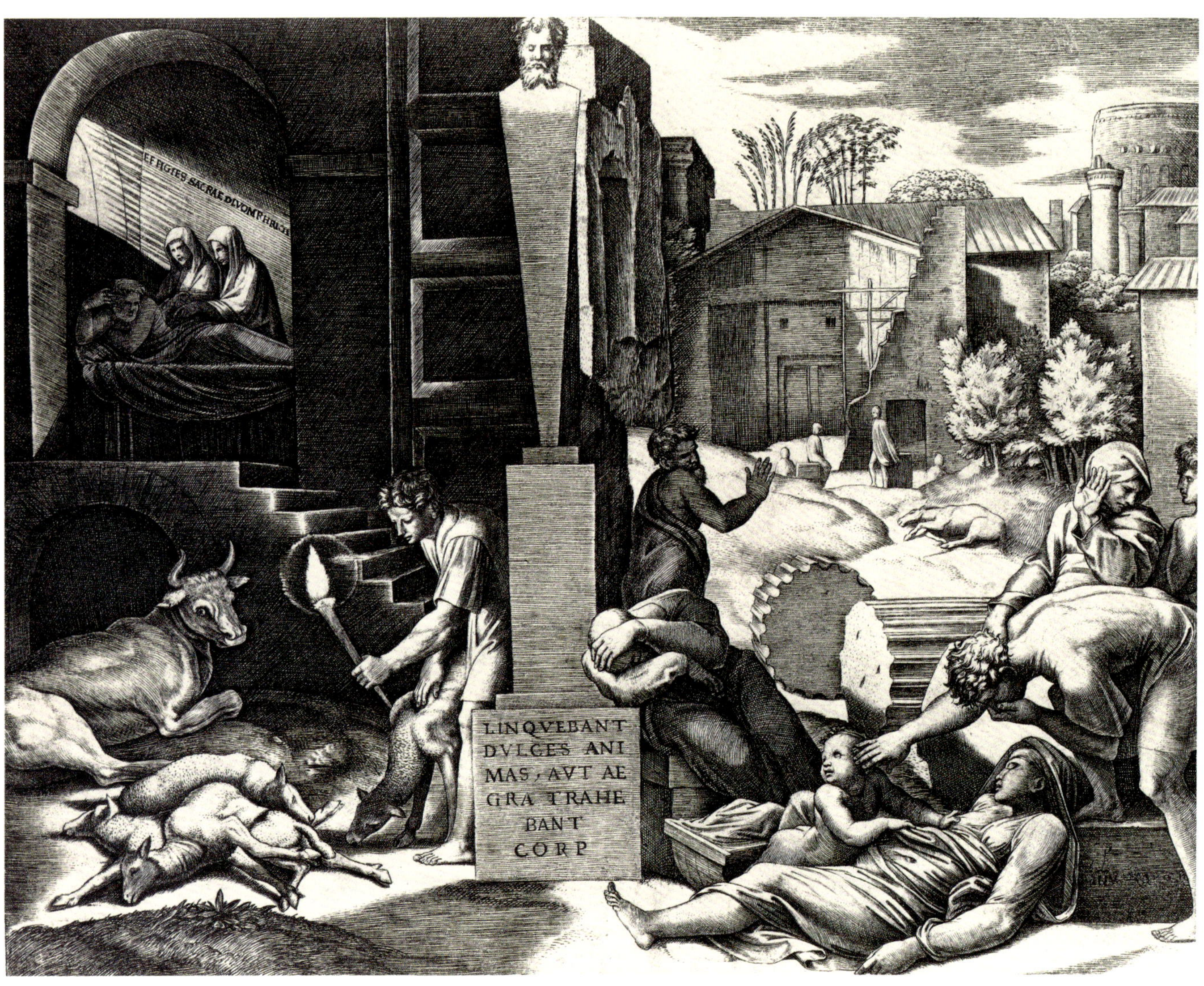
EFFIGIES SACRAE DIVOM PHRIGII
LINQVEBANT
DVLCES ANI
MAS, AVT AE
GRA TRAHE
BANT
CORP

5.
Marcantonio Raimondi after Raphael, *The Plague*, ca. 1514
Engraving, 40.6 x 55.9 cm
National Gallery of Art, Washington, D.C., Gift of W. G. Russell Allen

The Bolognese engraver Marcantonio Raimondi (ca. 1480-1534) was trained by a goldsmith. During a visit to Venice ca. 1506-08, he was inspired by the works of Dürer, which he copied so successfully that his works were sold as originals. After a stay in Florence, Raimondi settled in Rome, where he arrived in 1510 or 1511. There he became friends with Raphael, whose drawings he often engraved. Raimondi became the most influential Italian engraver of the Renaissance, achieving unprecedentedly nuanced effects of texture and tone.

Raimondi's print reproduces in reverse a still extant drawing by Raphael, who probably created his work to be engraved. The subject is taken from Virgil's *Aeneid*, Book III, which describes a sudden outbreak of the plague that struck the refugee Trojan community on the island of Crete. A vignette at the upper left depicts the subsequent dream of Aeneas, in which the Phrygian household gods that he had carried from Troy told him that Italy, not Crete, was his divinely ordained destiny.

Raimondi's prints disseminated Raphael's designs throughout Europe. This engraving of the plague, familiarly known by its Italian title *Il Morbetto* (the little disease, little referring to the small size of the engraving), was one of the most influential depictions of the plague in early modern European art. Its compositional details and figural groups – especially the dying mother and child in the foreground, which was taken from Pliny the Elder's ekphrasis of a famous Greek painting by Aristeides of Thebes – reappeared in numerous later plague paintings in Italy, France, and elsewhere. This exhibition includes examples by Caroselli, Sweerts, and Tiepolo.

6

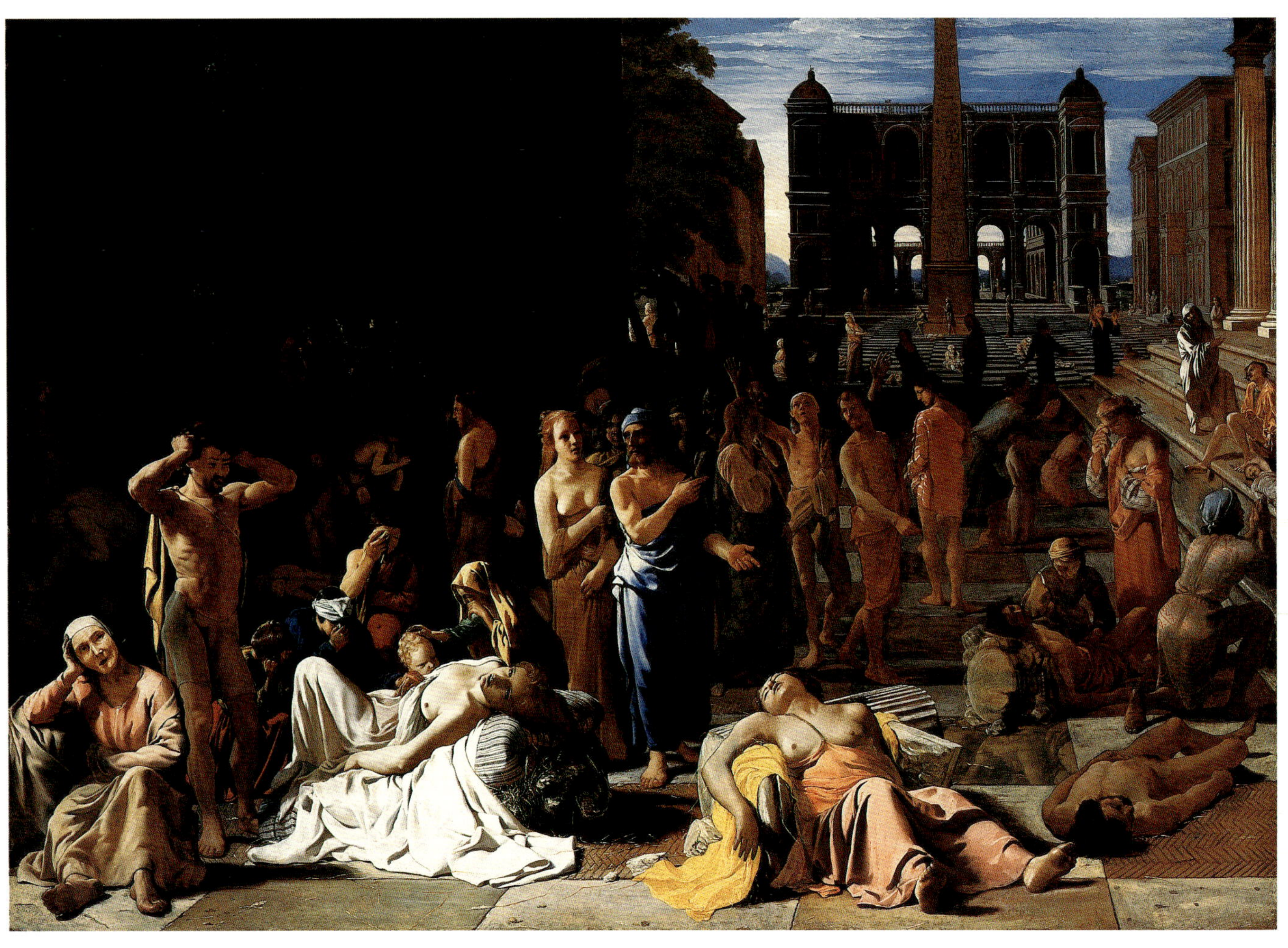

6.

Michael Sweerts, *Plague in an Ancient City*, ca. 1652-54
Oil on canvas, 118.75 x 171.45 cm
Los Angeles County Museum of Art, Gift of the Ahmanson Foundation

The Flemish painter Michael Sweerts (1618-64) was born in Brussels, but moved to Rome in 1646, where he remained until after 1652. Influenced strongly by Caravaggio, Pieter van Laer, and the Dutch *Bamboccianti*, he specialized in portraits and genre scenes. Sweerts returned to Brussels by 1656, where he joined the painters' guild in 1659. In 1660 he joined a Catholic missionary group called the Société des Missions Etrangères (the Society of Foreign Missions), and in 1661 accompanied them on a mission to Asia. He left the order in 1662 in Tabriz (Persia), and spent his final years in Persia and India. He died in the Indo-Portuguese capital of Goa in 1664.

This panoramic scene of a plague in antiquity is Sweerts's most ambitious and monumental painting. Bathed in dramatic lighting and rendered in cool colors with thin transparent glazes, it depicts the appalling devastation of the plague. The cityscape derives from Sebastiano Serlio's design for a tragic stage from Book II of the *Architettura* (Paris, 1545). Sweerts's tragic theme is set in a piazza filled with figures in classical poses and drapery. The dead and dying are surrounded by figures kneeling in prayer, crying out in anguish, or awestruck with horror. The motifs of the infant suckling his dead mother, in the left foreground, and the man holding his nose, in the right middleground, derive from Marcantonio Raimondi's engraving after Raphael, known as *Il Morbetto* (cat. 5), which was one of the most influential plague compositions in Italy. The woman on the far left rests her head on her hand, in a pose traditionally associated with melancholy.

Sweerts's classicizing painting was once attributed to Nicolas Poussin, and indeed pays homage to the French master's *Plague at Ashdod*, executed in Rome in 1630. Caroselli's copy of Poussin's painting is on view in the exhibition (cat. 1). Whereas the precise plague theme treated by Poussin and Caroselli is well known, Sweerts's theme has been exceedingly difficult to identify. *Plague in an Ancient City* was long thought to represent a pestilence that beset Athens in the fifth century B.C., but there are many discrepancies between Thucydides's account of the Athenian plague and the details of Sweerts's composition. Therefore, some scholars have suggested that Sweerts intended to depict a generic classical scene in order to comment on early modern experiences of the plague, such as the one he endured in Rome from 1648-50, or a meditation on the horrors of the disease in general.

In his essay in this catalogue, Franco Mormando proposes a new interpretation of Sweerts's image, which focuses on the contrast between pagan and Christian responses to the plague during the reign of the fourth-century Roman Emperor Julian "the Apostate." This contrast, Mormando argues, is underscored by the two-part composition, which is cast in shadow on the left, or pagan side, and is far better lit on the right, or Christian side. Mormando discusses in detail the complex iconography of the painting, which was probably conceived as a warning to heretics and Catholics alike to adhere to the teachings of the "true" Catholic faith or suffer the consequences of God's wrath.

7

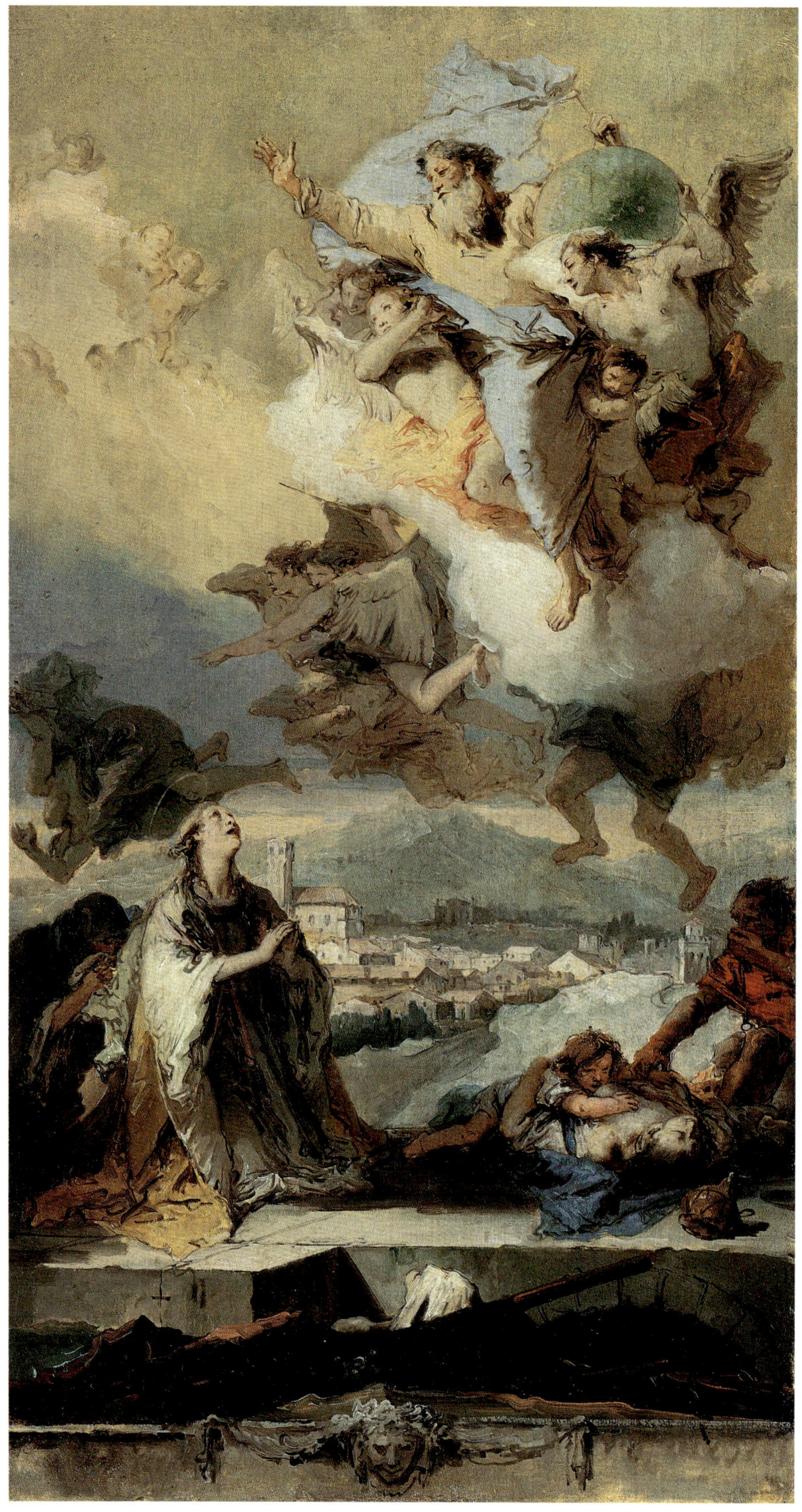

7.
GIOVANNI BATTISTA TIEPOLO, *Saint Thecla Praying for the Plague-Stricken*, 1758-59
Oil on canvas, 81.3 x 44.8 cm
The Metropolitan Museum of Art, New York, Rogers Fund, 1937

Giovanni Battista Tiepolo (1696-1770), the leading Venetian decorative painter of the Settecento, was one of the most sought-after Italian painters of his day. A prolific artist, he worked extensively on fresco commissions for both palaces and churches in Northern Italy, Franconia, and Madrid, where he died. His frescoes are often distinguished by impressive illusionistic effects typical of the sophisticated and playful taste of eighteenth-century elites.

Tiepolo's highly affective *Saint Thecla Praying for the Plague-Stricken* commemorates one of the most virulent outbreaks of the plague in early modern Italy, that of 1630. In that year, the town government of Este established in its cathedral a new altar dedicated to Saint Thecla, patroness of the city, beseeching her to deliver its inhabitants from the plague. Saint Thecla of Iconium was a follower of Saint Paul who suffered many tortures but survived to become a famed healer. Like many patrons of cities her intercession was invoked during times of plague. The cathedral's original ex-voto painting of 1630 was replaced in 1759 by Tiepolo's splendid altarpiece, for which this painting is the *modello* (sketch). Tiepolo's *modello* combines his hallmark fluid handling and subtle *colorito* – here marked by delicate yellows, grays, and blue, and overall golden tonality – with a spiritual depth and emotional poignancy unusual in his oeuvre.

In Tiepolo's *modello*, Saint Thecla intercedes on behalf of the town of Este, depicted in the background; the saint, kneeling on a bridge, is surrounded by death and desolation. Flanking her on the extreme left and right, two figures hold their noses in response to the stench of death, but also to protect themselves from the miasmic air that was thought to cause the plague. In the right foreground, beside Thecla, a child clings to its dead mother, an artistic tribute to another work in this exhibition, *Il Morbetto* (cat. 5). In contrast to this pitiful vignette is the message of hope and salvation provided by the triumphant entry of God the Father, who, in response to Thecla's prayer, appears in an effulgence of light at the upper right of the composition.

8

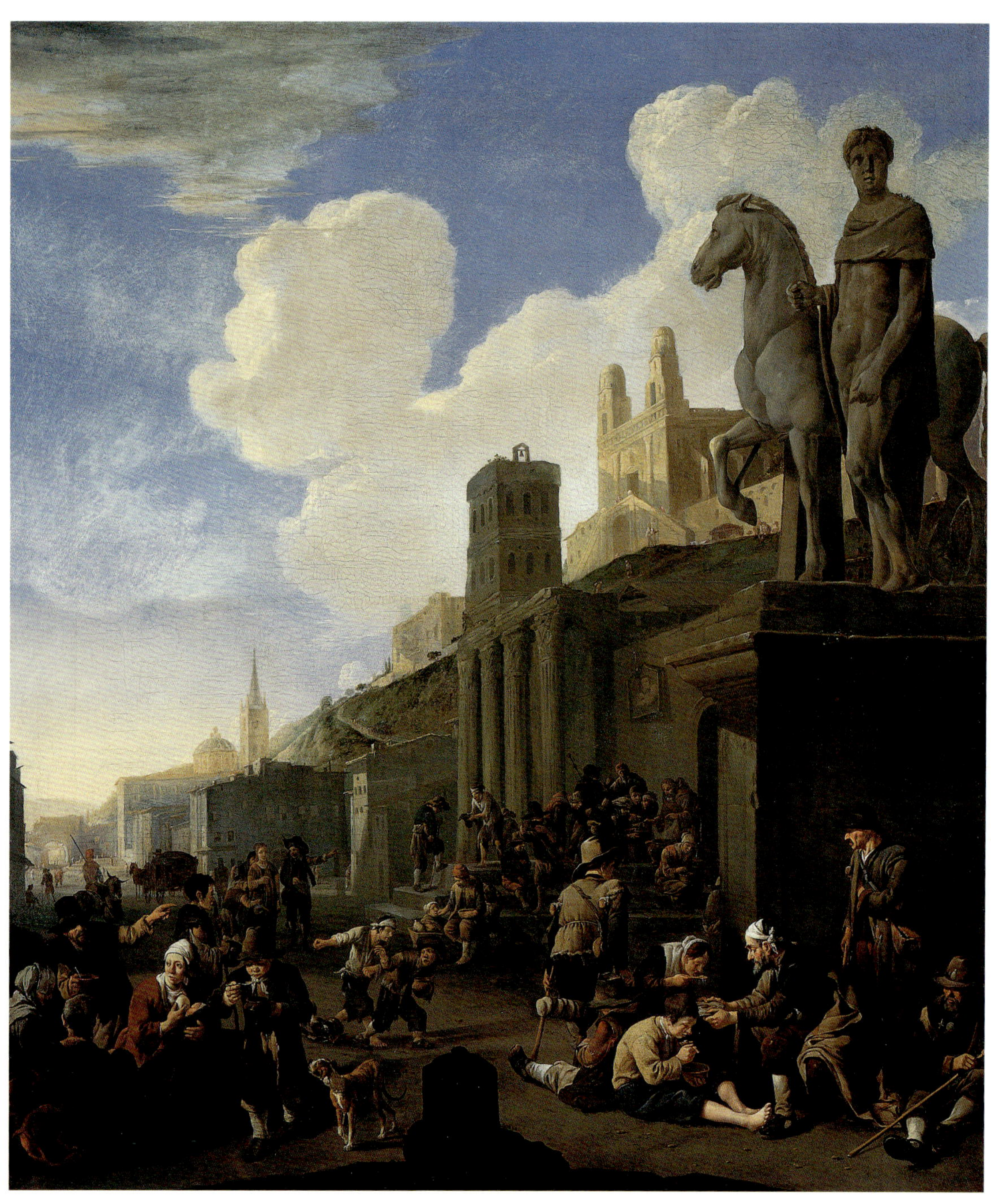

8.
JOHANNES LINGELBACH, *A Street Scene with a Capriccio of Roman Buildings*, ca. 1652
Oil on canvas, 61 x 91.4 cm
Worcester Art Museum, Sarah C. Garver Fund

Johannes Lingelbach (1622-74) was born in Frankfurt and later lived in the Netherlands. He was active in Rome 1644-50. In Rome, Lingelbach fell in with a group of Northern genre painters known as the *Bamboccianti,* who focused on scenes of everyday life among the city's poor and working classes. Although he moved to Amsterdam in 1653, Lingelbach continued to produce Roman street scenes well into the 1660s.

This scene is set in the Via del Babuino, near the Piazza di Spagna, where Lingelbach lived between 1647 and 1648; the artist, however, takes some liberties with topography to include more of Rome's famous monuments than one could actually see from that vantage point.

The *Street Scene with a Capriccio of Roman Buildings* is a celebration of one of the seven corporal acts of mercy: feeding the hungry (the others are: burying the dead, visiting prisoners, dressing the naked, offering hospitality to pilgrims, relieving the thirsty, and caring for the sick). A Franciscan friar is shown distributing soup to a throng of peasants who have gathered in the middle ground. Other figures are distributed throughout the canvas, including pilgrims, an amputee, a woman breastfeeding her child, and members of the aristocracy being approached for alms. The striking difference between the luminous Mediterranean sky above and the shadowy streets below highlight the poverty and suffering of the peasants. The seven corporal acts of mercy were closely associated with the realities of the plague, since famine was one of the plague's consequences, but also since it was generally believed that the plague was visited upon humankind as punishment for sins and to make people penitent.

9

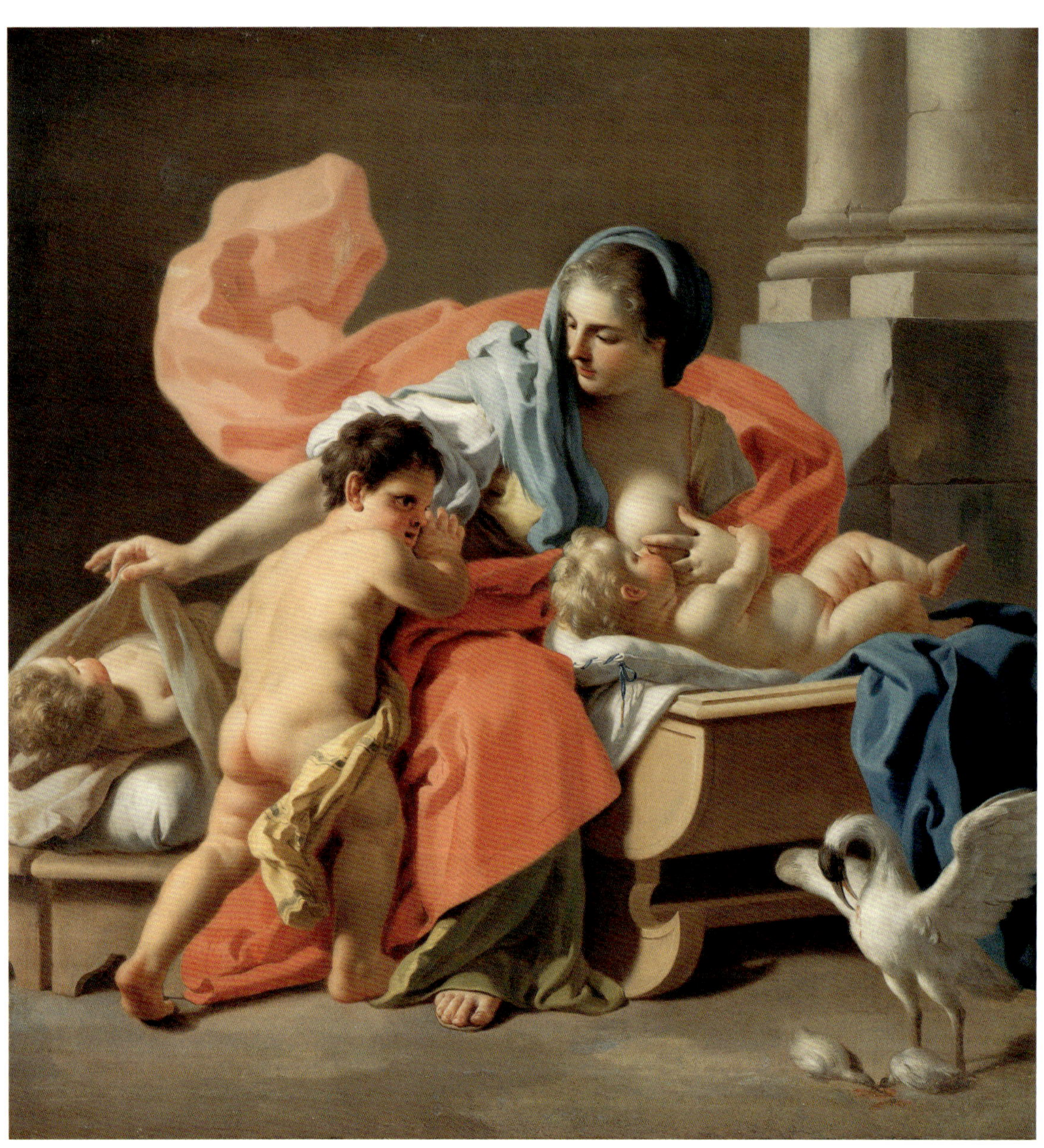

9.
FRANCESCO DE MURA, *Allegory of Maternal Love (Charity)*, ca. 1743-44
Oil on canvas, 139.54 x 134.62 cm
Art Institute of Chicago, Preston O. Morton Fund for Older Paintings

Francesco de Mura (1696-1782), a prominent Neapolitan painter of the Settecento, received his initial training from Domenico Viola, before becoming Francesco Solimena's favorite student. As a young artist his style was closely related to the grand Baroque manner of Solimena. By the late 1720s De Mura developed a more refined classicizing style, although some of his later works are rather Rococo in effect. During his long career, de Mura was active as a frescoist in Naples and Turin, where he painted both religious and mythological cycles in addition to easel paintings. De Mura ran a large workshop, and exerted a great deal of influence on artistic developments in eighteenth-century Naples.

De Mura's delicately painted *Allegory of Maternal Love (Charity)* may have been executed in Turin for the House of Savoy. It depicts the principal theological virtue, charity, or love of God and one's neighbor. By using the traditional motif of a woman suckling and caring for three tender infants as the primary focus of his painting, de Mura rendered the allegory emotionally accessible, hence its association with maternal love. In the lower right corner, a pelican is shown feeding its defenseless young with the blood streaming from its pierced breast. This motif, also traditional, was associated with charity and had a christological significance: it symbolized the Savior's sacrifice on the Cross, which made human salvation possible. The *Allegory of Maternal Love* typifies de Mura's style of the 1740s, when he painted many such allegories incorporating similarly monumental, idealized figures portrayed with extreme elegance and a blond tonality inspired by works of the Bolognese school.

10

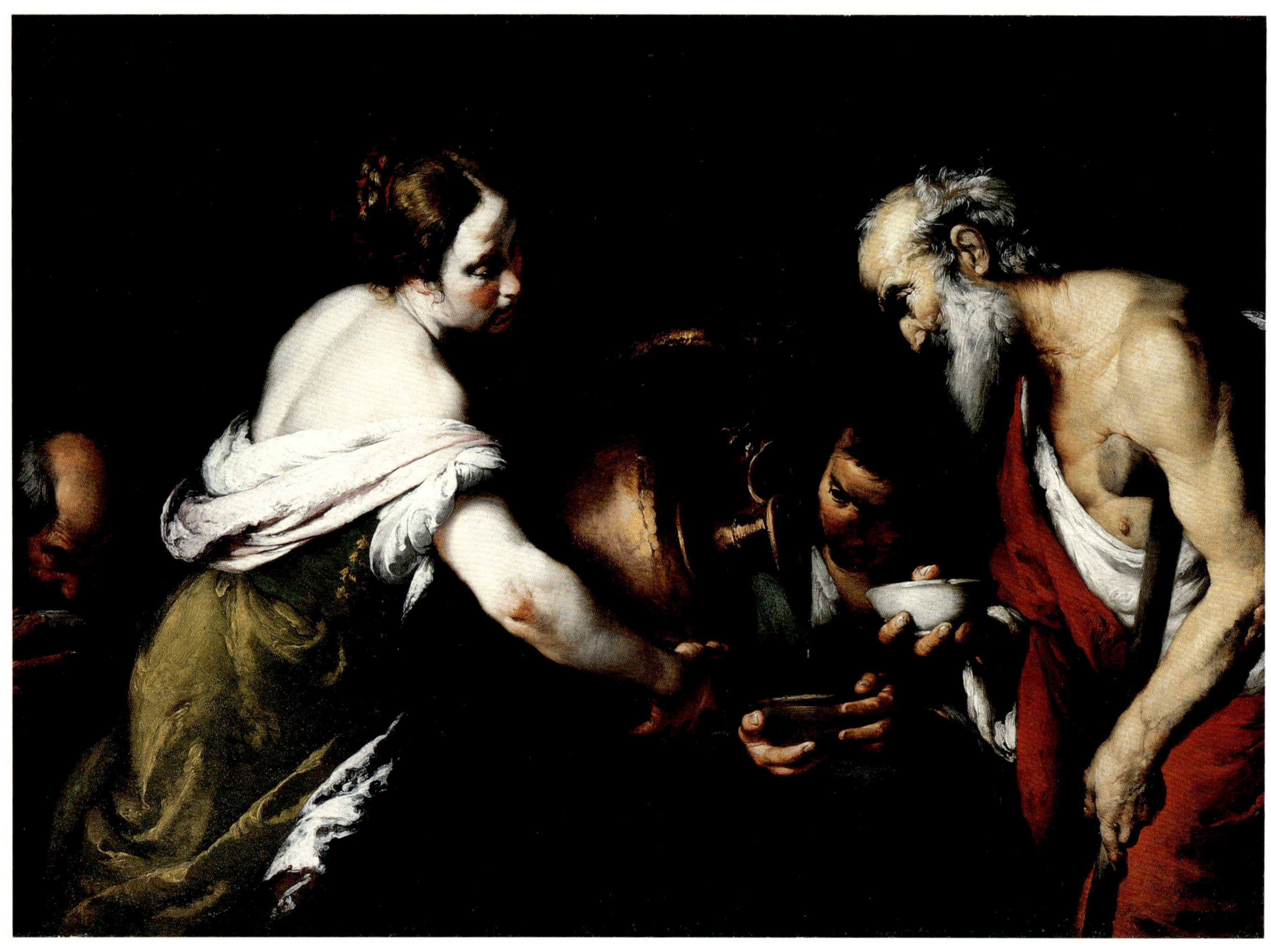

10.
Bernardo Strozzi, *An Act of Mercy: Giving Drink to the Thirsty*, 1616-18
Oil on canvas, 133.35 x 189.23 cm
Museum purchase, Collection of the John and Mabel Ringling Museum of Art, The State Museum of Florida

The Genoese master Bernardo Strozzi (1581-1644) is considered one of the greatest painters to have made the transition from Mannerism to Baroque in the early seventeenth century. Strozzi became a Capuchin friar in 1598, and was known throughout his career as *Il Cappucino*, and later as *Il Prete Genovese*. Influenced by Rubens, who was in Genoa in 1607, Strozzi himself became a leading member of Genoa's artistic scene. Strozzi's early works were dominated by a powerful chiaroscuro, but his palette became lighter after he moved to Venice, where he helped revive an interest in the city's painterly tradition. Strozzi was a versatile artist, known for genre scenes, portraits, and religious themes. He was influential on artistic developments in his native Genoa as well as in Venice, where he lived from 1630 until his death in 1644.

The painting in this exhibition is among the best versions of this theme, which the artist painted several times in his career. It is one of the Acts of Mercy identified in the Matthew, 25 (see cat. 8). Acts of charity were frequently painted in the early modern period when pestilence and poverty were ubiquitous. Strozzi was a member of the Capuchin order, a reform branch of the Franciscan order based on the strict observance of poverty and devoted to serving the poor and suffering. Thus Strozzi would have been particularly sensitive to the social and moral dimensions of this theme. During the plague, economies were driven to collapse or near-collapse, and quarantines prevented poor people from working, exacerbating their poverty. Charitable acts were more necessary than ever during calamitous times.

Strozzi presents us with an intimate scene in which the figures are pushed up close to the picture plane and rendered with much naturalistic detail. The woman in the center pours water from a heavy brass jug into the bowl held by a poor boy while an old man, leaning on a crutch at the extreme right, awaits his turn. At the far left, another elderly man drinks from his cup. The quiet but intense drama of the scene is enhanced by the chiaroscuro, which draws our attention to the figures and obscures any potentially distracting setting.

11

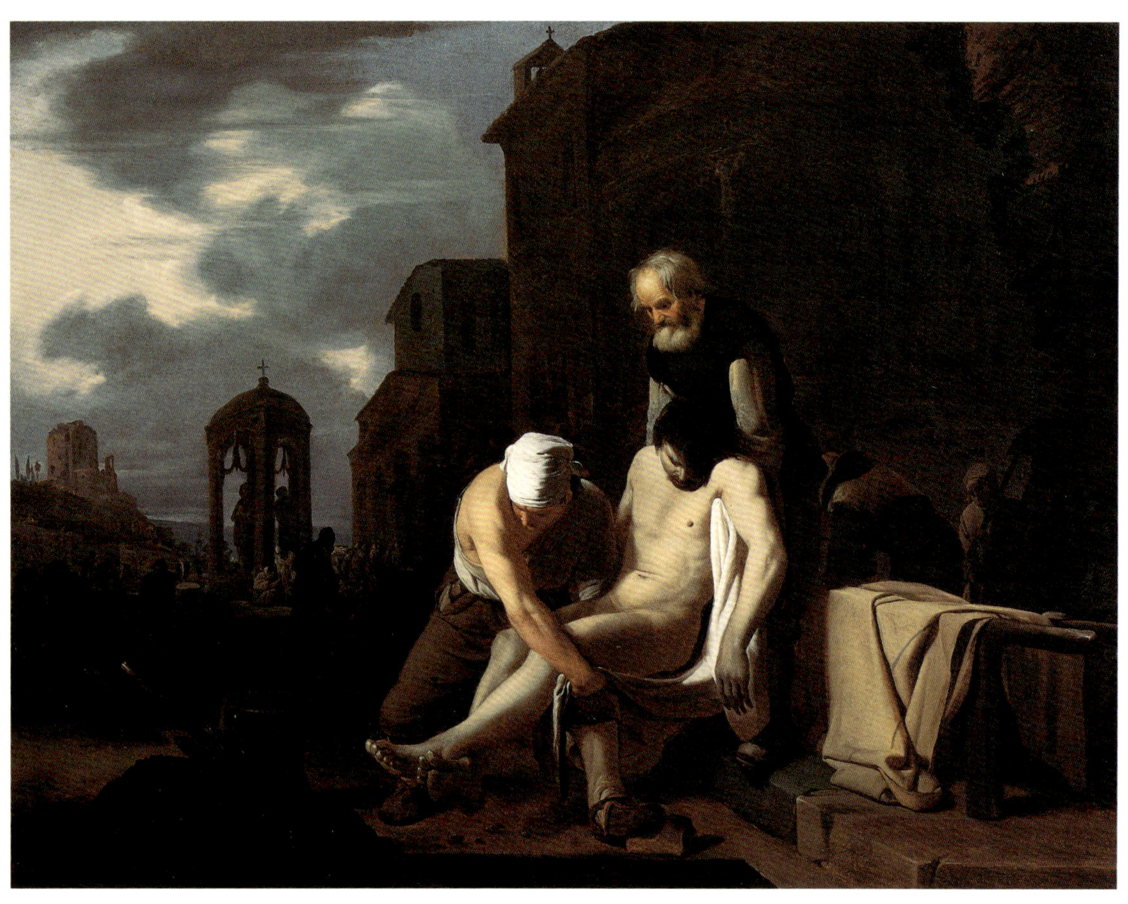

11.
MICHAEL SWEERTS, *Burying the Dead*, ca. 1646-52
Oil on canvas 74 x 99.1 cm
The Wadsworth Atheneum Museum of Art, Hartford
The Ella Gallup Sumner and Mary Catlin Sumner Collection Fund

Michael Sweerts (1618-1664) was born in Brussels, but moved to Rome in 1646, where he remained until after 1652 (see cat. 6). Painted during his Roman sojourn, Sweerts' *Burying the Dead* is a didactic rendition of one of the seven corporal acts of mercy. The somber tonality of Sweerts's painting and his concentration on the pallid flesh of the dead man also make the picture a *memento mori*, that is, a reminder of mortality. Of all the Seven Acts, burying the dead was naturally most closely associated with the plague. Indeed, burying the dead is not mentioned in Matthew 25, but was added to the Gospel list during the Middle Ages in response to the bubonic plague. Sweerts was very familiar with the pestilence, as a terrifying plague struck Rome while he lived there. Sweerts's canvas reminds us of the body of Christ, since the pose of the dead man recalls that of the dead Savior in Caravaggio's *Entombment* (for the Oratorian church of S. Maria in Vallicella in Rome), and also resembles that of Christ in Michelangelo's Vatican *Pietà*. The generic Roman setting is intended to make it familiar to the viewer, thus enhancing the immediacy of the need for charity.

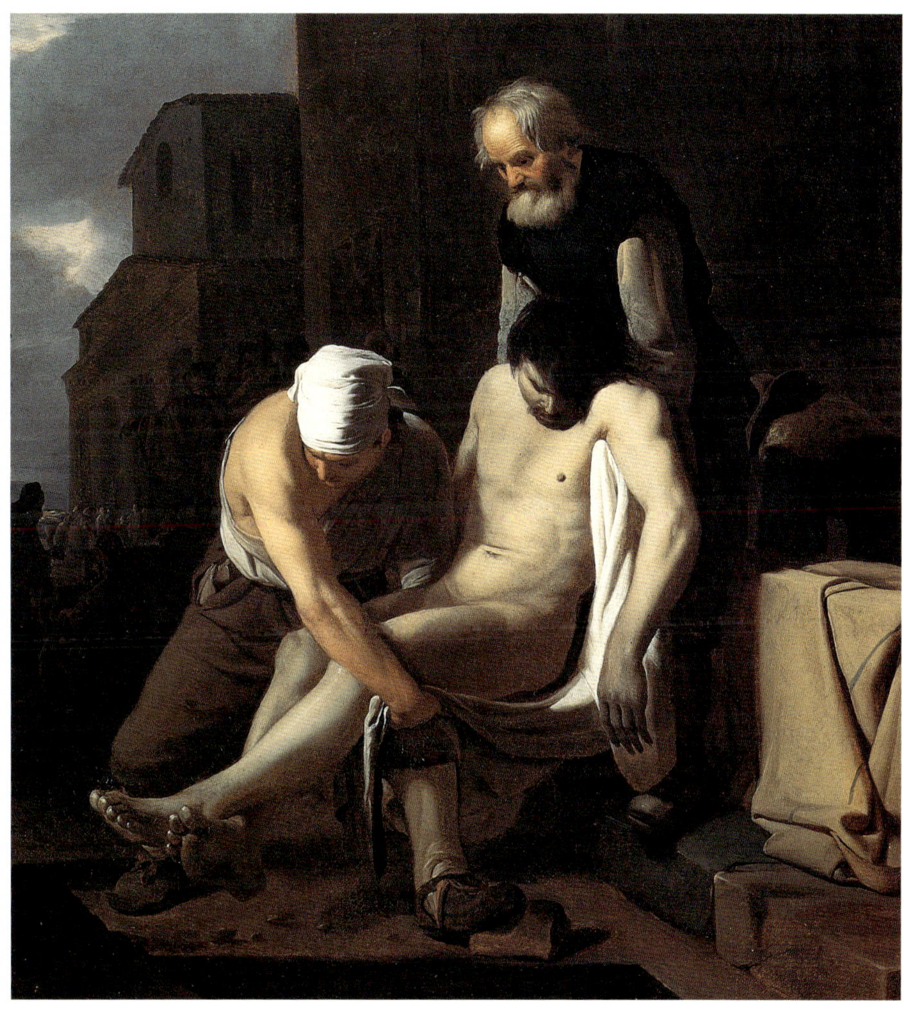

12

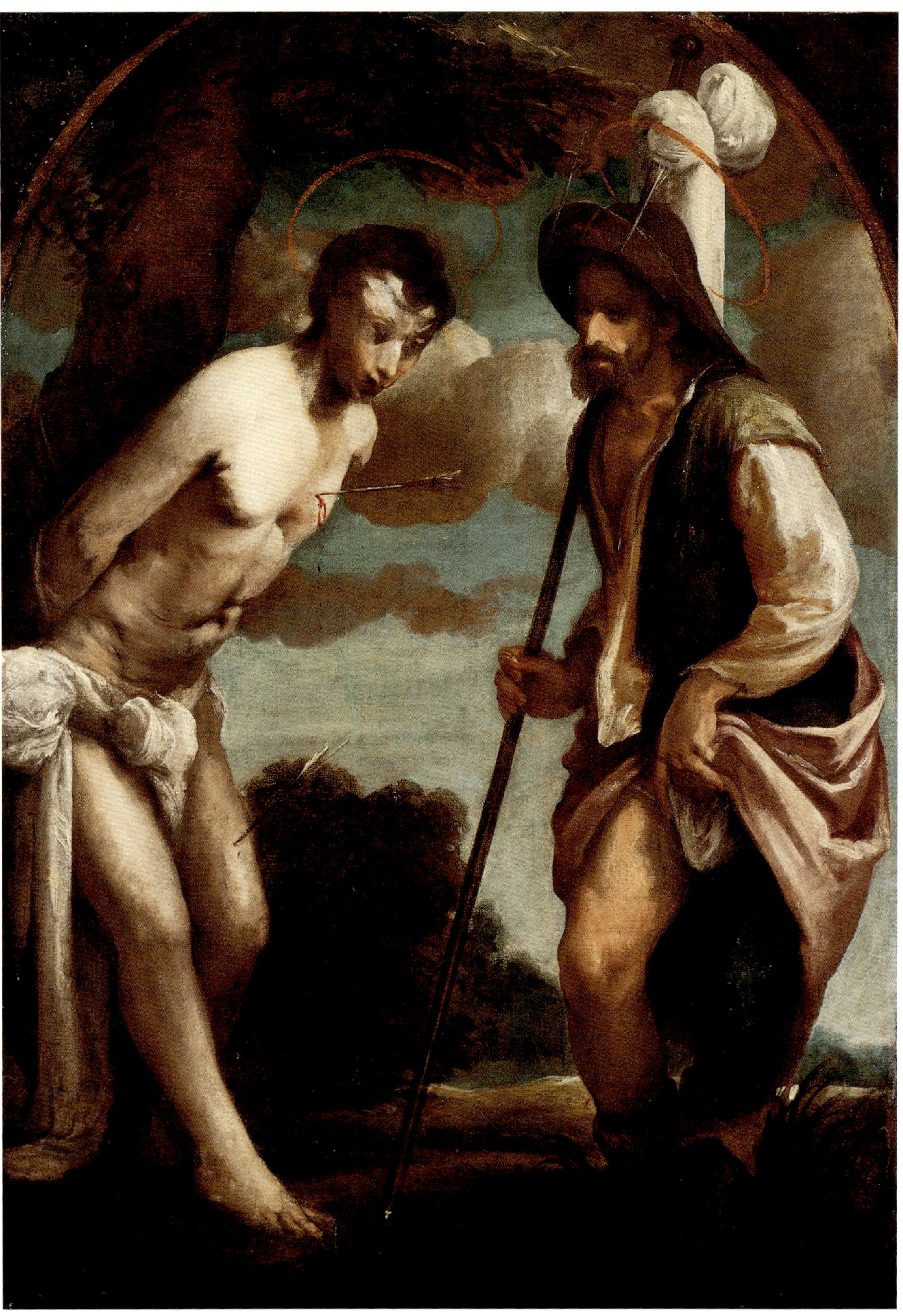

12.

Jacopo Bassano, *Saints Sebastian and Roch ([verso] The Madonna of Mercy with Saints Anthony of Padua and John the Baptist)*, ca. 1551
Oil on canvas, 104.1 x 76.2 cm
The Francis Lehman Loeb Art Center, Vassar College, Poughkeepsie, New York
Purchase, Betsy Mudge Wilson, Class of 1956, Memorial Fund, Gallery Lasson, London

The Veneto painter Jacopo da Ponte (ca. 1510-1592), known as Jacopo Bassano after the town of his birth, was a member of a large artistic family. Jacopo first trained with his father Francesco Bassano the Elder and then went to Venice to study with Bonifazio de' Pitati. Jacopo was a prolific painter of religious scenes and portraits, which are characterized by highly naturalistic passages, including unidealized human figures, animals, and landscape settings. Jacopo was the father of Francesco the Younger and Leandro, both of whom were successful painters of the Venetian school.

This painting is a ceremonial banner that must have been executed as an ex-voto. On the verso are painted the plague saints Sebastian and Roch, indicating that the work was commissioned in time of plague; on the recto the Madonna of Mercy, a cult of the Virgin traditionally invoked for intercession during the plague, is shown with saints Anthony of Padua and John the Baptist. On stylistic grounds, this painting has been dated to around 1551 and plague had broken out in the Bassano area in the late summer of that year. Although the banner's original patron is unknown, it is possible that it was commissioned by a confraternity whose patron saints were Anthony of Padua and John the Baptist. Bassano's processional painting is an exceptionally fine and rare example of a Renaissance banner. Its condition is expecially remarkable, since it would have had to withstand the elements.

On the verso of the banner, Saint Sebastian is shown on the left pierced by two arrows and bleeding profusely from the wound in his chest. His nearly nude body contrasts strikingly with the heavily clothed figure of Saint Roch, on the right, who turns toward Sebastian and raises his clothing to reveal the plague bubo on his right thigh. Although small in scale, the painting is executed rather broadly, probably due to its ephemeral nature. Indeed, Sebastian's face seems to have been treated with some haste. Jacopo Bassano had a large workshop, and the variety of hands detectable in the painting suggests that two assistants helped him paint this banner.

13

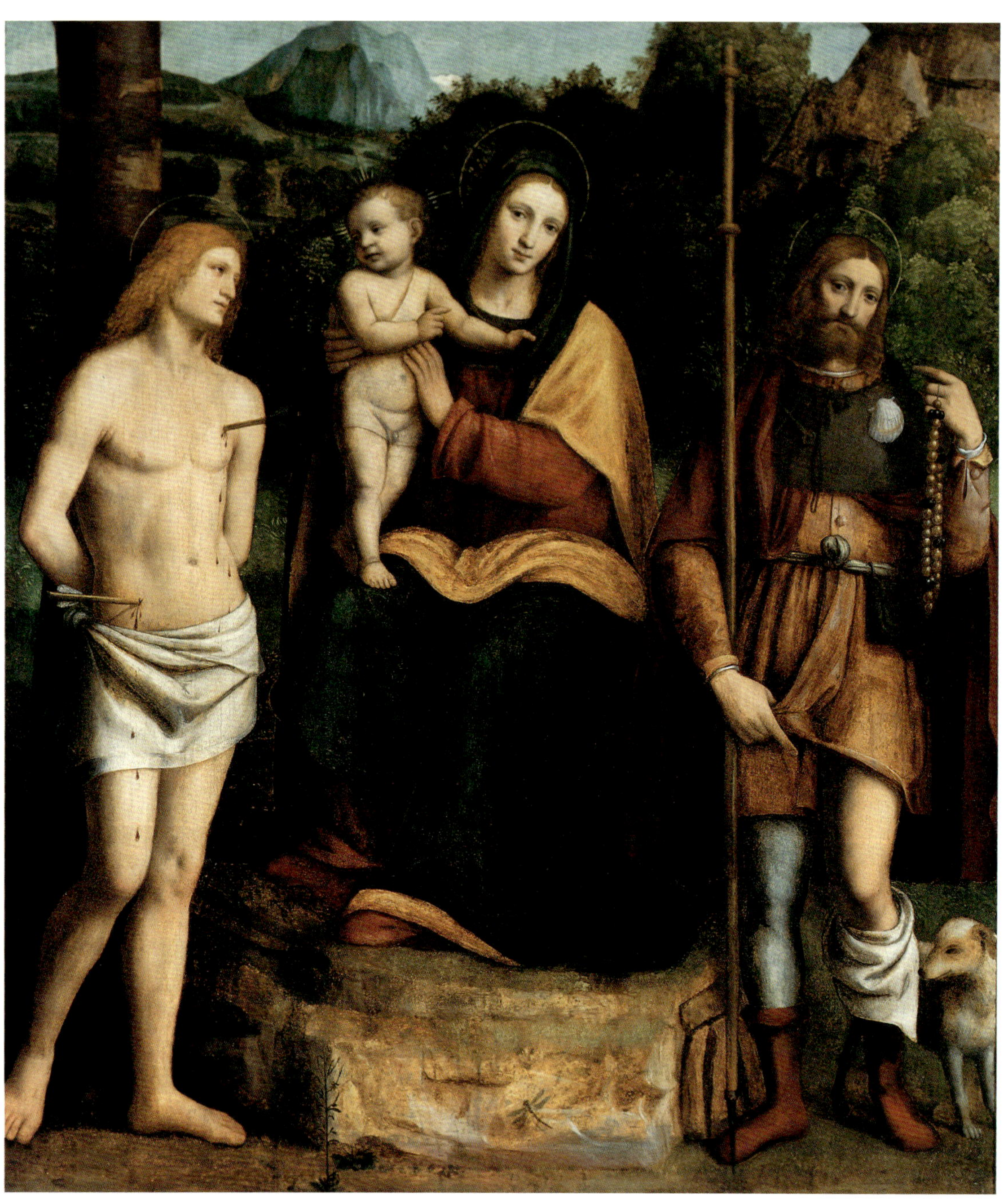

13.
BERNARDINO LUINI, *Madonna and Child with Saints Sebastian and Roch*, ca. 1520-26
Oil on panel, 173.36 x 154 cm
Bequest of John Ringling, Collection of The John and Mabel Ringling Museum of Art, The State Art Museum of Florida

Bernardino Luini (1480/85-1532) was a leading Lombard painter of the early Cinquecento whose serene classicism, delicate *sfumato*, and idealized figural types were influenced by Leonardo da Vinci. Luini is thought to have visited Rome. This seems likely because his handling of space and principles of design betray the influence of Raphael's paintings in that city, although Luini's rather static treatment of human figures is at odds with the more fluidly graceful poses of Raphael's figures. Luini worked in both fresco and oil and received many important commissions for religious and secular cycles in Lombardy.

Luini's *Madonna and Child with Saints Sebastian and Roch*, like many paintings of the Renaissance, combines the figures of the Virgin and Child with saints from different periods of history. Roch and Sebastian were the most universally invoked plague saints in Europe. According to legend, Sebastian was a soldier in the Roman army who had survived being shot with arrows as a punishment for his Christian faith. In later centuries, when plague was often imagined as arrows sent by God as punishment for sin, Sebastian's aid was seen as especially effective. Roch was believed to have been a Frenchman from Montpellier who, around the year 1400, went on a pilgrimage to Rome. In Italy he was said to have survived not only plague but also famine. Like Sebastian, Roch became a much implored saint by those seeking to survive outbreaks of epidemic disease. Mary was also thought to be an especially effective intercessor and other saints were believed to refer their requests to her. Thus the figures in Luini's painting were often represented together as particularly powerful intercessors on behalf of humankind during perilous times.

In Luini's beautiful and tranquil painting Jesus and Sebastian exchange a loving glance while the Madonna looks out at the viewer. Saint Roch, who also looks out at the viewer, points to his plague bubo with one hand and holds a rosary with the other. The dog at his feet is the animal that brought him bread while he was recovering from the plague in the wilderness. On Roch's chest is seen the pilgrim's scallop shell, and he carries the pilgrim's staff.

14

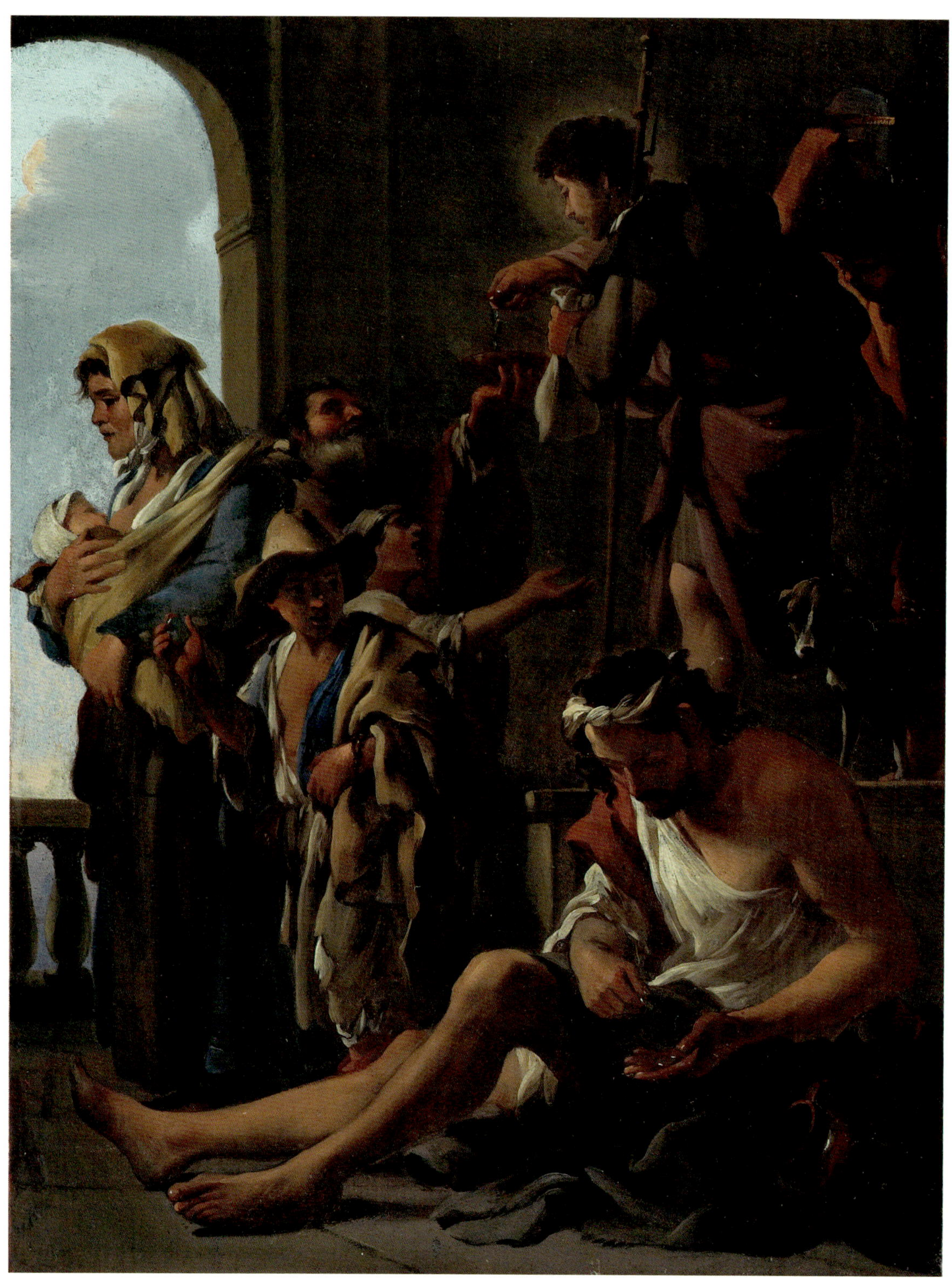

14.
JAN MIEL, *Saint Roch Distributing Alms to the Poor*, date unknown
Oil on panel, 25.1 x 18.4 cm
Art Gallery of Ontario, Toronto, Gift from Corporations' Subscription Fund

Born near Antwerp, Jan Miel (1599-1664) moved permanently to Italy by the mid-1630s. In Rome, he was influenced by Pieter Van Laer (called *il Bamboccio*), and became one of several Northern European artists, known as the *Bamboccianti*, who specialized in painting low-life street scenes in Rome.

At first glance, this painting may seem to be a simple genre scene of Charity. However, on closer inspection, one notices that the figure standing on a raised platform on the right and holding a pilgrim's staff has a halo of light around his head; this is Saint Roch, accompanied by his dog at the right. Saint Roch was universally invoked for assistance during the plague as he was believed to have contracted it after having left his native Montpellier in France on a pilgrimage to Rome, but to have recovered from the pestilence. After his recovery, Roch stopped in several Italian towns where he cared for the poor and sick, including plague victims.

This painting is an excellent example of Miel's signature style in which religious scenes are interpreted with a down-to-earth naturalism and attention to genre details. Miel includes peasants of all ages, from the infant in its mother's arms to the elderly man reaching up toward the saint. The relatively dark palette accented by warm tones heightens the intimacy of the scene and the quotidian nature of the plague.

15

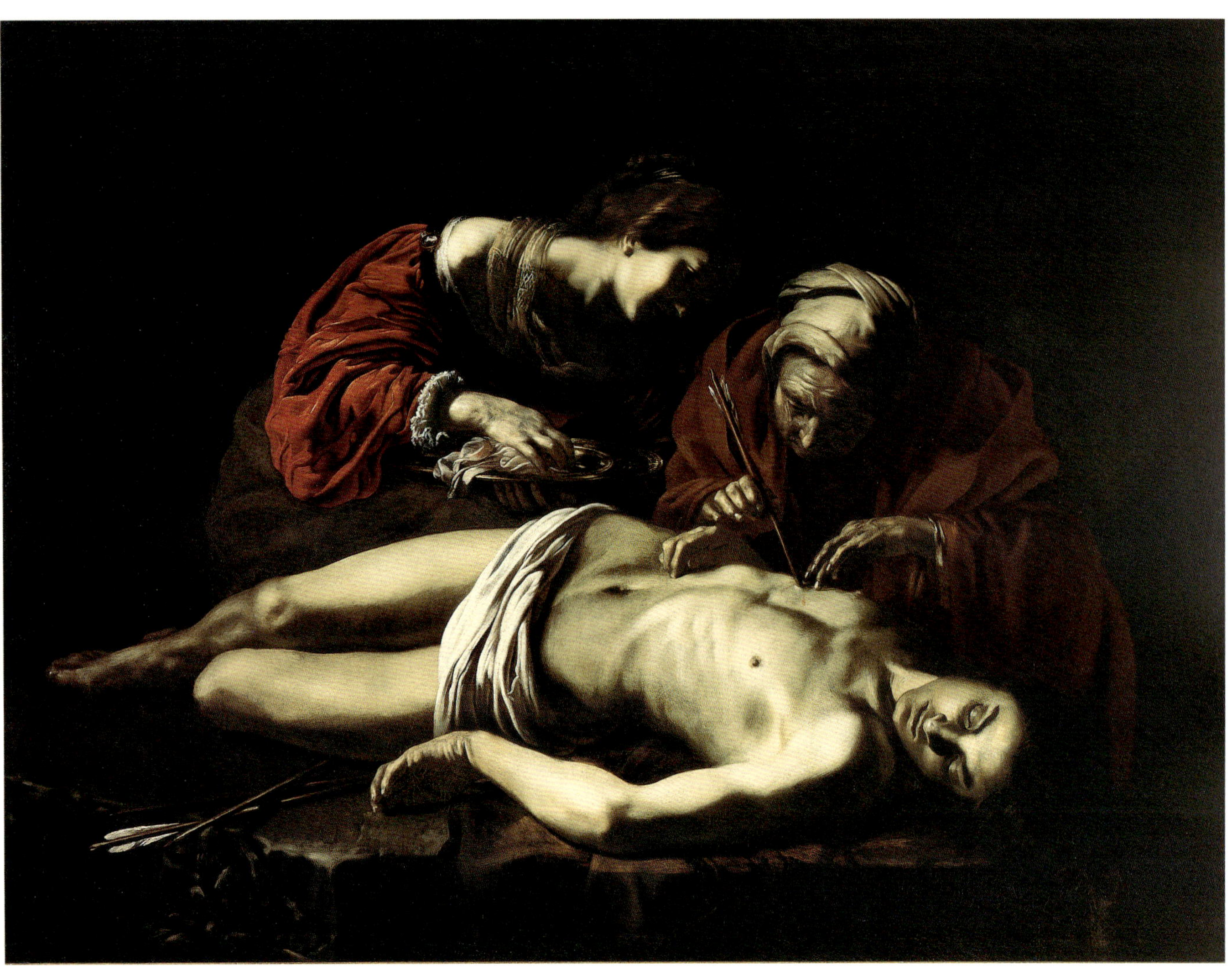

15.
NICOLAS REGNIER (attributed to), called Niccolò Renieri, *Saint Sebastian Attended by the Holy Women*, ca.1626
Oil on canvas, 124 x 166.5 cm
Iris and B. Gerald Cantor Center for Visual Arts at Stanford University, Mortimer C. Leventritt Fund

Nicolas Regnier (1591-1667) was a Franco-Fleming born in Mauberge (Flanders), and he studied in the Antwerp studio of Abraham Janssens. Regnier is known to have lived in Rome between 1621 and 1625, and may have been there as early as 1615. Joachim van Sandrart mentioned in his *Teutsche Academie* (1675-79) that in Rome Regnier followed the method of Bartolommeo Manfredi, the noted *caravaggista*. While in Rome, Regnier also knew the French painter Simon Vouet, and worked for the famous collector Vincenzo Giustiniani.

The early Christian martyr Sebastian was usually depicted in the Renaissance with his body pierced with arrows, but in the Counter-Reformation period the theme of Saint Sebastian cured by Saint Irene, which emphasized charity toward the afflicted, became very popular. Charity and good works, such as Irene's cure of Saint Sebastian, helped one on the path to salvation with the assistance of divine grace. According to legend, Irene was a Roman widow who nursed Sebastian when he had been left for dead, and she is therefore a patron saint of nurses.

Regnier shows Saint Sebastian's body laid out in dramatic proximity to the viewer. An aged and wrinkled Irene carefully removes an arrow from Sebastian's side while a younger woman prepares to clean the wound. The immediacy of the scene, the prominence of the unidealized figures, and the intensely dark setting are typical of Regnier's style, which drew considerable inspiration from that of Caravaggio.

16

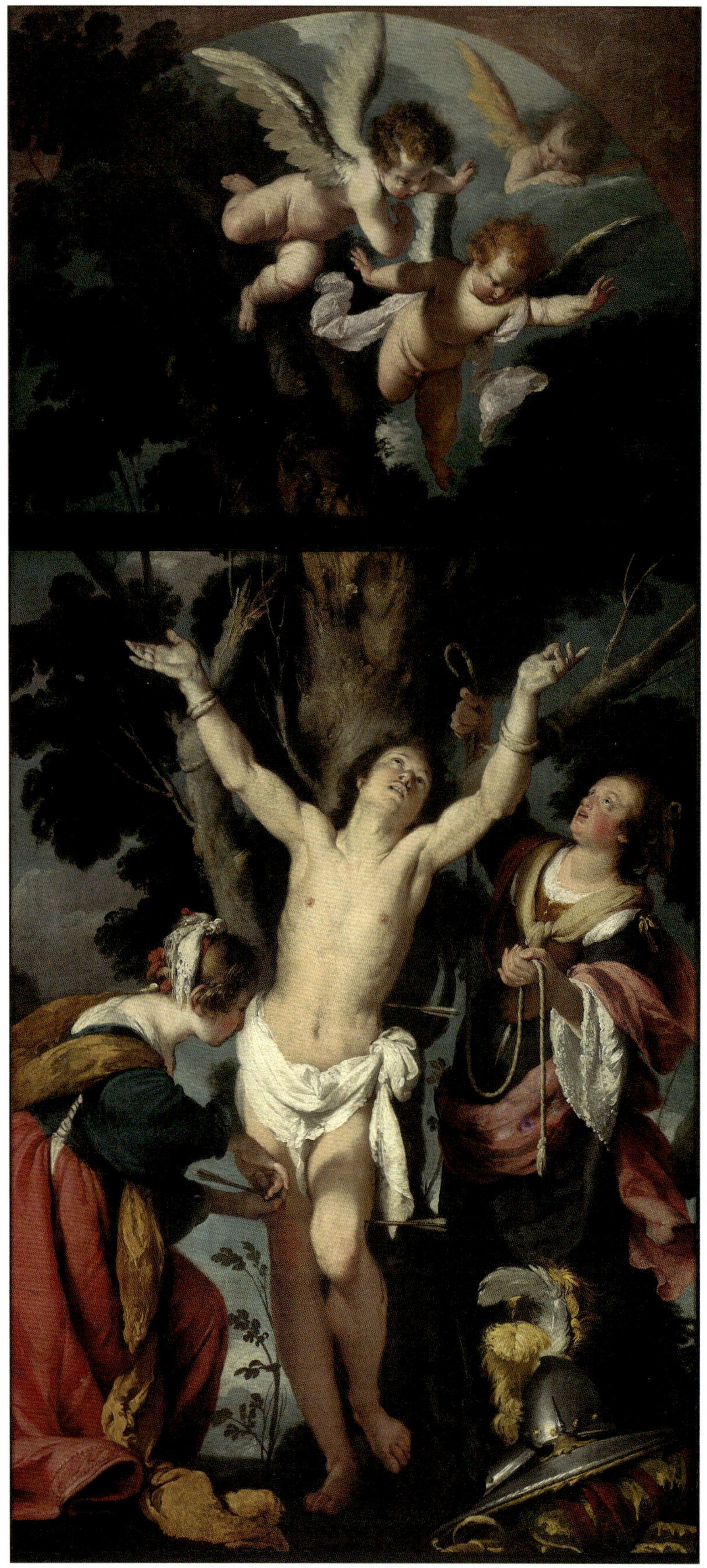

16.
Bernardo Strozzi
Saint Sebastian Tended by Saint Irene and her Maid, ca. 1636
Oil on canvas, 167 x 118 cm
Museum of Fine Arts, Boston
Charles Potter Kling Fund and Francis Welch Fund

Three Angels
Oil on canvas, 75 x 121.5 cm
Museum of Fine Arts, Boston
Henry H. and Zoe Oliver Sherman Fund

Here the Genoese friar (see cat. 10) treats the same theme undertaken by Regnier (cat. 15), with its relationship to charity and good works. Strozzi apparently had an abiding interest in the theological virtue of charity, since he dealt with the theme on numerous occasions. His most noteworthy series of charity allegories includes his early *Carità* from the Galleria di Palazzo Rosso in Genoa (1610-20) and three autograph copies, one in the Richmond Museum of Art (ca. 1620), and two later ones in private collections. He also painted a triple allegory of the theological virtues formerly in the Villa Donà delle Rose, Venice, that included another charity.

Strozzi's interest in the theme of charity may have led him to the commission for *Saint Sebastian Tended by Saint Irene and her Maid* (ca. 1636), the Venetian altarpiece that inspired this version. Painted during his sojourn in Venice, at the height of his maturity and at a time when he was immersing himself in the Venetian painterly tradition, the model is a full-length altarpiece for the church of S. Benedetto e Scolastica in Venice. Standing almost nude with his hands raised toward heaven in supplication, Sebastian anchors the picture in the center and the tree behind him echoes his profile. On the left, on her knees, Irene delicately removes one of the arrows from his leg while her maid unties Sebastian's left arm on the right. Since the eighteenth or nineteenth century, the Boston version was missing its top, leading scholars to suspect that the work was incomplete. In 2004 the crown was reunited with the rest of the canvas, and this is the first traveling exhibition in which the painting is displayed as a whole. The figure of Saint Sebastian is almost identical in the two paintings, and the attendant figures are very close as well, with only slight changes in the position of their heads. There are also subtle differences in the still-life arrangement at lower right, particularly in the placement of the helmet, shield, and tunic.

Like the Venice version, the Boston canvas is noteworthy for the monumentality of the figures, a nod toward Venetian tradition. Similarly, Strozzi reminds us of Veronese in the vertical composition and the figure of Irene. Scholars have compared the tree to that of a lost altarpiece by Titian of the Death of Saint Peter Martyr. Strozzi would later repeat Sebastian's face almost exactly in his *Saint Anthony of Padua* (ca. 1637-40) in the Venetian church of S. Nicolà da Tolentino. Like the Venetian version, the Boston version has been dated to around 1636, when the Venice plague of 1630-31 would have still been a vivid presence in the collective memory of the city.

17

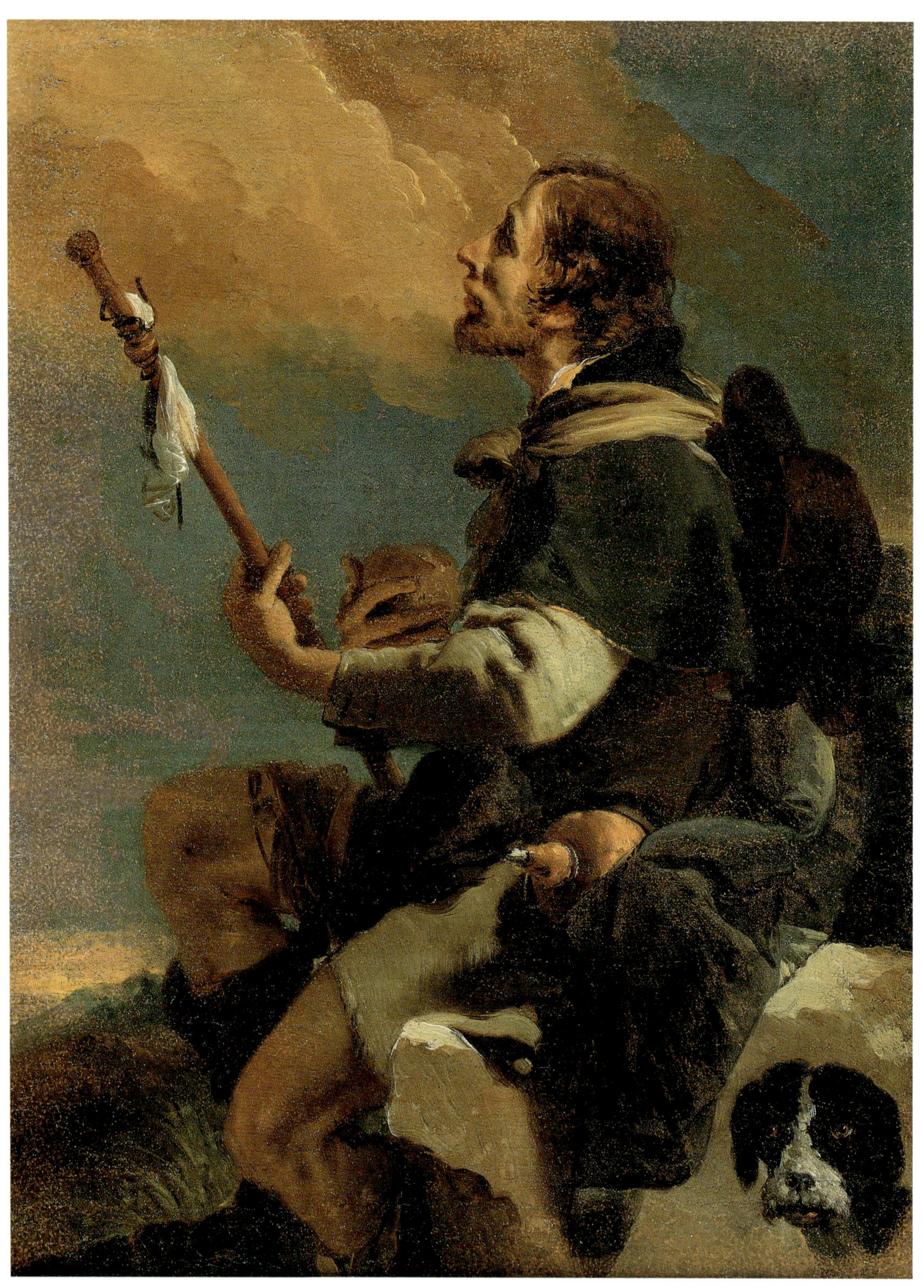

17.
Giovanni Battista Tiepolo, *Saint Roch*, ca. early 1730s
Oil on paper on canvas, 45.1 x 34 cm
The Philadelphia Museum of Art, John G. Johnson Collection

Tiepolo painted many small-scale canvases of Saint Roch, some of which were commissioned by the Venetian confraternity, or *scuola*, dedicated to the plague saint. The varying quality of these small paintings suggests that members of Tiepolo's workshop were probably involved in their production. In his book *Tiepolo. The Complete Paintings* (New York, 2002), Filippo Pedrocco illustrated twenty-one of the most accomplished versions of the theme, all of which have distinctively different compositions. Pedrocco dated these paintings to the early 1730s, before the master's work at the Villa Loschi in Vicenza.

The Philadelphia *Saint Roch* is among Tiepolo's most graceful and affective treatments of the theme. The saint is seated outside, silhouetted against the sky, a monumental conception that belies the work's small format. He holds his pilgrim's staff, while, at the lower right, the dog who fed him during his illness looks out at the viewer. As Saint Roch gazes upward toward heaven, light bathes his face and highlights exquisite passages of the brushwork characteristic of Tiepolo's painterly style.

18

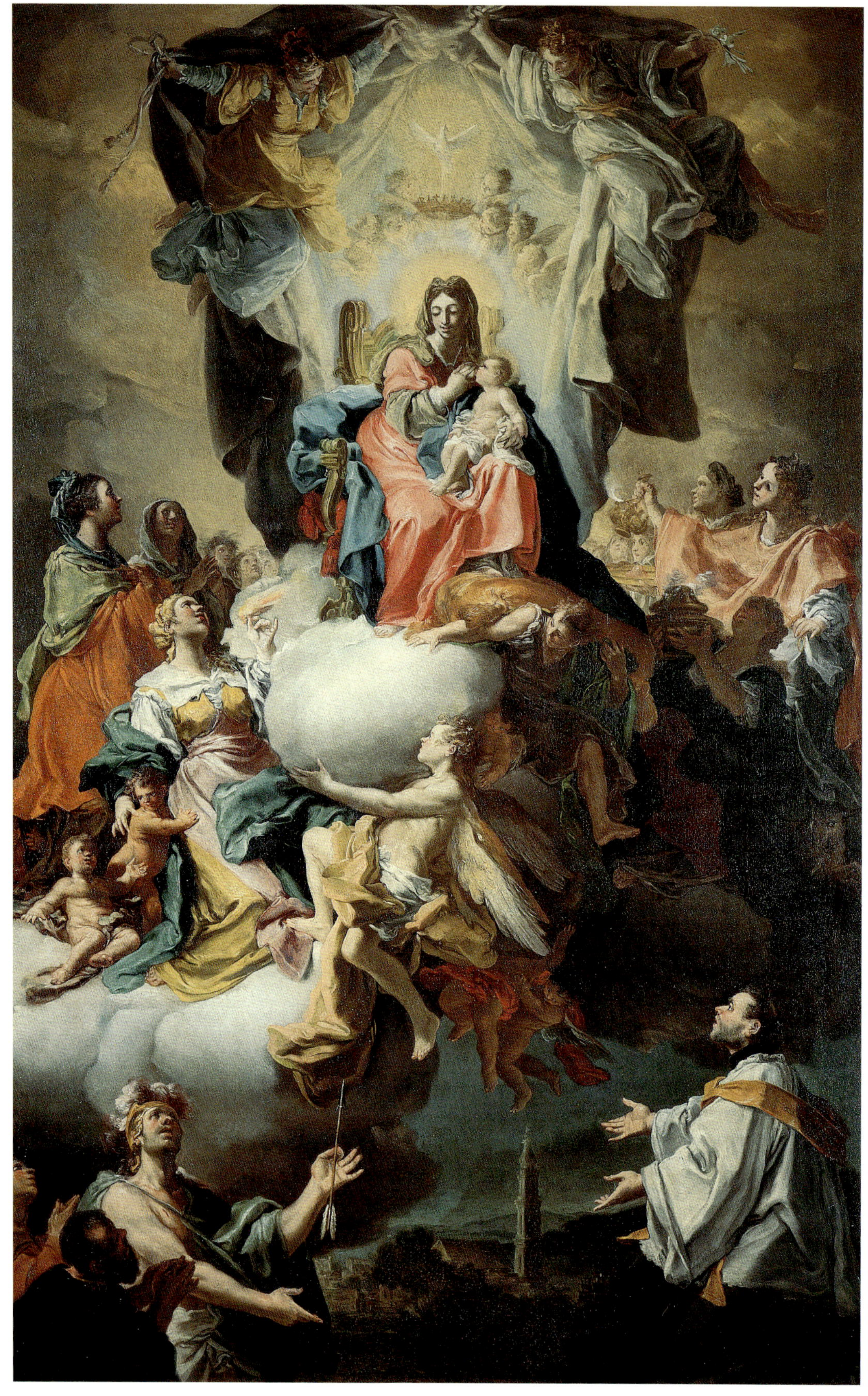

18.
DOMENICO ANTONIO VACCARO, *Madonna and Child with Saints Roch, Sebastian, and Francis Xavier*, 1730
Oil on canvas, 121.9 x 91.4 cm
Worcester Art Museum, Sarah C. Garver Fund

The Neapolitan artist Domenico Antonio Vaccaro (1605-70) was the son of Lorenzo Vaccaro and studied with Francesco Solimena. Active as a sculptor, architect, and painter, Domenico Antonio became one of the leading exponents of the Southern Italian Rococo. He created some of the most important sculptural and architectural projects of early eighteenth-century Naples, for which he was praised in particular by Bernardo De Dominici, the Settecento art critic.

A vivid portrayal of the role of saints as intercessors against the plague, Vaccaro's *modello* (sketch) features three of Italy's most important plague saints, Roch, Sebastian, and Francis Xavier, who appeal to the Madonna and other saints to release the Neapolitan town of Marigliano from the plague. At the top of the canvas, the Madonna and Child sit under a *baldacchino* of drapery supported by two angels, while a white dove, signifying the Holy Spirit of the Annunciation, hovers above them in the golden light of heaven. The Madonna is seen nursing Jesus and accompanied by three female figures representing the virtues of Faith, Hope, and Charity. The Holy Spirit is closely associated with charity and love, and in Vaccaro's painting the nursing Mary is herself a charity figure. To the right of the Madonna and behind her appear many saintly intercessors, including Saints Agnes and Agatha on the left. During times of plague, preachers and other spiritual writers gave courage and hope to the Christian community by reminding them of the promised joys of heaven, the company of Mary and the saints.

Vaccaro's painting is grounded in a specific place, the town of Marigliano, which is depicted at the bottom of the composition. In this zone, closest to the viewer's eye level, three intercessors are given pride of place. At the right is Francis Xavier, a Jesuit saint canonized in 1622. Francis Xavier was a popular plague saint in Naples and also one of the founders of the Society of Jesus, an organization especially committed to caring for the sick during times of pestilence. On the left are depicted the much older, universal plague saints, Roch and Sebastian, along with a donor in prayer. Sebastian holds aloft two plague arrows, and, like Francis Xavier, looks upward at the Madonna, beseeching her help on behalf of the townspeople of Marigliano.

19

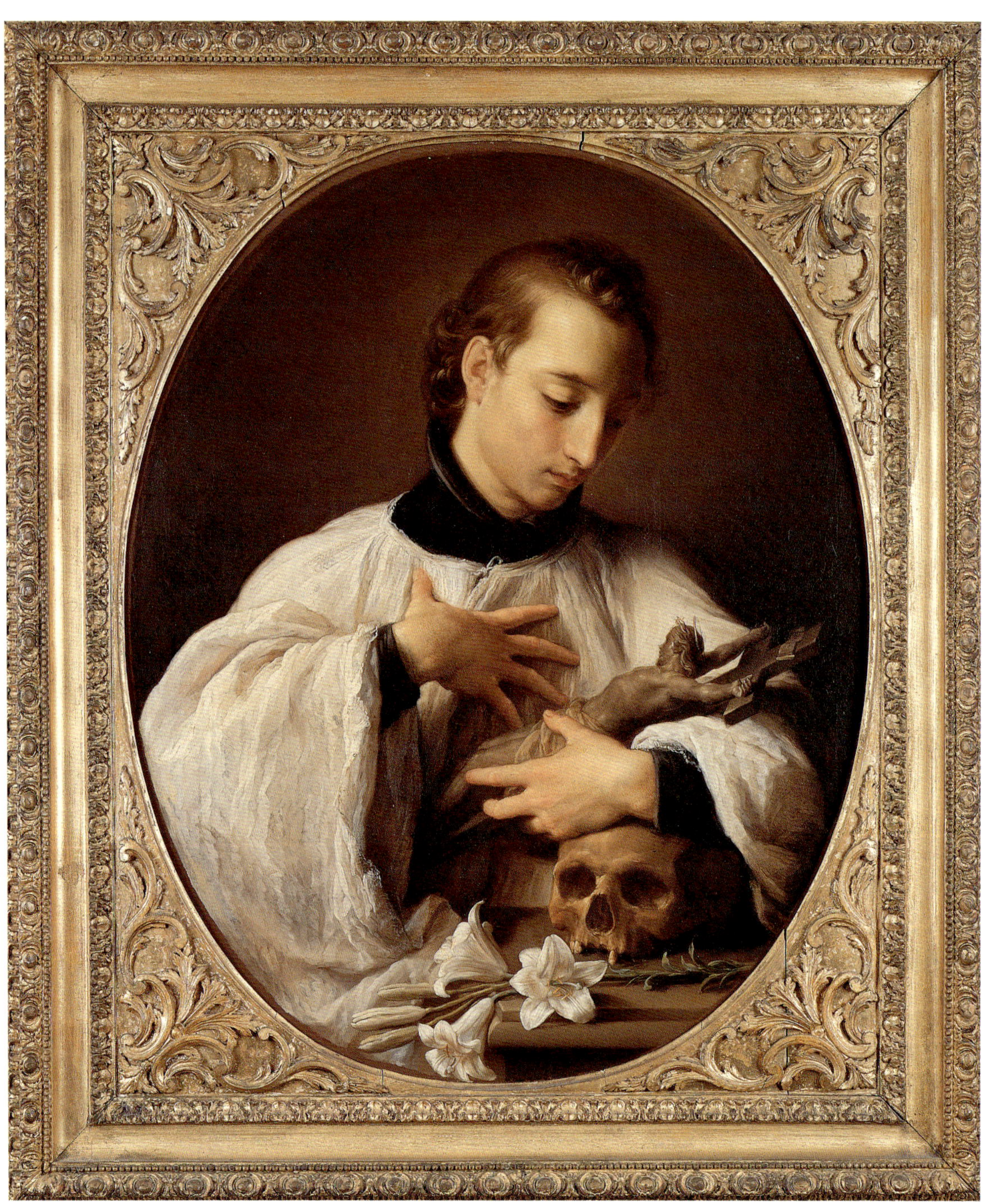

19.
POMPEO BATONI, *Saint Aloysius Gonzaga*, ca. 1744
Oil on canvas, 79.1 x 63.8 cm
Private collection, New York

Together with the German Anton Raphael Mengs, Pompeo Girolamo Batoni (1708-1787) was a leading painter of eighteenth-century Rome, where he moved from his native Lucca in 1727. Batoni was particularly inspired by ancient art and by that of Raphael and was in great demand as a portraitist of foreigners on the Grand Tour. In Rome he was curator of the papal collections. Many of his portraits show the sitters in Roman archaeological settings or with ancient sculptures. He also painted mythological, historical, and religious subjects. In addition to receiving numerous commissions from English travelers, he worked for Catherine the Great of Russia.

Batoni's oval devotional portrait of aristocrat-turned-ascetic Luigi (Aloysius) Gonzaga (1568-91) is a fine example of the master's elegant, sentimental style. The saint is shown half-length and close to the picture plane. Saint Luigi Gonzaga is in prayerful contemplation of a crucifix, which is lovingly cradled in his left arm, while his right hand rests on his heart, a reminder of the emotional and spiritual intensity of his devotion to the Passion of Christ. Luigi wears a white surplice, symbolic of his clerical status of acolyte, one of the minor orders leading to the priesthood, which premature death prevented him from attaining. Two traditional symbols are in the foreground: the skull is a reminder of Luigi's disdain for transient things of this world and of the inevitability of death, while the bouquet of lilies signifies the perpetual virginity the youth vowed to the Virgin Mary in 1578 and again at the conclusion of his Jesuit novitiate in 1587.

Batoni depicts the saint as an adolescent, although he actually died at the age of twenty-five. This youthful depiction follows hagiographic tradition promoted by the Jesuits at the time of Gonzaga's death in order to emphasize the dramatic contrast between Luigi's youthful physical appearance and his mature, heroic spiritual stature. In addition, after his canonization in 1726, the Church officially designated Luigi the patron saint of adolescent boys because he had died as a student. Saint Luigi's youthfulness was heightened to facilitate their identification with him. Such boys studied in the Jesuits' numerous secondary schools throughout Europe. For these students, Luigi was offered as an exemplar not only of chastity but also of charity, for he had died as a result of fearless and zealous service of the victims of the plague during an outbreak in Rome in 1591. During this plague, Saint Luigi carried plague victims on his own back to the hospitals of S. Maria della Consolazione and the Spirito Santo. As a result, Saint Luigi was considered a plague martyr.

20

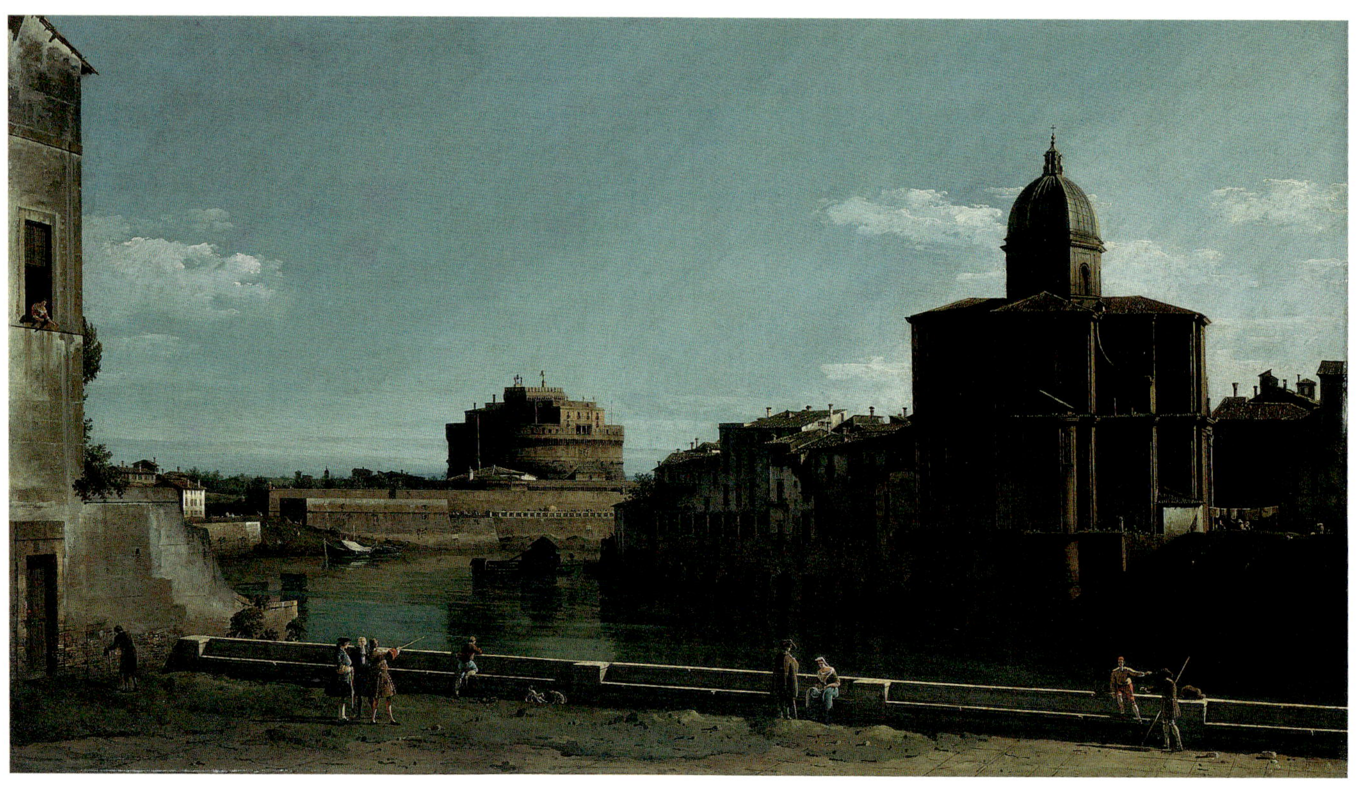

20.
BERNARDO BELLOTTO, *The Tiber with the Church of San Giovanni dei Fiorentini, Rome*, ca. 1742-44
Oil on canvas, 85 x 146 cm
Toledo Museum of Art, Purchased with funds from the Libbey Endowment, Gift of Edward Drummond Libbey

Bernardo Bellotto (1721-1780) was a Venetian painter and draughtsman who was active in Dresden, Vienna, and Munich for much of his career. His style is very similar to that of his uncle, Canaletto, and outside of Italy he signed his works *"de Canaletto."* In the 1740s, before leaving Italy, Bellotto traveled to Rome and through Northern Italy, where he painted his first imaginary idealized views. In comparison with Canaletto, Bellotto used a cooler palette, and had a stronger feeling for landscape and sky. Yet Bellotto also had a great fondness for architectural views and urban settings. In 1767 he moved to Warsaw in the service of King Stanislas Poniatowski, and he remained there for the rest of his life.

Bellotto's sedate and sunlit view of early eighteenth-century Rome shows the influence of his famous teacher and uncle Canaletto in its close attention to detail and genre interest. Yet Bellotto's personal style is also clearly emerging here, as seen in his more pronounced chiaroscuro, greater interest in the volumes of the buildings, and the lack of bright color accents. Bellotto's view across the Tiber shows in the center the Castel Sant'Angelo (that is, the Castle of Saint Michael the Archangel), a papal fortress/prison created from the second-century imperial Roman monument, Hadrian's Tomb. At the right, silhouetted against the sky, is the imposing church of S. Giovanni dei Fiorentini, the Florentine church in Rome, which is seen from the back.

The Castel Sant'Angelo is Rome's most important plague monument. In 590, Pope Gregory the Great led a penitential procession around the periphery of Hadrian's Tomb in order to placate God's wrath during an outbreak of the plague. According to pious legend, during the procession Saint Michael the Archangel appeared atop the monument sheathing his sword to show that God had been appeased and the plague was at an end. In gratitude for this miraculous deliverance, Hadrian's Tomb was renamed the Castel Sant'Angelo, and eventually a statue of Saint Michael was placed at its summit, as seen in Bellotto's painting. It is for this reason that Saint Michael appears in many plague-related paintings and on the frontispieces of early modern plague treatises. In addition, an angel sheathing a sword became a symbol of the end of the pestilence. Another prominent feature of Bellotto's canvas is the Tiber River, which in times of plague became the intense focus of the city's health initiatives; it was then thought that corrupted air, or a miasma, caused the plague, and stagnant waters and rotting detritus in the river and on its banks were seen as major threats to the city's welfare. This may account for the melancholy mood of Bellotto's painting.

21

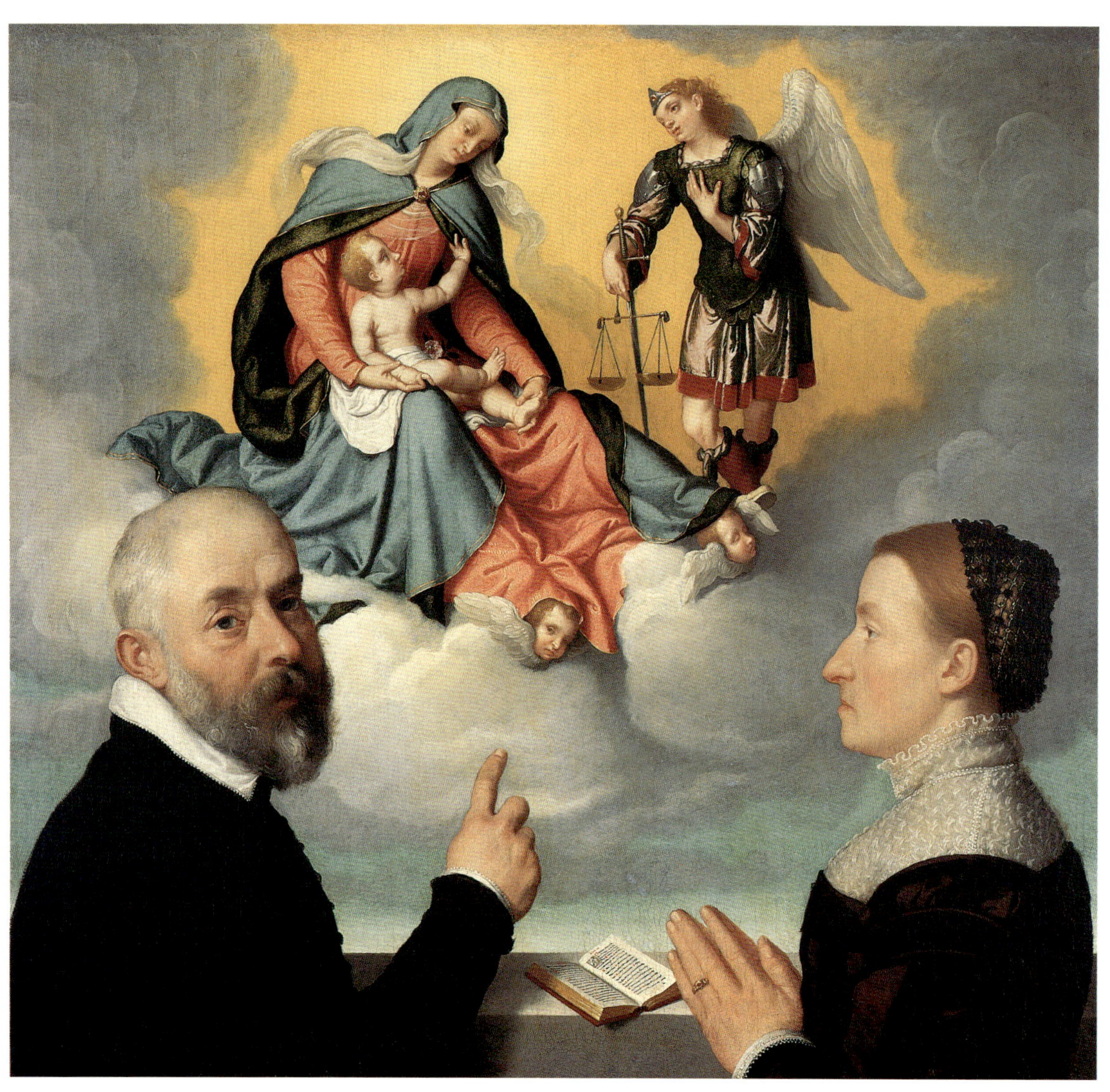

21.
Giovanni Battista Moroni, *Two Donors in Adoration before the Madonna and Child and Saint Michael*, 1557-60
Oil on canvas, 35 x 89.5 cm
Virginia Museum of Fine Arts, Richmond, The Adolph D. and Wilkins C. Williams Fund

Giovanni Battista Moroni (1520/24-1578), a Lombard painter, was born in Albino near Bergamo and studied in Brescia with the well-known Renaissance religious painter Moretto. Moroni worked mainly in Albino and nearby Bergamo. Although Moroni painted religious subjects, he is best known as a portrait painter. Indeed, he received many portrait commissions from the local gentry of North Italy and they are remarkable for their naturalism, psychological depth, and dignity.

In this compelling painting, Moroni combines a devotional scene with his hallmark naturalistic portrait style. In the foreground, a man and his wife are seen in an attitude of prayer, wearing the somber yet elegant black clothing popular in Spanish Lombardy of the Cinquecento. The woman, seen in profile, her hands brought together, has a breviary resting before her. Her husband looks out with a penetrating glance at the viewer while pointing toward a miraculous appearance of the Virgin and Child and Saint Michael the Archangel, who hover in the clouds above and are silhouetted against a bright golden light.

Neither the identities of the sitters nor details of the commission are known, but it is likely that this painting is an ex-voto piece painted in time of the plague. The work is generally dated to ca. 1557-60, which corresponds to the immediate aftermath of a plague that took its toll in Northern Italy from 1556 to 1557. It could be that Saint Michael the Archangel, who is shown in the upper right of the painting holding the scales, is the name saint of the male donor. In addition, however, Saint Michael's presence may indicate that this painting was commissioned in thanks for the couple having lived through the plague. The presence of the Virgin and Child in combination with Saint Michael lends further support to this plague connection, as the Madonna's aid was also invoked against the pestilence. The figures of the donors, which are rendered more naturalistically and vividly than the rather conventional holy figures, are placed closer to the viewer as models of Christian piety.

22

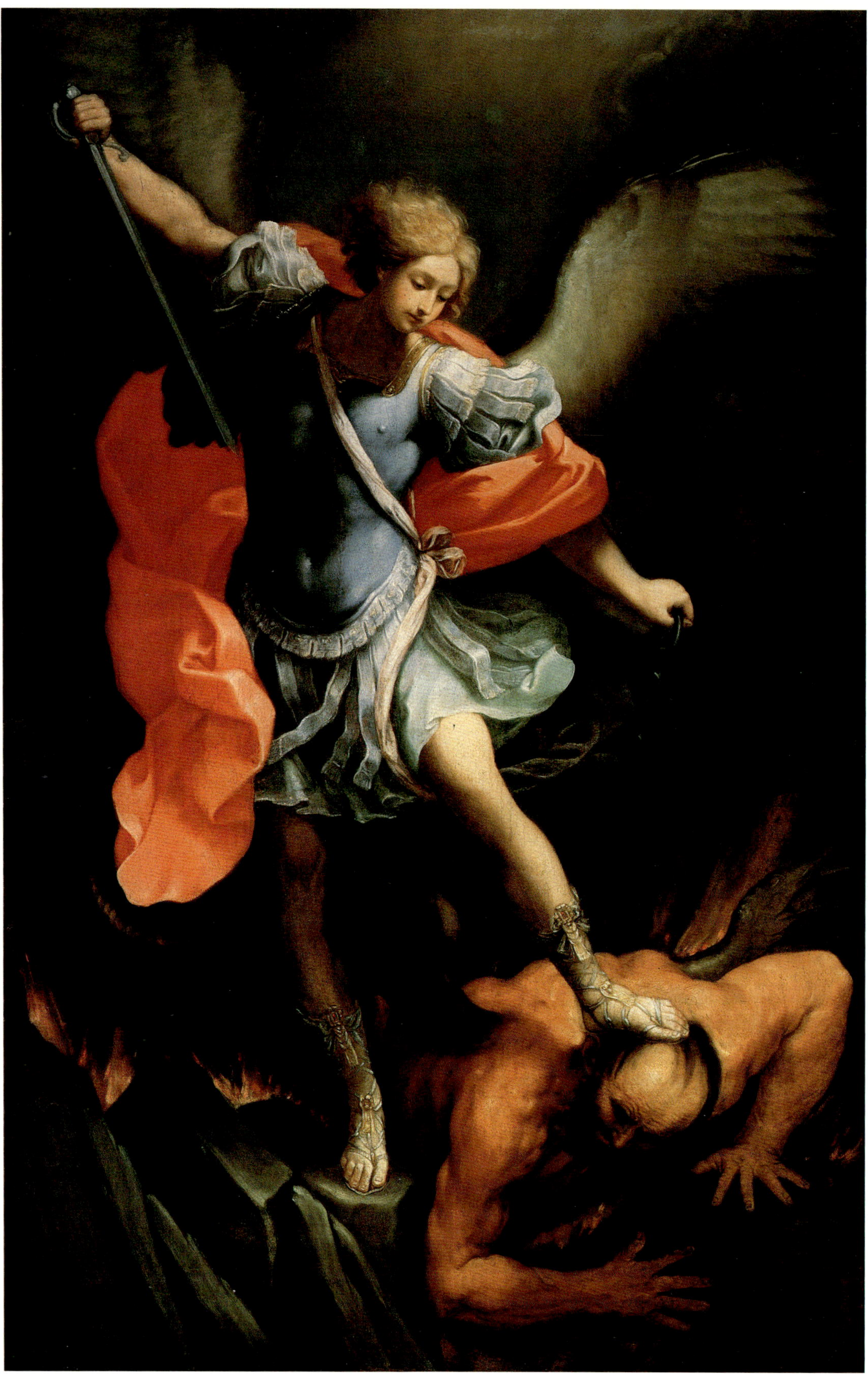

22.
Giovanni Andrea Sirani, *Saint Michael the Archangel Overcoming Satan*, late 1630s
Oil on canvas, 279.4 x 188 cm
Bob Jones University Museum and Gallery, Greenville, South Carolina
From the Bob Jones University Collection

The Bolognese artist Giovanni Andrea Sirani (1610-1670) studied first with Giacomo Cavedone and then entered the workshop of Guido Reni, where he worked as one of Reni's favored assistants until the master's death in 1642. Although Sirani was active at least until about 1665, little is known about his career and commissions. He was the father of the renowned painter Elisabetta Sirani.

Sirani's *Saint Michael the Archangel Overcoming Satan* is a faithful copy of Guido Reni's celebrated and influential altarpiece of ca 1635 in the Roman church of S. Maria della Concezione, which was inspired by Raphael's treatment of the theme now in the Louvre. Saint Michael's role as a propagandistic symbol for the Roman Catholic Church's battle against Protestantism and heresy has recently received much scholarly attention, but in seventeenth-century Italy, Saint Michael was equally, if not even more widely, known as a saintly protector against the plague and other deadly diseases. (See cat. 20.)

Pope Urban VIII Barberini controlled the patronage of the high altar of the Capuchin church for which Reni's *Saint Michael the Archangel Overcoming Satan* was executed, and it is possible that Urban also commissioned Reni's altarpiece, on which Sirani's painting is based. In 1623, Urban's coronation as pope was held at his request on the feast of Saint Michael (September 29) in thanksgiving to the archangel for Urban's deliverance from a near fatal disease. In addition, the altarpiece dates to the immediate aftermath of the great plague of 1630, which, although sparing the city in the end, gripped Rome with terror of contagion for over a year.

23

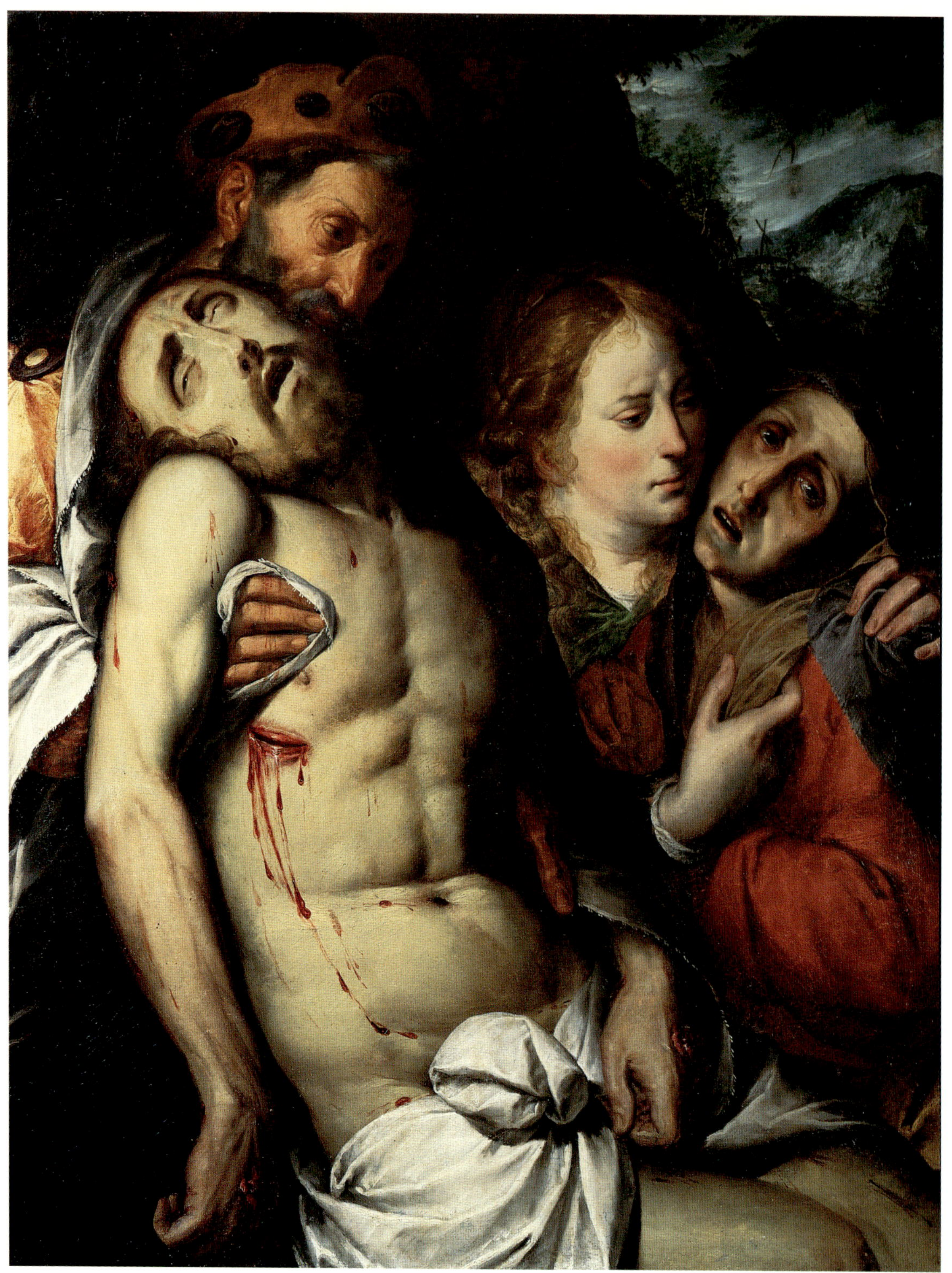

23.

Ortensio Crespi (attributed to), *Lamentation*, ca. 1610-14
Oil on canvas, 98.4 x 77.1 cm
Richard L. Feigen & Co., New York

Ortensio Crespi (ca. 1578-before 1631) was the younger brother of the famous Milanese painter Giovan Battista Crespi, called "Il Cerano," with whom he sometimes worked. Known paintings by Ortensio include a *Madonna degli Aranci* in the church of S. Marco in Novara, a *Saint Francis* in the Museo di Castelvecchio in Verona, and contributions to the fresco cycle in the Chapel of Pilate Washing His Hands (XXXIV) at the Sacro Monte (Holy Mountain) of Varallo, a popular shrine in Piedmont.

Because early modern Catholics believed that the plague was sent as a scourge by God on account of the sins of humankind, penitence was seen as a necessary means of placating God's ire. In addition to participating in penitential processions, prayers on the Passion of Christ were considered effective vehicles for atonement. Paintings such as Ortensio Crespi's *Lamentation* were sites for contemplation on the suffering of Christ and reminders that his sacrifice brought the promise of salvation in troubled times. During the plague of 1576-77, Carlo Borromeo, who was Archbishop of Milan, set an example by his devotion to the Passion of Christ and encouraged the faithful to pray on the Passion as well. One of Borromeo's favorite prayers was that of the Capuchin preacher Mattia Bellintani da Salò, called the Corone spirituali, or Spiritual Crowns. This prayer reached a crescendo with the contemplation of Christ's death, lamentation, and entombment, and encouraged the worshiper to focus on the horror and pain of the wounds in the Savior's body.

This painting by Ortensio Crespi is very close in style to works by his famous brother Il Cerano. It is a highly immediate, emotional depiction of the earthly suffering of Christ in which the viewer is confronted with the gaping wound and bloodied body of the Savior's corpse, as well as the agonized reaction of his mother, Mary, who swoons on the right. Even nature seems to respond to the figures' grief, as seen in the very painterly and dramatic landscape at the upper right.

24

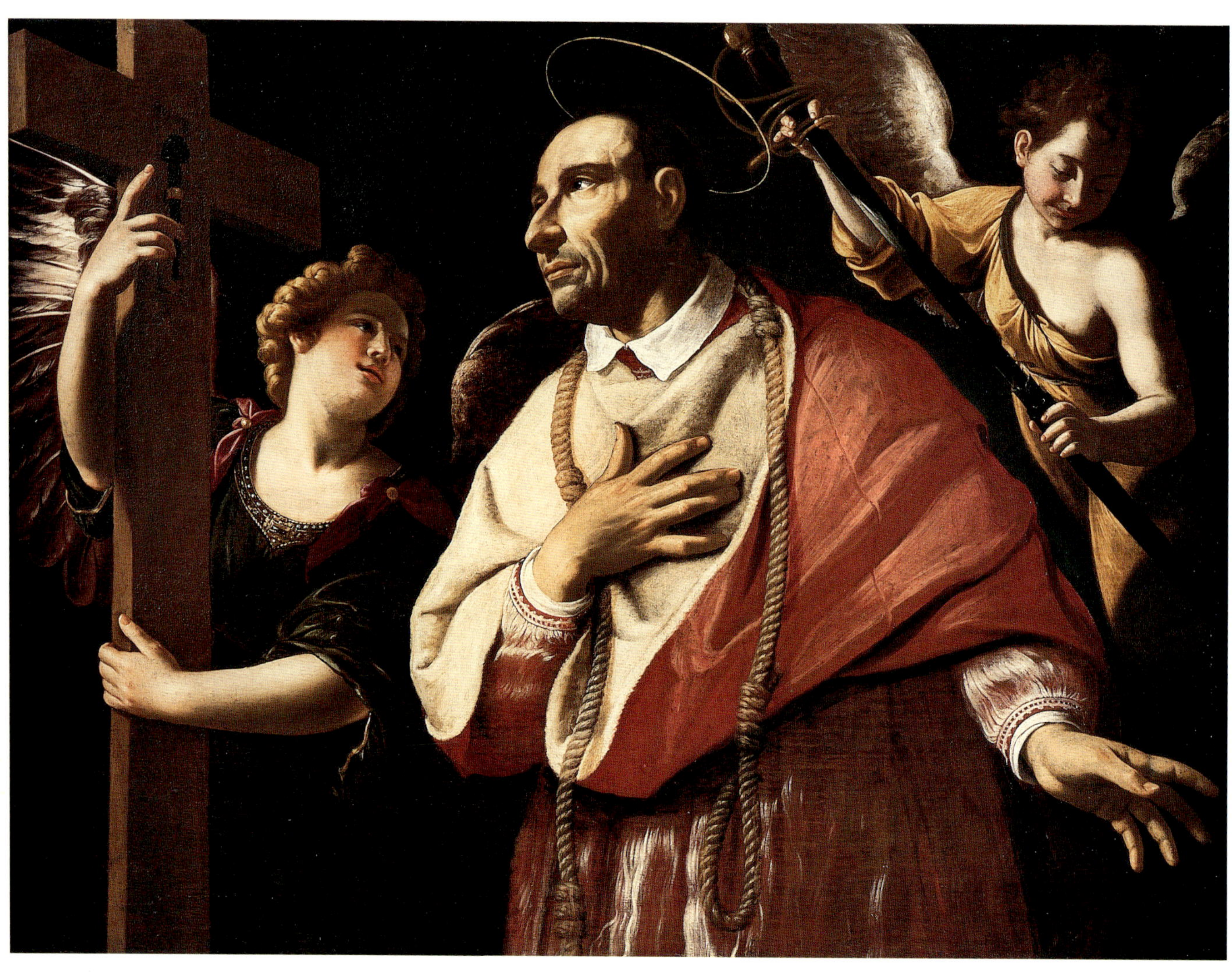

24.
Antiveduto Grammatica, *Saint Charles Borromeo and Two Angels*, ca. 1619-21
Oil on canvas, 96.5 x 127 cm
Van Ackeran Collection of Religious Art, Greenlease Gallery, Rockhurst University
A gift of the Robert C. Greenlease Family

Antiveduto Grammatica (1571-1626), born of a Sienese family, enjoyed a successful career in Rome and in 1593 became a member of the Accademia di S. Luca in Rome, and in 1604 of the Congregazione dei Virtuosi in the same city. Influenced by Caravaggio's tenebristic style, Grammatica's art appealed to some of Caravaggio's patrons, including Cardinal Francesco Maria Del Monte and Marchese Vincenzo Giustiniani. Grammatica's shop specialized in genre scenes and small religious pictures.

Grammatica's *Saint Charles Borromeo and Two Angels* shows the saint contemplating Milan's precious relic of the Holy Nail as he beseeches God for mercy on behalf of his diocese during the plague of 1576-77. During the pestilence, Borromeo led several penitential processions barefoot with a noose around his neck in imitation of the condemned Christ. All the while Borromeo contemplated the Holy Nail (it had long before been fashioned into a horse's bit, hence its odd shape), which he had affixed to a large cross that he carried in procession. In his biography of Borromeo, published in 1592, Carlo Bascapè stated that Borromeo undertook the penitential processions in emulation of Saint Gregory the Great during the plague of 590 in Rome.

Grammatica's painting was inspired by earlier ones by Andrea Commodi, Simon Vouet, and Orazio Gentileschi that created a compelling devotional image from historical events recorded in official biographies of the saint and in the *Acta Ecclesiae Mediolanensis* (*Acts of the Church of Milan*). In Grammatica's devotional image, an angel on the left embraces the cross and points to the Holy Nail, at which Saint Charles looks with reverence and humility, while a second angel on the right sheathes the sword to indicate that the saint's prayers have been answered and the plague has run its course. Grammatica's monumental figures, set close to the picture plane, are heightened by strong chiaroscuro effects, adding drama and emotion.

25

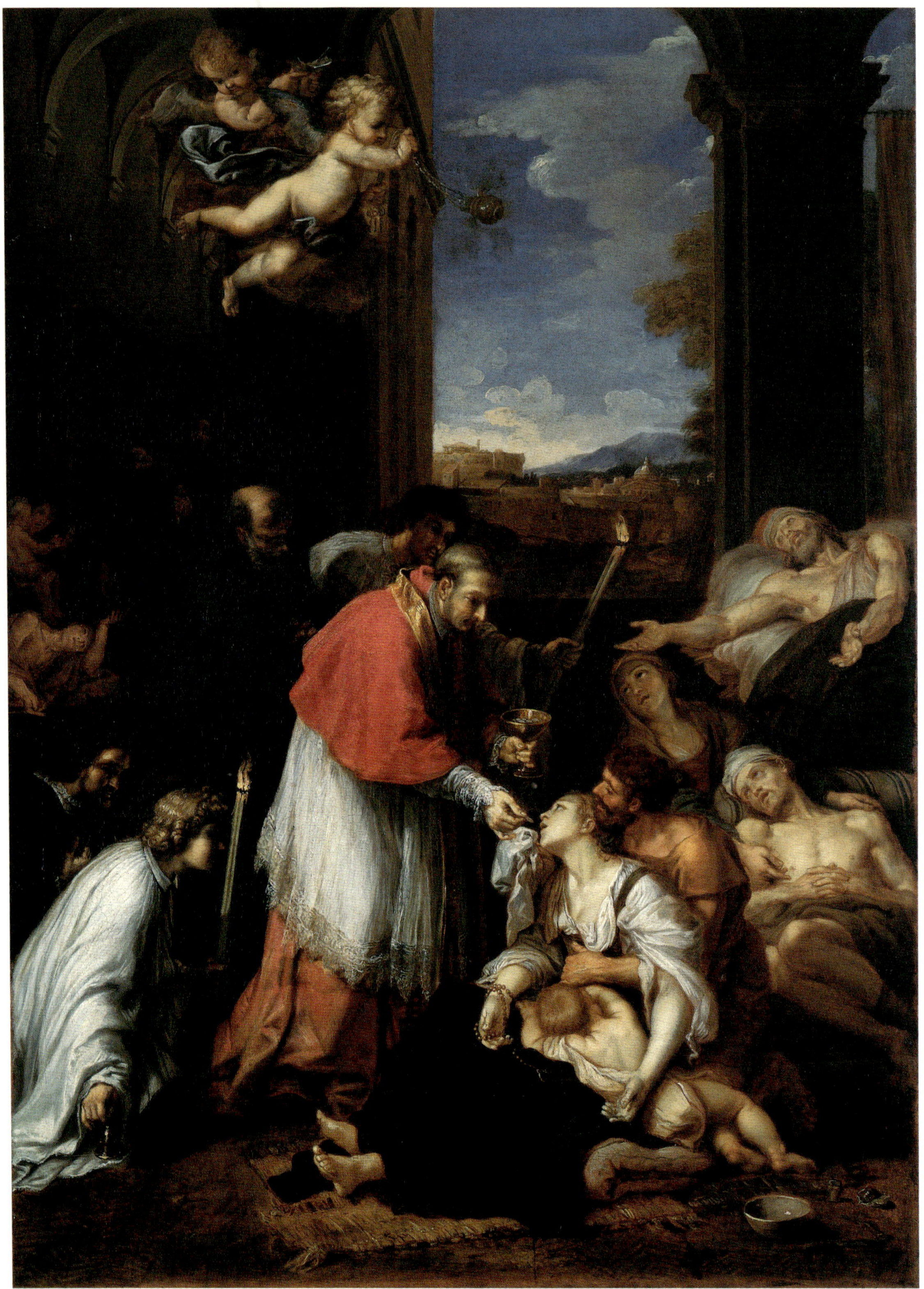

25.
PIERRE MIGNARD, *Saint Charles Borromeo Among the Plague-Stricken of Milan*, ca. 1647
Oil on canvas, 125 x 91.5 cm
Musée des Beaux-Arts de Caen

The noted French painter Pierre Mignard (1612-95), like his rival Charles Le Brun, studied with Simon Vouet. Mignard later moved to Rome in 1635, where he lived until 1657, studying the predominantly Bolognese style of the day, including the works of the Carracci and Albani, and of his own countryman Nicolas Poussin. After returning to Paris, although Mignard received some decorative commissions, including the dome of the Val-de-Grâce (1666), he was in highest demand as a portraitist. Toward the end of his life, particularly following Le Brun's death in 1690, Mignard received many important royal decorative commissions. He succeeded Le Brun as "premier peintre," and went on to hold important positions at the French Academy, which he had long refused to join.

Mignard's celebrated painting in the exhibition depicts Carlo Borromeo, who, as Archbishop of Milan during the plague of 1576-77, gained a reputation as a living saint due to his selfless material and spiritual care of the plague-stricken. Mignard depicts one of the most popular themes in the saint's iconography, his administration of the sacraments to plague victims in the lazaretto and camps of huts outside Milan's city walls. The painting is a *modello*, or sketch, for a competition for the commission of the high altarpiece of the Barnabite church of S. Carlo ai Catinari in Rome, the first church in that city to be dedicated to the saint. Although Mignard lost the competition to Pietro da Cortona, whose *San Carlo's Procession of the Holy Nail* (1667) is still in situ on the high altar, the French artist's painting was highly influential, both north and south of the Alps, due to various reproductive engravings.

Mignard shows Carlo Borromeo, standing in the center of the composition, wearing the scarlet vestments of a cardinal and surrounded by clerical assistants. He is offering the host to a plague-stricken woman whose child lies across her lap and grasps her desperately while a man supports her from behind. This motif derives from Raimondi's engraving after Raphael (cat. 5), known as *Il Morbetto*, one of the most widely copied vignettes in European plague imagery. The composition as a whole was inspired by two monumental altarpieces of the Last Communion of Saint Jerome by Bolognese artists, Agostino Carracci and Domenichino, as befits its intended role as a large public altarpiece. Mignard's painting shares with Carracci's and Domenichino's paintings the unidealized depiction of the figures, the gravitas of the scene, and the painterly, tranquil Bolognese landscape in the background.

26

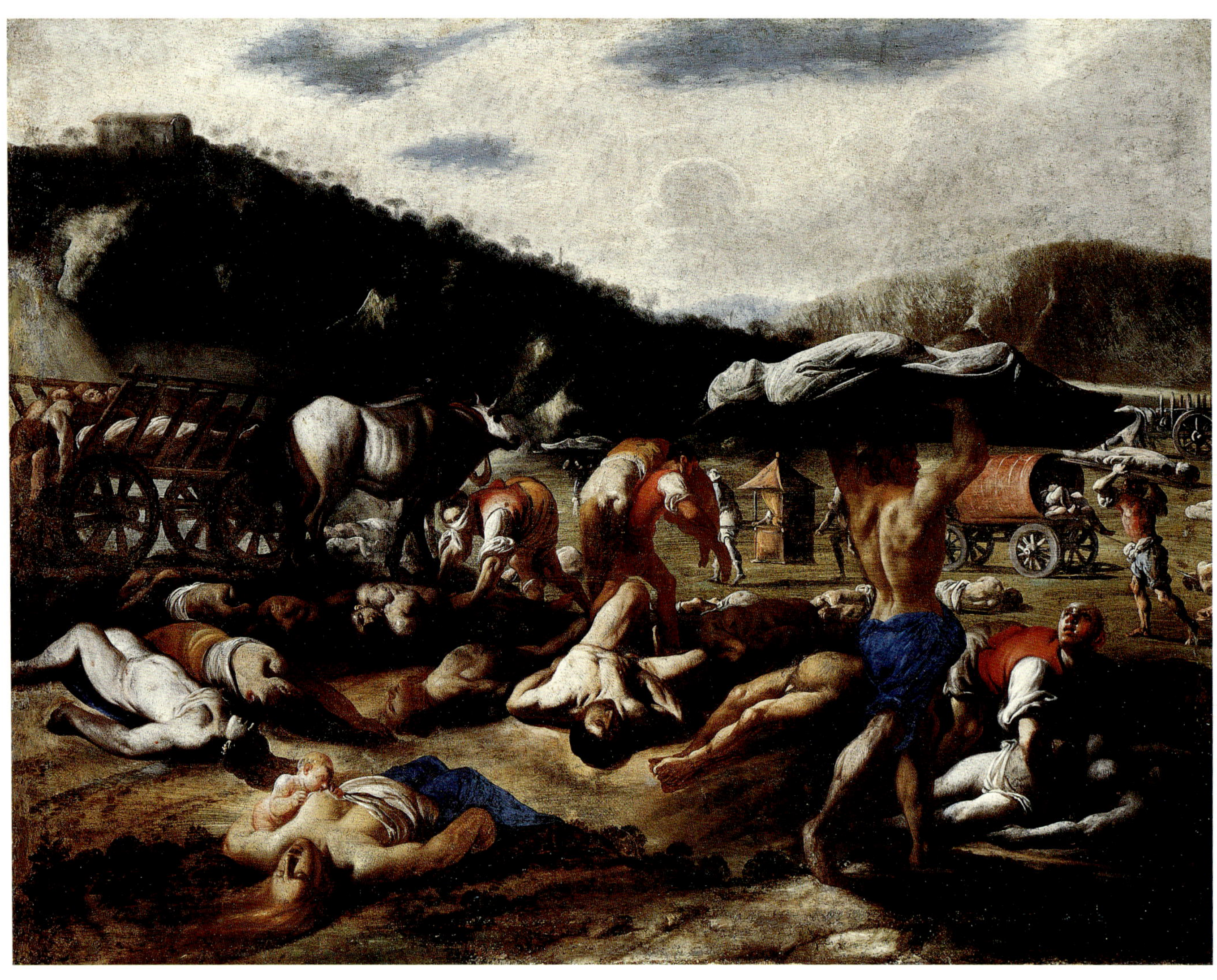

26.
CARLO COPPOLA, *The Pestilence of 1656 in Naples*, after 1656
Oil on canvas, 193 x 251.5 cm
Princeton University Art Museum, Caroline G. Mather Fund

The Neapolitan painter Carlo Coppola (active 1640-60) was a prominent student of the famous battle painter Aniello Falcone, and together with Micco Spadaro, Marzio Masturzio, Andrea di Lione, and Salvator Rosa, he helped develop the genre. Coppola experienced battle firsthand as well. During the Masaniello insurrection of 1647 in Naples, he and his fellow artists Rosa and Falcone formed an armed band called the Compagnia della Morte (Company of Death) to avenge the deaths caused by the Spanish rulers of the city, fighting by night and painting by day. His immediate experience with death and destruction finds its way into his view of the plague.

Coppola's scene of pestilence is a rare depiction of a contemporary plague, that of 1656 in Naples. Combining the panoramic scenery and human interest usually associated with the genre paintings of the Roman *Bamboccianti* with the blunt depiction of human misery, this painting shows one of the worst pestilences ever delivered upon Naples. Although the plague was a constant reality in the early modern period, few artists chose to paint actual scenes of contemporary plague victims, preferring instead to focus on the more positive images of divine intercession. This kind of journalistic image, more associated with print culture, is therefore an extremely valuable document, showing us details such as the corpses wrapped in shrouds and the oxcarts that traveled through city and country alike to gather bodies. One debt to print culture is quite specific: the infant trying to suckle its dead mother at the lower left is a quotation from Raimondi's engraving *Il Morbetto* (cat. 5), which was frequently used by plague painters as a model. Appropriate to the painting's morbid subject matter are Coppola's dark palette and the graphic depiction of death and suffering.

27

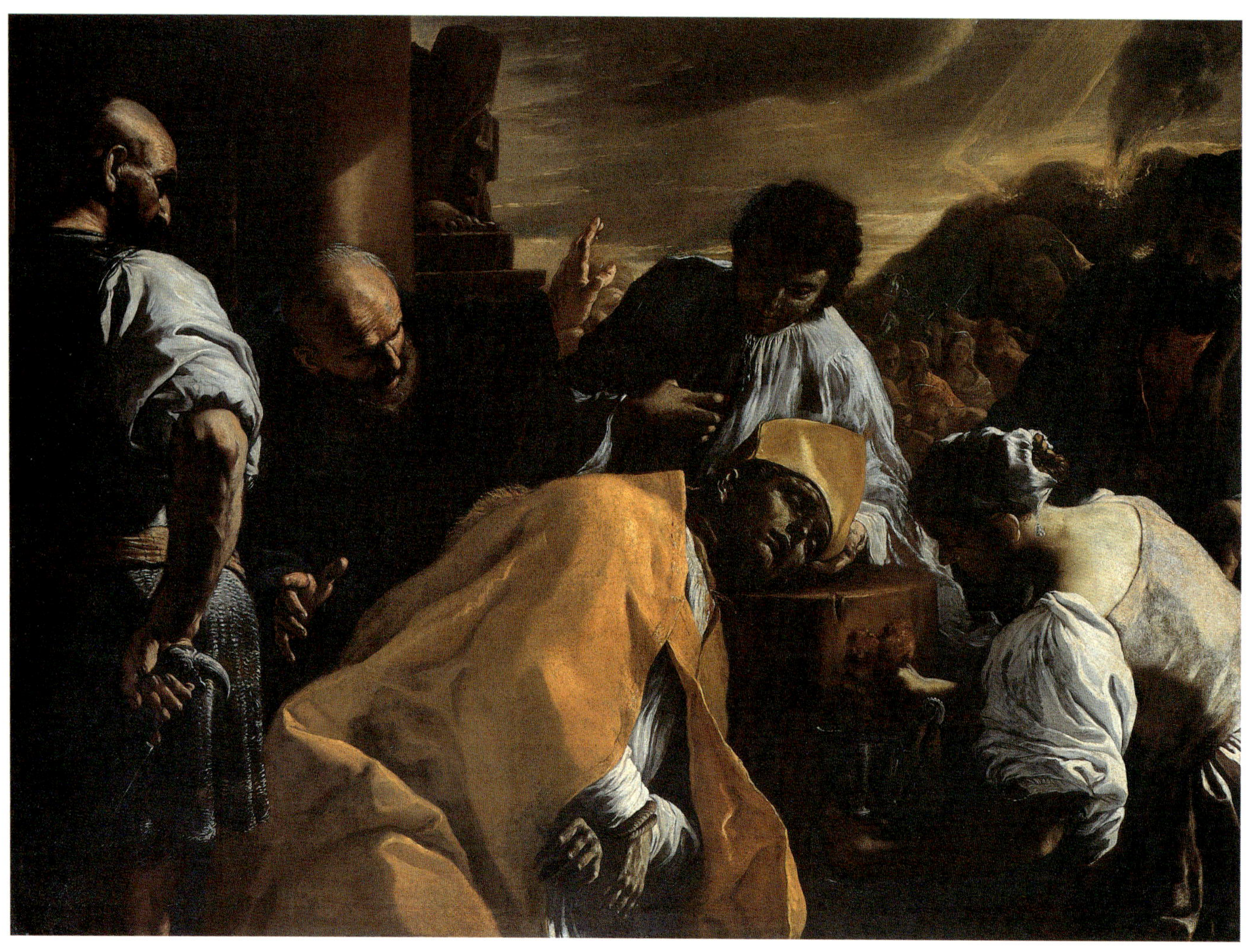

27.
Mattia Preti, *The Martyrdom of Saint Gennaro (Januarius)*, ca. 1685
Oil on canvas, 154 x 200 cm
National Gallery of Art, Washington, D.C., Patrons' Permanent Fund

Also known as the Cavalier Calabrese, Mattia Preti (1613-1699) was born in Taverna (Calabria). An extremely productive painter, Preti spent his career traveling around many different parts of Italy, possibly Spain and Flanders, and Malta, where he died. His first stop after leaving his native town was Rome, where he lived with his brother and fellow painter Gregorio. Although Preti's earliest works are scenes of musicians and card-players in the caravaggesque vein, he later produced full-scale frescoes and large canvases on religious subjects. After succeeding Lanfranco as decorator of the church of S. Andrea della Valle in Rome (1650-51), Preti undertook another ecclesiastical commission in Modena, and then moved to Naples in 1653, where he received such important commissions as the seven frescoes (now lost) commemorating the plague designed for the city gates, and many other paintings considered the finest of his career. Preti moved to Malta in 1661, where he painted altarpieces and frescoes for various churches, incuding Valletta Cathedral, until his death there in 1699.

Preti's canvas features Saint Januarius, a fourth-century bishop of Benevento who was beheaded at Pozzuoli along with his companions after he endured tortures under the Emperor Diocletian. Januarius, or Gennaro, is the main patron saint of Naples, and the relics of his head and blood are kept in the city's cathedral. According to legend, the saint's blood miraculously liquefies several times a year when brought into proximity with the head. On occasions when the blood does not liquefy, it is believed that disaster will strike, as in the case of the plague of 1527. Following this event, the citizens of Naples vowed to erect a treasury chapel for Januarius's precious blood to spare them from future pestilence. This chapel, part of the cathedral, was however only begun in 1608. Naples was one of the most plague-stricken cities in Italy, and after 1527 Januarius became the city's premier plague saint. In the seventeenth century he was frequently featured in paintings made as ex-votos for plague victims by such artists as Luca Giordano and Francesco Solimena (cat. 29).

Preti's canvas focuses directly on the martyrdom of the saint, sparing no horror. The saint's decapitated head rests on the crude executioner's block, while his blood runs into a cup held by Eusebia, the woman who is credited with preserving this precious relic. The darkened head of the dead saint and the somber lighting of the scene are contrasted with the brilliant gold of Januarius's cope and miter and the brilliant lilac of Eusebia's dress. The unmitigated gore of this scene reflects Neapolitan tastes of the time, when this type of direct representation of martyrdom had been popularized by Jusepe de Ribera, suggesting that the work's original patron came from that city

28

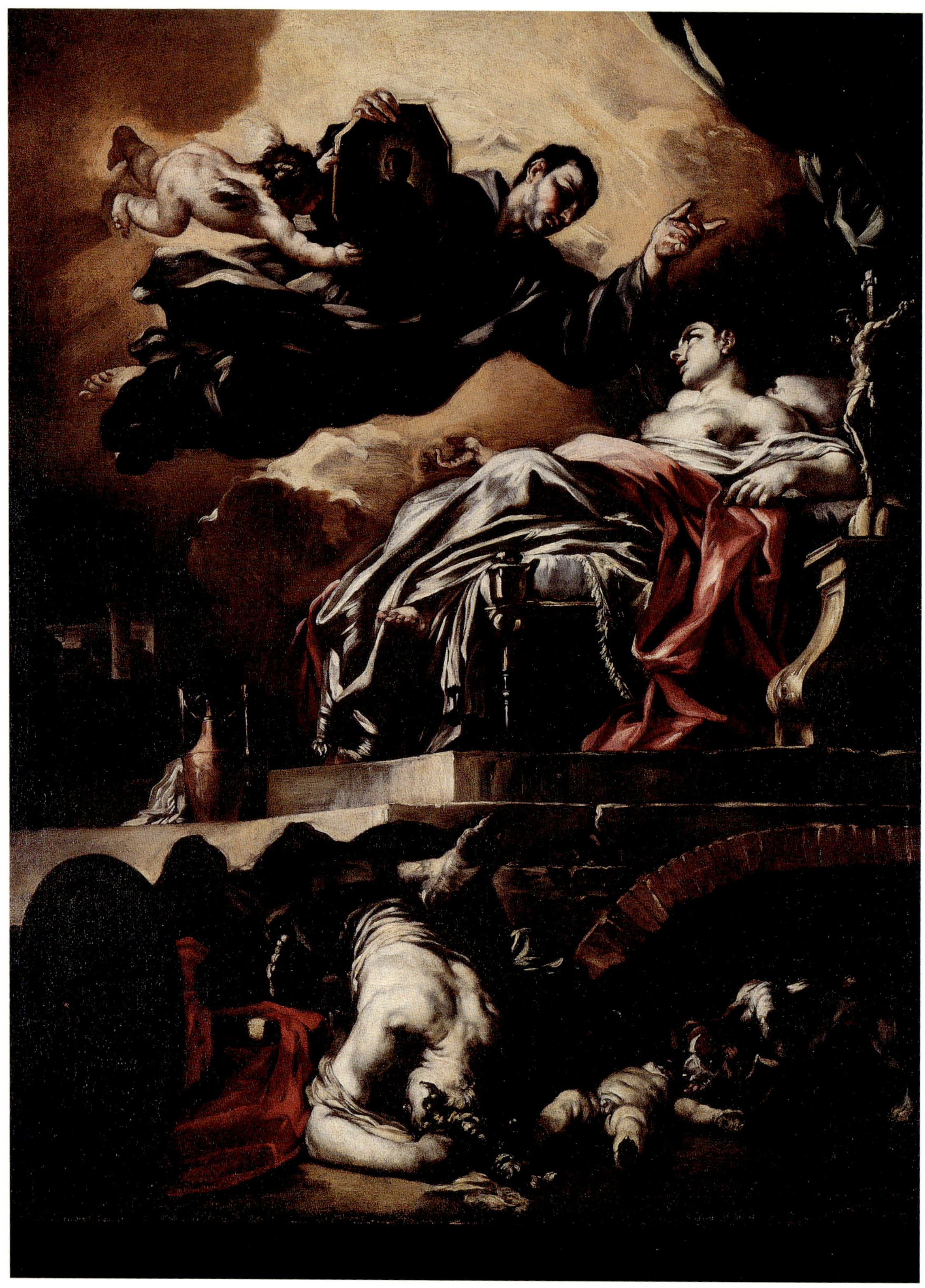

28.
Francesco Solimena, *The Miracle of Saint John of God*, ca. 1690
Oil on canvas, 93.3 x 72.9 cm
Williams College Museum of Art, Museum Purchase, John B. Turner '24 Memorial Fund, Karl E. Weston Memorial Fund

Francesco Solimena (1657-1747), the great Neapolitan artist and son of the naturalistic painter Angelo Solimena, was the most famous painter in Europe in the early eighteenth century. Francesco moved from Nocera to Naples in 1674, where he studied briefly with Francesco Di Maria. Although Di Maria seems to have been his only teacher, Solimena was greatly inspired by Luca Giordano. Throughout the 1670s and early 1680s Solimena was influenced by Giordano's Venetianizing color and light effects, but directly afterward he became more influenced by Pietro da Cortona in his broad gestures and physiognomic types. Among Solimena's most famous works of the 1670s are the frescoes for the Chapel of the Martyrs in the Gesù Nuovo, which, although totally repainted and only partly restored, represented a high point in his synthesis of the styles of Giordano and Emilian art. Solimena's first large-scale independent project was the fresco cycle of 1680 for the monastery of S. Giorgio in Salerno, which again represents an assimilation of the styles of Giordano and Cortona. From that point on Solimena received prestigious commissions for major fresco cycles and oil paintings. In 1702, he went to Rome, seemingly for the first time, where he was inspired by the works of Domenichino, Reni, Guercino, and particularly Carlo Maratta. He then returned to Naples, where he had a highly successful career until his death in 1747.

Solimena's painting is a *modello*, or sketch, for a still extant altarpiece at the Ospedale della Pace (Hospital of Peace) in Naples. It depicts Saint John of God (1495-1550), a Portuguese mystic who lived and worked in Spain and founded in Granada an order of brothers devoted to the care of the sick. After his death, the order spread elsewhere, including to Italy. With the number of miraculous cures attributed to him growing, John of God was canonized in 1690. Solimena shows Saint John of God freeing the city of Naples from the plague. Although the bare-breasted woman lying in bed has previously been identified as a personification the city of Naples, Sheila Barker argues in her essay in this catalogue that she is likely meant to represent Isabella Arcelli, a teenager who was miraculously cured of the plague in Rome in 1656 through the spiritual intervention of Saint John of God, to whom she had prayed before going to sleep. This miracle was officially recognized during the saint's canonization proceedings.

Below the reclining figure of Isabella Arcelli, close to the viewer, are the dead bodies of plague victims. Solimena unflinchingly depicts the foreshortened corpse of a little boy who has attracted the attention of a dog. Dogs and cats were suspected carriers of the plague, and, as a result, were often slaughtered en masse. The healing power of sacred images and the intercession of saints is underscored by the image at the top of the composition of Saint John of God appearing to Isabella Arcelli in a golden cloudburst, holding an image of himself to gaze upon for healing.

29

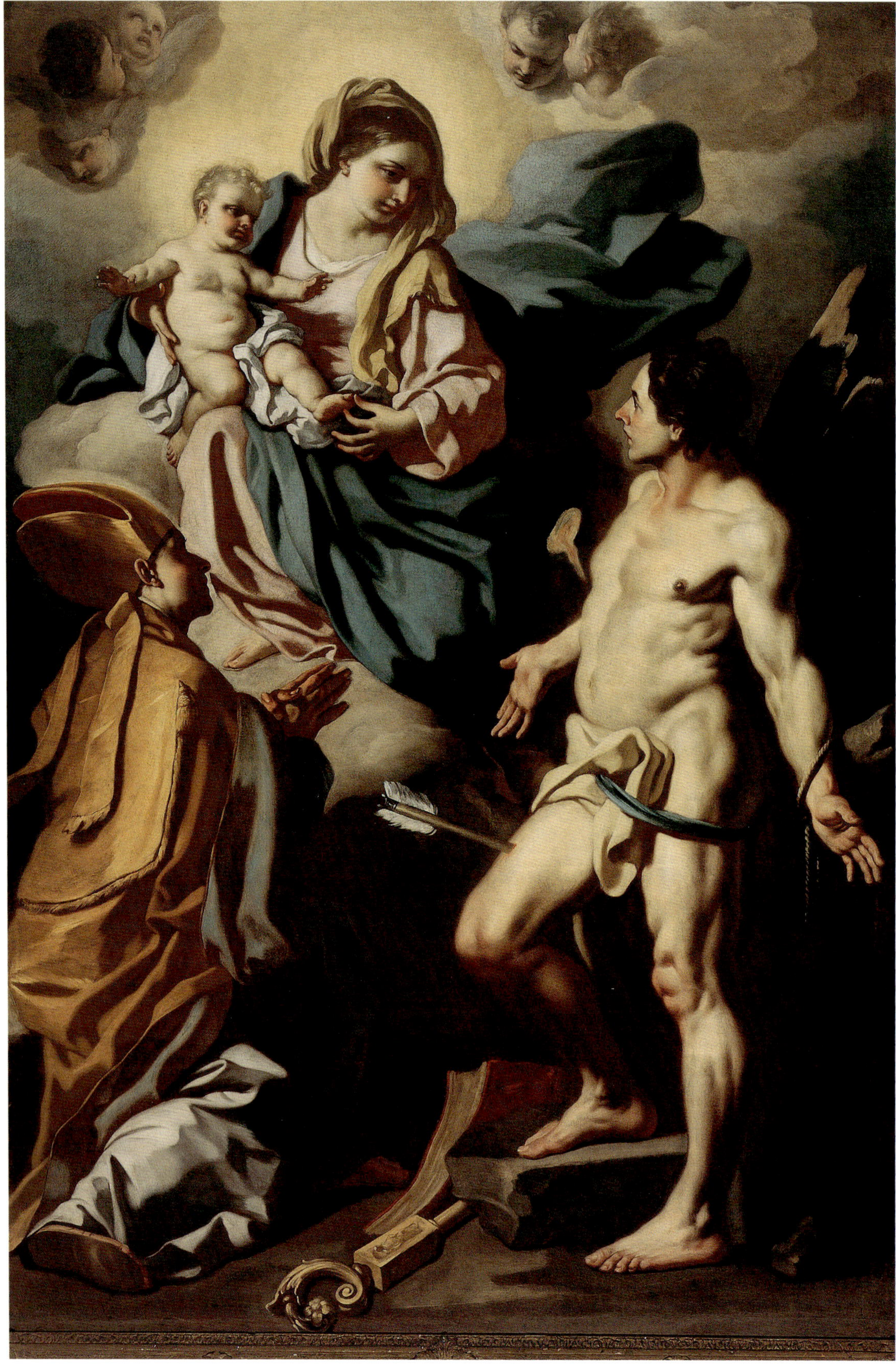

29.
Francesco Solimena, *Madonna and Child with Saints Januarius (Gennaro) and Sebastian*, ca. 1700
Oil on canvas, 254 x 175.3 cm
Milwaukee Art Museum, Gift of Friends of Art

This painting has been dated to ca. 1700, immediately before Solimena left Naples for Rome. In it the Madonna and Child are seen together with Saint Januarius, Naples' patron saint, and Sebastian, both of whom were principal plague saints in Italy. Mary was thought to be an especially influential intercessor with her son, and other saints were thought to refer their requests to her. In this painting Sebastian displays his arrow-pierced flesh to the Virgin and Child while Januarius kneels in prayer before them. These two saints bring suffering humanity to Mary and Jesus for healing.

This large painting incorporates the figure of Sebastian, who rather than being represented as a slim, graceful youth, as in many paintings of the period, is rendered as an insistently muscular, mature man. Sebastian gazes at the Madonna and Child, while Januarius, on the other side of the composition, kneels before them forming a graceful arc-like composition. The physiognomy and flowing drapery of the Madonna recalls the style of Pietro da Cortona, as do the pastel colors and rosy clouds. The figure of Januarius is distinguished by his glowing golden robes, which draw attention to this more local hero.

30

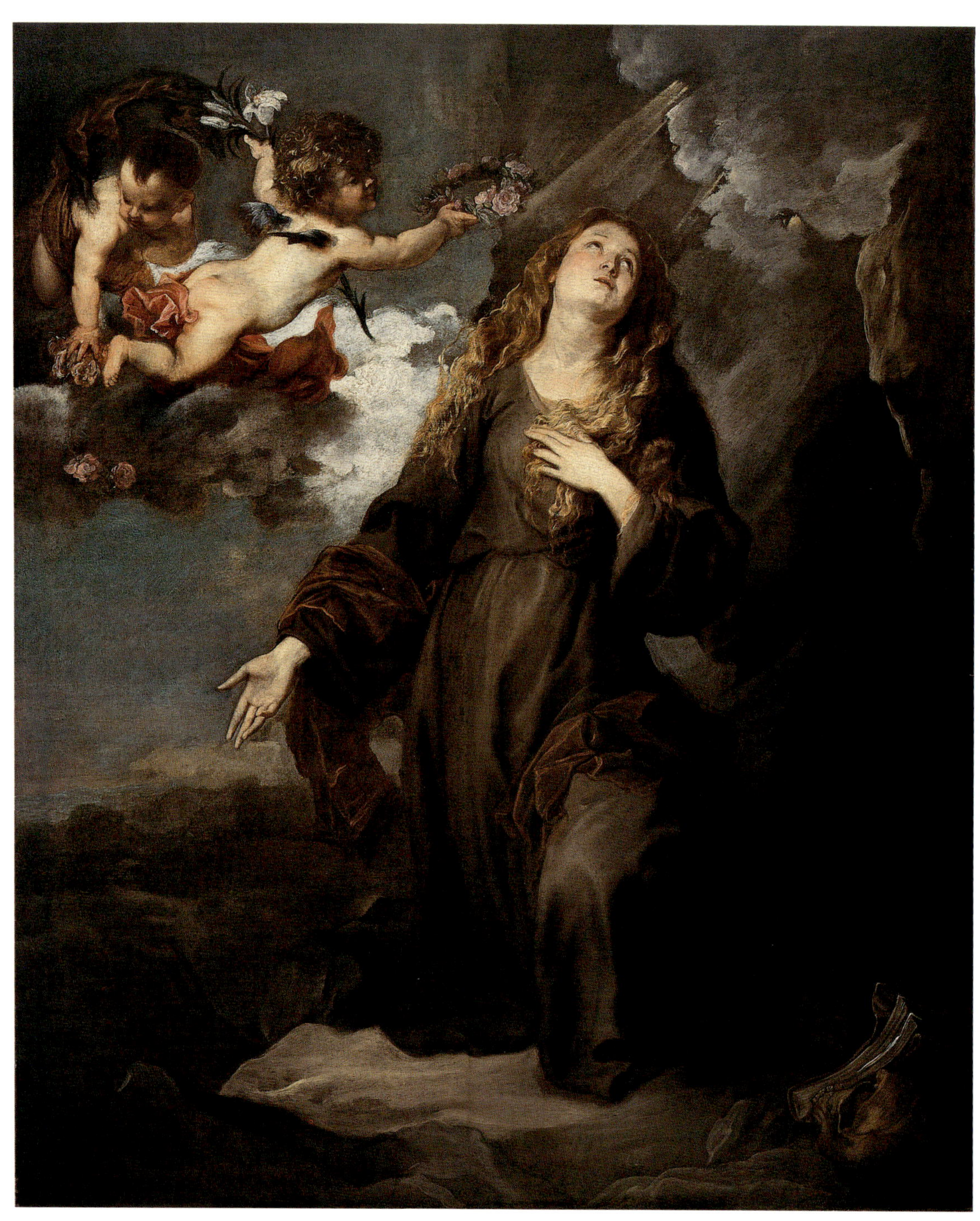

30.

Anthony van Dyck, *Saint Rosalie in Glory*, 1624
Oil on canvas, 165 x 138 cm
The Menil Collection, Houston

The Flemish painter Anthony van Dyck (1599-1641) was trained in Antwerp by Hendrick van Balen and subsequently became Rubens's chief assistant. Between 1621 and 1627, van Dyck was in Italy, where he traveled widely in the North and visited Bologna, Florence, Rome, and Genoa. In Genoa, like Rubens before him, van Dyck received important commissions for portraits of the leading merchant families. In the spring of 1624, at the invitation of the Viceroy of Sicily, van Dyck moved to Palermo, where he would remain until early September of 1625. He then returned to Genoa, where he was active as a painter until leaving for Antwerp in the winter of 1627. In Antwerp van Dyck had a distinguished career, mainly as a portraitist. In 1632 he went to England, where he was court painter to Charles I Stuart. Some of his most famous paintings represent members of the Stuart court and royal family. He was knighted by Charles I in July of 1632 and died in England in 1641.

Rosalie was a twelfth-century holy woman who spent the latter part of her life in solitary prayer on Monte Pellegrino near Palermo. Though some churches were dedicated to her in the following centuries and a handful of paintings of her are known from the Middle Ages and the Renaissance, her cult first flourished in the seventeenth century. In July 1624, her reputed remains were discovered in a grotto on Monte Pellegrino. Since May of that year, Palermo had been suffering from a severe outbreak of the plague, and Rosalie quickly became a favored intercessor against the pestilence. Van Dyck arrived in Palermo shortly before the outbreak of plague. During his few months in Palermo van Dyck almost single-handedly created the iconography of Rosalie as a plague saint, by combining Rosalie's traditional attributes – such as the crown of roses, the book, and the skull – with a pose and symbolism associated with the Virgin Mary, Mary Magdalene, and Saint Francis of Assisi.

In this dramatic painting, loosely inspired by a 1624 version by the Palermitan painter Vincenzo La Barbera (1605-1637), Rosalie wears the brown habit of the Franciscan order. A red cloth lies over her right arm. Her left hand lies over her breast in a gesture of acceptance of divine will as she looks up to the golden light of heaven. With her right hand, she gestures toward a distant view of Monte Pellegrino and the city of Palermo, for whose liberation she prays. The angels at the top hold a lily, a symbol of purity, and a crown of roses, indicating her name. At the lower right of the composition lies a skull, a symbol of her penitence but also a reminder of death during the plague; the book underscores her devotion. The setting and the saint's pose may have been inspired by Guido Reni's interpretations of such solitary saints in prayer as Saint Francis of Assisi and Mary Magdalene. The expressive, painterly handling reflects van Dyck's interest in Venetian painting.

31

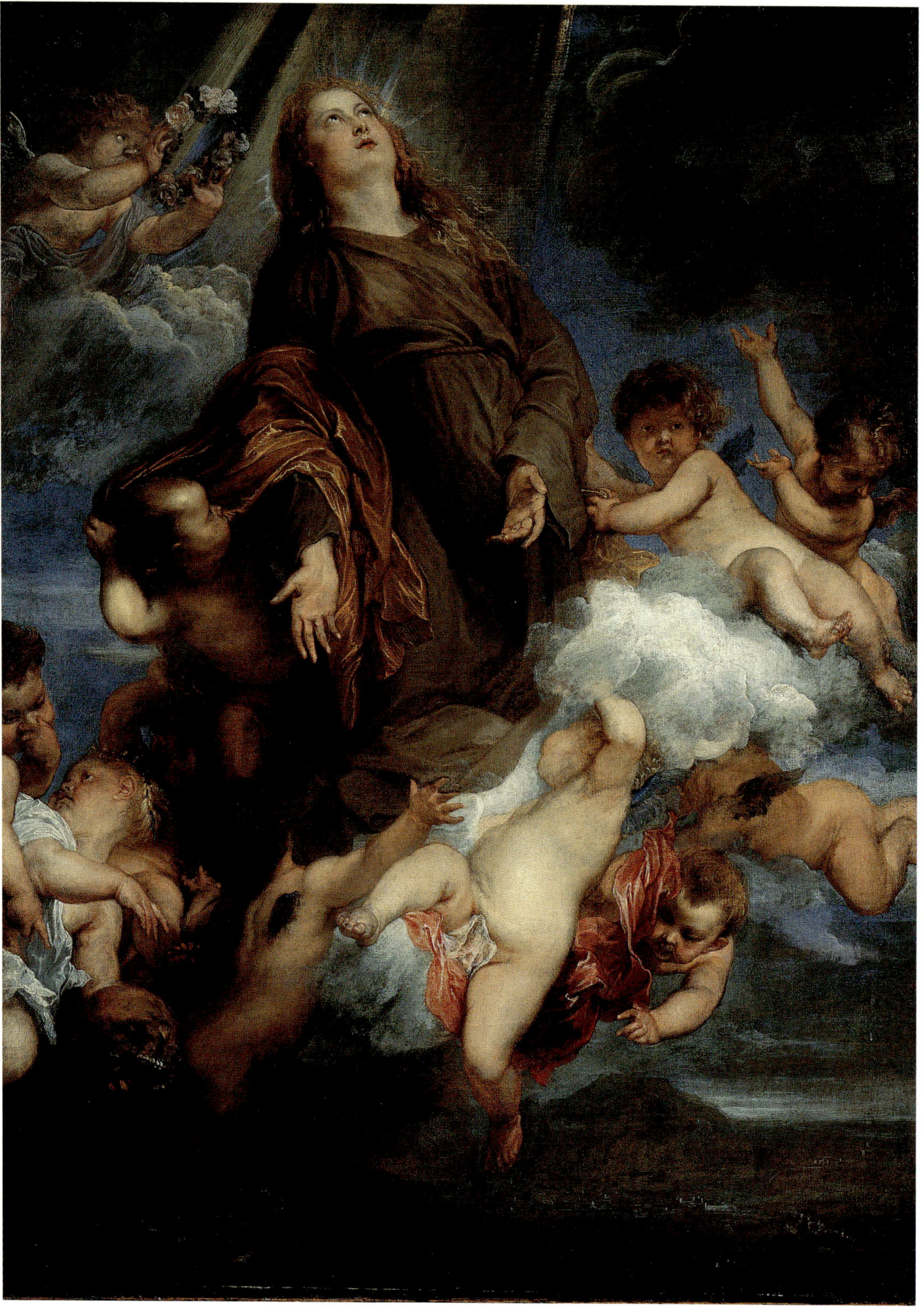

31.
Anthony van Dyck, *Saint Rosalie Interceding for the Plague-Stricken of Palermo*
Oil on canvas, 99.7 x 73.66 cm
The Metropolitan Museum of Art, Purchase, 1871

With *Saint Rosalie Interceding for the Plague-Stricken of Palermo*, the greatest of van Dyck's treatments of the theme of Rosalie in Glory, the artist has abandoned all references to the composition of La Barbera's 1624 canvas. Here van Dyck has referred instead to the iconography of the Assumption of the Virgin – in fact his own *Assumption* at the National Gallery in Washington (1628/32) has a very similar figure type. This version is likely to be the first of the series in which Rosalie is borne heavenward by angels and clouds, and her figure probably served as the model for the Rosalie in the *Madonna del Rosario* (1628) at the Oratorio del Rosario in Palermo.

In this canvas, Rosalie's whole body faces right for the first time, although her hands still point down toward the left, as in the Menil version and the original version at the Ponce Museum of Art. A single angel remains from the Menil canvas on the left, holding a crown of pink roses over Rosalie's head. The lights of the city of Palermo and the profile of Monte Pellegrino – much more prominent in his earlier treatments of the subject – are barely visible in a badly worn passage in the lower right of the canvas. The skull also appears here, borne aloft by an angel on the lower left. Chromatically, this work differs from the Ponce and Menil canvases, in that luminous light blues pierce through the clouds in the background. The satin veil that hangs over Rosalie's right arm and the shock of pink fabric intertwined in the lower pair of angels add a touch of luxury.

Neutron autoradiograph studies undertaken during the 1990s revealed that this painting was executed directly over a sketch van Dyck had made of a self-portrait. There is a copy of the Metropolitan canvas in copper at the Galleria Regionale della Sicilia. This new prototype of Rosalie in Glory served as a model for several Southern Italian and Spanish works, including Jusepe de Ribera's *Assumption of the Magdalene* in the Museo de la Real Academia in Madrid and his *Apotheosis of Saint Januarius* in the monastery of the Discalced Augustinians in Salamanca, as well as Pietro Novelli's *Apotheosis of Saint Cajetan* in the Theatine church in Palermo. Van Dyck painted a copy of this canvas, now in the Alte Pinakothek in Munich, whose quality and strong impasto scholars have praised.

32

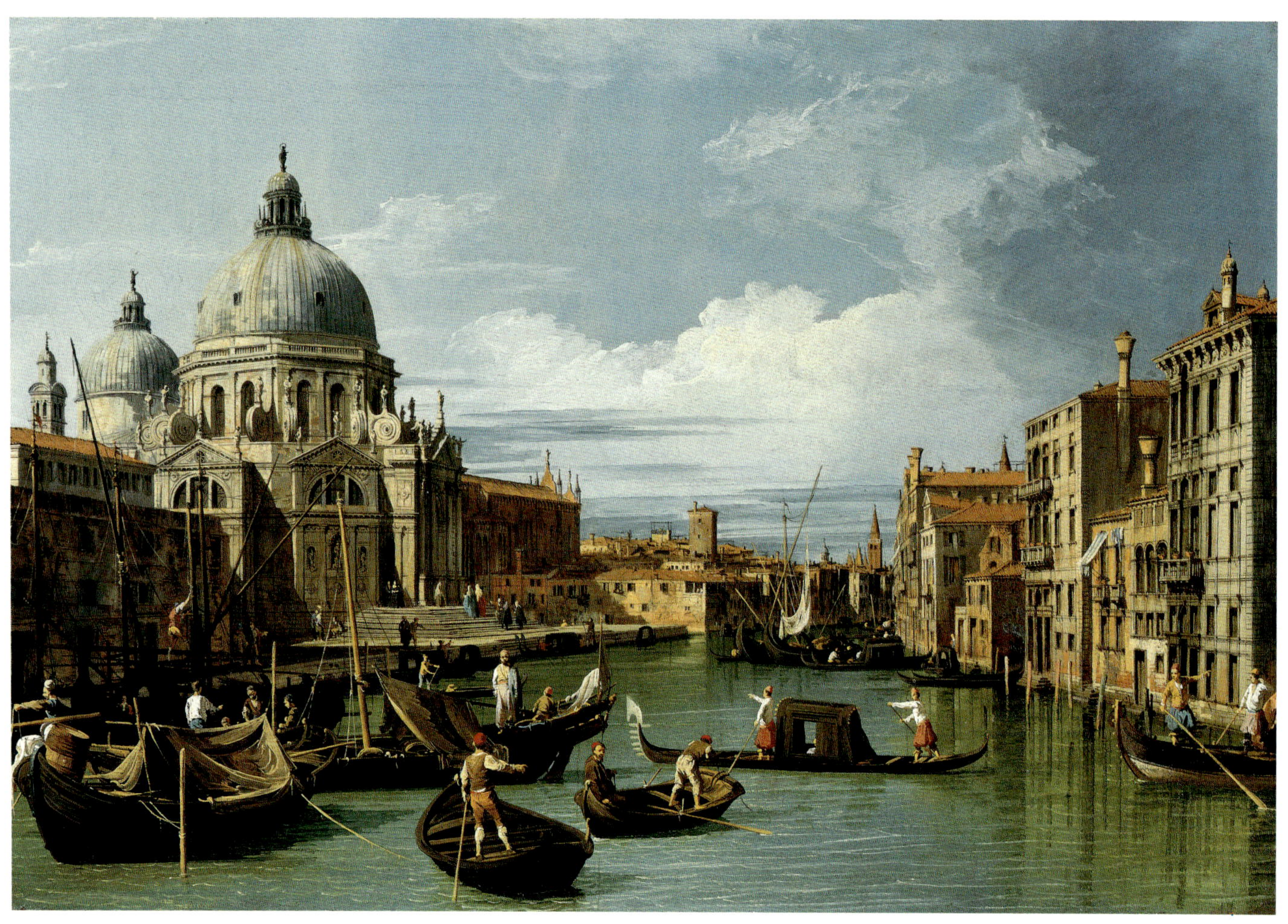

32.
Canaletto (Giovanni Antonio Canal)
Entrance to the Grand Canal with Saint Maria della Salute, 1730
Oil on canvas, 50.8 x 73. 7 cm
Museum of Fine Arts, Houston, The Robert Lee Blaffer Memorial Collection, gift of Sarah Campbell Blaffer

Giovanni Antonio Canal, called "Canaletto" (1697-1768), was an internationally renowned Venetian painter of the canals and major monuments of his city. He trained with his father and with Giovanni Paolo Panini. His works were particularly popular with aristocrats making the Grand Tour, especially in the 1730s. Joseph Smith, British consul in Venice and one of the artist's major patrons, helped sell Canaletto's paintings to an international clientele, who appreciated both his *vedute* (views) and *capricci* (imaginary views). Canaletto worked for about ten years in London, beginning in 1746, before returning to Venice.

The church of S. Maria della Salute, seen in Canaletto's painting, is one of the most monumental plague ex-votos ever built. Commissioned by the Republic of Venice in 1631 from Baldassare Longhena, the massive church overlooking the Grand Canal was built in thanksgiving for Venice's deliverance from the plague of 1630, one of the worst pestilences ever to visit Italian soil. S. Maria della Salute was also the focus of a celebration every November 21, in which the citizens of Venice constructed a pontoon bridge across the Grand Canal to allow a procession to enter the church in commemoration of the end of the plague (see cat. 33). In his beautiful painting, Canaletto represents the church and palazzi along the Grand Canal with great accuracy and precision, including a delightful array of gondolas and other boats. The light-filled canvas with the shimmering water of the canal characterizes Canaletto's popular Settecento style.

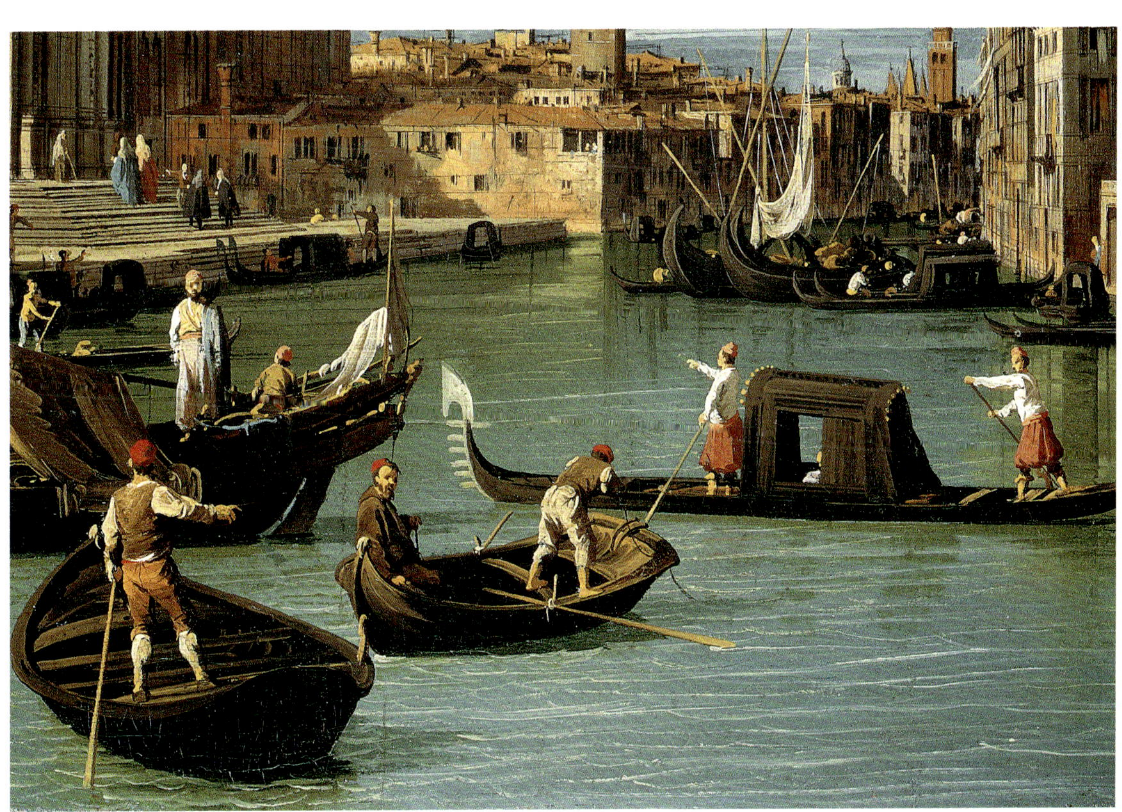

33

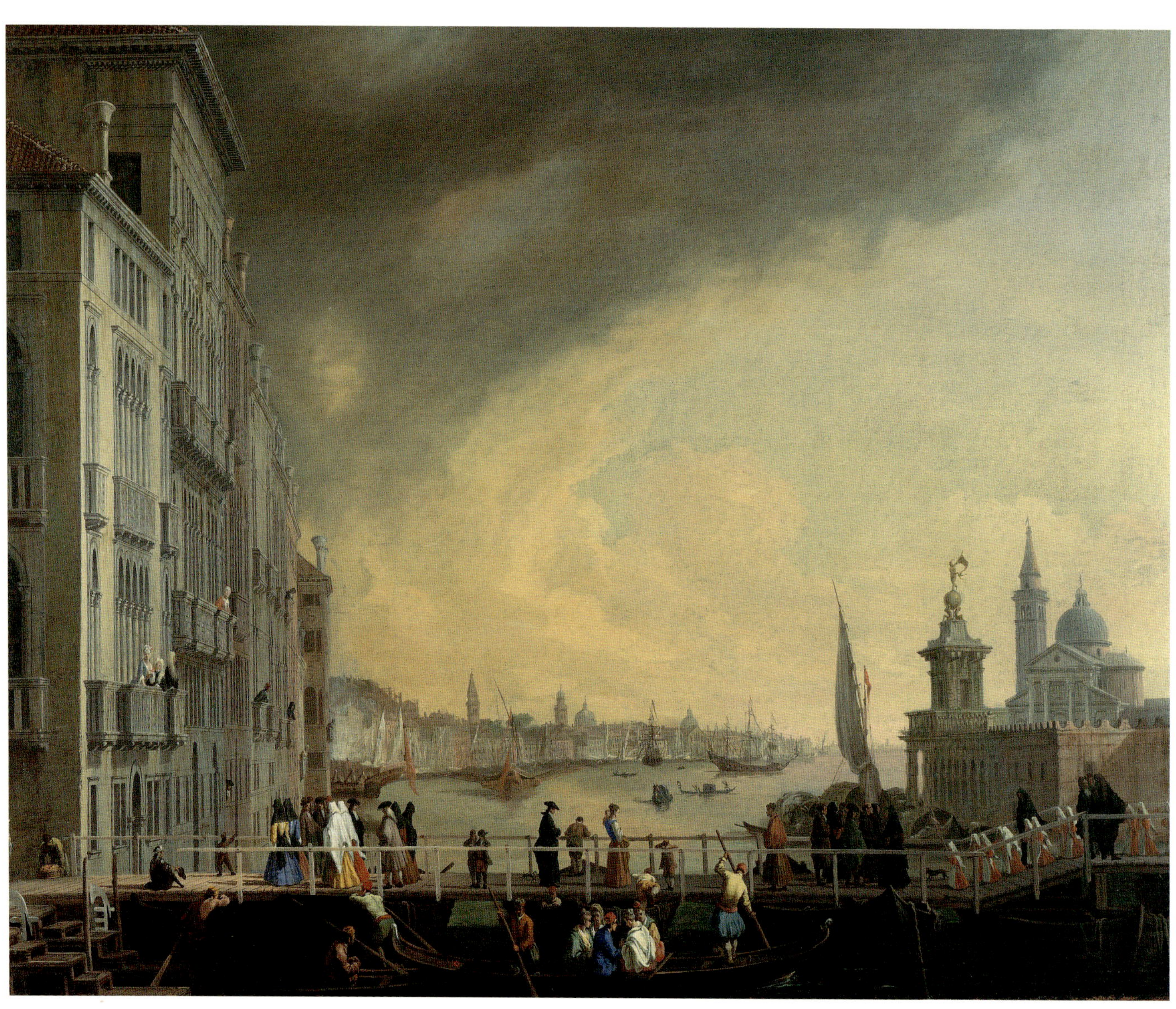

33.
Luca Carlevarijs, *The Feast of S. Maria della Salute*, 1720
Oil on canvas, 111 x 139 cm
The Wadsworth Atheneum Museum of Art, Hartford, The Ella Gallup Sumner and Mary Catlin Sumner Collection Fund

The Italian painter Luca Carlevarijs (1663-1730) also worked as a printmaker and architect. He is generally considered the first important painter of the views of Venice. He began his career with a series of engravings of 1703 of architectural views of Venice and he continued with paintings of various diplomatic scenes and ceremonies set in the canal city. Many of these paintings were taken abroad, thus helping popularize Venetian *vedute*.

Carlevarijs's *The Feast of S. Maria della Salute* provides a rare record of an annual festival mounted by the city of Venice on November 21 in commemoration of the city's deliverance from the plague of 1630. Although it is just outside the field of vision in Carlevarijs's painting, the church of S. Maria della Salute was itself commissioned as an ex-voto in celebration of the end of the same plague. Carlevarijs's canvas is full of genre details, including people traveling by gondola, noblemen and women promenading, and a procession of nuns and schoolgirls, and it brings the ex-voto nature of S. Maria della Salute alive in a way that a mere view of the church could not. Ominous gray clouds sweep in from the left, not only suggest the season, but may also serve as a reminder of the tragic plague of 1630.

As Cesare Ripa's widely disseminated handbook of allegorical imagery, the *Iconologica*, explains in its description of the personification of Pestilence ("a yellow complected woman in a beige garment with a garland of dark clouds around her wild hair"): "Her yellow color suggests infects of the body, for this color is always found in the pus that forms. The clouds around her head and the beige color of her dress represent the bad air and the appearance of the sky when pestilence comes."

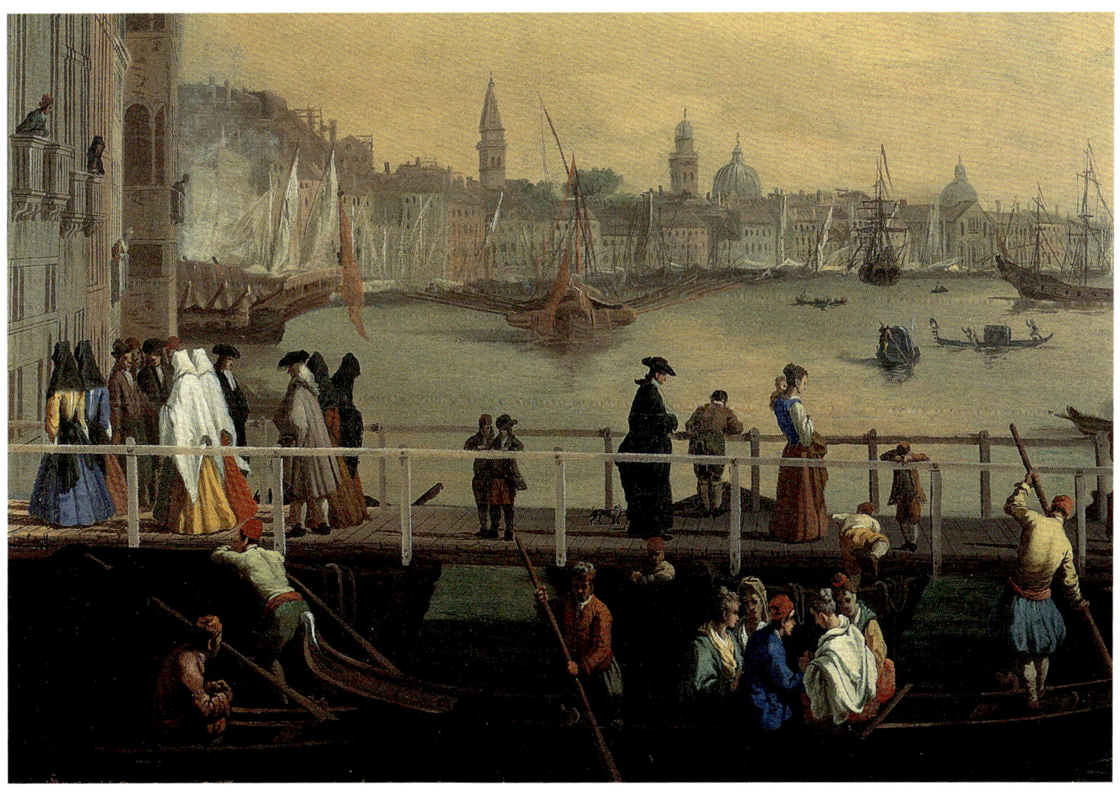

34

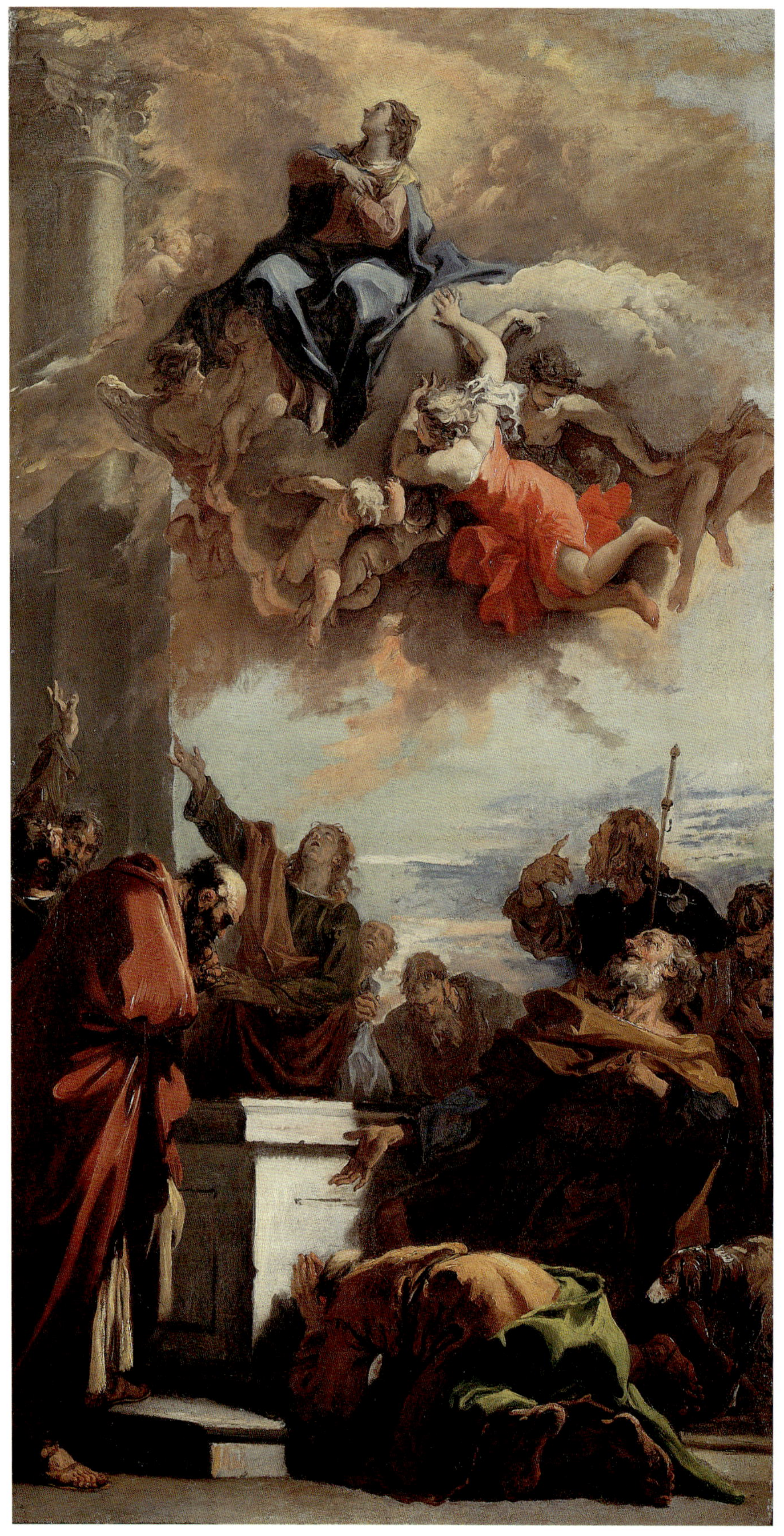

34.
Sebastiano Ricci, *The Assumption of the Virgin*
Oil on canvas, 131.4 x 64.1 cm
Museum of Fine Arts, Springfield, The James Philip Gray Collection

Sebastiano Ricci (1659-1734), whose style was indebted to the Renaissance painter Paolo Veronese, was a leading painter of his day, and influenced the great Settecento painter Giovanni Battista Tiepolo. Like many of his Venetian colleagues, Ricci enjoyed an international clientele, and was active in Vienna, Paris, and London (1712-16).

During the post-Tridentine era, the Virgin Mary was considered to be the chief intercessor with Christ and God the Father for physical and spiritual illnesses, and the iconography of her assumption into heaven was one of the most popular of the Baroque – even into the eighteenth century when memories of Protestant attacks on the Madonna's legitimacy had faded into history.

Ricci's version of the Assumption was executed in 1708-12 for the church of S. Maria Assunta in Clusone, near Bergamo, for which this version is a *bozzetto*, or sketch. In a traditional representation of the scene, Ricci depicts a group of figures gathered around Mary's empty tomb watching her ascend into heaven. One of the figures holds a pilgrim's staff and may be identifiable as the Apostle Saint James. However, the dog in the foreground suggests instead that the figure is Saint Roch. Roch's feast day was August 16, the day after the Feast of the Assumption, and the two celebrations may have been popularly conflated. The two are also linked together through their associations with curing. It was thought that Mary was assumed into heaven in both soul and body, and so like the Resurrection of Christ and the Raising of Lazarus, the Assumption of Mary would have offered hope to the afflicted, in both this life and the next. The sketch is done with the loose handling and lighter colors typical of the Venetian Settecento.

Ricci returned to the Assumption in one of his last works, an altarpiece painted just before his death in 1734 for the Karlskirche in Vienna, for which a *bozzetto* exists in the Budapest Museum.

35

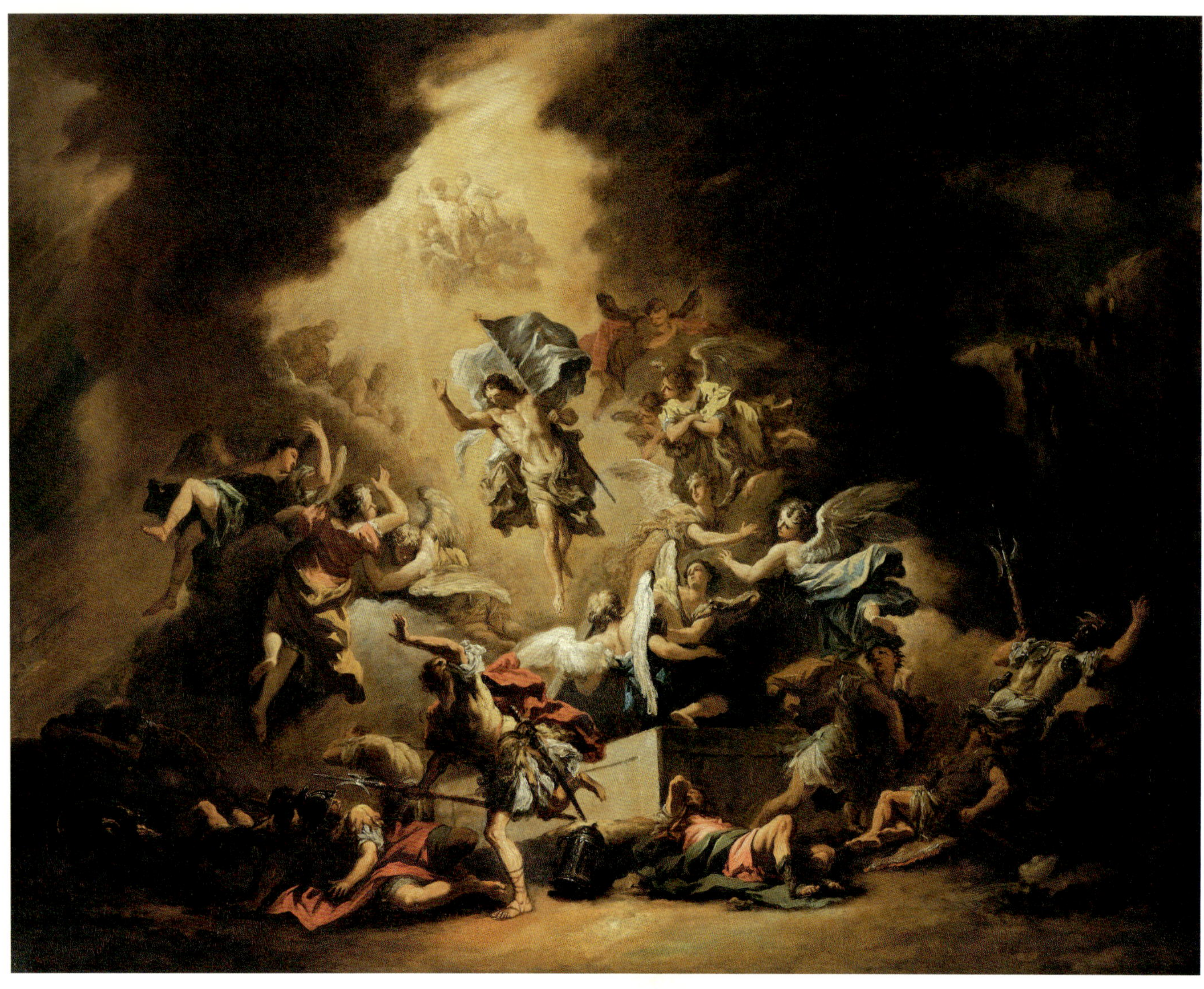

35.
SEBASTIANO RICCI, *Resurrected Christ Surrounded by Angels*, 1706-16
Oil on canvas, 100.6 x 126 cm
Columbia Museum of Art, Gift of the Samuel H. Kress Foundation

This painting is one of two extant *bozzetti*, or sketches, executed in preparation for Ricci's fresco for the apse of the chapel at Chelsea Royal Hospital in London. The *bozzetto* is an excellent example of the artist's mature style, characterized by fluid brushwork, luxuriant *colorito*, and theatrical monumentality. This elegant and powerful depiction of the resurrected Christ was meant to convey to the sick and the dying a vivid message of hope in the midst of their tribulations, with a promise of deliverance and recovery, if not in this life, then certainly in the next. During times of plague, preachers and spiritual treatise-writers pointed to the resurrected Christ as the guarantor of this central tenet of Christian doctrine.

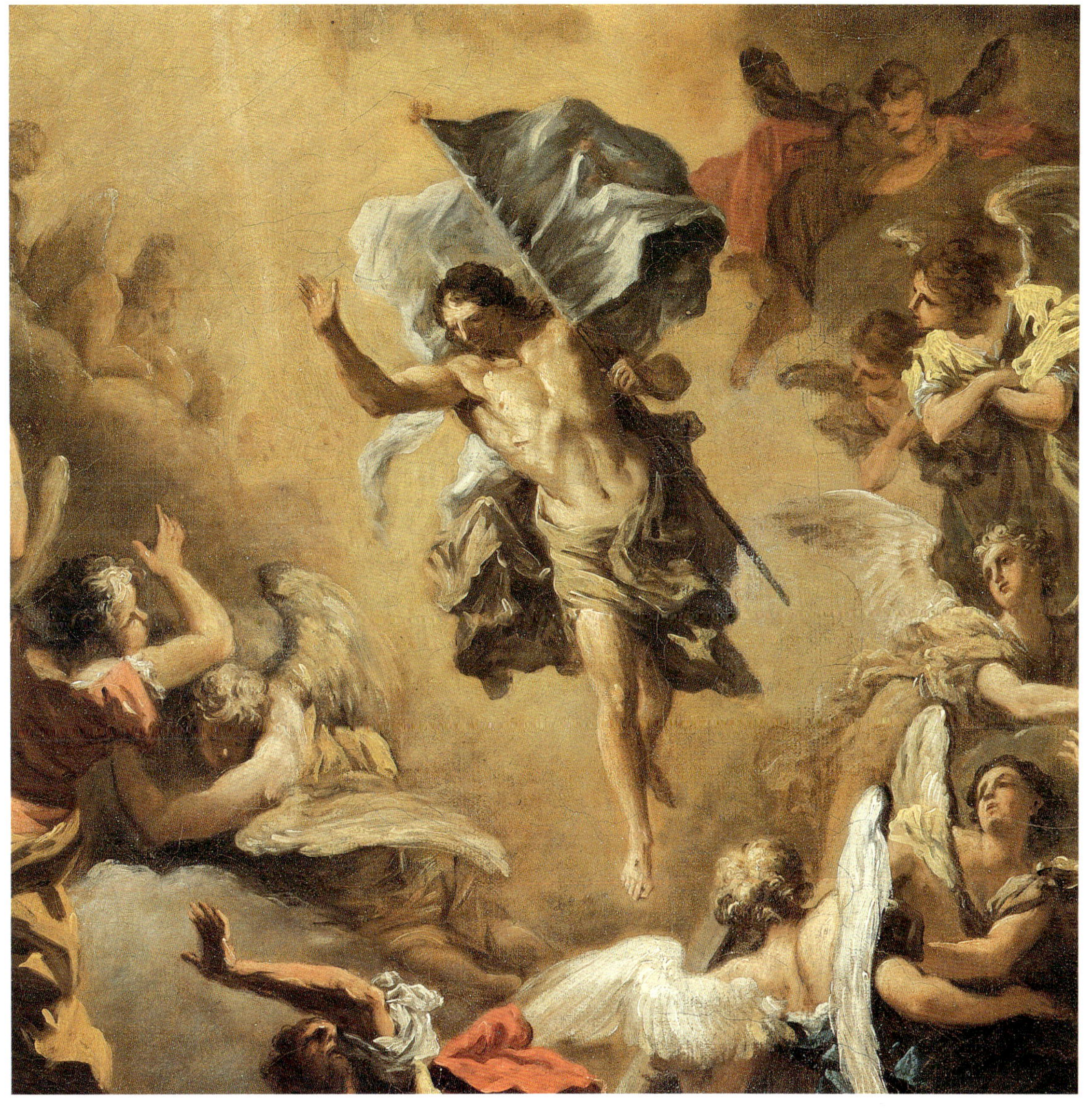

36

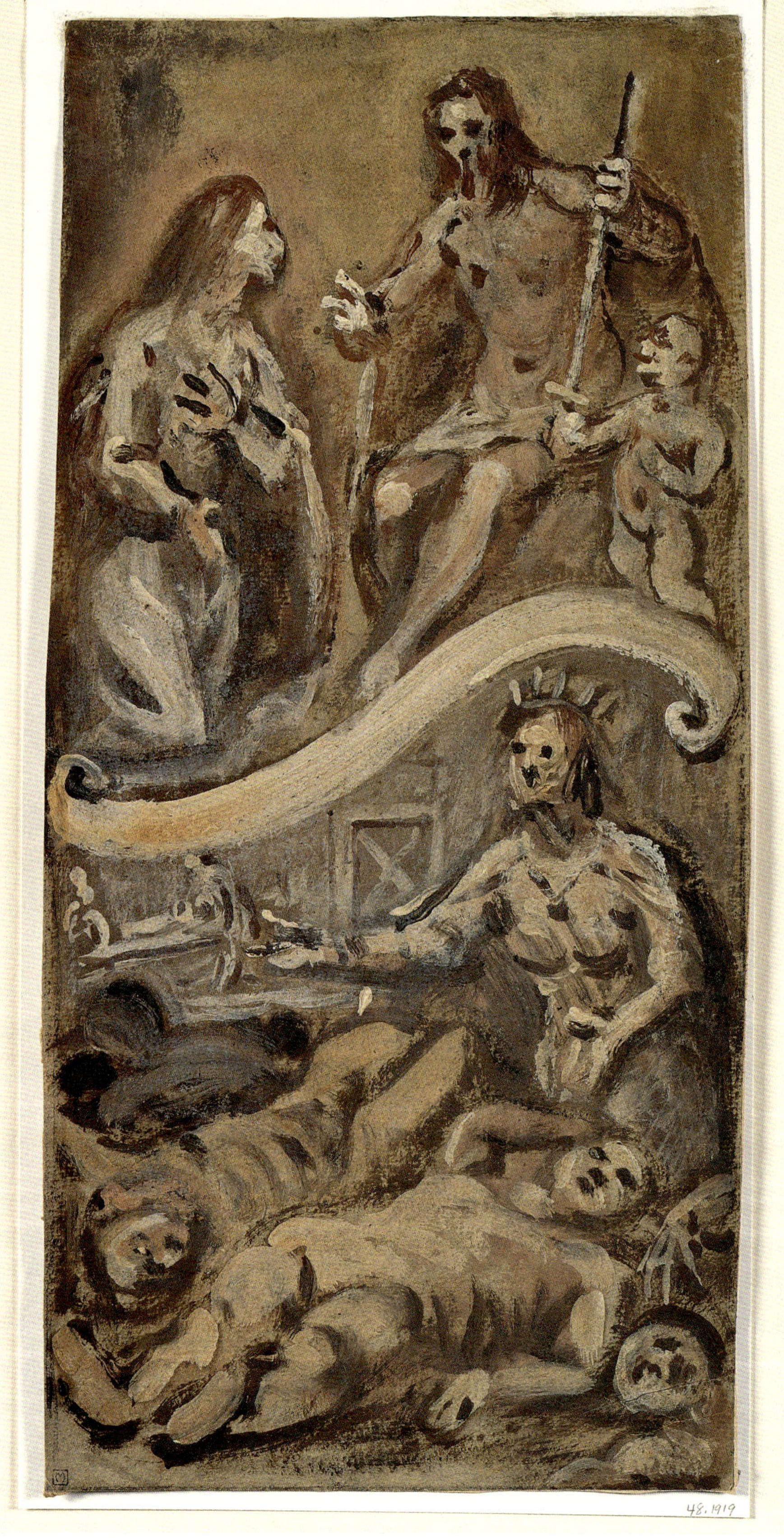

36.
Domenico Tintoretto, *Sketch for a Plague Banner: The Virgin Supplicating Christ for Plague-Stricken Venice*, 1630-31
Brush and red, brown, cream and pink oil on grayish brown prepared paper; 40.2 x 20 cm
Princeton University Art Museum, Gift of Frank Jewett Mather, Jr.

Domenico Tintoretto (1560-1635) was the son of the more famous Jacopo Robusti, called Tintoretto (1518-1594), one of the leading figures of the Venetian late Renaissance. Domenico studied with his father and entered the Venetian painters' guild at the age of seventeen. He assisted his father in painting cycles at the Sala del Collegio and the Sala del Senato in the Doge's Palace, and went on to work at the palace independently, coming to specialize in dramatic battle scenes such as his *Battle of Salvore*. Even after firmly establishing his own reputation, Domenico continued to collaborate occasionally with his father. Domenico made the transition to sacred painting in the 1580s and 1590s with altarpieces for S. Andrea della Zirada and S. Giorgio Maggiore, and a Crucifixion for the Scuola dei Mercanti.

Domenico's sketch for the plague banner – the final oil version is in the church of S. Francesco della Vigna in Venice – was executed on the occasion of the horrific Venetian plague of 1630-31, and the terror this event inflicted upon the city can be seen in the drawing itself. Unusually for plague imagery, which tended to shy away from the macabre, Domenico's scene is full of death, from the undertakers who cart off dead bodies in the middle ground to the corpses in the foreground and a striking depiction of an abandoned house, its windows boarded up, that had once belonged to plague victims.

37

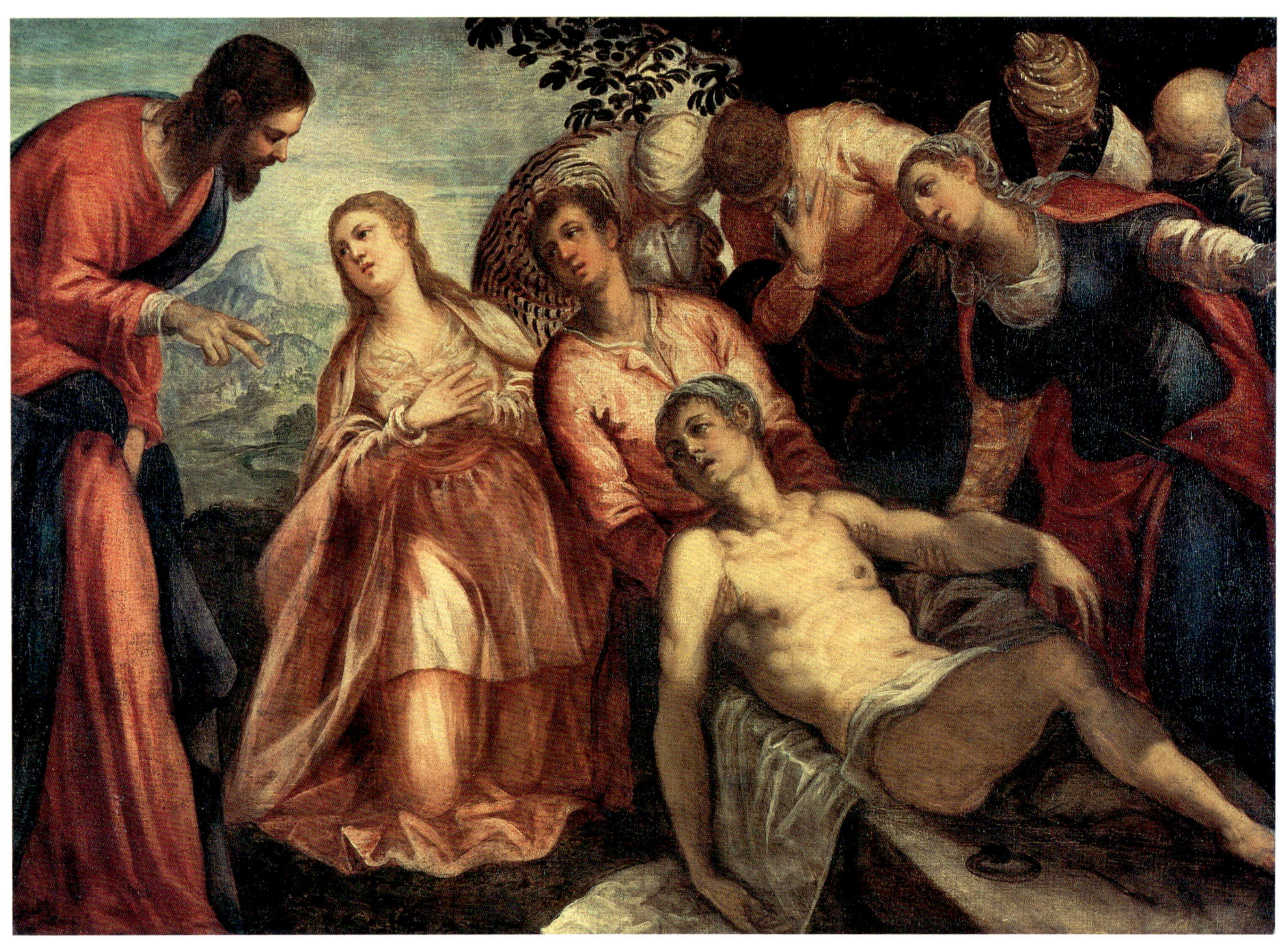

37.
Jacopo Tintoretto, *The Raising of Lazarus*, ca. 1556-57
Oil on canvas, 107 x 147 cm
Maryland Province of the Society of Jesus at the Jesuit Center, Wernersville, Pennsylvania
Courtesy of the Reading Public Museum, Reading, Pennsylvania

Jacopo Robusti, called Tintoretto (1518-1594), was the leading religious painter of late Cinquecento Venice. Little is known about his training and earliest years, although he seems to have worked briefly for Titian as a young man. In 1565, Tintoretto joined the Scuola di San Rocco, a lay charitable organization named for St. Roch, for which he had begun executing a large painting cycle in 1564. Throughout his career Tintoretto worked extensively on religious commissions in his native city. Three of Tintoretto's children – Marietta, Domenico, and Marco – were painters, and served as assistants in their father's large workshop.

Recently rediscovered, this painting is one of several versions of this theme by the Venetian artist. It represents a scene from the New Testament book John 11: 1-34 that was often depicted in times of plague, Jesus's miracle of raising Lazarus from the dead. Beginning in the eleventh century, "Saint Lazarus" acquired the role of a heavenly protector against leprosy and the plague. Medieval legend melded the identity of the resurrected Lazarus of John 11 with that of the poor, sore-covered beggar of the same name in Jesus's parable of Dives and Lazarus in Luke 16: 19-31. When Lazarus, poor and covered with sores, begged for food at Dives's lavishly set table the rich man refused him sustenance. Later, after both men had died, it was only Lazarus who gained salvation. Leprosy gradually died out in Europe but bubonic plague continued, and Lazarus became associated with the latter. Tintoretto's painting is generally dated to ca. 1556-57, a plague year in Venice.

In Tintoretto's painting the recumbent Lazarus is beginning to come to life. His sisters, Martha and Mary, and other companions gaze reverently toward Christ, who appears on the left, his right hand outstretched in a gesture of benediction. The painterly handling and the bold palette, ranging from pale shimmering pinks to highly saturated reds and blues, are typical of Tintoretto's style of the 1550s. The dark trees on the upper right push the figures up closer to the viewer, lending immediacy to the group.

Index

Marilyn Rowland

Photo Credits

Alinari/Art Resource, New York: figs 28, 29, 30, 47

The Art Institute of Chicago, Greg Williams, Reproduction: cat. 9

Sheila Barker: figs. 3-13

Bayerische Staatsgemäldesammlungen, Munich: fig. 45

© Gerard Blot, Réunion des Musées Nationaux/Art Resource: fig. 65

Osvaldo Böhm: figs. 54, 56, 58

© copyright The Trustees of British Museum: fig. 53

Cameraphoto/Art Resource, New York: fig. 66

M. Lee Fatheree: cat. 15

Courtesy of the J. Paul Getty Museum: cat. 8

Eric Lessing/Art Resources, New York: figs. 51, 59

Los Angeles County of Art, photograph 2004 Museum Associates: fig. 61, cat. 6

© 1983 The Metropolitan Museum of Art, cats. 7, 31

Ministero per I Beni e le Attività Culturali: figs. 19, 20

©Museum of Fine Arts, Boston: cat. 16

© copyright 2004 Board of Trustees, National Gallery of Art, Washington: cats. 5, 27

© copyright National Gallery of Canada: fig. 64

© copyright National Gallery, London: cat. 1, fig. 63

Réunion des Musées Nationaux/Art Resource: figs. 65, 68

Larry Sanders, cat. 29

Scala/Art Resource, New York: fig. 26, 31

Soprintendenza ai beni aristici e storici – Napoli: figs. 32-35

Victoria and Albert Museum: fig. 44

© Virginia Museum of Fine Arts, Katherine Wetzel: cat. 21

Bruce White, © 2004 Trustees of Princeton University, cat. 26, 36